Planning Sustainable Transport

Transport choices must be transformed if we are to cope with sustainability and climate change, but this can only be done if we understand how complex transport systems work. Straightforward choices are never made between one transport mode and another; door-to-door movements of both people and freight use combinations of different modes of transport.

This book offers a cross-disciplinary overview of transport systems and the ways in which they interact with urban and regional planning decisions and environmental issues. It offers a thoughtful critique of existing methodology and policy, raising issues, providing facts, explaining linkages and, particularly, stimulating debate. The book methodically explores the definitions, trends, problems, objectives and policies of transport planning. In particular the author looks at land use as a major determinant of the nature and extent of the demand for transport, concluding that the management of land use has to be a key element of any sustainable transport policy.

Planning Sustainable Transport will be essential reading for today's transport specialists, planners and property developers. It will also be useful to postgraduate students in planning and related disciplines.

Barry Hutton, now retired, was the founding Head of the Department of Town and Country Planning at the University of the West of England. In parallel with his academic work, he was a consultant appearing as a professional witness at many planning inquiries. As a member of the design team for Mosborough, Sheffield, he wrote a computer simulation of gridded road and public transport networks that was to be selectively adapted for Milton Keynes. He went on to help establish the Egyptian National Institute of Transport, was part of a project researching and creating a computer prediction of the speed-sensitive fuel consumption rates of cars in Edinburgh, and accepted an invitation from the United Nations to prepare a 'Sustainable, Multi-Modal Transport Plan' for Kosovo.

Planning Sustainable Transport

Barry Hutton

First published 2013
by Routledge
2 Park Square, Milton Park, Abingdon, Oxon, OX14 4RN

Simultaneously published in the USA and Canada
by Routledge
711 Third Avenue, New York, NY 10017

Routledge is an imprint of the Taylor & Francis Group, an informa business

© 2013 Barry Hutton

The right of Barry Hutton to be identified as author of this work has been asserted by him in accordance with sections 77 and 78 of the Copyright, Designs and Patents Act 1988.

All rights reserved. No part of this book may be reprinted or reproduced or utilised in any form or by any electronic, mechanical, or other means, now known or hereafter invented, including photocopying and recording, or in any information storage or retrieval system, without permission in writing from the publishers.

Trademark notice: Product or corporate names may be trademarks or registered trademarks, and are used only for identification and explanation without intent to infringe.

British Library Cataloguing in Publication Data
A catalogue record for this book is available from the British Library

Library of Congress Cataloging-in-Publication Data
Hutton, Barry.
Planning sustainable transport / Barry Hutton.
pages cm
Includes bibliographical references and index.
1. Transportation–Planning. 2. Transportation–Environmental aspects.
3. Transportation and state. I. Title.
HE193.H88 2013
388'.049–dc23
2012044459

ISBN13: 978-1-84971-390-0 (hbk)
ISBN13: 978-1-84971-391-7 (pbk)
ISBN13: 978-0-203-43606-6 (ebk)

Typeset in Baskerville by
Keystroke, Station Road, Codsall, Wolverhampton

Contents

List of figures		vii
1	The definitions: sustainability	1
2	The definitions: transport	19
3	The definitions: planning	29
4	The trends: travel and haulage	48
5	Fuel consumption and emissions of greenhouse gases (GHG)	68
6	Location and land use	89
7	The problems: congestion	101
8	The problems: interchanging and trans-shipment	141
9	The problems: the space budget	153
10	Transport costs	159
11	Sensing success and failure	175
12	Managing the environmental impacts	185
13	Mobility and accessibility	202
14	Controlling costs	219

15	Supporting the economy	239
16	Road vehicle design	256
17	Public transport	261
18	Tolls, taxes and tariffs: fares, fines and fees	321
19	Transport demand prediction	339
20	The need for a new methodology to estimate travel demand	379
21	Planning sustainable transport: the agenda	392
	Bibliography	412
	Index	421

Figures

1.1	CO_2 equivalent (CO_2-e) conversion factors	6
1.2	A selection of the 'strategy indicators'	13
2.1	Transport rhythms in a hypothetical freight case	26
3.1	Traffic flows on the M25	35
3.2a	Edinburgh, west and northwest suburbs (1928)	38
3.2b	Edinburgh, west and northwest suburbs (1964)	39
3.2c	Edinburgh, west and northwest suburbs (2000)	40
3.3	The linear, end-state planning process	44
3.4	The recursive, flexible planning process	47
4.1	The growth of personal travel, freight, traffic and real GDP per head (1953–2009)	48
4.2	The growth in the vehicle population (1953–2009) (as an index to show relative growth)	49
4.3	The percentages of households with or without the use of a car (1951–2009)	50
4.4	Number of households in Great Britain (1951–2010)	51
4.5	Descriptive statistics drawn from the 2001 census for examples of typical developments illustrated in Figures 4.6, 4.7, 4.8 and 4.9	52
4.6	Scottish tenement housing (1890s)	53
4.7	1930s housing	54
4.8	Housing on previous farmland: the virtual city	55
4.9	New flatted development on vacated industrial land within the city	56
4.10	Personal travel: total distance travelled, trip length, trip speed and total travel time	57
4.11	Freight: tonnes shifted – tonne-kilometres by major mode	59
4.12	Freight: tonnes lifted – tonnes loaded on to the major modes	59
4.13	Freight: mean carry distance	60
4.14	The overall capacity of the lorry fleet	64
5.1	Emissions of CO_2 equivalent (CO_2-e) by various fuels	70
5.2	Emissions of CO_2-e released by the petrol burnt in an average car as a function of its speed	71
5.3	The European standard fuel consumption test (80/1268/EEC)	72
5.4	Fuel consumption by a 1.8-litre petrol car during the EU test cycle	73
5.5	Emissions of CO_2-e as a function of speed	74

viii Figures

5.6	Emissions of CO_2-e by heavy goods vehicles as a function of speed	75
5.7	Lorry and container capacities	75
5.8	Emissions of CO_2-e per kilometre by average buses as a function of speed	76
5.9	Rail freight case studies	79
5.10	Out-turn performances of some British passenger trains	83
5.11	Emissions of CO_2-e per passenger-kilometre by an average bus as a function of the number of passengers	85
5.12	Emissions of CO_2-e by a 44-tonne gross weight articulated lorry (OGV2) at differing speeds and load factors	86
7.1	An intuitive, but incorrect, speed–flow relationship for an urban street	103
7.2	Space-headway related to speed	104
7.3	Time-headway related to speed	105
7.4	The general relationship between speed and flow	106
7.5	Density of traffic in vehicles per kilometre of road related to traffic speed	107
7.6	Speed–flow relationship reported by the Road Research Laboratory (1965)	108
7.7	An example of the 'official' relationship between flow and speed	109
7.8	Passenger car unit factors	110
7.9	Space-headways associated with the speed–flow relationships shown in Figure 7.7	110
7.10	The general relationship between speed and flow	112
7.11	The hybrid speed–flow relationship	114
7.12	The nominal capacities of rural roads	118
7.13	The nominal capacities of urban roads in vehicles per hour	119
7.14	Types of conflicting movement	121
7.15	Simple crossing conflict on two one-way roads	122
7.16	Complex crossing conflict	122
7.17	Crossing and merging conflicts	123
7.18	Conflict points at an uncontrolled four-legged crossroads	124
7.19	Conflict points at a simple roundabout	125
7.20	Conflict points at a junction controlled by simple traffic signals	125
7.21	Gaps accepted by 50 per cent of drivers at a minor road junction	127
7.22	The supply of five-, six- and eight-second gaps as a function of flow	129
7.23	Time taken to travel one kilometre	131
7.24	Indices of change in personal transport in London	134
7.25	Growth in traffic (measured in vehicle-kilometres) in London and southeast England compared with country-wide growth	135
7.26	Mean trip lengths and speeds	135
7.27	Overall growth in traffic in Great Britain	136
9.1	Indicative modal capacities (persons per hour)	153
9.2	Space-hours required and relative productivity	154
9.3	A sample train diagram showing two trains with dwell times at a station stop	157

Figures   ix

10.1	Car costs for a petrol car priced new at £14,000 and driven 24,000 kilometres per year	161
10.2	Depreciation of a car with a purchase price of £14,000, a life of 10 years and zero salvage value	162
10.3	The financial costs per year of the ownership of a car with a purchase price of £14,000, a life of 10 years and zero salvage value	163
10.4	Amortisation: sample annual repayment on a loan of £1000	165
10.5	Mode capacity, costing and emissions	166
10.6	Time budget for a hypothetical bus operation	169
10.7	The allocation of the 8760 annual life-hours of the hypothetical bus working as in Figure 10.6	170
10.8	Distribution of total annual costs for the hypothetical bus operation shown in Figure 10.6	171
12.1	Vehicle excise duty charged as a function of CO_2 emission rate (2012)	191
12.2	The modelled impacts of long-term emissions of CO_2-e	192
12.3	Greenhouse gas emissions (2006)	199
13.1	Hansen accessibility: journey 'costs' (kilometres)	214
13.2	Hansen accessibility: deterrence values = ('costs')$^{1.3}$	215
13.3	Hansen accessibility: accessibility factors = population/('costs')$^{1.3}$	215
14.1	Estimated annual costs for a 17-tonne two-axle truck	226
14.2	Estimated costs per vehicle-kilometre for a 17-tonne two-axle truck	227
14.3	Estimated marginal and average costs per vehicle-kilometre for a 17-tonne two-axle truck	228
14.4	Estimated cost per tonne-kilometre as functions of the load factors for three sample trucks	230
14.5	Work and subsidy on British Railways, 1994 and 2010	235
15.1	Flow chart for a Land-Use Transport Interaction Model	247
15.2	National Trip End Model: zones and study areas	250
17.1	Total cost per horse tram-kilometre (1880 prices)	266
17.2	Maximum distance between service stops as a function of top speed	275
17.3	Person-kilometres (billions) by bus and rail	277
17.4	Percentage of travelled person-kilometres by mode	278
17.5	Route workings and passenger boardings for a selection of local government areas	279
17.6	Census data showing use of mode for the journey to work for the examples given in Chapter 4	280
17.7	The vicious circle	284
17.8	The Nottingham Zone and Collar experiment (1975–1976)	287
17.9	Comparative journey times and costs from Bilborough/Wollaton to Nottingham city centre	289
17.10	Passenger journeys and distances on British railways	308
17.11	Numbers (thousands) commuting to the City of London in the morning peak in 2009, by main mode of travel	313

Figures

17.12	Trends in commuting mode used to access the City of London (1996–2009)	314
18.1	Supply and demand for trips	332
18.2	Effects of capacity changes	335
19.1	The hypothetical traffic at a simple four-legged, two-way road junction	340
19.2	The origin and destination (O+D) matrix from Figure 19.1	341
19.3	The origin and destination zone structure for Kington	342
19.4	The original but flawed origin and destination (O+D) matrix for Kington	343
19.5	The Kington road network, including O+D zones, dummy links and road proposals	345
19.6	Comparison between flows estimated from the Kington O+D matrix shown in Figure 19.4 and the actual flows measured by moving car observer	346
19.7	Numbers of car trips from the house per household per 24 hours	347
19.8	A demonstration O+D matrix showing the number of trips starting and finishing in each of four zones	349
19.9	A demonstration O+D matrix by gravity model showing the distances in kilometres between zones	350
19.10	The effective deterrent distance = (the ground distance)^N	350
19.11	A demonstration O+D matrix by gravity model showing the effective deterrent distance = (distance in kilometres between zones)$^{1.3}$	351
19.12	A demonstration O+D matrix by gravity model showing the 'likelihoods' of making a journey from one zone to another	351
19.13	A demonstration O+D matrix by gravity model showing the 'relative likelihood' of making a journey from each origin zone to one or other of the destination zones	352
19.14	A demonstration O+D matrix by gravity model showing the final synthetic O+D matrix	352
19.15	Theoretical diversion curves	358
19.16	The classic economic theory of supply and demand curves	369
21.1	A recursive, flexible planning process	393

Chapter 1
The definitions
Sustainability

The Brundtland Report

The Brundtland Report (1987) defined sustainability as:

> Ensuring that development meets the needs of the present without compromising the ability of future generations to meet their own needs.[1]

This definition implied a continuous process rather than an event or a quality. It acknowledged the need to use the earth's resources to meet the basic human needs of shelter, food and warmth for an increasing number of people. Brundtland did not suggest a reversion to a primitive life to ensure that the inventory of the earth's resources is left more or less as we find it but it did urge that the minimum impact should be made upon the resource stock. The Report emphasised four sustainable policies to ensure that the needs of future populations are not compromised:

1　Resources are used efficiently to minimise the depletion of finite resources.
2　Any wastes are disposed of with minimal damage to the environment so that the continuing natural renewal of the resource base is unimpeded.
3　The growth in world population is slowed.
4　'Development' is spread more evenly around the global population.

'Development' in this context means expanding global production, partly to even out standards of living across the world, and partly to satisfy the needs of an expected increase in global population. This expansion of production may only be achieved by more factories consuming more raw materials, backed by more offices, shops and transport, trends which Brundtland accepts as unavoidable but which should be kept to a minimum. This implies that damage must be recognised and quantified; otherwise its management and minimisation would be impossible.

The Brundtland Report did not hide the fact that some 'painful choices' would have to be made. Massive, unsustainable increases in production and consumption would be needed if the inequalities between the developed and the developing world were to be removed by bringing global consumption per head up to the levels now enjoyed by highly developed countries. Consequently, one plank of the sustainable policy suggested by Brundtland must be to ensure that current standards of living are spread more evenly. The Report argued that if this were not done, countries with lower living standards would strive to raise them by copying the economies of the richer countries, forcing up prices of energy and raw materials and then raising their consumption to unsustainable levels. It is arguable that this assertion, now a quarter of a century old, is becoming true. China, striving to emulate the West, is consuming more energy and raw materials, forcing global prices up and tending to create the very unsustainability feared by Brundtland.

Brundtland stressed that sustainability is more complex than a focus upon the reduction of pollution or even avoiding excessive environmental damage, intricate though these problems may be. If the headlong increase in the use of raw materials and energy is to be slowed, then existing production must be spread more evenly: that may well be seen to be a moral issue – an injustice – with some societies hogging more than their 'share' while others strive to keep pace. But Brundtland argues that it is more than a moral argument – it is in the interests of the richer nations to curtail their consumption in order to damp down the aspirations of poorer countries and so slow the rate of exploitation of the finite global resources. The 'painful choices' to which Brundtland draws attention are therefore painful to those who may have to forgo continuing increases in their standards of living but they are also painful to political leaders who have to run the risk of being pilloried and then rejected for placing the interests of the planet above the immediate interests of their own electorate.

This conflict between the long-term interests of future generations all over the world and the short-term interests of the existing inhabitants of the richer countries is, perhaps, the core problem facing us and it is important to recognise that it is not a problem of science or technology but of politics, attitudes and aspirations.

The Rio Conference

The Brundtland Report was published in 1987 under the auspices of the United Nations and, after a gap of three years to enable each national government to establish a response, the UN organised a summit conference in Rio de Janeiro to address sustainability. The product was 'Agenda 21', an international protocol defining global sustainable policy. Although few dared to say so, the problems and policies outlined in Brundtland required a global response but global political cooperation was not up to the challenge and, although Agenda 21 was the product of an unprecedented international conference, and although many nations signed up to the protocol, implementation was left to individual countries. Agenda 21 was recognised more in posture rather than in practice.

At the Rio Conference the international community made the problem of sustainability more tractable by shifting the emphasis away from the broad problems of poverty and the global disparities in standards of living, towards the issue of climate change. In effect it redefined 'sustainability', abandoning the broad Brundtland meaning, and concentrating on pollution, greenhouse gases and climate change. Clearly, this is a very important global problem and is one element of sustainability as defined by Brundtland, but climate change is much less politically sensitive than moving wealth from the advantaged to the disadvantaged.

The British government responded to Agenda 21 with *Sustainable Development: The UK Strategy* (1994).[2] The report was the first sign that the British government were more conscious of the immediate political dangers of reining in growth than of the long-term problems of sustainability. The Foreword, written by John Major, the then Prime Minister, made it very clear that the intention was to attempt to be all things to all men:

> 150 states committed themselves at the Rio conference to make future development sustainable – not to turn their backs on growth – but to ensure that the price of growth did not become an intolerable bill for future generations.

This was to become a common theme that actions to promote sustainability and climate change need not restrict growth, a theme reiterated by successive governments and articulated and expanded at length 12 years later in Stern's 'Review of the Economics of Climate Change' – not, it will be noticed, the 'Economics of Sustainability' but 'Climate Change': by 2006, 'sustainability' had been politically morphed into 'climate change'.

John Major's Foreword carried another message that was to repeat itself:

> The Agenda 21 was not just for government but for business, for organisations and for individual men and women.

A flag that the government intended to lead from the back, responding to public concern rather than setting a clear agenda for itself.

The Minister for the Environment, John Gummer, wrote an introduction with a completely different tone and intent, pointing out:

> that man lived on earth as a conqueror, dominating, controlling and exploiting the natural environment and that this could not go on without irretrievable damage since effects we could ignore when they were confined to the actions of a few, became intolerable when they were spread more and more widely.

He was also at pains to point out the effectiveness of the Clean Air Act (1956), hinting at the distinction between this decisive and effective legislation, an example of a government governing rather than establishing a camouflage net of committees and advisory groups.

Sustainable Development: The UK Strategy provoked a cloud of objectives and policies. Those for development were concerned in the main with satisfying the demand for new housing:

- promote attractive and convenient extensions to urban areas;
- in locations which minimise energy consumption;
- encourage brownland development;
- sustain the rural environment;
- engage developers.

And those for transport:

- influence the rate of traffic growth;
- provide a framework for individual choice in transport which enables environmental objectives to be met;
- increase the economic efficiency of transport decisions;
- improve vehicle design to minimise harmful emissions.

In the UK, as in many other countries, Agenda 21 appeared as 'Local Agenda 21' (LA21) to be set and implemented by local councils adopting the above targets rather than by national legislation. Devising LA21 policies was encouraged and supervised by the Sustainable Development Commission, a company limited by guarantee and effectively a wholly owned, arm's-length subsidiary agency of the British government. Although no doubt the Sustainable Development Commission would object to the suggestion that their arm's-length agency status was a way of taking sustainability out of the direct responsibility of Her Majesty's Government, there can be no doubt that it removed sustainability from the list of front-line political issues. The detachment of the Sustainable Development Commission from government was completed on 31 March 2011 when it was abolished, the related website dismantled and the documentation buried in the national archive.

In Britain the focus on pollution was emphasised by a second document published in 1994, this one by the Royal Commission on Environmental Pollution.[3] (The current political urgency of sustainability is indicated by the abolition of the Royal Commission on 1 April 2011, 24 hours after the Sustainable Development Commission was disbanded.) The objectives set by the Commission were to:

- ensure that an effective transport policy at all levels of government is integrated with land-use policy and gives priority to minimising the need for transport and increasing the proportion of trips made by environmentally less damaging modes;
- achieve standards of air quality that will prevent damage to human health and the environment;
- improve the quality of life, particularly in towns and cities, by reducing the dominance of cars and lorries and providing alternative means of access;
- increase the proportions of personal travel and freight transport by environmentally less damaging modes and to make best use of existing infrastructure;
- halt any loss of land to transport infrastructure in areas of conservation, cultural, scenic or amenity value unless the use of the land for that purpose has been shown to be the best practicable environmental option;
- reduce carbon dioxide emissions from transport;
- reduce substantially the demands which transport infrastructure and the vehicle industry place on non-renewable materials;
- reduce noise nuisance from transport.

In line with this general policy, LA21 set these explicit objectives for local councils:

- reducing fuel consumption;
- reducing the use of other finite resources;
- reducing the irreversible change in climate due to the emission of greenhouse gases;
- reducing other pollutions which cause long-term, irreversible damage;
- reducing the risks of damage to human health and quality of life;
- reducing the impacts upon natural and semi-natural habitats and upon areas of cultural and amenity value;
- promoting land-use patterns which depend for their viability on transport systems which will have one or more of the above effects.

Both of these lists, although ambitious, concentrated upon aims that may be delivered locally or nationally; they are local components of the global issue and much less politically contentious than dealing with global disparities in standards of living. That is not to say the lists were devoid of contention: today there is considerable scepticism about the nature, causes and relevance of climate change and about the impacts of policies designed to deal with them. Local councils lost their enthusiasm for LA21 policies, although many retained their concerns with rubbish, landfill and recycling: Brundtland had been diluted to less contentious, although still undeniably important issues. Despite sustainability and climate change being phased out of mainstream political concern, the issue is still an important one: Brundtland's stance is still appropriate and all the subsequent words, policies and postures, although now in the background, still have validity. Much of the content of this book is focused on just how the above two lists of objectives, taken directly from the Report on Transport and the Environment published by the Royal Commission on Environmental Pollution, might be delivered.

The Kyoto Protocol

The Kyoto Protocol[4] was signed in December 1997 and was to come into force in February 2005. Although ambitious, it confirmed the selection of climate change as a more tractable abstraction from the broader concerns of Brundtland and of the Rio Protocol. It also relied on the principles of market forces, perhaps because price mechanisms were seen to be the best or even the only way of delivering global policy. Even then, it was ratified by only 37 countries and so was both narrower by subject and weaker in political drive than the Rio Protocol.

The Protocol was concerned with 'greenhouse gases' (GHG), those gases which are thought to cause global warming by preventing some of the energy received from the sun from being reflected back into space, causing the earth's atmosphere to heat up in exactly the same way as the inside of a greenhouse. There are a number of greenhouse gases, some occurring naturally such as carbon dioxide (CO_2), and others which are by-products of industrial and other human activity. The total volume of greenhouse gas in the earth's atmosphere is rising due mainly to the burning of fossil fuels to create energy, but partly because new, potent synthetic greenhouse gases have been added to the atmosphere, gases such as those escaping from air-conditioning and refrigeration units.

The Kyoto Protocol, in common with many other documents and reports, uses 'CO_2 equivalent' (CO_2-e) as a measure of a mixture of greenhouse gases. This gives the number of grams of CO_2 which would have the same effect on solar irradiation, global warming and climate change as one gram of one of the other GHGs. Figure 1.1 shows the standard tariff of factors published by the British government.

The stated objective of the Kyoto Protocol was 'to promote sustainable development'[5] but the prime focus was actually to reduce the global emission of GHG, seen as a necessary, although incomplete, step towards a sustainable future. The protocol set out to achieve this by setting targets for the reduction of emissions of GHG by each country. These targets were in terms of a percentage reduction in CO_2-e from a nominated base year.

Greenhouse gas (GHG)	Chemical formula	Factor to convert GHG to CO_2-e (grams of CO_2 creating the same warming effect as 1 gram of GHG)
Carbon dioxide	CO_2	1
Methane	CH_4	21
Nitrous oxide	N_2O	310
HFC-23	CHF_3	11,700
HFC-32	CH_2F_2	650
HFC-41	CH_3F	150
HFC-125	CHF_2CF_3	2800
HFC-134	CHF_2CHF_2	1000
HFC-134a	CH_2FCF_3	1300
HFC-143	CH_3CF_3	300
HFC-143a	CH_3CHF_2	3800
HFC-152a	CF_3CHFCF_3	140
HFC-227ea	$CF_3CH_2CF_3$	2900
HFC-236fa	$CHF_2CH_2CF_3$	6300
HFC-245fa	$CH_3CF_2CH_2CF_3$	560
HFC-43-10mee	$CF_3CHFCHFCF_2CF_3$	1300
Perfluoromethane (PFC-14)	CF_4	6500
Perfluoroethane (PFC-116)	C_2F_6	9200
Perfluoropropane (PFC-218)	C_3F_8	7000
Perfluorocyclobutane (PFC-318)	$c\text{-}C_4F_8$	8700
Perfluorobutane (PFC-3-1-10)	C_4F_{10}	7000
Perfluoropentane (PFC-4-1-12)	C_5F_{12}	7500
Perfluorohexane (PFC-5-1-14)	C_6F_{14}	7400
Sulphur hexafluoride	SF_6	23,900

Figure 1.1 CO_2 equivalent (CO_2-e) conversion factors

Source: Reproduced from Department for the Environment, Food and Rural Affairs (DEFRA) (2010).

Two policy strands were arranged to achieve this:

1 Each national government was to establish a raft of policies designed to reduce pollution by GHG emissions.
2 Market forces were to be mobilised imposing an additional cost upon firms emitting GHG: that cost was set by creating a nominal price per tonne of CO_2-e.

Market force is an important mechanism to discuss since it reoccurs in a number of guises in transport policy-making, as a proposal to charge for using roads, as the underpinning principle in awarding franchises to operate trains, in providing bus services and in 'the polluter pays' policy.[6] The principles are discussed at more length in Chapter 18, 'Tolls, taxes and tariffs: fares, fines and fees' but for now it should be noted that there are wide differences between real markets, like those for cornflakes or overcoats, and a contrived market such as that developed at Kyoto for CO_2-e. The official website of the United Nations Framework Convention on Climate Change (UNFCCC), the body under whose auspices the Kyoto Conference and Protocol were arranged, declared: '*Carbon – a new commodity is born.*' In this case 'carbon' was being used as shorthand for 'one tonne of CO_2-e', not the element carbon itself. The new 'commodity' born in the Kyoto protocol was actually a licence to emit one tonne of CO_2-e, not the gas itself, a licence that firms could buy and sell. Such a licence is not 'a commodity', something that people would find useful and beneficial, like overcoats or cornflakes. This breaks two fundamental principles of a 'market'. First, the function of price in a true market is to ensure near equilibrium between supply and demand, rising prices tending to choke off demand while simultaneously increasing supply, and falling prices tending to increase demand while reducing supply. The supply and price of licences to emit CO_2-e by the tonne is fixed by a bureaucracy charged with the long-term aim of restricting pollution by reducing the number of certificates, not to respond to the market signal carried by changes in price. Second, the emission of a tonne of CO_2-e is a disbenefit – it is an anti-commodity – a benefit to nobody. Polluting is a form of antisocial behaviour, and licensing antisocial behaviour seems to be a strange piece of legislation. Some years ago the smoke from domestic coal fires in Great Britain was seen to be harmful to public health, and Clean Air Zones were imposed by law in which coal fires were banned: the government of the day would have been justly criticised if they had auctioned off certificates legitimatising the smoky fires lit by those who could best afford to buy the necessary certificate.

Nevertheless, the Kyoto Agreement established the number of tonnes of GHG to be emitted by each of the countries signing the Protocol. This tonnage was arbitrary. Each country was then entitled to sell permissions to pollute to industrialists through a national 'market': the supply was initially fixed within the protocol and countries were obliged to progressively reduce the supply over time in order to creep towards the long-term objective of preventing the worsening of climate change due to GHGs: that mechanism is, of course, the complete opposite to the workings of a normal market. This suggests that carbon trading is not a market at all but is a method of rationing a finite, limited ability by selling it to the highest bidders. In times of great shortage, such as food and petrol in the Second World War, it would have been inconceivable to sell petrol or food coupons to the highest bidder.

A 'carbon credit', namely a permit to emit one tonne of CO_2-e, was priced at €17.12 on the European Union market at the end of March 2011 and was on the rise due to the problems with nuclear powered generating plants in Japan and the expected repercussions throughout the world: the need to generate electricity from burning fossil fuels was anticipated to drive up the demand for carbon credits.

This book argues that the Kyoto Protocol, together with many other objectives used by the British governments (among others), are little more than postured aspirations, since there are no technical methodologies to measure the effectiveness of policies and actions supposed to deliver them. Much of the following content points to the weakness or absence of measures to assess the potential and the actual effects of 'sustainable' policies and actions. To set aims and to then design policies to deliver those aims, without the means of assessing whether the aims have been delivered or not, is not so much a matter of poor management as a complete absence of management. Without sensing the potential outcomes of actions, decision-makers are working in the dark, driven by hope, by guesswork and, all too often, by an ideology based on a faith in the efficacy of market forces.

The shifting balance between government and business in delivering policy

The gap between aspirations and the lack of ways in which policies and actions may be seen to deliver those aspirations, both before and after decisions are taken, is well illustrated by the British government's major policy statement on sustainability, *Securing the Future*.[7] This was thought to be important enough to have ranked a Foreword from the Prime Minister, Tony Blair, the final paragraph of which read:

> We have spent a long time getting to grips with the concept of sustainability. I want to declare a moratorium on further words. I want this new strategy to be a catalyst for action to secure our future.

Sustainability is a global issue, demanding a global approach. There is a fundamental dichotomy behind creating a global approach, a dichotomy that appears in many issues and at many scales. It is usually characterised as the difference between 'top-down' and 'bottom-up' approaches but, more accurately, it is the distinction between composing a large-scale strategy by a combination of a number of smaller scale, often individual, decisions or, alternatively, applying an overarching large-scale decision to smaller scale component areas. One example is the difference between creating the budget for an organisation by simply combining the budgets of its component departments or, alternatively, setting the overall budget and then dividing it among the departments. A resolution of this conundrum is discussed in Chapter 3, on the definition of planning, in which it is argued that decisions should be made and progressively refined by oscillating between scales – between the 'top' and the 'bottom'.

The difficulty with global issues such as sustainability is that there is no global authority with the power to implement policy: there is no 'top'. Therefore any strategy is perforce no more than the sum of the decisions and actions of individual states. The only readily available global process to convert policy into action is the market with individual behaviours being driven by price and cost rather than edict. This is in contrast to each national jurisdiction where market forces are modified by government creating and managing a currency, imposing taxes, making and enforcing law, in addition to itself taking action. In recent years there has been considerable debate about the extent to which state administrations should intervene in their local markets, but the debate has never extended into the possibility of interventions being made by a global administration. There is a body of international law but it is a compendium of bilateral and multilateral treaties rather than a body of law applying to every country and enforced by an international agency. This leaves market forces as the sole universal mechanism, a reliance which is clearly related to the now almost universally held belief, not only in the power of market forces, but in their ability to deliver the wisest of decisions.

A belief in the power of the market has come to dominate the world, gathering strength between the two World Wars and now suffusing nearly every culture and activity. There are two major components:

1   That decisions are best made by individual people and firms driven by their own self-interests. This is usually presented as individuals making 'choices' – 'choice' being an extremely important word in modern culture. This emphasis upon individual choices is supported by a theory that the sum of individual choices creates the best possible outcome: human behaviour is likened to that of bees and ants, and claims abound that modern electronic social networking facilitates wise individual decisions by providing a plethora of information.[8] It is as though twittering is able to replicate both the dance routines of bees and the pheromones of ants and, ultimately, to generate the sorts of political pressures achieved in storming the Bastille or the Winter Palace.
2   That choices are best presented and marshalled by price and market force.

These twin notions are threaded through modern sustainable and transport policy-making: they are the frame for this book. The implementation of British policy on sustainability, when stripped of the posturing and rhetoric, rests upon two propositions:

1   That individuals and firms should make their own decisions on whether to restrict their consumption of energy or recycle their waste, etc.
2   That the task of government is, first, to proclaim policy objectives and then to expect firms and individuals to make choices which, when taken together, will deliver those objectives. The myriad choices made by individuals and by firms is driven in the desired direction by adjusting the cost either by taxation to increase the cost of behaviours deemed to be undesirable (e.g. the tax on petrol), or by subsidy to reduce the cost of the choices which will serve to deliver the government's set objectives (as with solar panels).

The government is effectively withdrawing from making difficult, accountable decisions and is constructing frameworks within which the decisions by firms and individuals will be merged into a desirable collective action. This disperses responsibility and accountability and has shifted the nature of government away from governing, often by edict, towards a more 'business-driven' approach in which policy is delivered by the hidden hand of price and cost; business style has invaded state administration to such an extent that the task of government is often referred to as the management of 'UK plc'.

That the combination of the manipulation of price and cost, together with competition between private companies is a universal way of creating efficient systems, is now so strong that it is almost impossible to gainsay it – questioning the power of market forces is virtual heresy. The other side of the same coin is the powerful belief that government and all its activities is inherently inefficient and undesirable and should be minimised.[9]

This was not always the case, and the shifting balances between a government style setting and enforcing law, and a business style assessing value by comparing cost and revenue, has been particularly strong in transport. Public transport by rail, tram and bus was originally established by private companies but the Victorians were troubled that competition might not deliver the most efficient systems – there was an implicit query as to whether the objectives of private companies were coincident with wider national interests. The fear of prices being set by monopolies led to the control of fares, tolls and freight rates by successive Acts of Parliament stretching right back to the Statute of Winchester (1285).[10] The legal concept of the King's Highway, mentioned *en passant* in the Statute of 1285, is of continuing importance:

> [A] highway is a way over which there exists a public right of passage by all Her Majesty's subjects at all seasons of the year, freely and at their will to pass and re-pass without let[11] or hindrance.

'Let or hindrance' included the setting up of gates and the imposition of tolls: the right to pass and repass over the whole highway network free of tolls or charges has existed for over 700 years. It may only be varied by a very specific Act of Parliament[12] which not only enables the imposition of a toll but also fixes how much it should be.

The Victorians were also very concerned about safety and stringent rules, and procedures were imposed covering the structure and operation of vehicles. For example, the Tramways Act of 1870 (a Public Act) established the terms of individual Private Acts, each giving the right to a nominated private tramway company to construct tram tracks along specific public roads but only under the strict supervision of the local magistrates who had the power to license the trams and the operating staff, and also to set the fares. The Act also made it compulsory, after 20 years in the ownership of the tramway companies, for their tracks and cars to be offered for sale to the local council. The implicit assumption was that if there were to be a monopoly, then it would be best managed by local magistrates or councils in the public interest rather than a company in the interests of its shareholders. Factories, mines, railways and shipping were all heavily regulated and many city authorities themselves owned and operated gas, electricity, water and sewerage systems, all utilities with a natural monopoly. None of these crucial urban infrastructures was initiated solely by private companies but they were driven by Victorian government at both local and national levels.

During the 1914 to 1918 War, the British government took the operation of the railways under its direct control, anticipating that private companies would not best serve the national interest and found that rivalry between companies had not created an efficient, profitable service. In consequence, over 120 private railway companies were forcibly amalgamated in 1921 into four major groups. This was not nationalisation: the assets of the railways remained private property but it was an acknowledgement that the objectives of private companies did not comfortably map on to the public interest. The preamble to the Railways Act (1921) made it quite clear:

> With a view to the reorganisation and more efficient and economical working of the railway system of Great Britain railways shall be formed into groups in accordance with the provisions of this Act.

The concern that rivalry did not automatically deliver an efficient transport system was emphasised by the London Transport Act of 1933 which established the London Passenger Transport Board. The Act stated that the general duty of the Board was to:

> [E]xercise their powers under this Act as to secure the provision of an adequate and properly coordinated system of passenger transport for the London Passenger Transport Area, *while avoiding the provision of unnecessary and wasteful competitive services* (emphasis added).

In the Second World War the major elements of the transport system were once again taken into state control, confirming the view that private businesses (even those established under the 1921 Act) were unlikely to meet the needs of a country at war. After the war, it was recognised that the railway system could not be profitable and the shares became almost worthless. The shareholders were put out of their misery by the whole system being taken into state ownership.

Transport history shows that transport (and much else) was facilitated by the state passing the necessary enabling and regulating legislation, with the subsequent control contrived by a sometimes complex combination of public and private ownership and management: today's emphasis upon the superiority of lightly regulated business rather than government to deliver transport services was not evident for much of the past.

Market forces have very considerable merits but they are not omnipotent, and their role in delivering sustainable transport, even in the simplified form of reducing climate change rather than the wider objectives set out in the Brundtland Report, is questionable. There are two massive stumbling-blocks:

1. Many of the qualities bound up in sustainability are not saleable commodities with a proper market to balance supply and demand through price.
2. Attempts to create a false market, such as that for carbon credits, are inherently ineffective and open to manipulation. The strength of market forces is to bring

demand and supply into equilibrium but the objective of sustainable policies is to reduce the harmful impacts of some particular human behaviours by edict, ration or taxation and to do so at minimal expense. There is no equilibrium to be struck unless, that is, the harmful impacts can be quite artificially 'priced' so that the cost of sustainable polices may be weighed against a nominal price of disbenefits such as poor health, flooding, droughts, crop failures and all the other prospective results of climate change. In addition, false markets tend to be ill disciplined and prone to fraud due to prices having to be set not by a properly functioning market but by administrators. Their manipulations are not always in the public interest. Recent (2012) evidence of the manipulation of energy and financial markets may not have been conclusively proven but it is, at the least, discomforting.

Securing the Future, the then Government's policy published in 2005, listed no fewer than 68 'Strategy Indicators': a selection of them is shown in Figure 1.2. The indicators were measures of year-on-year changes to be detected as the presumed consequences of 'Public Service Agreements' (PSA): these were bundles of policies and actions to which various government departments had committed themselves (these 'Agreements' were abandoned, some in 2007 and the rest in 2010, evidence enough of their worth) but their existence for 10 years illuminates how the then government sought to address sustainability.

Although *Securing the Future*, the 'Public Service Agreements' and the 'Strategy Indicators' are all history, they represent a style of government that is still with us. It is a style borrowed from management theory, a subject developed in the 1970s with many schools of management established in universities and polytechnics, all offering Masters degrees in Business Administration (MBA) and hosting conferences and short courses, many sponsored by large firms. This work was supported by myriad publications: the National Library of Scotland catalogue has 5201 book titles with 'management' in them, the vast majority of which were published in the past 40 years.

This flood of departments, courses and books disseminated a style which seems to have two primary roots: first, the use of computers, especially, spreadsheets,[13] and, second, market theory, and the use of the price mechanism. Harvey[14] suggests that the emphasis on the use of price mechanisms (e.g. the carbon trading instituted in the Kyoto Protocol) was promulgated by the Mont Pelerin Society, including Milton Friedman and Friedrich von Hayek, the fathers of neoliberalism, with a commendable emphasis on 'freedom' but an emphasis taken to excess. Not only did they argue that the individual should be 'free', meaning subject to minimal restriction by law, but that this freedom should extend to 'legal persons' including all firms, even the global companies able to manage the markets in which they sit and also able to manage their own taxation.

The theory of management has focused on the use of spreadsheeted numbers in management, very often the use of monetary measures such as profit or unit cost but also using numerical ranking and scoring. Such scoring and ranking, often dubbed 'performance indices' or, as in *Securing the Future*, 'Strategy Indicators', is frequently used to assess managerial performance: examples are the OFSTED assessments of

UK government strategy indicators	Related Public Service Agreements (PSA) and other relevant policy statements
1 Greenhouse gas emissions: Kyoto target and CO_2 emissions **2 CO_2 emissions by end user:** industry, domestic, transport (excluding international aviation)	**Defra PSA 2, DTI PSA 4, DfT PSA 8** To reduce greenhouse gas emissions to 12.5% below 1990 levels in line with our Kyoto commitment and move towards a 20% reduction in carbon dioxide emissions below 1990 levels by 2010, through energy efficiency and renewables
4 Renewable electricity: renewable electricity generated as a percentage of total electricity **5 Electricity generation:** electricity generated, CO_2, NO_x and SO_2 emissions by electricity generators and GDP	**Defra PSA 2, DTI PSA 4** To reduce greenhouse gas emissions to 12.5% below 1990 levels in line with our Kyoto commitment and move towards a 20% reduction in carbon dioxide emissions below 1990 levels by 2010, through measures including energy efficiency and renewables
6 Household energy use: domestic CO_2 emissions and household consumption	**DTI White Paper:** *Our Energy Future – Creating a Low Carbon Economy*
7 Road transport: CO_2, NO_x, PM_{10} emissions and GDP **8 Private vehicles:** CO_2 emissions and car-km and household final consumption expenditure **9 Road freight:** CO_2 emissions and tonne-km, tonnes and GDP	**DfT PSA 6, Defra PSA 8** Improve air quality by meeting the Air Quality Strategy targets for carbon monoxide, lead, nitrogen dioxide particles, sulphur dioxide, benzene and butadiene **DfT PSA 7, Defra PSA 2, DTI PSA 4** To reduce greenhouse gas emissions to 12.5% below 1990 levels in line with our Kyoto commitment and move towards a 20% reduction in carbon dioxide emissions below 1990 levels by 2010, through measures including energy efficiency and renewables
24 Land use: area used for agriculture, woodland, water or river, urban (contextual indicator)	
25 Land recycling: (a) new dwellings built on previously developed land or through conversions; (b) all new development on previously developed land **26 Dwelling density:** average density of new housing	**ODPM PSA 6** The planning system to deliver sustainable development outcomes at national, regional and local levels through efficient and high-quality planning and development management processes, including through achievement of best value standards for planning by 2008

Figure 1.2 A selection of the 'strategy indicators'
Source: Department for the Environment, Food and Rural Affairs (DEFRA) (2005), ch. 7.

14 Sustainability

UK government strategy indicators	Related Public Service Agreements (PSA) and other relevant policy statements
32 Economic output: gross domestic product	**HMT PSA 1** Demonstrate by 2008 progress on the government's long-term objective of raising the trend rate of growth over the economic cycle by at least meeting the Budget 2004 projection
33 Productivity: UK output per worker	**HMT PSA 1** Demonstrate by 2008 progress on the government's long-term objective of raising the trend rate of growth over the economic cycle by at least meeting the Budget 2004 projection **DTI PSA 1, HMT PSA 4** Demonstrate further progress by 2008 on the government's long-term objective of raising the rate of UK productivity growth over the economic cycle, improving competitiveness and narrowing the gap with our major industrial competitors **DTI PSA 6** Build an enterprise society in which small firms of all kinds thrive and achieve their potential, with an improvement in the overall productivity of small firms **Defra PSA 4** Reduce the gap in productivity between the least well-performing quartile of rural areas and the English median by 2008, demonstrating progress by 2006, and improve the accessibility of services for people in rural areas **DCMS PSA 4** By 2008, improve the productivity of the tourism, creative and leisure industries
36 Households and dwellings: households, single-person households and dwelling stock (contextual indicator)	**ODPM:** *Housing Policy Statement, The Way Forward for Housing* **ODPM PSA 5** Achieve a better balance between housing availability and the demand for housing, including improving affordability, in all English regions while protecting valuable countryside around our towns, cities and in the Green Belt and the sustainability of towns and cities
55 Mobility: (a) number of trips per person by mode; (b) distance travelled per person per year by broad trip purpose	**DfT PSA 3** By 2010, increase the use of public transport (bus and light rail) by more than 12% in England compared with

Figure 1.2 Continued

UK government strategy indicators	Related Public Service Agreements (PSA) and other relevant policy statements
56 Getting to school: how children get to school **57 Accessibility:** access to key services	2000 levels, with growth in every region **DfT:** 'Walking and cycling: an action plan' **ODPM PSA 4** By 2008, improve the effectiveness and efficiency of local government in leading and delivering services to all communities **Defra PSA 4** Improve the accessibility of services for people in rural areas
58 Road traffic accidents: number of people and children killed or seriously injured	**DfT PSA 5** Reduce the number of people killed or seriously injured in Great Britain in road accidents by 40% and the number of children killed or seriously injured by 50%, by 2010 compared with the average for 1994–98, tackling the significantly higher incidence in disadvantaged communities
67 UK international assistance: Net Official Development Assistance: (a) per cent of gross national income (comparison with selected countries); (b) per capita (comparison with selected countries)	**DfID PSA 3** Improved effectiveness of the multilateral system, as demonstrated by: • a greater impact of EC external programmes on poverty reduction and working for agreement to increase the proportion of EC official development assistance (ODA) to low-income countries from its 2000 baseline figure of 38% to 70% by 2008 • ensuring that 90% of all eligible heavily indebted poor countries committed to poverty reduction that have reached decision point by end 2005 receive irrevocable debt relief by end 2008. Joint with HMT PSA 8 • international partners working effectively with poor countries to make progress towards the United Nations 2015 Millennium Development Goals. Joint with HM Treasury • improved effectiveness of United Nations agencies and the humanitarian aid system
68 Well-being: (well-being measures to be developed)	

Figure 1.2 Continued

schools, the counting of gifts of flowers, chocolates and of thank-you letters to nurses and the performance indices behind the payment of banking bonuses.

Two major spin-offs are apparent from such performance indices. First, the setting of 'targets', usually arbitrary values of a performance index which may be used to proclaim success. The second is equally pernicious: the development of computer models to predict and even manipulate future performance indices.

Targets in practice are particularly vulnerable to manipulation. Railway operating companies are set targets for the number of trains that arrive on time but the data are notoriously and blatantly fixed. Arrival times at intermediate stations are discounted entirely, so a train may be late at every station along its route but still be scored as 'on time' because it is not late in arriving at the final destination: to help achieve this, trains are calculated to have arrived 'on time' if they terminate within five minutes of the scheduled time and, to provide a little extra comfort, timetables often provide extra time along the final leg of the route. The setting of any target will inevitably cause managers to identify ways in which the data may be manipulated to achieve a good score. When this is done the effect of target setting is not what was intended and targets may have a reverse effect.[15]

The second spin-off is the use of computer models to forecast future performance by the use of:

> Pseudo-mathematical formulae providing models of behaviour that never quite fit what actually happens, in a way which resembles the physical sciences gone wrong: instead of equations describing reality, equations are used which describe ideal conditions and a theoretical reality of a type which never occurs in practice. Many disciplines suffer badly from envy of the physical sciences, of a world in which $f = mv$ means exactly what it says: academic economics has a particular case of physics-envy. Assumptions of rationally modelled behaviour are a big part of this wrong turn.[16]

Conclusion

The burden of this chapter is that the basic concept of sustainability is simple and the definition proposed in the Brundtland Report is succinct and clear:

> Ensuring that development meets the needs of the present without compromising the ability of future generations to meet their own needs.

However, it is a global objective, and there is no effective global authority providing the necessary leadership and initiative to drive the global policies necessary to reach this objective. Consequently, policy and its implementation must be left to national governments either acting alone or in consortia bound by agreement. The consortia may be broadly based, as with the European Union, or specific, as with Rio and Kyoto. In any event, the task is substantial and the means of addressing it limited, not by technology but by the confused political will. A combination of unwillingness and inability has led governments to resort to two levers:

1   market forces using prices and costs which are manipulated by taxation or set by a bureaucracy;
2   management theory based on scoring, targets and performance indices.

Given the limitations of these levers in setting and delivering objectives which have no true market value, the definition of sustainability has been made more deliverable by rendering it down to climate change, and within that, to the management of greenhouse gases.

So far as transport is concerned, the amount of GHG is largely a function of the energy used. In the main this is the petrol and diesel burnt in internal combustion engines but there is some consumption of electricity sourced from nuclear or renewable sources. Otherwise the energy comes from burning fossil fuel. This suggests the possibility of using the reduction in energy use as an acceptable objective, not only in its own right but also as a proxy for other objectives. For example, if the reduction of the conversion of land from agricultural to urban use is to be an objective, as has been identified in a number of past reports and policies, then if the measures taken to do that are successful, it will result in mean journey length being held in check which will partially stem the increases in vehicle kilometres which will, in turn, cut energy consumption. The relationship is a chain of rather indeterminate consequences but using fuel consumption as an indicator of the effectiveness of overall policy does seem to be a viable objective.

It is therefore suggested that the minimisation of the total transport fuel burn should be the inclusive objective of the efficacy of sustainable policy in the diluted form as it now stands, rather than the full Brundtland definition.

Notes

1 World Commission on Environment and Development (1987, p. 8). This report is usually referred to as the Brundtland Report, named after the Commission's Chairman.
2 HM Government (1994).
3 Royal Commission on Environmental Pollution (1994).
4 United Nations (1998).
5 United Nations (1998), *Article 2*.
6 See e.g. Department of Transport (1994), Para 1.11.
7 Department for the Environment, Food and Rural Affairs (DEFRA) (2005).
8 As an introduction to a considerable literature, see Surowiecki (2004); Lal (2006); Leadbeater (2009); and, for absolute prejudice, Goldberg (2007).
9 The nature and source of these ideas are explained in Harvey (2005).
10 Webb and Webb (1913).
11 *Oxford English Dictionary*: Old English 'let' meant to hinder or prevent.
12 Since 1797 British Acts of Parliament have been divided into Public General Acts which apply to everybody, everywhere, and Private Acts which apply only in specified circumstances: they are therefore commonly used to waive the prohibitions of Public Acts in particular circumstances. The King's Highway, defined before Parliament even existed, works as if it were a General Act capable of being waived by a Private Act (to legitimise a toll bridge, for example).
13 The most popular of the original spreadsheets, LOTUS 1-2-3, precursor of Microsoft's Excel, was published in 1983.

14 Harvey (2005).
15 Witness the famous example of a target maximum time for hospital emergency admissions to be left on trolleys before being moved to a proper bed. Managers took the wheels off the trolleys and called them beds.
16 Lanchester (2010, p. 117).

Chapter 2

The definitions

Transport

The *Oxford English Dictionary* offers a very restrictive definition of 'transport':

> To take or carry (people or goods) from one place to another by means of a vehicle, aircraft, or ship.

This definition is restricted in two undesirable ways:

1. Walking, the fundamental means of transport, would be excluded if movement were confined to mechanical means of transport, be they vehicles, aircraft or ships. Although escalators, conveyor belts, lifts and a panoply of mechanical handling equipment are not seen as 'vehicles', they transport people and goods for important, if not lengthy, distances. Transport should be defined to include all movement by all means.
2. The definition should not be restricted to the movement of people or goods. In Victorian times the source of domestic energy was carried by train and coal carts but is now brought to most homes by gas pipes and electricity cables: an obvious means of transport has been replaced by the less obvious. Similarly, most information now surges electronically through a global web of wires and cables, leaving a minority to be carried from place to place by messengers, postmen and commercial travellers. The definition of transport therefore needs to include the movement of:
   - people;
   - commodities (including raw materials, part-finished goods and liquids);
   - information;
   - energy;
   - waste.

The essence of transport is movement to a more desirable location.

The transport system

The transport system enabling this desirable movement is a collection of networks, vehicles and hardware all working in some sort of concert. The component networks are combinations of:

- Tracks, including footpaths, pipes, wires, air- and sea-ways as well as roads and railways.
- Vehicles, including anything with wheels.
- Interfaces between one method of transport and another.
- Power supplies, including on-board energy sources and their replenishment as well as external sources linked to vehicles by cable.
- Control systems, both formal (air-traffic control, railway signalling, mandatory traffic controls) and informal (conventions and 'rules of the road').
- Systems of ownership, regulation and management.
- Mechanical handling equipment, including escalators, cranes, conveyors, fork-lifts, even wheelbarrows.
- Hardware enabling commodities to be bundled into unit loads so they may be handled more efficiently. These include:
  - Pallets: small, simple platforms roughly a metre square, often made of wood, which may be loaded with goods and which are designed to be lifted by fork-lift trucks. Pallets are not stackable because the upper loaded pallets would weigh directly upon the loads below.
  - Stillages: small, sturdy metal cages with four legs, the feet of which are designed to make them stackable. Stillages must be moved and stacked by fork-lift trucks.
  - Cages: these are wheeled so may not be stacked but they may be pushed by hand or towed in trains by a small tractor.
  - Crates: usually small and light enough to be lifted and carried by hand when filled. Stackable and often designed for particular products as with beer crates.
  - Boxes and cartons: boxes are strong enough to be stacked but not very high.
  - Drums, barrels, etc.: to hold liquids. May be rolled but more usually are moved by fork-lift truck.
  - Containers: this used to be a generic term but it now means a large metal box designed to be stacked on-board container ships. Containers have to be extremely strong because at sea the sometimes violent movement causes a loaded container to exert considerable dynamic force upon those underneath it. Containers are consequently very heavy, even when empty. This makes them comparatively inefficient when being carried on land.

    It is useful to view many freight consignments as a sort of Russian doll structure: inside an international container there may be a number of pallets. Shrink wrapped on to each pallet may be a number of boxes; each box may contain a number of cartons; each of the cartons may contain a number of similar commodity items. Therefore any unit load may well be an amalgamation of sub-units. Shippers go to the expense of creating unit loads from sub-units just in order to make physical handling, checking and accounting easier: this advantage is particularly apparent if mechanical handling equipment is deliberately matched with the size, shape and weight of the unit loads it has to handle.

This list of network components is complex but the complexity is necessary. In

Chapter 1 it was argued that the minimisation of the energy used in transport and of the consequent CO_2 was the touchstone of a sustainable transport policy: reaching this objective depends upon an understanding of the complexities of the transport system. As a demonstration, it is often argued that a major step towards sustainability would be a policy to switch freight from road to rail, a suggestion driven primarily by the known lower costs and pollutions per tonne-kilometre for freight on rail rather than on road. Two levels of complexity throw doubt upon this policy as a general proposition:

1 The vast majority of freight consignments are moved between locations which cannot be directly served by rail, presenting a stark choice between:
    either
    - loading the consignment on to a lorry;
    - hauling it for the entire movement from origin address to the destination;
    - unloading;
    or
    - loading the consignment on to a lorry;
    - hauling to a railhead;
    - trans-shipping on to a rail wagon;
    - hauling the wagon to another railhead;
    - trans-shipping on to another lorry;
    - hauling to the destination;
    - unloading.
2 The second level of complexity lies in the nature of the trans-shipments from lorry to railway wagon. At its simplest, this may just be a matter of manhandling:
    - a labourer has to lift one unit load from within the overall consignment;
    - it has to be carried the relatively short distance from lorry to wagon;
    - placing it in the railway wagon;
    - the labourer has to return to the lorry.

The time taken between lifting one unit and the next is called the cycle time and this determines the productivity of the labourer and so the cost of the trans-shipment. Even so, the productivity depends upon the consignment being in an easily handled form: labourers are able to work all day lifting about 50 kg and nearly all societies have a unit of weight at about this size (the Imperial, pre-metric unit was a hundredweight (cwt = 112 lb = 50.8 kg): sacks and bags of many products commonly conformed to this weight).

It may be possible to reduce the cost of trans-shipment through slick, efficient handling but that depends upon the use of effective handling equipment and compatible unit loads, such as a combination of pallets and fork-lift trucks. If this is to be done, loads have to be unitised at the very beginning of the journey. Handling equipment costs money to acquire and operate, costs which must be spread over the loads handled. The additional cost will depend upon the total throughput – high and consistent volumes will justify the purchase of specialist handling equipment and will minimise the handling cost per unit shifted.

There are two conclusions which are important as generalisations:

1   The costs per metre shifted over the micro-distances covered in loading, unloading and handling are far greater than the haulage costs over the major stages of the journey and may well be the tipping factor in the choice of transport. For example, the cost of moving a sea-going container from the dockside on to a ship is approximately the same as that container being carried 5000 kilometres at sea.
2   An entire end-to-end movement is composed of a chained sequence of handling and of haulage but the handling itself also consists of mini-sequences of lifting, movement and placing. The entire end-to-end sequence and its component mini-sequences are inherently complex, and any transport policy, sustainable or not, must take this into account.

This subtle complication was demonstrated by some research into the possible development of the south side of the Humber estuary.[1] A factory making agricultural fertiliser used a granular raw material imported through the Port of Immingham, just 8 kilometres away. Power for the factory came from an on-site plant burning coal brought in from the Yorkshire coalfield, about 120 kilometres to the West. To the researchers' surprise, the granular raw material was moved the 8 kilometres from the dock to the factory by rail and the coal was hauled 120 kilometres by lorry. This was in direct contradiction to theory, which suggested that the low cost per tonne-kilometre by rail would make it the natural choice for the coal's long journey but the savings per tonne-kilometre by rail over lorry for the short distance from dock to factory would be insufficient to offset the costs of loading and then unloading the railway wagons. It transpired that the comparative haulage costs by road and rail were irrelevant: the crucial difference was in handling costs. The imported granular material could be craned out of a ship's hold and dropped into a hopper poised over the railway track. Railway wagons could then be loaded by gravity – the cheapest form of energy. Gravity was also used to unload the trucks; they were shunted over a pit and the doors in the bottom of the truck were opened and the granules fell into a chute feeding a conveyor belt.

The coal was quite different. The throughput was not sufficient to warrant anything more than a stockyard surrounded by a concrete wall within which the coal was stored as an extensive, flat heap about 2 metres high. It could then be retrieved as required by a modest, tractor-mounted shovel. This arrangement meant that each 20-tonne load of coal arriving from Yorkshire had to be delivered to a point 3 or 4 metres from the previous delivery. That could be done easily by eight-wheeled tipper lorry but not by railway wagon. It would have been possible for wagons to deliver their loads by gravity at a specific point as was done with the imported granules and, with some additional equipment, their loads could be pushed out to pile up along the flanks of the railway track, but it was impossible to deliver the coal by rail to the stockyard, each wagon-load just 3 or 4 metres from the previous one. That fact alone made the choice of tipper lorry rather than train inevitable. The case was a parable showing why transport policy cannot be based upon simplistic analysis of the comparative costs of movement over the major haul distances: the micro-distances involved in handling are very significant, and sometimes commanding.

Transport 'modes'

In the transport literature there is an almost universal distinction between 'modes' of transport: for example, the National Transport Model divides personal travel into journeys by car drivers, car passengers, rail, bus, walking and cycling,[2] distinctions that are both confusing and crude for three major reasons:

1. It confuses between tracks and vehicles: railways are a combination of specialist vehicles and very particular tracks, a combination that is clear and almost justifies rail being called a 'mode'. Nonetheless, a confusion remains between passenger and freight trains, each requiring different terminals and operating conditions, problems which may be solved by creating specialist lines: metro systems and the French TGV carry passengers only but the great majority of the North American railways are freight only.
2. Roads are a network of tracks with pedestrians and cyclists threading their way through a complex mixture of freight and passenger vehicles of very different performances. Some road capacity is lost to parked and stopped vehicles and to road-works accessing the sub-surface pipes and wires. Overall there is little definitive linkage between the track and the vehicles or between traffic and the people and commodities being moved. Hence neither the road network nor the flow of traffic on it may sensibly be seen as a 'mode'. The melange of different activities makes it difficult to separate them out, in turn making it very difficult to reach logical and effective decisions about how to manage the road network: the bickering about the need for bus lanes is an example.
3. The distinction between modes is not only confused but also crude. The National Transport Model and the official statistics use these definitions:
    - *Trip:* a one-way course of travel with a single main purpose.
    - *Mode and main mode:* trips may include more than one mode of transport, and each mode is recorded as a stage within that trip. When 'main' mode is used in the title of a table or chart this allocates information for the whole trip to the stage used for the greatest length (in distance) of the trip. When 'mode' is used this refers to information for individual stages of trips.

In fact most of the data in the National Travel Survey are for trips by 'main' mode, the mode used for the longest segment of the journey: the remainder of the journey is ignored.

Assigning a journey to the 'main' mode has led to the crude fiction that people make travel choices based solely upon the relative qualities of the available modes for the lengthiest, 'major' part of the trip, ignoring all the other aspects of the journey. This is completely at odds with the way in which people actually use the transport system. With the two exceptions of trips undertaken entirely by foot and by taxi, no trips are made end-to-end by a single mode: even car trips require an element of walking from a parking place to the destination. As a minimum, public transport trips involve a walk to a bus-stop or station and another walk to the destination. Contrary to the official statistics, nobody, but nobody, travels anywhere solely by bus – to do so, one would have to live at one bus-stop and work, shop and go to school at others. When planning or making journeys people have to consider the relative merits of alternatives which are all strings of segments including walking, interchanging, waiting and/or finding, capturing and retaining a parking space. People have to assess the risks of congestion and delay, how to cope with baggage, children and buggies, how to make sense of timetables, fares and booking, where to find somewhere to padlock a bike, or buy refreshments. The actual driving or riding along the 'main' mode is the easy part, just as sitting in an aircraft, not knowing or caring exactly where you are, is a relief after having to cope with checking in, departure boards and so on.

This official fiction that choices are made between 'main' modes on the simple criterion that one 'main' mode is better than another runs deep: the government's sustainable transport policies are based on promoting 'smart choices' between using public transport rather than a car as the 'main' mode.[3] Chapter 19 discusses the computerised models based upon this premise, models which predict travel demand and so influence policy decisions. For the time being, a short reflection upon how one's own personal travel choices are made will make it obvious that anticipated walking and waiting times within a complete end-to-end trip weigh heavily upon travel choices. One's own perceptions of entire end-to-end journeys influence the choice of destination as well as how to get there. The commercial success of the major supermarket chains rests upon easy parking to attract business away from shops where parking is difficult. Our personal choices clearly include parking problems and getting our shopping home, not just the balance between the actual journey by car or by bus. In general, the ease of travel on the 'main' mode itself is one contributory element in travel decisions but it is far from decisive.

Interfaces at which movements switch between one means of transport and another are a crucial part of any transport system. If the transport system is seen as a collection of 'main' modes there is an inevitable tendency to overlook the interfaces at which one mode inter-connects with another. This then fails to recognise the crucial importance of the delays and difficulties of interchanging as a powerful determinant of travel choices.

Inter-modal and multi-modal movement

It is very common for freight movements to involve trans-shipments: much of global production relies on international, sea-going containers to move semi-finished and finished products around the world. The containers and the matching handling equipment are designed to reduce trans-shipment costs between the ship and the landward transport of road, rail and inland waterway. This use of containers as a unit load common to more than one journey segment is termed 'inter-modal transport' and is characterised by the use of more than one 'mode' to move freight along the complete journey from start to finish, including the handling at trans-shipments by using containers with standard dimensions and handling characteristics to minimise handling costs. The fundamental characteristic of inter-modal freight is that the modes are complementary rather than competitive.

This very obvious, sensible idea of movement by combinations of mode has failed to take root in passenger transport theory. The basic problem has been quite obvious for over 40 years (Chapter 19 identifies 1968 as the date when it became apparent). Perversely, the passenger transport system is perceived as a set of self-contained, semi-autonomous rail, bus and road sub-systems, all mutually competitive, rather than complementary. A search of the Department for Transport website or a trawl of their publications over the past five decades will show document after document focused upon the problems and policies of particular modes. In 1998 the then government published what was intended to be a pivotal White Paper on transport policy: *A New Deal for Transport: Better for Everyone*.[4] It was supported by a string of 'Daughter Documents' on buses, walking, railways, ports and pedestrians, one for each of the individual 'modes'.

The failure to understand that the transport system is seen by its users as a single entity composed of complementary modes is due to inertia among the professionals responsible for creating the methodology used to predict personal travel. They have failed to see that all movement, not just freight movement, is 'inter-modal'. Personal travel is called 'multi-modal' rather than 'inter-modal', indicating that travel choices are perceived to be made between multiple competitive 'main' modes rather than combining modes into end-to-end journeys. This has been disastrous since the mistaken prediction of the amount of personal travel and of the conditions and subsequent costs of that travel has been driving transport policy and investment, resulting in poor decision-making and creating difficulties in addressing sustainability or any other coherent policy. For a while, politicians talked about 'joined-up policy-making' but there is no methodology by which this may be achieved.

Transport rhythms

All methods of transport have implicit rhythms, the combination of frequency and load size. This concept may be demonstrated using the example of shifting freight from road to rail. Let us assume a traffic consists of standard-sized pallets loaded with cartons which are stabilised on the pallet by shrink-wrapped polythene sheeting. They are taken from a warehouse by a single fork-lift truck and loaded on to a lorry with a floor area able to take 26 pallets. Let us assume it takes an average of two minutes for the fork-lift truck to locate the next pallet, lift it, take it to the lorry and place it, and then another 30 seconds to return: that gives a cycle time of 2.5 minutes. It will take $26 \times 2.5 = 65$ minutes to load the lorry.

Now let us presume it is a 50 km drive to the railhead and the lorry can achieve an average speed of 40 km/h. That gives a drive time of 75 minutes in both directions. We will also assume it takes another 65 minutes to transfer all 26 pallets to a rail wagon. The cycle time of the lorry is 65 minutes' loading time + 75 minutes' drive time + 65 minutes to unload + 75 minutes' return drive time = 280 minutes. If there are 60 pallets per rail wagon and 10 wagons, that is 600 pallets per train load. It will take 23 return journeys by the lorry to fill the train and that will take a total of 6440 minutes or 4.5 days. The three rhythms are shown in Figure 2.1.

Of course these rhythms are merely the product of the assumptions and if the assumptions had been different, so would the rhythms. However, irrespective of the

26 Transport

Method	Load (pallets)	Frequency
Fork-lift	1	1 load every 2.5 minutes
Lorry	26	1 load every 280 minutes
Train	600	1 load every 4.5 days

Figure 2.1 Transport rhythms in a hypothetical freight case

precise arithmetic, there are three important generalisations common to any set of assumptions:

1   The throughput is the same by all methods – in the above contrived example, all three methods carry 600 pallets in 4.5 days, the train in just one movement, the lorry in 23 return trips and the fork-lift truck in 600 separate movements.
2   All methods of transport have a rhythm: some, such as conveyors and escalators, run continuously and carry small incremental loads: others, like lifts and cars, run intermittently but frequently, carrying quite small loads, and still others, like trains, aircraft and ships, run infrequently but with large loads.
3   Wherever there is an interface between two methods of transport there is inevitable waiting – this is not evidence of inefficiency but an unavoidable consequence of disparate rhythms. In the above example, the fork-lift truck moves one pallet every 2.5 minutes' cycle time. The other 25 pallets which make up the lorry-load have to wait. As the loading proceeds, the place in which the pallets are forced to wait will be progressively moved from the warehouse to the lorry. The lorry itself will have to wait for the entire 65 minutes it takes to load it. Meanwhile the entire train of 10 wagons is doing nothing, waiting to be loaded: it will wait for 4.5 days.

For the journey from warehouse to train each pallet will be on the move, either by fork-lift truck or by lorry, for just 77 minutes: that is just over 1 per cent of the total time it takes to load the train – for 98.8 per cent of the time pallets will be unmoved, waiting to be loaded.

Goods in transit cost money: they are owned by somebody, having been bought or manufactured at some expense. They represent a capital investment using money borrowed from shareholders or lenders who will expect a return on their investment. The waiting time is therefore costly and the higher the value of the goods the more costly waiting time becomes. It is a truism that the speed of movement and the minimisation of waiting time is increasingly important as the value of consignments increases. In the above example, if the pallets were loaded with computers, the 4.5 days' transit time would be damning, but tins of chopped tomatoes could dawdle without crippling expense.

This problem of the inherent delay at interfaces between disparate rhythms affects passenger travel as well as freight. People walk to bus-stops and arrive in an intermittent dribble but the bus takes them away en masse. Consequently, bus-stops, a numerous but comparatively minor component of the transport system, are interfaces at which some waiting is inevitable. That waiting may be extended if the service is infrequent or unreliable – the rhythm of the buses is either slowed down or disrupted. The impact of the wait is commonly mitigated by providing a shelter, and the opportunity is often taken to combine this with advertising. This is taken one stage further at railway stations and airports in which more people spend more time: there, shops and cafés to soak up waiting times have become common.

As with freight handling, some interchanges are so complex and busy that micro-modes and micro-movements became important. Escalators, travelators and lifts all have their own intrinsic rhythms and associated interfaces: ancillary hardware in the form of trolleys and small electric vehicles for mobility-impaired people are often provided. At airports there are shuttles serving parking places and, at some airports, mobile lounges to serve the aircraft. The interface relies on passenger-handling equipment not dissimilar to the freight-handling equipment in inter-modal freight.

Interfaces between rhythms, coupled with the associated waiting and micro-movements, can be even more complex. In some instances the rhythms are so disparate that very extended waits are unavoidable. For passengers this is soaked up in hotels: airports have numerous related hotels and in the railway era all the mainline stations had an associated hotel – railway companies used to build and operate them. Even small railway stations often had a nearby pub called The Railway Arms or The Station Inn, reflecting the fact that waiting time was expected when changing from the pedestrian to the railway rhythm.

For freight, the disparate rhythms were accommodated in warehousing, goods sheds, etc. Ports with goods arriving and departing by ship with their inherent very slow, steady rhythms out of step with the quicker, shallower, landward rhythms of train, cart or lorry, needed massive floor space for warehousing.

Both hotels and warehousing, acting as the necessary buffer stores between rhythms, need still more micro-movements from the incoming method of transport into store and out again. For passengers this is usually by hotel shuttle, although in some places it is by travelator or a short walk. For freight it is an extra handling micro-segment. These hotels and warehouses acting as buffer stores are elements in the cost of movement and they are therefore an element in the overall transport system.

As the above example of an inter-modal traffic by lorry and train shows, long waits are not confined to the passengers and goods-in-transit. The handling equipment and vehicles themselves have periods of idleness forced upon them. For over four days the railway wagons are part-filled, waiting for the remainder of the load. The same is true of the lorry; it sits there being progressively loaded for a total of 23 times 65 minutes = 25 hours and another 25 hours being unloaded: that is, 46 per cent of the total lorry time spent on the task. (Again, the crucial point is not the seemingly exact figure of 46 per cent but the principle that loading and unloading creates significant lorry waiting time.)

Sometimes the waiting time during which goods are stacked in stationary vehicles can be deliberately extended, using the vehicles as small warehouses. Retaining a vehicle to be used as storage attracts an additional charge called demurrage. In today's cost-conscious world vehicles are turned around as quickly as possible to avoid demurrage but on the pre-Beeching railways it was common. Domestic coal was delivered by coal wagons to stations and held in the wagons for days, sometimes weeks, while the coal was gradually bagged and delivered. Clemens (2007) mentions the single weekly wagon from Nottingham to Lyme Regis carrying the stock replenishment for the Boots store there: much of the load was left in the wagon to be taken to the shop as and when the shelves needed refilling, something that must have been quite common for many small branch shops.

There is one final twist in the story of the interfaces between different rhythms. Before containers and unitisation came to dominate international freight transport, the break in rhythm was called a 'break of bulk', the place at which large but not necessarily homogeneous loads were broken down into smaller loads compatible with landward transport. Typically, then as now, manufacturing is best managed as a continuous process but the inputs of raw materials and components are delivered in surges, creating the need for operational storage to smooth out the intermittent deliveries into the continuous needs of production. Similarly, the continuous output cannot be delivered to customers in an unremitting, continuous trickle but has to be temporarily stored before being delivered in surges. Operational storage is an inherent part of all manufacturing.

It made sense to combine the operational storage needed to smooth manufacturing and the buffer storage needed to marry up the differing transport rhythms: then handling and the goods held in store could both be reduced. It thus made sense for many manufacturing plants to be sited in or near transport interchanges: the most obvious was 'port-related' industries in which flour mills, sugar refineries, etc. were set up in or near ports. The trend is less obvious now but it is still there: much of the electronics industry is sited near airports since their high-value goods need minimal transit times and are commonly air-freighted.

The historical patterns of land use, of industry and of transport interchanges were intertwined. Many towns and their trade were sited at points where trans-shipment was cheapest and easiest, not just at ports but at road bridges at the heads of the navigation of rivers, for example. It was common to site warehouses at such points in which to store goods as one rhythm melded into another. Today, the lower disparities of rhythm associated with consignments by lorry being so much smaller than by trainload, interchange warehousing is more related to the logistics centres sited at or near motorway junctions. The issue is presented in more detail in Chapter 8.

Notes

1   Harris *et al.* (1966).
2   Department for Transport (2009).
3   Cairns, Goodwin *et al.* (2004).
4   Department for the Environment, Transport and the Regions (1998).

Chapter 3

The definitions
Planning

The *Oxford English Dictionary* offers two definitions of the word 'plan':

1. *A large-scale, detailed map of a small area.* In common perception this is often a drawing of the layout of an existing building or, more commonly, a proposed development, perhaps just one building or, more likely, a larger area. The area may be quite complex; for example, the line of a proposed road.
2. *A scheme for accomplishing a purpose proposed.* This is essentially a list of actions which, when completed, will achieve a defined purpose.

These two definitions, although quite different, one a drawing and the other a series of actions, are clearly related. The drawing of a proposed development encapsulates the purpose of the plan and implies a set of actions, digging the foundations, building the walls, etc., which will accomplish that purpose.

The nub of planning of any sort, be it planning a town, planning one's own career or planning the economy, is the definition of purpose: without clearly defined objectives, the necessary actions cannot be sensibly arranged; nor can it be known whether the plan is being implemented effectively, or even at all.

The definition of objectives is absolutely crucial to effective planning: without them, actions are merely blind fumbles in an attempt to do something, no matter what, or, much more likely, to be seen to be doing something. This essentially purposeless action often has a hidden agenda: the real objective is for decision-makers to be seen to be active; moreover, the lack of an explicit, achievable objective has the very attractive, additional merit of hiding any failure to make a worthwhile difference – no explicit objectives, no sense of failure to meet them!

This rather cynical approach has already been hinted at in Chapter 1. The Brundtland Report set the sustainability agenda very widely, including an aspiration to address poverty by redistributing production and consumption rather than expanding it. But the subsequent Rio and Kyoto international conferences, while paying lip-service to the objective of global sustainability, actually redefined the problem by, first, making it a local rather than a global problem and then by massaging the broad Brundtland objectives down to an emphasis on the one issue of climate change and greenhouse gases. This effectively pushed the larger, thornier problems of the global inequalities of wealth and of the depletion of natural resources into the background.

Many people will argue that this selection of a component, tractable issue, rather than the less tractable problems of the global disparities of wealth, may have been undesirable but, nonetheless, inevitable: they will quote the dictum that 'politics is the art of the possible',[1] and that there is no sense in inviting failure by attempting the impossible, particularly no political sense, where so much now rests upon reputations and postures polished by press releases and the media.

Town and country planning

In Britain, 'planning' is often used as a shorthand for 'town and country planning', a comprehensive, country-wide system of land-use planning created by the Town and Country Planning Act of 1947. The objectives were set out in a preceding White Paper and were breathtakingly ambitious:[2]

> Provision for the right use of land in accordance with a considered policy, is an essential requirement of the Government's programme of post-war reconstruction. New houses, whether of permanent or emergency construction; the new layout of areas devastated by enemy action or blighted by reason of age or bad living conditions; the new schools which will be required under the Education Bill now before Parliament; the balanced distribution of industry which the Government's recently published proposals for maintaining active employment envisage; the requirements of sound nutrition and of a healthy, well-balanced agriculture; the preservation of land for national parks and forests; and the assurance to the people of enjoyment of the sea and countryside in times of leisure; a new and safer highway system better adapted to modern industrial and other needs; the proper provision of airfields – all these related parts of a single reconstruction programme involve the use of land, and it is essential that their various claims on land should be so harmonised as to ensure for the people of this country the greatest possible measure of individual well-being and national prosperity.

These aims were debated in Parliament while the Second World War was still raging and far from being won.[3] The White Paper and the consequent 1947 Act bore traces of past concerns over public health, housing, unemployment, social security, preservation and conservation, agriculture, transport and public welfare. This comprehensive approach had been prompted by the two major public traumas of the recent past: first, the economic privations of the 1930s, and second, the continuing World War of the 1940s. But the mood and style of the day had been caught three years earlier during Britain's darkest hour: the issue of *Picture Post*[4] of 4 January 1941 was a blueprint for the Welfare State. The issue was quite remarkable: totalitarian governments reigned over the whole of Europe; every centimetre of the coastline from the north of Norway to the Pyrenees was held by the Nazis; the United States was aggressively neutral; Germany and Russia were bound together in a non-aggression pact; the British Army had been evacuated from Dunkirk leaving most of their armaments behind; and, although the Battle of Britain had been won and had put a stop to daylight raids and the immediate threat of invasion, the night-time blitz continued. As this issue of *Picture Post* was being written, Bristol was reduced to a smoking ruin. Enemy bombers droned overhead at night and enemy submarines prowled British territorial waters. Britain was isolated and vulnerable. Despite all that, here was a popular magazine publishing a plan to be put into effect once the War had been won: it was audacious, defiant confidence.

Among sections in *Picture Post* on health, unemployment, education, agriculture, housing and leisure there was an article on town planning that listed objectives which were to appear, after some redrafting, in both the 1944 White Paper and, subsequently, the 1947 Act:

- everyone to live in cheerful, healthy conditions;
- slums to be demolished and replaced;
- civilise the industrial towns;
- plans to build housing, schools, hospitals, industry and transport.

Picture Post asserted that all this could not be achieved by haphazard, piecemeal actions but would have to be overseen by government. This is totally at odds with modern policy implementation which relies on a confusing mixture of budgets, initiatives, agencies and contracted private companies, but it was very understandable for its time. Wars of the devastating complexity of the Second World War cannot be waged, let alone won, by uncoordinated decision-making: to ask individuals to fight the Nazi threat in the hope that the sum of their decisions would be successful is a fanciful idea. Government was everywhere, directing industry; deciding who should be in the military and where the others should work; rationing food, clothing, fuel and raw materials; controlling the transport system and managing the 'War Effort'. Government was 'planning' and controlling the entire economy. Today's fight against global warming and pollution does not have the sense of urgency, nor the coherence driven by the pressing need for survival that dominated the 1940s.

This poses the question why that wartime intrusion into daily life was acceptable; why the restrictions upon personal and corporate freedoms did not spark widespread dissent. The answer is found not so much in the text of *Picture Post* as in the advertisements:

- 'Doubtless you already own a radio – make do with it for the time being. If you really need a new one you will be glad to know a few new instruments are trickling through but government contracts take precedence.'
- 'Food is a munition of war. Don't waste it.'
- 'Don't let coughs keep you off duty: take Kay's cough mixture.'
- 'Yesterday it was an office block: today a mass of rubble, but HP sauce is always the same.'

There was palpable sense of common purpose, some of it a simple, unthinking wish to survive, but much of it was a realisation that, if the country were to survive, society had to work in concert, not in competition: 'pulling one's weight' or 'doing one's bit' was a constant personal concern. 'Keep calm and carry on' was more than a passing giggle; and, of course, such socially cohesive concerns were used to assess the behaviour of others.

The conclusion should be not just that 'planning' must have clear objectives but that those objectives need to be embraced by enough people to create a common purpose in delivering them. Therein lies a paradox: the emergence of a sense of 'common purpose' is not dependent exclusively upon coincident thinking by a significant number of individuals: it must be more than that. There must be a core agreement, not only about objectives, but about the actions needed to achieve those objectives and that concurrence will only gel given an element of leadership. A collection of like-minded individuals may provide the seed-bed for action but the cooperation and mutually supportive actions necessary to deliver such common aspirations must be orchestrated. In the Second World War there was a very clear common objective but the actions required to reach it were choreographed and articulated by leaders such as Churchill, Eisenhower and members of the government, Parliament and the military.

This adds a further crucial component to a planning process: there must be a system to define and then implement objectives. The 1947 Town and Country Planning Act did this by creating mechanisms which are still in use today, although, after some modification, not all of it constructive:

- Those wishing to 'develop' land had to obtain planning permission from the local planning authority (the local council). 'Development' was comprehensively defined as:

    The carrying out of building, engineering, mining or other operations in, on, over or under land or the making of any material change in the use of buildings or other land.[5]

    To make the need for permission quite unambiguous, the Act had two supporting regulations:
    1   *The Use Classes Order.* A list of defined uses enabling the definition of 'a material change of use' to be a change from one class to another: permission was not needed for a change of use within a class. The order has been almost continuously tinkered with, tinkering that, for example, enables petrol filling stations to be local convenience shops as well.
    2   *The General Development Order.* This was a particularly clever piece of legislation. There are many trivial changes in use – the erection of a garden shed or loft conversion – but, instead of exempting these trivialities from the need for permission (which would have made the Act itself applicable in some instances and not in others, creating possible legal disputes over the distinction), the Act required everything to acquire planning permission, but then gave automatic, deemed permission for any trivialities listed in the General Development Order. It was a very neat way of turning a negative

process (these trivialities are exempt from the need for permission) into a positive one (these trivialities do need permission but it will be given automatically).
- Legal persons (meaning individuals, firms or other organisations) may apply for planning permission but permissions are granted to the property, not to the applicant. Hence if a property changes hands, any granted permissions will go with it and not be retained by the seller.
- Applications must be quite specific, showing a plan of the exact site and of what is being proposed.
- Applications may be granted, or granted subject to specific conditions or refused, but a refusal or the imposition of conditions must be supported by explicitly stated reasons.
- Those reasons must refer to the provisions of an approved plan, itself composed of a map or maps, coupled with a statement of policies; such as that all proposed buildings must be no higher than x metres, or no nearer than y metres to another building. This ensures that applications are not determined on whimsy but are clearly related to a known plan which must have been subject to public consultation and approval by the local planning authority.
- Refusal to grant permission or to impose conditions may be appealed with all the arguments and documents in the public domain.

The link between land-use planning and transport

All movements start and finish at specific addresses at which there is a land use and, very probably, buildings with permission for the floor space to be used for particular activities. This sounds draconian but it does not imply that every square metre of floor space has to have a certified use: Town and Country Planning Law is concerned primarily with change of use, not with the use itself. With some minor, unimportant exceptions, a legal right exists to continue the current use of both land and floor space; permissions are only required for changes from the existing use, and even then only if there is to be a move from one use-class to another or if the proposal is not covered by an automatic 'deemed' permission.

The planning system is unable to control the demand for transport by edict but it can influence patterns of transport by managing the changes in land use. In the jargon, land uses are said to 'generate' movement. Some places, such as shopping malls, will generate much coming and going but others, such as individual homes, comparatively little. In some areas of dense development there may be a cluster of small generators which will collectively produce a lot of movement; some places may generate movements by a mixture of transport methods, including pedestrians, buses, lorries, bikes, cars, etc.; others, like petrol filling stations, may be quite limited in the range of transport methods. Some, such as 24-hour shops, will generate movement throughout the day, and others only intermittently or even seasonally (e.g. the Wimbledon tennis courts).

One quite common reason for refusing planning permission is because the expected number and style of movements could not be accommodated by the local transport system, either because the local networks would be unable to cope with the extra flow or because the local configuration would be unsafe due to poor sight distances at the site accesses. For these reasons, for refusal to be legally valid there would have to be transgressions of the policies and criteria set out in the approved plan.

This posed, and still poses, a technical issue. For a refusal based on lack of capacity or poor access to be legally valid, there has to be some quantification of the problem: it is not sufficient to allege that a proposed development would generate too much traffic. For a refusal to withstand an appeal by the applicant against the refusal, there has to be, first, some sort of estimated generation by the proposed development and, second, a measure of how much extra traffic, if any, may be absorbed by the local network. The second issue, essentially about network capacity, is quite technical and complicated and will have to wait until Chapter 19. But estimating the movement generated by a proposed development may be done quite simply by using the TRICS[6] database or some other, similar tariff.

There also needs to be some reassurance that the capacity of the water, gas, electricity and sewerage networks will also be able to cope with the increased demand, and this too needs methods of calculating the extra loads and establishing that there is enough unused capacity to deal with them.

This gives a clue to another type of problem mentioned previously in Chapter 1. The additional demands for transport and utility services generated by one comparatively small development may be within the network capacity, but a combination of demands from a number of comparable developments might be overwhelming: this could be a tripwire if there is a discontinuous stream of separate but similar applications. This is another facet of the perception of whether a large issue is the sum of smaller issues or whether a small issue is a subdivision of a larger one. It may be epitomised by the raw sewage from one rural cottage being discharged into a stream having no terrible effect, but if a whole village does the same thing, the stream will be polluted beyond recall. For this reason planning cannot work on precedent: if permission is granted for one new house, it does not follow that subsequent applications should be given permission. In general, the aggregation of small issues may well create a problem which is not just of a different scale but of a different nature. It was once neatly encapsulated:

> The aggregate of decisions made by individuals may produce a situation that has a feed-back effect upon the individuals who make them, modifying the satisfactions that they had hoped to achieve.[7]

The link between transport and land-use planning

The causal relationship in which land use generates movement can be reversed. Permission to develop a site is unlikely to be sought unless it is served by all the necessary communications and transport services. It follows that if the transport, communications and utility systems are extended, opportunities to develop those sites with improved services may well be taken up. The classic case is the M25, the motorway which in 1986 completed the encirclement of London, enhancing the accessibility of a swathe of land through the Home Counties.

Section between junctions	Date opened	Forecast flow	Actual flow 1992	Multiplier (forecast to actual)
1–2				
2–3				
3–4	February 1986	69,000	76,000	1.10
4–5	February 1986	69,000	78,000	1.13
5–6				
6–7				
7–8				
8–9	October 1985	55,000	107,000	1.95
9–10	October 1985	62,500	109,000	1.74
10–11	December 1983	75,900	129,000	1.70
11–12	October 1980	82,800	146,000	1.76
12–13				
13–14	August 1982	97,100	162,000	1.67
14–15	December 1985	103,000	152,000	1.48
15–16	September 1985	100,000	143,000	1.43
16–17	January 1985	87,000	120,000	1.38
17–18				
18–19				
19–20	October 1986	59,500	110,000	1.85
20–21	October 1986	59,000	113,000	1.92
21–22	October 1986	41,500	106,000	2.55
22–23	October 1986	56,500	114,000	2.02
23–24				
24–25				
25–26	January 1984	70,000	106,000	1.51
26–27	January 1984	76,000	95,000	1.25
27–28	April 1983	69,000	107,000	1.55
28–29	April 1983	60,000	93,000	1.55
29–30	December 1982	61,000	89,000	1.46
30–31				
31–1				

Figure 3.1 Traffic flows on the M25
Source: Data taken from Department of Transport (1994) fig. 5.1.

The forecasts shown in Figure 3.1 were made using the then standard methodology: a computer map of the road network without the new road was loaded with existing traffic volumes. The new road was added to the map and, assuming that traffic would switch from the existing roads to the new one if it made for a quicker journey, the flows were reloaded on to the enhanced network. These flows were then increased according to the expected rate of traffic growth. The forecast therefore contained an element of 'extra' traffic due to the trend of increasing car ownership and use. The flows predicted for each section of the M25 were therefore based on a combination of two sources of change: first, traffic changing route from the older roads to the new one because it afforded a faster journey, and second, the overall trend towards more traffic due to increased car ownership and use.

However, Figure 3.1 shows that traffic on the M25 was more than had been forecast and, on some sections, much more. The Department of Transport speculated that some of the unexpected additional traffic was due to a combination of the new road enticing some people to make more or longer car journeys and some people to switch from other 'modes'; in other words, that the size and nature of generation rates in the areas served by the M25 had changed. However, it was also believed that some of the extra traffic was due to new developments of land which was now more accessible. The data at hand did not show the weights of the various possible components of the unexpected increases but the data did conclusively show that the construction of the M25 had itself created extra traffic.

It is slightly shocking that this conclusion was thought to be rather daring at the time. That new transport infrastructure can create extra movement had been seen before at many other times and in other places. The development of the areas served by the extension of London's Metropolitan Railway was thought to be so likely that the company bought up the land to be served by the new railway and made a considerable profit from the increases in value due to the improved accessibility. In the 1930s new roads were funded in part by buying a wider strip of land than was necessary to accommodate the road and funding the road construction costs by selling off the extra flanking plots for houses or factories. The development of the land accessed by the new railroads in the Wild West of America is not just a matter of record but the basis of quite a few Westerns. More recently, land near airports and motorway junctions has both increased in value and in its power to generate traffic due to its excellent accessibility.

It is clear that the value and rate of development of land has a self-referential relationship with the levels of service delivered by the transport, communications and utilities networks. The relationship works in one sense by taking up the as-yet unused capacity in the local networks and it works in the opposite sense when the networks are improved, inducing the development of land which is now better served. This confused relationship is difficult to unravel, and the M25 is a good case in point. It was initially built as a 2×3-lane motorway but it generated so much additional traffic due to new development creating extra traffic that it has become congested, presumably then choking off further generation: the M25 has switched from facilitating development to constraining it. The congestion created political pressures, resulting in a widening of the M25, lifting the constraint but creating more development and more traffic and more congestion: once again capability flipped into constraint. It is a process that has been compared to throwing food to pigeons: the more food, the more pigeons, and so the food per pigeon remains constant.

This relationship is another facet of a major planning issue that has already been touched upon: is overall development the sum of a number of separate sites or is site development a subdivision of overall development? It would appear that site development is manageable by the planning system overseeing each application but the criteria, enshrined in the approved Plan, may well fail to pay sufficient attention to the sum of many site applications. On the other hand, large step improvements to the transport networks such as the Metropolitan Railway or the M25 create a backdrop to a surge in applications. This is a substantial issue in predicting the outcomes of any capital expenditure on the transport system: should the objective be left at seeking some optimal balance between the transport system and the patterns of land use or should the target be sustainability or climate change characterised by the minimisation of CO_2? If keeping CO_2 in check is to be the target, then the methodology of assessment needs to be modified. It is this issue that occupies much of the rest of this book.

The changing structure of urban areas

The interplay between changes in the transport system and in the patterns of land use is well demonstrated by the changes that have occurred in the size and structure of urban areas. Figures 3.2a, 3.2b and 3.2c show a time series of maps of the western suburbs of Edinburgh. There is no particular significance in the dates – 1928, 1964 and 2000 – nor in the choice of West Edinburgh: the maps happened to be at hand. More or less the same story could be demonstrated with maps of other Edinburgh suburbs, or similar maps of any British city.

In effect, these three maps are just three still frames taken from a movie of continuous urban development. The story behind the movie is one of changing patterns of the relative ease of movement and of the differences in accessibility that were created. The 'panhandle' of development marked 'A' was originally a line of factories powered by the rushing waters of the Water of Leith. Energy from water wheels had to be transmitted from source to point of use by belts and pulleys, a system that is mechanically efficient in a vertical rather than horizontal direction, leading to tall factories with a comparatively small footprint and with the machinery located on a number of floors. With the river banks dominated by a string of water-powered factories, the housing for the workers had to be elsewhere, although, of course, within walking distance. The river was fast and shallow, good as a source of energy but hopeless for transport, so raw materials and products had to be carted along the parallel road which then became the spine of the housing. Hence the panhandle development that is still evident today.

The development at 'B' occurred later, and demonstrates the continuing interplay between transport and land use with shifting constraints and opportunities driven by changing accessibilities. By this time energy from water wheels had been supplanted by coal-powered steam-engines. Energy still had to be moved within a factory by belts and pulleys, retaining the need for tall factories with small footprints and a high density of jobs per unit area but now the factories had to be sited alongside the railways where coal could be delivered cheaply. The railways already existed but were built to serve the centres of early Victorian cities and so they were radial. Area 'B' is a neat parable of transport investment being first attracted by development (railways to the centre), followed by development being attracted to the transport (building factories at the trackside) and then followed by more transport investment attracted to the developed factory site (the building of direct connections into individual factories).[8] With rail-side land dominated by coal-driven industry and a high density of employment, but with people still walking to and from work, housing had to be high-density too, in conditions that came to be called 'slums'.

Figure 3.2a Edinburgh, west and northwest suburbs (1928)
Source: Reproduced from the Ordnance Survey sheet with the permission of the National Library of Scotland.

A big jolt occurred towards the end of the nineteenth century. Cheap mass urban transport by electric tram[9] meant that large areas of land became accessible to anybody who could afford the tram fare, and, with increasing prosperity, that came to include most people. Developers were quick to build new housing on the land brought within acceptable journey times of the city centre and of the industrial inner suburbs, and cities expanded at an unprecedented rate for the first three decades of the twentieth century.

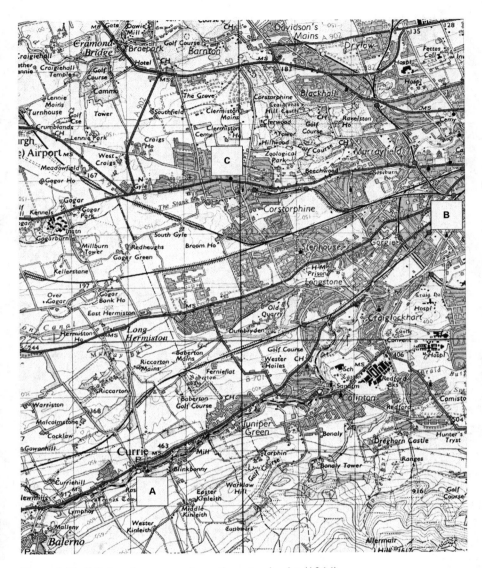

Figure 3.2b Edinburgh, west and northwest suburbs (1964)
Source: Reproduced from the Ordnance Survey sheet with the permission of the National Library of Scotland.

However, the expansion was unevenly distributed. Tramways are a considerable capital investment and must be used intensively with frequent, well-filled trams if they are to make financial sense. This high level of service provides very high accessibility levels to land within easy reach of a tram route, in contrast with other land, but tram

Figure 3.2c Edinburgh, west and northwest suburbs (2000)
Source: Reproduced from the Ordnance Survey sheet with the permission of the National Library of Scotland.

financing only allowed for comparatively sparse tram networks: there was no sense incurring the high cost of more routes if they jeopardised the patronage on the existing routes. Northeast Edinburgh, marked 'C', was not served by tram at all until 1923 when the line to Corstophine was opened. The road from the City Centre to Blackhall and on to Cramond never carried trams and was left with spot developments around the railway stations.

The high but selective accessibility provided by tram routes led to a new trend in the geography of urban areas. To this day the old tram routes in Edinburgh and elsewhere are still lined with small shops attracted by the high footfall of people using the trams. The demand for new, improved housing was high but the land liberated by the trams was limited, creating characteristic housing forms. In England this was terraced housing, usually with small gardens front and back; in Scotland with its different law on land tenure, the form was the walk-up tenement of the type shown in Figure 4.6. The tram era demonstrated the symbiotic nature of land use and transport: trams needed high levels of patronage and served limited areas. Those areas were developed at densities that provided the levels of demand to sustain the trams.

But this was to change. The next still from the movie, Figure 3.2b, the map for 1964, shows a different urban form. The trams had disappeared from Edinburgh's streets seven years previously but their effect on Edinburgh's geography had waned substantially before that. In 1928 18 per cent of journeys by public transport in Edinburgh were by bus but 12 years later the percentage had risen to 30 per cent. Buses had the considerable advantage over trams in that they did not have to carry the very considerable cost of the track. That released them from the financial necessity of running very intensive services. Buses could work profitably at lower frequencies and this meant in turn that they could provide a much denser network of routes extending into a much wider area. That extended acceptable levels of accessibility to the areas within the city that trams had not previously covered and also brought public transport to peripheral areas previously not served at all. The proliferation of bus routes in the 1930s improved accessibility to extensive areas of land, enabling cities to extend significantly. The demand for housing was still high but with so much land available for development, housing could now be built at much lower densities spread over much wider areas, as exemplified by the area flagged as 'C'.

This produced the 1930s housing boom typified by semi-detached housing and bungalows, many with quite substantial gardens: a density never before seen. Much of the undeveloped land of Northwest Edinburgh (seen in the 1928 map in Figure 3.2a) had been developed by 1964. Beyond the area shown in the maps, Edinburgh's girth increased as public transport extended into the periphery. However, one characteristic remained. All public transport tends to be radial, although the more flexible finances of buses did allow for a few tangential routes. The city centre remained the shopping and commercial core with the inner suburbs retaining their emphasis upon industry and employment. This configuration created a strong radial, and rush hours became a feature of public transport in all major cities.

The use of public transport peaked in 1950 and began to wane as car ownership and use became more common. Cars have created a completely different urban form exemplified by the last of the maps (see Figure 3.2c). In many respects cars are the complete antithesis to public transport, which runs necessarily on set, mainly radial routes to a timetable, and therefore provides selective accessibility to a restricted number of places at particular times. Cars are, in effect, infinitely frequent and able to take people in any direction at any time. Public transport works best if journeys are concentrated in direction and with good loadings. Cars work best if travel is diffused over all directions and with as little concentration by time and space as possible; otherwise they precipitate congestion.

Individual vehicles make virtually everywhere constantly accessible. Consequently they make a mass of land so accessible that it is open to the possibility of development. But cars have one very considerable disadvantage apart from their inability to provide high rates of flow without congestion. They need parking space. An average car spends roughly 98 per cent of its life parked up.[10] The footprint of an average car is roughly 12 square metres, but it will require 20 square metres of floor space when parked off-street because it will need its share of circulation space. Probably more telling, when parked on the street, a car needs about 5.25 metres of kerb space. Road and kerb space of this size is in very limited supply in city centres.

This creates a paradox. City centres, the places of the greatest need of accessibility, are not readily accessible by car, partly owing to congestion on the approaches but mainly because of the difficulty in finding, capturing and keeping a parking place. In contrast, wherever the need for accessibility is much lower, cars are more able to provide it. But the paradox becomes an enigma. The inability of city centres to cope with cars has been resolved by drivers using the almost infinite flexibility of car use to go somewhere else in preference to going to the city centre. It seems that car use not only creates congestion and parking problems but also provides their solution by drivers choosing to go somewhere less congested and with plenty of parking space. It is this mechanism that has changed urban geography. This echoes the issue that has already been raised: are large decisions little more than aggregated, small, individual decisions or are the small, individual, tactical decisions a by-product of large, corporate, strategic decisions? In the case of individual motorists eschewing the city centre in preference for some alternative, that alternative has first to be developed by some corporate decision. Private transport choices must be made after land-use choices.

The first modern, self-service supermarket was opened by Sainsbury's in Croydon in 1950, although it had no car-park and shoppers still had to carry their bags of shopping home on the bus.[11] Nevertheless, it triggered a trend, and the supermarket companies, realising that a supermarket without a car-park was in a financial straitjacket, sought sites in the suburbs. These were in short supply, a supply still further restricted by local planning authorities being antagonistic due to the traffic implications, coupled with an awareness that decentralisation might undermine the viability of town centres. The turning point in Britain was in 1979 when the newly elected government ordered a presumption in favour of planning permission being granted unless there were substantial reasons for refusal. The underlying, but unstated, theory was that the desire of the individual to shop by car was politically more important than the sustenance of town centres. By 1972 the applications to build out-of-town supermarkets, hypermarkets, shopping malls, factories and warehouses had begun to roll in. Individual travel choices had been facilitated by, first, government policy on land-use planning, and, second, by company decisions to develop the suburban and out-of-town sites which became available as a result.

Figure 3.2c has a shopping mall marked at 'D' but nearby are three other examples of the changes in urban geography wrought by the escalation of car use. There is a 'business park' just across the road consisting of office blocks backed by car-parks. These are insufficient and the roads are choked with parked cars. This problem spreads into the adjacent industrial estate. In contrast to the tall factories of yesteryear, these are all single story. Each piece of machinery is now individually powered by electric motors, making the central power source and the associated belts and pulleys a thing of the past. Without the need to distribute power from a single source, the main control upon factory design is now the movement of goods within the factory, often by fork-lift truck, and that needs solid, flat floors.

The third piece of evidence of the effect of car use is the housing built near South Gyle Station. Unlike the housing on the other side of the railway, built when the bus was the major mode of urban travel, the new housing is at a much lower density with a complex, open, road network. Most of the houses are detached with gardens.

Not shown on the sample maps but also the product of car use are the out-of-town housing developments usually connected to villages and country towns some way away. They are part of the new 'virtual city', disaggregated and scattered around the countryside, linked to the city by commuter car trips: they are exemplified by the type of development shown in Figure 4.8.

In conclusion, the past 100 years have seen a progressive loosening of the fabric of the city. The tightly packed Victorian city in which people walked from place to place and goods were carried by train and then distributed by local horse and cart has been supplanted by a loosely packed, dispersed collection of land uses in which parking has proved to be a major determinant. The city has spread, covering a far wider area and creating the need for longer journeys. Those journeys are much less tidal than they used to be and are diffused in time and space, making them difficult if not impossible to make by anything other than a car. The property values in the city centres have been retained and, with them, the intensity of use which, through the consequent congestion and parking problems, force them to continue to rely on access by public rather than private transport.

The stark problem which has to be addressed is how to create and implement a sustainable transport policy within an urban geography that has developed over the past 50 years or so to accommodate the car and which now very often demands the use of a car. It is a problem unlikely to be resolved easily, quickly or with the wave of some magic wand.

The planning process

The seeds of the British planning system were sown many years before the 1941 issue of *Picture Post*, the White Paper on land use or the 1947 Town and Country Planning Act. Plato's *Republic* introduced the notion of an ideal Utopia: Romans planned their towns; kings set out grand legacies like Versailles; the new cities of North America were formally geometric as were new settlements founded by many landlords in Britain – Ullapool was laid out as a grid long before Milton Keynes. Utopian planning as a solution to filth, squalor and social problems of the emerging industrial cities was put into practice in the factory villages of New Lanark and Saltaire. The later Garden Cities movement was a deliberate attempt to provide idealised living conditions, both physical and moral, for the workers in the growing industrial cities. But it was Geddes[12] who spelt out a planning process, rather than remedial objectives, with his seminal proposition: '*Survey, Analysis, Plan*'.

This became almost a planning mantra and suggests a logical sequence of survey (to identify problems), analysis (to establish their size and nature) and plan (to do something about them). However, Geddes did not think officials should do this in sequence: he thought there should be a continuous process of public participation, of suggestion, counter-suggestion and debate facilitated by an ongoing public exhibition and forum. He even established one in Edinburgh with a *camera obscura* atop of it. The 1947 Act did incorporate a considerable element of public participation: draft plans have to be published, sent out to public consultation and considered at a public inquiry before they are approved. It is a lengthy and convoluted business, frequently decried, but the criticism is too often directed at the system rather than the principle.

The system as it stands echoes the ancient ideas of utopia: the planning of a city some years ahead in which the problems of today have been resolved. This is termed 'End-State Planning' in which a 'Plan' of what the city will look like in some future design year is created in response to the perceived problems of the existing city. The flow chart is shown in Figure 3.3. This is a linear process just as the stylised Geddes suggestion of 'Survey, Analysis, Plan' but, unlike Geddes' suggestion the public are not asked to contribute to the Plan, only to comment and validate it well after the draft has been completed

In practice the process in Figure 3.3 is flawed:

- There is a tendency for the problems and solutions to be paired, making the Plan little more than a compendium of compartmentalised projects.
- In the period between identifying the existing problem and the design year, the nature, importance and urgency of the problems is likely to change.
- The identified resources available to implement the projects will also change.
- The Plan will fragment and become redundant due to its inherent inflexibility.

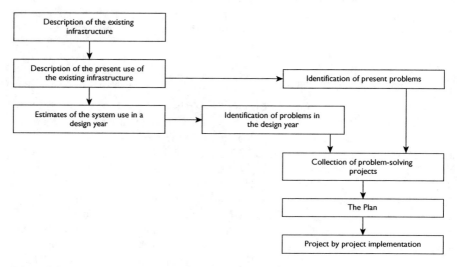

Figure 3.3 The linear, end-state planning process

Linear plans to deliver semi-utopian 'end states' are invariably overtaken by events and are often doomed to sit on a dusty shelf along with their predecessors, all tending to address yesterday's problems and rendered impotent by their inability to adjust and re-prioritise the project list as circumstances change.

This criticism is particularly true of transport planning. Due mainly to the dominance of 'modes' in official thinking, transport planning is too often characterised by a wish-list of mode-specific projects for which all or part of the funding melts away. The archives show regular White Papers defining sets of projects which have never come to fruition.

Planning as management: steering by iterative correction

It is sobering to realise that some of the most important technical steps forward are made to meet the needs of warfare. Not just trivia like cardigans and Wellington boots, but crucial abilities such as making workable cylinders and pistons for steam-engines using the techniques for boring cannons; or the mass production of internal combustion engines, lorries and aeroplanes in the First World War; or the creation of computers, operations research and cybernetics in the Second World War. It is not so much the creation of fundamental ideas but the hastening of design and development. The thought sneaks in that perhaps the wartime suspension of market forces, competition and the price mechanism as the tools to manage the country might have something to do with it: perhaps effort then goes into delivering what is needed rather than what is profitable.

Weiner (1948) developed practical work on gun laying in the Second World War into a theory of system control of everything from animals, to machines and to national governments. The crucial idea was 'feedback': having defined an objective, a track of the changes needed to reach that objective must be made and then actions must be taken to implement the step-by-step changes necessary to follow that track. The effects of these actions must be monitored and the results compared with the track as designed; if reality conforms to the desired track then all is well; if not, the deviation must be corrected by modifying subsequent actions. This is the fundamental notion of 'error actuated feedback', the basis of control systems.

This is essentially steerage. Aircraft pilots are given destinations and routes. Using satellite positioning technology, they know where they are, and, if this is not where they should be (perhaps due to cross-winds), the plane has to be steered to correct the error. If the plane is on autopilot this will be done automatically with the position of the plane being scanned second-by-second and the necessary changes made. Sensing the deviations from the planned route and making the necessary corrections may be a blur of very fast, small, incremental steps, but, on occasion, the destination and route may have to be changed, perhaps because a passenger is taken seriously ill; or an engine malfunctions; or the destination airport is struck by an emergency. First, a new objective and a track leading to it will have to be defined and a few very substantial and deliberate reactions made to steer the plane on to this new track. This facet of steerage is crucial – it allows for the possibility of the defined objective itself being changed, a possibility which does not sit too well with an objective of creating a utopia. The steerage process is enabled by a 'system' composed of sensors to monitor changes in the 'system state', servos (mechanisms that create changes in the system state), a communications net carrying information from the sensors and instructions to the servos, and controllers that set the objective, the desired track, and send instructions to the servos. In the aircraft example the satellite navigation system acts as the sensor; the servos are the plane's flaps and rudder; the communications are the combination of the on-board hydraulic and electronic networks, together with the radio messages; and the controlling mechanism a combination of the pilots, air-traffic controllers on the ground and on-board electronics. In all, this amounts to a subtle mixture, giving, in combination, a 'system'.

Adam Smith (1776) had grasped the essence of cybernetics well before Weiner:

> Systems in many respects resemble machines. A system is an imaginary machine invented to connect together in the fancy those different movements and effects which are already in reality performed.[13]

Error actuated feedback and steerage are the implicit characteristics of the market: shifts in prices are the messages transmitted to both suppliers and consumers to steer production and consumption to an equilibrium: Adam Smith's 'Invisible Hand' is actually steering. The problem with a reliance upon market forces is not that the error actuated feedback mechanism is faulty but that the objective, and therefore the track, remains implicit: the assumption is that the aggregate of consumer desires and the self-interested actions they take to satisfy those desires is itself a suitable objective. That precludes other objectives such as winning a war, or addressing climate change or global inequality.

It is clear that 'end-state' planning (shown in Figure 3.3) cannot be a flexible cybernetic system since there is no feedback and so no ability to understand whether the objectives and actions specified in the Plan are appropriate, effective, or even possible, and hence no ability to update or modify them. If we are to address environmental issues, climate change or global inequalities by local, national or international policies, we need a system which is flexible and responsive. 'End-state' planning, as created by the 1947 Act with the end state defined by an approved Plan, is no longer fit for purpose.

McLoughlin (1969) suggested a cybernetic systems approach and this, in combination with a report by the 'Planning Advisory Group', had a partial effect through the 1971 Town and Country Planning Act but the possibility of monitoring and flexing the objectives of Plans was still not understood. This was probably because the implicit objectives were still those of post-war Britain, still a response to the twin trauma of the 1930s depression and the 1940s violence, still national rather than global goals.

It is here argued that, if the current global economic, climatic and military instabilities are to be addressed, objectives will have to shift in their natures and priorities and we will need to establish mechanisms by which this may be done. A proper planning system incorporating feedbacks is necessary: such a system is shown in Figure 3.4.

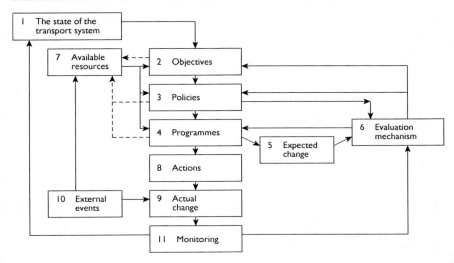

Figure 3.4 The recursive, flexible planning process

This flow chart is not merely a proposed system: it explains the structure of the rest of this book, with each of the remaining chapters being related to one of the numbered boxes.

Notes

1. Otto von Bismark (1867).
2. Ministry of Housing and Local Government (1944).
3. It was debated in Westminster at the same time as the Battle of Arnhem was being lost.
4. This was a weekly magazine carrying large numbers of photographs. In an era without television it took the place of the news and current affairs programmes. It was hugely popular, selling close on two million copies a week, and was handed around in barracks and air-raid shelters until it was in shreds.
5. Town and Country Planning Act 1947, Section 12(2).
6. **T**rip **R**ate **I**nformation **C**omputer System, a database created in 1989 by a consortium of local authorities to show the measured numbers of trips generated by developments. Many new developments are monitored by local authorities after they have been built and reported to the database. The data are presented as trip rates per square metre of floor space, per employee or using some other unit rate.
7. Hibbs (1974).
8. Even as late as 1956 there were 144 places in Edinburgh and another 82 in Leith at which rail freight could be handled (British Transport Commission 1956). Now there is none.
9. Perversely, Edinburgh's trams were not initially electric but hauled by sub-surface cables. They were converted to electricity in 1922 (Hunter 1999).
10. The average annual distance covered per car is about 13,000 km, and if the speed averaged over the year is 70 km/h, then the car is being driven for 185 hours: about 2.1 per cent of the year.
11. Or tram! Trams stopped right outside until 7 April 1951.
12. Geddes (1915, p. 286).
13. Smith (1795).

Chapter 4
The trends
Travel and haulage

Figure 4.1 shows the increases over the past half-century in passenger movement (measured in person-kilometres), the movement of freight (measured in tonne-kilometres) and road traffic (measured in vehicle-kilometres). It also shows the improvement in the average standard of living (measured in real gross domestic product (GDP) (£) per head), at once both the cause and the effect of the rise in traffic and transport. The data are portrayed in the form of 'indices',[1] since this enables the trends to be compared despite the different units of measurement.

There is a major shortcoming in the vast majority of the official data from which this and later figures are drawn. The crucial short links between the different parts of start-to-finish movements are excluded in their entirety. Figure 4.1 does not include walking at all and, in the later figures which do include walking, they only take into

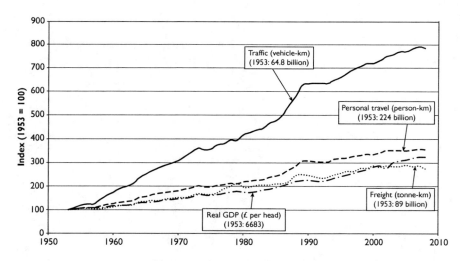

Figure 4.1 The growth of personal travel, freight, traffic and real GDP per head (1953–2009)

Source: Department for Transport, *Transport Statistics for Great Britain* (2011), tables TSGB0101 (person-km), TSGB0499 (tonne-km) and TRA 9901 (veh-km); *Social Trends* #39 (2009), p. 64, table XX.

account movements made entirely on foot, and not those vital parts of journeys such as walking from a car-parking place to the actual destination or from the start of a journey to a public transport pick-up point. Unless noted otherwise, movements are credited to the 'mode' used for the longest segment within an overall movement: other segments by ancillary modes are ignored. This overlooks elements of door-to-door movements, such as walking to the final destination or changing from one mode to another, which may themselves be minor distances but are major influences upon choices and decisions. If policy is to influence transport choices for the better, the minor, incidental elements within a journey should be included in the raw statistics and their analysis.

The growth of traffic and the overall movement of passengers and freight kept more or less in step but with different rates of growth, as shown by the different slopes of the curves in Figure 4.1. The prime driver was the real (GDP) per head, an indicator of rising standards of living. The GDP is the sum of the prices paid for all the goods and services produced and consumed but it is severely affected by inflation: for example, the total GDP in 1952 was £15,983 million and that for 2009 was £139,587 million, nine times as much, but, in reality, the total goods and services used in 2009 was only about three times that in 1952; the rest of the nine-fold apparent increase was due to rising prices. The rising GDP shown in Figure 4.1 has been corrected for inflation to create a measure of real GDP and is shown as the GDP per head of population – it is a measure of the rise in the standard of living and so in the average disposable income.

Figure 4.2 shows where some of that money was spent. The number of private cars rose 10 times: from 2.7 million in 1953 to 27 million in 2009. Over the same period the number of goods vehicles, excluding vans, was almost constant at 450,000, but

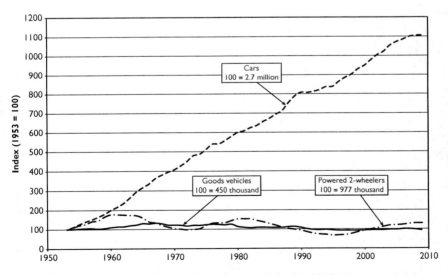

Figure 4.2 The growth in the vehicle population (1953–2009) (as an index to show relative growth)

the amount of freight carried increased considerably (see Figure 4.11). This was due to a combination of larger lorries replacing smaller ones and more intensive use of the vehicles. Figure 4.2 also shows that the number of 'powered two-wheelers' (PTW) (solo motorcycles, mopeds and scooters) stayed fairly constant at around 900,000 but with rather more fluctuation than with the goods vehicles.

The ten-fold increase in the numbers of cars was not spread consistently over the population and the variations give important clues on past and future trends. Figure 4.3 gives some idea of the distribution of the rapid and extensive growth of car ownership over the nation's households.[2] In 1950, only 15 per cent of households had the use of a car with a tiny minority (1%) owning more than one. Post-war austerity had begun to wane by 1960, and the number of households with the use of a car had doubled in just ten years. For the next ten years car ownership accelerated apace until, in the late 1960s, just over half of all households owned a car or cars. After 1970 the proportion of households owning only one car remained almost constant at about 43 per cent, and that figure is still true in 2011. The significant changes were the continuing decline in the numbers of households without a car, down to the current figure of about 25 per cent of households, and a corresponding rise in the proportion owning more than one car, currently about one-third of households.

The almost constant proportion of households with one car is interesting. The households within this category should not be thought of as a stable group: over the past few years they have changed constantly as some households, having acquired their first car, have joined, and others have left to become two-plus car households. This process, in which a population remains numerically or proportionately constant while the constituent membership fluctuates, is called 'churn'.

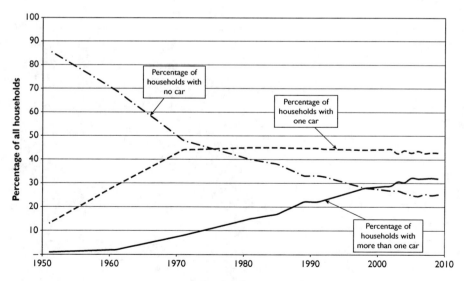

Figure 4.3 The percentages of households with or without the use of a car (1951–2009)

In the case of household car ownership, there was more churn than just a movement of households from one car ownership category to another. Figure 4.4 shows that the number of households has itself changed rapidly: the numbers of people, household sizes and the related increase in the number of households per 1000 population are presented as indices but with 1951, the census year, as the base. The increase in the number of households is usually termed 'household fission' and is due to much younger people leaving home to form their own independent households and, at the other end of the household life cycle, older people living independently rather than with their children. Consequently the number of no-car households shown in Figure 4.3 which was once dominated by families in the middle of the household life cycle, but with insufficient income to acquire a car, is now dominated by small households containing people in either their first or their last household.

The increase over the past 60 years of some 40 per cent in the number of households per 1000 population and of over 60 per cent in the absolute number of households is related to yet another aspect of churn. This increased number of households has driven up the demand for housing but the response has been neither uniform nor constant: the churn is complex and untidy, more shaken than stirred.

There are data on the expansion of urban land: Bibby and Shepherd (1997) is a particularly good source, not just in the data themselves but as a lesson in how data may be analysed in different ways to produce contradictory results. But their data, taken from the census, are averaged over large areas within which the variations are so wide that the average misrepresents the detail of actual developments.

The story of the nature of urban expansion is best told through specific examples. Figure 4.5 shows comparative data for four detailed areas, two as examples of development before the expansion of car ownership, and two from the first decade of the twenty-first century. Figures 4.6 to 4.9 give some idea of the visual character of these four examples.

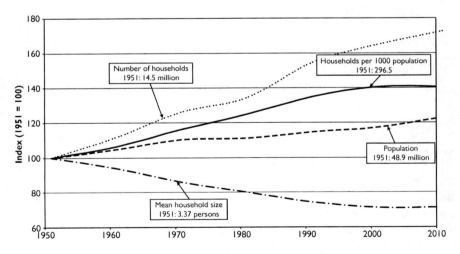

Figure 4.4 Number of households in Great Britain (1951–2010)

Date constructed	1890s	1930s	2000	2005
Visual characteristics in:	Figure 4.6	Figure 4.7	Figure 4.8	Figure 4.9
Distance to the city centre (km)	2	4	25	3
Persons/hect	287.88	59.57	48.16	53.63
Dwellings/hect	139.39	29.89	15.43	36.69
Persons/hsld	2.11	2.01	3.16	1.62
Car/hect	92.93	22.80	27.71	33.52
Cars/household	0.68	0.77	1.82	1.01
Cars/person	0.32	0.38	0.58	0.63
% by 'soft' mode	42.11	14.44	17.69	18.40
% by public transport	23.16	17.69	10.06	19.79
% by motor	20.70	25.27	50.47	37.15

Figure 4.5 Descriptive statistics drawn from the 2001 census for examples of typical developments illustrated in Figures 4.6, 4.7, 4.8 and 4.9

Notes: The distinction between 'hard' and 'soft' measures and policies seems to have arisen in the late twentieth century. 'Hard' measures affect a product itself (for public transport, frequency, reliability, etc.) and 'soft' measures are attempts to mould perceptions of the product (particularly marketing). The distinction was later adapted to distinguish between motorised and non-motorised travel modes (walking and cycling).

The percentages by mode do not sum to 100%. Those unaccounted for either work from home or are not at present working or studying.

The first example (Figure 4.6) is a typical Scottish tenement, a four-storey block of flats of a size and comfort that belies their reputation, built in the 1890s just before cheap, frequent trams began stopping at the end of the street. In England the contemporary form was the nineteenth-century two-storey terrace still to be seen in the inner suburbs of the major cities. Today, car ownership per person is low but, since the population density is very high, the car population per hectare is three times that in later developments and is reflected in the severe parking problems shown in the photograph. The City Council manages parking demand by issuing a rationed number of costly permits, but even then car users have difficulty finding a parking place. The parking problem is insoluble: demand will always be greater than supply. Not only is keeping a car tinged with problems but an alternative bus service at the end of the street is very efficient, and is reflected in the high use of public transport for the journey to work.[3] The use of the soft modes – walking and cycling – is also high, a reflection not only of the low car ownership per household, but also of the proximity to the city centre.

The second example (Figure 4.7) is of a 1930s development built at the time when motor-buses were beginning to provide accessibility to large tracts of land outside the Edwardian city and the number of dwellings per hectare fell to roughly a quarter of what they had been in Victorian development. This was driven, not by larger dwellings but by creating gardens, both back and front. The example was contemporary with the ubiquitous semi-detached houses built all over England in the 1930s but which were not built in such large numbers in Scotland where similar densities were achieved using bungalows on small plots or, as in this case, maisonettes. At the time car ownership was low but cars were precious, so the more expensive houses

Figure 4.6 Scottish tenement housing (1890s)

Persons per hectare	Dwellings per hectare	Persons per household	Cars per hectare	Cars per household	Cars per person	% j-to-w by 'soft' mode	% j-to-w by public transport	% j-to-w by motor vehicle
287.88	139.39	2.11	92.93	0.68	0.32	42.11	23.16	20.70

Note: j-to-w = journey to work; 'soft' modes = walking and cycling

were built with integral garages. Today these garages are typically used as garden sheds, and cars are parked in what were originally front gardens or in the street. The comparative ease of parking is reflected in car ownership being approximately 20 per cent higher than in the Victorian tenements but, since the density of households is much lower, the pressure upon parking space does not require council management. Walking and cycling accounts for only 14 per cent of the journeys to work, the lowest of all the examples; this may well reflect the age of the people living in this style of property as well as the distance from the city centre. Nonetheless, only a quarter of journeys to work are by car.

The two examples in Figures 4.6 and 4.7 are shown to illustrate the types of development before new housing had to be designed around accommodating the car but, nonetheless, now have to cope with a substantial car population. Following the explosion in car use shown in Figure 4.2, new housing displayed two contrasting effects. First, the car had to be accommodated by the deliberate inclusion of a parking space. Second, the ability of the car to move in almost any direction and at any time opened up many previously inaccessible areas to development. This enabled the use of agricultural land for housing, extending the built-up area of the city deep into the surrounding countryside, stopping only at the limit imposed by the time that commuters were willing to dedicate to their journey to work.

Figure 4.7 1930s housing

Persons per hectare	Dwellings per hectare	Persons per household	Cars per hectare	Cars per household	Cars per person	% j-to-w by 'soft' mode	% j-to-w by public transport	% j-to-w by motor vehicle
59.57	29.89	2.01	22.80	0.77	0.38	14.44	17.69	25.27

This effect is displayed in the third column of Figure 4.5 and the related photograph in Figure 4.8, an example of new development on former agricultural land. It is an extension of a small village 25 kilometres to the east of Edinburgh and would not have been built, had it not been for the accessibility provided by the car. The houses are mainly detached in their own gardens, with both garages and space to park within the plots; the housing density is just one-ninth of that displayed about 100 years previously, shown in the first column of Figure 4.5. Car ownership is very high – almost two cars per household – and 3.16 persons of all ages per household reflects the occupation of the fairly large houses by families, producing a comparatively low car ownership per person despite the high ownership per household. The low number of dwellings per hectare brings the count of cars per hectare down, notwithstanding the high levels of ownership. Parking on driveways and in garages results in virtually no on-street parking. The journey to work by public transport, walking and cycling appears to be quite high but this is mainly due to schoolchildren either walking to the primary school less than one kilometre away or using a bus to travel to the nearest secondary school 17 kilometres to the east. The percentages veil the reality: the reported 50 per cent of journeys to work by car is lower than might be expected in an area with almost two cars per household but the percentage has been diluted by the journeys to school on foot and by bus. There are

Figure 4.8 Housing on previous farmland: the virtual city

Persons per hectare	Dwellings per hectare	Persons per household	Cars per hectare	Cars per household	Cars per person	% j-to-w by 'soft' mode	% j-to-w by public transport	% j-to-w by motor vehicle
48.16	15.43	3.16	27.71	1.82	0.58	17.69	10.06	50.47

270 actual journey-to-work trips by car, an average of 1.5 per day per household, many more than suggested by the fairly low percentage.

Figure 4.9 shows modern flats built on a former rail-connected industrial site only two kilometres from the city centre. The density of dwellings per hectare is far lower than the tenements of yesteryear but greater than the maisonettes of the 1930s. This is attained by building higher so that the share of the developed space credited to each dwelling is quite low but gardens are sacrificed to provide parking and road space: in fact the footprint of the flats is smaller than the parking space provided for the residents. These flats are targeted at young people setting up their own households. The mean household size of 1.62 persons shows a mixture of singles, people sharing and newly marrieds – there are few buggies but a high proportion of small, zippy cars. It is only a short walk or cycle ride to the city centre, and one-fifth of the journey-to-work trips are by these 'soft' modes while another one-fifth use public transport (there are 18 buses per hour serving a stop four minutes' walk away). Despite the efficient public transport and the convenient walk or bike ride, the majority still go to work by car. There is an average of over one car per household, significantly higher than the ownership rate in the nineteenth-century tenements where there is a dearth of parking. There must be a suspicion that the attractiveness of living in these modern flats is more to do with the easy parking than the quality of the flats themselves.

The trends show that cars are extremely popular; otherwise three-quarters of all households would not have striven to acquire one and the examples emphasise two

56 Travel and haulage

Figure 4.9 New flatted development on vacated industrial land within the city

Persons per hectare	Dwellings per hectare	Persons per household	Cars per hectare	Cars per household	Cars per person	% j-to-w by 'soft' mode	% j-to-w by public transport	% j-to-w by motor vehicle
53.63	36.69	1.62	33.52	1.01	0.63	18.40	19.79	37.15

aspects of the very substantial effects of the increase in car ownership and use over the past 50 years or so:

- First, the need to park cars is both a constraint upon the design of new housing and a constraint upon car ownership and use within older housing. Where parking problems abound, car ownership and use are suppressed, forcing the use of the alternative soft modes and public transport.
- Second, paradoxically, although cars create parking and congestion problems, they also provide a solution. Being able to provide transport at virtually any time and in any direction, they are able to offer accessibility to tracts of previously inaccessible land now developed at a density that solves the parking problem, as typified by Figure 4.8. Moreover, this disperses development and spreads traffic over a wider area: this does not solve the congestion problem, but it does make congestion less objectionable than it would otherwise be.

The conclusion is that the parking problems apparent in the older city and exemplified in the first two examples are the root cause of the new styles, densities and locations of the developments in the second pair of examples. Developments of this sort are spread over the whole country and have loosened the weave of the urban fabric, changing the size and nature of urban areas. The functional city, defined as the area containing both the homes and the workplaces of its inhabitants, now enfolds surrounding villages and hamlets to form the 'virtual city' bound together by car-commuting. Just as toothpaste cannot be put back in the tube, so these effects of the explosion in car ownership and consequent fundamental changes in urban form cannot be reversed.

The increase in the numbers of cars and in the spread and discontinuity of urban areas has created not just more journeys but also longer journeys. Figure 4.10 shows the annual averages per head of population.

The National Travel Survey, from which Figure 4.10 has been derived is based on quite low sample rates and has been affected by changes of definition so that some of the detailed fluctuations in the graph in Figure 4.10 may not be significant but the overall trend is quite clear. Throughout the 1970s and 1980s and well into the 1990s there were substantial increases in the amount of personal travel (measured in kilometres per year), in the average trip length and in the average speed. In large measure the increased speed compensated for the increased trip length so that the average trip time was actually reduced until recently. As with many official data, these figures are based on the 'main' mode used and therefore exclude any ancillary modes used within trips: this means, in particular, that the distances and times spent walking as incidental parts of trips are ignored.

Despite this flaw, the data resonate with the data showing the growth of car ownership and use. Although the data displayed in Figure 4.10 do include longer journeys, the majority reflect travel within the virtual city. The increases in total and trip distance are compatible with urban areas becoming larger as car use made more

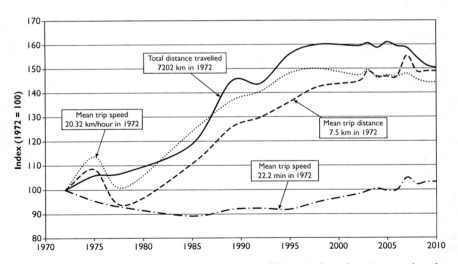

Figure 4.10 Personal travel: total distance travelled, trip length, trip speed and total travel time

Note: Averages per head of population, per year.

land accessible, creating a looser, more dispersed, decentralised urban form. With that came more diffuse movement, spreading traffic over more time and space with less congestion than there would otherwise have been and sustaining mean travel speeds.

These trends are echoed by the trends in freight transport. Figure 4.11 shows the changes, in tonne-kilometres by the major freight modes over the past 60 years: just as personal travel by car expanded by about eight times (Figure 4.1), so road freight has expanded by about five times. This does not mean that lorry movements have expanded exactly in step, since the lorry fleet now comprises much larger vehicles and their operation has changed radically. The freight statistics are difficult to interpret. The usual distinction is between tonnes shifted (the total carry measured in tonne-kilometres shown in Figure 4.11) and tonnes lifted (the aggregate load measured in tonnes shown in Figure 4.12). The mean distance carried (in kilometres) may be derived from dividing the tonnes shifted by the tonnes lifted and is shown in Figure 4.13.

Figure 4.11 shows that, although road freight has increased five-fold over the past 60 years and rail now carries about half of what it used to, the switch from rail to road accounts for only a small minority of the growth in road freight. The major cause is the tripling of the total freight tonne-kilometres. The expansion of water transport has nothing to do with the resurgence of the canal system: that has been driven by leisure boating, not by freight traffic. The growth has been in coastal shipping, due partly to the movement of containers from one British port to another and partly to major changes in the energy industry with a major shift from domestically produced to imported coal together with imported oil and gas. This is also reflected in the exponential increase in the use of oil pipelines.

Figure 4.12, showing the tonnes lifted by the same modes as those in Figure 4.11, elaborates the same story. The total number of tonnes lifted has expanded but to a much lesser extent than the tonnes shifted, suggesting that the kilometres travelled by each tonne have increased faster than the tonnage carried.

Figures 4.11, 4.12 and 4.13 all combine to display a mixture of short-term effects and long-term trends. In the early 1960s the then Minister of Transport, Ernest Marples, instigated two intertwined strands of policy. First, he laid an emphasis upon roads and traffic: the Lancaster and Preston bypasses had been opened in 1958 as the initial sections of what was to become the M6 and, in the following year, Marples ceremoniously opened the first stage of the M1 between London and Rugby. Contracts were signed for many additional miles of motorway and plans laid for the improvement of much of the ordinary trunk road network. Marples did not confine his attention to the road system between towns but also commissioned Colin Buchanan to write a report on traffic within towns.[4] Coincidentally he appointed Dr Richard Beeching as Chairman of the British Transport Commission, created in 1948 as the administrative hub of the nationalised transport system created as part of the post-war Welfare State. Beeching was charged with winding up the Commission. This was the effective demise of the perception of the transport system as an interrelated whole and the adoption of free-standing policies for each of the major modes. The Commission had disbanded by January 1963 and Beeching then became Chairman of the new British Railways Board with the remit to turn the railways

Travel and haulage 59

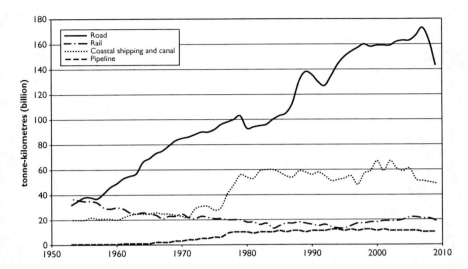

Figure 4.11 Freight: tonnes shifted – tonne-kilometres by major mode
Source: Department for Transport, *Transport Statistics Great Britain* (2010), table 4.1.

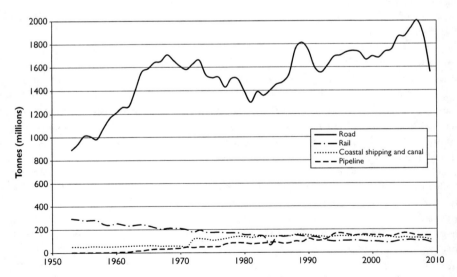

Figure 4.12 Freight: tonnes lifted – tonnes loaded on to the major modes
Source: Department for Transport, *Transport Statistics Great Britain* (2010), table 4.1.

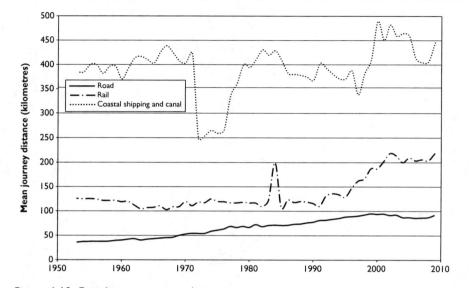

Figure 4.13 Freight: mean carry distance
Source: Department for Transport, *Transport Statistics Great Britain* (2010), table 4.1.

into a commercially viable operation. Beeching's report on how this might be done[5] caused a political storm, since it proposed to shut many lines and stations, scrap swathes of rolling-stock and withdraw from the unprofitable haulage of general freight.

A debate still rages over whether the 'Beeching Report' was an act of vandalism or an acknowledgement of reality. It is arguable that Marples had a hidden agenda to move government funding from subsidising the railways to investing in roads, but it is not certain whether this was done as part of a comprehensive, although hidden, transport policy, recognising that road freight was superior to rail, or whether it was a reflection of a more fuzzy ideological stance dividing policies into one for the nationalised, subsidised, monolithic rail system and another for the more flexible, competitive, road freight system.

The changes precipitated by Marples' policies for roads and Beeching's for railways had their roots some years previously. Prior to 1956 all heavy goods vehicles (those over 3 tons) were limited to a blanket maximum speed of 20 miles per hour, restricting their capacity for work and forcing up costs. The removal of the limit enabled hauliers to reduce their prices at a time when rail was required to charge using a fixed tariff per tonne-mile,[6] making the railways uncompetitive. They were already losing traffic to lorries well before Marples and Beeching. More importantly, the widespread post-war switch to electricity to drive industry meant that factories no longer had to be powered by a system of belts and pulleys driven by a central steam-engine: each machine could now be separately powered. This not only changed factory design from multi-storey buildings with small footprints to extensive single-storey buildings, but energy could be brought to the factory door by cable instead of by coal cart from the nearest rail-connected coal yard. The location of manufacturing industry began to be affected by the flexibility of cables and lorries to serve any address in the same way that cars were affecting housing. That flexibility not only released the locational ties to places served by rail but enabled the development of areas that could not possibly be served by rail, a trend that could not and cannot be reversed.

Two examples may be cited to show the effects of the simultaneous improvement of the road system, the withdrawal of rail freight services and the redrawing of urban geography: first, the distribution of products from suppliers to retailers, and second, the supply of energy.

Retail distribution

The original system was for carriers to act as traders, owning the goods they carried, buying at source and selling direct to customers, covering the costs of cartage out of the difference between the purchase and selling prices. That arrangement changed with the development of canals and then railways: they acted as carriers of other people's goods. Then the tendency became for retailers to order small quantities from manufacturers or wholesalers to be shipped either 'cash on delivery' (COD) with carriage being paid for by the supplier who included it in the price charged to the customer or by customers buying at a 'factory gate' price and arranging the costs of 'carriage, insurance and freight' (CIF) themselves. Stocks were held both by the supplier and by the retailers in small quantities restricted by the available storage space at their shops. Stocks of some more esoteric goods with slow turnover were held by local wholesalers who could order enough of each item to satisfy demand in their locality, and then bundle a number of different items for one delivery to retailers. It is this intermediate function that has come to dominate modern distribution, as is well described by Quarmby.[7]

The current system is dependent upon large logistics centres which have been built at places well served by the motorway and principal road network. These have three major functions:

1 They receive bulk deliveries from product suppliers direct from factories and ports. These inward products are usually carried in homogeneous bulk from a single source.
2 The products are then stored in the logistics centres to form buffers between the surges in delivery and the day-to-day dispatches to the shops.
3 The lists of products ordered by each shop are picked from the storage racks and consolidated into loads comprising a wide range of different products, destined for a specific shop.

This system has a number of defining characteristics:

- The habit of shoppers 60 years ago going nearly every day on foot to a small, local 'pantry' shop and carrying a bag or two of shopping home has almost disappeared. Most households now have the space and money to buy fridges and deep freezes and to keep them well stocked – the 'pantry' has migrated from small, local shops to the household. Shopping is now a weekly or even monthly activity, buying far more than can be carried home on foot. Food shops have to have large car-parks and so have had to be built where space is available, either on the edge of urban areas or on vacated industrial land. To match modern consumerism and be commercially viable, such shops have to have the space for many product lines and are far bigger than their in-town ancestors. With multiple products being sold and with the high turnovers generated by customers filling their trolleys with a week's shopping or more, there is a need for levels of stock high enough to prevent stock-outs. To provide the necessary storage space within the shops themselves would be expensive: it is more efficient to concentrate stocks in the logistics centres, each one providing stocks for a number of shops.

- For this arrangement to work efficiently and for the risk of stock-outs to be minimised, the shelves in the shops have to be replenished frequently and reliably. This is dependent upon a combination of the use of barcodes, telecommunications and computers. Each shop is able to monitor its sales through point-of-sale scanners, cross-checked by inventories of the shelves. Stocks should always be able to meet demand up until the next delivery with a few, but not too many, to spare.[8] Computerised lists of the items necessary to replenish the shelves are transmitted to the logistics centres and the items picked and loaded into roll cages which are then dispatched direct to the shop by lorry.
- There are two major underlying objectives:
    1   Stocks, both in the logistics centres and in the shops themselves, should always be large enough to cover the demand between one delivery and the next but not so large that the interest payable on the borrowing needed to cover their capital value is unacceptably high.
    2   Haulage costs are minimised. Costings are discussed in Chapter 14 but the touchstone is to ensure that lorry loads are as large as possible. The current maximum permissible gross lorry weight is 44 tonnes[9] but a lorry may be 'full' before this maximum is reached. A 44-tonne articulated lorry has a loadable floor area of just over 30 square metres and a volume of 75 cubic metres. Manhandling to load and unload is slow and expensive: 'roll-cages', with a footprint of about 0.65 square metres, are used to subdivide a load into units capable of being wheeled in and out of the lorry. The floor area of a full-sized articulated trailer is able to accommodate about 50 cages, each containing up to 400 kg. This 'full load' of 20 tonnes is well below the maximum payload of 29 tonnes.

    Maximum loading also requires a minimal number of dropping-off points, preferably just the one. This not only minimises the total time that the lorry and driver are unproductively stationary during loading and unloading but also avoids inefficient partly loaded running between drops.
- Attaining these objectives depends upon deliveries being made to a planned timetable. Quarmby asserts that reliable delivery times are dependent upon

lorries using dual carriageways for much of their journey. Lorries do not have the acceleration to use the marginal overtaking opportunities common on single-carriageway roads and are therefore vulnerable to variations in the traffic flow. Speeds and transit times on dual carriageways are far more predictable, and disruption of the crucial delivery timetables much less likely, so reducing the risks of stock-outs.

The logistics and supply chains feeding the retail industry have been organised around a combination of trends:

- a fundamental change in urban geography with larger shops set in swathes of parking space and residential areas dispersed at lower densities;
- a radical change in shopping habits with less frequent but larger loads to be carried home;
- the use of cars for travel between the new residential and retail geographies;
- major improvements to the inter-city road network including the construction of dual carriageways;
- the construction of logistics centres at optimal locations served by the improved road network;
- the restructuring of supply chains, not only within the retail industry but throughout production and distribution, transforming the simple haulage industry into logistical end-to-end supply chains incorporating haulage, storage and stock control;
- changing the characteristics of the lorry fleet to carry both large, homogeneous loads from suppliers to distribution depots and large consolidated mixes of products from distribution depots to shops;
- the reorganisation of the location ownership and management of stocks.

These trends are linked in a whirl of cause and effect, difficult to analyse as a chain of action and reaction and now impossible to unravel or reverse.

As shown in Figure 4.2, the number of heavy goods vehicles has remained almost constant for many years but, as shown in Figure 4.14, the capacity of the fleet (measured in the aggregate tonnage of the gross vehicle weight (i.e. the weight of the lorries together with their payloads)) has increased substantially due mainly to smaller, rigid lorries being replaced by larger, articulated vehicles.

The fleet has managed to cope with the five-fold increase in tonnes shifted as shown in Figure 4.11. This has been achieved not just by extending the capacity of the fleet but by dual carriageways increasing average speeds, by more efficient scheduling and by the reduced partloaded and empty running enabled by modern logistics reducing drops per journey and aggregate loading and unloading times.

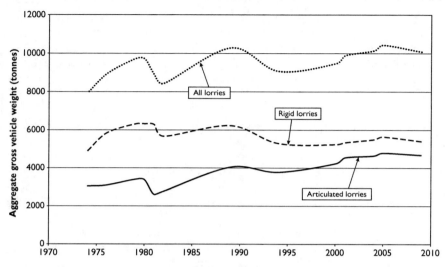

Figure 4.14 The overall capacity of the lorry fleet

Source: Department for Transport, *Transport Statistics Great Britain* (various issues and tables).

Energy distribution

The second example of how the trends in freight have changed is the events that have moulded the distribution of energy. In the first half of the twentieth century gas, electricity and water were seen to be unavoidably monopolistic – it was clearly uneconomic to install competitive networks of pipes and cables. The reorganisation of local councils in 1888 was largely premised upon their role in providing public utilities, namely water, sewerage, gas, street lighting and electricity. Many councils built the necessary distribution infrastructure at public expense but many took it further, building gasworks and power-stations as well as reservoirs and sewage treatment plants: reminders are everywhere in the cast-iron manhole covers which still bear the initials of the councils responsible for their installation. Some councils used private companies working under contract (for example, the Gas Light and Coke Company in London) – in any event, local legislation was always needed to authorise the necessary way-leaves, trenching and plant.

The use of electricity grew rapidly, and it became clear that small local power-stations could not cope with large fluctuations in demand. The problem was addressed with political urgency: as early as 1919 a National Electricity Supply Corporation was established and managed by appointed Commissioners. In 1926 this was extended by the creation of the Central Electricity Board and the start of the construction of the National Grid running at 132kV. This ensured that every small town did not have to have its own power-station but could draw current from a network fed by a smaller number of larger stations sited in or near the major cities. These stations were all thermal, burning coal.

At that time there was no national gas network. Coal gas (later to be called town gas) was made in much smaller, local works: even quite small places had a local plant (for example, in 1952, Cornwall had 28 gasworks, serving individual towns right down to a population as small as 2,700 (Padstow)[10]).

During the Second World War the massive increases in the demand for power from industry, despite disruptions to the network due to bombing, could only be met by flexible, almost ad-hoc arrangements driven by the imperatives of the war effort rather than accountants' analysis sheets. The nationalisation of the energy (and transport) industries was, in part, ideological – a belief in state organisation as a Labour Party principle. But for those many people who were strangers to socialist rhetoric, formal nationalisation was little more than a carry-over from the previous six years of state-driven war effort during which market forces left to themselves were seen to be intrinsically incapable of orchestrating food rationing, or the provision of gas masks and air-raid shelters or the cohesion and complexity of D-day.

The newly nationalised electricity industry set about improving the system. Power was brought to remote villages and farms until virtually every property throughout the country was connected to the mains. New generating capacity was constructed but research had shown that very large power-stations were thermally more efficient than smaller ones. Most of the pre-war stations within or near cities were closed and replaced by massive megawatt stations located away from the areas of consumption and nearer to the coalfields.

This had very considerable implications for the railways. No longer was energy carried as coal from pits to a large number of small, urban power-stations. Now it was carried in large, fixed formation trains from pits to a small number of large power-stations. The National Grid was massively enhanced to link the new generating plant to consumers. Energy was now transported by wires rather than by railway wagons.

Power is lost during transmission: wires heat up as current passes along them and some energy is inevitably wasted. This waste is the product of the distance, of the size and nature of the cables, of the voltage and of the amount of energy carried (the wattage). The enhanced grid was built to move energy in bulk at 400kV, halving the transmission losses per kilometre incurred by the older 275kV system. The cost of moving millions of tonnes of coal by train had been changed to the cost of transmission losses on the National Grid and had a very substantial influence on railway finances.

The reduction of railway freight revenue was emphasised by further shifts in the nature and geography of the movement of energy. Domestic heating had traditionally been provided by open coal fires. Setting and feeding the fires was laborious and expensive, and domestic heating was usually confined to just one living-room. Families congregated in that room and helped to keep it warm with their own body heat.[11] As standards of living rose, domestic heating developed from a coal fire in one room to central heating. At first this was either solid fuel or oil (both delivered by road), or gas (delivered by pipe). All that changed fundamentally in the early 1970s as natural gas from the North Sea replaced coal gas. The change required no less than the modification of every gas fire, cooker and boiler in the country as well as the entire infrastructure. The job was accomplished without too much fuss, and on time and in budget. It was a stunning refutation of the belief that a nationalised industry is intrinsically inefficient: efficiency everywhere rests on precise, explicit objectives.

The change to natural gas emphasised the shift in the movement of energy away from railways. No longer did coal have to be moved from the pithead to millions of domestic fireplaces; no longer did every railway station have its coal yard and local coal merchants to cart coal to everyone's front door. No longer did trains of coal wagons deliver their loads to the thousands of local gasworks. The cash flow generated by coal traffic on the railway faded, and it could be argued that the 'Beeching' cuts had proved to be justified. The residual, but important, traffic was the bulk, comparatively short-haul, fixed rail movements from the pithead to the few megawatt power-stations. This traffic remains, but the reduction of the mining industry to a shadow of its former importance as the prime source of national energy has extended the typical haul: this is no longer from the pitheads but from specialist ports through which coal is imported with a haul to power-stations which, perversely, were originally sited to minimise the distance from mine to furnace.

Coal traffic is declining in importance with the construction of combined circuit gas turbine (CCGT) stations fed by the now ubiquitous yellow pipes bringing gas from under the North Sea or further afield. This new CCGT technology does not show the economies of scale that were apparent in the days of coal-fired stations and so can be smaller and distributed nearer to centres of consumption. Generation is becoming more dispersed again, a geography facilitated by inputs of raw energy by pipe and outputs by wire. The trend is being emphasised by the efforts being made to harvest renewable energy. Wind farms and plants driven by tides and waves are naturally dispersed but tend to be located well away from centres of consumption. The transport of energy is changing yet again with diametrically opposed trends. Imported energy is concentrated at the ports of entry irrespective of its mode: cables and pipes come ashore at a few discrete points, and bulk carriers of coal, oil and natural gas dock at specialist ports. In contrast, the generation of renewable energy is dispersed over time and space. End uses are spread, but very unevenly: cities are expanding and the distribution networks must keep pace. Secondary[12] and tertiary[13] industries are dispersing to locations best served by road: cars and car-parking for employees and lorries and logistics centres for freight.

The trends over the past half-century are clear. Passenger and freight movement has increased prodigiously with the major growth in road traffic by lorry and by car. But that traffic is far more dispersed than it used to be: houses, factories and shops are more spread out; cities have grown outward and are discontinuous, virtual cities – the weave of the urban fabric has loosened. The change has been facilitated by cars and lorries being able to get to any address in the country. Perversely, a major component in this insidious revolution is not the need to cope with the growth in traffic, the moving vehicle, but the need to cope with parking, the stopped vehicle. The car-parking space needed by modern shops, schools, workplaces, universities and offices is a major determinant of the form and density of development.

Notes

1 To make an index, a base year has to be chosen to act as a benchmark – in this case the choice fell on 1953. The measurement for that year, in whatever the appropriate units might be, is awarded an index of 100. Thereafter the index for each of the following years is calculated by comparing the measured number for that year with the comparable measurement for the base year: thus, for example, the index for GDP in 1986 is 200 which means GDP per head in that year was twice that in the base year of 1953.
2 The definition of a 'household' is a group of people (not necessarily blood-related) sharing a dwelling: the crucial test is whether they habitually take meals together.
3 Journeys to work include journeys to study (students of all ages).
4 Published as *Traffic in Towns* (Ministry of Transport 1963a) – The Buchanan Report.
5 *The Reshaping of British Railways* (Ministry of Transport 1963b) – The Beeching Report.
6 Transport fares and charges still bore the marks of Victorian legislation based on a fear of monopoly. Fares were fixed per mile (which is why railway timetables still show the mileage between stations). Railways were also legally bound as 'common carriers' to accept any load offered to them, a duty that was lifted in 1953.
7 Quarmby (1987).
8 The technique is called 'just-in-time' with the shelves being replenished just before the last item is sold. This reduces stock costs but stock-outs may only be avoided if delivery times are exact.
9 For articulated vehicles 15.5 metres long and subject to meeting conditions on the number and spacing of axles, 'road-friendly' suspension and engine emissions are to a European standard.
10 Cornwall County Council (1952).
11 Humans irradiate about 100 watts per hour, so a family of four is the equivalent of a small, rather dull electric fire.
12 Manufacturing.
13 Service and distribution.

Chapter 5

Fuel consumption and emissions of greenhouse gases (GHG)

Sustainable objectives

Chapter 1 argued that reducing the production of greenhouse gases (GHG) was not only an end in itself but could stand proxy for other aspects of sustainability. One way of lessening the pollutions from transport is by reducing the number of vehicle-kilometres and a potent way of doing this is to reduce average journey length. This is best achieved by controlling the spread of urbanisation by the development of agricultural land. Hence a policy to control GHG has a related effect upon sustainable agricultural policy.

This extension of the case put forward in Chapter 1 for using the control of GHG as the touchstone of sustainability is to argue that one comparatively simple objective may carry a number of other objectives upon its back. This rests upon accepting an imperfect, simple measure to monitor an extensive, complex system, outflanking arcane arguments about how to measure the effects of each sustainable policy and how to balance their relative merits and demerits. Multiple indexes of performance have bedevilled transport planning over the years: the reduction of aggregate journey time and accidents (giving both debatable monetary values) with coincident minimisation of environmental impacts (to which values are impossible to give without provoking somebody's wrath) have been the prime measures of the viability of transport schemes. This has led to vehement arguments about both the measures themselves and the tariff of offsets and balances between them – the destruction of how many trees and houses is acceptable to 'buy' reduced travel time? The forthcoming conflicts over high-speed rail routes will occupy thousands of argumentative hours and cause explosive rises in blood pressure, most of which will be about conflicting objectives, how to measure them and how to offset the merits of one against the merits of another.

The proposal of one simple touchstone, the control of GHG emissions, is an attempt to circumvent most of such confusion, but it has to be recognised that the touchstone can only be partially successful. It is, perhaps, too simple and too crude to stand proxy for a bundle of complex objectives. For example, it would open the door to an argument that the best way to minimise GHG emissions is for people to stay at home and wear warm clothing. This would be to make the very common error of confusing a measure designed to monitor actions with a target. This confusion is rife in many areas of policy: in the 1980s higher education policy used cost per student as a measure of efficiency. The cost per degree awarded was a reasonable measure of efficiency but it was then transformed into the target of minimising, rather than reducing, the cost per student. This, being a target rather than a metric, transcended all else, and universities closed courses and, sometimes, whole departments in science and engineering which had intrinsically high unit costs. The modern use of spread-sheeted budgets, costs and 'efficiency savings' as targets has supplanted the definition of desirable operational outputs with the spread-sheets confined to ensuring good value for money rather than minimal expenditure.

GHG emissions are being suggested as a way to monitor and assess sustainable transport policies, but the minimisation cannot be a target trumping other objectives such as providing a transport system to meet society's needs without unnecessary, superfluous emissions.

GHG and CO_2 emissions

CO_2 is not alone in affecting climate by adsorbing heat from the sun and failing to irradiate it back into space. This 'greenhouse' effect is magnified by some other, minor GHG and it is usual to convert their effects into a quantity of pure CO_2 that would have had the same impact upon global warming: this measure is termed 'CO_2 equivalent' (CO_2-e) (Figure 1.1 gives the rates to convert each GHG into its CO_2-e). The Carbon Trust asserts that the combustion of a litre of petrol will produce 2.331 kg of CO_2-e,[1] whereas the Department of Energy and Climate Change quotes 2.7329 (sic),[2] 17 per cent greater. In both cases the majority of the CO_2-e produced comes from the 2.023 kg of pure CO_2: the balance comes from the nominal effects of the other GHG.

There is something bizarre about quoting a figure to an accuracy of four decimal places when different government agencies publish values that disagree by 17 per cent. One of the banes of the spread-sheet mentality is spurious accuracy: if a quantity cannot be measured with a constant accuracy to ensure that its value is quoted definitively, then using a value to four places of decimals in a spread-sheet is an unwarranted sleight of hand which, like as not, has a purpose. If the government has pledged to reduce CO_2-e (which it has, in the Kyoto Agreement) or if licences to pollute are bought and sold (which they are, in Carbon Trading), then the final place of decimals has an arithmetic significance which is unrelated to the actual physical effects. The precise climatic effect of one gram of nitrous oxide (a minor, but potent, GHG) is, perhaps, approximately the same as that of 300 grams of pure CO_2 but, even then, we cannot know that a gram of CO_2 has a precisely measurable, long-term effect upon global warming. To quote spurious accuracies invites argument over the exact number, an argument which then delays acceptance of the existence of a powerful risk that aggregate CO_2-e has had, and will continue to have, a cumulative impact upon climate, a risk that is not dependent upon the exact arithmetic.

Figure 5.1 shows the parameters used by the Department of Energy and Climate Change: their accuracy, or lack of it, will not threaten the general argument, nor the policy analysis that follows. The emission of CO_2-e per kWh gives a comparison of the relative effects of the various fuels.[3] Some of the figures seem to be counter-intuitive,

Energy source	Units	Kg of CO_2-e per unit	Kg of CO_2-e per kWh
Electricity from coal-fired thermal power stations*	tonne	2642.7	0.37455
Natural gas	Cu. m.	2.2240	0.20322
LPG	litre	1.6786	0.24127
Gas oil	litre	3.5477	0.32331
Fuel oil	tonne	3766.5	0.31108
Burning oil	tonne	3750.1	0.29247
Diesel	litre	3.1787	0.30099
Petrol	litre	2.7329	0.28455

Figure 5.1 Emissions of CO_2 equivalent (CO_2-e) by various fuels
Source: Carbontrust.com.
Note: * The average CO_2-e emissions per kWh are falling as an increasing proportion of electricity is generated from natural gas and renewables.

particularly the fact that electricity appears to produce more CO_2-e per kWh (0.37455 kg) than diesel (0.30099 kg), contradicting the common assumption that replacing diesel trains and buses with electric trains and trams is environmentally desirable. However, the figure for electricity includes the inefficiencies of power-stations and also the transmission losses between generation and use: in contrast, the figure for diesel does not include the emissions caused by refining and transporting.

Fuel consumption and CO_2-e emissions: cars

Predictable rates of CO_2-e emissions are clearly vital if the total CO_2-e is to be used as the touchstone of sustainability. If a litre of petrol is poured into a tray and set alight,[4] the combustion will create 1.38 cubic metres of CO_2-e, weighing 2.73 kg. Burning the petrol in a vehicle's engine rather than wasting it in an open tray, will make little difference: the quantity of CO_2-e produced will still be substantial. The 50 litres of petrol in the tank of a family car will create 136 kg of CO_2-e, weighing rather more than the driver.

The fuel used by motor vehicles is a function of speed. Most cars have an optimum speed of about 55 km/h. At lower speeds the engine works less efficiently but, at higher speeds, power is wasted in pushing tonnes of air out of the way. The combination of these twin effects creates the shallow 'bathtub'-shaped curve shown in Figure 5.2.

Figure 5.2 contrasts three methods of estimating the CO_2-e emissions in grams of CO_2-e per kilometre for an average car with a 1.8-litre petrol engine. The TAG and VMM curves are both derived from models of petrol consumption in millilitres per kilometre as it varies with speed. The consumption has then been converted into CO_2-e emissions at 2.729 grams per millilitre.

The TAG curve[5] is the model used by the British government to predict the fuel consumption of an 'average' car with a petrol engine. It is self-evidently very wrong: when a vehicle is stationary with the engine running, fuel is being burnt and CO_2-e released but the distance covered is zero, giving an infinite emission of grams of CO_2-e

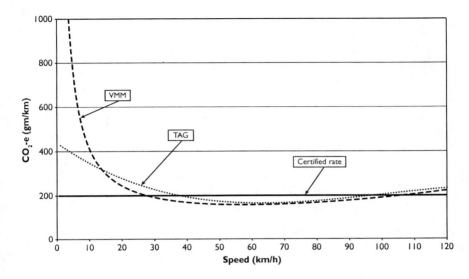

Figure 5.2 Emissions of CO_2-e released by the petrol burnt in an average car as a function of its speed

per kilometre, not the 438 predicted by the TAG curve. This infinite rate of consumption when a vehicle is stationary with the engine idling is shown correctly by the VMM curve.[6] Both curves show a similar L-shape – one gives an optimal speed of 58 km/h and the other 63km/h – but the TAG curve shows emissions at speeds of more than 40 km/h to be approximately 20 per cent greater than the VMM curve. As shown in Chapter 19, the rate at which fuel is used or saved is a crucial input to economic assessments of schemes designed to improve traffic flow and the TAG curve, showing a basic error in consumptions at speeds of 10 km/h or less, has biased the assessments against reducing urban congestion. The magnified fuel consumption at speeds over 20 km/h has created a similar but opposite bias in favour of improving traffic flow at speeds typical of the open road. In contrast, the VMM curve shows that fuel consumption, together with the consequent output of CO_2-e, doubles if the speed falls from 30 km/h to 10km/h and doubles again if it falls to 5 km/h. This is crucial to the creation of sustainable transport policy.

In contrast, the constant straight line rate of CO_2-e emission is the certified rate printed on British vehicle registration documents as a characteristic of the make, model and year of manufacture. In fact, as both the TAG and VMM curves show, real on-road rates are anything but constant. However, the official rate printed on the registration document is not intended to give the on-road performance but to compare the performance of one car as against others under strictly controlled, standard conditions. Despite that intention, the given constant rate can very easily be misleading, being the rate measured in a laboratory with the car on rollers while being subjected to a European standard pattern of theoretical speeds and accelerations

72 Fuel consumption and greenhouse gases

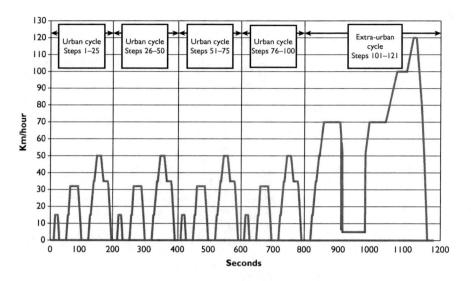

Figure 5.3 The European standard fuel consumption test (80/1268/EEC)

(shown in Figure 5.3). Not only do real on-road rates vary but they are generally higher than the laboratory rates.

The European standard test lasts 1180 seconds, divided into 121 steps. There are five elements, four identical simulations of start-stop urban driving and one of extra-urban driving. Examples of every make, model and variation are tested and the consumption rate averaged over all 121 steps of the entire cycle. This fuel consumption rate, measured in millilitres per kilometre, is then converted to the CO_2 emission per kilometre that appears on British car registration documents by using the standard production of CO_2 per litre of fuel. It must be re-emphasised that the purpose of the test is to provide comparisons of different cars by using a rigorous, standard test carried out in standard conditions: it is only vaguely related to real, on-road performance. Figure 5.4 shows the fuel burn per second by a particular, sample car with a 1.8-litre petrol engine as it is led through the pattern of speed changes shown in Figure 5.3.

Averages are used as generalisations to represent a variable quantity but, although averages are good representations of symmetrical changes in the value of a variable, an average may be a poor, misleading representation of asymmetric variations. It may well lull the senses into believing that it is properly representative. In general, averages should be considered with benign scepticism no matter what arcane arithmetic is used to create them. As an example of the problems that may arise, Figure 5.4 shows the changes in a car's fuel consumption (incidentally, it shows that for every second during which the car is stationary, the engine still burns 0.35 ml petrol, an infinitely large rate of burn per kilometre). During the 1180 seconds of the test, the car 'travels'[7] 11.013 km at an average speed of 33.6 km/h and burns 854.9 ml of petrol at an overall rate of 77.63 ml/km. However, if the total fuel burn is estimated by assuming

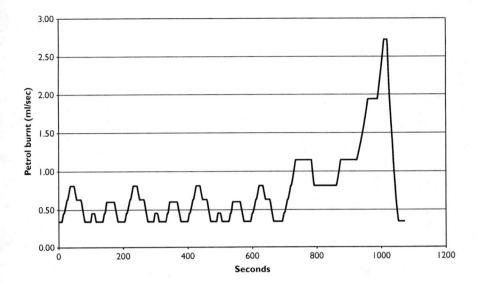

Figure 5.4 Fuel consumption by a 1.8-litre petrol car during the EU test cycle

Note: This figure has been derived from Figure 5.3 by modelling fuel consumption and CO_2-e emission rates as a function of speed using the VMM model. It will be seen that there is a positive fuel burn even when the car is at rest.

that the average speed (33.6 km/h) is a good representation of the complete cycle, a speed at which the consumption is 66.5 ml/km, the result is an estimated total burn of 732.4 ml, 14 per cent less than the actual, metered burn. This small example demonstrates a simple but universal truth: if real variations are individually calculated and then summed to create an overall result, it will usually differ from bundling all the variations into an average and then using that to create a total.

Using a theoretical hybrid of the VMM and TAG curves displayed in Figure 5.2, Figure 5.5 shows the estimated average CO_2-e emission rates for average cars and vans (light goods vehicles) with either a petrol or a diesel engine.

The indicative rates of CO_2-e emissions shown in Figure 5.5 are far from exact and should be used with care. Consumption varies continuously over a wide range as vehicles accelerate and brake. Many modern cars have dashboard displays showing both the instantaneous and average rates of fuel consumption: the instantaneous rate will only fleetingly align with the average rate and both are likely to be very different from the constant rate printed on the registration document.

Sustainable policy-making must take two important generalisations into account:

1   The lower the constant rate of emitted CO_2 per kilometre reported in the official registration document the better. Although this is no more than a laboratory rate created to compare vehicles rather than a variable rate found in real driving, it

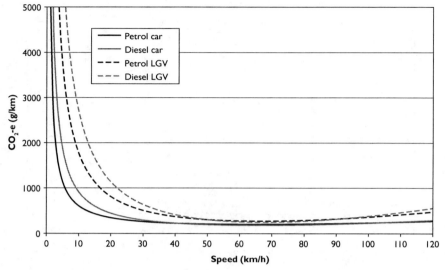

Figure 5.5 Emissions of CO_2-e as a function of speed (estimated by a theoretical hybrid of the TAG and VMM models)

locates the L-shaped curves seen in Figure 5.5: the curve for a vehicle with a low reported consumption will be markedly L-shaped and tucked well into the bottom left of the graph but a vehicle with a higher reported consumption will display a curve set more to the top right and with a less pronounced L-shape: this is because smaller engines lose some of their mechanical efficiency when working harder at higher revolutions per minute but larger engines tend to be in larger vehicles with larger frontal areas which need to spend more energy at higher speeds to push their way through the air.

2 The penalties of congested speeds are substantial, suggesting that sustainable policy should target the problems of congestion. Chapter 7 argues that the best approach to this objective may well be counter-intuitive.

Fuel consumption and CO_2-e emissions: road freight

Figure 5.6 displays the fuel consumption of loaded heavy goods vehicles as defined by TAG: 'other goods vehicles' are bundled into two groups: OGV1 with two or three axles and OGV2 with four or more axles.[8]

Figure 5.7 hints at another problem in making generalisations which veil very important variations. Many freight statistics assume that a 'fully laden' lorry is carrying the maximum payload measured in tonnes. In fact a lorry may by 'fully laden' because the floor-space is entirely taken up or, less often, because the load occupies all the available volume. The true extent of 'fully laden' lorries being below their maximum gross weight is not known but has an importance in the analysis of part and empty loading. The haulage industry has to provide many more apparent

Fuel consumption and greenhouse gases 75

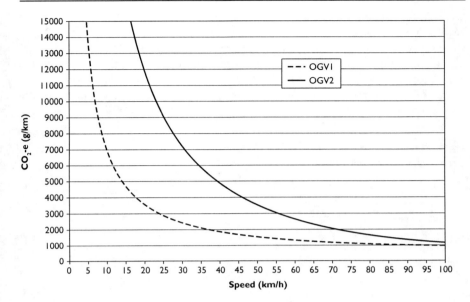

Figure 5.6 Emissions of CO_2-e by heavy goods vehicles as a function of speed (estimated by a theoretical hybrid of the TAG and VMM models)

		Floor area (m^2)	Volume (m^3)	Gross weight (kg)	Tare weight (kg)	Payload (kg)
OGV1[1]	Dropside	11.35		7500	3800	3700
	Box	13.49	31.84	7500	4000	3500
	Box + tail-lift	13.49	31.84	7500	4500	3000
	Curtain sided	14.38	32.80	7500	4300	3200
	Curtain sided	20.34	52.06	18000	7500	10500
	Box + tail-lift	20.83	51.24	18000	8000	10000
OGV2[2]	Articulated (4-axle)	52.30	260.00	38000	14000	24000
	Articulated (5-axle)	52.30	260.00	40000	14000	26000
	Articulated (6-axle)	52.30	260.00	44000	15000	29000
Containers	20-foot	14.40	33.20	30480	2170	28310
(Demounted)	40-foot	29.00	67.59	30480	3750	26730
Roll-cage		0.625	1.06	650	50	600

Figure 5.7 Lorry and container capacities

Notes:
[1] Other goods vehicles.
[2] Other goods vehicles.

tonne-kilometres than are actually used to cover running part-loaded or empty, much of it unavoidable,[9] and also to cover the fact that many lorries are 'fully laden' even though they are not up to the maximum permissible tonnage. The CO_2-e emissions are mainly a function of engine size and speed, and the overall fuel use and emission is far greater than is seemingly needed by the tonne-kilometre carried. Although an additional tonne of cargo does make a difference to a lorry's performance, overall emissions are not related to tonne-kilometres by neat and tidy arithmetic.

Fuel consumption and CO_2-e emissions: road passenger transport

Figure 5.8 shows a fuel consumption curve for an 'average' passenger carrying vehicle (PCV) as defined in TAG but the definition neglects to say how the average was created. As with the curves in Figures 5.5 and 5.6, this curve has been calculated by a theoretical combination of the TAG and VMM models. Pinning fuel consumption rates on double-decker buses is difficult, since they operate in widely different circumstances. As with all vehicles driven directly by internal combustion engines, they consume fuel at an infinite rate when stationary and very high rates when moving intermittently and slowly in congested traffic. The mix of bus-stops and of congestion is very variable, making it difficult to identify generalised rates.

Transport for London estimates the average operational consumption to be 0.28 litres per kilometre but the technical press[10] cites instances double this figure. A fully laden double-decker is able to carry around 6 tonnes of people – a report to the Department of Transport[11] suggests that a full load of passengers increases

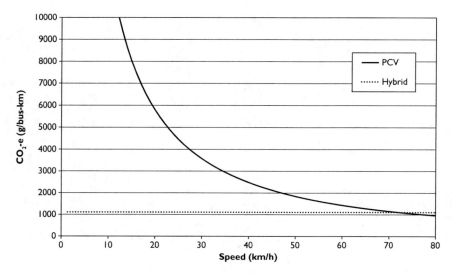

Figure 5.8 Emissions of CO_2-e by average buses as a function of speed (estimated by a theoretical hybrid of the TAG and VMM models)

consumption by less than 10 per cent, although this is magnified by speed. Only a minimal proportion of bus-kilometres are driven at speeds above 40 km/h and so a generalised, representative rate of 0.55 litre of diesel per bus-kilometre is likely to be inaccurate but acceptable. At the rate of 2.64 kg of CO_2-e per litre, this emits 1.45 kg of GHG per bus-kilometre, a rate that will vary with speed and, in reality, is unlikely to be precisely accurate at any given instant.

Within the past five years or so the transmission of power from the bus engine to the wheels has developed in a radical direction, leading to a reduction in the fuel used, but also breaking the link between speed and pollution. The theory behind the 'hybrid bus' has been known for some time, but it is only quite recently that such buses have entered service. The theory has been delivered by modern electronics providing sophisticated controls of the on-board production and use of power. Hybrid buses are driven by an electric motor drawing its power from a bank of batteries. These are charged by a generator driven by a much smaller diesel engine than those fitted to the traditional diesel buses. The smaller engine in the hybrid runs at an efficient, constant speed, generating the electricity to be stored in the batteries until it is needed to power the bus. This basic design may have some variations: smarter electronic controls may link the diesel-driven generator directly to the electric motor, bypassing the batteries, whenever it is more efficient to do so. Still other variations enable the diesel engine to be uncoupled from the generator and paired directly with the wheels, as in existing buses. The reason behind these variations is that electric motors are very good at starting the bus from stationary and at moving it along at low speeds, but direct mechanical linkage is more efficient at higher speeds.

In any event, the diesel engine in a hybrid bus does not have to have the brute strength to overcome the inertia of a fully loaded stationary bus; nor does it have to propel the bus at the slow, congested speeds at which diesel engines are inherently inefficient: electric motors are better at doing both of these things. An engine the size of those in 1.5-tonne delivery vans is sufficient to keep the batteries charged. The hybrid bus therefore evens out the supply of power and the fuel burn, releasing the engine from the need to supply power at the instant that it is needed. When the bus is stationary it does not consume power at all, although it does continue to produce power to be stored in the batteries until it is needed. The L-shaped curve relating power production to speed becomes redundant, replaced by a constant such as that shown in Figure 5.8.

Hybrid buses have another, very important attribute: regenerative braking. The electric motor normally used to drive the bus may be used as a very efficient brake. When the power from the batteries to the motor is switched off, the momentum of the bus may then be used to continue to turn the motor, converting it from a motor into a generator, creating electricity to be fed back into the batteries and braking the bus as it does so. This replaces the traditional friction brakes which convert the momentum of the bus into heat which is then blown away and wasted.

Transport for London reports that hybrid buses now in service are using 40 per cent less fuel than buses with normal mechanical transmission. This comes from a combination of regenerative braking and using the attributes of the electric motor to heave the weight of the bus and its load from stops. From an environmental point of view it not only reduces pollution but keeps much of it away from congested streets where the diesel engines of normal buses work so inefficiently.

The disadvantages of hybrid buses are that they are more expensive to buy, weigh more and are complicated, interposing very smart automated electronics between the driver and the bus. This must be an admitted potential hazard but one with rather fewer implications than the electronics interposed between modern aircraft and their pilots.

Fuel consumption and CO_2-e emissions: rail

Consumption rates on railways are fraught with complexity. Power is derived either from diesel consumed on the train itself or from electricity generated elsewhere and incurring transmission costs from the power-station to the trackside. Power consumption rates are spread over a wide range depending upon speeds, loadings, gradients, etc. Over recent years passenger trains have gradually changed from being a string of unpowered coaches hauled by a single locomotive, to a rake of carriages with power units at each end and then to sets of coaches, each with its own power pack. Freight trains have continued to be locomotive hauled, although very heavy trains are sometimes topped and tailed with locos at each end. This is a variation of the practice in other parts of the world where radio-controlled locomotives are distributed along the length of very long, heavy trains to prevent destructive stress upon the coupling between a single locomotive and the train it is hauling.

These different configurations make it difficult to identify common measures: certainly consumption per train would be useless, since trains vary greatly in their length and capacity. Load factors (the weight of the actual load as a proportion of the maximum capacity) and the consequent fuel consumption per tonne or person carried are also very variable. It would be easy to take the annual fuel consumption and divide it by the total passenger- and tonne-kilometres to calculate an average rate of consumption but this would not create a criterion by which to judge the relative merits of policies and actions. The need is for an estimate of future consumption as affected by some potential policy or action, not a measure of past average performances.

A study of the transfer of traffic from road to rail in Scotland[12] focused on two specific forms of traffic: the haulage of goods packed into seagoing containers and the movement of cement powder in bulk. The same locomotive type was used in both cases, consuming 4.35 litres of diesel per train-kilometre, emitting 13.83 kg of CO_2-e as it does so. Figure 5.9 shows that the container train consisted of 12 wagons, each carrying two containers. The cement train had 31 short, four-wheeled wagons, making a train length comparable to that of the container train. The capacity of sidings and passing loops would have limited overall train length: although this is not reported, it may be assumed that both trains are of the maximum possible length.

The 40 per cent difference in the GHG emission per tonne of payload between the container (0.0216 grams per payload tonne-kilometre) and the cement (0.0125) trains is not due to the load carried but to the hardware used to carry it. Seagoing containers have revolutionised shipping practices and costs but they have to be exceptionally strong to withstand the weight of other containers stacked on top of them on the quayside and in the ship. When a ship is at sea the effective weight of a container is

	40-ft containers	Bulk cement	Australian test train		Swiss electric train
Loco (tonnes)	130	130	328		
Wagons	12	31			13
Tare (tonnes)	152.4				
Containers	24				
Tare (tonnes)	242.4	131.75			232.5
Gross (tonnes)	883.92	1240	2700		
Payload (tonnes)	641.52	1108.25			1027.5
Train (tonnes)	1013.92	1370	3028		1260
Diesel litres/ train-km	4.3505	4.3505	15.4000	kWh/ train-km	14.5530
Diesel litres/ pay tonne-km	0.0068	0.0039		kWh/pay tonne-km	11.8676
Diesel litres/ train tonne-km	0.0043	0.0032	0.0051	kWh/train tonne-km	0.0116
Kg CO_2-e/ litre diesel	3.1787	3.1787	3.1787	Kg CO_2-e/ kWh	0.4470
Kg CO_2-e/ train-km	13.8290	13.8290	48.9520	Kg CO_2-e/ train-km	6.5052
Kg CO_2-e/ pay tonne-km	0.0216	0.0125		Kg CO_2-e/ pay tonne-km	5.3048
Kg CO_2-e/ train tonne-km	0.0136	0.0101	0.0162	Kg CO_2-e/ train tonne-km	0.0052

Figure 5.9 Rail freight case studies

multiplied as the ship rides the waves. This dynamic effect may be easily demonstrated: if a hammer weighing no more than a tin of beans is rested upon your hand you will feel the weight on your skin and no more, but if your hand is hit by the same hammer it will hurt due to the weight being magnified by the speed at which the hammer is moving. You will feel this effect even if the hammer has moved through quite a short distance and is not travelling that fast when it hits your hand; the lurching of a ship being battered by a storm does not make the containers move up and down very quickly but the jolting magnifies their momentarily effective weight, an effect they must be heavy and strong enough to withstand.

The 24 seagoing containers on the train in the case study weigh a total of 90 tonnes and the wagons that carry them have to be sturdy too: each weighs another 7.5 tonnes, giving a total of 242 tonnes even when the train is entirely empty. The loco weighs another 130 tonnes, giving an overall weight of the empty train of 372 tonnes. When fully laden with each of the 24 containers packed with the maximum 26.7 tonnes of cargo, the train carries a 641-tonne payload, giving a total weight of train and cargo of 1014 tonnes. In contrast, the cement is carried in 31 much lighter, self-contained wagons, each weighing 4.25 tonnes when empty, leaving more capacity for a 1100-tonne payload. This is 75 per cent greater than that on the container train and creates the substantial difference in the fuel burn per payload tonne-kilometre.

No figure used to represent a range of different values will ever be universally applicable – there will always be differences between any estimate used in predicting the effectiveness of policies and decisions and the later, real data. This is particularly true in transport where speeds, flows and fuel consumptions are constantly changing. It has already been noted that the fuel burn of road vehicles fluctuates from moment to moment, with the real, instantaneous rate of consumption coinciding only fleetingly with any representative constant. The problem is to select a representative quantity that does not mislead either by hiding crucial variations (such as the rates of road vehicle fuel consumption tending towards the infinite at low speeds) or by being hopelessly optimistic (such as the rate printed on registration documents). Even where data appear to be accurate and verifiable, there are likely to be differences over time and space. For example, a flow of traffic may be counted accurately to be 600 vehicles an hour, giving a rate of 10 vehicles per minute, but very few minutes, possibly none, will see exactly 10 vehicles pass by. Moreover, even if the flow per hour is constant (which is unlikely), the minute-by-minute fluctuations will be different at different times and at different places along the road. Identifying a constant to represent a complex, ever-changing quantity is fraught with difficulties, and there will be unavoidable differences between any chosen representative value and the real quantity at particular times and places: these differences and variations are neither a sign of inaccuracy nor a sign of invalidity but reflect implicit statistical problems. The usual device is to use an average, but averages themselves have to be constructed and used carefully to ensure they do not mislead. The restless disparities between real and representative data often unsettle engineers and scientists thirsting for accuracy who then focus upon refining and modifying representative quantities to a level where they may appear to be more 'accurate' but are useless in decision-making, often because they require more input data which are themselves intrinsically variable: for example, any attempt to account for the minute-by-minute variations in traffic flows will require more complicated and questionable data to be fed into the calculation.

The differences between the container and cement trains are illuminating. The loaded container train may emit 0.0216 kg CO_2-e per tonne of payload but it would be foolish to use this figure to estimate the emissions of other trains, since it is very dependent upon the hardware being used (heavy containers and wagons) and upon the load factors: similar trains with empty or lightly loaded containers will have significantly different rates. The very different 0.0125 kg CO_2-e per tonne of payload of the cement train gives a hint that emissions related primarily to the train, not to its cargo. If the train is empty, half-full or fully laden it will emit more or less the same amount of CO_2-e per *train*-kilometre although the emission per *cargo tonne*-kilometre will vary enormously.

The emissions are due to the train's journey: the load factor makes a difference to the arithmetic behind the emission per payload tonne but not to the overall quantity of the emission. Rather than use emission per payload tonne-kilometre as a representative quantity, it is more useful to use the emission per gross fully loaded *train tonne*-kilometre when it is. This reflects the capacity provided by the train together with the nature and weight of the wagons and locomotives being used. The container train returns 0.0236 kg CO_2-e per gross train tonne-kilometre while the cement train achieves 0.0101 kg, despite the same type of locomotive being used for both trains. Significantly, these rates are an exact reflection of relative gross train weights when fully laden. This suggests two policies: first, train hardware should be as light as possible; second, the capacity should be as well used as possible. The first policy will reduce the energy used per train-kilometre and the second will ensure that energy is spent productively.

There are very few studies providing similar detail to the container/cement cases. The difficulty is magnified by rail freight companies appearing to believe that data collection is expensive and unnecessary, and then hiding whatever data are collected behind 'commercial confidentiality'.[13] The focus seems to be upon the out-turn fuel consumption per payload tonne-kilometre: this is understandable, since the prime concern of the freight operating companies is to study recent past performance in a quest to control operational cost and revenue rather than identifying representative quantities to be used in estimating future emissions.

There is confusion over the CO_2-e emissions by electric trains. It is true that the different means of the generation of electricity have different and distinctive rates of CO_2-e emissions: coal-fired power-stations emit far more CO_2-e per generated kWh than those burning natural gas, while renewables emit none. The average CO_2-e per generated kWh has reduced significantly over recent years due mainly to the increasing use of natural gas in place of coal and to the use of renewables. Some studies of electricity used by the railways have attempted to distinguish between the fuels used in generation and have also attempted to account for the transmission losses between power-stations and trains. This ensures that the estimation of the emitted CO_2-e per kWh used by trains is complex and confusing – a further example of 'accuracy' being unhelpful.

The exploration, extraction, refining and distribution costs of diesel are not converted into emissions and scored against diesel trains – they are properly scored against the oil industry. Similarly, one kWh has the same effect in powering a train as another, regardless of its source. To lay the arithmetic of CO_2-e per kWh at the door of the railways produces unhelpful complexities that may be argued over in detail while more fundamental issues are glossed over. It is quite sufficient to take representative emissions and use them to illuminate policy.

The results of two other test trains are also reported in Figure 5.9. The Australian test was with diesel locomotives that were almost identical to those used in the container/cement study but over a much more hilly route. The result is not incompatible with the earlier study.

A Swiss test train weighing 1260 tonnes drawn by an electric locomotive and traversing gradients of up to 1.2 per cent (1 in 80) consumed an average of 0.0116 kWh per gross train tonne-kilometre,[14] a figure reduced by regenerative braking.[15] Using the mean British rate of 0.444 kg CO_2 per kWh[16] at the point of generation and adjusting it upward by 1.0064 to convert from CO_2 to CO_2-e, the consumption of the 0.0116 kWh reported in the Swiss case will create 0.005 kg CO_2-e per gross train tonne-kilometre. Network Rail have reported computer simulated data based on a nest of assumptions.[17]

This estimated a power consumption of 0.021 kWh per gross train-kilometre for a train similar to that in the Swiss test: this is 80 per cent more than the Swiss train's 0.0116 kWh, a figure that may well be the result of the British train being hauled by a simulated aged locomotive without regenerative braking and the Swiss train hauled in reality by a brand-new TRAXX model with up-to-date regenerative braking. An estimated emission of 0.005 kg CO_2-e per gross train tonne-kilometre appears to be a robust assumption for future generations of electric freight haulage.

A comparable diesel freight train produces 2.7 times as much CO_2-e per gross train tonne-kilometre (0.0136) and a fully loaded 44-tonne articulated lorry 5 times as much (0.02551 kg CO_2-e per gross vehicle tonne-kilometre). There is no gainsaying that these comparative multipliers are inaccurate and should be viewed with care: they are the product of a chain of estimates and assumptions about very variable quantities. No doubt some people will argue that such generalisations are incredible and should be ignored, but the differences are so large that their ranking and scale is unlikely to be wrong: inaccurate perhaps, but not misleading. Other people are likely to come to the opposite conclusion, arguing that if lorries produce five times as much CO_2-e per tonne-kilometre as an electric freight train, 80 per cent of GHG emissions could be saved by transferring freight from road to electric railway. That would be true if all freight were carried between addresses served by rail but that is never going to be the case. Chapters 8 and 10 consider the opportunities and constraints for the use of rail and for reaping some of the benefits of its efficient use of energy.

For passenger trains the confusion between emissions per passenger rather than per train appear to be entrenched but the solution is easier to perceive. The 10 a.m. train from Edinburgh to London will consume energy and create CO_2-e, no matter whether every seat is full or empty. It is true that if all 554 seats were occupied by 60 tonnes of obese tourists rather than, say, 25 tonnes of fashion models, power consumption would rise but probably by less than making an extra intermediate stop. The energy used is proportional to the gross weight of the train, including passengers, but they and their luggage are only a small proportion of the total train weight. Trains vary in their capacity and weight, and so the important parameter is the capacity (the number of persons at full load) and the gross train weight per person.[18] This is not a constant.

Figure 5.10 reports the findings of research by the Railway Safety and Standards Board into the performances of some British passenger trains, both diesel and electric. It shows that power consumption and the resultant GHG emissions per train-kilometre are very variable but performances per tonne- and place-kilometre are similar, apart from a very marked difference between diesel and electric trains: electric trains emit approximately 50 per cent of the GHG emissions of diesel trains. The other generalisation is that high-performance trains such as the French TGV (Eurostar) and the German ICE have the higher emissions expected as the price of their performance.

The data suggest two policies similar to those advocated for freight transport: first, the important metric is the GHG emission per seat, regardless of whether that seat is occupied or not. Second, the mechanical efficiency and fuel consumption of trains is a function of their loaded weight. This suggests the following:

	Places	Tonnes	Fuel (per train-km)	Fuel (per place-km)	CO_2-e (kg/ tonne-km)	CO_2-e (kg/ place-km)
			Diesel (litres)	Diesel (litres)		
170 Turbostar (2-car)	119	91.4	0.908	0.0076	0.0316	0.0243
170 Turbostar (3-car)	164	133.7	1.362	0.0083	0.0324	0.0264
180 (Adente)	268	254.8	2.626	0.0098	0.0328	0.0312
220 (Voyager)	188	185.6	2.256	0.0120	0.0386	0.0381
221 (Tilt)	246	282.8	2.952	0.0120	0.0332	0.0381
125 (2+7)	541	447.0	4.761	0.0088	0.0339	0.0280
125 (2+8)	617	480.6	5.491	0.0089	0.0363	0.0283
			Electricity (kWh)	Electricity (kWh)		
357 (ElectStar)	282	157.6	8.798	0.031	0.0250	0.0140
460 (Juniper)	274	164.0	8.768	0.032	0.0240	0.0143
IC225	554	476.0	17.728	0.032	0.0167	0.0143
390 Pendolino (9-car)	439	460.0	17.560	0.040	0.0171	0.0179
390 Pendolino (11-car)	591	562.0	20.685	0.035	0.0165	0.0157
Eurostar[a]	750	721.0	41.250	0.055	0.0257	0.0247
ICE 3M[a]	430	435.0	28.380	0.066	0.0293	0.0296
SET[b] III (el)	696	438.0	33.000	0.047	0.0338	0.0213
SET[b] III (bi)	309	249.0	66.000	0.214	0.1188	0.0958

Figure 5.10 Out-turn performances of some British passenger trains

Source: Railway Safety and Standards Board (augmented).

Notes:
[a] High-speed trains.
[b] Proposed British Super Express Train.

- Trains should be built with the lowest possible weight per seat. There is clearly a balance between passenger comfort and train weight per place: providing sufficient knee room, lavatories, buffets, adequate luggage space, etc. reduces the number of places and pushes up the weight per place. Providing air-conditioning, sound insulation, etc. pushes up the train weight.
- Seat occupancy should be maximised.

Sensible representative figures would appear to be 0.033 kWh (0.0148 kg CO_2-e) per seat-kilometre for normal electric trains and 0.060 kWh (0.026 kg CO_2-e) for high-performance electrics. A reasonable representative consumption for diesel trains appears to be 0.01 litres (0.32 kg CO_2-e) per seat-kilometre. There will always be specific examples and occasions when these generalised assumptions will be wrong, but they are unlikely to be so wrong that they lead to poor decision-making.

Fuel consumption and CO_2-e emissions: air

There is a plethora of data about aircraft and their performances: one of the most useful references focuses upon the fuel burn and emission per 'available seat-kilometres' (ASK) and 'available tonne-kilometres' (ATK).[19] The report rejects the use of emissions per passenger- or tonne-kilometre on the grounds that such quantities are dependent on load factors – on how much of the capacity is occupied. The paper argues that 'the load factor is not a technical property of the aircraft but a measure of the operational efficiency of the airline'.

The survey arrives at a sensible, robust generalisation of 4.55 litres per aircraft-kilometre. In truth, there will be variations away from this representative quantity: short-haul flights burn more, since burn rates increase during take-off. Weather conditions cause burn rates to fluctuate during all flights, quite apart from the variations among makes and models.

Aircraft burning around 4.5 litres per aircraft-kilometre are big enough to carry 400 passengers[20] or 113 tonnes of freight, or combinations of the two. This returns either 0.01 litre per seat-kilometre (0.36 grams CO_2-e), no matter whether the seat is occupied or not, or 0.04 litres per tonne-kilometre of payload capacity (0.29 grams CO_2-e), no matter whether the capacity is used or not.

Rates per vehicle-, person- and tonne-kilometre

The problems of distilling representative quantities to be used in predicting the future effects of potential decisions from a heap of data on past performance are fraught. Many people in the transport industry believe that the real need is to identify the GHG emissions per person- or tonne-kilometre. It is argued that vehicles, be they cars, lorries or trains, only move to carry people or goods and there is no significant benefit to be gained from vehicle movements unless they are carrying a load of some sort. This may be true, but it hides the problem of then identifying representative loads from which the representative future per person- or tonne-kilometre may be derived. The arithmetic can fluctuate wildly depending on the load: a 1.8 petrol-driven car emits about 162 grams of CO_2-e per car-kilometre at 30 km/h. A lone driver will then account for 162 grams of CO_2-e per person-kilometre but a load of five people will reduce this to 32 grams per head. The immutable fact is that the emission is generated by the car-kilometre, not by the person-kilometres of those in the car.

This is emphasised in Figure 5.11. This shows the effective CO_2-e emission per passenger-kilometre given the speed and the number of passengers. The fuel burn and emissions are for an average passenger carrying vehicle (PCV – a bus or coach) estimated by the government's TAG model[21] and shown in Figure 5.8, but using four sample speeds, 5, 10, 15 and 20 km/h, rather than the whole speed range.

When the rates in Figure 5.11 are compared with those for a car shown in Figure 5.5, it appears that GHG emissions per person-kilometre by PCV are less than those

Fuel consumption and greenhouse gases 85

by a car occupied by just the driver, providing, at a speed of 5 km/h, that there are 22 or more passengers on board or, at 20 km/h, 16 or more. At first sight this appears to be a sensible metric but it has two practical difficulties:

1   Figure 5.11 shows a very wide range and complicated pattern with rates per passenger-kilometre sensitive to both speed and loading. The combination of assumptions on vehicle size, speed and occupancy can shift the calculated emission rate from very low to very high values almost at choice. The use of such data in predicting future rates would depend on predictions of both speed and the numbers of passengers, quantities so volatile that credible future estimates would be almost impossible.
2   Most importantly, the graph does not, and cannot, show the effects of one extra passenger upon the bus. It cannot do so because, although the extra weight of an additional passenger will have an effect on consumption, that effect will be almost imperceptible.

This is a crucial problem when considering policy-making. Conventional bus services are provided to a timetable: the costs and emissions made are unrelated to the number of passengers carried. Hence, the emissions per *passenger*-kilometre are a fortuitous by-product of the numbers of people who happen to use the service: emissions per *vehicle*-kilometre are a product of the services provided and are fixed for as long as the timetable is in operation. If a person uses, or does not use, a timetabled bus, the service costs and pollutions are completely unaffected.

The same problem arises in freight transport. Some haulage is timetabled with committed emissions independent of loads, but the rest is essentially demand-responsive.

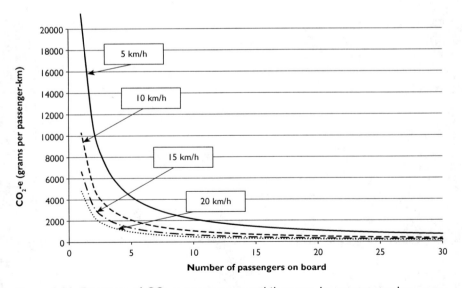

Figure 5.11 Emission of CO_2-e per passenger-kilometre by an average bus as a function of the number of passengers

Predicting the proportions of total lorry-kilometres that were timetabled would be impossible, but the need for some prediction is clear. A number of studies were commissioned to predict the effect of raising the maximum gross vehicle weight to 44 tonnes,[22] and there are likely to be future studies into the possibility of transferring some freight from road to rail. The need is for a forecast of the number of lorry-kilometres and their CO_2-e emissions, given a set of circumstances which may be dictated by government (e.g. altering taxation or the regulations on lorry sizes) or by local decisions (e.g. to build freight handling depots). Some will argue that load factors and tonne-kilometres will be important, just as the numbers of passengers and passenger-kilometres have been thought to be important. Figure 5.12 gives some clues as to the importance of load factors: it tells the same story as bus occupancy. Emissions per tonne-kilometre are significantly influenced by load factors but perhaps by not as much as may have been thought, and, in any event, speed is a far greater influence, suggesting, once again, that policies and actions to reduce congestion will be more effective in reducing pollution than policies to improve load factors.

The conclusion is clear. The forecasting of GHG emissions, forecasts to be used in assessing the effects of possible future policies and actions, must be based on two components: the number of vehicle-kilometres and the rate of fuel consumption and GHG emission per vehicle-kilometre. Load factors and tonne-kilometres may be components in forecasts of vehicle-kilometres, but using a metric of GHG per tonne-kilometre would be entangled in a thicket of assumptions and a forest of different rates like those hinted at in Figure 5.12. Simple emission rates per vehicle-kilometre will also provide protection against technological change. Hybrid buses and cars are already on the road and hybrid vans and trucks must be in the offing: they will change

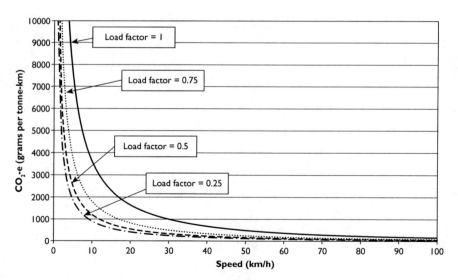

Figure 5.12 Emission of CO_2-e by a 44-tonne gross weight articulated lorry (OGV2) at differing speeds and load factors

the economics of the freight and distribution industry with knock-on effects on load factors, empty running, etc.

Summary

The task of those planning sustainable transport is to predict and assess the effects of changes to the transport system, no matter whether those changes are deliberate policies or actions, or organic shifts produced by the aggregation of myriad individual choices. Generalised, representative rates of fuel burn and GHG emissions are necessary in making those predictions and assessments. In general the emissions are from vehicles, trains and planes, not from people. The better the design, the less GHG is discharged per seat- or tonne-kilometre of capacity. Lowering the total GHG emission is then a product of, first, reducing the numbers of vehicle-kilometres (a matter of managing urban and economic geography) and, second, striving to use the provided seat- and tonne-kilometres to best advantage.

This chapter has focused upon emissions per vehicle-, train- and plane-kilometre, arguing that emissions per unit of load is not a useful planning metric, since load factors are volatile and so difficult to forecast. As Peeters *et al.* have said, 'the load factor is not a technical property of the aircraft but a measure of the operational efficiency of the airline': a truism that applies throughout transport.

Notes

1 See www.carbontrust.co.uk/cut-carbon-reduce-costs/calculate/carbon-footprint.
2 See www.defra/DECC/GHG Conversion Factors for Company Reporting in Table 1.1.
3 A watt is a tiny unit of instantaneous energy, roughly equal to a tennis ball travelling at 23 km/h, energy of which you would be suddenly very conscious if the ball hit you. Energy is usually measured in larger, more tangible units: kilowatts (kW = 1000 watts), megawatts (mW = one million watts) or even gigawatts (GW – a thousand million watts). Power is energy delivered over a sustained length of time: a kilowatt-hour (kWh) is a flow of 1000 watts lasting one hour and is the energy consumed by a small electric fire left on for an hour.
4 It should be noted that this is a theoretical suggestion and should not be verified in practice; particularly indoors.
5 Department for Transport, *Traffic Assessment Guidance, Unit 3.5.6*, Paragraph 1.3.5.
6 Kirby and Hutton (2003).
7 Remember: the car is in the laboratory on rollers.
8 See Highways Agency, *Design Manual for Roads and Bridges* (DMRB), Volume 7, Section 2, Part 1 for the definitions.
9 For example, tankers supplying petrol filling stations are obliged to return empty, although the effect may be reduced by minimising the number of stations served per trip and by crafty scheduling.
10 See, e.g. the Volvo website which quotes 0.55 litres/kilometre.
11 Davies and Mayer (2003).
12 Department for Transport (2010).
13 See, e.g. Department for Transport (2012b).
14 Bombardier Ltd. Sales information for their TRAXX locomotive.
15 Many electric trains are able to use their motors as generators when rolling downhill. This acts as a brake while also feeding energy back into the electricity supply network.

88 Fuel consumption and greenhouse gases

16 www.earthorganization.org. This is less than the official government rate of 0.545, which includes transmission and distribution losses.
17 Network Rail (2008).
18 Capacity is usually given in the number of seats, but sometimes public transport is designed to accommodate standing passengers, so the number of 'places' rather than 'seats' is appropriate.
19 Peeters *et al.* (2005).
20 This is another variable that is difficult to pin down. Some Airbus 330-300 aircraft have 295 seats, others 440.
21 Department for Transport, *Traffic Assessment Guidance, Unit 3.5.6*, Paragraph 1.3.5.
22 See e.g. McKinnon (2005).

Chapter 6

Location and land use

The quandary of the interactions between transport and land use

Nothing is both produced and consumed in the same place.[1] The inputs to each productive process (no matter how primitive or advanced) have to be gathered together at a single location and the outputs taken to other places to be used: there may be neither production nor consumption without transport. Transport planners have traditionally analysed movements, the traffic flows, the tonne- and person-kilometres, but, more recently, the places at each end of movements (in transport planning jargon, the 'origins' and 'destinations') have been the focus of a more detailed concern.

The economy and people's behaviour are ever-changing. New firms, new houses, new schools and new shops are developed, older buildings and sites are redeveloped, new freight flows flower and old ones wither, people change jobs, form different relationships and move house. The geography of the multitude of origins and destinations is ever-changing. The transport system has to cater for the second-by-second movement of people, goods, waste, information and energy, as well as for the slower, insidious shifts of the places where these movements begin and end. The prime difficulty is how to understand the shifting patterns of both the origins and destinations and of the traffic they generate in ways that enable forecasts to be made of the likely effects of policy decisions. Earlier chapters have suggested that the overarching objective of sustainable transport policy should be to reduce the emission of greenhouse gases (GHG) but achieving that objective depends on decisions based upon credible forecasts of their effects, forecasts which must address both the nature and volume of movement and the geography of the places between which that movement takes place. There is an insistent quandary as to whether the locations of origins and destinations affect the volume and nature of movement or whether the characteristics of movement affect the locations of human activity – which is the cause and which is the effect.

The definitions of accessibility and mobility

By definition, the transport system must ensure that all origins and destinations are *accessible*. Initially this seems to be a useful concept but, as it stands, it is absolute.

Nowhere is totally inaccessible: man has been to the top of Everest, to both Poles, to the wreck of the Titanic and everywhere in between: places cannot be divided into the accessible and the absolutely inaccessible. To be useful, accessibility has to be relative, showing that some places are easier to get to than others.

Transport, the medium through which accessibility is provided, plays a dual role. It both provides accessibility and, as the transport network changes, moulds the differentials in accessibility between one place and another. Transport infrastructure develops in the long term but in the short term the characteristics of the working transport system change minute-by-minute as congestion and timetabled departure times come and go. In general, land uses are relatively stable but the transport system is comparatively volatile: relative accessibility is a changeable quantity.

Initially, relative accessibility may be thought of as an attribute of place. Mobility is the other side of the same coin: it is the ability of a person, firm or function to move to a more desirable, probably more accessible, location. The movement may be to a very temporary place and may be repeated over time, as in trips to the shops, but movement may be a once-in-a-lifetime shift to an almost permanent alternative location, such as moving house or relocating the entire Post Office Research Establishment from Northeast London to Suffolk in 1975. Production depends upon the collection of raw materials and the other inputs at a specific site, but some production has a fixed location – it is immobile. Coal-mines and quarries are bound to the local geology: transport can do no more than serve them by transporting their output to more convenient places. Primary production, with its fixed geography, demands that the transport system be constructed to serve it, whereas secondary production (i.e. making things) is more mobile[2] and may be sited where the transport system delivers the most advantageous costs. Even primary production is not absolutely fixed. Coal in remote, comparatively inaccessible places will be left untouched, while more accessible mines will be developed. The distinction will be made on cost grounds: if the transport system can be extended to reach remote coal deposits at acceptable cost then they will be developed; otherwise they will be left untouched.

Mobility, as a concept, is more usually applied not to industries but to specific people or groups whose ability to move is restricted. The restriction may be owing to people's personal characteristics – they may be physically or financially disabled or, perhaps, just uninformed. There may be barriers due to the nature of the transport system – steps or poor service levels. This suggests an interaction between mobility and accessibility: poor accessibility together with restricted mobility may trap some people but liberate others. Living in a remote, relatively inaccessible place without the use of a car creates an overwhelming difference to those who do have the mobility provided by the combination of a car and uncongested roads. The lack of mobility may be a constant, irretrievable, day-to-day problem, as it is with those confined to a wheelchair, or it may be a problem that is resolvable by a cataclysmic act such as making a permanent shift to another location where the restrictions are looser. A British politician once saw the solution to unemployment as 'getting on your bike to look for work'. This imagined a non-existent mobility: for example, ex-coal-miners who had bought their own homes at rock-bottom prices from the National Coal

Board, but whose homes were now worthless and impossible to sell, were effectively trapped in their pit villages; bikes were of little use in moving children to a new school, buying a house, getting a mortgage, etc.

Isochrones

Crude accessibilities may be shown graphically by isochrones: these are imaginary lines passing through all the places that may be reached from a particular journey origin within a specified travel time. As a demonstration, assume somebody is standing at a point in the very middle of a large area of flat grassland: Windsor Great Park will do as a model. If that person walks at a constant 5 km/h, in five minutes they will be 417 metres from the starting point, irrespective of which direction they take. The five-minute isochrone will be a perfect circle 417 metres in radius centred on the origin. The ten-minute isochrone will be a concentric circle 833 metres in radius. A radial line crossing the isochrones at right angles will indicate the walking speed: the isochrones are 416 metres apart, the distance covered in the five-minute time difference between the five- and ten-minute isochrones and confirming the walking speed at 5 km/h.

If there is a boggy area in one direction, forcing the walker to negotiate around it, the isochrones will be contorted, losing their circular shape by being flattened and brought closer together in the area beyond the bog.

If the example is assumed to be in an area with a dense network of roads and alleys rather than in a grassed, if slightly boggy, park, the isochrones will lose the precision of their circular shape, showing a jagged outline because point-to-point distances[3] are extended in some directions by the need to steer through the streets and footpaths, but in other directions the route will be straighter along more direct roads. The isochrones will be almost but not exactly circular – quasi-circular.

If the isochrones were to represent the distances covered through an urban street pattern at a particular time of day, those for 8 a.m. will not be all that different from those at 10 p.m., although, if the case study were in an area of the city in which there were throngs of pedestrians at some time but not at others, the isochrones would have reduced diameters and be more closely spaced at such times, reflecting the reduced walking speeds due to the crowds.

If the journey starting point were a bus-stop, the shape and nature of the isochrones would be radically different. The overall speed of urban buses is three or four times' walking speed, pushing the 15-minute isochrone 3.75 kilometres away along the line of the bus route but remaining at 1.25 kilometres away in all the other directions in which walking is the only option. The isochrone will have lost its circular shape and become quasi-linear – lozenge-shaped – reflecting the fact that buses work more efficiently than walking but only along the line of their routes. The efficiency of all public transport is directionally specific, creating quasi-linear isochrones aligned to their routes, a completely different signature to the quasi-circular isochrones associated with constant walking speeds regardless of direction.

There is a more fundamental – not to say awkward – attribute of public transport isochrones. Public transport services run intermittently, and would-be passengers have to wait for the next service. This waiting time extends the overall journey time, reducing effective journey speed and deforming the isochrones still further. The picture is now of dynamic isochrones that pulse, extending and retracting along the line of the bus route like heartbeats on a hospital monitor and, like heartbeats, the pulse is to a rhythm: the rhythm of heartbeats is set by human physiology but for bus services it is the timetabled headways[4] between buses. Most bus services do not run at night: waiting times extend into infinity and isochrones revert to being quasi-circular with the radius set by walking speed.

Changing patterns of land use and transport

Chapter 2 defined transport as a combination of vehicles and tracks. In early civilisations human porters or beasts of burden carried their loads along paths established by no more than habit. Humans have a limit on how much they are able to carry for any distance: 50 kg[5] at 4 km/h may be topped by nimble Sherpas and yomping paratroopers, but is a reasonable limit for common manhandling and portering. This is roughly a very modest 2 tonne-kilometres per day per porter. Even in the days of slavery when the cost of a porter was little more than their food and shelter, every tonne-kilometre was expensive. Pack animals are able to carry about four times as much as a man: a burden of 200 kg at walking pace gives 8 tonne-kilometres per day per animal at the cost of feeding it and employing somebody to lead it.

Effective tonne-kilometres per day depend in part upon the terrain to be crossed. Average speeds and productivity may be improved by upgrading the track, draining boggy areas, and building bridges over streams and rivers. A common mark of civilisation is that the responsibility for the definition, maintenance and improvement of tracks is arranged by the 'state'.[6] Edward I, the ruler of the thirteenth-century English state, decreed in the Statute of Winchester (1285)[7] that the responsibility for the maintenance of a public right of way rested upon the owners of the land it crossed. However, the same statute made tolls illegal, preventing landowners from charging those using the right of way and effectively imposing a tax upon landowners. The Statute created the 'King's Highway', a network of rights of way open to public use without charge and also arranged for its maintenance. The responsibility for defining, maintaining and paying for the road network still rests with the state, although the debate about how it should be done and to what extent market forces should play a role has shifted from Winchester to a rather confused alliance between Whitehall and Brussels.

The road network, at first no more than primitive tracks, affected the isochrones. Movement along the tracked rights of way was more efficient than going cross-country and so the isochrones were drawn out along its routes. Land transport using pack animals on the crude tracks of the 'King's Highway' was still unavoidably expensive. Water transport was far more efficient. Towpaths along navigable rivers enabled a horse to haul a barge loaded with 50 tonnes, producing 2000 tonne-kilometres per day, 250 times the productivity of the horse used as a pack animal and a thousand times more productive than a human porter. Such productivity was only possible along rivers maintained to provide a suitable depth of water, flanked by a towpath and provided with wharves at which freight could be transferred from land to water. The costs of both construction and maintenance were covered by laws permitting the imposition of tolls at precisely specified places, exceptions to the general rule that tolls were illegal. Improvements to the transport infrastructure were facilitated and protected by law, providing and enabling context for initiative and enterprise – a combination of state and business.

The efficiency of the transport network enhanced by the use of navigable rivers may be shown by adapting isochrones to represent not just the simple travel time, but productivity measured in cost per tonne-kilometre with the 'cost' expanded to include the provision of 'vehicles', be they enslaved porters, pack animals or barges, together with any payments of taxes and tolls authorised and imposed to cover track costs. This adaptation transforms isochrones into heavily contorted 'cost contours' reaching out along the roads and waterways where speed and capacity loadings combined to reduce costs per tonne-kilometre. The contours were dynamic, changing their shape as the transport network developed but also pulsing hour-by-hour as caravans of pack animals and barges departed on their journeys. This complicated variation over clock time may be accounted for by including an average waiting time in the list of costings in place of the actual, but quite variable, waiting time: the average will be inaccurate for any particular consignment and will be generally representative of all consignments, but it will replace the pulsing cost contours with stable, slightly inaccurate ones.

Seagoing sailing-ships could carry more than river barges and could also use free wind power, but costs were extended by the crew needed to work the ship and by the long, slow detours to find usable wind. Nevertheless, productivity measured in tonne-kilometres per unit cost of building, maintaining and working ships was far better than land transport.

There is now a clearer picture of accessibility. Places served by good transport will have extensive, although irregular, areas within the cost contours centred upon them: places with poor transport links will have tightly drawn contours, demonstrating that they are relatively 'inaccessible'. 'Accessibility' becomes a matter of the area contained within a cost contour.

The real concern is not accessibility in itself but relative accessibility. A location near to a wharf or port will have lower transport costs than other sites at which the expensive overland carry by porter or pack animal is greater. Footloose productive functions were then best sited at accessible places with minimal transport costs. Consequently ports and wharves became growth centres, driven not so much by their absolute accessibility as by the advantages of comparative accessibility. This might suggest a principle that development is an effect of the transport system, or, at least, of the differences in costs due to transport being more efficient in some directions than in others. Unfortunately things are not that simple.

Improving navigable rivers will cost money, a cost incurred in anticipation that it will be beneficial, perhaps to somebody who has a right to charge tolls, perhaps directly to people whose goods will be carried along the river. In any event, the improvement will be driven by freight flows that are already in existence or are anticipated. Those flows will be generated by land uses. Cause and effect have been reversed: production and land use are not being located at accessible places created by the transport network and defined by the cost contours: the transport network and the related cost contours are being developed to serve land uses.

The transport system and patterns of land use may be seen as the product of cyclical feedbacks where the outcome of one change prompts other changes which then modify the initial change. This feedback cycle disrupts the notion of a simple, linear connection between a cause and its effect. Cause and effect swop places. Moreover, the swops may not be in a simple time series: one development may have effects which occur at differing times, and which prompt a swirl of swops between different causes and different effects, creating a complex tangle of trends, events, causes and effects which is difficult to unravel.

The early industrial revolution is a good example. The fundamental attribute of manufacturing on an industrial scale is the use of power. The initial source of industrial power in Britain was water wheels married to those rivers with sufficient flow to work them. Early industrial iron-making required water power to work the bellows needed to achieve the high temperatures for smelting, and to work the hammers needed to beat out impurities and to fashion the iron into usable products. It also needed charcoal as fuel and considerable volumes of ore. Early iron-making was located by suitable watercourses, in forests where charcoal could be made and near ore deposits. The Weald in Southern England provided all these inputs and was the initial centre of the iron industry.

Technical innovations in the late eighteenth century supplanted charcoal with, first, coke and then coal, enabling the industry to become more footloose and to move from the Weald to places such as the Coalbrookdale/Blists Hill/Ironbridge complex in Shropshire, a place at which coal was mined nearby and could be delivered at minimal transport cost. The surge in the production and availability of iron provided the raw materials from which to build steam-engines which were then used to blast air into the furnaces and to power the hammers and rollers needed to fashion the metal. This outdated the need for water power and its tied locations: a good example of the recursive feedback with one development triggering another. The supply of cheap iron then enabled the production of rails, which, together with locomotives engineered from earlier stationary steam-engines, gave rise to the railways. A horse may produce 2000 tonne- kilometres per day if used to pull a barge but that depends upon there being a river or canal which, by their nature, are able to serve very few places. A horse can haul a loaded one-tonne cart along a smoothed, surfaced road, producing 50 tonne- kilometres per day, better than an unsurfaced road but still below the productivity of barge traffic. If the cart is put on crude wooden, rails, friction is reduced to the level at which a horse may haul 2500 kg and deliver around 150 tonne-kilometres per day. Metal rails, manufactured by the emergent iron industry, produced a steep increase in efficiency: in 1805 a trial on the Surrey Iron Railway showed that a single horse could haul 5000 kg at 5 km/h, a rate of 250 tonne-kilometres per day. Replacing the horse with an early, crude steam locomotive enabled 50 tonnes to be moved at 11 km/h, an output of 5500 tonne- kilometres per day, over 600 times the productivity of a pack horse[8] and even superior to barge traffic where friction is minimal but speed is very restricted. The telling advantage of railways was not just in their combination of loadings and speed but because they could be built in many more places than waterways, albeit at some considerable capital cost which had to be covered by the freight rates.

Railways enabled the iron industry to break free from locations dictated by the geography of its inputs and to spread to wherever the inputs could be amassed and the outputs delivered to end-users. Although the economies of scale and specialisation led to the concentration of some parts of the industry at a few, very particular places, other parts proliferated country-wide. The names cast into old manhole covers show that many were made in local casting yards.

Three conclusions have been reached:

1 Transport flows and their origins and destinations are inextricably intertwined.
2 Neither the transport network nor the locations of production 'cause' the other but the relationship is complex, with cause and effect reverberating against each other, constantly exchanging places.
3 Effective transport planning must attempt to unravel the processes of changing transport demands and land use if it is to achieve the objectives set for it.

Urban development

There is an endemic link between accessibility, transport costs and commercial success, a link which is more subtle and explicit in modern times but which has always been in the background. It is the major explanation why seaports have always hosted industries making use of the low transport costs by water. From very early times ports and trans-shipment points have been the crystallisation points of urbanisation.

Relative accessibility works at a local scale too: production needs working people. Until just over a century ago, working people had to live within a maximum of five kilometres or so walking distance of where they worked. At first this was no great hardship: much of production was in cottage industry and small workshops – many people lived literally on top of their work. As production became more sophisticated and work became more specialised, larger groups were organised. Once mechanical power was deployed within factories, the concentration of workers at factory sites grew, and grew swiftly. If all the most accessible land was taken by productive industry, land for dwellings had to meet two criteria, one negative and one positive: it had to be within walking distance of the workplace but did not have to be so accessible that it attracted industry.

In the late nineteenth century freight transport was largely dependent upon the railways for the major part of end-to-end movements with expensive and inefficient collections and deliveries by horse and cart.[9] If entrepreneurs intent upon building a factory, brewery, food-processing plant, etc. made a list of all the locations from which they wished to draw fuel and raw materials and of the delivery points for their products and then totalled the transport costs, there would have been a startling difference between the aggregate transport cost to and from a site with its own private railway siding and other sites requiring cartage to and from a railway goods depot.

That cartage was not only expensive in itself but the carts and the manhandling on and off them imposed a strong constraint on the size and packaging of consignments. Accessibilities were spread over a wide range and were dominated by rail freight facilities. Relative accessibility ensured that urban areas had a tightly woven fabric, with industry clustered along and as close as possible to railways and with housing packed around it: twice a day the pavements rang with the clatter of working people's boots and clogs.

A change in this noise marked a major development in urbanisation. The Tramways Act (1870) granted a country-wide permission to construct tramways within the public highway subject, first, to a separate, specific private Act to cover each particular scheme, and, second, to the local magistrates fixing the fares and licensing each tram, each driver and each conductor. For the next 30 years or so trams were drawn by horses at little more than walking pace and at expensive fares which had to cover the cost of the horse, the crew, the vehicle and the track. The routes wound their way through the richer parts of major cities, carrying people willing to pay quite high fares to travel only a little faster than they could walk. The users of horse trams were the well-off with a taste for ostentation – horse trams were the BMW SUVs of their day.

All that changed in the decade straddling the turn of the century. Horse trams were replaced by heavier, faster and cheaper electric trams: for the first time, ordinary working people were able to live beyond walking distance from their place of work. The effect was radical, extensive and astonishing. As electric tramways extended from the Victorian city into the surrounding countryside, many square miles of land became accessible for the first time. Urban isochrones changed their shape, reaching out well beyond the edge of the Victorian city and driving Edwardian housing into what had been countryside.

It was another example of the confusion between cause and effect. Tram tracks and the electric power supplies were expensive, and dense route patterns did not develop – usually a limited number of radial fingers extended out from the Victorian town centre. The expense could only be covered if the trams were heavily used at fares low enough to be within the means of working people. That demanded very frequent, well-used services,[10] and that required housing densities which could sustain the required levels of demand. The form that emerged was terraced housing or tenements with some, very restricted, if any, garden space. Transport technology and costs were in a close symbiosis with housing development.

Cheap urban travel by electric tram and rapid urban growth marked the first ten years or so of the twentieth century, but the nature and rate of change were overtaken by even more radical urban transport technologies. The First World War prompted the swift development and use of internal combustion engines. At the beginning of the war local, flexible transport depended upon people's feet and the hooves of horses with the addition of the steel rails of railways between cities and tramways within them. Four years later the cavalry were sitting in petrol-powered tanks, supplies were delivered by lorries and flight had become a commercial reality. After the war, ex-army lorries were bought cheaply by enterprising ex-servicemen and converted into buses, often to be run in competition with more conventional bus services managed by companies which were, in the main, owned by the older tram or railway companies, or by municipalities.[11]

In the 1920s bus fleets expanded, competing with the trams, although usually not as a direct alternative. Buses, running on free, public roads, were relieved of the heavy costs of track provision and maintenance and, with that relief, did not have to carry very high loadings in order to justify and cover track costs. Buses did not have to run at tram frequencies and their route networks were consequently very different. Whereas trams were necessarily confined to a few high-cost, high-frequency radial routes, buses could provide a much more prolific network but at much lower frequencies. The result was a complete redrafting of the isochrones and journey cost contours. The long radial fingers of tram systems were supplemented by bus routes bringing less frequent services to much-extended areas. Yet another explosion of house-building occurred, this time at the lower densities epitomised by the 1930s semi-detached housing with small front and back gardens.

The post-1918 revolution in public transport and in housing location and density had its counterpart in freight transport. Motor lorries began to appear on urban streets, intermingling with carts and horses. But motors had a cost disadvantage: they consumed fuel while stationary. In 1951 British Railways still owned 3300 horses used to collect and deliver small consignments, and horse-drawn carts were used for small domestic deliveries such as milk and coal until the 1960s. Nonetheless, the flexibility and productivity of lorries for local distribution widened the cost contours and gradually untied the close attachment between industrial location and rail freight services. Long-distance freight was still largely the province of the railways, partly because 'heavy goods vehicles' (anything over 3 tons) were restricted by law to a maximum of 20 miles an hour and partly because the road system had not been improved sufficiently. The locational effect of road freight transport was therefore largely to be seen in the spread of urban manufacturing from the previous concentrations near railways to more widespread distributions, a spread in keeping with the wider nobilities provided by the expanding bus networks catering for a more dispersed journey to work.

There were changes too in the hidden, less conventional modes of transport. The foundations for the National Grid were laid by Act of Parliament in 1919, heralding a gradual shift from coal and stationary steam-engines to electric motors in powering industry. Electricity travels at the speed of light and the concept of cost contours for the supply of electric energy seems almost irrelevant: but it is not totally immaterial. Overhead or underground power lines require capital investments which do increase with distance, and so there is an effect upon cost that varies with distance and should be included in accessibility. The costs of supplying water and removing waste are also minor influences but can provide important barriers and thresholds.

The two World Wars stimulated the development and adoption of internal combustion engines which had fundamental effects upon passenger and freight transport and facilitated radical changes in the shape and size of urban areas. Rather less obviously, communications technology, a fundamental aspect of military operations, changed beyond recognition. Radios and telephones had been invented before the outbreak of the First World War but their development was driven forward by the war. Similarly, cathode ray tubes and television pre-dated the Second World War but the needs of war drove the development of radar and then computing. The transport of information was to release other constraints upon location, origins, destinations and movements. Not only do we no longer have to go to a travel agent to buy travel tickets but the operators are able to adjust their prices in bewildering real time.

War gave transport yet another dimension. Modern war is a complex mixture of technology, procurement and supply. In the Second World War this engendered a new dimension to the transport industry – logistics, defined as the 'management of the supply of goods from the point of origin to the point of use'. Reliable supplies of fuel, food, ammunition and medical products both enabled and constrained military action. Usually logistics is represented as a set of 'supply chains', one chain for each product. The chains begin with product manufacture and continue in a sequence of storage, trans-shipment, carriage and delivery. The chains have to encompass not merely transport but warehousing, including the placing and retrieval to and from storage, and trans-shipment. A chain may include movement by various modes and in variously sized consignments.

Logistics is primarily concerned with the efficient management of these multiple chains and is dependent upon a swift and reliable flow of information back up the chain to control transport and storage. Goods in transit and in storage represent idle capital – they have to be paid for but their value cannot be realised until they are delivered. A major logistics objective is to minimise the time between the purchase made at the start of the supply chain and the sale at its end, an objective that may be characterised as minimising the value of products in transit or store. A common touchstone is the 'just-in-time' principle. Using the shelved products in a supermarket as an example, there should always be sufficient supplies to satisfy immediate demand without stock-outs but not so much that capital is tied up unproductively. The theory is that just as the last of a product is sold off the shelf, a new delivery is shelved. In order to achieve that trick the shelf contents will need to be constantly monitored and the supply chain managed right back to the supper to ensure that neither the shelves nor the intermediate warehouses are ever empty, nor that they are overloaded. There is far more to logistics than transport.

It follows that for supermarkets and most industries, 'accessibility' involves communications and a choice of locations at which a range of products may be delivered and then consolidated into loads for specific locations – complex warehouses now called distribution centres. It is a far cry from the days when orders were sent by post and delivered by horse and cart in a plethora of small consignments. Supply-chain efficiency needs well-managed transport but it also requires warehouses, supply depots and storage to be located in well-chosen places and of a size that matches the volume and nature of the products passing though them. Small, badly located depots will add to logistical costs: over-large depots will generate extra lorry mileage. Supply-chain efficiency depends upon choosing the right number and placement of depots in addition to the deployment of lorries. It is yet further evidence of the untidy jumbling of cause and effect: are distribution depots related to the transport system or is the transport system managed to serve the distribution depots?

The modern definition of accessibility

Chapter 19 discusses the link between transport policy and the methodology used to define and predict travel demand. It argues that there have been two major policy shifts: the 1968 Transport Act attempted to create a local coordinated transport policy and network covering all modes. The techniques to predict travel demand responses to changes in the multi-modal transport system could not cope: they had been designed to predict road traffic, and adaptations to cater for public transport proved to be unable to support political decision-making. The attempt to devise local transport policies decayed back into policies focused on roads and, in particular, inter-urban trunk-roads and motorways.

The second revolution was longer-lasting. In 1993 it was finally realised that transport policy could not rest upon predicting demand and then trying to cater for that prediction, a policy dubbed 'Predict and Provide'. A new policy of 'Travel Demand Management' was adopted with the intention of managing demand to fit into the system capacity as it was or as it may be with comparatively minor adjustments. 'Managing demand' required perceiving the transport system as a whole and not as primarily a road system with some lesser modes catering for specific movements.

This time the methodology to predict travel demand did change. The 'Predict and Provide' regime had concentrated upon movement itself, particularly road traffic, but 'Travel Demand Management' necessarily moved the focus to the origins and destinations of movements – to the land uses where decisions about mode and route were made. Spatially the focus shifted from transport infrastructure and its capacity (what needed to be provided) to land-use patterns and the transport opportunities that were provided there: 'transport landscapes' is the term used in Chapter 19. That is, a focus of the accessibility of particular sites and much of the consequent transport planning activity was upon the provisions to be made for developments proposed within the planning system. It was common to impose planning conditions to enhance the transport landscape perceived at new sites by requiring facilities for buses and bicycles. Site accessibility by mode became a policy objective.

In the next decade this mutated to a concern about accessibility by particular groups of people, namely the disabled, the unemployed, etc. This turned the focus back to the infrastructure and transport services available: whether steps or ramps or information, etc. were either preventing travel or imposing a surcharged cost of time penalties.

Accessibility has therefore come to have two meanings and two focuses: first, accessibility to a particular place, usually characterised by a particular function (the site of a proposed development or of a hospital). Second, ease of access by particular groups of people: this usually related to their mobility and the barriers restricting their mobility, barriers which could be removed or reduced by modifications to the transport system. The two foci may overlap. How is the mobility of a group of people to be enhanced to enable them to access a particular place or function? The difference may be demonstrated by signature patterns of isochrones. The pattern representing the travel landscape viewed from a particular place will reflect the services available, their frequency, reliability and cost: those services will include journeys by car. Those isochrones will be adjusted for groups with specific characteristics: they will be contorted by barriers similar to the boggy ground example at the beginning of this chapter, except that the barriers will be invisible to those outside the group.

Notes

1. An overstatement: in the life of a hunter-gatherer, 'gathering' could qualify as both production and consumption in situ, just as those grazing pick-your-own fruit farms are able to eat a few strawberries there and then.
2. The usual term is 'footloose'.
3. These are usually called 'as-the-crow-flies' or 'airline' distances.
4. Bus services are often described by their frequency (x buses per hour) but headways (minutes between one bus and the next) give a better measure, since it *should* equate directly with the maximum waiting time and, if it does not, the discrepancy is a measure of service reliability.
5. Most civilisations have a unit of weight of about 50 kg. The imperial measure was a hundredweight (112 lb = 50.84 kg). In ancient China the dan was 49.9 kg. The Babylonian talent was 60.6 kg.
6. The meaning of the 'state' is not confined to modern notions of government. It means any organisation able to impose rules of law and levy taxes. Over time this has included monarchies, the church, local lords, republics, local councils, etc.
7. Webb and Webb (1913).
8. For more detailed data on the productivity of horse-drawn transport see Robertson (2003, p. 31, table 6).
9. Steam traction engines did exist but they were heavy and expensive, and their use was confined to large, indivisible loads on roads able to bear their weight.
10. A tram ran every three minutes on the 20 km-long route from Central London south through Croydon from 04.46 to 23.52 and the Edinburgh Tramways Manager asserted that if you just missed catching a tram, the next one was always in sight (Cooper 1977).
11. Many of the major local authorities in Britain had become public transport operators almost by accident. The 1870 Tramways Act required tramway companies to offer their systems for sale to the local authority after 20 years of company operation. Many local authorities took advantage of this provision and, having become tram operators, it was logical to extend into bus operations.

Chapter 7

The problems
Congestion

Gridlock: the political imperative

For many people, public and professional alike, the major transport problem is ever-worsening traffic congestion leading to eventual gridlock. In 1999 John Prescott, the then deputy prime minister responsible for transport policy, began the Foreword to *Breaking the Logjam*, the government's public consultation document on congestion, with:

> Everybody hates traffic jams. They cost time and money. They pump out pollution. They take the pleasure out of driving.[1]

He ended with:

> On recent trends, traffic is due to grow massively in the next 20 years. If we don't act now, we will be heading for gridlock.

Prescott was restating a long-held view. As early as 1853 William Malins wrote:

> It must be obvious that the constantly accumulating number of omnibuses, wagons and conveyances of all sorts will, if it continues for two or three years, render London insupportable for the purposes of business, recreation and all ordinary transit from place to place.[2]

Almost 100 years later the London and Home Counties Traffic Advisory Committee reported:

> Saturation point has been reached . . . traffic has outgrown the capacity of the streets.[3]

This widespread view of congestion is a package of interrelated ideas:

- Roads have a finite capacity – if the actual volume of traffic is below the capacity of a road then congestion will be kept at bay but, if greater, congested queues will form as traffic struggles through bottlenecks.

- Such congestion is costly and undesirable.
- The delays have become worse over the years and will get still worse as the volume of traffic continues to increase.
- The worsening congestion will eventually lead to a complete gridlocked standstill.

The word 'gridlock' first appeared in the United States in the 1970s to describe heavy congested gridiron roads. If a queue at one junction tails back to the preceding one it will precipitate queues on the entry roads which will then tail back to other nearby junctions until all the roads and junctions within a series of gridiron blocks are locked solid. Gridlock is now more generally used to mean any dense, almost stationary, traffic.

It is a short step, often taken in dinner party and pub chatter, to suggest that congestion is best solved by increasing road capacity, a suggestion advocated in rather more erudite ways by the motoring lobby.[4] However, urban road widening is extremely expensive, disruptive and politically fraught. Faced with that problem, the government, together with many others,[5] argue that congestion is best reduced by imposing charges upon motorists for using congested roads, claiming that this would be a 'win-win' policy because not only would charges reduce the volume of traffic, but they would generate a considerable and reliable cash flow to be spent on improving the transport network. This approach is underpinned by the idea that every road has a finite capacity but the flow should be restricted by price to match the capacity rather than improving the network to create the capacity needed to cope with the flow.

The nature of traffic flow and congestion

The assertion by the London and Home Counties Traffic Advisory Committee that 'Saturation point has been reached . . . traffic has outgrown the capacity of the streets' feels intuitively right. It suggests that if the actual flow is less than a road's capacity there will be no congestion, but if the flow is greater, traffic will be delayed and the delay will build up until gridlock. This theory, illustrated in Figure 7.1, is actually wrong, despite being intuitively right.

A moment's thought makes it obvious why Figure 7.1 must be wrong – if traffic speed is zero due to gridlock, then flow must also be zero, and the real curve must curve back on itself to pass through the point of zero speed and zero flow at the bottom left-hand corner of the graph. However, one thing is almost right – real traffic speeds do decrease as flow increases but there has been persistent misunderstanding about whether this reduction in speed is due to the increase in flow or whether the increase in flow is due to the reduction in speed. The normal convention when drawing graphs such as Figure 7.1 is that the cause (usually called the 'independent variable') is plotted on the horizontal axis and the effect (the 'dependent variable') on the vertical axis. By this convention, Figure 7.1 implies that traffic flow is dependent upon speed, a mistaken premise that pervades official documents.

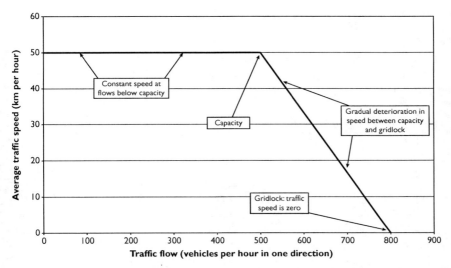

Figure 7.1 An intuitive, but incorrect, speed–flow relationship for an urban street

Simple flow theory

The basic principles of traffic flow are exceedingly simple. In a theoretical flow of identical vehicles along a single lane of road with no possible overtaking, drivers would be obliged to allow sufficient space between their vehicle and the one in front to ensure that, if it made an emergency stop, there would be sufficient time and space to stop behind it without any danger of crashing into the back of it. Flow is therefore characterised by the space between vehicles (the space-headway) and the time between them (the time-headway), two quantities which are interrelated by speed. As the Highway Code[6] reminds us, there are two components in the safe headways between vehicles:

1. *Drivers' reaction time.* This varies from person to person and from one circumstance to another, but these variations may be built into an assumed, representative figure: the Highway Code uses 0.67 seconds as a reasonable time between an event (the brake lights coming on in the preceding vehicle) and a driver's foot hitting the brake pedal.
2. *The braking distance.* This depends on the speed of the vehicle at the time when braking starts and the rate at which the vehicle decelerates. The rate used in the Highway Code is 6.5 metres/sec/sec.[7] The actual individual rates included within this representative average will vary according to the characteristics of the road surface, the tyres, and, to some extent, driving style and skill. For safety's sake, each vehicle must be able to stop at least one metre behind the one in front. An assumption of a standard vehicle length of 4.5 metres plus an assumed safety margin of one metre between vehicles once they have stopped gives a total of

5.5 metres between the front of one stopped vehicle and the front of the one stopped behind it.

Three assumed representative figures determine the arithmetic of the relationship between traffic speed and flow but they do not affect the principle behind the relationship. If different values were to be assumed the result would be numerically different, but the nature of the relationship would remain:

- driver reaction time = 0.67 second;
- braking rate = 6.5 metres per second per second;
- vehicle length = 4.5 metres.

The space-headway, shown in Figure 7.2, is the distance between the front of one moving vehicle and the front of the following one, and is composed of the front-to-front space between vehicles once they have stopped, plus the distance moved during the driver's reaction time (which depends upon the vehicle's speed) plus the braking distance (which is very strongly speed related).

Figure 7.2 obeys the convention of plotting the cause (the independent variable), in this case speed, on the horizontal axis and the effect (the dependent variable), the braking distance, on the vertical axis. It will be seen that at a speed of zero, the distances covered during the reaction and braking times are both zero (since both are dependent on speed) but the total space-headway is a positive 5.5 metres, the distance between the front bumpers of stationary vehicles.

Figure 7.2 shows how space-headway increases with speed, partly because the vehicle will travel further during the driver's reaction time but mainly because the braking distance increases in proportion to the square of the speed.

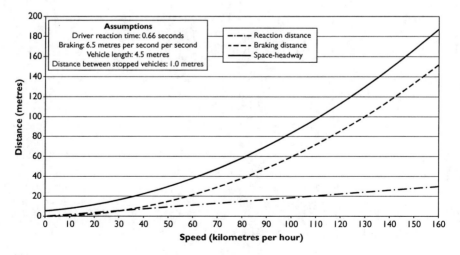

Figure 7.2 Space-headway related to speed

Somebody standing on an over-bridge with the single lane of uniform traffic passing underneath could measure the time-headway elapsing between vehicles passing under the bridge. The result of the observations are plotted in Figure 7.3, the shape of which is the product of two contrary influences imposed by speed:

1   If cars were spaced at a constant distance apart, no matter how fast they were moving, rather like the bottles on a brewery conveyor belt, the flow would be exactly proportionate to the speed. The space-headway would be constant but the time-headway would reduce as the conveyor belt speeded up, creating an increased flow per hour.
2   However, vehicles in a traffic flow are not constantly spaced. As Figure 7.2 shows, braking distances and space-headways increase with speed. Although increased speed means that space-headways will be covered more quickly, this effect is overwhelmed at speeds over about 30 km/h by the need for ever-increasing braking distances. This drives up both space- and time-headways at an increasing rate.

Thus far the analysis has focused upon time- and space-headways since these are the fundamental quantities in traffic flow: both are functions of speed, and Figures 7.2 and 7.3 are shown correctly according to convention, with the independent variable, speed (the 'cause'), on the horizontal axis and the dependent variable, the headway (the 'effect'), on the vertical axis. However, flows are usually quoted in vehicles per hour rather than in headways. The relationship is simple: (flow/hour) = (3600/time-headway in seconds). Figure 7.4 is merely a redrawing of Figure 7.3 to show flow in vehicles/hour rather than in headways.

The shapes of the curves in Figures 7.3 and 7.4 show a telling characteristic. A uniform time-headway of 3 seconds gives a flow of 3600/3 = 1200 vehicles per hour,

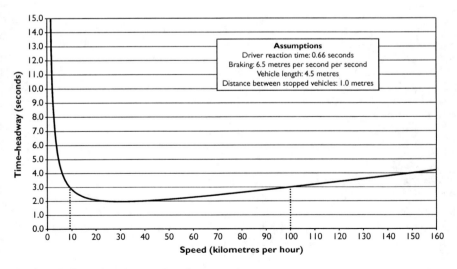

Figure 7.3 Time-headway related to speed

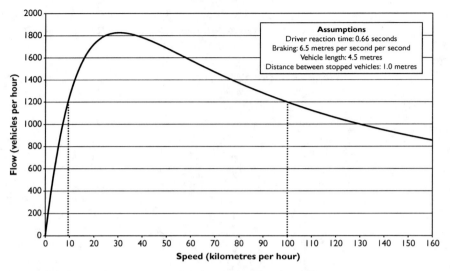

Figure 7.4 The general relationship between speed and flow

and Figures 7.3 and 7.4 show this to occur at both 9 and 100 km/h, although these two speeds show other, very different features. An observer on an over-bridge with a flow of 1200 vehicles per hour passing under it at 9 km/h would look down for most of each 3-second time-headway on the roofs of vehicles moving slowly about 2 metres apart. In contrast, looking down on the same 1200 vehicles per hour but now moving at 100 km/h, there would be a roughly 78-metre gap between vehicles, and for most of the time the observer would be looking down at the unoccupied road surface rather than at vehicle roofs.

Figure 7.5 shows the relationship between speed and vehicle density, measured in vehicles per kilometre of traffic lane. As speeds increase so does the safety distance between vehicles, and so the number of vehicles per kilometre is reduced. An observer on an over-bridge would see a flow of one vehicle every 3 seconds (1200 vehicles per hour) moving at 9 km/h and then the same flow but at 100 km/h as a massive contrast in the density of vehicles – fast vehicles would have 78 metres of space between them but the slow flow would have only 2 metres between vehicles. Vehicle density instinctively appears to be a measure of 'busy-ness' – roads covered almost entirely in traffic look 'busy' but, in fact, may be carrying very low flows. The differences between two flows of 1200 vehicles per hour, one very slow-moving and the other quite fast, may be seen (or experienced) in reality as either slow-moving, dense traffic (e.g. 9 km/h and 136 vehicles per kilometre) or faster, more spaced-out traffic (100 km/h and 12 vehicles per kilometre). The maximum density will occur when traffic is stationary: a uniform traffic of 4.5 metre-long cars stopped with 1 metre of space between them will show 182 vehicles per kilometre.

The idea that roads have a 'capacity' is both intuitive and beguiling: if pint tumblers and dustbins have a finite capacity, it makes apparent sense to think that roads do too

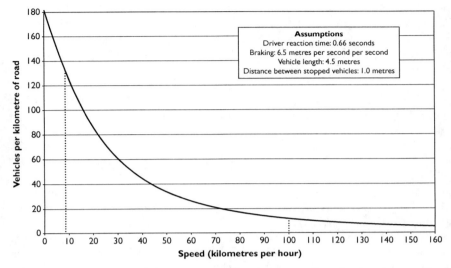

Figure 7.5 Density of traffic in vehicles per kilometre of road related to traffic speed

and, moreover, to believe that congestion will occur if that capacity is exceeded. So far the analysis hints that the capacity concept may be helpful but not in the absolute sense that a pint glass has a finite maximum capacity. Figure 7.4 shows a maximum flow of 1830 vehicles per hour at 30 km/h, providing that all vehicles are driven in file along a single road lane, each driver copying the behaviour of the driver in front. That precise number reflects the presumed representative reaction time, deceleration rate and vehicle length: any other assumed values will produce a slightly different maximum flow and optimal speed, but the shape of the curve will remain the same and will show a similar maximum. If speed falls below or rises above the optimum, flow will be reduced.

In reality, such presumed uniformity of vehicles and driving is impossible: driving styles and vehicle performances vary and will drag the optimum flow with them, suggesting that maximum capacities and optimal speeds will vary from time to time and from circumstance to circumstance.

The argument presented thus far is that speed is the independent, controlling variable and therefore it defines capacity. This is an accepted truth in calculating the capacity of tracked systems: railway capacity is seen to be related to the time-headways between trains and to the speeds and the signalling systems that determine those time-headways. In contrast, traffic analysis has always found that speeds and time-headways are uncomfortable determinants of capacity, and for very good reason. Road improvements are expensive and the budget is very limited, creating a continuing focus on whether road schemes offer good value for money. The prime justification for road improvement is that it will improve the speed of traffic. To calculate increases in speed clearly requires a methodology to estimate traffic speeds before and after a road has been improved, and this creates an almost unavoidable spotlight on the ways in which traffic speed will react to any changes in traffic flow. This spills out into a presumption that the relationship between flow and speed is that the flow affects speed, not vice versa. There is a plausibility behind this presumption: numerous research studies show that increases in flow are *associated* with decreases in speed and vice versa, but this falls well short of proving that reductions in flow *cause* an increase in speed.

The initial British research into traffic was undertaken by the government's Road Research Laboratory (RRL) and was reported in a substantial series of research reports. Many of the early reports were compiled into a seminal book, *Research on Road Traffic* (RRL 1965). Page 108 sets out the space- and time-headway analysis of the speed–flow relationship,[8] correctly identifying speed as the prime determinant of flow as substantially reported in the above Figures 7.2, 7.3, 7.4 and 7.5. However, 14 pages later, *Research on Road Traffic* showed the flow–speed relationship reproduced in Figure 7.6[9] making the fundamental error that speed was the product of flow rather than the other way round. The error was made desirable by the need to link reductions in flow with increases in speed in order to assess the effectiveness of road improvement schemes and it was made possible by fitting curves to empirical field data, plotting flow on the horizontal axis as though it were the cause, and speed on the vertical axis as though it were the effect. Unlike the initial analysis based on the variations in space- and time-headways due to speed as reproduced in detail above, there was no supporting theory to explain why volume should be the independent variable and speed the effect. This is not surprising, since the premise that speed is a product of flow is wrong.

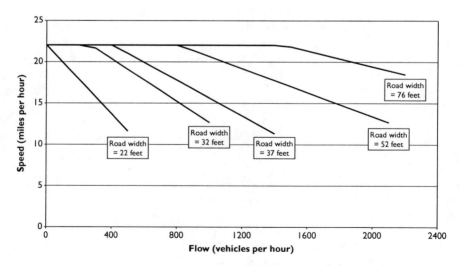

Figure 7.6 Speed–flow relationship reported by the Road Research Laboratory (1965)

Source: Reproduced from Road Research Laboratory (1965), fig. 6.5.

Figure 7.6 was created by fitting the curves to empirical data collected on the streets of London. The misrepresentation is that flow has been plotted on the horizontal axis as though it were the independent variable (the 'cause'), although this was unsupported by any theory describing the mechanism by which speed may be seen to be a function of flow. The observed data are undisputed – the error is in the assumption that speed is the result of the flow rather than vice versa.

Despite the lack of credible theory, numerous important documents have been based on the fundamental error that speed is a function of flow rather than the reverse. The first was Technical Memorandum T5/67[10] which held that a reduction in traffic volume would produce a predictable increase in speed, despite the complete absence of theory as to why this should be so. The assertion was made purely upon the basis of curves fitted to empirical data.[11] The modern version is shown in Figure 7.7, a reproduction of the speed–flow relationships, currently postulated by the British Department for Transport, for a rural single carriageway and for an urban A-road.[12]

The shape of the curves in Figure 7.7 bears a strong resemblance to the intuitive curve in Figure 7.1 and to the fitted curves in Figure 7.6, but there is a significant difference: the horizontal axis is not in vehicles but in 'passenger car units' (pcu) (Figure 7.8). This is a further demonstration of the pervasiveness of the concept that roads have a finite 'capacity'. Various types of vehicle are assessed to use different amounts of that 'capacity' because they have different abilities to brake and accelerate: cars are allocated a pcu value of 1.0 but articulated lorries are reckoned to use 2.9 times the amount of the available capacity as a car. Hence, if a road has a 'capacity' of, say, 870 pcu/hr, then it could be used by 870 cars or by 300 articulated lorries, or by some mixture of vehicles summing to 870 pcu/h.

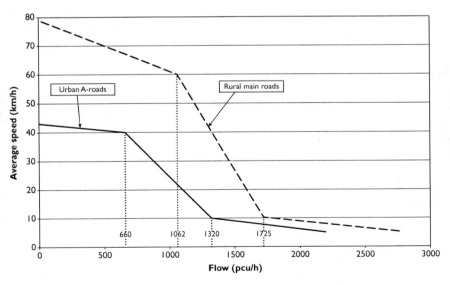

Figure 7.7 An example of the 'official' relationship between flow and speed

Congestion

Vehicle type	PCU factor
Car	1.0
Light goods vehicles (vans)	1.0
Rigid goods vehicles	1.9
Articulated goods vehicles	2.9
Public service vehicles	2.5

Figure 7.8 Passenger car unit factors
Source: Department for Transport, WebTAG Unit 3.9.5, table 8.

The speed–flow curves shown in Figure 7.7 are two of a number of hypothetical speed–flow relationships used by the British Department for Transport in FORGE.[13] The irregular shape of the curves suggests that they are hypothetical, fully supported by neither theory nor data: moreover, they are, in part, impossible nonsense. This is shown in Figure 7.9 where the flows shown in Figure 7.7 have been converted into headways.

Figures 7.7 and 7.9 display identical data, but the vertical axis on Figure 7.7 shows average speed, whereas that in 7.9 shows average space-headway. In both cases all cars move at the average speed, since an enabling assumption has been made that the flow is completely homogeneous. The conversion from representing the flow by its speed into its headway is done by first changing the flow from the pcu/h shown in Figure 7.7, and then into time-headways (in seconds), then into space-headways (in

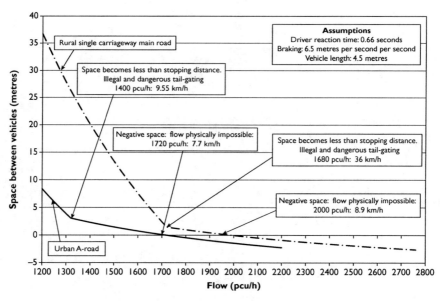

Figure 7.9 Space-headways associated with the speed–flow relationships shown in Figure 7.7

metres), and finally, given that the vehicles are a uniform 4.5 metres in length, into the space between the back of one car and the front of the next. For example, in Figure 7.7 the rural main road curve shows a flow of 1725 pcu/h moving at 10 km/h (2.8 metres/second). Assuming the flow is entirely of uniform cars, a flow of 1725 cars per hour gives an average headway of 2.09 seconds: in that time a car moving at 2.8 metres/second will travel 5.9 metres. Since space-headways are measured from the front of one vehicle to the front of the next and all vehicles are presumed to be 4.5 metres long, this gives (5.9 − 4.5 = 1.4 metres) from the back of one car to the front of the next as they are moving. That is illegal and dangerous tail-gating.

Higher flows given by the rural single carriageway curve are even more bizarre. The curve suggests that 2760 cars per hour could move at a speed of 5 km/h (1.37 metres/second). A total of 2760 cars per hour is a flow running at a headway of 1.3 seconds: this gives a space-headway of 1.8 metres between the front of one car and the front of the next. Since cars are 4.5 metres long this suggests that the distance between vehicles would be *minus* 2.7 metres and therefore cars must be mounting one another three deep like orgiastic elephants.

Figure 7.9, and Figure 7.7 from which it is derived, are bizarre because the belief that traffic speeds are a consequence of traffic flow is taken to a demonstrably impossible degree. This impossibility is the combined product of two misconceptions:

1   That there is some unexplained process by which traffic speeds dictate the flow of vehicles per hour.
2   That this process may be extrapolated beyond the realms of reality.

Figure 7.7 and the theory behind it show a deep, but mistaken, belief that flows are the product of speed. The importance of this cannot be overstated: if traffic speed and, by implication, congestion is due to the amount of traffic, then speeds may be enhanced by restricting traffic – that is the fundamental thinking behind road-user charging. But if that premise is not true (and the argument being offered here is that it is not) and flow is dependent upon speed, then any policy to reduce congestion must be to improve speed per se, not to reduce volume.

Definitions and measures of speed

The thorny question of how speed might be improved requires a definition of what is actually meant by 'speed'. Vehicle speeds vary from place to place, from time to time and from vehicle to vehicle, and the speeds shown in the figures thus far are implicit averages, although, since the flow is assumed to be unrealistically homogeneous, all vehicles conform to the average. The lifting of the assumption of homogeneity poses the question of what speeds contribute to an 'average speed'.

Traffic engineers recognise a number different speed measures:

- *Spot speeds* are measured as vehicles pass a fixed point – a spot. The readings from a fixed radar speed meter are 'spot speeds' and may be included in an average speed at the one specific point on the road. That raises a secondary problem over

112 Congestion

the times of the year at which the raw data are collected. We are back to the common problem inherent in all averages: they may be representative of the measured speeds but any one actual speed may be way off from the average.

- *Running speeds* are the speeds at which traffic actually moves along a length of road. This could be measured by timing a series of vehicles over the road length. Two different sorts of variation will be included within the average: first, every vehicle will vary its speed along the length of the road and so the timing of each vehicle will itself be an average of the range of speeds at which it moves; and second, to represent a complete flow along the length of the road, those averages will in turn have to be averaged.
- *Journey speeds* are similar to running speeds but include the time during which vehicles are stationary rather than actually on the move. The periods during which vehicles are stationary are usually called 'delay' times, so giving running time + delay time = journey time, and this, together with the distance covered, will give the journey speed.

The hybrid flow–speed/speed–flow curve

Figure 7.10 shows exactly the same data as Figure 7.4 but now, defying the convention that the causal independent variable is plotted on the horizontal axis, it has been put (wrongly) on the vertical axis to conform to the manner in which speed–flow relationships are normally presented.

Figure 7.10, in common with Figures 7.2 to 7.5, is founded upon a simple theory of flow based on a set of enabling assumptions:

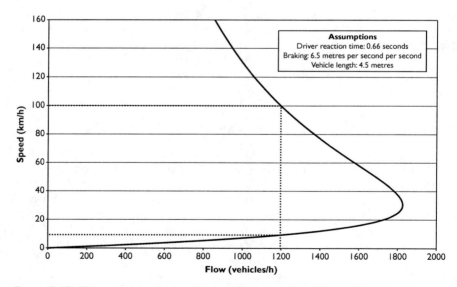

Figure 7.10 The general relationship between speed and flow (also shown, more conventionally, in Figure 7.4)

- All vehicles are identical cars 4.5 metres in length.
- The flow is along a single lane.
- There is no overtaking.
- The space- and time-headways between cars are uniform.
- The implication then must be that all cars in the flow are driven in exactly the same way with each driver copying the person in front.

These assumptions are reasonably valid for congested urban traffic. Overtaking is usually impossible either because the road is too narrow or there are oncoming or turning vehicles. Consequently, drivers are forced to follow and copy the person in front. The uniform size and performance of vehicles within the flow is an invalid assumption for real flows, but this does not mean that the principle behind the theory has to be abandoned. Longer vehicles with different braking and accelerating characteristics will reduce the volume, but not the basic criteria of reaction times and stopping distances which determine volumes. It is argued that the theory behind Figure 7.10 is valid so long as road width and traffic density prevent overtaking and force follow-my-leader driving, up to a theoretical limit of about 1800 vehicles per hour at around 30 km/h. In reality this sort of traffic may be seen in the peak hour on very densely trafficked urban motorways such as the M4 westward out of London. Because drivers take risks in tail-gating, real observed speeds and flows can be higher than those suggested by the theory. Driver behaviour overcomes the fundamental stopping distances shown in Figure 7.2 and vehicles travel too quickly and too closely for safety – it is in these conditions that driving has been likened to formation flying with strangers.

The traffic speeds shown in the figures are actually the average speeds of the vehicles within the flow. In flows where speed is dictated by the vehicle in front, the variations between individual vehicles will be due to little more than differences in vehicle performance rather than driver choice, and the spread of speeds[14] will be quite small. Traffic engineers call this 'forced flow'.

Figure 7.10 shows that, in theory, forced flow in a single lane with vehicles tailing one another at 160 km/h (100 m/h) could run at about 900 cars per hour and still be able to make emergency stops without concertina crashes, but such flows are rarely seen, even on German autobahns. Hints of what high-speed forced flow would be like may be seen (together with the consequences) on very tight racing circuits like Monaco or Indianapolis, but real highway speeds are limited by law and common sense. Normally, higher speeds are only to be seen on derestricted roads with overtaking opportunities, either because they are multi-lane or because gaps in oncoming traffic allow overtaking; the assumptions of no overtaking and follow-my-leader driving upon which flow theory has been based so far are then no longer valid. Once the flow loses its homogeneity, the theory becomes more complex, needing to take into account the probability of opportunities to overtake, a calculation that has to include the local characteristics and geometry of the road.

Where overtaking opportunities are minimal and the flow is pinned to a single lane with follow-my-leader driving, the flow theory based on stopping distances as a function of speed still applies, but where overtaking is possible the theory becomes

114 Congestion

inappropriate – the determinants of flow become very variable. The single-lane speed–flow theory flickers on and off as overtaking opportunities present themselves, releasing drivers from the need to copy the speed of the driver in front, then disappear again, reimposing the need to drive in single file. As it does so, the range of speeds contained within the average flickers in rhythm, since overtaking implies that the average speed includes a mix of faster and slower vehicles.[15] It could be argued that the flickering is between times and places where flow is a function of speed and where speed is a function of flow, or between 'forced' and 'free' flow – 'forced' where drivers are obliged to copy the speed of the vehicle in front and 'free' where they are not. Many textbooks attempt to resolve the clash between forced and free flow by using a hybrid curve such as that shown in Figure 7.11.

Figure 7.11 is actually a combination of two curves with quite different characteristics. The dotted 'free-flow' curve represents the flows when drivers are able to overtake and drive at speeds of their choice. The freedom fades as the traffic flow increases. In low flows, at the left end of the dotted curve, drivers are free to drive as fast as prudence and the law will allow, maintaining their speeds by overtaking the slower drivers. Comparatively few vehicles spread over a wide range of individual speeds will create a high average speed, with a large spread between the slowest and the fastest drivers. As flows build up, the number of slower vehicles to be overtaken increases but the number of overtaking opportunities reduces, and the faster drivers are increasingly impeded by the slower ones. This reduces both the average and the spread of speeds. When traffic is really congested, overtaking becomes almost impossible and all vehicles then have to travel at the speed of the slowest: such follow-my-leader driving is the prime characteristic of the solid 'forced-flow' curve and the

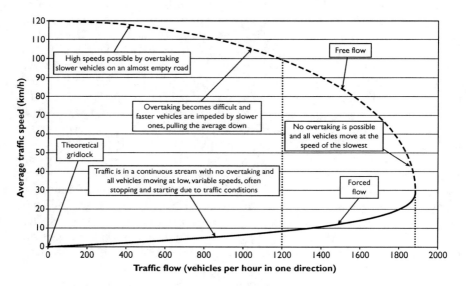

Figure 7.11 The hybrid speed–flow relationship
Source: Adapted from Hobbs and Richardson (1967), Vol. 2, p. 25.

average now represents a large number of vehicles, all moving at more or less the same speed.[16]

The dotted 'free-flow' curve is actually a modification of the solid 'forced-flow' curve which itself is just a reproduction of Figure 7.10. It should now be plain that the mutation of the solid 'forced-flow' curve into the dotted 'free-flow' curve is a result of overtaking. It has already been established that the opportunities to overtake are a product of the road width and geometry, and are particular to local road characteristics. This implies that the dotted curve cannot be precise but will vary in position and shape according to local circumstances. This is exactly the premise behind the 1965 research shown in Figure 7.6: this shows a family of curves covering a number of road widths. Research on road traffic shows how these relationships could be further modified by measures of 'curviness',[17] sight lines and flows in the opposite direction – by measures of local characteristics. The curves in Figure 7.6 are stylised versions of the dotted 'free-flow' curve with the smooth curve replaced by an angular crank. Most importantly, they are the product of statistical curve fitting rather than the theory based upon enabling assumptions used to create the solid 'forced-flow' curve.

The stark criticism of the current 'official', but impossible, speed–flow relationships shown in Figures 7.7 and 7.9 is really because the dotted 'free-flow' curve shown in Figure 7.11 and its ancestor in Figure 7.6 have been thoughtlessly extrapolated to take the place of the solid 'forced-flow' curve.

The instability of maximum flows

These two conditions – on the one hand, forced flow, where average speed represents a narrow range of speeds, speed determines flow, and, on the other, free flow where the average speed has a wider spread – merge around the maximum possible flow, shown in Figure 7.10, as about 1800 vehicles per hour per lane within which driver behaviour will tend towards being homogeneous because the opportunity to do anything other than follow the car in front is very limited. The actual maximum varies widely according to the characteristics of the road (width, curvature, junctions, etc.) and of the traffic (percentage of heavy vehicles, buses, etc.), and it is usually far lower than 1800 vehicles per hour. More importantly, the maximum, no matter what its size, is unstable, and rarely achieved in practice. When traffic on a free-flowing road builds up towards the maximum, some event will usually provoke a queue, and the flow will jump from the dotted free-flow curve down to the same traffic volume but now at a much slower speed on the solid forced-flow curve. This jump will be familiar to many motorway drivers: traffic can be going quite fast but with all vehicles travelling at more or less the same speed, spaced out to give drivers the time to react should the vehicle in front brake: flow will be on the dotted curve just before the maximum. Suddenly, the flow collapses into dense traffic, moving slowly, nose-to-tail: flow has collapsed on to the solid curve. The volume in vehicles per hour is often more or less the same with very similar time-headways but traffic speeds are reduced to a crawl, space-headways shorten drastically and the density of vehicles per kilometre of road shoots up. It is the practical effect of the theory that the same flow in vehicles per hour can happen in low-speed, dense traffic and in higher speed, spaced-out traffic. In both cases the time-headways are the same but the space-headways are radically different.

The event that prompts the jump from free to forced flow may be one of many. High-speed, high-volume driving, with vehicles travelling at similar speeds in front, close behind and on each side, can be very intimidating. It only takes one driver to break out of the pattern to provoke a slow-moving, bumper-to-bumper queue. That driver may be intimidated or just prudent, leaving a longer space between the vehicle in front, or may have to change lanes to take an exit road, or be driving a heavy vehicle slowed by an up-hill gradient. Once a slow-moving queue has formed it cannot disperse until the flow of vehicles leaving the front of the queue is greater than the number of vehicles joining the back. This is why some motorway and main road queues seem to have no apparent cause: the queue was initially created some time previously and the cause has since vanished, but the queue has remained because the rate at which drivers leave the front is less than the rate at which other drivers arrive at the back.

This poses the question of the rate at which drivers may drive away from the front of a standing queue. Matson and colleagues (1955) argued that on average drivers take 2.4 seconds to realise that the vehicle in front is pulling away, to engage gear, release the brake and start to follow (pedantic purists may claim that often handbrakes are not on, etc., but the data showed that vehicles cross a start line every 2.4 seconds – a maximum flow of 1500 cars per hour).

More recent work by Kimber *et al.* (1986) concluded that the basic rate at which vehicles started from a dead stand at traffic-lights was 1940 cars per hour (a time-headway of 1.9 seconds). In part, the difference may be due to the green traffic signal being a prompt to drivers to react quickly, enabling them to hurry by cutting headways. The lack of signals when starting from the front of a normal, standing queue forces drivers to comprehend, unaided, that the vehicle in front is beginning to move forward and this may account for the lower rate of discharge from the front of the queue. However, the difference is more likely to be due to the inherent difficulty of identifying a valid average or other value to represent a widely ranging variable. If a maximum discharge rate from the front of a standing queue is assumed to be 1800 pcu/h (a time-headway of 2 seconds) it will be inaccurate in many actual circumstances, but not inaccurate enough to be misleading. This then may be adopted as the maximum capacity of one lane of good-quality road without any impediments to normal flow such as sharp bends, signals, pedestrian crossings, parked or turning vehicles, etc.

Figure 7.11 shows a maximum flow slightly in excess of this (1827, to be precise), but this is because the curve assumes that vehicles are on the move and the capacity is set by braking and the relevant headways rather than starting from a halt.

Lack of capacity and congestion

It may now be seen that there are two fundamentally different types of congestion:

1. The first is caused by the capacity of a length of road being less than the volume of traffic trying to drive along it. All vehicles creep forward, nose-to-tail, at a more

or less constant, common speed, so there is little variation from a low average. This is typical of congestion on otherwise free-flowing, inter-urban roads and will be found in practice to be related to free-flow conditions (good speeds with long space-headways and low traffic densities) deteriorating very quickly into forced-flow (low, congested speed, short space-headways and high traffic density). In these circumstances the measure of mean speed would be the mean spot speed or, more likely, the mean running speed.

2   The second is caused by traffic having to stop to give way to other traffic within a road network rather than along a single length of road. The consequent flow is intermittent, traffic stopping and then surging forward in untidy pulses. Each driver has to vary speeds over quite a wide range, from complete stops up to occasional spurts of higher speeds. The low average is derived from wide variations in speed as traffic makes its way through the network. This is completely different from the low averages on inter-urban roads which are due to a much more uniform slowness. This pattern of speeds will include delays, and so the mean speed will be the mean journey speed.

It would be simple to define the capacity of any road as the maximum uncongested flow – to use the absence of congestion as the criterion of capacity. Although that is an attractive theory, it would be very difficult to use when planning roads to carry predicted flows: that requires a tariff, giving the maximum flow that may be carried by roads of designed dimensions without the risk of congestion. In Britain these definitions of capacity are published in the *Design Manual for Roads and Bridges*.[18] It should be emphasised that these nominal capacities are arbitrary points chosen on the speed–flow curves to be used in design and assessment. They are chosen to represent a flow that may be accommodated without undue risk of congestion, but many roads will carry flows greater than their nominal capacity simply because drivers will choose to drive at smaller, but still acceptable, headways.

Rural road capacity

Figure 7.11 shows that the maximum possible flow on the nose of the curve at the conjunction of the solid and dotted curves cannot be used to define capacity, since it is usually unattainable and, even when it is reached, it is unstable. Usually traffic conditions make the leap from free to forced flow at a flow rate well below the maximum. Consequently an arbitrary volume has to be chosen as a nominal capacity. Free flow, as characterised by the dotted curve in Figure 7.11, occurs for much of the time over a good proportion of the rural road system. Capacities vary from place to place and from time to time, influenced by width, curvature and the weather, so there is never an easily defined capacity; but whenever flow is less than the possible maximum, traffic will be comparatively steady with drivers often able to choose their speeds rather than having to copy the driver in front.

The official capacities of rural, derestricted roads[19] are held to be dependent upon two main attributes: the type of road and the percentage of heavy vehicles. Three road types are quoted and their flow–speed characteristics are shown in Figure 7.12:

118 Congestion

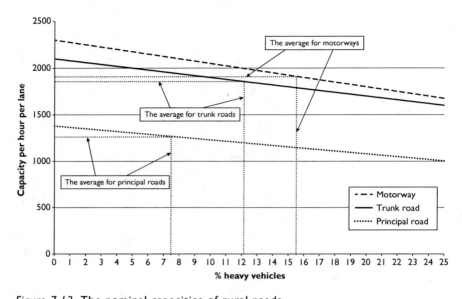

Figure 7.12 The nominal capacities of rural roads
Source: From Highways Agency, *Design Manual for Roads and Bridges*, Vol. 5, Section 1, Part 3, Annex D.

1   Trunk roads – primary A-roads between cities. These are usually shown on maps in green with a (T) after the road number.
2   Principal roads – the other A-roads, usually mapped in red.
3   Motorways – dual carriageways with no flat junctions, no frontage access and no pedestrians. These are usually mapped in blue.

Of course capacities do not really depend upon this official designation: the categories are actually proxies for the numbers of flat junctions, frontage accesses, parking and pedestrian crossing points and the other causes of interruption and delay. Motorways have fewest interruptions and ordinary A-roads the most.

Heavy vehicles slow the traffic down, particularly on hills, and this reduces capacity. Since motorways carry the highest percentages of heavy lorries, the effect on flow is more noticeable than on other roads. Figure 7.12 has put these effects together and shows that the average capacity of a motorway is 1900 vehicles per hour per lane, for a trunk road the average capacity is 1858 and for a principal road 1250. [Note: these are only average figures to be used as guidelines; the precise capacity will be different for different roads and for different times. Rain can reduce capacity by 10 per cent and, if the actual number of heavy vehicles is different to the average, there will be a substantial effect upon capacity.]

	Speed limit km/h (mile/h)	Junctions	Access to property	Parking + loading	Road width (m)	
					6.75	7.3
Urban motorway	100 (60)	Multi-level	None	None		4000
Main road	60 (40)	Less than 2 per km	Limited	None	1320	1590
Main road	60 (40)	More than 2 per km	Residential only	Restricted	1260	1470
Main road	50 (30)	More than 2 per km	Full access to frontage	Unrestricted	1110	1300
Shopping street	50 (30)	More than 2 per km	Full access to frontage	Unrestricted	900	1140

Figure 7.13 The nominal capacities of urban roads in vehicles per hour
Source: Reproduced from Department of Transport (1999) Traffic Advice Note TA 79/99.

Urban road capacity

Figure 7.13 shows some of the nominal capacities for urban roads. Estimating the capacity of urban roads is fraught with problems: road junctions, accesses to flanking property, pedestrian crossings, parking and freight deliveries all reduce the volume of traffic that a road can take. This is the practical face of the conditions represented by the solid forced-flow curve in Figure 7.11: flow is determined by speed, and speeds are suppressed by vehicles having to negotiate the hazards of a busy urban road. This implies that congestion on a road beset with junctions, frontage access, parking, etc. will occur at a much lower flow than on stretches of plain road, even if the width and other characteristics of the road itself are the same.

Urban congestion is more the product of the numbers and actions of other road users than of the characteristics of the road. This creates the perverse effect of reducing road capacity at the very time when the amount of traffic wishing to use it increases. In general, both capacity and flow vary continuously throughout the day but the variation is contrary – as the flow increases the capacity declines. This perversity has an unavoidable conclusion: congestion on urban streets is inevitable, at least to some extent or another. The task is to ameliorate the degree of congestion and the number of people affected by it.

In truth, Figure 7.13, together with its source, Traffic Advice Note 79/99, provides nominal values which hide very wide variations in reality. The Note itself points out:

> The potential capacity of a road will not be reached if either the capacity of junctions along the road or the capacity of the adjoining network is lower than that of the road in question (para 2.3).

Since urban roads have innumerable junctions, the capacities shown in Figure 7.13 are rarely reached. As the above quotation implies, the capacity of an urban road network is not determined by the capacity of the roads themselves but by the capacity of the junctions. This reduces Traffic Advice Note 79/99 to nothing more than a chimera – it is normal for the capacity of an urban road junction to be less than the sum of the capacities of the roads leading into it.

It should be noted that the official nominal capacities reproduced in Figure 7.13 do not map on to the FORGE speed–flow relationships reported in Figure 7.7. The reason given by the Department for Transport is that the FORGE relationships are 'nominal' assumptions to enable economic assessments: they are, nonetheless, literally incredible.

Junction capacity

Junction capacity is an arcane and complex topic but there are some simple, general principles which apply not only to roads but also to other modes of transport. A risk of collision exists wherever movements merge, diverge or cross. These risks for trains and aircraft are minimised by controllers with an overall view of events, but reducing the risks for road traffic depends upon individual drivers responding to unfolding events as they see them. In any event, the risks of accident are reduced mainly by ensuring that there is plenty of space between vehicles and this need cuts route capacity, no matter whether it is on a road, railway, flight path or shipping lane.

At road junctions the risk of collision is greatest at 'conflict points', points at which drivers leave, join or cross other traffic. Drivers do their best to assess the relative speeds of other vehicles and the changing patterns of the gaps between vehicles, gaps which may be used by drivers to make their own manoeuvres. It is a fraught, complex and potentially dangerous business. Decisions and actions have to take place within a 'conflict area' centred upon the conflict point but which may be both extensive and variable.

The diverge

As shown in Figure 7.14, the simplest conflicting movement is the diverge. A driver preparing to turn out of a stream of traffic has to slow down, causing following drivers to avoid rear-end collisions. The decisions of drivers within the stream are quite simple, based on straightforward observations of the vehicle in front plus judgements about its rate of deceleration. If the turn-out is sharply curved, the exit speed has to be low and the effect of the necessary deceleration on following vehicles is greater, but the risk of actual collision is comparatively low and the area of conflict is confined.

The merge

The merge is rather more complex. Drivers entering the traffic stream have to observe, comprehend and predict the speeds and spacing of vehicles in the flow they wish to join. It becomes almost second nature for drivers to do this but it actually needs considerable experience, skill and judgement to get it right. There are risks of provoking heavy braking in the flow being joined and also the possibility of rear-end

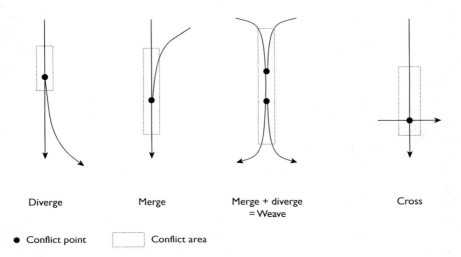

Figure 7.14 Types of conflicting movement

collisions if the joining vehicle is unable to accelerate up to the speed of the main flow in time. This risk is severe if the speed of the joining vehicle is well below the speed of the joined flow. This is why motorway slip roads are designed without sharp curves and with acceleration lanes – if a merging vehicle is moving at approximately the same speed as the traffic to be joined, the risk of provoking heavy braking is avoided and the joining vehicle may move across into a relatively short gap.

The weave

The weave is a sequence of a merge and then a diverge and is rather more than the sum of the two. The crucial characteristic is the difference in speeds: first, between the two merging flows, and second, between the two diverging flows. If all four flows have similar speeds, drivers are able to make good judgements about what time- and space-headways are acceptable and which are too dangerous to use. Substantial differences in speed make for poor judgements and high accident rates. Irrespective of the differences in speed, high speeds will ensure that the severity of collisions will be substantial, and not just the number of accidents but the number of injuries will rise.

Crossing movements

Crossing movements present drivers with more complex and risky situations. Figure 7.15 shows the simplest, but comparatively rare, movement of one flow crossing through another single, unidirectional flow. As with merging, drivers have to observe the speeds and vehicle spacing in the flow to be crossed and, in the knowledge of their own acceleration rates, decide when and whether to cross. The crossing conflict area is comparatively small and the exposure to risk is for quite a short time, but the

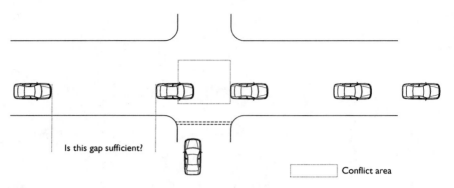

Figure 7.15 Simple crossing conflict on two one-way roads

intensity of the risk is considerable – the danger is not of a rear-end collision but of a sideways-on crash with a high probability of personal injury.

Most crossing movements are not as simple as crossing a one-way road. Drivers usually need to cross over traffic moving in both directions, as shown in Figure 7.16, a manoeuvre involving a much larger conflict area. Drivers have to observe both streams of traffic to be crossed and assess whether the gaps between vehicles in both streams are going to coincide long enough for them to make their manoeuvre – decisions which are difficult and hazardous.

Even more complex and dangerous is a right-turn out of a side road to join the lane on the far side of the road, as shown in Figure 7.17. The stream to be crossed (moving

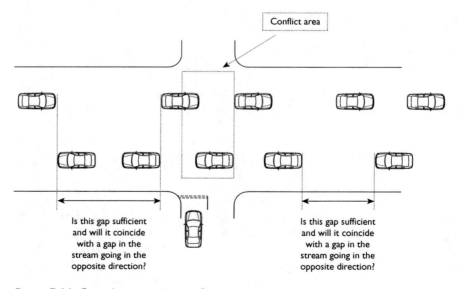

Figure 7.16 Complex crossing conflict

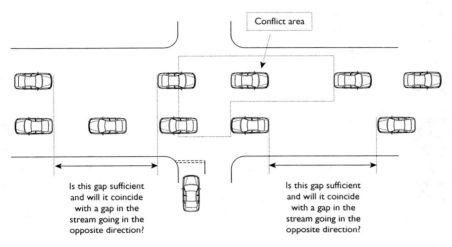

Figure 7.17 Crossing and merging conflicts

from right to left in Figure 7.17) has to be observed and assessed in a search for a long enough gap between vehicles to cross through. The stream to be joined (moving from left to right in Figure 7.17) has to be assessed for a gap long enough to allow the driver to join the stream and then accelerate quickly enough to avoid causing a rear-end collision: this need extends the conflict area. The driver then has to assess whether the crossing gap in the near-side stream and the merging gap in the off-side stream are going to coincide long enough for the manoeuvre to be made. It is a decision fraught with difficulty and danger which most drivers take with time and care.

Most urban junctions are more complex than the comparatively simple cases shown in Figures 7.15, 7.16 and 7.17. There are more possibilities of turns and, very often, possible conflicts with pedestrians as well. The numbers, sizes and positions of conflict areas are extensive and ever-changing: moreover, the significance of each is emphasised by the volume of traffic moving through it, and the characteristics of that change. In busy urban areas drivers are presented with a massive number of decisions in an almost continuous stream, and a mistake in any one of them can lead, at best, to the loss of a no-claims bonus and, at worst, to a funeral.

Although individuals are largely unaware of what is happening in their heads, it takes a significant time for human beings to observe, analyse, understand and then decide what to do. The more complex the situation, the longer it takes. The less experience, the longer it takes. The greater the influences of tiredness, hunger, anger or distraction, the longer it takes. It is a tribute to the awareness and care taken by the majority of drivers that the accident rate is not higher than it is.

That awareness and care is reflected in the time that most drivers give themselves by dropping their speed as they pass through conflict areas. The more complex and busy a junction, the more time the drivers take to assess the situation, decide what to do and then do it, time that they buy by reducing their speed. As drivers slow down, giving themselves the time to make good, safe decisions, they reduce average traffic speed. As seen on the solid curve in Figure 7.11, this cuts down the rate of traffic flow. It is clear that the stop-start congestion seen in urban areas is primarily due to the need for drivers to slow down through the conflict areas at junctions. If urban congestion is to be reduced, a major policy would appear to be to lessen the number and complexity of decisions confronting drivers, a daunting task, since it would need the simplification of junctions combined with a reduction in their number.

Traffic engineers try to increase flow by managing conflict points, either reducing them in number or spacing them out so that drivers are more able to concentrate on them one at a time. Figure 7.18 shows the conflict points at an uncontrolled four-legged crossroads with all four legs carrying two-way flows: at every one of the 32 points there is the risk of collision, a risk which drivers will try to minimise by slowing down and giving themselves more time to comprehend the situations confronting them. Slowing down implies increasing the time-headways and reducing the flow, and so the numbers and severities of conflict points have a direct influence on actual capacity.

Drivers' decisions and the time needed to make them may be made easier by using one or other of two basic techniques. The first is to build a junction that spreads the conflict points over the area, separating them and so presenting decisions to drivers one at a time, simplifying the decisions to be made and giving drivers more time to make them. Figure 7.19 shows how a roundabout achieves this.

As shown in previous figures, each conflict point represents a conflict area within which drivers have to make decisions which, if faulty, may cause an accident. The risks are increased with traffic speeds and volumes, and with complexities due to overlapping conflict areas which force drivers to make multiple, crowded decisions. Roundabouts and more extensive one-way systems not only reduce the number of conflict points but, by spacing them out, reduce their complexity, enabling drivers to make quicker, less risky decisions and to minimise space- and time-headways.

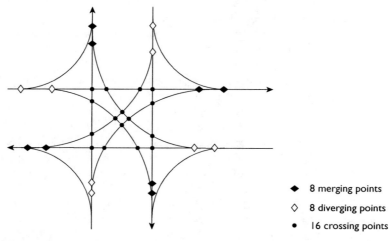

◆ 8 merging points
◇ 8 diverging points
• 16 crossing points

Figure 7.18 Conflict points at an uncontrolled four-legged crossroads

Congestion 125

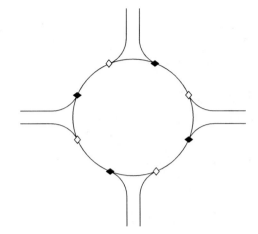

- ◆ 4 merging points
- ◇ 4 diverging points
- ● 0 crossing points

Figure 7.19 Conflict points at a simple roundabout

However, roundabouts have disadvantages which become particularly apparent in urban areas. They demand expensive space and are difficult and dangerous, both for pedestrians (due to the almost constant flows on the entries and exits) and for cyclists (due to their vulnerability when mixing with weaving traffic).

Traffic signals also reduce the nature, number and complexity of conflict points and areas but achieve this in time rather than in space. Figure 7.20 shows a simple signalled junction. By alternating between one set of simplified conflict points and another, stopping some flows entirely while permitting others, traffic signals reduce the number and complexity of the conflict points and areas through which drivers

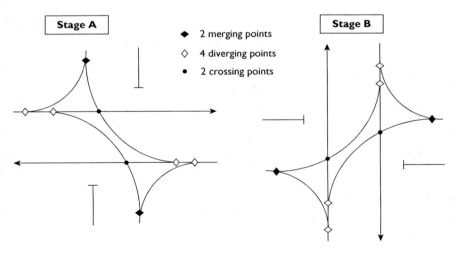

Figure 7.20 Conflict points at a junction controlled by simple traffic signals

have to pass. They effectively ration the capacity of the road space within the junction by denying any capacity to some flows from time to time while devoting all available capacity to others. The objective is to allow the maximum total number of all vehicles per hour through the junction, an objective reached by simplifying the decisions to be made by drivers.

Drivers' decision times

Simple reaction times have already been introduced as one of the key elements in traffic flow. Figure 7.2 and its later derivatives show a mean driver reaction time of 0.66 seconds. This is taken from the illustrations of braking time and distances quoted in the Highway Code and is the assumed representative time taken by drivers to start braking in an emergency. But this is the time to react taken in response to an extremely simple event – the brake lights on the vehicle in front being illuminated

In the seminal study by Matson et al.,[20] drivers' response times were analysed into four component activities:

1 *Perception (P):* the finite time taken for an image to be perceived by the brain for what it is – it might be the vehicle in front braking, a child running across the road, or any other event.
2 *Intellection (I):* the time taken for the brain to analyse the image and to estimate what might happen in the next second or so. This depends more on experience than intelligence. If the brake lights of the vehicle in front go on, experience makes the connection with the need to brake quickly, but an untoward event such as something falling off or out of the vehicle in front has to be analysed and understood before a response is selected. Complexity and variability increase the intellection time and so situations such as that shown in Figure 7.17 (making a right turn from a side road into a two-way flow) require an immense amount of on-the-spot analysis of the apparent gaps in the flows in both directions, whether they are lengthening or shortening, what speeds other vehicles are doing, the risks of collision, whether the predicted behaviours of other drivers are reliable, etc. At the end of the intellection time a driver will have selected a course of action, perhaps from a number of perceived possibilities, although the selection may not have been at an entirely conscious level: responses to a child running across the road, for example, may be swerving to left or right, or just trying to brake very sharply, but the choice is likely to be made by reflex rather than by conscious deliberation.
3 *Emotion (E):* this is not really a component but a modification of the previous two components. Preoccupation with ongoing personal arguments or decisions may have produced stresses and angers that extend normal intellection times. Some preoccupations may be avoidable: using mobile phones or even listening to a debate on the radio can reduce driver concentration and lengthen intellection times. Other events may be accidental: a child being travel sick or a diverting event such as a fight outside a shop. Emotions may have been affected by alcohol or other drugs, whether or not on prescription. In all, there are a wide range of effects upon intellection times which prevent any accurate, definitive generalisation of

response times, but law, practice and convention are able to bring them within acceptable envelopes. Currently there is concern about the use of mobile phones, with debates about their use extending response times well outside an acceptable envelope and calls for their use to be further restricted by law.

4   *Volition (V):* this is the time taken for the action identified in the intellection phase to be implemented: for messages to be sent from the brain and for muscles to work to brake or steer. This time may be extended by disability; hence the need for tests on eyesight and other medical conditions before licences to drive may be granted, but volition, like intellection, may be temporarily affected by drugs.

More recently, response times have been analysed[21] in ways that are similar to this original PIEV analysis, but the fundamental idea remains that more complexity in the decisions confronting drivers creates longer response times, heightened accident risks and reductions in capacity.

Gap acceptance

Drivers need time and space in which to respond to events as they see them and to manoeuvre accordingly. To do this they would need to drive through conflict areas while they are actually empty of other vehicles, so drivers need to recognise and use gaps in the flow of traffic. Figure 7.21 shows some seminal data on the gaps accepted by 50 per cent of drivers when presented with a junction similar to those shown in Figures 7.16 and 7.17. There is a plethora of later studies using more sophisticated statistical techniques to identify variations away from averages such as those shown in Figure 7.21, but they all demonstrate the fundamental principle that the more complex the movement to be made, the longer drivers take to make their decisions and therefore the longer the gap needed in the flow to be joined or crossed. The corollary is that decisions may be quicker and flows higher if drivers are presented with simple layouts with a minimum number of well-spaced decisions.

This is particularly apparent in Figure 7.21. Fifty per cent of drivers emerging from a side road with a 'Stop' sign guarding the junction and making a left turn accepted a gap of 6.5 seconds or more but if they made a right turn they were much more selective and needed gaps of 8.3 seconds or more. The extra 1.8 seconds reflects the

Movement from minor road	Minor road drivers presented with a 'Give Way' sign	Minor road drivers presented with a 'Stop' sign
Left turn	4.6	6.5
Straight across	5.5	6.7
Right turn	6.4	8.3

Figure 7.21 Gaps accepted by 50 per cent of drivers at a minor road junction (seconds)
Source: Road Research Laboratory (1965), table 9.1.

extra time needed to assess gaps in both the flow to be crossed and the flow to be joined, to estimate whether the gaps were going to coincide and whether there would be sufficient time and space to accelerate up to the speed of vehicles in the flow to be joined. This is the intellection time in the PIEV analysis.

The supply of gaps

Observing traffic from the roadside will show that vehicles are not normally evenly spaced, as was assumed for the sake of simplification in the flow theory of Figures 7.2 to 7.5, although it will be very close to being absolutely regular in slow-moving congested flows dominated by nose-to-tail, follow-my-leader driving. These notions may be expressed in another way: in congested traffic the headways between pairs of vehicles will be very similar, with minimal variations away from the average and a consequent low standard deviation.[22] The time-headways in a flow will appear as gaps to drivers manoeuvring through conflict areas and a congested nose-to-tail flow will have no gaps long enough for any merging, or crossing manoeuvres to be made. A few drivers within the congested flow may make diverging movements and provide minimal, chancy gaps, but otherwise the supply of gaps will be minimal and the discharge from side roads will be almost blocked.

In free-flowing traffic there will be quite wide variations from the average headway with an almost, but not quite, random distribution of gaps akin to that given in Figure 7.22 which shows the influence of the flow upon the number of gaps equal to or longer than three illustrative lengths: the curves should be interpreted with care at lower flows, since the gaps may be considerably longer than five, six or eight seconds, enabling them to be used by more than one manoeuvring vehicle. The curves show important lessons: as flows increase the number of longer, usable gaps reduces and act to cap the numbers of movements from the side roads. They also show that at even quite high flows, longer gaps still appear – eventually.

Figure 7.21 showed that right-turn movements require a longer gap than left turns and Figure 7.22 shows that the supply of such longer gaps is restricted. This lower supply is further magnified by the size of the flows within which a gap has to be found. Figure 7.17 showed the conflict area through which a right-turner has to pass, crossing the flow moving from right to left and then joining the flow moving from left to right. This requires gaps in each of the flows to coincide. In practice there has to be a length of time (a gap) during which no vehicle enters the conflict area, either from the left or from the right. The random Poisson model of gaps, upon which Figure 7.22 is based, need not be concerned with direction, so the two main road flows may be added together and the necessary gap (about 8 seconds in Figure 7.21) found in the combined flow; this represents the coincidence of gaps in both directions of flow combining to give an overall gap sufficiently long for the manoeuvre to be made. In contrast, the shorter 6.5-second gap to make a left turn is only required in the flow in the one direction (right to left). It follows that right turns are much more demanding than left turns, partly because they require a longer gap but mainly because that longer gap must be found in the combined flows in both directions.

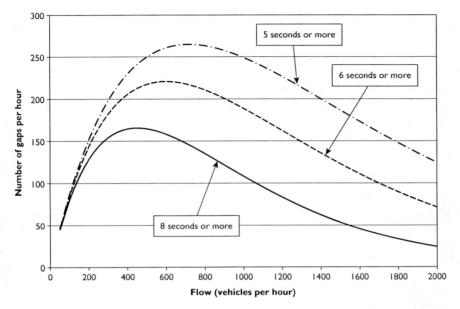

Figure 7.22 The supply of five-, six- and eight-second gaps as a function of flow

Note: These curves are based on a random Poisson distribution of gaps.

Tackling congestion[23]

This chapter began with quotations showing political attitudes towards growing congestion. Prescott's definition of congestion appears to extend beyond 'gridlock' to include the 'delays' in which drivers are obliged to travel at speeds below their aspirations. The government sought to emphasise the importance and urgency of dealing with congestion by asserting that it cost £15 billion per year.[24] This figure, or one like it, crops up repeatedly and has a long history. The government quotes the source as *Moving Forward – a Business Strategy for Transport* published by the Confederation of British Industry in 1995, but this in turn used an unacknowledged source produced two years earlier by Newbery.[25] Long before that, Reynolds and Wardrop (1960)[26] argued that 10 per cent of the costs of road transport were wasted due to congestion. Their estimate was based on the premise that average speeds should be 30 mile/hour in urban areas and 40 mile/hour in rural areas. Any speeds below these figures were deemed to be 'congested', and the extra time and fuel costs incurred were summed to create an annual cost of about £200 million. Using such benchmark speeds seemed to be unquestioned at the time but they were, nonetheless, foolish. It does not need any sophisticated analysis of field data to understand that traffic on urban streets thronged with pedestrians, with stopping buses and delivery vehicles, with parked cars and with traffic threading its way through multiple conflict areas, is not likely to maintain an average speed equal to the legal maximum. On the contrary, delays forcing speeds well below the legal maximum are endemic and unavoidable, posing the question of how inevitable, and therefore necessarily acceptable, delays are to be defined and what policies should be written to ensure that congestion is no worse than necessary.

More recently, the Department for Transport has retrieved the idea of a benchmark speed,[27] although it is now variable from place to place rather than being one or other of the fixed urban and rural speeds assumed by Reynolds and Wardrop in 1960. Speed data are collected along a sample of roads at varying times of day and night by using test cars.[28] In urban areas the benchmark average speed is defined as the speed in the middle of the night when traffic is very light. In rural areas the old 1960s presumption of an uncongested average speed has been retained, although there is a range of benchmarks set for various road types and speed limits.[29] The delays due to congestion are defined by the Department for Transport as the difference in the time taken to travel each section of road, first at the benchmark speed and then at the daytime, congested speed. The delays to the test cars on a small sample of roads are multiplied by the actual volumes of traffic and reported as the delay per vehicle-kilometre. The global total for the whole country is estimated from this small sample.

The data for 2006 to 2007 show an average delay of 1.31 minutes for every 16 vehicle-kilometres.[30] In that year there were 506.4 billion vehicle-kilometres, giving a crude estimate of 'lost' time as 41.2 billion vehicle-minutes. The average cost per vehicle-hour has been reckoned to be £11.28,[31] resulting in an annual cost of delay of £7.75 billion. This is considerably different to the £15 billion quoted in *Breaking the Logjam* but this does not imply that either figure is 'wrong' – instead it reflects the difficulty of making a global estimate of any quantity such as congestion which varies over so many dimensions. For the time being it is best not to put a price on congestion but to accept that it is a pernicious nuisance – as Prescott said:

> Everybody hates traffic jams. They cost time and money. They pump out pollution. They take the pleasure out of driving.

The national aggregate cost of congestion is not only difficult to estimate, it is not that useful in detailed decision-making: very large differences from the average occur from time to time and from place to place. Of more importance is the effect of congestion upon individuals. As Prescott implies, people see the problem as a waste of their personal time, measuring the effects of congestion by their watch rather than by their purse.

For transport planners the importance extends beyond congestion itself towards the attempts made by individual drivers to avoid its effects. Figure 7.23 shows that the time penalties for low speed are severe and get progressively worse as speed falls. It takes 1.2 minutes to drive one kilometre at the urban speed limit but it takes five times as long to cover the same distance at a congested 10 km/h. Broadly, the time taken to cover one kilometre doubles if speed drops from 50 km/h to 25 km/h, doubles again with a drop to 12 km/h and doubles yet again if speed falls to 7 km/h.

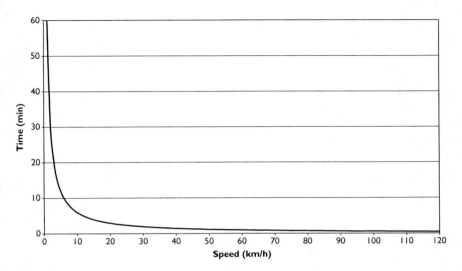

Figure 7.23 Time taken to travel one kilometre

At first sight this appears to be a compelling argument to agree with John Prescott,[32] with the RAC[33] and with many others that congestion is a bane, and that its eradication, or at least amelioration, should be a major objective. Unfortunately the argument is not that simple. When faced with low, congested speeds, individual motorists take avoiding action as best they can. They have five choices:

1. Use another route, avoiding the worst bottlenecks.
2. Make the journey at a less congested time.
3. Travel by a less congested mode of transport.
4. Go to a different destination with less congestion en route.
5. Endure the delay (no doubt making continuous complaints about the driver in front being the cause).

Route changes

This may be the sort of convoluted route beloved by taxi drivers, using back streets and side roads, or it may be more sweeping, perhaps using a ring road to approach a city centre from a different direction. These changes are inevitably self-defeating in the long run as more drivers switch route and provoke congestion at other points of limited capacity such as complex junctions. This serves to spread congestion over an ever-widening area.

Time changes

Leaving before or after the eye of the peak is a common reaction and results in the shoulders of the peak becoming progressively busier, extending the peak until congestion is apparent for much or all of the day. This spreads congestion over time rather than space.

Mode changes

This is more problematic, since it depends upon the availability of a mode which is subject to less delay. This is a fundamental issue to be considered later.

Destination changes

The choice may be made by an individual motorist, perhaps to go to an out-of-town shop rather than the high street or, in the longer term, even to take a job with a less congested journey to work. But the choice is often a corporate one, with firms choosing to locate in less congested areas, giving both their employees and their customers the opportunity to avoid delays. These choices are not made on a whim but are a fundamentally important effect of congestion which will be covered in later chapters.

Enduring the delay

Prescott was right: most people 'hate traffic jams'.[34] For some, the alternatives of different routes, times, modes or destinations are really impossible but many others *think* they are impossible without really considering whether this is actually the case.[35] Walking, with or without using public transport for part of the journey, may be rejected without even trying it. There may be real alternatives, hidden by a lack of awareness of their existence: many car drivers have little knowledge of public transport routes, timetables and fares, often asserting that the services are unacceptable without finding out whether this is in fact the case. A significant number of individuals join the hated jams, protesting that they have no choice, although they may well have chosen to live in a place which needs a long, congested drive to work. That choice is usually quite logical: their chosen lifestyle depends upon having a desirable house in a desirable place, often near a good school and upon driving to work in a warm, personal vehicle which often wraps them in a desirable status. The price paid for their lifestyle is the time and money spent in the hated, but endured, traffic jams.

Changes in route, time and destination are all driven by the quest to find less congested roads but such changes paradoxically spread congestion over more time and a wider area. Congestion becomes 'worse' because it is spread, but it does not get 'worse' by intensifying: speeds and volumes do not fall down along the solid forced-flow curve shown in Figure 7.11 into total gridlock. Despite the rhetoric, there appears to be a floor to congested traffic speeds, and total gridlock is rarely evident unless some unusual event has created it: this is not to say that severe congestion does not occur, nor that it is unimportant, but that it is not the demon it is often made out to be. It is also to say that it is endemic and that any politician aspiring to solve the problem is bound to fail.

For speeds and flows to be almost constant, there has to be a pool of drivers for whom a floor average speed is just about acceptable. If speeds drop below the floor, probably because some junctions are not coping well with the flows seeking to enter them, a sufficient number of drivers will avoid the congested areas and times to bring speeds back up to the floor. But if speeds improve, other drivers will join the queues to force speeds back down to the floor again.

If this assertion is right, the pool is probably a set of people making lifestyle decisions, people for whom enduring congestion is a cost of choosing where to live and how to travel. It is a cost they accept, perhaps unwillingly and noisily, but the fact that they are there, wasting their time in congestion, is largely a result of their own lifestyle choices, no matter how strongly they deny it: if the problems were really too much for them, they would not choose to be there. This is, admittedly, a dangerous argument because its strength has been depleted by having been used in cases where people are trapped without having any real choice – it has been used, for example, about those without a job: they are said to be 'unemployed because they choose to be'. And there may well be some people who are enduring congestion because they do genuinely not have a choice – because their skills tie them to a particular workplace, their job description ties them to a particular clock-in time and family obligations restrict their choice of home.

But change continues to happen: even patterns which appear not to change are actually undergoing continuous alteration. For example, the percentage of households owning only one car has been constant at about 40 per cent for some 30 years, but the composition of that 40 per cent has been changing the whole time as some households become car owners for the first time, swelling the percentage, but other households acquire a second car, bringing the percentage back down again. Similarly, as people move house or jobs they are replaced by other people with different patterns of behaviour, different lifestyles and different transport choices.

Goodwin calls these changes 'behavioural churn'.[36] Patterns of movement change, not by individuals changing their particular travel choices but because fundamental changes are made to their lives – they move house or retire, or switch jobs – and their places are taken by others with different lifestyles and choices. Hence, if a group of people apparently change route, travel time, mode or destination, it is probable that a good proportion of those changes will not be due to identifiable individuals making choices to change, but will be because incomers to the group with different choices are replacing others leaving and taking their personal choices with them. Much of the apparent effect will be due to behavioural churn.

Figure 7.24 uses London as a case study, focusing on the central area. The data are presented as indices covering the ten years 1995 to 2005 and are drawn from the annual *Transport Statistics Great Britain*. This is an important decade, since the congestion charge was implemented and changes were made to public transport fare structures, but whether these developments were the cause of the trends shown in Figure 7.24 is far from clear.

It will be seen that car traffic entering central London fell, although the total number of people travelling to the centre rose. The use of public transport rose and so did average traffic speeds. In the country as a whole there was a contrary and substantial rise in car traffic.

134 Congestion

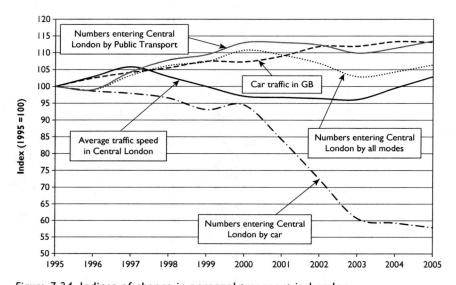

Figure 7.24 Indices of change in personal transport in London
Source: Data from Department for Transport, *Transport Statistics Great Britain*, table 0106.

Figure 7.25 expands a little on the comparison between London and elsewhere. Again the data are presented as indices but now London appears as 'Greater London' rather than the central area.

The trends shown in Figures 7.24 and 7.25, although specifically about London and the Southeast, suggest that people are appearing to make choices to circumvent congestion by moving to some other time or mode or place, although such changes may be due to behavioural churn rather than explicit personal choice. Time shifts result in the extension of peak-hour congestion, perhaps forcing other drivers below their acceptable floor speed and increasing the propensity to move to another location.

In the short term individuals are able to select homes and workplaces which reduce their congested driving, but their choices will be reflected in market-driven corporate decisions to develop housing in congestion-free areas and to build commercial developments where traffic and parking problems are lessened. Their actions change the shape and structure of urban areas. The past 40 years or so have seen offices and shops built in suburban and peripheral locations and housing developed in the surrounding countryside. These two trends have created the modern, extended virtual urban area, with traffic spread and diffused over wide areas with low numbers of road junctions per kilometre of road.

This restructuring of the city has resulted in journeys becoming ever longer as they interconnect dispersed, low-density housing with places of work and commerce which have been moved out of the congested city centre to locations served with parking and accessed by relatively uncongested roads. This has resulted in journeys ('trips' in the jargon) becoming extended; the data confirm this to be so.

Congestion 135

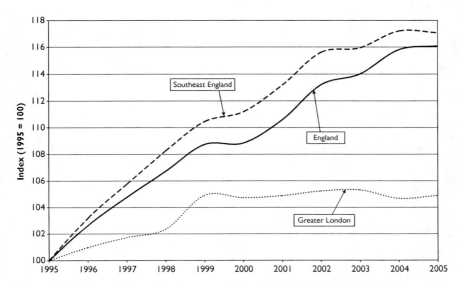

Figure 7.25 Growth in traffic (measured in vehicle-kilometres) in London and southeast England compared with country-wide growth

Source: Department for Transport, *Transport Statistics Great Britain* (2006), table 7.09.

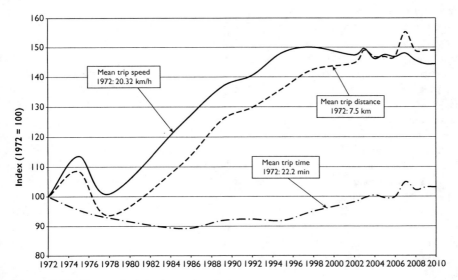

Figure 7.26 Mean trip lengths and speeds

Source: Department for Transport, *National Travel Survey* (2010), table NTS0101.

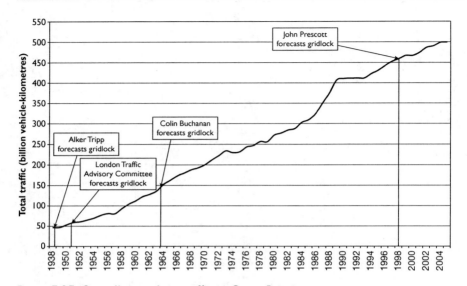

Figure 7.27 Overall growth in traffic in Great Britain
Source: Department for Transport, *Transport Statistics Great Britain* (various dates).

Figure 7.26 is not merely interesting for showing that the mean trip distance, irrespective of mode, has extended by 50 per cent over the last 40 years but that the time taken to travel that distance has been more or less constant at just over 20 minutes. This suggests that the choices being made, either by individuals as such or by a churning group of individuals, are not only to avoid congestion but also to maintain their travel times at a constant level.

This hints at a paradox. Figure 7.27 shows that traffic has increased ten-fold over the past 70 years and that during this time there have been repeated warnings of forthcoming gridlock – not merely congestion but massive runaway congestion. There is no denying that congestion has got worse but it has done so by being more widespread in time and space, affecting more people rather than affecting the same people more intensely. Nonetheless, the predicted complete thrombosis has not happened and this suggests that it is unlikely to happen in the future. Past trends in which individuals and firms have made myriad decisions to avoid congested areas, in the short term by driving elsewhere and in the longer term by building elsewhere, seem to have kept total failure of the traffic system at bay. Congestion has been tackled so well that a 1000 per cent increase in traffic has been accommodated, perhaps imperfectly but fairly effectively.

The sting in the tail

There appears to be a further paradox in the tendency for traffic to congest but not to congest absolutely. The capacity of urban road junctions seems to set a limit upon how much traffic may be accommodated: when that capacity is reached, delays and queues pull down journey speeds to levels that some drivers find intolerable. But then they use the flexibility of their cars to vary the times, routes and destinations of their journeys in a quest to outflank congestion, creating the paradox that vehicles cause congestion but they are also the means of mitigating its effects.

Governments make noisy affirmations that congestion is a major problem but they have been relatively unsuccessful in adopting policies to cope with it. This does not seem to be completely disastrous, since congestion appears to mitigate itself merely through individual and corporate decisions to avoid it by going somewhere else. 'Gridlock' therefore stays below the horizon, not because of effective government policy but by a cloud of separate, uncoordinated decisions.

The sting is that this process may appear to be more or less effective but it has potentially disastrous results. Spreading urban development over ever-increasing areas erodes the productivity of agricultural land by converting it into low-density housing and commercial development accessed by more road space. Those extensions of the road network are not just in major roads but also in considerable lengths of access roads. Such development produces ever longer journeys for which cars become almost a necessity and which are almost impossible to cater for by other means of transport.

Consequently, doing nothing positive and effective about congestion is inherently unsustainable because the problem will then be tackled by default through dispersed, piecemeal decision-making, resulting in dispersed, piecemeal development of ever more land. This has generated and will continue to generate increased, diffused travel, burning more fuel and producing more CO_2. This changes the nature of the problem to be tackled: it is not to reduce congestion per se but to do so with the added objectives of restraining the conversion of land from rural to urban uses and reducing the rates of traffic growth rather than stimulating them.

The hunt is then on for policies to achieve this. Increasing urban junction and road capacity is known not to work except in a smattering of trivial cases. Reductions of road freight would imply restricting deliveries to commercial properties, but, if urban areas are to retain their commercial functions rather than dispersing them around the surrounding areas, the ease of servicing and delivery needs to be enhanced, not restricted. That appears to leave only one option: to reduce the demand for urban travel by car.

Both government and lobbyists assert that this may only be achieved by some form of road user charging – by pricing traffic off urban streets. This suggestion is self-evidently impossible. The reason why congestion has an element of self-correction is that the delays and low speeds produce increases in cost and it is those high costs that drivers strive to avoid by avoiding congested areas, and it is the combination of those efforts that has resulted in the decentralisation and dispersal of the city. To accelerate and magnify the costs per urban vehicle-kilometre by imposing a surcharged tax or toll will only serve to enhance the congestion effect. It may well reduce urban traffic but will do so by exporting it to the suburbs and beyond in exactly the same way as has been done over the past 50 years or more. Such a policy is not only unsustainable but history has demonstrated it to be so.

This points towards a counter-intuitive policy. If the capacity of the urban road network cannot be increased and if reducing traffic by displacing it to suburbia and the surrounding rural areas is unsustainable, then policy-makers need to find another option. If improving traffic speeds, no matter how, attracts additional traffic until speeds revert to their previous levels, then the only avenue available is not to take action to change traffic speeds but to reduce the number of vehicles affected by those congested speeds. To do this requires urban road and junction capacity to be reduced rather than enhanced. If the theory is correct this will make congestion worse in the short term but will deflect traffic away until the floor speeds return. The difficulty is, first, to weather the political hurricane that would be whipped up, and, second, to ensure that travel is deflected on to sustainable transport, but, perhaps, that is really not so difficult. Figure 17.24 shows what has happened in London with concrete evidence of reductions in total traffic, of increases in traffic speed and a surge in the use of public transport, and all this in the most prosperous area of Britain with a high car-ownership rate. This seems to indicate that some things are right and effective, even if they may not have been entirely thought through and predicted.

Appendix 7.1

Moving Car Observer

The Department of Transport methodology for assessing and then justifying road schemes relies in very large part upon the putative value of travel time savings. These are calculated from the difference in travel time through the unimproved and improved networks – in 'before' and 'after' traffic flows. Obviously, the 'after' speeds and volumes must be based on estimates which are the product of modelling techniques (discussed in Chapter 19): these are open to question. The 'before' data should really be determined by field measurements, but there has been a historical tendency for this to be crudely done.

Objectors to road and traffic schemes have found that collecting their own 'before' data has provided a firm platform for telling criticism. The Moving Car Observer (sometimes called the Floating Car) technique provides a cheap and easy method of collecting good-quality, robust data by non-professionals.[37] It is also good for making estimates of fuel consumption and emissions as functions of speed.

The technique is based on one or more test cars, each containing three observers driving to and fro along a set route. The route is defined by a string of predetermined 'timing points'. These are the major road junctions and other constraints on flow such as pedestrian crossings or points at which the nature of flow changes: speed limits, ends of dual carriageways, etc. The distances between timing points must be known as accurately as possible.

One of the observers, armed with a stop-watch or lap-top, notes the times at which the car stops, starts or passes through one of the timing points. Since distances are known, this produces data on the journey and running speeds and the differences between them (the delays).

The second observer counts the vehicles that overtake the test car or are overtaken by it: this provides the basis for a correction to the speed data to align the behaviour of the test car with that of the traffic flow in general.

The third observer counts the vehicles moving in the opposite direction to the test car. Since the test traverses each section of the route twice, once in each direction, the counts of traffic in one direction may be related to the speed of the car as it passes in the other direction to give a good measure of flow. This precludes collecting flow data on one-way roads.

The technique produces accurate data about traffic speeds and delays but, as ever with traffic data, whether these are representative of 'typical' flow is always questionable. The flow data are of mean flows along a section of road, not flows past a point, and if the data are to be presented at a Public Inquiry, it is a good idea to make a static roadside count to provide some validation.

Since the traffic volume and speed is known along each section of the route, the fuel burn and pollution may be estimated.[38]

Notes

1. Department for the Environment, Transport and the Regions (1999) Foreword, p. 2.
2. Malins, first Chairman of the Metropolitan Railway, quoted in Barker and Robbins (1963, p. 106).
3. 'London Traffic Congestion'. London and Home Counties Traffic Advisory Committee (1951).
4. See Banks et al. (2007).
5. See e.g. Stern (2006).
6. www.direct.gov.ukdg/188029.pdf.
7. This may be difficult for some people to understand: 6.5 metres per second is the same as (6.5 × 3600 (the seconds in an hour) ÷ 1000 (the metres in a kilometre) = 23.4 km/h. Braking at 6.5 metres per second per second means that a vehicle's speed is reduced by 6.5 metres per second (23.4 km/h) for every second of braking time. Braking distance (B in metres) is calculated as the initial speed (S in m/sec) squared divided by twice the deceleration rate (A = 6.5 metres per second per second): $B = (S^2) / (2 \times A)$.
8. Road Research Laboratory (RRL) (1965, p. 196).
9. RRL (1965, p. 210).
10. Ministry of Transport (1967).
11. Curve fitting without adequate linkage between cause and effect can be laughably misleading. If the number of television sets is graphed against the numbers of cars it produces a plausible straight line, but the one does not affect the other. Other graphs would show that both have a common driver, household income.
12. Department for Transport (www.dft.gov.uk/webtag) National Transport Model: FORGE (Table 9).
13. FORGE (Fitting on Regional Growth and Elasticities), a component of the NTM (National Transport Model) (www.dft.gov.uk/webtag).
14. Statistically, the spread is given by the 'standard deviation' (usually represented by the Greek sigma: σ). If all speeds are the same, $\sigma = 0$. If they are nearly but not quite the same, σ will be a very small number. If the range from the smallest to the largest is wide then σ will be a much larger number.
15. And this increases the value of σ.
16. Statistically, the spread of data on either side of the mean is measured by the standard deviation, so this reduces as traffic thickens.
17. RRL (1965, p. 193).
18. Highways Agency (online).
19. Highways Agency, *Design Manual for Roads and Bridges*, Vol. 5, Section 1, Part 3, Annex D.
20. Matson et al. (1955, p. 20).

21 See Dorn (2000, pp. 195–216) and Toledo (2007, pp. 65–84).
22 This is a statistical measure of the spread to the values which contribute to an average.
23 This heading has been borrowed from the Scottish Executive's consultation paper (1999), the Scottish counterpart to *Breaking the Logjam* (1999) produced by the Department for the Environment, Transport and the Regions.
24 Department for the Environment, Transport and the Regions (1998, p. 5).
25 'The Economic Effect of the Recommendations of the Royal Commission Report on Transport'. *Economic Journal*, Vol. 105.
26 'Economic Losses due to Traffic Congestion'. *Traffic Engineering and Control*, Vol. 2, No 7: 406–408 (November 1960).
27 *A Measure of Road Traffic Congestion in England* (Department for Transport 2000). Available at roadtraffcongest2000.pdf on the DfT website.
28 The 'Moving Car Observer' technique is a very useful and cheap method of collecting traffic data and is described in an Appendix to this chapter.
29 Table 1 in roadtraffcongest.pdf on the DfT website.
30 *Road Statistics 2006* (Department for Transport 2007, table 3.1).
31 Department for Transport (2007a) Unit 3.5.6.
32 See Department of Transport (1999).
33 RAC Foundation (2007).
34 Department for the Environment, Transport and the Regions (1999, p. 2).
35 See e.g. Stradling *et al.* (1999).
36 Goodwin (2008).
37 Ministry of Transport (1965).
38 POOHSTIX (Peripetetic Observation of Half-street Traffic Intensity Xactly) is a package describing the methodology and includes lap-top software for the collection and analysis of data. Available from barry@hutton.name.

Chapter 8

The problems
Interchanging and trans-shipment

Neither freight nor passenger journeys are completed from beginning to end by a single mode. The only exceptions are the few personal journeys made entirely on foot, while all others include changes from one mode to another. At the simplest, these may be the switch from feet to wheels at bus-stops or in car-parks, although many mode changes are far more complex, particularly those in freight transport where handling between modes is an unavoidable and very visible problem. Typically, mechanical handling equipment designed to cope with standardised unit loads is used in switching from one mode to another. Such units may then be used to carry the freight on the major, long-haul modes as well as by the handling equipment between modes. Such methods are tagged as 'inter-modal'.

To some extent this is a very old idea. In the days when goods were heaved around by human muscle power, goods were often crudely unitised in bags or bottles to make handling easier. Words like 'cran' and 'bushel' still survive from the days when many goods were moved in units of about 50 kg, the weight a fit person is able to repetitively lift and carry throughout a working day. By the 1930s petrol and diesel engines were available and hydraulic systems were being developed to replace cables to work vehicle brakes and the landing gear, and control surfaces of aircraft. These technologies were combined in the development of the diesel-powered, hydraulically controlled fork-lift truck which came to play a vital role in the logistics of the Second World War. Vast tonnages of war material had to be transported, creating an emphasis on efficient handling, an emphasis that was enhanced by the military being not only the shipper but often organising the actual handling and haulage too.

Small goods like rifles or hand grenades had to be unitised, first by packing them in standard-sized boxes and then by stacking the boxes on small wooden platforms (pallets) designed to be lifted by fork-lift trucks. The much older ideas of packaging goods to make them easier to handle had been developed into a 'Russian Doll' model in which basic, simple packets were combined to make palletised units which were then amalgamated into truck, train or ship loads. The use of pallets and fork-lift trucks saved many thousands of scarce labouring hours.

Towards the end of the Second World War the US Army developed a larger unit, the Transponder, a standard box which could be filled with loaded pallets and then lifted on to a lorry or train by fork-lift truck or by crane on to a ship. In 1955 this idea was taken forward by Malcom McLean, an American trucking magnate, to create the modern standard shipping container, a steel box of 1280 cubic feet capable of taking a net load of 24 tonnes. The two seminal characteristics of McLean's design were, first, a standard way of fixing the container to a lorry or railway chassis, and second, sufficient strength to enable stacking one upon the other on-board ship where the ship's motion during a storm produces considerable dynamic loadings. The result was a revolution. The nature and costings of sea ports were changed fundamentally by the use of specialist cranes, fork-lift trucks and other mechanical handling equipment designed to cope with the known standard dimensions and fixings. The first sailing of a specialist ship dedicated to containers was in early 1956; in the little more than 50 years since then over 90 per cent of all international freight has come to be containerised.

Crucially, this revolution was driven by improvements, not in the transport modes themselves, but in the handling technology used at the interfaces between modes. Container ships may have reduced shipping costs, but their use was secondary, dependent upon the adoption of better methods to load and unload them.

Container ports: a demonstration case

Chapter 2 introduced the concept of transport rhythms, with each mode of transport having a signature rhythm composed of the size and frequency of loads. Container ships are able to carry thousands of containers: in British practice trains are able to carry 30 containers or more and lorries only one. A ship able to carry 10,000 containers will need to be matched with about 300 trains or 10,000 lorries to cope with the same throughput. It is rare for a ship to be completely emptied and reloaded at one port, but, as a demonstration example, it will be assumed that it takes three days. Matching the ship's load would need trains at 15-minute intervals, each carrying 33 containers, or lorries, each carrying one container, at 26-second headways. The three have very different rhythms, the ship with 10,000 containers every three days, the trains with 33 containers every quarter of an hour and lorries with one container every 26 seconds; but despite that wide difference, all three have the same, matching throughput.

There are two radical implications behind such disparities in rhythm. First, containers will be subject to significant waiting times between an inward container arriving by ship and leaving by the onward mode and between an outward container arriving at the dockside and leaving by ship. Second, these waiting containers must be stored somewhere.

All other things being equal, the average waiting time per container in the demonstration example would be 36 hours, a total of 720,000 container-hours during which both inward and outward containers are stationary, waiting to be moved along the next segment of their journeys. Some of this time will be spent on-board ship. If it were possible for loading and unloading to take place simultaneously and, as inward containers were unloaded, they were replaced immediately by an outward container, the ship would have 10,000 containers on board for the whole three days in port, although, as the hours passed, the container population would change by 'churn'. This would cater for the whole 720,000 container hours and the ship would be effectively acting as a container store for the entire three days it was at the dockside

In reality, some, but not all, the waiting container hours will be aboard the ship. It is quite impossible to organise loading and unloading so that every unloaded inward container is immediately replaced by an outward one: on-board containers are stacked on top of one another. Even if the rate at which the outward containers arrived at the dockside by lorry were constant at one every 26 seconds and if the inward ones left at the same rate, the need to sort them by destination would prevent immediate handling. Furthermore, if containers arrived by train in groups of 33, there would inevitably be some time before all 33 containers were lifted off, time during which the remaining containers would be awaiting their turn to be moved, keeping the train waiting and being used as a temporary parking place for waiting containers in exactly the same sense that the partially loaded ship is used to accommodate some container waiting time. But using vehicles, be they ships, trains or lorries, as temporary storage for longer than the minimal time necessary for loading and unloading is wasteful. Vehicles are made to move freight, not to store it: all vehicles cost money per hour but only earn money per unit of loaded distance. If they are stopped, for whatever reason, they are creating cost but earning nothing.

There are two aspects of leaving waiting containers on the vehicle used to move them:

1 There is the unavoidable need to leave containers where they are to await their turn to be handled on or off. This detains the vehicle, using it as a necessary short-term store.
2 This minimal time may be extended for other reasons, prolonging the detention of the vehicle and incurring additional cost.

The truism that expensive equipment designed to move loads costs money for every minute of its existence but only earns money if it is loaded and moving is at the root of Malcom McLean's revolutionary development of containerised transport. He separated the expensive parts of freight vehicles, the chassis and power units, from the cheap part, the simple, load-carrying box. By creating the design of a cheap standard-sized, stackable box with simple fixings, he not only enabled more efficient handling but also the use of the box as a store without incurring large financial penalties. Since containers are strong enough to withstand the pounding weight of other containers stacked on top of them at sea, they can also be stacked on shore to create what is in effect a large but very flexible warehouse. Consequently, the waiting that is implicit at interfaces between different transport rhythms does not need to be at the cost of detaining expensive transport vehicles but may be accommodated by stacking containers on dockside hardstanding.

The inevitable need to lift and lower the containers on and off ships, trains, lorries and, in many ports, barges, is a further, major complication demanding ancillary micro-modes of transport, designed to lift and place containers by using their standardised lift points. Container cranes with their high gantries able to clear ships' superstructures and spreader frames rather than hooks at the ends of the lifting cables serve to characterise container ports. The spreaders attach to the container tops using the same fixings as are used to attach containers to lorry or train chassis, keeping the container level as it moves. In common with all modes of transport, these cranes have their signature rhythms appearing as 'cycle times', defined as the time between beginning to lift one container and lifting the next. During the cycle time, the spreader has to be lowered and fixed to the top of a particular container which has to be lifted, moved horizontally and lowered, the spreader unhitched, lifted and moved horizontally back over the next identified container. The movements are quite slow, even ponderous, since a container cannot be placed safely and accurately if it is swinging around. Cycle times vary but 3.5 minutes is a reasonable representative average giving a rate of about 18 containers per hour.

Just one crane working at that rate is clearly inadequate. In the demonstration case of 10,000 containers being entirely unloaded, a ship would have to stay at the quayside for the best part of a year if its cargo were handled by just one crane. The purchase price of a ship of this size is approximately £65 million. Financing the purchase will cost in the order of £6.5 million per year, about £18,000 per day or £750 per hour with operating, crew and insurance costs on top: every hour at the quayside is expensive and every unnecessary hour is extremely wasteful. Port turn-around times are crucial and ships are worked as quickly as possible. This is achieved by using as many cranes as possible and, more recently, to use spreaders able to lift more than one container at a time.

This urgency to unload and load ships as fast as possible creates a problem to the rear of the line of cranes where inward and outward containers are lowered and raised. Unless they are moved as quickly as possible to and from the stacking yards there will be chaotic congestion. More equipment is necessary to do this. Straddle loaders are able to pick up containers, move them at speeds of up to 30 km/h and place them in stacks up to four high. These machines have widely ranging cycle times depending on the distance between the rear of the cranes and locations in the stack yards: there must be a sufficient number of loaders to keep pace with the cranes and still more to link the stack yards with the lorries and trains carrying the containers in and out of the port area. These loaders too have their own rhythms, cycle times and capacities.

The waiting time between each individual outward container arriving and then leaving a port will be divided over waits on the stationary delivery vehicle, in the stack yard, at the rear of the crane and then on-board ship. The length of all these waits will be a reflection of the disparities in the rhythms of the equipment use to move the containers: first, the original delivery mode, second, the loaders going to the stack yard, third, the loaders from the stack yard to the rear of the crane and, lastly, the crane itself. The port is therefore much more than just an interface between landward modes and ships; there have to be ancillary micro-modes and waiting areas. This creates an overall picture of a complex, constantly moving organism with a number of diverse components all working in some sort of rhythmic balance. Each component has its signature rhythms and costs. The micro-modes each impose a cost per container-metre, a cost which depends on the cycle times. Every minute freight spends waiting or being shifted imposes a stock cost. The sum of these costs is substantial: it has been estimated that the cost of moving an outward container from its delivery vehicle to its place on-board ship is about the same as carrying it 5000 kilometres at sea. Nonetheless, the fundamental advantage of the containers is that they have slashed handling costs from the days when handling used human muscles with their inherent poor unit loads and cycle times.

Inter-modal freight: the generalisation

All freight, whether containerised or not, has to be loaded at the start of its journey and unloaded at the end and, very often, it has to be trans-shipped at some point during the journey. Micro-modes, perhaps as simple as human porterage, have to be used for this handling and each micro-mode itself has implicit cycle times, rhythms and waits, all contributing to the overall cost. These handling costs, measured per kilogram-metre, will be disproportionately greater than the costs of the modes used for the major part of the journey. It therefore makes sense to minimise handling costs. This may be done in a combination of two ways which may work counter to one another. The first is to use specialist handling equipment but this is subject to the same general rule as all transport equipment: the costs are per hour but the benefit is per unit shifted. To keep costs down, handling equipment has to be kept busy, and this leads to the second way of reducing handling costs: by concentrating the work at a limited number of very busy, well-equipped interfaces.

This concentration will change the nature of the interface. The waiting to which freight is subjected has been shown to be the product of disparate rhythms, but waiting has another role too. Much of industrial production is a sequence of processes. Many products are assembled wholly or partly from parts bought in from suppliers who may be long distances away, even in other continents. Computers and cars are both examples: all computers contain chips which have been mass produced elsewhere. Modern car plants do not make cars; they put them together using components shipped from other factories. It is usual to refer to the flows of such parts as the 'supply chain' stretching right back to the factories, mines and quarries in which the component materials and parts have been produced. There will be an identifiable supply chain feeding a particular plant but many of the sources back down the chain will supply more than one plant, and so the chains are all interlinked into a complex supply network. That network is composed of a myriad factories, of sources of raw materials and of energy, all interlinked by modes of transport, handling and storage.

This whole network does not work continuously. The interfaces between rhythms cause inevitable interruptions but industrial production itself fluctuates too. The reduction of manufacturing costs sometimes requires long product runs during which more is produced than can be immediately sold. Demand also has peaks and troughs: production and consumption rarely march in step. The imbalances are smoothed out by creating stores in which excess production may be stocked and from which surges in demand may be satisfied.

The transport system itself creates a need for storage, partly because matching throughputs on modes with different rhythms require storage at the interface and partly because carrying goods in small consignments is much less efficient than hauling larger loads. Consequently, deliveries are typically made in surges, out of step with both production and consumption and needing buffer storage at both ends of the journey.

The overall picture is of a freight system that is not composed just of modes of transport and the interfaces between them, but of warehouses, depots and container hardstanding, some of which are needed to accommodate rhythmic differences between modes, some to allow consignments to be large enough to attract good haulage rates and many to smooth out the imbalances in the rates of production and consumption. Storage is not just a matter of finding and paying for suitable space but it also involves equipment to place and retrieve goods: storage creates a need for handling, and handling is expensive. Consequently it becomes sensible to minimise costs by combining the various needs for storage. This is best done by locating storage at transport interfaces where the storage needs generated by the characteristics of transport may be amalgamated with the need to smooth out demands and supplies within the supply chain.

Historically, when handling was dependent upon human porterage, many industries clustered around ports with dockside warehouses used to accommodate freight being trans-shipped and to damp down the fluctuations in the supply chain. Dock-related industries could be linked to the port by short hauls and minimal handling. In general, the need to minimise transport and handling costs attracted industry to locate in or near transport hubs, whether they be goods stations and yards, canal wharves or ports. That relationship is still in evidence, but it has weakened and the characteristics have changed under two very substantial trends:

1. The motor lorry combined with an extensive road network now provides a very flexible transport system able to reach any address in the country, so elements in the overall transport system such as storage depots are no longer tied to the capital-intensive infrastructure of the canals and railways.
2. The massive reductions in handling costs created by modern, expensive but intensively used handling equipment have revolutionised storage costs by changing the costs of placing and retrieving goods. The more particular use of handling machinery in combination with containers has completely altered the cost, speed and reliability of international freight.

These two trends have changed the geography of the global economy. With the ever-decreasing costs of international freight transport, manufacturing industry, previously located within the areas of high demand for their products, has migrated to areas of low wages: the savings in the wage bill have more than offset the increased distances which goods have to be transported, distances which no longer have the heavy cost implications they once had in pre-container days.

This fundamental shift in the industrial location has been accompanied by a related restructuring of industry. At one time much of industry was vertically integrated with factories designed to accommodate as much of the productive process as possible upon one site, minimising the use of external transport and handling. The best example was Ford's Dagenham car plant at which raw materials such as coal and iron ore were fed in at one end and complete cars rolled out of the other. Containerisation has provided reductions in the overall manufacturing cost by buying in components from external suppliers, often located in low-wage countries, rather than manufacturing in-house as part of an integrated line of processes. Such out-sourcing has moved production lines from unitary, vertically integrated factories to a dispersed, volatile spread of processes linked by containerised shipping rather than internal conveyor belts. The change has been accompanied by more than differences in transport patterns: many firms are now global rather than local, and the economic and political balances between countries have also shifted radically. The rise of China as a political, financial, industrial and economic power has been based on a growth in the manufacture of complete products, of components and of part-finished goods to be assembled elsewhere, a rise that has been fuelled by the rapidly reducing costs of containerised international freight.

Once ashore, containers may be hauled to virtually any address using the flexibility of road transport, an ability which has broken the tight bond between warehousing, industry and the ports. The old, dockside warehouses and factories have been almost universally converted into 'characterful' housing. Their place has been taken by inland container 'ports' at which containers are filled and emptied[1] and by very large 'distribution depots'. These are new, large warehouses sited to take advantage of the motorway and principal road network, and designed to make maximum use of modern, high-capacity handling equipment. Whereas the old dockside warehouses had been tall, multi-storey buildings served by cranes to lift goods from ground level and men to move the goods to and from their resting places, the new warehouses are single-storey, flat-floor buildings with goods on purpose-built racking, placed and retrieved by specialist fork-lift trucks. Typically, goods arrive in bulk from suppliers but leave in multi-product loads bound for a single or local group of destinations. This minimises the number of drops to be made together with the related part-loaded running between drops.

Three other interrelated developments have facilitated the restructuring and relocation of the freight and distribution industry:

1   The computer has had a radical effect. The organisation of storage depots and of container ports depends on real-time management by sophisticated computer programs without which the benefits of new mechanical handling techniques could not have been harvested.
2   The invention of barcodes has made the collection of data to be fed into such programs easy and cost-effective. Consignments from the very largest to individual items may be easily and cheaply identified. This makes it possible to micro-manage stock control and track items as they move through the transport system.
3   The Internet has enabled the global transfer of data between computers and has provided the means of managing entire supply chains.

The 'just-in-time' principle is that stock levels are constantly monitored and, when they fall to a level at which there is a risk of a stock-out, effectively creating a temporary break in the supply chain, an order to replenish is generated automatically for delivery 'just-in-time' as almost the last item is withdrawn from store and ensuring that availability is uninterrupted. The 'just-in-time' principle ensures continuous supply but with minimal stocks. This is important, since stocks represent idle money: they are an expense but provide an insurance against interruptions in the supply chain.

'Just-in-time' is achieved by scanning the barcode whenever an item is withdrawn from stock, inputting that data into a computer program which will calculate the consequent risk of stock-out and, if necessary, generating an order to replenish, which is sent to the supplier back down the supply chain. This may trigger other replenishment orders rippling further down the chain. The size of the orders and the response times will be dictated by the known rates of use. For every supply chain passing actual goods up the chain there is a matching information chain passing orders and other paperwork in the opposite direction.

Inter-modal freight: the conclusions

The focus has been upon handling micro-modes within the interfaces between the major long-haul modes. It is in handling that the major developments have been made since the 1940s, particularly in the adoption of containers and the means to move them. Handling over minor, even miniscule distances is, and always was, the most expensive part of freighting measured in cost per tonne-metre. The very large reductions in handling costs through the intense use of high-capacity handling equipment has altered both the nature and location of global manufacturing, and of local storage, warehousing and distribution. The prime argument is that freight transport is far more than long-distance haulage: it encompasses the handling and storage necessary in the complete start-to-finish movement.

Multi-modal passenger transport

Unlike freight, passenger journeys have rarely been analysed as entire start-to-finish movements including any necessary modal transfers. In the absence of any analysis of complete journeys, the focus has always been upon 'trips' by particular modes starting at the place at which the mode was entered and ending wherever the mode was left. This yields data about the separated segments of an end-to-end journey but, since there is no sense of complete journeys, it cannot be known which segments are linked together. By default, this leaves interchanging as an unstudied 'black box' between modes or, if it is studied at all, studied as a separate entity into which passengers enter and then leave as though negotiating the interchange were a journey in its own right rather than an integral part of an overall journey from a particular origin to a particular destination. This segmentation of journeys into their component stages is closely related to the historical methodologies used to predict the demand for travel. In the seminal methodology of the late 1950s the task was to predict the movement of cars rather than the movement of people. That precluded walking and public transport. Attempts were made to modify the methodology in the 1970s to include public transport, attempts which produced the myth of the 'modal-split'. This characterised travel choices as a preference for either cars or public transport, setting them as competitive alternatives between which travel demand was 'split'. This virtually precluded the inclusion of interchanging in the demand models of the day, a deficiency that is still with us.

The problem is well illustrated by the evidence given by Transport for London (TfL) to the Parliamentary Committee considering the proposal to build a new high-speed railway from London to Birmingham and beyond. The TfL evidence pointed out that the predictions of the numbers of passengers likely to use the proposed line were station-to-station forecasts with no consideration of how passengers were expected to get to or from the stations. Consequently the necessary improvements to the systems providing access to the new lines were being disregarded. Lurking in the background of this complaint was a very real concern over the funding of interchanges, particularly that at London-Euston, but the issue is more fundamental than that. Transport policy, even the structure of the Government Department for Transport, is divided by mode, leaving interchanges as a residual and relatively unattended issue.

The contrast with the analysis of freight transport is marked. Storage, handling and trans-shipment are integral parts of the freight analysis, but waiting, walking and using mechanical aids such as escalators, lifts and shuttles in interchanges are not included as integral parts of passenger journeys. The difference is flagged by the terminology: the term *'inter-modal'* is used in freight, a term which recognises the complementary uses of different modes and the problems and costs of switching from one to another. In passenger transport the corresponding term is *'multi-modal'*, where modes are presumed to be competitive alternatives rather than complementary methods linked together to make complete journeys. In consequence, the problems and costs of interchanging are overlooked.

The fundamental modal signature rhythms composed of combinations of load size and frequency are in evidence in passenger just as much as in freight transport. Walking is largely individual and more or less at random. Buses, on the other hand, carry groups of people at discrete times, usually fairly frequently, while trains carry even more people but at lower frequencies. The movements of pedestrians, buses and trains are very different and very characteristic. Delay and waiting is unavoidable at the interface between rhythms: people will arrive on foot at a bus-stop at variable, pseudo-random intervals but they will depart together at discrete times. Each individual will have to wait at the bus-stop, perhaps momentarily, perhaps for some time. The bus-stop is therefore not only a place of interchange but also a waiting place made necessary by the difference in rhythms in the arrivals on foot and the departures by bus. The importance of this is reflected in the provision of shelters and seats at many bus-stops and, very often, advertisements to capture the otherwise wasted waiting time. In contrast, at those bus-stops where people switch from being bus passengers to being pedestrians, a difference in rhythm that does not demand waiting, there are typically neither seats nor advertisements.

Railway stations have to accommodate more waiting, partly because trains have quite substantial capacities creating a high throughput of passengers, and partly because trains are generally of lower frequency than the means used to get to the station. Consequently, railway stations have to provide more waiting facilities, not just waiting rooms and displays of advertisements, but also refreshments, bookstalls and even shops.

In general, these waiting areas and facilities may be tagged as 'buffer stores' accommodating the delays which are inherent at the interfaces between disparate rhythms. Some interchanges, particularly airports, are even more complex, containing ancillary micro-modes of transport interposed between the main arrival and departure modes. Shuttle buses to serve long-stay car-parks, escalators, travelators, lifts and mobile lounges are all needed to transport people within the terminal in addition to the baggage-handling tugs, conveyors, etc. Airports are a hive of different supporting micro-modes, taking food to and waste from aircraft, refuelling, providing emergency services, etc. Not all of it is in continuous use but it is all necessary and creates substantial cost.

Some ancillary micro-modes, like conveyors and escalators, run continuously, but others (e.g. shuttle buses and baggage trains) are intermittent with a constraining rhythm of their own and a need for a buffer store in the form of transit lounges or baggage holding bays. Other supporting modes need very simple, informal storage/ waiting areas, like the uncluttered spaces at lift doors.

Passenger transport networks include a wide range of interchanges from the very simple bus-stop to the complexities of an international airport, but they carry the common characteristic of interfacing different rhythms and accommodating the consequent waiting time. However, there is one common interface that is set apart from this generalisation. Car-parking, both at the kerbside and in purpose-built parks, are places at which modes are switched, but pedestrian and car rhythms are very similar: neither are timetabled and movements may be at personal whim. Although the costs and inconvenience of waiting during the change between modes may not be a feature of car-parking, ancillary costs in time and possibly money are incurred in finding, identifying, capturing and keeping a parking space.

Interchanging by passengers, as with freight, does incur cost and is a factor in travel choices. But the choice mechanism is confused. Some costs are hidden: the costs of the provision and operation of the interchange are not charged to travellers but may be met by local authorities, operators, advertisers and those providing services such as shops or cafés. Travellers do have to spend time interchanging, but how they value that time is a moot problem. There have been a number of studies of the value of time: these are discussed in Chapter 10 together with their use in assessing the value of schemes to improve the transport system.

The perceived inconveniences of interchanging extend beyond the necessary waiting time and walking. Passengers burdened with luggage, children and infirmity have physical difficulties to surmount: finding the way through the interchange and finding reliable information adds to stress, particularly if services are disrupted and decisions on variations of routes and timings have to be made. Transport planners have called passengers 'self-moving freight', not meaning that they move themselves long distances, but that they make and implement real-time decisions about their journey during interchanges. Freight handling is always a managerial decision but passengers have to fend for themselves. This is in all probability the reason why comparatively little interest has been shown in the knowledge, perceptions and decisions that interchanging passengers make.

Conclusions

Transport professionals, particularly those working within government, view the passenger transport system and the use made of it as a collection of separate modes, cars, buses and trains with air and sea tacked on. As a consequence, the problems of interchanging are left relatively alone. This is a critical fault in policy-making and investment where the models and assessments of value for money are restricted to the use of specific modes for journeys made between the places where passengers board and alight.

This is not how individuals themselves perceive the transport system. As the design of travel planning software such as 'Traveline' demonstrates, people use the transport system to get from one particular place to another by whatever combination of modes suits them best: they perceive the transport system as a collection of interconnected services in which the modes are complementary, not competitive. There is an element of competitive choice, not between modes per se, but between routes and combinations of mode, including the interchanges between them. Nobody will travel on the proposed high-speed railway *from* London-Euston *to* Birmingham New Street: everybody will travel *through* Euston and New Street on their way to and from other, quite different places requiring interlinked journey segments by other modes. Those modes and the interfaces between them will influence travel decisions in combination with the new railway. The relative merits of Heathrow and Euston as interfaces will be an element in travel choices

The conclusion is that travellers perceive the transport system as an integrated network through which they choose the most attractive route and that modelling the travel demands that are to be better catered for by new transport investments should be predicted in step with those travellers' perceptions.

This network-wide perception of the transport system is already evident in inter-modal freight transport which does more than perceive that the network consists of complementary modes, but has focused on the micro-modes implicit in trans-shipment: transport costs and demands have undergone a revolution in the past half-century or so, not because of modal development but due to new methods of transferring freight between modes and in placing and retrieving goods in store: the focus has been on micro-movements measured in metres rather than long haul measured in kilometres.

A change is necessary in the professional and official perception of the nature of the transport network and of the uses made of it. The Transport Plan for Kosovo suggested that this perception should be reflected in the organisation of the Ministry of Transport. Long-term planning and investment (including the modelling of future demand) was to be organised within one department covering all modes embracing all means to transport people, freight, energy, information and waste. In that way all the services necessary to sustain new developments and structural changes to the economic geography of the country could work to the same, comprehensive objectives. Short-term, operational management was to be organised mode by mode but with an additional department to deal with interfaces of all sorts, including airports, railway stations and parking. This department was also to be responsible for managing inter-modal conflicts such as that between road traffic and the services by cable and pipe beneath the road network.

Note

1 The more usual, although inelegant, terms are container 'stuffing' and 'unstuffing'.

Chapter 9

The problems
The space budget

Smeed argued in his seminal paper on the space needs of urban traffic[1] that the transport infrastructure required space and that urban space was limited. He built a highly theoretical, abstracted model to investigate what the space budget might be. Smeed began with the table of indicative capacities (see Figure 9.1).

Figure 9.1 is a child of its time. The road 'capacities' are related to those produced by the Road Research Laboratory (of which Smeed was Director) and shown in Figure 7.6. In demonstrating a higher capacity at a speed of 16 km/h than at 24 km/h, Smeed is repeating the heresy that, as the traffic volume increases, so the average speed decreases as though this were a causal interaction. As explained in Chapter 7, the truth is not as Smeed suggests, namely that speed depends on flow, but the opposite, that flow depends on speed.

In the late 1950s and early 1960s the remit of the Road Research Laboratory, was to research roads and traffic, and it is no surprise that Smeed considers road capacities in terms of vehicles, converting them into flows of people by adopting representative occupancy rates. These reflect the attitudes of the time – the bus occupancy, at 32, is the contemporary mean loading over whole routes, including the lightly loaded route

		Vehicle	Car	Car	Bus	Train
		Occupancy	1	1.5	32	1000
Track	Width (m)	Speed (km/h)				
Urban street	7.3	24	610	915	6500	
Urban street	7.3	16	990	1485	11000	
Urban street	13.4	24	1970	2955	21000	
Urban street	13.4	16	2790	4185	30000	
Clearway	13.4	48	4400	6600	47000	
Motorway (per lane)	3.7	65	2000	3000	21000	
Railway	7	30	24			24000
Footpath (per metre)	1	2	2600			

Figure 9.1 Indicative modal capacities (persons per hour)
Source: Adapted from Smeed (1962), table 1, p. 137.

ends: this is prejudicially low for peak-hour travel in city centres. However, the paper was written at the dawn of the British motorway age when the confident prediction was that in the future every household would have at least one car and that the role of public transport was limited to provide the transport needs for those who had yet to acquire one.

Figure 9.2 is the author's modification of Figure 9.1 to give space needs in square metre-hours rather than in square metres as in Smeed's original paper. If a lane of road is 3.7 metres wide, one kilometre of road will occupy 3700 square metres of land. If the maximum hourly flow is 610 cars, this 3700 square metres of road space will carry 610 car-kilometres per hour, giving a road use of 6.07 square metre-hours of road space per car-kilometre.

Smeed used mean vehicle occupancies (the number of people they *did* carry) rather than their capacities (the numbers of people they *could* carry). This is in contrast with the road flows which were expressed in the numbers of vehicles that roads could carry at observed maximum flows rather than the averages they actually carried. This anomaly has been corrected in Figure 9.2, replacing the capacities quoted in vehicles in Figure 9.1 with capacities measured in the numbers of available person-spaces. Not only is this akin to the road capacities but it avoids making doubtful assumptions about average loadings.

There is no comparable column in Smeed's work to the final column of Figure 9.2: this shows the productivity per square metre-hour compared with that of a car on a normal, multi-use urban street. A lane of urban motorway dedicated to bus use would be nearly 20 times more productive. Great care must be used with such data since they may be quite misleading – for example, they assume that buses do not stop: a grave disadvantage for the passengers, but a naivety common to the assumptions made for all modes in Smeed's paper.

The paper from which Figures 9.1 and 9.2 have been drawn continued to assess theoretical land-use budgets for towns of variously sized working populations. Smeed's model is highly abstract but important, since it introduced the concept of 'land budgets', the amount and proportion of that which has to be dedicated to transport use. The paper was also unusual because it considered non-car modes on

Track	Lane width (m)	Lane capacity (vehs/h)	Places per veh	Space need (sq. m hour per place-km)	Relative productivity
Urban street (cars)	3.7	610	5	1.21	1.00
Urban street (buses)	3.7	200	90	0.21	5.90
Clearway (cars)	3.7	1400	5	0.53	2.30
Clearway (buses)	3.7	467	90	0.09	13.78
Motorway (cars)	3.7	2000	5	0.37	3.28
Motorway (buses)	3.7	667	90	0.06	19.68
Railway	3.5	40	1000	0.09	13.86
Footpath	1	2900		0.34	3.52

Figure 9.2 Space-hours required and relative productivity

an equal footing and particularly because it saw that car use was dependent upon parking space which formed a crucial component in the land-use budget.

There were a number of important conclusions:

- Not only does the amount of road space increase with the size of the working population (that much is entirely intuitive) but the *proportion* of the city area devoted to transport increases too.
- The mode of travel (represented by the space-hours needed per person-kilometre) has little effect upon small towns but is crucial in large towns. Hence, in small towns the difference between high use of cars for the journeys to work rather than walking or public transport makes very little difference to either the land-take or the mean journey distance but it does make very considerable differences in large towns.
- The effect of the space needed for parking is substantial and loosens the weave of the city structure, forcing the density of development down, not only because of the land-take for parking itself but also because it increases the need for road space for moving vehicles.

At the time, Smeed failed to emphasise the link between traffic flow and parking demand. The obvious purpose of travel is to reach a destination at which something is to be done: implicitly that requires stopping. Just as a train is useless without stations, so cars are useless without parking places, and Smeed's model should really have included a stronger arithmetical link between the space that cars need to move and the space they need to stop.

A car parked at the kerb or in a ground-level car-park needs around 12 square metres of space, more than its simple footprint since there has to be an ability for people to get in and out, and for the car not to be blocked in by others: this gives 830 parked cars per hectare. At the roadside a car will require 5.25 linear metres of kerb space, around 190 cars per kilometre. In town centres kerb space is a very limited commodity and has to cope with the demands for bus-stops, emergency access and for the servicing of flanking properties by lorries and vans, as well as for parking cars.

In multi-storey car-parks there is about one parking space for every 20 square metres of floor space, 12 square metres for the car space itself and an additional 8 square metres for circulation and manoeuvring. The number of floors is limited by the exit rates through the barriers and also by the capacity of the surrounding streets. If too many spaces are served by one exit there will be queues blocking circulation within the car-park and if the surrounding streets are inadequate there will be queues outside. As a rule of thumb multi-storey car-parks are limited to four floors, with each 20 square metres of car space requiring 5 square metres of ground space.

In the past the failure to match movement and stopping space has created bizarre plans. The 1962 plan for Manchester,[2] written, like Smeed's paper, in the days when the policy objective was to cater for unconstrained use of the car, suggested that all the major radial roads should be widened to form 'Clearways'. Any new buildings along the flanks of such roads were forced by conditions on planning consents to be aligned behind 'Improvement lines' which, in time and with the expected rate of the redevelopment of older buildings, would provide the space for widening without massive compulsory purchases. The plan was to provide access to the city centre by 23 lanes of radial clearways with a combined capacity of about 30,000 cars per hour. One hour's flow would have filled close on 36 hectares of ground-level parking or 60 hectares of multi-storey space with a combined footprint of 15 hectares. Providing that amount of parking together with the necessary access roads would have required the compulsory purchase and demolition of much of central Manchester, removing the buildings to which the 23 lanes of road were designed to give access. The plan was noisily adopted and quietly abandoned.

Driven by the desire to accommodate the car, many authorities insisted that new city centre buildings should include parking provision. The lack of wisdom in this policy was driven home in London's Victoria Street which was largely redeveloped in the 1960s. The new buildings were required to have basement car-parks, all of them too small to cater for the parking demand from the floors above them, but large enough to swamp the capacity of Victoria Street, making it very difficult to exit the car-park: cars were not just parked, they were trapped.

The Manchester Plan and the problems in Victoria Street served as a parable on the general foolishness of planning the constituent parts of an urban transport system in isolation and of the particular failure to see that car-parks are as much a necessity for a road network as stations are for a railway system. They are the interchanges at which switching from one mode to another takes place (car use to walking), switching that enables the completion of journeys from one specific place to another.

Stopping is a necessary part of all movement. Freight has to be delivered, and lorries must come to rest. As shown in the previous chapter, all modes, including the micro-modes covering very short distances, have to be linked to intermediate storage associated with loading and unloading. Vehicles have to remain stationary while this is done. The general term is 'dwell time': the time during which a vehicle has to remain motionless to allow loading and unloading. It is a necessary but expensive time during which not only the costs of the vehicle have to be covered but it is also probable that it will also occupy a part of the infrastructure, preventing its use by other vehicles. This applies to all modes in one way or another but is best illustrated by railways.

The frequency, time- and space-headways of trains are dependent upon the permissible speeds, upon the signalling system passing instructions to the drivers on when to brake, and upon the braking performance once the brakes have been applied. The analysis is similar to the discussion of road capacity in Chapter 7, but train drivers, unlike car drivers, do not have to react to the condition of the road ahead as they see it: in most cases trains are travelling too fast for them to stop within the distance drivers are able to see for themselves. Drivers rely in the main upon the intermittent trackside signals to tell them of the state of the track ahead, although continuous electronic communication is becoming more common.

In practice, the capacity of a railway track is determined primarily by the dwell times at stations. Railway timetables and track capacities are presented graphically as 'train diagrams': a hypothetical example is shown in Figure 9.3. This shows that headways, the prime determinate of capacity, are strongly related to the dwell time at the station. The effect of the dwell time is extended by the need to decelerate before

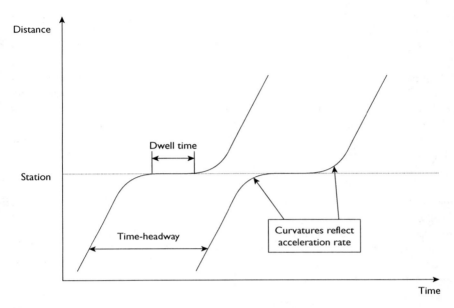

Figure 9.3 A sample train diagram showing two trains with dwell times at a station stop

the stop and accelerate back up to working speed after leaving the stop. Transport managers strive to minimise dwell times, since this increases the productivity of both track and vehicles. Long-distance trains have doors at each end of the coaches restricting loading and unloading speeds and extending dwell times. Stations dealing with such trains tend to have multiple platforms to provide the number of platform hours necessary to accommodate the extended dwell times. In contrast, suburban trains have multiple, wide doors enabling fast transfers of passengers and minimal dwell times, although at the cost of much-reduced seating. In consequence, stations dealing with trains with long dwell times have a much greater land-take than suburban stations characterised by short dwell times.

Although Smeed failed to expand his thinking into the space needs of stopped vehicles, he was very close to forging the link which has moulded the nature of urbanisation over the past 60 years or so. Twenty square metres of gross office space per member of staff is a fairly robust generalisation supported by data reported from the City of London, the West Midlands and Canberra. The gross office space includes circulation space, lavatories, stationery cupboards, etc., giving a ground-level footprint per employee of 20 ÷ the number of floors. The significance of this figure is that it is approximately equal to the floor space required to park a car in a multi-storey car-park, but the ground space needed for parking is greater, since car-parks are effectively limited to four storeys but offices are not. The generalisation is that workers in multi-storey office blocks cannot all travel to work by car, since their need for parking space cannot be met, at least within walking distance of their desks.

The arithmetic for the other major land use in city centres, shopping, is not so easy. There are data on the expected turnover per square metre and for the average spend per customer. These data will yield the number of customers, and this may be cross-checked against more modern data on footfall – the numbers of people walking into shops. However, the need is for dwell times in particular shop types, in shopping areas and in the car-parks they use. This would give the number of parking-space-hours used by shoppers, the number of times each space was used by different drivers during the course of a day and the accumulation of shoppers.

That the data are suspect may be sensed by looking around a shop during business hours and assessing whether one or two customers per 12 square metres (the on-street parking space required for one car) would generate the sales necessary to keep the shop in business.

The gist of the argument is not only that there is insufficient parking space to support full car access to the shops and offices which dominate city centres (that much is self-evident) but that the arithmetic behind land-space budgets, although not completely quantified, ensures that there is no way of ever providing enough. For the offices and shops in city centres to be financially viable they have to be fed with workers and spenders, but there is insufficient space to cope with their parking demand, a deficiency that is fundamentally intractable.

A combination of two trends has been apparent in coping with this dilemma:

1   Enough people to keep the city centre working have been using public transport to avoid the necessity of finding a parking space. In doing so they are using public transport as a solution to the parking problem, not as a solution to congestion; the focus is not on the problems of moving but on the problems of stopping.
2   The centre has been decentralised out to places where parking space can be provided. This has not only dispersed offices and shops but has changed their nature. Lower land prices have reduced the pressure to build high: the multi-floored city centre department stores of yesteryear have migrated to single- or double-storey suburban shopping malls.

The paradox of cars being the source of the parking and congestion problems which now beset cities but simultaneously being the solution by providing access to previously undeveloped land was noted in Chapter 6. The inexorable space budgets are at the root of the mechanism for changing city structure. For many people it is perceived as a change for the better. Shopping by car is flexible and convenient, enabling substantial amounts of goods to be carried home, but their convenience is being bought at the cost of longer journeys, more CO_2 bought through high fuel prices and the almost unavoidable need to endure the cost of acquiring, keeping and running a car.

Notes

1 Smeed (1962).
2 South-East Lancashire and North-East Cheshire Area Highway Engineering Committee (1962).

Chapter 10

Transport costs

It is common to use 'cost' and 'price' as synonyms: they are not. The price is the money a buyer hands over to a seller for a good or for a service. The cost is the money the seller had incurred in providing it, including, of course, the prices paid to others for the inputs that went into its creation. Prices and costs form a chain: each actor in a supply chain gains revenue from the prices paid for the goods and services they sell but also incurs costs of providing them, costs which include not only the prices paid for raw materials and labour but also for the transport and storage needed to deliver to customers at the right time and place.

The word 'product' is now used to cover both goods (tangible items like cars and petrol) and services (actions that are performed). This is unfortunate, because the distinction is very important. Goods like cornflakes may be stored on a shelf and taken whenever needed. Services cannot be stored: a bus company cannot run services during the night and store them, ready to be used in the morning rush-hour. Sometimes it is possible to store the resources which are to be committed to a service as a proxy for the service itself, rather like McDonald's staff who are kept in a holding room to be called upon to satisfy surges in demand, or extra buses are put on the road at peak times. It is therefore more telling to say that services themselves have to be created and immediately consumed at particular times.

In transport these particular times are very important: departure and arrival, delivery and transit times are major attributes of transport services. This fundamental trait makes it difficult to arrange effective competition at the point of use. Unlike shelved cornflakes which are constantly available, transport services, being time-specific, cannot be on constant offer, nor can competitive services be simultaneously available for selection. One company's bus leaving at 09.03 is not the same 'product' as another company's bus leaving at 09.05 – in economic jargon the two buses are not acceptable substitutes one for the other, in contrast to boxes of branded cornflakes stored side by side on the supermarket shelf, enabling one box to be instantly substituted for another on a consumer's whim.

This raises the rather more fundamental issue in transport of the definition of the 'product' being offered and bought. Is it a simple ride from a boarding point to an alighting point? Or is it a complete journey from start to finish, including the incidental ride? Or is the ability, not only to make the outward journey, but to return and perhaps return at a time yet to be decided? Or even return by a different route

160 Transport costs

with an intermediate call or two? Is the service being bought an actual journey made there and then, or is it an *ability* to travel using a network spread over time and space?

In the past tickets were bought for particular journeys and complex journeys were covered by a series of tickets. The car seems to have changed that. A car provides incidental access to the road network and an ability to travel more or less whenever and wherever people wish: the ownership of a car, a good, comes bundled with the use of an extensive road network. Public transport seems to have followed suit, selling its products, not as single ride tickets but as access to an entire network. This seems to have been initiated by public operators with network tickets such as the 'Carte Orange' in Paris, the 'Strippenkarte' in the Netherlands and the 'Fares Fair' passes (later the Oyster Card) in London. The 'product', defined by the tickets being offered and bought, has changed.

In common with other services, car travel cannot be stocked: a few kilometres cannot be reeled off when the roads are quiet, to be used later when they are busy, although the car itself can be parked, waiting to provide what is, in effect, an instantly available, infinitely frequent, service. Car owners are usually unaware of the cost per journey but more aware of the total outlay of the acquisition, ownership and use of their car, suggesting that the product they are buying is an ability to travel when and where they wish rather than a summation of the actual journeys made.

This adds another level of complexity to the 'product'. In buying access to a network, people are buying a very flexible, future ability, the nature of which has yet to be defined, whereas buying a single-ride ticket is, by definition, very well defined. This snaps the close link between the revenue gained from selling a product and the cost of providing it: that is a problem to be considered in more detail in Chapter 18. In the meantime, the focus will be upon unit costs which may then be summed to provide a costing of any service provision.

Car costs

The costs of acquiring, keeping and using a car are usually categorised into fixed and variable costs. Fixed (sometimes called standing) costs are those which have to be paid regardless of the distance driven. They are predominantly time costs paid per annum. Variable (often called running or operating) costs are those which are affected by the distance driven and are costs per kilometre. The Automobile Association publishes tables of current motoring costs for a range of cars of various purchase prices and degrees of use. Figure 10.1 gives the 2011 costs for a mid-range car covering 24,000 kilometres per year.

The precise numbers and percentages will change with the size and cost of a car and they will also change with the annual distance driven, but the rankings will remain. Figure 10.1 shows that over 67 per cent of the fixed/standing costs (33 per cent of total costs) are concerned with finance, but this is often a grave underestimate. The AA includes two categories of financial cost:

1. *The cost of capital:* personal money used either as a deposit or to cover all or part of the purchase price could have been invested in some interest-earning account instead: the interest forgone is an accountable cost.

	£ per year	Pence per kilometre	% of fixed cost	% of total cost
Fixed costs				
Vehicle excise duty (annual licence)	165	0.69	5.2	2.5
Insurance	805	3.35	25.2	12.4
Cost of capital	300	1.25	9.4	4.6
Depreciation	1873	7.80	58.7	28.8
Breakdown cover	50	0.21	1.6	0.8
Total fixed costs	**3193**	**13.30**	**100.0**	**49.1**
Variable costs			% of variable cost	
Fuel		9.02	65.3	33.3
Tyres		0.71	5.1	2.6
Maintenance		2.98	21.6	11.0
Parking and tolls		1.10	8.0	4.1
Total variable costs		**13.81**	**100.0**	**50.9**
Total overall cost		**27.11**		**100.0**

Figure 10.1 Car costs for a petrol car priced new at £14,000 and driven 24,000 kilometres per year

Source: AA car cost tables.

2 *Depreciation:* this is the loss on the book value of the car from one year to the next. The problem with depreciation is that it is furtive. It works continuously: book values decay month by month but owners only really become aware of the extent to which their car has declined in value when they come to sell or trade in. Then there is a tendency not to understand that the value of their car has withered and that they have lost about as much money during their ownership as they spent on fuel, but they perceive the trade-in value as a discount on a new, desirable replacement. Consequently the depreciation is perceived only after it has occurred, and even then its size and nature is not really appreciated.

Figure 10.1 omits what is for many people a massive, additional financial cost. Many cars are bought with a deposit, with the balance paid with borrowed money either through a hire purchase agreement or with a bank loan. The resulting repayments and interest do not appear in the AA data, reducing the size of the financial implications of car purchase and ownership. Car owners effectively pay twice for their ownership: first, the financial costs in buying the car are considerable, no matter whether they use their own money, sacrificing possible investment income, or whether they use somebody else's and pay loan charges. But, second, the vehicle bought at this expense becomes increasingly worthless.

Corporate accountants are obliged to value company assets, taking a formal account of their depreciating value. This 'writing down' of the book value of assets may be done by having them professionally valued, but that is time consuming and expensive. Alternatively, the estimated paper value of assets may be calculated using the initial value (the purchase price), an expected life of the asset, an estimated salvage value at the end of that life and a rate at which the value declines over the asset's lifetime from the purchase price to the salvage value. Given those figures, the depreciated paper value of an asset may be calculated using one or another of three main methods of calculating estimated depreciated values:

1. A constant rate with a fixed amount deducted annually from the assets value. This is arithmetically simple with anticipated overall loss (the purchase price less the salvage value) divided by the asset's expected life. It also gives a constant loss per year which is arithmetically convenient, even if it is not strictly accurate.
2. An annual percentage depreciation. In this case both the value and the amount by which it reduces changes each year. Furthermore, the final value never actually reaches zero.
3. The sum of the years. This is more realistic because the depreciation as a percentage of the value is higher in the years immediately after purchase but the effects of depreciation fade as the asset ages.

Figure 10.2 shows the depreciating book value of a car with the initial purchase price of £14,000, assumed in Figure 10.1, and a useful life of 10 years at the end of which the salvage value is zero. If the life were shorter, the curves would be the same shape but more upright, tending to be pressed against the vertical axis.

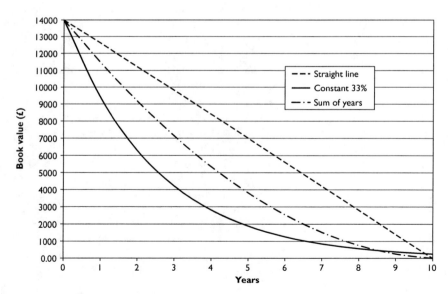

Figure 10.2 Depreciation of a car with a purchase price of £14,000, a life of 10 years and zero salvage value

However, book values are intended to estimate the capital value of assets, not the cost of keeping them: the actual depreciated book values cannot be used as an input to the calculated costs per kilometre. For that to be done the related annual loss in book value, effectively the cost of owning the asset, has to be calculated. Figure 10.3 shows the annual cash flow needed to maintain ownership of the asset: Figure 10.2 identifies the change in the value of capital assets – it is concerned with static money. Figure 10.3 shows the cash outflow needed to cover the costs of ownership.

Depreciation, no matter how it is calculated, is a method of resolving a fundamental problem that afflicts all accountancy and costing. Most activity combines the use of capital assets purchased with a lump sum at a single point in time, with continuous flows of materials and labour bought in as the need arises. The total cost per unit of production must include some representation of the capital cost, converting it from a single lump sum into a continuous flow that may then be added to the flows of payments for raw materials and labour. Depreciation, essentially a paper exercise, does this by adding the money 'lost' to depreciation from one year to the next to the costs of labour and raw materials: it changes a fixed capital lump sum into a running cost.

The methodology used currently to assess the value for money of transport projects uses the diametrically opposite approach to the resolution of the fundamental difference between lump sum capital costs and ongoing flows of operational costs. Rather than converting capital lump sums into continuous flows, it converts continuous flows into lump sums using a technique called 'discounted cash flows'. The purpose is the same – to enable lump sums and cash flows to be combined into a single measure of cost.

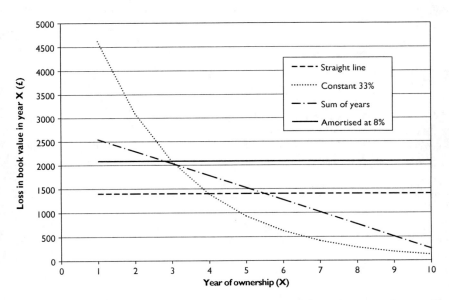

Figure 10.3 The financial costs per year of the ownership of a car with a purchase price of £14,000, a life of 10 years and zero salvage value

Neither depreciation (using the annual loss in capital value as an operational cost of owning an asset) nor discounted cash flow (converting annual cash flows into lump sums) are very satisfactory ways of combining once-and-for-all capital costs with continuous operational costs. There is a third way, one more in tune with reality. Most economic activity is funded by borrowed money: firms use money borrowed from banks and investors, paying them for their loans in interest, or, if the firm is using shareholders' money, in a share of the profits. If a bus company wishes to acquire a new bus it may well borrow the money and pay it back over the lifetime of the bus together with any interest payments. If it is a company with a healthy bank balance, it may 'borrow' the money from itself but it should still pay back with interest, just as the AA costings in Figure 10.1 allow for the loss of income from the interest which could have been earned if the money had been left where it was. Yet another alternative is not to buy the bus at all but to lease it from a company specialising in owning rather than operating buses, and pay 'rent' for its use: that is effectively borrowing money from the owners of the bus.

These options are similar to the choices made by individual people in acquiring somewhere to live. They may rent from a landlord, or buy with money borrowed on a mortgage from a bank or building society, or they may pay with their own cash and forgo the interest they could have earned had they invested their cash. In any event, they are converting the lump capital price into a continuous cash flow.

In general, these financial arrangements may be reflected by 'amortisation', a completely different principle to writing down the value of an asset. An initial loan covering the purchase price of an asset is made within an agreement to repay within a defined number of years and at a specified rate of interest. The repayment of the loan and of the interest upon it is combined into one, single debt, and a fixed, regular payment is calculated that will pay off the whole debt including all the interest payable within a specified time period.

To borrow £1000 to be repaid with interest at 8 per cent per annum over 10 years will cost £149.03 per year and, as Figure 10.3 shows, to borrow the £14,000 showroom price of a new car will commit the purchaser to pay £2086.42 per year for 10 years, a total of £20,864. To the borrower this arrangement, although expensive, is arithmetically very useful, since it sets an annual cost that is constant throughout the life of the asset. This stable expense may then be used to calculate financial costs per year, per week, per day or per kilometre. Although the amortised annual repayment is constant, in the early years most of it is used to pay off the interest, with the remainder used to pay off the actual loan. As the years go on the loan reduces, and so does the interest, allowing more of the fixed payment to be used as pay back. As a result, the outstanding debt reduces slowly at first, but then with increasing speed until it is discharged.

Amortisation very effectively transforms a single large capital investment into a regular cash flow by amalgamating all the financial costs together, so removing the need to calculate depreciation and related putative book values. By the end of the loan period the debt will have been completely discharged ready for a new loan to buy a replacement vehicle. It does not matter if, in practice, another method of financing the acquisition of an asset is actually used; the arithmetic of amortisation, shown in Figure 10.4, may be used to include capital items in the calculation of variable costs.

	Annual interest rate				
Years to repay	5.00%	6.00%	7.00%	8.00%	10.00%
2	537.80	545.44	553.09	560.77	576.19
4	282.01	288.59	295.23	301.92	315.47
6	197.02	203.36	209.80	216.32	229.61
8	154.72	161.04	167.47	174.01	187.44
10	129.50	135.87	142.38	149.03	162.75
12	112.83	119.28	125.90	132.70	146.76
14	101.02	107.58	114.34	121.30	135.75
16	92.27	98.95	105.86	112.98	127.82
18	85.55	92.36	99.41	106.70	121.93
20	80.24	87.18	94.39	101.85	117.46
22	75.97	83.05	90.41	98.03	114.01
24	72.47	79.68	87.19	94.98	111.30
26	69.56	76.90	84.56	92.51	109.16
28	67.12	74.59	82.39	90.49	107.45
30	65.05	72.65	80.59	88.83	106.08

Figure 10.4 Amortisation: sample annual repayment on a loan of £1000

Notes: These repayments are calculated by $R = ((P * i) / (1 - ((1+i)^{(-y)})))$
(where) R = the fixed annual repayment
        P = the amount borrowed and to be repaid
        i = rate of interest (as a number, not a percentage (8% = 0.08))
        y = years to repay.

Amortisation is arithmetically identical to the capital recovery factor (CRF), which is usually represented in a superficially different guise:

$$CRF = ((i*(1+i)^y) / (((1+i)^y) - 1))$$

CRF = capital recovery factor
i   = rate of interest (as a number, not a percentage (8% = 0.08))
y   = years to repay

This relationship yields a number between 0 and 1 which, when multiplied by the amount borrowed, gives the constant annual repayment to be made for each of y years.

General transport costs

Thus far, the cost characteristics and structures have been focused upon car ownership and use, but the same analysis may be used for all vehicles and for all methods of transport. Many of the continuously running transports, the various forms of conveyor together with pipes and wires, have very high capital but low operational costs. The total cost is therefore predominantly payments on the investment, much of which is irrecoverable: there is little salvage value in a trench with a sewer in it. Such infrastructure also has an indeterminate physical life – London's Victorian sewers and

Assumptions	Car	Diesel bus	Hybrid bus	Tram	Train Class 172	LGV 3.5 tonne
Purchase price (£)	16,000	192,000	300,000	2,000,000	3,400,000	21,000
Interest (per year)	8.0%	8.0%	8.0%	8.0%	8.0%	8.0%
Life (years)	10	15	15	30	30	5
Fuel consumption (litres or kWh/100 km)	8.5	40	12	500	90.8	12
Fuel (£/litre or kWh)	1.35	0.912	0.912	0.03	0.5	1.35
Kilometres per year	24000	35000	35000	70000	102000	56000
Mean running speed (km/h)	40	25	25	35	50	66
Mean journey speed (km/h)	30	9	9	20	45	55
Working hours per year	800	3889	3889	3500	2267	1018
Staff cost (£/head/year)	50000	50000	50000	50000	50000	50000
Fixed (£ per year)[1]	3329	24596	37213	179655	304013	6470
Variable (£ per km)[2]	0.190	0.457	0.206	0.215	1.287	0.241
Variable (£ per hour)[3]	0.0	25.0	25.0	50.0	44.2	25.0
Capacity						
Places	5	90	90	250	150	
Tonnes						1.625
TOTALS						
£ per year	7883	137806	141660	369705	535321	45420
£ per life-hour	0.90	15.73	16.17	42.20	61.11	5.18
£ per work-hour	9.85	35.44	36.43	105.63	236.17	44.61
£ per kilometre	0.3285	3.9373	4.0474	5.2815	5.2482	0.8111
Units (place-km or tonne-km)	120000	3150000	3150000	17500000	15300000	91000
£ per unit	0.0657	0.0437	0.0450	0.0211	0.0350	0.4991
CO_2 (kg per unit)	**0.0541**	**0.0141**	**0.0042**	**0.0089**	**0.0192**	**0.2348**

Assumptions	17 tonne 2-axle	44 tonne artic	Loco + 12 wagons	10000 container ship	Fork-lift	Human porter
Purchase price (£)	55,000	100,000	4,000,000	65,000,000	20,000	0
Interest (per year)	8.0%	8.0%	8.0%	8.0%	8.0%	8.0%
Life (years)	7	6	25	25	5	20
Fuel consumption (litres or kWh/100 km)	24	37.2	435	16750	12	0
Fuel (£/litre or kWh)	1.35	1.35	0.5	0.5	0.5	0.5
Kilometres per year	88000	140000	55000	270000	30000	6000
Mean running speed (km/h)	66	66	55	45	24	3
Mean journey speed (km/h)	55	55	50	40	15	3
Working hours per year	1600	2545	1100	6750	2000	2000
Staff cost (£/head/year)	50000	50000	50000	50000	50000	50000
Fixed (£ per year)[1]	13214	26332	474715	7089121	6509	0
Variable (£ per km)[2]	0.416	0.550	3.175	85.250	0.108	0.000
Variable (£ per hour)[3]	25.0	25.0	50.0	180.0	25.0	12.0
Capacity						
Places						
Tonnes	10.5	28	900	267000	3.5	0.05
TOTALS						
£ per year	89822	166996	704340	31321621	59749	24000
£ per life-hour	10.25	19.06	80.40	3575.53	6.82	2.74
£ per work-hour	56.14	65.61	640.31	4640.24	29.87	12.00
£ per kilometre	1.0207	1.1928	12.8062	116.0060	1.9916	4.0000
Units (place-km or tonne-km)	924000	3920000	49500000	72090000000	105000	300
£ per unit	0.0972	0.0426	0.0142	0.0004	0.5690	80.0000
CO_2 (kg per unit)	**0.0727**	**0.0422**	**0.0154**	**0.0020**	**0.1090**	**0.0000**

Figure 10.5 Mode capacity, costing and emissions

Notes:
[1] Includes Finance (amortised @8%), insurance and licence.
[2] Includes fuel, tyres and maintenance.
[3] Includes wages and overheads.

railways are well into their second century of work and now need physical but not financial maintenance: they were built with borrowed money but their physical life has outlived their financial liabilities. This appears to support the principle of amortisation, using the life of the loan rather than the life of the infrastructure as an input to cost calculations: this conveniently avoids the difficulty of calculating a nominal depreciation.

The vast majority of transport requires operating staff usually paid by time, although piece-rates per kilogram-metre or per item do exist (self-employed taxi drivers and some urban porters are examples), but such arrangements are rare. As a rule of thumb the working year may be taken as 2000 hours ($50 \times 5 \times 8$) with hourly rates hovering at around £12.50 (2012); this gives £25,000 per annum per member of the operating staff. The cost to the employer is substantially more: insurance, pensions, administration and supervision can double the total cost to £50,000 per employee per annum. By its nature, this can be no more than a guesstimate of an average over a very wide range.

Figure 10.5 shows the estimated costs of a sample of different modes of transport, but these figures are just estimates of indicative quantities: they veil wide ranges of different circumstances and should not be assumed to be definitive. The unit rates at the foot of each part of the figure are the important measures from which conclusions will be drawn, conclusions that will be quite robust, independent of any inaccuracies. However, it should be noted that Figure 10.5 is concerned with vehicle and movement costs – there are no allowances made for track costs, which are substantial for trams and railways and also for the road network, although these are less identifiable and explicit.

Vehicles exist for 8760 (365×24) hours per year, called 'life-hours' in the figure, every one of which costs money in fixed costs, mainly in amortised finance but also in licences and insurance. 'Work-hours' are those in which the equipment is staffed and capable of productive work, although the vehicle may be stationary, being loaded or unloaded or waiting to work: during these work-hours the total incurred cost is a combination of the life-hour and the work-hour costs. Whenever the vehicle moves doing productive work a third element of cost is added: the variable operational cost per kilometre. The work is measured in the provided ability to move unit-kilometres (place-kilometres for passenger vehicles and tonne-kilometres for freight). The actual out-turn cost per unit-kilometre carried is not shown in Figure 10.5, since it is very dependent on load factors which, even if known, vary across wide ranges.

It must be further emphasised that the numbers in Figure 10.5 are no more than indicative and should not be used without being checked against specific, local data. Given this refinement, these estimates may be used to indicate improvements in efficiency. Vehicles only earn their keep when they are transporting people or goods, but they have to stop to be loaded and unloaded and to be maintained, and so the ideal of earning revenue continuously is impossible. The nearest is the case of container ships which, with their long, uninterrupted voyages and slick port times, are able to create very large numbers of tonne-kilometres per year.

The majority of vehicles are also stationary for part of their lives because there is no immediate need to use them, incurring costs but with no opportunity to generate

Transport costs   169

income. This is most apparent with private cars which, typically, are parked and idle for 90 per cent of their lives, time during which the costs of finance, insurance and licensing still have to be paid. Motorists in general accept this waste of money as a price they are willing to pay to have a constant and flexible ability to travel on a whim without much forethought.

Commercial operators cannot afford to be so profligate, and have to keep their vehicles on the move and earning. As a demonstration, Figure 10.6 shows a hypothetical case study of one bus working on an imaginary route.

The left-hand column shows the arbitrary characteristics of the imagined route 10 km long and with 40 intermediate stops, approximately one every 250 metres.[1] The example shows the time cost of each of the stops composed of the times taken to decelerate from the line speed (40 km/h) to the stop and then to accelerate back up again (both using an acceleration of 1 m/sec/sec) together with an arbitrary dwell time at the stop of one minute. There is a layover time at each end of the route between the bus completing the journey in one direction and starting out on the return: this, too, is discussed later, since it not only provides a short rest for the crew but acts as an opportunity to recover from late running and assists in providing a reliable service.

	Route	Per cycle	Per 16-hour day	Per 300-day year
Number of cycles		1.0	7.0	2100.0
Distance travelled (km)	10.0	20.0	140.0	42000.0
Max speed (km/h)	40.0	40.0	40.0	40.0
Max speed (m/sec)	11.1	11.1	11.1	11.1
No. of intermediate stops	40	80	560	168000
Stop-to-stop distance (m)	243.9	243.9	243.9	243.9
Acceleration rate (m/sec/sec)	1.0	1.0	1.0	1.0
Time per stop				
Braking distance	61.605 m	5.05 km	35.36 km	10608.4 km
Braking time	11.1 sec	0.25 hr	1.77 hr	532 hr
Dwell time	60.0 sec	1.33 hr	9.33 hr	2800 hr
Acceleration distance	61.605 m	5.05 km	35.36 km	10608.4 km
Acceleration time	11.1 sec	0.25 hr	1.77 hr	532 hr
Time between stops				
Net distance at line speed	120.7 m	9.9 km	69.3 km	20783.2 km
Time at line speed	10.9 sec	0.25 hr	1.7 hr	520 hr
Route analysis				
Layover time	120 sec	0.07 hr	0.5 hr	140 hr
Dwell time	2400 sec	1.33 hr	9.33 hr	2800 hr
Running time	1356 sec	0.8 hr	5.3 hr	1582 hr
Cycle time	3876 sec	2.1 hr	15.1 hr	4522 hr
Mean journey speed (km/h)		9.3	9.3	9.3
Mean running speed (m/h)		26.5	26.5	26.5
Out of traffic (hr)			8.9	4238.0

Figure 10.6 Time budget for a hypothetical bus operation

The second column shows the time budget for one cycle of operation from starting the outward leg of one return journey to beginning the next: in general these data are in metres and seconds. The two columns on the right show the time budgets per day (assumed to be 16 hours) and per year (of 300 days): the data are in hours and kilometres.

Figure 10.6 is arbitrary, even trivial, but Figures 10.7 and 10.8, which are both derived from it, show important principles. The numbers themselves are probably unrealistic, but the principles behind their calculation are important.

Yet again, these figures are not authoritative but are provided as a demonstration of the principle of classifying cost, first, between fixed and variable costs by time and by distance, and second, by activity. These component activities have distinctive mixtures of fixed and variable costs which give clues on ways to improve productivity. Although Figure 10.8 is concerned with hypothetical bus costs, the general pattern has echoes for other modes too. The costs of consumables (fuel, tyres, etc.) are comparatively minor, although that is not to say they are unimportant: if margins are tight they may well be the difference between profit and loss. It is staffing costs that are dominant and an inspection of Figure 10.5 shows this to be true of most modes. The efficient and productive deployment of staff is clearly crucial and has been the drive behind single manning of buses and trains, the minimisation of ships' crews and, in particular, the use of capital equipment to replace manhandling: Figure 10.5 shows the costs and productivity of human porterage to be very poor.

This emphasises the major message of the previous chapter. It was the high cost and low productivity of port and stevedoring that stimulated the container revolution,

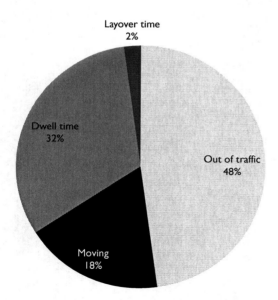

Figure 10.7 The allocation of the 8760 annual life-hours of the hypothetical bus working as in Figure 10.6

Annual cost rates	Fixed (£ per life-hour)	Variable (£ per work-hour)	Variable (£ per kilometre)	Total	
Out of traffic	2.81			2.81	
Moving	2.81	25.00	0.46	28.27	
Dwell time	2.81	25.00		27.81	
Layover time	2.81	25.00		27.81	
Annual costs					% of total annual cost
Out of traffic	11886.3	0.0	0.0	11886.3	**7.6**
Moving	4445.4	39550.0	19320.0	63315.4	**40.3**
Dwell time	7868.0	70000.0	0.0	77868.0	**49.6**
Layover time	393.4	3500.0	0.0	3893.4	**2.5**
	24593.1	113050.0	19320.0	156963.1	**100.0**
% of total annual cost	**15.7**	**72.0**	**12.3**	**100.0**	

Figure 10.8 Distribution of total annual costs for the hypothetical bus operation shown in Figure 10.6

a trend further emphasised by concentrating international freight flows in a comparatively few but very well-equipped ports providing minimal dwell times to load and unload. The dwell times in the bus demonstration case study account for more of the operating costs than anything else. The numbers may not be exact, but the message is important: minimal dwell time is a crucial objective in running any efficient operation. Historically, once staffing costs for buses were reduced by single-person operation, dwell times increased due to the driver having to sell and check tickets. That expensive increase in dwell times has been reversed by charging flat fares, by not giving change, by the use of passes and network tickets, and by off-bus sales. That surge and then reduction in dwell times was accompanied by providing separate doors for getting on and off, thereby minimising congestion at the fare box, but, in many instances, this has had to be abandoned to meet legislation on better wheelchair access. The sequenced changes from rear-platformed buses with two-person crews and single-ride tickets sold on board for cash, to single-person operation with minimal cash and on-bus transactions, has been interwoven with the desirability of reducing dwell times and gleaning more bus-kilometres from both equipment and staff.

The importance and sensitivity of dwell times were epitomised by minibus operations in Milton Keynes shortly after deregulation. On a 7.5-minute interval service operated by minibuses with poor door widths, steps up into the bus and cash ticket sales, one woman with shopping, two children, a buggy and no change inadvertently disrupted the complete service by taking over half the headway to get on and off the bus. With minimal layover times, the service was unable to recover proper uniform headways and all buses on the route became bunched into an ineffective convoy.[2]

Dwell times are extremely important for passenger train operation, with the numbers of doors and widths being matched to the numbers of passengers needing to get on and off the train. In general, the shorter the distances between stations and the shorter the mean journey distance, the greater the swirl of passenger movement at stations and the greater the aggregate door width along the length of the train. Long-distance trains tend to have doors only at the coach ends and need extended dwell times to cope with all the passenger movement to and from the platform. This has to be catered for by providing multiple platforms at stations along long-distance routes.

At terminals, dwell times are driven by more than the needs of boarding and alighting passengers. Trains have to be cleaned and reversed. In the past when the productivity of train sets was thought to be comparatively unimportant, trains were shunted out of terminals to be cleaned in nearby sidings, helping platform occupancy but creating many expensive shunting movements and occupying a considerable amount of the capacity of the approach tracks. In more recent years station times have been drastically reduced by abandoning the use of locomotive-hauled stock needing the locomotive to be uncoupled and shunted. At first this was done by having a permanently coupled locomotive at each end of the train and then by using trains with an unpowered driving cab at one end and a permanently coupled locomotive at the other, pulling the train in one direction and pushing it in the opposite direction. Still more recently the concept of the locomotive has been abandoned, replaced by each coach in the train being individually powered. All these solutions are enabled by the power units being controlled and coordinated remotely, albeit by an on-board driver. The need for cleaning has been met by a combination of swarming trains with cleaners as they stand at terminal platforms and by en-route cleaners. In general, train terminal dwell times have changed radically, with shunting and empty stock movements disappearing almost completely, releasing platform and approach track capacity but using some of the available platform hours for extended dwell times to enable cleaning.

Dwell times are crucial for freight trains too. Coal is loaded at ports and mines, and delivered at power-stations by gravity and without the train stopping – the 'Merry-go-Round' service, ensuring that the maximum is squeezed out of the train costs but at the capital expense of loading and unloading facilities. Trains serving container ports are turned round speedily by the use of cranes and fork-lift trucks, not just to avoid detaining the train but also to get the maximum throughput from the sidings.

The same pattern is true of aircraft: the airlines offering cheap fares are able to do so by cutting their dwell times to the absolute minimum. An aircraft on the ground does nothing but cost money.

The time budgets of vehicles, trains, ships and aircraft are controlling factors in their productivity. All equipment exists for 8760 hours per year, every one of which costs money whether the equipment is working or not. Figure 10.4 shows that a piece of equipment costing £1000 and with a 30 year life costs £89 per year in financial servicing alone. An aircraft worth, say £30 million costs £2.7 million a year in financial charges, about £300 per hour of its life, payable whether it is airborne with every seat occupied or mothballed. Unless it is flying, it cannot be creating income and therefore the flying hours are a heavy constraint upon its financial efficiency. Once in the air the load factor is crucial but it has to be flying before the load factor becomes important.

This is true for all transport equipment. Even a wheelbarrow represents money laying idle unless it is moving. The load factor is irrelevant for stationary vehicles. This emphasises the crucial importance of dwell times and, particularly, the dwell times related to loading and unloading. This emphasis is magnified when the costs of delays to the people or goods being carried are added to the costs of the delays to the vehicles carrying them. These are so important that ancillary micro-modes are often inserted into the chain of modes. An extreme example is the Suez–Mediterranean pipeline. Very large tankers deliver their infrequent cargoes to a terminal at the Suez end of the continuously running pipeline which connects to a similar terminal on the Mediterranean coast. Large tank farms at both terminals provide the buffer stores to cope with the wide disparity in rhythm. An extra micro-mode is inserted between ships and tank farms. High volume hoses and pumps span the gap between ship and tank farm. In themselves they are grossly inefficient, using many expensive high capacity pumps working in parallel but only doing so for comparatively short bursts of time, laying idle for much of their life. But their high cost minimises port time for massively expensive ships.

The same theory is apparent in airports where more expensive piers than are really necessary are provided to ensure that the risk of delaying very expensive planes is minimised, and also in container ports where the cranes are used inefficiently but they reduce the risk of extended port times for very costly ships. It is a characteristic shared by much mechanical handling equipment.

This all emphasises two vital aspects of transport: first, all transport is based upon a sequence of segments by mode and micro-mode; second, spare redundant capacity is vital to ensure delays are kept to a minimum. The corollary is that productivity of any one element within a modal chain is much less important than the efficiency of the door-to-door movement as a whole.

Conclusions

The costing grid shown in Figure 10.8 may be used for any mode of transport, although some will show a predominance of unfilled cells. Pipelines, cable networks and sewers will show the vast majority of their cost to be fixed costs per life-hour, itself a possibly complex amalgam of the amortised capital costs of enhancements, upgrades and repairs made necessary, not by the flow itself but by the need to create capacity.

This hints at a problem that so far has been neglected. For some modes of transport the distinction between track and vehicle is blurred: pipes and wires do not have 'vehicles', nor do conveyor belts, escalators, and other continuously running systems. Operationally they may be considered to provide an infinitely frequent service but financially the stationary 'track' and the moving 'vehicle' are inextricably intertwined. Since they run continuously, the distinctions between moving, dwell and layover times may be collapsed into a single working time. For many such systems service has to be stopped for maintenance, logged as 'out-of-traffic' or 'down-time', but most of the cable and pipe networks do not rest, working without interruption for the complete 8640 hours of the year.

174 Transport costs

For the traditional modes of road, rail, sea and air, track costs are difficult to establish both in theory and in practice. They are a combination of:

- plain route;
- interchanges, stations, ports and terminals;
- parking, stabling and anchorages;
- energy supply by wire or refuelling points;
- waymarking by buoys, lighthouses and signposts;
- real-time control systems by signalling, instruction and advice by radio.

Finding the levels of capital investment and reducing the amortised costs down to rates such as those shown in Figure 10.8 needs to be done, but warrants a major research project.

More constructively, the size and importance of the costs of layover, dwell times and down-times reinforce a general theme that had been developing from Chapter 1: that transport is not just about movement but must include parking, stopping, loading and unloading, and about interchanging and trans-shipping. The interfaces where this occurs are a crucial and often a constraining influence on the provision and use of the transport network as a whole.

Notes

1   This may be thought to be an unrealistically short distance between stops. However, it is typical of the stopping patterns of street trams in the 1920s and 1930s, and will be used later in a discussion about the balances between users' walking and riding times.
2   Evidence to Inquiry held by the Traffic Commissioner in April 1987.

Chapter 11

Sensing success and failure

Objectives

All behaviour is driven by motives of some sort or another. Motives may be quite simple and vague, almost unconscious. Watching a young child playing is intriguing – repeated attempts are made to put things inside or on top of one another. There is clearly a task to be achieved, and the child learns how to do it by repeated trials, errors and corrections. That can only work if there is a memory of the motive, of what has been done and of what the outcomes were, something which we and other animals do instinctively and unconsciously. Cyberneticists term the process 'error-actuated feedback'.

In Chapter 3 such trial and error was likened to steerage, first setting an objective and then defining a programme of actions to achieve it. Regular tests on progress towards the objective are made and, if there is a deviation away from the desired path, the action programme is adjusted to bring progress back on track. Chapter 3 extended the process beyond sensing whether events are actually moving positively towards the objective, to an understanding of whether the objective itself is really attainable. A child will find that efforts to build a tower from wooden blocks will repeatedly fail unless the first course is on a stable flat surface – that there are preconditions which, unless met, will cause failure no matter how much effort is put into trials and the analysis of errors. The lesson to be learned is not just how to steer towards an objective but how to recognise an unattainable objective.

That much is trivial, although it is a simplicity that appears to escape much political thinking. Unlike a child learning by trial and error in which the objective, the analysis of trials and the consequent decisions on what to do next are all in the child's own mind, society's decisions are made by groups of people, some deciding upon objectives, others defining courses of action, and still others detecting progress. These complexities are likely to be made worse by there being a number of simultaneous courses of action, some focused upon the same objective but others related to quite different objectives. Unravelling the effects of actions and then sensing whether they are creating positive progress towards particular objectives is the major task of good management.

Management by error-actuated feedback may fail due to an inadequate definition of effective actions, to poor implementation or to intractable objectives, but, within corporate organisations, there is the additional hazard of poor communication between those responsible for sensing change, those analysing the links between change and past actions, and those responsible for steerage by adjusting programmes of action. There is clearly more to cybernetic steerage than monitoring progress and correcting deviations, or even to understanding whether the objective is feasible: there has to be good communication between all parties.

Good communication is more than the simple transmission of information. Human beings tend to retain their initial individual learning behaviour and continue to interpret, evaluate and weigh up all incoming information just as they did in their early trial-and-error childhood days. They allocate levels of belief or disbelief to information using their own criteria, often sifting data to select items that support their own agenda while rejecting the others. Examples abound: collectivisation of Soviet farming in the 1930s was an abject failure evidenced by the deaths of thousands from starvation, but the official analysis was not that the policy was fundamentally flawed, but that it was being poorly implemented. More recent, more contentious examples, both military and economic, have filled newspapers and books.[1] There is always the possibility that individuals and sometimes complete groups will, perhaps silently, overwrite the corporate objectives with their own. There is no absolute protection against such perversions in the supply chain of information, nor in the programmes of actions, but the problem may be reduced by ensuring that people 'own' the agreed corporate objectives by making them clear and well understood throughout an organisation. Modern organisations try to achieve this by engendering a corporate identity through 'mission statements' and team-building exercises. Military organisations pre-dated their efforts by fostering regimental and group cohesion through uniform behaviour.

Transforming objectives into common purposes that pervade an organisation is a prerequisite for error-actuated feedback to work. Team building through problem-solving games (modern management theory) or by badging (military theory) are not the only ways: it may be done by awarding money (bonuses, piece rates, etc.) or by including team members in discussions both about the protocols of reaching decisions and about substantive issues (the traditional approach in academia[2]). As with so many things, generalised theory may be right, but successful practice will depend on operational detail. Paying people to work to a common agenda may or may not work: piece rates in the British motor industry of the 1960s and 1970s produced conflict rather than coherence and bonuses paid to senior managers in the banking sector have backfired on company performance. In contrast, employee partnerships such as John Lewis have created successful common purpose, probably by being inclusive rather than divisive. Bonding through discussion and the intellectual understanding of objectives, the totem of academic management, works for as long as people are aware that they are making personal contributions to decision-making but are absolved from personal responsibility for the decisions made. It relies further on ensuring that there is a uniform, collective memory: the bureaucracy of circulated minutes is well recognised in both government and business.

It appears that defining objectives and how they are to be achieved is only one aspect of management. There have to be methods by which progress, success and failure are detected and, most importantly, there has to be a communications web able to bind policy-makers, actors, sensors and evaluators into a system with a common, well-recognised purpose. Defining objectives is necessary but insufficient.

Criteria

Policy objectives such as 'to reduce CO_2 emissions' are very broad and unspecific, raising operational queries on how it is known when or even whether the objective has been reached. These queries may be expanded into 'to what degree has the objective been reached?', a query that is likely to provoke debate over whether the objective has been reached with sufficient effect to justify claims that the policy aims have been fulfilled. Pre-setting some sort of criterion will forestall such debate. Defining quantitative criteria which show the extent to which objectives have been reached has the additional advantage that they may be used as waymarkers to test the extent to which progress is being made as the action programme is implemented: they become an input to steering and modifying the programme.

The use of numerical and pseudo-numerical data within spread-sheets has revolutionised policy-making and implementation to include statistical targets. These not only specify objectives in numerical terms, actually supplanting the substantive objective with a numerical value, but also specify a track by which it is to be achieved. The European Union Directive on 'The Use of Energy from Renewable Resources' (1009/28/EC) (Annex 1) is an example: it requires the UK to produce 15 per cent of its energy consumption from renewable sources by 2020 and specifies the progress that has to made from the 2005 level (1.3%). The desired trajectory of change in the percentage of energy from renewable resources is defined as:

2011–1212	$(1.3 + (0.20 \times (15 - 1.3)))$
2013–2014	$(1.3 + (0.30 \times (15 - 1.3)))$
2015–2016	$(1.3 + (0.45 \times (15 - 1.3)))$
2017–2018	$(1.3 + (0.65 \times (15 - 1.3)))$

The Directive is an integral part of attempts to address the problem of climate change by reducing CO_2 emissions, and the example is not given in criticism of the policy, nor of the European Union's methods being used to deliver that policy: it is there as a demonstration of the distillation of policy into numbers which are then transformed into targets (the 2020 level of 15 per cent) and then into a path leading to that target.

Such theory is neat and sensible, but in practice there are pitfalls:

- There is a feeling of doomed earnestness – a hint of naive statisticians isolated in their offices, unaware of people's naughtiness. There is a history of the manipulation of field data and its analysis to ensure that statistical targets are met. It was found some years ago[3] that crime clear-up rates had been massaged by inducing criminals to admit to crimes they could not have committed and, worse, that some solved crimes were complete fabrications. Cooke *et al.*[4] quote Lipley as reporting ways in which patients were 'hidden' from the descriptive statistics on waiting in hospital emergency departments.

- More importantly, it is a massive problem to ensure that all parties whose actions and decisions will contribute to achieving the target are aware of it, aware of their own roles and are willing to accept responsibility. In an age where state regulation is held to be undesirable, the major tools are exhortation and fiscal measures, particularly carbon credits. These licences to emit CO_2 by the tonne only work to stimulate the use of renewables by penalising the alternatives. Implementation then becomes the responsibility of a large number of individuals and agencies coordinated by pricing and costing.
- Within this structure there is a jostling for resources, particularly money. The EU Directive on renewable energy, in common with many policy statements at all levels, does not consider the resource implications of setting and meeting the targets, yet it is virtually certain that any failure to achieve them will be justified by a lack of resources. This is likely to be both absolute (there turned out to be insufficient funding) and relative (the funding that was available had to be spent on more urgent issues).
- Criteria and waymarkers must be chosen carefully. They are rarely measures of the objective itself but are usually more easily monitored attributes acting as a contribution to, or a proxy for, the objective. The increased use of renewables is just one component of a policy to reduce CO_2 emissions but it may well be used as a gauge of the progress being made in the round, and this may mislead. If consumers believe, rightly or wrongly, that their consumption is sourced by renewables, they may be less concerned about energy thrift, weakening the link between the monitored quantity and the policy it is monitoring.
- Demand may be expressed indirectly through a third party. Renewable energy is an example: in switching on the kettle, consumers are unable to choose that it is boiled by renewable energy. That choice is made by their supplier, who may sense their customers' preferences but may not represent them. Although individuals may choose their cars for comfort, safety, etc., the choice of trains they use have to be made by the operator, not the traveller.
- In general, it is difficult to monitor preventions: collecting data to explain the reasons why some things are *not* done is extremely hard and is even more difficult to link definitively to a particular policy. The prime example is the reduction in car use. Given an assumption that journeys are going to be made by some means or another, reduction in car use is sensed by the increased use of the alternatives. That may not be true: some journeys may be abandoned and others consolidated into more complex journeys calling at a number of destinations. Certainly, as fuel prices have risen in recent years vehicle-km has fallen, but there has not been a commensurate rise in the use of public transport.
- It is tempting to use money as an indicator, partly because the data are usually easier to collect and partly because, as a society, we are accustomed to using money to value things. If there are a number of criteria associated with an objective, it is easier to combine or offset one against another if they are converted into a common currency. As will be shown later, this is sometimes done using real money: the cost table in the previous chapter (Figure 10.8) is in money that really has to be used to pay wages, buy fuel and pay insurance premiums. But at other

times pretend money is used: for example, people's travel time is given a nominal rate per hour, although no travellers pay a time charge, nor do they gain a cash benefit for travelling quickly. The manner in which each of us spends our 8760 hours of existence per year is not determined by a sense of financial profitability: 'wasting time' is not the same as losing money.

Pseudo-money requires a tariff of pseudo-prices: for example, in evaluating road schemes not only is the driver's time given a value but vehicle time and accidents have a nominal monetary value ascribed to them too. These values are defined by decree laid down in government documents and so, for example, the evaluation of the proposed London–Birmingham high-speed railway will incorporate standardised values and weightings. The wisdom and equity of this is discussed in Chapter 18.

- Numeric criteria may supplant the real objective for which it is the proxy and this is particularly true for measures monitored in cash. The aggregate cash value of the attributes being monitored becomes more than the monitored quantity and becomes an objective in its own right, so that policies are directed at maximising or minimising the monitored value or, alternatively, turning the monetised value into a rate (£/kilometre) and then optimising that rate.

This whole subject area has been heavily influenced by management theory which itself has sprung from the power and flexibility of computing. Spread-sheets first appeared over 30 years ago[5] and not only enabled numerical assessments of progress, success and failure but transformed them, spawning the use of binary attributes ('ticking the boxes') and the greater use of 'scaling' (the assessment of an event or quality on a scale of 0 to 5 or by the number of 'stars', etc.), with the primary intention of reducing assessments to numbers capable of being manipulated by spread-sheet arithmetic.

Optimisation and sufficing

Wherever quantitative values are used there is a tendency to strive for optima. Chapter 19 gives a discussion of the methods by which travel demand is predicted, methods which are predicated upon individuals seeking the quickest or cheapest routes. Similarly, one of the planks of much of economic theory is that consumers seek the 'best buy' or that firms strive for the highest profit. The practice of a constant quest for the 'most' or the 'best' may be questioned:

- Choices are usually made against a number of different criteria: a choice of route may be based on time taken plus the distance (longer but quicker routes). Multiple criteria imply ways in which each may be set off against the others.
- The scores against each criterion are a mixture of past experience and predictions which are vulnerable to actual events: road-works may upset an optimal choice.
- All possible alternatives can never be considered and the 'best' may be unknown.

- Optima can never be recognised even post hoc: the 'best' at any point in time is unknowable both before and after the choice has been made.
- Complex interwoven criteria are hidden in many situations, particularly complex and important ones. When buying a house or a car, or even a box of cornflakes, the criteria used and the information to hand on whether those criteria are met is fraught with difficulties.
- Past experience may have been distilled down into habits, laden with inertia, making decisions unresponsive to changing circumstances.
- Circumstances and attributes change in time and today's 'best' may not retain its superiority. Any review of past decisions will often raise queries as to whether they have been overtaken by events.
- Many choices are made by reaction rather than through thoughtful analysis, even of the available information: job interviews are renowned for the risks of making poor choices.

Decisions may well appear to be illogical to an analyst with a wide range of data, some of it beyond the knowledge of a decision-maker, although, at the time and with the knowledge and perceptions to hand, the decision may have been completely logical.

Amusingly, theorists familiar with models of decision-making premised upon optima are rarely able to explain the methodology behind their own choices of spouse or house: neither is usually the product of seeking an optimum. It usually boils down to making a list of attributes, seeking options, testing them against the list and selecting the option that satisfies the list. It is a process called 'sufficing', making a decision knowing that it may well not be the optimum, but which satisfies a specific list of criteria. Very few people actually write down the list: it may be impressionistic, held in the mind and well larded with anticipation rather than fact. The list is also likely to include negatives – attributes to be avoided. These have a tendency to be absolute rather than relative and so a bad quality cannot be set against some counterbalancing good qualities.

Assessments of policy options set out as a table of points for and against with each weighted to allow trade-offs was initiated by Nathaniel Litchfield in 1956[6] with the aim of identifying the best from a limited list of options, and not the best of all possible options. This carries an implication that the list is probably drawn up to include what are reckoned to be likely candidates for the 'best' and exclude those which are unlikely, and that presupposes some knowledge (or perhaps prejudice) in those responsible for drawing up the list.

Litchfield's seminal work grew into the concept of the 'Planning Balance Sheet',[7] a concept into which the idea of sufficing does not easily fit. The balance sheet is structured around ranking the extent to which a planning option delivers attributes, both good and bad, and allows for trade-offs. Sufficing is much more akin to ticking boxes, with scaled attributes being replaced by binary qualities that are either adequate or not. Hence they have an in-built threshold dividing the acceptable from the unacceptable, thresholds that have to be set before the scoring can take place.

Systems and conditions

A cybernetic system is a collection of components interconnected by linkages able to transmit information and instruction from one component to another. Crucial components are the sensors able to detect change and servos able to alter the configuration of various components. The word 'cybernetic' is derived from the Greek for steersman and was originally used in studies of the ways in which human bodies work. Various organs act as sensors, feeding information through the network of nerves to the brain where it is processed to create the five major senses, namely touch, taste, smell, sight and hearing, and also to other, more minor senses partially derived from the major ones: pain, balance, movement, temperature and proprioception. The latter is particularly important: it enables the brain to create a dynamic, three-dimensional map of the position of the limbs and other parts of the body. It is proprioception that enables human beings to put food and drink in their mouths, to scratch, to play musical instruments, to drive cars or, for a simpler example, to clap their hands over their heads. Muscles, working as servos to move the body's configuration, act under instructions from the brain, instructions transmitted to them through the network of nerves. Clapping one's hands out of sight over one's head involves the brain making the decision to do it (the objective), and then continuously sensing the difference between where the hands actually are and where they need to be to clap, and then sending messages to the muscles to reduce that difference – it is a constantly running error-actuated feedback, assessing what further movement is necessary to achieve the objective. Clapping one's hands requires the brain to monitor the hands and issue instructions to the muscles in an uninterrupted loop, but man-made systems are often unable to achieve such continuous monitoring, sensing the state of the system only intermittently: personal finances used to be sensed by monthly bank statements, the levels of engine oil were occasionally checked by the use of a dipstick. This intermittent monitoring is called 'polling', but electronic sensors are able to provide monitored measurements at very short intervals, reducing down to the infinitely small – effectively continuously, like the human body.

Clearly, all sensors, servos and communications must work in harmony. Too much alcohol impairs the controlling function of the brain and it is quite possible to try to clap one's hands over one's head but miss. There is a general condition for any error-actuated feedback to work: the decision-makers must have decided what needs to be done, the sensors must be capable of monitoring change, system-state information must flow through the communications network from the monitors to the policy-makers and from the policy-makers to the administrators, and the administrators must have the powers and the abilities to implement change. Without all components being in place and operational, system management cannot function.

However, even that is a simplification. Systems are nested within one another. The human body has digestive, respiratory, circulation, reproductive, immune, etc. systems, none of which work entirely independently. Cities have traffic, sewage, water, waste, energy and information systems supported by systems of law, ownership and government. The combination of systems has to work, if not in entire unison, then without undue mutual interference. For example, roads, canals and railways require land in narrow but very long strips, a configuration contrary to normal patterns of landownership and agriculture. From very early times the development of transport networks was inhibited by difficulties in buying strips of land from a large number of owners, many of them intent upon extracting extortionate prices. Roads, canals and railways did not and could not be created by the normal processes of land purchase within an open market. The state had to resolve the problem by modifying the normal legal system for buying and selling land. In the thirteenth century in Britain this was done by distinguishing between the ownership of land and the ownership of the right of way across it. It was the right of way that was acquired and legally defined by the state in the thirteenth century as the 'King's Highway', but the land under the Highway remained in the hands of the original owner. As the use of the road network increased, merely defining rights of way was insufficient: the roads needed repair and maintenance, tasks which, by the sixteenth century, were held to be the legal responsibility of the landowners themselves, but this proved to be unworkable and the responsibility had to be taken by the state in the form of the local parish. There it remains, although now with local authorities as successors to parishes.

The crucial point is that transport networks cannot be developed without legal systems being reformed to enable their construction – that the state, being the creator of the law and also responsible for ensuring that it is kept, is a vital member of the family of systems which, together, facilitate the fabric of civilisation.

The changes in the legal system itself may be seen as an aspect of error-actuated feedback. By the seventeenth century the King's Highway with its confusion over repairs and maintenance was proving to be inefficient, hobbling the development of the economy by imposing heavy transport costs. That 'error' was corrected by making possible the necessary land acquisition for properly designed and maintained toll roads through the Turnpike Acts, one for each proposed new road.[8] Parliament recognised that they were empowering the owners of the new toll roads to acquire land outside of the normal market procedure and, at the same time, were creating local monopoly advantages which then might be exploited. To forestall this problem each Turnpike Act specified maximum levels of toll. The state was not only enabling the new roads but was regulating them too. It was recognised that untrammelled market forces were not only unable to facilitate the necessary land acquisition but could also be misused to extract monopoly profit, a sophistication which has not made its way unscathed up until the present day.

The Turnpike Acts were the model to facilitate the building of canals. Once again, canals needed land in very thin parcels and Parliamentary Acts, one for each canal, specified the land required in great detail and also determined the legal tariff to be charged. Like the turnpikes, canals were open to be used by anybody paying the requisite toll. Unlike the turnpikes, the users had to acquire specialist vehicles, barges which could not be used elsewhere, and, once again, the transport system had to adjust, this time fairly simply. Many industrial users bought and operated their own barges and some bought more than they needed, leasing them out to independent operators. A complex structure developed in which the 'track' (the canal), the 'vehicles' (the barges) and their contents (the cargo) were often owned by three different sets of people, but examples of all possible combinations of ownership may be found.

The initial Railway Acts (Stockton and Darlington (1821), Liverpool and Manchester (1826)[9] were modelled upon the then canal practices, expecting the railway companies to own the line but other people to own and operate the trains.[10] William Huskisson, President of the Board of Trade, the government department responsible for the regulation of canals and railways, was a guest of honour at the Grand Opening of the Liverpool and Manchester. In common with most people there on the day, he had no idea how fast trains could travel, nor how long they would take to stop, failed to get out of the way of the famous Rocket, and was knocked down and killed. The error was plain and the feedback inevitable, although it came too late to save Huskisson: railway operations had to be systematically managed. The trains travelled so fast that drivers could not stop if they saw an obstruction on the track, and their line of sight had to be extended and enhanced by a signalling system, implying that the owners of the track had to operate it themselves. The open access that was a feature of roads and canals had been overtaken by technologies enabling much higher speeds.

Those speeds were risky and accidents common. The state, through the Board of Trade, thought it right to instigate a formal error-actuated feedback system to analyse and learn from every accident: the railway system became a collection of systems steering and managing the track, the signalling, the rolling-stock, accounting, etc., plus systems of ownership (the shareholders) and regulation. Government regulation was explicitly in the interests of the public, with safety being paramount. As an example of this role, in August 1873 the Scotch express derailed at Wigan station with heavy loss of life. It was a long train with many coaches reserved in their entirety for aristocratic parties on their way north for the opening of the grouse shoot. The error-detection system designed and imposed by the state went into action immediately, not to ascribe blame, nor to provide evidence for civil actions against those thought to be culpable, but to ensure that any errors were detected and corrected. It was discovered that a set of points had moved as the train passed over them. Parliament then introduced new regulations to fit mechanical locks worked from the signal box to all points of a similar nature. Those regulations were still in place at the time of the Potters Bar accident in May 2002 which was also caused by points changing as a train passed over them. There the similarity ended, because the error was not an inadequate design as it had been 130 years earlier but an appalling lack of maintenance. The response was not as crisp, decisive and effective compared with the Victorians. A confused jumble of police investigation of a presumed crime, a criminal trial, an official inquiry, an inquest and subsequent civil actions all concentrated on post-hoc analysis used to allocate blame. It seems to have been driven by a presumption that if those responsible for poor maintenance were penalised financially, they would be induced to do better in the future. The Victorians instructed companies to do better under pain of law.

This parable of the moving points is an example of a system (the railway) being a collection of intertwined subsystems with government being an integral part, providing objectives (a safer railway), communication (investigation, data collection, analysis and reports) and servos (making legally driven changes). State action after

August 1873 certainly reduced risks and saved lives. State confusion and indecision after the Potters Bar incident in May 2002 failed to put in place a legally enforceable maintenance routine and the same problem arose yet again in February 2007 at Greyrigg.

Two problems are apparent:

1 If systems are the joint responsibility of many parties, the communications between the various parts of the system have to leap across boundaries of responsibility at which there is potential conflict and changes in emphasis and priority.
2 If error and failure do occur, the system itself should be modified to ensure that the error is not repeated. That requires a focus on doing things better in the future, not a focus on the past to ascribe blame in the hope that it will be corrected without further feedback and compulsion.

It is doubtful whether money penalties for past errors, often specified in contracts between various parties within a system, are as effective in preventing future errors as instruction and organisational discipline.

Notes

1 See e.g. Tavis and Aronson (2008).
2 So cruelly parodied in Malcolm Bradbury's *History Man* (1975).
3 See Gill (1987).
4 Cooke *et al.* (2004).
5 VisiCalc (1979), Lotus 1-2-3 (1982), Excel (1987).
6 Litchfield (1956), reviewed in Taylor (1998, p.79).
7 Litchfield and Marinov (1977).
8 The first was passed in 1663 for a road in Hertfordshire.
9 Neither of the lines was constructed and opened until four years after the Acts were passed.
10 The person who operated the stage coach between Stockton and Darlington via the Turnpike changed the wheels on his vehicles and transferred them, still horse-drawn, to the new railway, where they were mixed in with locomotive-drawn coal trains.

Chapter 12

Managing the environmental impacts

Two major reports were published in Autumn 2006. They were not statements of government policy but they did act as good indicators of the priorities, objectives and methods of the government at the time. There has been no radical change since their publication, despite a change of government. Both reports were commissioned by HM Treasury, not by the departments of state directly responsible either for the environment or for transport. They were:

- the Stern Review of the Economics of Climate Change (October 2006);[1]
- the Eddington Transport Study: transport's role in sustaining the UK's productivity and competitiveness (December 2006).[2]

The reports were closely related. Although Sir Nicholas Stern's name was given to the Review of the Economics of Climate Change, it was not entirely his work. He chaired a committee with one foot in the Treasury and the other in the Cabinet Office, a position which must have been none too comfortable in the years of political strife between the Prime Minister and the Chancellor of the Exchequer. Sir Nicholas was also Chair of a committee advising Sir Rod Eddington in his study.

Both reports were children of their age, an age in which policy-making was dominated by economic theory, a domination which still remains:

- The titles themselves show that the prime objective was economic – to promote continued productivity and consumption at a global scale (Stern) and at national level (Eddington). The secondary objective was to minimise the environmental cost of that economic growth, with a focus upon climate change and, in particular, upon CO_2-e emissions. Neither report, nor the contemporary critiques of them, questioned this priority: there was no suggestion that the primary focus should or could have been upon the risks to the planetary eco-system, what should be done to address those risks and only then what the effect on the economy might be.
- The dominance of economic growth as an objective was matched, in both reports, by the use of economic theory, analysis and policy. This was not surprising. The reports were commissioned by the Treasury, and both Stern and Eddington shared the Treasury's faith in economic theory: Sir Nicholas Stern's CV showed

a career which included spells at the World Bank as an economic adviser to the government, and as a Professor of Economics; Sir Rod Eddington was a businessman of long experience culminating as Chairman of British Airways.

The Stern Review (p. 1) was quite clear about this focus upon economics:

> Climate change presents a unique challenge for economics: it is the greatest and widest-ranging market failure ever seen. The economic analysis must therefore be global, deal with long time horizons, have the economics of risk and uncertainty at centre stage, and examine the possibility of major, non-marginal change. To meet these requirements, the Review draws on ideas and techniques from most of the important areas of economics, including many recent advances.

To describe climate change as a 'market failure' presumed there was a 'market' for climate and also posed the question of the possible nature of a 'market success'. This focus upon the market mechanism was sustained in the proposed corrections to its 'failure'. Both reports advocated three major strands of action: first, the pricing of both carbon and the use of road space; second, research, development and the application of technology; and third, the removal of 'barriers' to behavioural change. Carbon pricing and road-user charging are market manipulations by the imposition of arbitrary extra costs; the 'barriers' to be removed are those which might inhibit responses to market forces; while the development and application of technology was rather more intransigent. The role of private companies was held to be crucial but they were recognised as a major source of the initial failure and so could not to be relied upon to deliver the necessary changes in technology on their own initiative: Stern advocated state expenditure on research, development and application. It is a tacit admission that market forces, left to their own devices, were not omnipotent. It also emphasised the weakness in Stern's call for long-term global horizons, attitudes that markets are not suited to take.

Stern's acceptance that the workings of some markets were flawed and required remedial action through state intervention and yet simultaneously advocating a reliance upon those market forces to deliver the prime objective of economic growth without creating climate change was a paradox repeated by Eddington, although in another context. He asserted that economic growth was contingent upon labour markets being concentrated to provide both choices of jobs for employees and choices of workers for employers, creating a link between economic and urban growth. He reported that the great majority of existing congestion (80%+) was in urban areas and accepted that economic and urban growth was bound to make it worse unless urban transport policy could address the problem effectively. He offered two solutions: the first was to impose road-user charging, and the second was to improve public transport, particularly bus services.[3] The report paradoxically suggested that this should be done by simultaneously introducing more privatisation and more regulation. The claim was made[4] that the competition/deregulation introduced in 1986 had improved the efficiency of the bus industry, 'cutting costs by up to 50 per cent', with the implication that more competition would yield further improvement. However, the very next paragraph admits that 'service levels post-1986 had been falling, fares had been rising, and patronage, with the exception of a few markets, had continued to fall'[5]: clearly privatisation/deregulation had been unable to prevent service deterioration. The paragraph then goes on to suggest that the necessary effective coordination between bus services and other public transport modes in large urban areas was critically dependent upon cooperation between operators and local authorities: that market forces of themselves were incapable of delivering the public transport service levels necessary to support the concentration of population and jobs in urban areas.

Both Stern and Eddington stumbled over the same problem: that an efficient transport system needs to be coherent and coordinated, qualities which cannot be delivered by multiple operators, each chasing their own individual objectives in the absence of external planning and coordination. It is a very old problem exemplified by the multiple main-line terminals in London and Paris where the railway systems were built by private companies, each acting in their own interests, in contrast to the single Hauptbahnhofs and Centraal stations in Germany and in the Netherlands resulting from imposed government control.

This problem should not be characterised as a straight conflict between market forces and state control, winner takes all. State intervention may be through ownership; through imposition of a price regime to replace the market; through the imposition of maximum prices; through retaining the market but manipulating it by subsidies or taxes; or through means unrelated to market forces – through legally imposed instructions, prohibitions, directions and standards.

Ownership has usually been accompanied by managing day-to-day operations, but ownership and operations do not have to be combined. After the nationalisation of the British railways in 1948 much of the freight rolling-stock was owned and maintained by the companies whose goods it carried, but was operated by British Railways. During both World Wars the railways remained in private ownership but were operated by the government. Pure market force, characterised by different companies offering different rates for comparable services, was suspended from the very inception of turnpike roads, canals and railways. Parliament saw that transport was inherently monopolistic, and fares and freight rates were imposed by all the Private Acts authorising the construction and operation of turnpikes, canals, railways, toll bridges and ferries. In 1842 (only three years after the opening of the first trunk route from London to Birmingham), the railway companies themselves established the Railway Clearing House responsible for publishing rates and fares between stations owned by different companies and also for distributing the revenues between the companies owning the various sections of the track along each route. It was an important demonstration that the prime commercial importance was for companies to offer the services of a network and that companies had immediately appreciated the need for cooperation rather than competition. Three years later, Parliament imposed network-wide maxima freight rates and passenger fares per mile, and five years after that the Railway Clearing House was brought under the supervision of the Board of Trade.

The history of transport legislation shows a constant recognition of the need to support or modify market forces in the provision of efficient transport services. The Victorians passed laws to ensure that ships were not overloaded; that the dangers of locomotive boilers exploding were minimised; that taxi drivers behaved responsibly; that fares and rates were not extortionate; that accidents, when they did occur, were learned from; that where local economic viability was threatened, subsidies were available through mail contracts. Victorian Parliaments were also good at specifying the bodies responsible for enforcing the legislation. Today we enjoy the environment and the civilisation that they and their successors ensured, not by state ownership nor by supplanting market forces but, in concert with private companies, by modifying the market to overcome its shortcomings.

The Eddington Report

This was the simpler of the two reports, being restricted geographically to England and Wales and also relying upon data from the Department of Transport archives to support the policy recommendations. These were as follows:

1. To meet the changing needs of the UK economy, Government should focus on improving the performance of existing transport networks, in those places that are important to the UK's economic success:
    - Government action needs to focus on tackling congestion, capacity constraints, and unreliability on existing networks.
    - In some limited circumstances, there may be opportunities to extend the network which offer good value for money, for example government may wish to explore the case for extending the reach of existing urban networks in order to deepen labour markets.
2. Over the next 20 years, the three strategic economic priorities for transport policy should be congested and growing urban areas and their catchments; and the key inter-urban corridors and the key international gateways that are showing signs of increasing congestion and unreliability. These are the most heavily used and economically significant parts of the network:
    - Look for signals of congestion, overcrowding and high productivity as high-level indicators that transport improvements may make a significant impact on economic growth and productivity.
    - Bring forward and assess a wide range of alternative options to address transport performance in these areas.
    - To achieve the greatest benefits from available funds, prioritise the options in these areas that offer the highest value for money, based on a full appraisal of their economic, environmental and social impacts.
3. Government should adopt a sophisticated policy mix to meet both economic and environmental goals. Policy should get the prices right (especially congestion pricing on the roads and environmental pricing across all modes) and make best use of existing networks:
    - In line with the Stern Review, prices across all modes should reflect the true cost to society, including congestion, overcrowding and environmental impacts – through appropriate fiscal, regulatory, pricing or trading instruments.

- Use road pricing as the most appropriate way to tackle congestion by introducing widespread, congestion-targeted road pricing to deliver the potential benefits cost-effectively; setting out the key decisions needed to unlock the vast potential of road pricing.
- Explore the potential for high value for money better use measures that encourage changes in travel choices or exploit the opportunities provided by new technologies reflecting the high returns available from some transport investment, based on full appraisal of environmental and social costs and benefits, the Government, together with the private sector, should deliver sustained and targeted infrastructure investment in those schemes which demonstrate high returns, including smaller schemes tackling pinch points.
- After considering the potential for pricing and better use, deliver sustained infrastructure investment where it offers strong returns in the three strategic economic priority areas.
- Do not be seduced by 'grands projets' with speculative returns.
- Implement proposals for additional runway capacity where the case is robust, having accounted for the environmental costs of emissions.[6]

In large measure, the Eddington Report provided support for existing policy and the means used to deliver it. Points 1 and 2 of the above résumé may be paraphrased into 'do what you are doing but better and faster'. More specific suggestions such as 'improve the key international gateways' are not supported by any definitions of what should be done, where, and using what criteria to test improvement.

Point 3 encapsulates the reliance upon market forces. The basic premise is that, providing 'all prices reflect the true cost to society' and that this premise is built into 'the fiscal, regulatory, pricing and trading instruments', the problems of 'congestion, overcrowding and environmental impacts' will be resolved. That is a heroic aspiration unsupported by any evidence.

The suggestion is also made that road pricing has 'vast potential' in addressing worsening urban congestion, this despite the evidence that the cost of driving in congested urban conditions has grown consistently with an equally consistent response of the decentralisation and expansion of urban areas as firms and individuals strive to escape from those escalating costs. Creating a step increase in the costs of urban driving through the imposition of road-user charging will just serve to accelerate that trend. Nobody drives in congested traffic for fun, so it must be presumed that the journeys are necessary, not to get from one address to another, but to get from one function (such as one's home) to another (such as one's work). If the journey becomes unacceptably slow and costly then the response is to change the address of 'home' and 'work'. Thus road-user charging will not reduce congestion by making traffic vanish but will instead push it to other places. Inexplicably, Eddington states:

> I have not examined land use policies in any detail given the scope of my study. Where there is significant new development, then it will be important for transport and land use to be developed together.[7]

The declared lack of concern about land use is strange and seems to be at odds with the assertion that any new development should address both transport and land use, although there is no supporting evidence of why this should be so, nor any suggestions about the reasons or means by which it should be done.

The Stern Review

The objective given in the Stern Review is clear: to reduce the risk of climate change by managing the long-term emission of CO_2-e but to do so without undermining global economic growth. Reaching that objective demands orchestrated decisions by hundreds of thousands of people, firms and governments who do not have a common purpose – they do not 'own' or even agree with the objective. The efficient lines of communication necessary to orchestrate decisions and actions do not exist. Communication within markets is through price signals but the signals are bedevilled by misinterpretation, by poor forecasts of future prices and by manipulation. The recent financial crisis is a parable. Millions of mortgage loans were made based on forecasts that the value of mortgaged properties would continue to rise, but past rises in values were generated by prospective buyers being given ever-larger mortgaged loans. The whole system was self-referential: easy mortgages drove up property prices, which then justified making easier mortgages. The endemic failure of market forces is evidenced by financial turmoil, by the profligate misuse of resources, by worsening pollution, by the destruction of natural habitats and by the terrible disparities in living standards. The message from the financial crises, from overwhelming debt burdens and from worsening poverty is deafening. It is not that market forces are completely inadequate: quite the reverse; they have a proven record in organising much of the local and global economies, but they are far from omnipotent: they have their limitations, and economists need to be far more sceptical – a little dissent would not go amiss.

However, the reliance upon economic theory and practice is now so wide, so deep and so general that it is held with the tenacity of the medieval belief in paradise: it has become an almost incomprehensible heresy to doubt the ubiquitous power of markets and price mechanisms. Polemics such as those by Kwarteng and Dupont[8] and Lal[9] fuel a belief in the power of unregulated market forces that reach the miraculous but the claims made are just amplifications of a more general belief in the power of markets and in the effectiveness of price mechanisms.

Figure 12.1 is intended to demonstrate the depth of the belief that behaviour may be influenced by price in delicate detail. The Treasury has set the cost of annual car licences to create differentials between cars with differing rates of CO_2 emission per vehicle-kilometre in an attempt to persuade people to run 'greener' cars. No doubt a Treasury official will be able to quote an elasticity[10] which shows that a difference in taxation amounting to the price of a daily bar of chocolate is really effective but there does not appear to be any evidence that their faith is justified. There is evidence that greener cars are being bought and that this trend has occurred following the changes to the taxation system, but there is no evidence to suggest that the one was due to the other: the choice of greener cars is more likely to be driven by the escalating price of petrol than by the small reductions in excise duty.

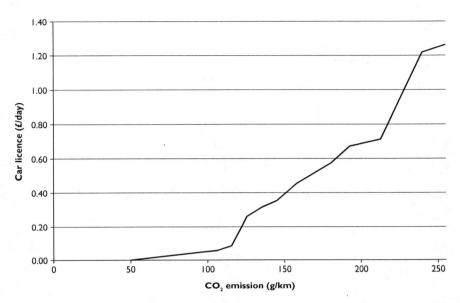

Figure 12.1 Vehicle excise duty charged as a function of CO_2 emission rate (2012)

This heavy reliance upon economic theory, mathematical models and pound signs is comparatively new. Previous concerns with pollution, culminating in the Clean Air Acts (1956 and 1993) and the Civic Amenities Act (1967) were not preceded by arcane debates about the evaluation of monetised costs and benefits, nor about what the impact might be on the economy, nor about the elasticities driving the effectiveness of charges and penalties. The legislation was direct and unequivocal: it specified pollutions (mainly smoke but also fly-tipping), made them illegal and enforced the law through the courts. Economic theory and practice played no part in either defining or implementing policy.

Reeling back even further, it would have been unthinkable for objectives in the Second World War to have been evaluated by the economic balance between their costs and benefits. Any suggestion that the decision to storm the Normandy beaches in 1944 should have been based on the balance between the estimated cost and the monetary value of prospective benefits now sounds outrageous, even stupid: at the time it would have been treasonable. But the Stern Review spells out a long, comprehensive list of physical threats to global civilisation caused by climate changes linked to the emission of CO_2-e, but it then goes on to assess the social cost to be £54 per emitted tonne of CO_2-e.[11]

There is a grave danger that this criticism of some of the content of the Stern Review will be countered by misrepresenting it. The doubt is confined to the use of economic models to define fiscal policies to address the problems of climate change, and is not concerned with the use of quantitative methods and modelling used in estimating the nature, extent and effects of climate change. Operational research was born during the Second World War, and statistical analyses of the effectiveness of bombing and of anti-U-boat strategies played a large part in the genesis of the sophisticated models that have been used in the Stern Review to estimate the long-term emissions of CO_2-e[12] and of their possible impacts.[13]

Figure 12.2, reproduced from the Stern Review, shows the predicted impacts of rises in CO_2-e upon the natural world. At the top of the figure are levels of CO_2-e in

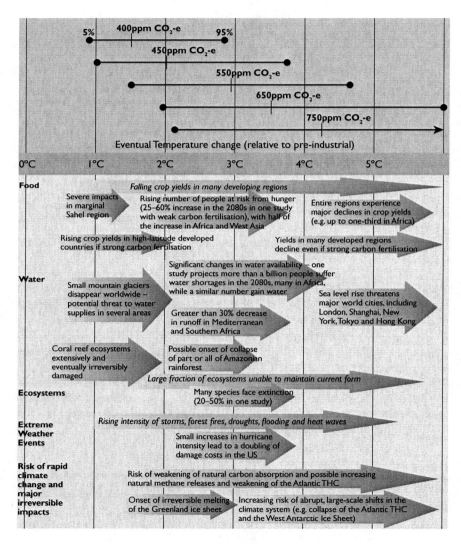

Figure 12.2 The modelled impacts of long-term emissions of CO_2-e
Source: Reproduced from Stern (2006), Executive Summary, fig. 2.

the atmosphere expressed as parts per million: they are sitting on bars showing the probabilities of their effect upon global warming, itself shown in average global temperatures in degrees Celsius over and above the benchmark of the estimated mean global temperature prior to the industrial revolution. The body of the figure shows the estimated effects upon the natural world.

Figure 12.2 has a paradoxical importance. The very existence and importance of climate change has to be demonstrated by statistics, models and forecasts; otherwise many people would just rely upon their own personal experience and others would scoff at the very idea, and yet the data presented in Figure 12.2, and in the text supporting it, are riven with implicit doubt. The very idea of a mean global temperature representing temperatures at all times of the year, all over the world is in itself open to debate, if not downright disbelief. That scepticism is enhanced by the suggestion that such an average can be known for three centuries ago in pre-industrial times, and with such certainty that it may be used in Figure 12.2 as a benchmark. The scepticism is compounded by forecasts of the increases in mean global temperature to be expected from that benchmark, forecasts made not by extrapolating an observed trend, but as an unconfirmed modelled function of the presence of CO_2-e in the atmosphere. On top of that wobbly foundation there is a prediction of CO_2-e levels and, on top of that, a prediction of what the effects might be.

The paradox is that the process outlined in Figure 12.2, and the data, statistics and models supporting it, are necessary to demonstrate the existence of global warming, but are themselves so imprecise and theoretical that they may be used to support arguments that global warming is a myth. This happened on publication of the Review. Sceptics and antagonists to the notion of global warming, of its causes and of its effects, set about casting doubts about the methodology, inputs and assumptions in the report and felt able to reject the conclusions. Global warming has become a scientific football to be kicked around a very large political playground with both sides using the Stern Review and other similar reports as evidence to support their preconceptions.

Figure 12.2 is not an accurate portrayal of a scientific truth but the lack of accuracy and the absence of a provable sequence of causes and effects is no reason to reject it. There is a trend in contemporary culture to demand proof positive: that, if the numbers and the computerised mathematical models do not *prove* that propositions are valid, the unresolved doubts are sufficient reason for them to be rejected. This is twisted logic. Propositions, theories and policies should certainly be rejected if they are disproved, but not if there is merely an absence of positive proof. There is a myth that Bertrand Russell argued that, if the presence of a chocolate teapot orbiting within the solar system could not be disproved, then one was obliged to admit the possibility that there was indeed such a thing.[14] It is a completely different proposition to interpreting the absence of an observable teapot as evidence that one did not exist. The problem becomes entangled with the chances of a proposition being right coupled with the risks of it being wrong, and that is partly down to preconceptions and prejudices. Moroney[15] points out that very few people have seen either a leprechaun or a bacterium and yet 99 per cent of people do not believe in leprechauns but do believe in bacteria. Given their experience and knowledge, they have guessed the odds of the existence of both, but their guesses are weighted by what they think are the risks of being wrong: disbelief in leprechauns may not be too harmful, but, from what is known, disbelief in bacteria may turn out to have been very unwise.

The mechanism of global warming displayed in Figure 12.2 is certain to be 'wrong' in detail but it encapsulates the principle that the CO_2-e in the global atmosphere is increasing and the climate is changing, and that these two trends are likely to be cause and effect. It also postulates that the quite small changes in climate will have very considerable effects upon the natural world and that modern industrial society is dependent upon the state of the natural world even if the close day-by-day linkage has been broken. Any debate over the detail of the mechanism displayed in Figure 12.2, or even whether the mechanism is right in principle should be set aside. The real question should be about risk: what if Figure 12.2 is wrong and any actions taken to cope with climate change turn out to have been unnecessary? The damage will have been confined to no more than a brake upon the growth of the global economy. On the other hand, if the concept of climate change as illustrated in Figure 12.2 is rejected, no matter for what reason, and then it turns out to have been right, the damage will have been done, the global economy will have been wrecked and human existence threatened.

The question is clouded by doubts over whether advances in scientific knowledge will provide a means to counteract any damage. The example of the effects of DDT, as spelled out by Carson,[16] is often cited: it is a very good example of error-actuated feedback. Carson showed that DDT and its effects were cumulative, and she was able to prompt the research that proved the accumulation would have catastrophic long-term effects. That knowledge and the political weight behind it allowed the problem to be nipped in the bud before the accumulation reached levels that were impossible to reverse. It was excellent work, but a poor model for the climate change issue now confronting us. DDT pollution was not so widespread that it was a global issue. DDT was pernicious because it entered the food chains of many fauna but its effects did not travel far beyond the places where it had been sprayed, making it susceptible to local control and national legislation. DDT also had a rate of decay, so a ban on more spraying allowed the existing stock within the natural world to slowly decline. CO_2-e, on the other hand, does not respect boundaries of any sort: national legislation cannot create national effects. CO_2-e is cumulative, but the effects are not directly upon natural systems themselves but alter the very nature of the global environment within which subordinate systems sit. Unlike DDT, climate change is global, pernicious, cumulative and probably irreversible. The risk of massive damage should not be dismissed just because too little is known about the risk.

The 'Polluter Pays' principle

Both Stern and Eddington emphasise a political principle that those who pollute should pay the costs of the damage caused by their pollution:

> it is essential, both from an economic and environmental perspective, that the environmental impacts of transport are fully reflected in decision making. The

transport sector, including aviation, should meet its full environmental costs. The conclusions in this Study therefore, are based on analysis which reflects environmental costs and benefits.[17]

This is yet another repetition of the mantra that price mechanisms are fundamentally capable of delivering desirable outcomes if only they are fed with the right inputs, that 'full' costs are imposed upon all economic activity. This notion has a long history in academic theory but made its initial, explicit appearance in government policy in 1994:

> The Government is committed to provide a policy framework which will help to ensure that people's transport decisions are compatible with environmental goals. A major element of this framework, as set out in the Sustainable Development Strategy, is to encourage people to take full account of the wider costs of their transport choices, such as the impact on the environment. In accordance with the polluter pays principle, the Government is putting a particular emphasis on steps which will bring the costs to the user more closely in line with their full costs. This will inform people's choices and, by putting a price on a cost where there is none at present, will be more economically efficient.[18]

This is a restatement of the economic theory that, given the right price signals, the innate choices made by individual human beings will aggregate into an efficient, desirable use of resources. The theory, propounded in 1776 by Adam Smith[19] as the 'hidden hand', depends upon human beings acting in a manner driven by a self-interested desire to maximise their 'satisfaction' from whatever resources they have available – to act as 'economic men'. The 'satisfaction' for an entrepreneur may be measured in large part by profitability sensed through the balance sheet, but satisfaction for an individual is not so easily defined. It will be a complex amalgam: some people will take shards of satisfaction from recycling their rubbish, seeing it as a tiny but worthwhile contribution to sustaining society and the planet. Market economists, convinced that the price mechanism is so universally competent that any restrictions upon it are necessarily harmful, will argue that it is possible to ascribe a monetary value to the satisfaction gained by fulfilling that small duty to society.[20] The basic principle behind the theory is that satisfaction may be aggregated and then maximised, although the units used to measure satisfaction need not necessarily be either money or pseudo-money. This suggests that every individual has in their heads an implicit tariff quantifying and ranking each source of satisfaction, so making it possible to sum them all to a total. Maximisation may be achieved by trading off one satisfaction low in an individual's tariff against another standing rather higher. This is the idea of 'opportunity cost' in another guise: an 'opportunity cost' is an action which is forgone in order to adopt an alternative – perhaps a family has to choose between a skiing holiday or having the outside of their house repainted, making the continued tattiness of their house the opportunity cost of their skiing.

The concept of opportunity cost carries with it an implication of a constraint forcing a choice between one option and another: choosing both is precluded. That in turn presumes the presence of a finite, limited resource to be spent on either one or the other. In a world of real money rather than pseudo-monetary[21] tags tied to various qualities, this constraint would be disposable income. However, satisfactions measured in pseudo-money have no such constraint: people can amass or spend unlimited amounts of pseudo-money. Recycling rubbish as a semi-altruistic act cannot be easily related to disposable income, although it could be made to have some relevance: if the collection and disposal of domestic rubbish to landfill were subject to a charge but recycling rubbish was free, then the real cost of rubbish disposal could be reduced by recycling. This bumps up a general problem: recycling is not the only way of reducing the amount of waste sent to landfill, and charging would encourage the alternatives, increasing fly-tipping and engendering an interest in the black art of shifting cost on to somebody else – using other people's bins, packing the free recycled collection with non-recyclable material, using cheaper but irresponsible alternative collectors, personally taking rubbish to landfill after building up and storing enough to make the journey worthwhile. In poverty-stricken areas the solution is brutally apparent – just avoid all costs by letting rubbish stay where it is.

But real cash is not the only constraint. In previous chapters there has been an emphasis upon time. Personally we each have 8760 hours per year, neither more, nor less – it is an absolute constraint applicable to everybody on the planet. The opportunity cost of recycling rubbish is about 30 minutes a week which could have been spent watching television or just daydreaming. Using time as a metric together with each individual's tariff of preferences upon how time is best spent, it begins to make sense to measure the 'cost' of each activity in person-minutes with a fixed daily summation of 1440.

But that is not what Eddington, Stern and other theoretical economists are suggesting. Under the principle that the 'polluter pays', they suggest that the state should impose a tax equal to the cost of any environmental damage, so increasing the out-of-pocket cash cost of travel (and, presumably, also of energy consumption and other potentially polluting activities) to cover the costs imposed upon other people living on the planet. In a fantastic theoretical world this 'damage tax' should be paid to all those, present and future, who suffer dis-benefits from the pollutions imposed upon them. This would create a 'market' in which the production and the unwitting consumption of pollutants would be brought to an equilibrium. Of course, that theoretical world can never exist. In its place the 'damage tax' would have to be paid to the state, which would then spend the money as parliamentary whim dictated.

This proposal has a massive problem quite apart from the actual collection and deployment of the new tax. The amount of tax to be charged would have to satisfy two different and unfathomable criteria. First, the tax would have to be set to a level ensuring that polluters were effectively deterred from polluting. Second, it would have to bear some relation to the emitted pollutants and with the effects, quantified over time. That would be technically difficult but politically impossible. Devising numerical models formalising and costing a working version of Figure 12.2 which was both technically robust and acceptable to every jurisdiction throughout the world is an unattainable objective. Without the policy being politically accepted worldwide and being demonstrably effective, it would be impotent.

Insisting that the 'polluter pays' is a beguiling suggestion, but the question of who pays how much to whom for what is not easily answered.

Towards a Sustainable Transport System[22]

A little under a year after the Stern and Eddington studies were published, the government produced the White Paper which translated the suggestions into policy proposals. It acknowledged that Eddington had reported that an efficient transport network was necessary to support the economy and that Stern had emphasised that global warming would have to be addressed if the global economy was to grow, but that the cost of doing so was well within the compass of the budget.

The White Paper was clearer than many of its predecessors. It stated that the broad tasks were to:

- state the above policy goals with clarity;
- identify the transport challenges;
- measure the outcomes and their support of the goals;
- make a detailed geographical analysis to identify specific pressures;
- generate options to address those pressures;
- select the options that deliver the best value for money in the context of sustainable development.

It then broke entirely fresh ground, taking a view of the transport system which was radically different to that of both Stern and Eddington. It began by focusing on the users of the transport system rather than on the attributes of the system itself:

> People travel daily and want a system that gets them from A to B safely, securely and without damaging the environment. If there are problems on their journey, they want to be told about them. They want predictable end-to-end journey times, and expect to travel in reasonable comfort and get a good quality of service. Businesses rely on transport not only so their workforces and customers can use it, but to ensure their goods can be transported quickly and cheaply. Reliability of transport networks, including international networks, is a high priority for freight. This wide range of aspirations means that transport is necessarily complex, but the Government's agenda can be summarised in five broad goals.[23]

The first phrase is revolutionary. The Stern and Eddington studies had been commissioned when Alastair Darling was Secretary of State for Transport but he had been replaced in June 2006 by Douglas Alexander who received the reports in late 2006, only to be replaced himself six months later in June 2007 by Ruth Kelly. The foundations of the White Paper *Towards a Sustainable Transport System* must have been laid when the contents of the Stern and Eddington reports were known but as yet unpublished, but the bulk of it must have been written during Alexander's short rule. Kelly signed the White Paper in October 2007 and much of it echoed some of Stern and the majority of Eddington, including 'urban congestion charging with the generated cash flow spent upon improving urban public transport'.[24] But the enthusiasm was muted: money was set aside in a 'Transport Innovation Fund' to support any local authority wishing to explore local congestion charging, a proposal which most councillors were likely to accept only if it were thrust upon them by coercive national legislation. That major plank of the policy platform suggested by Stern and Eddington was effectively removed.

Apart from that, the White Paper paid the same lip-service to climate change, reciting how important it is but referring it to the government's committee on climate change. There is now discussion about how overall energy and fuel consumption may be reduced through active policies.

However, one phrase keeps popping up in the White Paper: 'predictable end-to-end journey time' is seen as an objective, although the phrase does not always fit with the general flow of the text in which it is found. One thing is clear: that predictable journey times for complete journeys from start to finish are seen as a touchstone of policy to improve urban public transport. The great deficiency of the policy is that, apart from the objective, it is completely unspecified. Nonetheless, the phrase does reflect an awareness of the transport system as a whole, including the interfaces along journeys. Unfortunately, it was an awareness which seems to have been confined to Ruth Kelly herself.

Delivering a Sustainable Transport System[25]

This was published a year after Ruth Kelly's White Paper. By then she had resigned after a little over a year in the post and had been replaced by Geoff Hoon, who was to resign in turn after an even shorter term in office.

The new document proclaimed itself as a discussion paper upon how transport policy should be derived. Hoon's Foreword (p.5) states:

> We still want to cut transport's carbon footprint. It is wrong to think that, in a time of economic difficulty, we can put the climate change agenda on the back burner for a while. We cannot. Global warming requires urgent action. And the Stern report leaves no doubt about the massive economic price we would pay if we failed to address it. But Stern also stresses the importance of tackling climate change in the most economically efficient manner. That means preserving freedom of choice, facing people with the true carbon cost of those choices, forcing the pace of technological change, and helping people reduce their need to travel or switch to lower-carbon modes. It does not mean rationing transport demand by constraining the capacity of our transport networks.

The priority could not have been stated more clearly: the problems of climate change were secondary to those of the economy. Moreover, the government sought to shift the responsibility of coping with pollution by greenhouse gases on to individuals who, it was hoped, would respond to price signals based on the 'true carbon cost of their choices'. However, the document fails to produce any proposed actions to achieve

Managing the environmental impacts 199

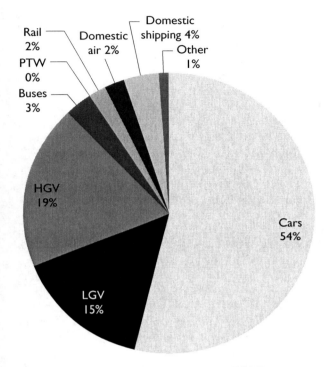

Figure 12.3 Greenhouse gas emissions (2006)
Source: Reproduced from Department for Transport (2008), p. 14, fig. 1.1.

this. There is a pie chart showing the percentages of greenhouse gas emissions by various transport modes, reproduced here in Figure 12.3. It shows that about 90 per cent of the otherwise unquantified emissions come from road transport, but the paper is silent upon how the problem might have been addressed. Contrary to its title, the paper does not spell out how a sustainable transport system could have been delivered.

The Haddington case study

Delivering a Sustainable Transport System was the culmination of a number of documents which were long on diagnosis of the problems of climate change but short on policies and actions designed to have an effect. The disparity between posture and action is illustrated by events in Haddington, a small Scottish market town 25 kilometres to the east of Edinburgh.

Scotland has had its own government since 1999 and published a 'Climate Change Delivery Plan' in 2009 which was far more ambitious than the British government's Plan. More than that, the ambitions were expressed in binding legislation: the Climate Change (Scotland) Act (2009). The policies are as follows:[26]

- improvements in energy efficiency of petrol and diesel vehicles, and increasing uptake of hybrid and electric engines with supporting infrastructure;
- smarter measures, including reduced travel and modal shift to less carbon-intensive modes of transport (e.g. public transport) and active travel (e.g. walking and cycling);
- demand management including road space reallocation;
- changes to the pattern of development to reduce the need to travel;
- efficient driving: through improved driving behaviour (e.g. eco-driving, car sharing or lower speed limits);
- sustainable biofuels;
- improved energy efficiency of new ships;
- more widespread uptake of improved vehicle efficiency in vans and HGVs;
- more widespread adoption of eco-driving;
- speed limit reductions on motorways.

This agenda may only be delivered by ensuring that all decisions by government departments and agencies conform to the above list of policies. The East Lothian Local Plan was subject to a Local Public Inquiry, as required by statute, in August 2006. It included a proposal to build 750–1000 dwellings on the western flank of Haddington. The Plan contained no proposals for increasing the number of jobs in the locality nor any evidence that there was a need for housing for those already working in the vicinity. The Council's case was that the Approved Structure Plan for Edinburgh and the Lothians (within which the Local Plan had to sit) contained a requirement for 750 dwellings in Haddington and that therefore the issue was beyond question. It transpired that in the creation of the Structure Plan the expansion of the employment in Edinburgh had been estimated and was the basis of the need for new housing. Since the available land in Edinburgh itself was very limited the Plan concluded that the majority of new housing would have to be the three surrounding local authorities. This was where the first fundamental mistake was made. The Climate Change (Scotland) Act (2009) had yet to be passed but the issues of energy, emissions and climate change were already known. Nonetheless, the total demand for housing was divided among the three local authorities without regard to the transport and energy implications. It appeared that it was pro-rata with existing populations, presumably because the council taxes on new housing would be a welcome increase in Council income and there was a political necessity for this to be done 'equitably'.

The Structure Plan accepted that the focus of employment growth would be in western Edinburgh, concentrated not far form the airport and, since the need for 750 dwellings in the Haddington area was already held to be beyond question, the Inquiry was presented with a fait accompli that condemned a good proportion of the new Haddington residents to commuting across the diameter of Edinburgh.

The Council presented evidence that the new housing could be served by public transport but this did not estimate how many people would go where. It just explained that an hourly bus service to Edinburgh city centre was possible by diverting an existing route (a route that has now been withdrawn by the bus company as being uneconomic). This paucity of consideration of transport was the second fundamental error. Evidence was given to the Inquiry on the likely car commuting, fuel consumption and emissions but it was ignored in the Report of the Inquiry despite being related directly to a well-published aspect of Government policy. Any further debate on the transport issues was crushed on the grounds that a Transport Plan was being prepared by another statutory body (South East Scotland Transport Partnership) and the matter was therefore sub-judice.

The whole procedure engendered a feeling of tired cynicism. The Government's own policies and aspirations on energy and transport had been pointedly ignored, many buried in procedural blather about being too late (after the Structure Plan) or too early (before the Transport Plan). The moral of the story is that policy lists like that in the Climate Change (Scotland) Act (2009) are worthless unless the administration in its entirety, including all agencies and out-sourced contractors, acts in concert to deliver. Posture alone is inadequate.

Notes

1. Stern (2006).
2. Eddington (2006).
3. Eddington (2006), Executive Summary, Paragraph 1.163.
4. Eddington (2006), Executive Summary, Paragraph 1.164.
5. Eddington (2006), Executive Summary, Paragraph 1.165.
6. Eddington (2006), Executive Summary, Paragraph 1.180.
7. Eddington (2006), Executive Summary, Paragraph 1.123.
8. Kwarteng and Dupont (2011).
9. Lal (2006).
10. Elasticities are measures of the sensitivity of consumers to price. It is equal to the percentage drop in sales divided by the percentage rise in price. Thus, for instance, if the price of petrol rises by 2 per cent and the amount sold falls by 1.6 per cent the elasticity is 0.8.
11. Stern (2006), Executive Summary, p. xvi.
12. Stern (2006), Box 1.2 on p. 9 and the references from which it is drawn.
13. Stern (2006), Chapter 6, p. 157, Part 2, fig. 6.5.
14. His argument was about the existence of a *china* teapot.
15. Moroney (1951).
16. Carson (1962).
17. Eddington (2006), Executive Summary, p. 5.
18. Department of the Environment (1994), Paragraph 1.11.
19. Smith (1776).
20. See Freidman and Freidman (1980, p. 213), 'The environment'.
21. A reminder: pseudo-money seems to be a currency but cannot be spent or banked. The Department for Transport WebTAG Unit 3.5.6, table 1 sets the value of time to be £26.73 per hour, but if five minutes are shaved off your train journey you do not have an extra £2.23 in your pocket which you may spend on a cup of real coffee – it is pseudo-money.
22. Department for Transport (2007).
23. Department for Transport (2007), Paragraph 10.
24. Department for Transport (2007), Paragraph 31.
25. Department for Transport (2008).
26. Scottish Executive (2009), Paragraph 5.6.

Chapter 13

Mobility and accessibility

The definitions

Mobility and accessibility are two very similar concepts attracting similar policies, but they need to be clearly distinguished. Accessibility applies to places, identified either by their geographical location or by the activities taking place there. Mobility is concerned with people, either as individuals or as groups, their mobility being defined by the range of places and functions which they perceive to be accessible. Personal mobility is constrained by available time and money, by physical abilities, and by the extent and nature of the transport system. Accessibility concerns locations, and it too depends on the nature of the transport system within which they are located, the available terminal facilities (including car-parks, bus-stops and stations), and the services provided through the system.

An individual's mobility may be assessed by using the isochrone analysis, introduced in Chapter 6, to estimate the destination they are able to reach within an arbitrarily defined time from a particular starting point, usually their home. This defines the opportunities provided by the 'transport landscape' as they see it. Maximum mobility is a quasi-circular area of a radius defined by the mean speed of a car or taxi. At its limit, this area could conceivably cover the whole country, but the area becomes far more confined once the constraints of the individual's time and cash budgets are imposed. Areas accessible on foot and bicycle will also be quasi-circular, walking radii limited if medical conditions hamper speeds, and cycling radii reduced to zero for those without the ability to ride a bicycle. An individual's complete transport landscape will be an amalgam of the areas and places accessible by all the modes open to them. The areas reachable by modes other than on foot, bicycle, by car or taxi will be irregular rather than quasi-circular due to route availability and interface characteristics.

The shape of isochrones changes over time. In the very short term the isochrones and the areas they contain will pulse in step with service frequencies – in the middle of the night when services stop, headways and waiting times are effectively infinite and the shape of the accessible area shrinks to nothing. Longer time frames will alter the shapes as public transport routes, frequencies, reliabilities, fares and the characteristics of interchanges are modified. Changes in the nature of the transport system will have an effect: kneeling buses[1] giving easier boarding will improve the transport landscape for those with physical disabilities, in wheelchairs or with prams and buggies. For them modifications to interfaces, replacing steps with escalators or lifts, may cause considerable revisions of their perception of complete end-to-end journeys.

It is all too easy to group people into stereotypes. Some people are permanently disabled but everybody has periods of disability. The prospect of infirmity due to age awaits us all, but a youthful twisted ankle or 22 kg of holiday suitcase or a bag of shopping brings temporary disability. Of major importance is the change in mobility due to having to care for young children. Negotiating the transport system with a pram, buggy or toddler imposes an effective disability on most people at some time or another. Perhaps transport planners should be required as part of their professional accreditation to write a report on their experiences of a day's travel pushing a pram, even if it is empty. The overall picture is one in which the population of the 'disabled' is churning constantly as people join and leave, sometimes in the short term, sometimes in the long term.

Cash budgets may form a constraint upon the possible use of modes and therefore upon mobility. Cars and taxis offer almost limitless theoretical mobility but only to those with bottomless pockets and, even then, parking problems may create a ceiling that cannot be easily broken. Lack of disposable income creates economic disability and immobility. Glyncorrwg is at the head of a blind valley in South Wales. The prime employer was a mine and the majority of the miners had bought their own homes from the National Coal Board at knock-down prices. The mine closed in the early 1970s, destroying the local economy. The lack of alternative employment and the isolation of the village meant that houses were unsaleable, trapping families in their worthless homes. Even looking for work was nigh-on impossible: the nearest employment exchange was in Port Talbot, an expensive 80-minute bus ride away. The great majority of people, although fit and healthy, were as effectively disabled as if they were dependent upon broken wheelchairs – their mobility was negligible and many collapsed into a torpor of despair.

Mobility is a fairly simple concept, but creating an operational measure by which to assess the effectiveness of interventions to improve it is difficult. One general approach is to provide definitive, mandatory standards for the dimensions of steps, etc., such as those published by the Department for Transport.[2] Standards such as these do not require any monitoring of their local effectiveness, only of whether they are adequate as a general standard. The introduction to *Inclusive Mobility* does make the point that everybody is susceptible to being disabled from time to time and that the benefits of standardised staircases, etc. will not be confined to the long-term physically disabled but will be useful to everybody as they drift in and out of disability. However, it is the personal, long-term, physical disability at which most mobility policies are directed. The 'blue badge' scheme which exempts drivers with a certified disability from some parking regulations and may entitle them to use reserved spaces is an example. Fares may be discounted or even abolished for some groups: in Scotland, all travel by bus and coach, both long and short distance, is free to everybody aged 60 or over, whether disabled or not, and also to the medically disabled of all ages. This theoretically pushes the isochrone defining mobility to every town in Scotland, if not to every address.

A distinction must be made between such concession schemes and the discounts provided by 'senior' and 'student' railcards. These are marketing methods designed to increase revenue by protecting the full fares paid by those not claiming discounts[3] rather than improving individuals' mobility.

Resources are always limited and must be deployed to best effect. That poses the problem of how to measure the value for money of projects and investments designed to improve mobility. That is probably the wrong problem to address: the bus fare concessionary scheme has undoubtedly increased mobility, particularly in Scotland where free travel is more general than in England. In 2009 the Scottish scheme cost £200 million and was open to 1.1 million concessionary pass holders, £180 per year per head, about 50p per day. This poses the question of whether pass users get, on average, 50p of daily benefit. This is not defined by travel for which they would have paid 50p had they not held a pass, but by travel which they would not have been able to make had it not been for the pass. That transforms the question into 'Has travel worth £200 million been made which would have been suppressed without passes?' That question, too, is difficult, if not impossible, to answer, but it shifts the focus away from improvements to mobility, changes that would be hard to measure and even harder to justify, towards reducing the barriers to mobility – in other words, to design policy to reduce immobility rather than to enhance existing mobility. Since mobility is a very personal quality, dependent upon personal economics and personal fitness, that would shift the focus from a general provision to a selective targeting of those encountering physical or economic barriers to travel. It may then be appropriate to link schemes enhancing mobility to individuals' economic standing, through the tax system and to certified medical conditions, akin to disabled parking permits.

Shifts in the government's role

Since the early 1980s governments of all shades have been placing ever greater emphasis on the greater use of competitive pricing, combined with privatisation and outsourcing operations to contracted businesses. The ability of market forces to manage and coordinate activity effectively and cheaply has been claimed regularly; sometimes it appears to some extent that ideology supplants evidence. Responsibility for policy and action has been increasingly divided and compartmentalised, often by devolving responsibility from central to local government and from government to agencies and other 'partners' bound by contract rather than the traditional disciplines of personal employment. This has been associated with a change of scale from the strategic to the local and a change of time frame from the longer to the shorter term. It has also ensured a necessary multiplicity of organisations, objectives and budgets to deliver policy.

This shift has been at its strongest in transport. The Road Traffic Act (1930) tightly regulated the bus industry through a system of authorised fares together with licences for routes, buses and operating staff. In 1968 the bus industry was reorganised into municipal operators providing local urban services together with the subsidiaries of a new, state-owned National Bus Company mainly running longer distance, inter-urban routes but also serving some urban areas. In 1986 this structure was completely unpicked: ownerships were fragmented and privatised, and, outside London, fares and routes were left to be defined by the market. It epitomised the radical change in the balance between the state and market forces.

The railways received similar but far from identical treatment through the Railways Act (1993). This split British Railways, a single, monolithic, state-owned organisation, into a range of companies, some operating trains, others owning them and still others subcontracting maintenance, servicing, etc. British Railways had been created in 1948 by the nationalisation of four major railway companies which had themselves been formed by government edict in 1923 through the enforced amalgamation of 93 private companies. The changes of both 1923 and 1948 followed times of war during which the government had taken direct responsibility for coordinating railway operations, although ownership remained with the private companies. In both instances government had taken control because the internal market between railway companies was incapable of satisfying the needs of wartime traffic.

The change in scale and time frame of transport planning

The shift towards devolving responsibility for public transport was accompanied by shifts in the focus of land-use planning. Longer term, strategic planning lost emphasis, to be replaced by development control at site level. The two trends – first, changing the structure of the transport industry, and second, shifting the emphasis of land-use planning – combined to change transport planning and the methodology used to support it. Transport planning became less concerned with delivering major, expensive schemes requiring the use of extensive demand models and far more concerned with the traffic implications of the development of particular sites. Planning applications had to be accompanied by a 'Traffic Impact Analysis' prepared by the applicant. This supplanted the previous arrangements in which local authority staff had assessed the traffic implications as an integral part of making decisions on whether to grant or refuse permission. Later, the 'Traffic Impact Analyses' were extended to include walking, cycling and public transport, and were renamed 'Transport Impact Analyses'. Although it will be denied strenuously by those writing such documents, these analyses shifted from being tests of the suitability of the development to being advocacies supporting the application. Subsequently, applications for smaller sites no longer had to be accompanied by documents showing the transport implications, but developers of substantial sites were required to submit audits and statements in support of their planning application describing the ways in which their proposals were to be linked to the transport system and how these links were expected to be used.

Planning Policy Guidance Note 13: Transport (PPG13)

Within this atmosphere of change as the role of government shifted and as the nature of land use and transport planning altered, the government produced a radical change in the objectives of transport policy, although it was more radical in the statement than in the application. PPG13,[4] published in 1994, declared a shift in transport policy from 'Predict and Provide' to 'Travel Demand Management', a change from providing a network to meet predicted demand towards managing demand to fit the network. Surrey County Council had provided an overture by reaching the conclusion that solving traffic problems, principally those of congestion, could not be achieved by building more road space.[5] Road improvements designed to improve existing flows seemed to generate additional traffic, diluting their effectiveness. This was confirmed by a weighty government report prepared by SACTRA[6] showing that road improvement policies were in part self-defeating with the expected value for money eroded by extra traffic; in the long term the problem appeared to be outstripping the solution.

In theory, the previous methodology of predicting future flows by applying growth rates to the existing measured flows and then using those predictions to design and evaluate road schemes to provide more capacity ('Predict and Provide') should have been supplanted by entirely new methods of predicting the effects of attempts to manage travel behaviour. However, that change in methodology would have been dependent on an understanding of two crucial mechanisms:

1   If travel demand were to be managed by inducing people to make journeys by means other than the car, there has to be an operational model of people's choices between using a car for a journey and using some alternative combination of modes. This, in turn, depends, first, upon realising how complete end-to-end journeys are perceived, including the walking, waiting and interchanging, suggesting that walking is an integral part of all travel and not a separate mode used all the way from start to finish, the assumption usually made. Second, it depends on understanding that the interfaces between modes are critical components of the transport system.

2   The causes of the incessant changes in land use and urban structure. These are constantly, insidiously shifting, driven by individual and corporate quests for improved accessibility. Over recent decades the geographical distribution of residential, retail and commercial development has profoundly altered, but transport planning methodology has failed to analyse these changes with sufficient rigour to be able to predict them. The fault is best demonstrated by the repeated advocacy of road-user charging as a solution to transport problems on the assumption that, if using a car were made more expensive, people would use other modes: history shows this to be a false assumption. Over the years urban car use has become progressively more expensive due to fuel costs, parking charges and congestion, but the popular response has not been to switch modes but to move the ends of the journey to less congested places where travel is cheaper and less of a hassle. Road-user charging will reduce traffic in the places where charges are imposed, but only by displacing it to places where the costs are lower, accelerating the urban decentralisation and dispersal which are already apparent. It will relocate the problem, not solve it, and, incidentally, create longer journeys, more urbanised land and more pollution. There is evidence that the London congestion charge has achieved its intention of reducing traffic in

Central London but traffic in the outer suburbs and Home Counties has increased at a greater rate than in the rest of the country. It is a major failing of transport planning theory and practice that there is no way of knowing whether this is cause and effect or not.

In the absence of reliable predictions of people's reactions to managed changes in their transport landscapes and of the causal links between transport and land use, no model of managed travel demand could be developed and attention switched to the provision of accessibility.

The emphasis upon accessibility planning

The task of transport planning is to provide the most effective spread of accessibility that can be wrung out of the available resources. Transport infrastructures and services cannot provide uniform accessibility to all addresses. This is due partly to the simple, unavoidable consequence of geography: ports may only develop where the coastline is suitable and large cities cannot be built in mountainous terrain. But it is also a reflection of the necessarily limited extent of the transport system. The task of selecting beneficial extensions to the system is made both more complex and easier by the tendency for firms and individuals to locate in clusters at places matching their needs. The task is made easier due to the 'Matthew effect':[7] economic activity tends to cluster around places with good accessibility and it makes sense to improve that accessibility still further rather than spend resources on improving the accessibility of other, more sparsely developed places in the hope that it might generate new clusters. But the task is made more difficult because clustering is self-referential: better accessibility will attract more use of the transport infrastructure, but continuing increases in use may cause overloads and congestion, eroding accessibility. It is a puzzle that confronts many activities: success can foster failure as usage levels tip from the economies of scale into the diseconomies of scale. A small shop will be more effective with an increasing customer base but the effect will first fade and then reverse as it becomes too busy and too crowded. It happens at a personal level too: people perform with increasing effectiveness as they work harder or longer, but the improvement has a maximum beyond which there is too little time to do everything properly. It has been tagged the 'Goldilocks effect'.[8] The relationship between accessibility and development may therefore be characterised as a dynamic conflict between the Matthew and the Goldilocks effects.

The revised objective of manipulating travel demand to fit the transport network could not be delivered directly: that would have required policies and actions with the predictable effect of managing demand, but no mechanisms for making such predictions existed in 1994 when PPG13 was published: it still does not exist. The previous travel demand models used to provide the 'predictions' against which 'provisions' were tested were concerned with complete journeys from origin to destination, but only by a single, uninterrupted mode. They were intrinsically incapable of predicting seamless inter-modal travel that was needed to assess the success of demand management. An alternative had to be found.

The alternative was to duck the problem by focusing on improving access, particularly access to new development, implying an emphasis on journey ends rather than on the complete journey. The assumption was that if places were effectively served by non-car modes, people would use those modes and, in concert, would manage their own aggregate travel demands. It was another instance of definitive, instructive government designed to deliver firm policy being supplanted by aggregations of personal choices.

Transport Impact Analyses, accompanying planning applications and designed to inform the decision whether to grant or refuse permission, were reconstituted to include some consideration of sustainability, provoking another change of name to 'Transport Assessments'. The change of name covered more than the inclusion of aspects of sustainability. The Department for Transport's *Guidance on Transport Assessment*[9] sets out their form and purpose:

> **Para 4.1** A detailed Transport Assessment will be required where a proposal (as described within a planning application) is likely to have a significant transport and related environmental impact.
>
> **Para 4.3** Transport Assessments should address the following issues:
> - Reducing the need for travel, especially by car
> - Sustainable accessibility
> - Dealing with residual trips
> - Mitigations.

This is a good parable demonstrating the ongoing, but largely unsung, changes to the role of government. The purpose of the original Traffic Impact Analysis was to ensure that new developments would not overwhelm the local road network: they reflected a basic policy of restricting development to match the capacity of the road network and were required to provide numerical evidence that the traffic generated by the proposed development could be loaded on to the local roads without provoking problems. That was an implicit criterion which, if transgressed, could and did lead to refusals of planning consent. In contrast, Transport Assessments require the issues in Para 4.3 to be no more than 'addressed'. The applicant has to show that the process has been complied with, not that it has resulted in evidence that specified criteria have been met.

Guidance on Transport Assessment is a strange document. It establishes the purpose of an Assessment:

> **Para 1.2** A Transport Assessment is a comprehensive and systematic process that sets out transport issues relating to a proposed development. It identifies what measures will be taken to deal with the anticipated transport impacts of the scheme and to improve accessibility and safety for all modes of travel, particularly for alternatives to the car such as walking, cycling and public transport.

It then jumps from the 'issues related to a proposed development' to the actions necessary to deliver the government's strategic objectives, a leap from the local, immediate issues to the national, long-term objectives:

Para 1.11 The desired actions are given as:
- new capacity, where it is needed and justified on environmental and social grounds;
- locking in the benefits of new capacity through measures such as high occupancy vehicle lanes and tolling, where appropriate;
- the Government leading the debate on road pricing and the opportunity this gives to motorists to make better choices;
- better management of the network;
- using new technology, so the travelling public can make smarter journey choices.

In terms of enhancing local travel, this implies:
- freer-flowing local roads delivered through measures such as congestion charging;
- more, and more reliable buses enjoying more road space;
- more demand-responsive bus services that provide accessibility in areas that cannot support conventional services;
- looking at ways to make services more accessible, so that people have a real choice about when and how they travel;
- tackling the environmental impacts of travel by encouraging more sustainable travel choices through promoting the use of school travel plans, workplace travel plans and personalised journey planning, and encouraging people to consider alternatives to using their cars;
- creating a culture and improved quality of local environment, so that cycling and walking are seen as an attractive alternative to car travel for short journeys, particularly for children.

Although this list of actions is desirable, it is not at all clear how individual site developers are able to deliver them: the list cannot be the criteria by which an application may be granted or refused.

The document goes on with another list, this time of the issues to be addressed in the Assessment:

Para 1.19 In preparing a Transport Assessment the following considerations will therefore be relevant.

Encouraging environmental sustainability:
- Reducing the need to travel, especially by car – reducing the need for travel, reducing the length of trips, and promoting multi-purpose or linked trips by promoting more sustainable patterns of development and more sustainable communities that reduce the physical separation of key land uses.
- Tackling the environmental impact of travel – by improving sustainable transport choices, and by making it safer and easier for people to access jobs, shopping, leisure facilities and services by public transport, walking, and cycling.

- The accessibility of the location – the extent to which a site is, or is capable of becoming, accessible by non-car modes, particularly for large developments that involve major generators of travel demand.
- Other measures which may assist in influencing travel behaviour (ITB) – achieving reductions in car usage (particularly single occupancy vehicles), by measures such as car sharing/pooling, High Occupancy Vehicle (HOV) lanes and parking control.

Managing the existing network: Making best possible use of existing transport infrastructure – for instance by:
- low-cost improvements to the local public transport network and using advanced signal control systems, public transport priority measures (bus lanes), or other forms of Intelligent Transport Systems (ITS) to improve operations on the highway network. It should be noted that the capacity of the existing public transport infrastructure and footpaths is finite, and in some areas overcrowding already exists.
- Managing access to the highway network – taking steps to maximise the extent to which the development can be made to 'fit' within the available capacity by managing access from developments onto the highway network.

Mitigating residual impacts:
- Through demand management – using traffic control measures across a wide network to regulate flows.
- Through improvements to the local public transport network, and walking and cycling facilities – for example, by extending bus routes and increasing bus frequencies, and designing sites to facilitate walking and cycling.
- Through minor physical improvements to existing roads – it may be possible in some circumstances to improve the capacity of existing roads by relatively minor physical adjustments such as improving the geometry of junctions etc. within the existing highway boundary.
- Through provision of new or expanded roads – it is considered good transport planning practice to demonstrate that the other opportunities above have been fully explored before considering the provision of additional road space such as new roads or major junction upgrades.

As with the previous lists, these targets cannot be delivered by the applicant. The resolution to this conundrum is that, although the developer is responsible for writing the Transport Assessment, the responsibility for implementing it may well rest with other 'partners and stakeholders' including, but not limited to, the local authority whose legal duty it is to grant or refuse planning permission. This not only enables horse-trading – it demands it. The flavour of the process is implied by:

Para 1.20 Consideration of these matters should take place at an early stage in the process of preparing a development proposal. Work on developing the Transport Assessment can then help inform, and be informed by, discussions about the location of the site and the scale and mix of uses proposed.

The implication is that developers do not apply for planning permission but negotiate for it. Such a regime cannot deliver firm policies, since delivery can be no more than the sum of decisions reached through negotiations between a number of disparate parties, each with its own objectives and priorities. Since many of those parties will not view environmental objectives as important or urgent, even if they have been nominally accepted, the negotiations are unlikely to set much store on the reduction of pollutants. The tenor of Transport Assessments is made clear in this paragraph:

> **Para 4.6** . . . The Transport Assessment should indicate the transport aspects of the proposal, how the proposal will help to deliver the aims and objectives of the development plan, and how it responds to relevant Government planning policy guidance and statements.

Developers are not required to conform to government policy but to demonstrate how their proposals might 'help to deliver the government's aims and objectives'. This is an incentive to strike a posture of compliance without necessarily meeting the government's wishes and also to minimise any suggestion that the proposals were contrary to government policy. It is certain that no developer is going to do anything other than minimise the risk of refusal and avoid providing any evidence to support a refusal should a planning appeal and inquiry ensue. This paragraph sums up the basic objective behind Transport Assessments:

> **Para 4.51** The key issue is the need to ensure that development proposals strive to achieve nil-detriment ('no worse off') to the strategic network, for the opening year and appropriate horizon year.

If there were any real importance and urgency in fulfilling the policy objectives set out in Paragraph 1.19 and reproduced above, the 'key issue' would be rather more ambitious than 'nil-detriment'.

The whole document epitomises the changes that have occurred in the way in which the government expects to realise its policies and targets. The traditional view, that the state made general, strategic policy, implementing it through a combination of legal regulation and the deployment of state expenditure, has been replaced by the view that policies are best delivered through an aggregate of decisions made by individuals, firms and corporate bodies. In practice, it is simply a conflict between top-down, explicit government and bottom-up, implicit government. This was not a party political divide. New Labour were as committed to minimal regulation coupled with devolved decision-making as were the Conservatives.[10]

The emphasis upon the delivery of government policy by the aggregate of informal, personal decisions was made by the later 'Smarter Choices' campaign.[11] This advocated the adoption of 'Travel Plans' by individuals, firm and schools. These could not be binding and were an element in an awareness campaign to induce the use of cars to be forgone. It has not met with general success.

Scepticism about the likelihood of government policy being delivered by myriad personal decisions may well attract criticism based on a distinction between personal freedom and state compulsion. Of course there has to be both: there is little debate that murder and violence should be the concern of the state and not be left to individuals within vigilante groups. On the other hand, state control over criticisms of the state is important evidence of the erosion of freedom. The boundaries between the legitimate and illegitimate concerns of the state are a major presence of today's political landscape, but the scepticism over Transport Assessments and over the whole spectrum of sustainable policy is not about whether the state should have policies or not; it is about whether those policies should be enforced by law or left to personal choice. The wearing of seat-belts, the use of mobile phones while driving, restrictions on noise and chemical pollutants are all invasions of personal freedom that some people resent to the extent of flaunting them. Nonetheless, laws have been written and enforced: the alternative would have been to inform the population, perhaps reinforcing the information with impositions of tax, but allowing individuals to make their own choices akin to the choices provided by the Victorians over tobacco and alcohol.

One fundamental aspect of the problem is whether the policy objective is absolute or relative; whether the target is solution or mitigation. If it is absolute, then compulsion appears to be unavoidable. Leaving outcomes to the sum of unknowable personal choices will mitigate the problem, but to an unpredictable degree. The view of earlier chapters was that the nature and extent of climate change is not absolutely predictable, but that there is a considerable risk of irreversible global damage. Wise counsel would seem to be to plan for the risk to be high because if that assumption turns out to be wrong then little damage will have been done, but if we do little or nothing and that turns out to have been wrong, then we will have damaged the planet beyond repair. In that case, it seems to be irresponsible for the government not to be decisive, writing policies and ensuring that they are put into effect by state action, not by personal choice. If that is so, documents such as *Guidance on Transport Assessment* are totally inadequate in protecting our future. We need much more robust, firm legislation similar to that on air and noise pollution, legislation that defines and legally imposes standards of behaviour.

The theory of accessibility

The dictionary definition of accessible is simply 'within reach'. The something which is in reach must be either a place or a function located in a place: it is the destination. This leaves open the questions of from where, by whom and by what means it is reachable. The seminal answers to those questions were provided by Hansen.[12] 'From where' is from everywhere else – from all possible journey origins; 'by whom' is everybody who might make the journey from any one of the possible origins to the target destination; and 'by what means' does not matter because the important attribute of the journey is the 'cost', not the hardware used.

Hansen's paper, in common with the theory of the time, took the 'cost' of journeys to be either the physical distance from origin to destination, or the time taken to make the journey or an amalgam of the time and the out-of-pocket expense, a metric that requires time to be given a cash value. This amalgam is called the 'generalised cost' and it may be expanded to include waiting and walking times, comfort, safety, etc., all of which must be listed in a tariff used to convert them into cash equivalents (actually pseudo-cash equivalents because money does not change hands: for example, if a journey is uncomfortable the traveller is none the richer by the cash value placed upon comfort).[13]

The other feature of Hansen's analysis is that the 'cost' of a journey, no matter how it is measured, is seen to be a deterrent to making the journey. If a journey is very 'expensive' because it is slow, or involves awkward interchanges, or the fares are high, then the likelihood of making the journey is lessened, but quick, cheap journeys are much more likely to be made. Hansen also accepted the principle that the deterrent effect becomes increasingly strong with the length of the journey so that a journey costing, say, 10 units (as measured in pounds, minutes, pseudo-pence; it matters not) will have a greater deterrent effect than twice the effect of 5 units. This effect is reproduced arithmetically by raising the cost to a power. If that power is assumed to be 2, as it is with Newtonian measures of gravity, then the deterrence is the square of the measured cost – a journey costing 3 actual units has an apparent equivalent effect upon people's perception of the journey as would 9 units. Empirical studies showed the power to be rather less than 2 – somewhere around 1.20; nevertheless, estimates of accessibility using journey cost raised to a power are still called 'Gravity models' even if the power is other than 2.

Hanson was really calculating probabilities (chances or bets) of journeys being made from one of the possible origins to the target destination. He argued that the probability increased with the number of people at the origin who might make the journey (the more people, the more journeys), but the probability decreased with the deterrence effect (the longer or more expensive the journey, the fewer journeys would be made). This conflict between the tendencies to make journeys or fewer journeys may be estimated by a simple division ((the number of people who might make a journey)/(the deterrence)). This is just a number that will grow with the numbers of potential travellers at the origin, but reduce with the deterrence of the journey.

If a similar number is calculated for all the possible origins, and all those numbers are added together, the destination may be labelled as an 'accessibility score'. That in itself would be meaningless, but if the same calculation were made for all the possible destination places, each one being given an accessibility score which was the sum of the probabilities from each of the possible origins, then the scores could be ranked in order, showing that some places were more accessible than others and, moreover, the degree by which they were more accessible. To make such an estimate, an analyst would have to divide an area into zones, ascertain the population of each zone, establish the generalised cost of travel between the zones, calculate the probability index for each pair of zones (the origin population divided by the deterrence), sum the indices for each destination and then rank them. When Hansen wrote his paper in 1959 that was quite a tall order – computers had only just come on to the market, but this was just the sort of project for which they were suited.

The Hansen measures reflect the capabilities of the transport system in providing access, but then weight those capabilities by the numbers of people who might use them, numbers which are themselves weighted by the 'cost' of the journey: they are therefore good measures, although very general. They have the desirable quality of placing considerable emphasis upon journey 'cost': when these costs become excessive, the probability of journey-making (the numbers of potential travellers divided by the deterrence) tends towards zero, placing some origins beyond reach.

The generality of Hansen measures as explained thus far is not intrinsic to the method. It is possible to stratify the population at any particular origin by counting the numbers of schoolchildren or those needing to access outpatient departments. It is also possible to be selective about modes and combinations of modes of transport, establishing the 'costs' of transport by each, but it always needs to be borne in mind that this method produces comparative, not absolute results. Thus it may be used by commercial companies to select sites, working out the Hansen factors for each and establishing the most preferable. The preferable locations of in-town 'local' supermarkets are determined in this way.

In practice, Hansen measures are normally calculated using a matrix. The convention is to place the origins down the side so that there is one row for each origin, and the destinations along the top with one column per destination. Figure 13.1 shows a hypothetical demonstration matrix with the populations of each of the origin zones in place and the cells of the matrix showing the journey costs between all origin and destination pairs. These are symmetric, the normal pattern when costs are quoted in distances; other measures of 'cost' (travel times, generalised or composite costs) commonly show differences between movement in one direction or the other.

'Costs' are given in inverted commas to remind readers that journey costs are not necessarily measured in cash or even pseudo-cash: they may be distances (as they are in Figures 13.1–13.3) or times, or some combination of various journey attributes as in generalised costs. Figure 13.2 shows these journey costs as they are weighted by the power of 1.3 to emphasise the increasing effect of the journey 'cost' with increasing distance. Figure 13.3 shows the further weighting by the 'size' and attractiveness of the destination, as indicated by its population.

The journey costs may be those of a particular mode or of an inter-modal combination, including the cost penalties of negotiating interfaces. The pattern of costs (and the subsequent pattern of accessibilities) across the matrix reflects the shape of the isochrones: cars, walking and cycling have quasi-circular isochrones and the patterns across the matrix are fairly uniform, but with one very important

Origin		Destination zone					
Zone #	Population	1	2	3	4	5	6
1	950	0	3	3	10	13	13
2	1200	3	0	3	6	7	6
3	600	3	3	0	12	10	8
4	350	10	6	12	0	4	11
5	750	13	7	10	4	0	6
6	875	13	6	8	11	6	0

Figure 13.1 Hansen accessibility: journey 'costs' (kilometres)

Mobility and accessibility 215

Origin		Destination zone					
Zone #	Population	1	2	3	4	5	6
1	950	0.00	3.74	3.74	15.85	21.71	21.71
2	1200	3.74	0.00	3.74	8.59	10.33	8.59
3	600	3.74	3.74	0.00	19.73	15.85	12.13
4	350	15.85	8.59	19.73	0.00	5.28	17.77
5	750	21.71	10.33	15.85	5.28	0.00	8.59
6	875	21.71	8.59	12.13	17.77	8.59	0.00

Figure 13.2 Hansen accessibility: deterrence values = ('costs')$^{1.3}$

Origin		Destination zone					
Zone #	Pop.	1	2	3	4	5	6
1	950		254.20	254.20	59.94	43.75	43.75
2	1200	321.10		321.10	139.77	116.16	139.77
3	600	160.55	160.55		30.42	37.86	49.48
4	350	22.08	40.76	17.74		66.31	19.70
5	750	34.54	72.60	47.32	142.10		87.35
6	875	40.30	101.91	72.16	49.24	101.91	
	TOTAL	578.57	630.03	712.52	421.47	366.00	340.05
	Rank	3	2	1	4	5	6

Figure 13.3 Hansen accessibility: accessibility factors = population/('costs')$^{1.3}$

variation – matrices showing journey costs and accessibility by car will show journeys to urban centres to be relatively more 'expensive' as the penalties of congestion and parking play an increasing role.

Public transport matrices will show the complete opposite. Since public transport is largely radial, serving town centres better than elsewhere, there is a bias in public transport 'cost' and accessibility matrices towards access to central areas being relatively 'cheap'. That tendency is reinforced by public transport journeys between suburbs often requiring a deviation and change of route in the town centre, with the additional 'cost' making such journeys relatively 'expensive'.

The differences between car and public transport matrices are telling: if the car/public transport ratios are calculated cell by cell, there will be a different ratio for each origin–destination pair. Cells representing urban centres will be biased towards public transport reflecting the relatively high car 'cost' due to approach congestion and parking and the relatively low public transport 'cost' due to routes being radial and frequencies at their best. Even then, the car 'cost' may be the lower, helped by the need to walk to a bus-stop and wait there for a bus, a burden avoided when using a car. On the other hand, public transport avoids the burden of finding, capturing and keeping a parking space. That advantage will be reflected in the car/public transport 'cost' ratio, a ratio which may be further enhanced if public transport can be protected from congestion.

There are three very important conclusions to be drawn from this analysis of the differences and rationale of 'costs' and accessibility:

1 Comparisons between modes cannot make sense unless the comparison is for complete journeys including the incidental walking, waiting, interchanging, parking and congestion.
2 Isochrones vary over time, pulsing with service frequencies, with the raising and lowering of barriers, perhaps due to changing personal circumstances, perhaps to the nature of the transport system.
3 Blanket policies covering entire areas are inappropriate. The car/public transport ratios vary widely, reflecting the strengths and weaknesses of both. Given urban structure and geography as it now stands, public transport cannot provide acceptable levels of service for many journeys and unselective policies to manage travel demand will fail, but cars are unsuited to journeys in and to urban centres. Travel demand management depends for its credibility and effectiveness on selecting journeys, modes and places where it will work: there are no prizes for flying in the face of reality.

The effects of density

The contrary Matthew and Goldilocks effects of the clustering of transport demand are made the more complex when considered in the context of mode. Chapter 6 was concerned with the impacts of changing accessibility upon land use and cites the example of the M25. The construction of this motorway made a step change in the accessibility of swathes of the Home Counties, leading to both the development of many new sites and the redevelopment of many existing ones, intensifying their use. The consequent increases in traffic overwhelmed the capacity of the new motorway which became notoriously congested, choking off further improvements in accessibility and leading to vociferous demands for the capacity of the road to be increased, even though it had only recently been completed and opened: the Matthew effect writ large and overwhelming Goldilocks (see p. 207 above).

One of the major developments served by the M25 is Heathrow Airport. The expansion of the airport's activity was not due to the M25, although, had the motorway not been built, its growth may well have been stunted. Airports are not simply interchanges between ground and air: they spawn a wide range of services for the aircraft, for the airlines, for the staff and for the passengers. Just as port-related industry clustered around seaports a century or so ago, so modern industry dependent upon air freighting expensive components clusters around modern airports. There are about 100,000 jobs within the immediate airport area and many others within the vicinity.

Roads and cars cannot cope with that number and density of journeys to work. Road capacity at about 1500 cars per hour per lane cannot keep pace, even with high car occupancy rates, but, more tellingly, sufficient parking could not be provided within acceptable walking distances from either the workplace or the check-in. At first, public transport access to Heathrow was limited to extensive bus services, but in December 1977 the Piccadilly tube line was extended to the airport: it provides 12 trains per hour at a capacity of 1238 places per train,[14] a total of 14,800 places per hour. This service was supplemented by a second line, the Heathrow Express in 1998 with four trains per hour, each with 414 seats.[15] The two lines together provide a capacity of 16,500 places per hour, the equivalent of two lanes of motorway used solely by fully laden five-seater cars, a flow that would require 3.6 hectares of parking space for every hour's flow. This simple arithmetic hints at a fundamental difference. Cars need space to move and to park, and are therefore unsuited to provide access to areas developed to high density. That proposition may be reversed – that high densities are unsuited to cars. As car ownership and use has grown, so densities, measured in terms of origins and destinations per hectare, have steadily declined: the examples given in Chapter 4 demonstrate this case.

But the reverse is true for public transport. To operate without subsidy, public transport needs to carry a payload, a level of demand that has to be attracted by a combination of frequency, reliability and spread of stops. That combination has to be supported by high densities of development. A similar but contrary dichotomy is true for moving vehicles. Any concentration of traffic on particular roads, junctions or destinations precipitates congestion, so traffic is best dispersed over the road network. Concentrations of demand on public transport create the frequencies that retain expanded demand – Heathrow Airport is a demonstration: two rail services provide service levels that can only be sustained by a high density of demand but also those high levels of demand may only be satisfied by tracked systems. The link between density and mode is self-referential. It seems that the Matthew effect dominates in public transport while the Goldilocks effect drives road traffic.

The patterns of accessibility and mobility are constantly changing and the dynamic link between density of demand and the modes catering for that demand are always shifting. The prime source of the changes is car ownership. Over the past years the expenditure on maintaining and improving the road network in Britain had been, roundly, £8 billion per year. Approximately £30 billion per year has been spent on buying new cars. If the spend on other new vehicles is included, the ratio is of the order of £5 being spent on vehicles for every £1 spent on the road network carrying them. To that should be added the private investments of site developers in car-parking (in terminal facilities), an overall investment that is creating ever-increasing personal mobility and accessibility, not just as an absolute measure but, more importantly, relatively to public transport. This suggests that transport policies with sustainable objectives must have related policies on density and location of development. It also emphasises the suggestion that transport policy must be spatially differential, focusing on public transport where the size and density preclude adequate parking provision but accepting that car use elsewhere will be the choice of most people. The infinite frequency and flexibility of cars is undeniable.

Notes

1. 'Kneeling' buses are those with adjustable springing to the front wheels, enabling the step height to be reduced when the bus is stationary.
2. Department for Transport (2005a).
3. In theory, some people may have been willing to pay more for a product than the price actually charged, a benefit enjoyed by the consumer at the expense of lost revenue by the provider, a benefit termed the 'consumer surplus'. To increase total revenue, firms charge a high price but then discount it for those who are unwilling or unable to pay that price. Thus 'senior' and 'student' railcards are devices to sell tickets at a lower fare better suited to them, but retaining the high fares for those willing and able to pay them. Traditional stylised child fares, excursion tickets, etc. are driven by the same theory.
4. Departments of the Environment and of Transport (1994).
5. The draft county structure plan (1993) contained an explicit objective *not* to meet the full demand for travel, particularly during the peak hours and in town centres.
6. The Standing Advisory Committee on Trunk Road Assessment (1994).
7. The Gospel according to St Matthew, chapter 13, verse 12: 'For whosoever hath shall be given and he shall have more abundance: but whosoever hath not, from him shall be taken away.'
8. From the children's story in which Goldilocks deems things are either too much or too little until she settles for things being 'just right' – a happy medium.
9. Department for Transport (2007a).
10. Although there were divisions between Old and New Labour which were apparent in transport policy-making. Paradoxically, the transport White Paper *A New Deal for Transport: Better for Everyone* (Department for the Environment, Transport and the Relgions 1998) bore a title suggesting the focus was on the individual but contained top-down strategies defined by government while the legislation, particularly the 2000 Transport Act, sang the counterpoint, concentrating on devolved decision-making.
11. Department for Transport (2005b).
12. Hansen (1959).
13. Purists will claim that it may well be possible to buy more comfort by travelling first class or by car, and therefore the extra cost of doing so has been 'saved' if the discomfort has been endured. Such 'savings' are imaginary and cannot be spent.
14. www.tfl.gov.uk.
15. www.heathrowexpress.com.

Chapter 14

Controlling costs

Accounting for intangibles

Sustainability does not, and cannot, have a commercial value. At the meta-scale a price cannot be placed upon the risk of damaging the planet's future; at the individual scale, personal health and future well-being cannot be bought and sold at a market value. It follows that the commercial mechanisms of market forces and profitability alone will be unable to deliver the desired objectives. This is far from unique: the word 'war' seems to be used politically to mark out those areas of policy in which market and price mechanisms are muted or even absent. The 'wars' on terrorism, on drugs, on communism, on crime are extremely expensive but do not attract stern questions about their value for money: they enjoy almost open cheque-book finance.

There is a political and public perception that non-commercial actions are an open invitation to waste, inefficiency and possible corruption, a perception supported by an undeniable history of incompetence within organisations which lack proper financial discipline. But that history is evident in organisations supposedly driven by profit as well as in others: the financial sector is littered with dead and crippled companies brought down by poor financial discipline. The recent financial crash prompted by sub-prime mortgages but magnified by excessive government expenditure, is a demonstration of the constant need to link explicit, attainable objectives with proper accounting. The common error is to define 'proper accounting' by maximising differences between revenue and expenditure, but that is impracticable whenever 'revenue' is intangible. The woes of the financial sector were magnified by poor evaluations of risk, intangible before an event but all too tangible after.

A modern device to resolve this problem is to 'value' such intangibles in an arbitrary pseudo-currency; for example, a death in a road accident is valued at £1,535,510.[1] There is even a mechanism by which this figure may be updated. This is numerical economics run riot.[2] Those advocating the use of such numbers argue that it is necessary in order to prevent excessive expenditure on road safety but the arithmetic is extremely shaky. It rests entirely upon predicting deaths: first, without proposed safety measures, and second, with them. The difference between these two predictions is held to be the 'saving' in deaths and is 'valued', in the official methodology set out in government documents, to the nearest £10. The probability of both 'without' and 'with' predictions being correct is negligible and, even if they were (something that nobody can ever know), nobody will have benefited financially. It is an indefensible statistical fig-leaf.

That is not an argument against any attempt to assess and control expenditure. On the contrary, producing desirable effects at minimum cost is vital: the mistake is to convert the intangible and unpredictable into some quasi-currency and then to relate it to real money expenditure. Extending the example of deaths in road accidents, the circumstances which create potential accidents are well known: they are statistically related to the number of conflict points, the volumes of traffic passing through them and vehicle speeds. Such data may be used to create an index of risk which does not have to be 'valued' by tagging it with pseudo-monetary 'cost'. The task is to reduce the index of risk at an acceptable expenditure. What is 'acceptable' cannot be some blanket, arbitrary figure because the cost of safety measures and their effectiveness will vary from site to site: hence the cost per unit reduction in risk will range widely. The nub of this argument is that a methodology for assessing the effectiveness of policy decisions and of the expenditure they incur is vital, but tariffs to place monetary or pseudo-monetary values on the effects are not. This carries an implication that attempts to aggregate benefits should be avoided: the prime purpose when using a value for road deaths is to allow the purported reductions in deaths credited to a road improvement scheme to be bundled together with other benefits, particularly the savings in travel time. It is a strange metric reported as money but in neither case is the money spendable, and in both cases the value is a statistically derived representative value that has been arbitrarily assigned. The ratio between the two (£1,535,510 for a death and £26.43 per car driver hour or £17.00 per cyclist hour[3]) shows that a death has the same value as 90,000 hours spent riding a bike but only 58,000 hours of driving a car. If sustainability were to be 'valued' in the same bizarre game there would be a figure showing how many human deaths would equate to risking the death of the planet. In truth, there is no reason to aggregate benefits of road schemes. There is no possible trade-off of the sort implied by the ratios of 'values' ascribed to different benefits, and so it would be reasonable to keep time savings and reductions in the risk of accidents in separate metrics without the implied weightings of allocated 'values'. In planning sustainable transport, the effect of reducing CO_2 is not precisely known, the risks are not known and a monetary evaluation of those risks is not only impossible but would be foolish. Taking the emission of CO_2 as the touchstone, our policy should be to reduce it at a sensible, payable expenditure and leave it at that.

Nonetheless, some accounting of the cost of delivering objectives is necessary. Unaccountable costs and open cheques are inevitably abused no matter whether they are subsidies designed to do no more then cover operational deficits, or monopolies, private or public, where revenue comes too easily and lax accounting fails to justify expenditure. However, controlling accountable costs is easier said than done: even the definition of 'cost' is problematic. Monetary costs are the expenditures without which delivery of the objective would be impossible. Some of these will be historical capital costs that are difficult to count; many will be operational costs and consumables that are easier to account, but may be difficult to debit to particular actions. Still others will be impositions upon other people for which they have to pay in some currency or another. The military call these impositions 'co-lateral damage': economists call them 'externalities'. They are the incidental side-effects of projects, the costs or disbenefits of which are borne by people external to the project promoters. For example, a bypass or a new railway may well impose pollutantss of all sorts upon people living nearby. Any compensation or the cost of mitigations such as noise barriers effectively monetise some part of the externalities but the rest are just imposed upon those affected.

This raises the general question of whether such impositions should be debited against the project to enable some notion of either the absolute project cost, or relative to the costs of other schemes. There seems to be a very weak case for excluding externalities: it implies a bias against those who have intangible costs thrust upon them and in favour of those who benefit directly from the project, a conflict that may be characterised by partiality in favour of people and freight moving through an area and against the people and activities within it. The contrast seems to be primarily between the benefits derived from the explicit objectives driving a project and the ancillary effects which are implied by the project, but not the objectives in themselves.

Both of these categories will have both gains and losses which may be set against one another to produce a net count: given that the prime objective driving transport schemes is to improve accessibility by reducing travel times, there will always be a minority effect of some travel distances and times being increased due to diversions, severance, etc. It is the net change in accessibility that is the measure of success in reaching the objective. The same must be true of the ancillary effects: some will be beneficial, the removal of pollutants from the bypassed roads to be used to offset the 'costs' of pollutants upon people and property near the bypass itself.

Two propositions have now arisen:

1   That effects may be divided into two major categories, those which represent the actual prime objective and those which do not.
2   That both of these categories must be net, with the negative effects (costs) being offset against the positive effects (the benefits).

The third aspect of contemporary methodology[4] is whether all the net effects in both categories should be bundled together to create a composite net 'cost'. If that is to be done, then all effects have to be brought to a common unit of account (usually money) using a tariff of conversion factors ('prices'). That tariff is difficult to create and even more difficult to justify, since it implies relative values that may be unpalatable – for example, a time saving of just one minute by each car driver in one year's flow on one lane of motorway has roughly the same value as somebody's death.[5] The unpalatability increases if the common unit of account is used to offset some qualities of a project against others (perhaps 'selling' the environment to 'buy' motorists time savings), but such disapproval is hollow, since bringing everything to a common measure of account has no purpose other than aggregating, offsetting and so prioritising the various costs and benefits. If that process is unacceptable there is no real need to combine effects, no need to have a common unit of account, no need for a tariff to convert time savings and accidents and pollutants, all measured in their appropriate units, into common but artificial units. Putting a pound sign in front of a number does not make it real money: real money can be banked and credited to be used later to pay for any choice of good or service. If that cannot be done then it is not real money. Similarly, unless conversion factors are verifiable by simple, direct experiment, as with conversions of imperial into SI units, the tariffs are bound to be questionable and to produce values which are not completely compatible with measurements made initially in the appropriate units.

The conclusion has to be that objectives should be achieved at the lowest 'cost' in each of a number of categories and units. Of course it is unlikely that minimal 'costs' will be achievable simultaneously in all categories and that decisions will have to be made using implicit weightings attached to each category. However, it is right that the weightings should be allowed to vary from case to case.

It is rather like choosing a house to buy. Even if they are not written down, there will be rankings under a number of headings: the living space, the kitchen, the bathroom, etc., and each heading will have a weighting, although it may be no more than a prejudice. However, the weightings themselves will vary from one potential buyer to another.

Accounting for expenditure in real money

Costs and benefits measureable in real money using real prices and expenditure are less contentious than scoring intangibles, and, although easier to cope with, are not without their problems. The difficulty of combining large single capital costs with day-to-day operating costs has been addressed in Chapter 10. There the suggestion was made that depreciation should be abandoned in favour of amortisation with a presumption that all capital is borrowed, perhaps from a variety of sources with the amount borrowed having to be paid back together with the interest over the working life of whatever asset was bought with the loan. This gives a fixed annual payment which may then be easily combined with the operating costs to give a total annual cost. Figure 10.5 used this to provide estimated costs per year, per work-hour and per tonne- or seat-kilometre of available capacity.

Repaying the loan with interest over the operational life of an asset makes sense for vehicles and other assets with a known life and, perhaps, with a salvage value at the end of that life. However, some acquisitions have an indeterminate life or a life at the end of which there is no salvage value, preventing the period of loan from being aligned with the life of the asset. A good example is the track bed and bridges of a railway or rapid transit line. The track itself will have a finite life which may be estimated and the annual amortised cost calculated. Unless both the engineers estimating the life of the track and the accountants arranging the loan are blessed with extraordinary good luck, the loan will not be discharged at exactly the same time as the track comes up for renewal, but the disparity will not be important: the renewal will be covered by a new loan in an extended, slow cycle of regular renewals linked to updated amortised costs. But the structural right of way, the bridges, cuttings, embankments and drainage will not require complete renewal, just routine, fairly predictable maintenance. Nor will they have any residual or salvage value – pre-used embankments never appear on 'e-bay': they exist, more or less, in perpetuity rather like Roman aqueducts. Such semi-permanent capital expenditure is usually called 'sunk cost': the money has been spent but is irretrievable.

It is theoretically possible to raise a loan with no discharge date but upon which the interest is payable in perpetuity. Although debts may be traded, enabling lenders to retrieve at least part of their loan earlier than had previously been arranged, this is usually a costly arrangement. Very long-term commercial loans stretching out into perpetuity are therefore uncommon. For commercial companies the more usual way of gathering long-term capital is to sell shares entitling the shareholders to 'dividends', namely a proportion of the company's profits, rather than interest. Dividends cannot be predetermined but are a residual after prearranged costs have been paid out of the company's revenue, so making the out-turn expense of capital provision by shareholders unpredictable. In making calculations of cost, it is better to assume that share capital is, in fact, a loan upon which a standard rate of interest is payable and then calculate a post-hoc adjustment once dividends have been declared. In practice this means that all share capital, irrespective of source or of use, is treated as though it were an interest-only mortgage.

To some extent even this does not help in making useful cost calculations, since sunk costs cannot really be tied to particular historical expenditures. For example, the Forth Bridge was built in 1890 by an independent company with the construction costs met by the sale of shares. In 1921 these shares were compulsorily purchased and given to the LNER company. With the nationalisation of the railways in 1948, the LNER shares were compulsorily purchased and became the property of the state. However, their ghost remains. The costs of the compulsory purchases were covered by extending the National Debt which is largely in the form of Government Bonds, the holders of which are entitled to an annual payment of interest. A miniscule proportion of the current National Debt is actually the sunk cost of the Forth Bridge. The National Debt also contains faint traces of earlier railway construction: a financial archaeologist should be able to find a flicker of debt due to the 1825 Stockton and Darlington Railway, even though part of it is now disused and the original shareholders together with their shares are long gone. In 1863 the shares were bought by the North Eastern Railway whose shares were then compulsorily bought and given to the LNER in 1921, only to be acquired by the state in 1948 by the same extension of the National Debt that brought the whole railway system, including the Forth Bridge, into national ownership. The interest payments upon debt incurred by sunk costs cannot be sensibly added into contemporary costings: they are there, but no action is possible to shed them and they cannot be manipulated to improve efficiency. They are an unaccountable burden – a financial gene.

Many capital items with a long life and no salvage value represent sunk costs, but are closely related to other capital assets which do require maintenance and, perhaps, renewal. Track, for example, has to be laid over embankments and through cuttings and tunnels which are sunk capital, but the track itself has a need to be maintained and renewed, incurring continuing cost. In the days when British Railways was a single coordinated organisation, each line was categorised by the speeds and axle weights it could accommodate with the signalling designed to cope with the necessary braking distances, stopping patterns and frequencies. These specifications required expenditure on maintenance and upon capital renewals and enhancements. Joy[6] estimated the out-turn track costs at 1.03p per passenger-kilometre and 0.13p per tonne-kilometre for freight. These representative averages were used to estimate the savings from line closures, estimates which proved to be overblown – in the event the savings turned out to be far below the estimates.

As a prime component in the privatisation of British Railways, all the track and signalling was gifted in May 1996 to a new company, Railtrack plc, the shares of which were sold on the stock market. Revenue, profits and dividends were to be generated by charging the train operating companies for the use of the tracks. As with all cases of firms outsourcing services, this became a very complex contractual arrangement with Railtrack striving to ensure that the costs of track maintenance, renewal and upgrading were covered by the revenue. The system failed for reasons that seemed to be as complex as the organisation itself. A major element was that the contracts between Railtrack and the operating companies (TOCs) not only defined the ways in which the charges for the use of track were to be paid, but also defined the levels of service to be provided by Railtrack and the financial compensation to be paid to the TOCs should there be a failure to deliver the service. It appears that the financial structure was not mapped on to the costs of maintaining track in a safe condition, and a major accident was traced to poor and widespread track conditions which could not be quickly corrected. This caused the imposition of speed limits and the consequential payments of compensation that swept Railtrack into bankruptcy.[7] The company assets and duties were then transferred to a new company, Network Rail Ltd, under the auspices of the state, and which has no shareholders.

TOCs are still charged for track use on a tariff set by the Office of the Rail Regulator after consultation with the TOCs: such 'consultations' are invitations to lobby on the prices set in the tariff and tend to be a form of negotiation. The rates are published by Network Rail[8] as prices per locomotive-mile (the locomotive in the example of the container haulage in Figure 5.9 is charged £43.72 per locomotive-mile), together with prices per passenger train-mile and per 1000 gross tonne-miles (kg-tm) for freight wagons (the container wagons in the example are charged £0.9492 per kg-tm when loaded and £1.5534 when empty). These rates are computed from a formula using axle-loadings, bogie design and commodity carried, etc., and are set to reflect the estimated track wear: there are differing rates for every type of locomotive, wagon and coach.

These charges are no more than selective tolls as were used on eighteenth-century turnpike roads and canals, where charges were varied: so much per animal on the hoof, per waggon, per human, etc. Such tolls are yet another way of converting the cost of a capital asset into the cash flow related to an operating cost. Movement is being made easier by renting part of the capacity of a capital asset in the ownership of another party. Transport operators renting vehicles and equipment rather than owning them has become increasingly common, although it has always been a facet of the transport world. At the start of the canal age, the canal company owned the capital asset of the canal, together with the locks and the water supply necessary to maintain a navigable depth. The ownership of the boats was spread: some bargees owned their own boats but others rented boats from hire companies. Similarly, some companies whose goods were carried on the canal owned their own boats while others used hire companies. Later some canal companies did own and operate their own fleets. There were three categories of commodities to be owned: the canal itself, the boats and the freight.

There were four groups of owners: the canal company, the boat hire companies, the freight shippers and the boat owners. On top of this there were the boat operators who could be individuals owning or renting their own boats or they could be operating companies with a number of boats. Virtually all combinations of ownership and operation were to be seen. This complexity is apparent today but on the roads and railways rather than the canals: many lorries, buses and trains are not owned by the companies operating them but by vehicle-leasing companies. The lease may include servicing and maintenance bundled in with the rental cost, an arrangement now quite common on the railway in which train manufacturers build bespoke maintenance depots and contract to make a set number of fully operational trains at the start of each day. It is another example of the fragmentation of previously monolithic, vertically integrated companies dependent upon tasks being managed through industrial discipline, being broken up into smaller, specialist companies performing the tasks under contract. This trend is apparent right down to employee level where some people are self-employed with a legal contract with the company for which they work rather than being an employee managed through industrial discipline.

This increasing complexity of industrial organisation serves to shift management from day-to-day ad-hoc tasks to creating contracts and systems of rules and responsibilities to bind a network of agencies into a working whole. Efficiency, with its touchstone of cost reduction, is becoming increasingly a matter of creating contracts and systems: this, in turn, seems to be shifting the managerial time-frame in conflicting directions. On the one hand, day-to-day detailed management is being replaced by out-sourced contractors, lengthening the time horizon from the immediate to the short term, but, on the other hand, the shift from in-house capital investment to bought-in suppliers shortens the time horizon from the long to the mid-term. This seems to have changed our definition of 'the future'. The careless corporate and individual debt of the early twenty-first century, the pension crisis, the demise of long-term careers, all seem to indicate that the future is a lot nearer and more adjustable than we thought. The focus on sustainability, necessarily long-term, appears to have been driven into the shade by the immediate concerns of the economy, the markets and government debt.

Marginal and average cost theory

Ensuring that transport works with maximum efficiency with objectives being attained at acceptable cost needs the application of some theory. Fixed costs have to be paid as standing charges and are independent of the amount of work done. Variable costs are pro-rata with the output. However, the distinction is not tidy and mutually exclusive: in the end, nearly all fixed costs can be made variable to some extent or another. Staff costs are awkward: employees cannot be easily laid off at slack periods

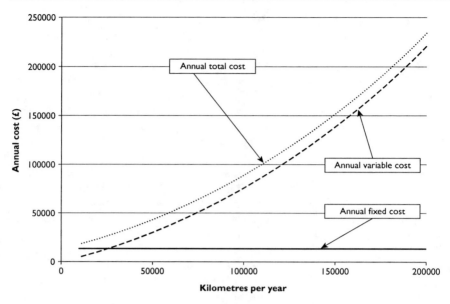

Figure 14.1 Estimated annual costs for a 17-tonne two-axle truck

and, for the short term at least, are effectively fixed but in the long term staff numbers may be adjusted by shedding or recruiting staff.

Figure 14.1 shows the estimated aggregate cost of running a 17-tonne two-axle truck as in Figure 10.5. The wage costs have been inflated to £25 per hour to cover management costs, insurance, sick-days and holidays, etc. The personal working year has been assumed to be 2400 hours (300 working days at eight hours per day). The working year of the truck assumes a mean speed of 55 km/h. Total wage costs to cover the truck working year are weighted by the ratio between the truck and personal working years: where the truck works more than the personal year of 2400 hours, the age bill is increased to cover overtime and/or extra staff; where it is less, the wage bill is reduced on the assumption that staff will be deployed on other work. The wage bill in this case has been made into a variable cost. The dotted total cost curve is the simple sum of the solid fixed cost and dashed variable cost curves.

Figure 14.2 converts the data in Figure 14.1 from total annual cost to cost per vehicle-kilometre and is more telling. There is one counter-intuitive aspect: the variable cost appears to be constant and the fixed cost appears to be variable. A moment's thought will show why: fixed costs are set for the year and are independent of the distance covered, and therefore reduce per vehicle-kilometre as the truck covers more distance over the year. On the other hand, the variable cost, which includes both fuel and wages, varies in tune with the distance covered but at a fixed rate – hence the straight line.

Figure 14.2 demonstrates a transport truism: the bigger the distance travelled in a year, the greater the annual cost, but the smaller the unit cost per vehicle-kilometre.

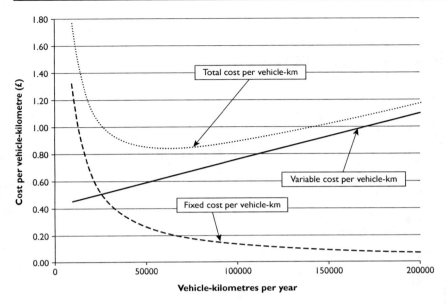

Figure 14.2 Estimated costs per vehicle-kilometre for a 17-tonne two-axle truck

This provides a principle of good management: if unit costs are to be kept low then vehicles should maximise the distance covered per year. That may be put in another, more pithy way. Transport revenue depends upon the passenger- and tonne-kilometres carried and so a stationary vehicle cannot create revenue but will always create cost.

Figure 14.3 introduces a new idea – that of marginal cost, defined as the extra cost imposed by the delivery of one more unit of production – in this case just one more vehicle-kilometre. It is shown in the figure as a straight line, although this is a quirk of the simplifications and assumptions built into the example. The operating costs per kilometre are a constant, the wages per vehicle-kilometre have been assumed to increase smoothly with distance and driving times but the component financial costs decrease. The combined effect is that the marginal cost of each successive vehicle-kilometre increases but at a constant rate.

The other curve in Figure 14.3 is the average cost which is exactly as it says – the total cost of producing a number of vehicle-kilometres, including all fixed and variables, divided by the number of units produced. The shape of this curve is typical – it is commonly called a 'bathtub' curve, a shape that reflects the fact that the contribution of fixed costs to the cost of each unit declines as production increases but that effect is eventually overwhelmed by the increases in cost caused by production having to strain to produce more. In this case this effect is represented by overtime and then extra staff, but there would also be higher maintenance costs as the truck was worked around the clock.

Figure 14.3 also shows a shaded rectangle, the area of which is the number of vehicle-kilometres times the average cost – it is a graphical representation of total cost.

228 Controlling costs

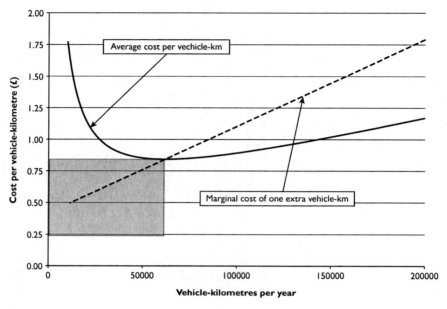

Figure 14.3 Estimated marginal and average costs per vehicle-kilometre for a 17-tonne two-axle truck

It is shown on the figure at the point of minimal average cost, a point at which the marginal and average costs are the same. This is an arithmetic certainty in all cases for so long as the average cost curve is progressively smooth with no quirky twists. It is certain because if the cost of one extra unit (the marginal cost) is less than the average cost then producing it will reduce the average and vice versa. The marginal cost curve always cuts the average cost curve at its minimum.

Traditional economic theory goes on from this theory of costings to the theory of revenue which uses the similar concepts of average and marginal revenue with marginal revenue declining as production increases due to price cuts and discounts having to be offered to sell the extra production. It is a matter of common sense to see that maximum profit is achieved if marginal cost is equal to marginal revenue because producing and selling one more unit will cost more to produce than the extra revenue it creates, whereas producing and selling one less unit will reduce revenue by more than the cost of producing it.

However, the analysis of revenue depends upon 'costs' and 'revenues' being in the same currency. That may well be true of pencils and cornflakes, but it cannot be true of transport. There is not only the thorny problem of accident deaths and injuries but also of local and global, short- and long-term environmental damage. Even if these can be reduced to risks, probabilities or other quantities, such numbers cannot be converted into real monetary values. Profitability and 'value for money' are concepts that cannot help socially responsible decision-making.

Shorn of some mechanism to 'balance' the sums of costs and of 'revenues', it remains to estimate costs as accurately as possible and to minimise them while still striving to achieve policy objectives. Figures 14.1 to 14.3 clearly show that minimising total cost is a poor strategy – it is average cost that has to be targeted. Some of the components are difficult or impossible to change: the cost per pound borrowed cannot be changed radically. Loan charges are really only reduced by lowering the amount borrowed. In recent years this has been increasingly achieved by leasing equipment rather than buying it. This, in effect, is still borrowing money, but from the leasing company rather than directly from a financial house. In many cases this may be more expensive: the annual cost of the lease may be more than the interest that would have been paid on a straight loan. On the other hand, the lease may cover depreciation and replacement, releasing lessors from acquisition costs – the lease continues beyond the life of particular assets which are automatically renewed and updated as appropriate. The choice between purchase and leasing may also be influenced by the costs of maintenance and overhaul being borne by the leasing company rather than by the lessors. That will release an operator from having to provide and maintain buildings and equipment which may not be fully utilised. There do not appear to be any generalisations about the best or cheapest choice apart from the observation that outsourcing the provision and maintenance of capital assets depends upon detailed, enforceable contracts rather than in-house management and discipline, and consequently problems may well sink into an expensive, legal dispute.

In a similar vein insurance is also a matter of negotiation. Very large companies often bear some of the risk themselves: companies with large vehicle fleets will not insure against accident damage, bearing the cost of any repairs within their day-to-day expenditure but retaining insurance against large claims for personal injury, etc.

Monitoring variable costs

Variable operating costs are best kept in check by constant monitoring: this will provide updated figures on the recent costs of consumables per unit of production, providing managers with clues and targets for improvement. This is no more than 'good housekeeping', probably dependent upon good databases and spreadsheets.

Wages are a rather different variable cost. Each full-time equivalent employee delivers around 2000 working hours per year. The managerial task is to ensure that those hours are as productive as possible. A common error is to perceive a workforce as a collection of individual employees, each working to their maximum efficiency: it is a mistake corrected many years ago by the Military. First the Navy and then the Army realised that very little is actually achieved by individuals working by and for themselves. Success depends upon working together as teams. Soldiers are not driven by a personal bonus to support their comrades; they work in cohesive groups bound by morale, a fact recognised and nurtured by the military. It is also a fact recognised in the past by industrial pioneers such as Titus Salt and Robert Owen and, today, by many German and Japanese firms. It is a thread woven into much of the transport industry, sometimes almost by accident: the old London Transport Passenger Board staff[9] or those of the Great Western Railway[10] seemed to see themselves to be communally responsible for delivering a public service: sometimes it has been deliberate – part of a brand image.[11] The recognition that efficiency is facilitated by cooperation rather than divisive separation means ensuring that mutually supportive working groups rather than individuals are monitored and managed: it is a question of maximising output rather than minimising cost.

Figure 14.4 shows the estimated cost curves for a range of 'load factors', defined as the tonne-kilometres which are carried as a proportion of the tonne-kilometres which could have been carried had the truck been fully laden. A 17-tonne rigid truck can carry about 12 tonnes of cargo although, as shown in Chapter 5, many trucks are fully laden when carrying less than this maximum weight: a truck may be fully loaded if the whole truck floor is occupied with pallets or with free-standing packages, or if the volume of the truck is full of comparatively low-density freight. In consequence it is unrealistic to think that the full work rate of a truck's maximum payload can be carried for every vehicle-kilometre of its working time. Although that maximum may be out of practical reach, an optimum at which the unused tonne-kilometres are minimised should be aimed for.

Figure 14.4 should not be thought to be accurate: the costs are estimates which may not be true of every truck or of every practical application. However, the principles behind the figure are true: first, that load factors are a very strong determinant of cost and, second, that the effect of increasing load factors wanes: the reduction in cost between a load factor of 0 (representing a track running empty) and 0.25 (running some combination of being a quarter full for all of the time or running completely full

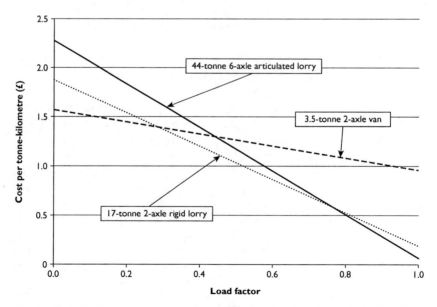

Figure 14.4 Estimated cost per tonne-kilometre as functions of the load factors for three sample trucks

for a quarter of the time) is very substantial. The difference between a load factor of 0.75 and 1.0 (the unattainable theoretical maximum) is far, far less.

This implies that striving for the optimum means reducing empty and part-loaded running to the minimum. Some empty running is unavoidable. Return loads are always difficult: finding ad-hoc backloads is facilitated by websites[12] and sometimes backloads are impossible – a concrete mixer lorry cannot bring anything back from site to the mixing plant. Large haulage companies are better placed, particularly if they have a spread of depots – another example of the Matthew principle in which size attracts growth. Modern communications linking computerised information bases with drivers on the road has helped, as have the common uses of handling equipment such as roll-cages. These may be used in conjunction with the ubiquitous standard curtain-sided lorries to transport a maximum range of goods. McKinnon[13] shows that empty running as a proportion of all running is declining, but much of it is unavoidable.

Part-loaded running is unavoidable whenever deliveries and collections have to be made at a number of addresses – whenever a 'load' is actually a combination of a number of consignments to be dropped at a number of destinations. The cost per vehicle-kilometre is lower when running empty – multi-axle vehicles are able to save on tyre costs by lifting the wheels clear of the road and fuel costs are slightly lower but assuming a constant cost irrespective of load will not invalidate the analysis. The cost per tonne-kilometre rather than per vehicle-kilometre clearly depends upon the size of the load. Chapter 10 considered costs per unit capacity regardless of how much of the capacity was used.

Figure 14.4 continues the estimated costs of lorries from the previous figures; however, the principles are the same for all modes. They are as follows:

- The greater the capacity of the vehicle the lower the cost per unit-kilometre when it is fully laden – in Figure 14.4 the lowest cost per tonne-kilometre is for the 44-tonne articulated lorry carrying its full payload of 28 tonnes with costs per tonne-kilometre less than one-tenth of the 3.5-tonne van.
- However, the greater the capacity of the vehicle the greater the penalty for underloading: if loaded to 60 per cent of its capacity, the 44-tonne articulated lorry costs as much per tonne-kilometre as a fully laden van and more than a 17-tonne lorry running almost half-empty.
- Load factors are not confined to points in time: they may represent average loadings during a day's work. A vehicle leaving a depot in the morning fully laden but returning empty later on in the day will have an average load factor of well under 1.
- The combination of those three characteristics points towards some specialisations. Larger vehicles are economical if used for long distances with constant, high loadings but lose their advantage if run part-loaded and if intermediate stops for loading and unloading extend dwell times at the cost of running times. A high-cost, high-capacity vehicle loses more money when it is stationary than a smaller vehicle. It makes sense to use smaller vehicles for short distances with intermediate drops, even though the cost per tonne-kilometre of capacity when on the move is high.

- Amassing a large load takes longer than smaller loads, and traffic which requires minimal transit times is best hauled with vehicles that do not have to delay their departure in order to consolidate an economic payload.

Redundancy

'Redundancy' has a common social meaning in which workers surplus to needs are dismissed, but it also has a specific meaning in engineering – a reserve strength not normally used but there to withstand abnormal excesses. The original Tay Bridge was a minimal structure with no inbuilt redundancy and, once weather conditions exceeded the norm for which the bridge was designed, it collapsed, by terrible chance taking a train with it. In reaction, the Forth Bridge was over-engineered, with some parts of it unstressed and 'unused' for all time.

All systems, particularly transport systems, need to include some redundancy in order to retain service levels should the system come under pressure. Commuter lines have to be able to withstand the rush-hour even if capacity is underused at other parts of the day. Lorries have to be available to meet unpredictable demands. Emergency services have to have the equipment to deal with emergencies which, hopefully, may never happen. Seaside councils have to have a enough deckchairs to cope with a sunny bank holiday. Ships have to have enough life-vests and rafts, although it is hoped that they will not be needed.

High-value and perishable goods need minimal transit times which make it worthwhile to deploy more expensive means of transport. For example, newspapers are perishable in the sense that interest in their content quickly fades and transit times from the presses to sales points must be minimal: small, part-loaded vans are appropriate, even though much of their capacity is unused and the cost per tonne-kilometre is considerable. Many activities display other needs: public transport needs to be reliable, appearing and arriving at the expected times. The transport system as a whole has to cope with fluctuating, surging demand, some of it predictable, like peak hours, some not, like abrupt changes in fuel prices driven by war.

The problem is not recognising the possibility of surges and perturbations but working out what surplus or rarely used capacity should be provided to cope with them. It is another facet of assessing the value of intangibles of the justifiable insurance against disruption. This has been a growing problem. Computer systems, especially spread-sheets, have been deployed to an ever greater extent to cost and assess activity, making the provision of redundant or unused assets vulnerable to 'cost savings' – the costs may be identified but their benefits are hard to evaluate. This seems to have particularly affected public transport. Under-used double track has been reduced to single, removing emergency back-up and making timekeeping susceptible to even small disturbances. Overhead wiring on the East Coast mainline was designed down to a cost and, like the Tay Bridge, is able to withstand storms but not hurricanes – the earlier West Coast electrification was more expensive but sturdier. As a result, high winds cause disruption, delay and cost to the East Coast line but not to the West Coast. If bus services are to be regular and reliable they must be able to cope with disruptions, and the best way of achieving that is to provide 'layover' times at route ends, minimising the knock-on effects of late arrivals upon subsequent departures. But layover times, with their costs unmatched by revenues, appear to be 'inefficient' – an identifiable cost with only a vague, fickle, but nonetheless valuable benefit.

The conclusion must be that minimising cost should not be an objective in itself but should be a measure by which efficiency is recognised. The objectives of service quality, including the ability to cope with disruptions, to maintain reliability and response times should be targeted and costs should be a criterion of efficiency in reaching those objectives, but cost should not itself be an objective.

Subsidy

There is a link to redundancy. The word 'subsidy' is derived from the Latin, subsidium, a body of troops held in reserve to cope with unforeseen events or disruptions – troops which had no set objective but were ready to be deployed to make good failures or to pursue ancillary objectives. The modern definition and use of 'subsidy' has a whiff of disapproval – sums of money granted by government to sustain unprofitable activity or to reduce prices to below their market values. Many intangible qualities, like an unpolluted atmosphere, or freedom, do not have market values and so their sustenance must depend upon subsidy. The great danger is that without the checks and balances normally provided by market accountancies, subsidies may be abused – some will argue are bound to be abused. This has been particularly true of nationalised industries held to be the foundations of the economy: in the past and in many countries the subsidy was an open-ended deficit subsidy. The nationalised industry did what it had to do under essentially political direction and the out-turn cost was paid by the government. It is the same structure as the defence and intelligence services enjoy today: there are budgets and questions are asked, but *force majeure* is deployed to cover retrospective expenditures.

Often these purchases are of intangibles devoid of a market price, but the urge to tag them with a pseudo-market price in pseudo-money does not ease the problem of assessing whether the subsidy meets its purpose: far better to measure the needs and the effects upon those needs directly.

As with redundancy, many qualities within civilisation provide security and reliability. Most people only rarely call upon the emergency services but are assured by their ability to do so should the need arise. Thus the 'product' is much more than the number of fires attended or cats rescued from trees or admissions to A & E: the 'product' is the sum of the unused ability to ask for these things to be done should that be necessary. The sense of security given by such unused ability does not have a market value: one could be created using social surveys in combination with pseudo-money, but it would be a game to convince few people. Far better so say that an hourly bus service will be provided within 500 metres of everybody's front door (or some similar objective) and then strive to provide that performance objective at minimal cost rather than fix an affordable subsidy and splash it around in response to whims or lobbying. A good example of this approach may be seen in the TransPerth Corporate Plan.[14] Less than a quarter of costs were covered by the fare revenue. The 'Net Community Expenditure' of $A105 million was used to:

Provide in the most efficient and effective manner, urban transport services for the overall benefit of the general community in accordance with Government policy.

That was expanded and interpreted to mean:

- Providing mobility to those without access to private transport.
- Making the Perth Central Business District and other centres accessible to all.
- Reducing the consumption of non-renewable fuel resources by providing means of transport which are more energy-efficient than cars.
- Easing congestion and reducing pressure for expensive road building, improvement and maintenance, by providing transport modes which are more efficient users of road space than private cars.

Each of these objectives was paired with a monitored measure, but there was no attempt to ascribe pseudo-monetary values to them with the intent of equating their sum to the $A105 real cash subsidy.

Implicit subsidy has been a feature of transport from the very earliest times. Civilisation depends upon mobility and trade: it was not merely the horse and then the wheel that were the foundations of civilisation but passable tracks and roads for them to move along. Roman roads were built by the state without any commercial mechanisms. That continues to this day everywhere: there are some enhancements for which tolls are charged, but the roads providing access to individual addresses throughout the world are built and maintained at state expense without any mechanism to equate the costs with explicit benefits – they are subsidised. Any other system would be politically unacceptable and practically unworkable: it is beyond the limit of the capabilities of the market-based price mechanism.

That provokes the question of where those limits lay. The privatisation of the UK railways initiated by the Railways Act 1993 was driven by an ideology – a belief that economic efficiency could only be provided by market-driven price mechanisms. The power of that belief, articulated by think-tanks such as the Adam Smith Institute[15] and the Centre for Policy Studies,[16] fuelled a political stance which stood in the way of the definition of desirable levels of service and of the ownership and management best able to deliver that service. In its place was a stark objective of privatisation in the belief that this would of itself provide the best mix of services. It was the same sort of difficulty as had afflicted nationalisation in 1948 – a lack of any definition of the improvements in performance that were expected to flow from the proposed action. The two were totally different ideologies, but in both cases the ideology became the objective rather than the means to achieve performance objectives. As it has turned out, privatisation has moved the subsidy of British Railways from about 5 per cent of annual cash flow in 1990 to about 38 per cent in 2010.[17] Those advocating privatisation will argue that the railways are now far busier than they have ever been, and that therefore privatisation has been 'successful'; so it has, if the objective had been to sell more passenger-kilometres, but that was not the avowed intent of privatisation. As Figure 14.5 shows, in the 16 years since privatisation, the subsidy

	1994	2010
Passenger-km (billion)	39	64
Tonne-km (billion)	13	19
Transport-km (billion)	52	83
Net government support (£ billion 2010 prices)	2.2	7.6
Support per transport-km (£)	23.6	10.9

Figure 14.5 Work and subsidy on British Railways, 1994 and 2010

paid to the railways has more than tripled; thus, if the objective of privatisation was to reduce the drain on government finance it has been an expensive failure, but if the objective was to increase the work done by the railways, particularly with regard to passenger-kilometres, then it has been a considerable success. In the absence of any declared objective, success or failure is an irrelevant question.

Prior to privatisation, British Railways had changed its structure, organising itself into a number of separate but related businesses. In part this was a reflection of ongoing changes in the business world and in part the current political climate. In industry the tendency from the very beginning of the industrial revolution had been for businesses to strive for growth, but to do so, in the main, by vertical integration. The apogee was the Ford motor plant at Dagenham which ingested basic raw materials and discharged fully finished cars, but many firms tried to incorporate as much of the production as possible into one long chain of processes converting simple inputs into complex outputs. This required very short movements of raw materials, components and part-finished work within large industrial sites.

From the 1970s onwards this changed: business still sought growth but from horizontal rather than vertical integration. Companies amalgamated, sometimes retaining previous brand names and using badge engineering to distinguish products which were actually very similar. In step with this change, the nature of industry changed from in-house manufacturing to the buying in of part-finished modules and components: many plants shifted the emphasis from manufacturing to assembly. This change which saw the virtual demise of native car manufacture in Britain may be linked to radical changes to transport costs. First, on land, road freight costs fell, enabling some of the manufacturing processes to be dispersed, replacing in-factory handling with road freight. The British car industry became notorious for hauling part-finished bodies and truck loads of engines from one part of the country to another – it was as though the production line had been strung along the road system. Second, and a much more important change, international freight rates fell substantially as a result of containerisation. Part-finished products and components could now be made wherever labour was cheapest, and manufacturing become a sequence of processes strung along international supply chains. This shifted the focus of international trade from the previously dominant bulk haulage of basic raw materials to the movement of components. It incidentally shifted the nature of transport away from bulk towards inter-modal traffic.

In parallel with the technical and geographical spread of manufacturing and of the change in emphasis from national economies served by the internal transport networks to the global economy facilitated by international inter-modal transport, there was a political drive to separate off functions, to disentangle parts of what had previously been monolithic structures. Large, vertically integrated organisations had become unfashionable. In Britain, the NHS became a pattern of hospital trusts: schools became financially more autonomous and there was a move to separate the track and infrastructure from railway operations. This was epitomised by the European Directive 91/440 which instructed member countries to separate the management of the track and infrastructure from the operation of the trains. Contrary to the rhetoric of those advocating rail privatisation, the Directive did not require either function to be the task of private companies, but it did serve the objective of enabling more than one operating company to provide services – to facilitate competition. In part this was an expression of the faith in competition to provide efficient services, but it was also an attempt to bring the railways into line with the road network where the track was provided by the state and the services using the track by a multiplicity of organisations. As one senior European explained, the objective was to enable the choice of sending a consignment of timber from Finland to Gibraltar by a range of companies providing both road and rail services offering different rates on an otherwise equal footing.[18] It was an argument based on theory and ideology rather than on practicability.

This is tinged with irony, since it is the premise upon which railways in Britain were initially organised. It took the horrific death at the opening of the Liverpool and Manchester Railway of Huskisson, the government minister responsible for railway legislation, to demonstrate that providing a railway for individual companies to operate was an impossible option. Trains travelled so fast that drivers could not respond safely to conditions beyond their personal vision. Signalling was vital, and that addition to the infrastructure back in 1829 implied a close relationship among the characteristics of the trains (braking distances and frequencies), the characteristics of the infrastructure (speed limits, signal spacing and sighting) and the abilities of the drivers. Everywhere in the world, railways were henceforward organised as combinations of the design and management of the infrastructure with the design and operation of the trains.

The detachment of infrastructure from operation on the roads model does not appear to have had any clear objectives, apart from theoretically enabling competition among operators, but that objective is a mirage. The basic requirement for effective competition is substitutability: competing products must be equally acceptable. But that is impossible with transport services: for example, passengers arriving at Gatwick Airport intent on travelling to London have the choice of trains operated by two different companies, but they work to different timetables, thereby hobbling substitution. Most people will choose the next train, irrespective of its price, colour, comfort or any other attribute – always assuming that people know there is a choice to be made. On the other hand, separating infrastructure from operation has clear disadvantages which the European Commission is forced cope with: it harks back to signalling and Huskisson's untimely death. The Commission has plans for a standardised electronic signalling system but it needs the combined actions of all the infrastructure companies and all the train builders and operators – the differences between infrastructure and operating, recently made, now have to be bridged.

The problems have become entangled with subsidy, both in principle and in practice. British privatisation established an independent infrastructure company, Railtrack, which was intended to be funded profitably by track access charges paid by the operating companies to whom contracted subsidies were awarded. The arrangements anticipated that privatisation would engender efficiencies that would eventually render subsidies unnecessary. As Figure 14.5 shows, this has not happened so far; nor is it likely to unless trends take an abrupt turn. However, the premise upon which Railtrack was founded proved to be false. Those who advocate separate infrastructure companies and, moreover, that they should be given a remit of commercial profitability, will argue that the financial failure of Railtrack was due to bad management rather than the remit itself being impossible.

This byzantine accounting appears to be a complexity without coherent objectives. The 2012 Command Paper[19] specifies the government's objectives to be to:

- offer commuters a safe journey;
- facilitate an increasing amount of travel;
- support local public transport;
- transport millions of tonnes of freight.

These are postures rather than policies, akin to the objectives of making the sky bluer and the sea warmer – there are no measures by which the success or failure of such policies may be sensed, and hence no ability to know whether the £8 billion per year is being used wisely or not.

Finally, the role of competition needs to be defined. The traditional view is that monopoly can extract abnormal profits by being able to charge high prices: the obverse of that view is that competition, in providing an alternative product, will bring prices down to a level at which the revenue covers all costs plus enough return on the employed capital to provide the necessary commercial incentive for firms to stay in the market. This argument is extended to include service levels, reliability, etc., so competitive firms are driven to provide whatever customers want. The argument rests fundamentally upon the products offered by competing firms to be entirely substitutable. But firms constantly strive to overcome this need by emphasising that their particular product is not substitutable by any other – it is 'new', does its job more thoroughly or without so much work by the user or, simply, is packaged and branded in an identifiable way. Companies strive to lift their product out of the general market and into a smaller enclave with monopolistic tendencies.

That is much easier to do with stockable products. As far as the railways are concerned, competition is more apparent in selling online tickets than in running trains. Providing substitutable alternatives is exceedingly difficult. Nonetheless, British privatisation of the public transport industry has been based on the notion of the provision of competing services at the point of consumption. Practice has leant away from the theory to become completion behind closed doors for the contractual right to run a monopoly. On the railways, operations are delivered by a franchise system in which competitive bids for the franchises are assessed against the minimal subsidy demanded to run the service. It is a costly, complex arrangement in which licences to operate limited monopolies are subject to a modified Dutch auction. The same sort of system worked for those bus routes for which a subsidy is paid but these are comparatively few and within minor restricted markets. For the most part the administrative structure of registering commercial routes facilitates competition in pre-journey choices by the use of timetables and websites such as Traveline rather than crude competition at the bus-stop. The underlying mistake in the legislation is the belief that 'the product' is a journey from a boarding point to an alighting point. Few journeys are as simple as that – there is always a return, perhaps by a different route, perhaps at a range of possible times. The product is more likely to be a pass, a network card or a multi-ride ticket, and that places high emphasis upon flexibility. Competition is then between networks, not between rides.

Notes

1. Department for Transport (2009), Paragraph 2.1.5.
2. There is a – probably apocryphal – story of an academic transport economist standing with his wife in front of an automat selling travel insurance and asking her at what level of compensation she would find his death acceptable. One hopes she replied with a miniscule sum, putting the man and his question in their place.
3. Department for Transport (2011b), Paragraph 1.2.10, table 1.
4. Defined in detail in Department of Transport (www.dft.gov.uk/webtag).
5. 2000 (cars per hour per lane) × 8 (hours per day) × 300 (working days per year) = 4.8 million cars per year; 4.8 million minutes = 80,000 hours @ £26.43 per hour = £2 million. A death is valued at £1.5 million.
6. Joy (1973), ch. 9, 'The track cost question'.
7. The story is well told in Wolmar (2001).
8. www.networkrail.co.uk (2010), Track usage price list.
9. See Collins (1977).
10. See Bryan (2004).
11. For example, Eddie Stobart's trucking company.
12. For example, www.ecohaulage.com.
13. McKinnon and Piecyk (2010).
14. TransPerth (1990). TransPerth is the public transport provider in Perth (Western Australia). The Plan is now updated year on year.
15. See Irvine (1988).
16. See Gritten (1988).
17. Modern Railways (May 2010) *Statistical Mess Perpetuated.*
18. A personal conversation with a Danish economist explaining why infrastructure should be separated from service provision.
19. Department for Transport (2012a).

Chapter 15

Supporting the economy

Transport and economic activity

It is a truism to say that all production involves transport. Primitive hunter-gathering people's use of transport was trivial – people walking, stalking, gathering and carrying their catch back to wherever it was to be consumed. Even today, some transport is just as trivial – grazing supermarket shelves or portering documents from one desk to another – but the principle still stands: the economy is composed of trillions of actions, each requiring the positioning of the necessary inputs of labour, energy, capital equipment and component materials, and the carrying away of the product to wherever it is to be used. The distance to be moved may be anything from a matter of a few strides with a load carried in the arms or balanced on a head, or it may be thousands of kilometres by ship or plane. Nothing and nobody of any use can stand still for long.

Much of the history of civilisation has been focused upon making movement easier by building and using the means of carrying things; first the tracks along which movement could take place, then the vehicles to move along the tracks, then the energy to power that movement, and then systems of control and organisation of the movement. The transport system cannot be ubiquitous; it has to link selected places. Some activities are tied to particular places: coal cannot be mined wherever the mood takes people, crops cannot be grown on rocky, mountainous slopes. Most of primary industry (the gathering of basic raw materials, farming and fishing) is geographically fixed and must be served initially by simple, dedicated routes. Secondary industry (production fed with raw materials) and tertiary industry (processing information) is not tied to precise locations and may be located wherever the inputs can be amassed to best advantage. The extra movement then attracts the development of the network to better serve the needs of the activity.

The dynamic picture is of a civilisation with constantly growing primary and secondary industry linked together by an ever-more complex, efficient transport network. This was initially composed of no more than a disjointed pattern of simple routes serving primary production, but it developed slowly through the construction of ports and roads followed by investments in ever-new transport technologies, until today the global movement of people, freight, energy, information and waste pulses through a transport fabric of interwoven real and virtual threads. Primary, secondary and tertiary industry throughout the world is served by an infrastructure of roads, ports, sea- and airways, pipes and wires all thrumming with movement.

Over most of history the drive to develop the transport system was to provide better and cheaper movement for existing traffic: if that then stimulated new activity then so much the better, but that was not the immediate objective. From Roman ports and roads, through the turnpike, canal, railway and motorway ages, the basic motive was to carry existing movement more efficiently. Of course, the improvements to the transport network did change the economic geography, but that was incidental, not the basic purpose. The British motorway system, like the investment in railways a century before, was a remedial policy correcting the inadequacies of the road network. However, both the railways and the motorways changed the absolute and relative patterns of accessibility and so changed the geography of development. A good example is the concentration of warehousing and distribution depots in the vicinity of Junction 18 on the M1, all built on land which would have remained as farmland had it not been for the proximity of the motorway. Such development was not a reason for the construction of the motorway but became an unintended, if nonetheless welcome, result.

Policy objectives

The traditional policy of providing better roads for existing traffic was clearly stated in *Roads for the Future*:

> The aim is to provide a comprehensive national system of trunk roads on which commercial traffic and private cars can move freely and safely and on which congestion and the frustration and economic costs it creates will have been virtually eliminated.[1]

This is the 'predict-and-provide' policy in a nutshell. A radical change in policy arrived in 1980 shortly after the election of the new Conservative government:

> The first priority of the Government is national economic recovery. We have to strike a balance. New road schemes can bring undoubted economic advantages. Exports can reach their markets more quickly; goods can be distributed more efficiently; traffic can flow more easily and fuel can be saved.[2]

Although the document went on to repeat the objectives and methodology of 'predict and provide', that opening paragraph suggests a new emphasis upon stimulating economic activity and, by implication, doing so in particular places and along particular routes. In effect, this was arguing for the provision of more road capacity, not to cope with the problems of existing traffic, but in anticipation of future traffic being generated by road improvement. This policy was focused upon access to ports and to areas in which heavy industry was under economic stress. There was also an emphasis upon building bypasses around known bottlenecks. Overall, the policy was contrary to that of ten years earlier: then the aim had been to provide a comprehensive, national system, but now that very general aim had been replaced by a policy to improve accessibility selectively and to do so specifically for freight.

This policy was reasserted and strengthened nine years later by a further policy document,[3] which set out a programme of over 500 schemes at an estimated total cost of £23 billion with the same aim of improving the competiveness of British industry in world markets by providing more efficient and cheaper inland road haulage.

Both the 1980 and 1989 policy statements suffered from the same deficiency: no suggestions were made in either document about how the expected stimulation of the economy could be forecast or monitored, and so the effectiveness of the proposed programme of road improvements could never be sensed. Rather than proposing a new methodology to match the new objective, the old assessment methodology was retained. It had been developed over the previous 20 years to assess the value for money of 'predict-and-provide' schemes designed to improve flow and hasten journeys, not to stimulate the economy. The new policy was clearly very concerned with freight traffic but this was virtually ignored in the modelling. Furthermore, the retained 'predict-and-provide' methodology assumed a fixed land-use pattern, usually based on the local authorities' statutory plans, despite economic stimulation demanding the development of new economic activities on well-served sites. There was a gaping hole in the methodology to assess the effectiveness of policies and schemes.

Although some would deny it, that gaping hole is still there. The twin changes in policy, first from 'predict and provide' to 'travel demand management' and then from the improvement of existing traffic flows to the stimulation of the economy, provoked some development of Land-Use Transport Interaction Models,[4] designed to predict the changes in land uses wrought by changes in accessibility, but this work has not yet developed into an ability to assess the relative abilities of transport schemes to improve local economies – that is, to assess whether government policy is working at all, let alone working effectively.

Interrelating transport, land use and economic activity

It has to be recognised that creating a comprehensive model incorporating both the changes in accessibility and in land use wrought by improvements in the transport system is an immense task. Over 50 years ago the Buchanan Report stressed:

> the close interlocking between questions of land-use, on the one hand, and transport and movement on the other, applies all the way from the widest questions of regional planning and the distribution of population and employment, to the detailed design of city centres. This is extremely important and points the need for the closest co-operation between everyone working in these fields. We think this applies to the internal organisation of central departments, and the whole range of local authorities. But most important of all is the need for a new synthesis of minds amongst those professionally engaged on these problems. A much improved concept of professional collaboration is needed, with a greater emphasis on mixed-team working.[5]

A number of local ad-hoc inter-professional groups were established soon after the Buchanan Report was published, but these groups had no power and no agreed agenda. In the mid-1960s a group of like-minded professionals and academics arranged a series of 'Urban Studies Conferences' in Oxford which succeeded in debating the nature of a 'General Urban Model' combining both land use and transport, but made no grounds for building one. A major, but not the only, problem lay in a cultural chasm between engineers and town planners. Engineers cannot leave their structures open to chance and have to design and construct accurately: consequently, engineers have a tendency towards determinism – if a structure is well designed and constructed then it will not collapse. Planners live in a much more fuzzy world where mistakes in calculations do not result in physical collapse but neither do correct calculations ensure a definitive outcome; planners tend to see the arrival of firms, jobs and traffic at development sites as non-deterministic, rather like throwing dice. By the mid-1960s traffic engineers had already built travel demand models of considerable arithmetic complexity requiring the use of computers, but land use was always an input, usually fixed by the definitive statutory plan, never an output, preventing models from reflecting the ways in which transport and land use swop places as the driving and driven forces in urban development. The Oxford dream of a General Urban Model could never have been as precise and deterministic as the engineers would have wished, but nor could it have been sufficiently intuitive and probabilistic to satisfy the planners. The notion withered on the vine.[6]

Twenty years later, the Transport Planning Society was established as a learned society to provide a forum within which planners, engineers and others could discuss the nature, extent and practice of transport planning, defined widely enough to include not just movement, but also the places between which movement takes place. The Society has made a name for itself in transport planning education and in disseminating good practice, but it has not succeeded in welding transport and land-use planning into a methodological unity.

Guidance on the Methodology for Multi-Modal Studies (GOMMMS)

GOMMMS[7] was published in 2000 and the government commissioned a series of studies as to its specification. These were supposed to build a new approach to transport planning but were fundamentally flawed from the very start. Some will argue that this is unfair criticism, since the Multi-Modal Studies were not designed to marry transport and land use: they were designed to expand the modelling of transport demand to cover all modes rather than being confined to private cars. GOMMMS seems to have been prompted by the new Labour government's reaction to the previous government's adoption of 'travel demand management' as the touchstone of transport policy.

Two problems had appeared in the wake of PPG13 and the switch from 'predict and provide' to 'travel demand management':

1   If travel demand is to be 'managed' by inducing the use of other modes in preference to the car, then those other modes have to replace the entire door-to-door

journeys that would have been made by car. That necessarily involves chains of segments using combinations of the other modes. At its very simplest, the combination has to be a public transport ride together with walks to and from the journey ends. Journeys are intrinsically inter-modal (using modes in combination by interchanging from one to another) rather than multi-modal (choosing one mode from a multiplicity of competitive alternatives).

2   Neither cars nor public transport are able to serve all addresses: car use in highly dense areas is difficult, expensive or even impossible, due to the intrinsic lack of parking space. In contrast, low-density areas are unable to sustain the service frequencies that make public transport viable. It follows that managing density through managing development has to be an integral part of 'travel demand management'.

GOMMMS is woefully inadequate on both counts. It is blinkered by retaining the basic architecture of the previous 'predict-and-provide' methodology and then adapting it to the multi-modal needs of 'travel demand management'. The problem is evidenced by the definition of 'mode' as taken from that in the National Travel Survey (NTS):[8]

Trips: The basic unit of travel, a trip, is defined as a one-way course of travel with a single main purpose.

Stages: A trip consists of one or more stages. A new stage is defined when there is a change in the form of transport or when there is a change of vehicle requiring a separate ticket.

Mode/main mode: Trips may include more than one mode of transport, and each mode is recorded as a stage within that trip. When 'main' mode is used in the title of a table or chart, this allocates information for the whole trip to the stage used for the greatest length (in distance) in the trip. When 'mode' is used this refers to information for individual stages of trips.

These National Travel Survey definitions are unhelpful:

- Many trips do not have a single main purpose and if minor purposes are excluded (diversions to take children to school or supermarket shopping on the way home), some important explanations of behaviour are missed.
- Defining stages by ticketing ignores network tickets such as Oyster, day-tickets, etc.
- Actually very few tables or charts in the NTS outputs refer to stages – they are nearly all of 'main' modes and it is this simplification that is adopted in GOMMMS, ignoring the ancillary, but possibly defining elements within trips.
- NTS recognises seven major modes: walking, car/van, rail (including London Underground but excluding the Docklands Light Railway), light rail (including Docklands and the Glasgow Underground), local bus, cycling and other. 'Other' is really puzzling: it includes motor cycles, camper vans (which are trivial in

numbers but need parking space) and taxis (which are neither trivial nor need parking space), together with non-local buses and air travel. Using NTS definitions to plan airport access must be a testing task – much of it is by one or other of the 'other' modes.

The worst problem concerns walking: since the walking segments in any inter-modal journey are bound to be shorter in distance than other parts of the journey, they cannot appear as 'main' mode unless the entire journey is made by foot. Hence walking as an integral part of trips is overlooked and, once that is done, any hope of predicting and monitoring effective ways to manage travel demand is lost, since individual perceptions of the problems of travel are heavily influenced by the segments that have to be made on foot.

GOMMMS simplifies the list of modes found in the National Travel Survey:

> Given a multi modal context, it can be expected as a minimum that car, public transport, and non-motorised modes will need to be distinguished.[9]

This retains the long-held view that choices are made between using a car or not: and yet it is a view that is constantly disproved by the actions of the very individuals who hold it. The choice is not between car and an alternative but between making journeys including or excluding the use of a car. Car use entails avoiding or enduring congestion, finding, capturing and retaining somewhere to park and getting from there to the final destination. Not using a car includes walks to, from and within the transport system plus waits, uncertainties and lack of information. It is true that travel choices are made between competing alternatives, but it is not the competition between a car and some alternative to the car but between two journeys perceived in their entirety, one involving the use of a car and the other not.

Travel choices and their implications are important, since all economic activity is dependent upon businesses finding, capturing, occupying and developing locations served by all the means to move the necessary people, goods, information, energy and waste, a fundamental process in which transport is both servant and master. The continuous interaction between land use and transport suggests that modelling should be by a dynamic model akin to a movie in which each still frame represents a point in time. That is a difficult notion to put into practice, although it does seem to have been managed by the authors of video games such as SimCity. It is also being developed for practical use at the Centre for Advanced Spatial Analysis.[10]

The dynamic nature of urban geography has to be understood even if it cannot be accurately reproduced in a computer model, since moulding the size, shape and nature of the city is an inherent aspect of sustaining the local, national and global economies. GOMMMS expressly excludes such an idea:

> A good simplification in multi-modal forecasting is to treat the total number of trips as being constant within each planning scenario but – at least in principle – to model changes in mode and destination in response to changes in generalised cost which arise from both congestion and the impact of policy action.[11]

This paragraph suggests that the number of generated trips in each area is fixed, but the mode used and the destination may change in response to the relative generalised cost. This is mistaken on two counts:

1   If the economy is effectively stimulated, the number of trips cannot be fixed.
2   The choices of both mode and destination cannot be driven by a simple comparison between the generalised costs of two competitive main modes.

While criticism of GOMMMS on the grounds that it is not designed to cover land-use changes may be a little unfair, the criticism that the remit should have included land-use changes remains. Perversely, GOMMMS contains a section on Land-Use Transport Interaction Models (LUTIs),[12] although their use conflicts with the assertion that the number of trips should be fixed. Nevertheless, GOMMMS summarises the reasons for including land use on computer models of future transport demand rather well:

> 2.2.2
>
> Land-use is of relevance to 'transport' for at least three reasons:
>
> - land-using activities and the interactions between them generate the demands for transport;
> - those activities and interactions are to a greater or lesser extent influenced by the availability of transport;
> - the linkages between transport and activities may be important to the appraisal of transport strategies – especially when trying to consider whether the transport system is providing the kinds of accessibilities that activities (i.e. people and businesses) require, rather than simply providing mobility.

The unit then goes on to make further, rather more complex points:

> 2.2.9
> - the land-use impacts of a transport change may extend far beyond the spatial scope of the transport proposal itself – they can extend at least as far as the area in which the transport change affects accessibility, and secondary effects may extend further;
> - a great deal of locational change takes place through changing occupation of existing buildings, with changes in either the density or the nature of the occupation (for example, one type of business replacing another, or retired persons occupying housing previously occupied by families with children);
> - the value of property is an important influence on its occupation; if improvements in transport increase the demand for space in a particular location, the resulting increases in rents may affect households or businesses who have no direct interest in the transport change itself; and
> - it follows from the above points (a) that in many cases changes in composition are likely to be more significant than changes in totals – for example,

changes in provision for commuter travel may have a significant impact on where the working population and its dependants live, but a much smaller impact on the distribution of the total population (as households without workers move into the areas that the workers are leaving); and (b) that significant land-use effects may occur within the market for existing property, with no new development and no formal change of use, and therefore beyond the control of the planning system.

This is good theory, but the Guidance has wandered into the very labyrinth that stymied the proposals for the General Urban Model back in the 1960s. Figure 15.1 gives the flow chart of a Land-Use Transport Interaction Model given in GOMMMS.[13]

Figure 15.1 is an attempt to mime the actual development process so far as it is known rather than create a model that produces helpful results. This resonates with the 1960s debate over the General Urban Model between the engineers' desire for 'accuracy' (although by now the engineers have been replaced by mathematical economists) and the planners' contention that such precision is impossible. The flow chart defines a process that has to be driven by an immense dataset describing the geography of a pattern of zones, each of which is necessarily a crude average of all the locations within it:[14]

- employment by work zone (stratified by industry);
- employment by residential zone (stratified by industry);
- floor space by zone by type;
- rental values by zone by type;
- household incomes by zone;
- zone-to-zone matrices of the journey to work;
- zone-to-zone matrices of the supplies of goods and services to consumers;
- development under construction in the base year of the forecast.

These data have to be related to each other by a set of eight relationships (elasticities):[15]

1　units of labour per unit of production (by industry);
2　unit of services required per household;
3　matrices of the inputs and outputs (measured in units of employment) between sectors of industry;
4　household expenditures by household type and zone;
5　arithmetic relationships between number of employees and the floor spaces they occupy, by zone and by industry;
6　arithmetic relationships between rental values per unit space (and so per employee);
7　dispersal factor for the journey to work by employees by industrial sector and zone;
8　dispersal factor for the distribution of goods and services by industrial sector and zone.

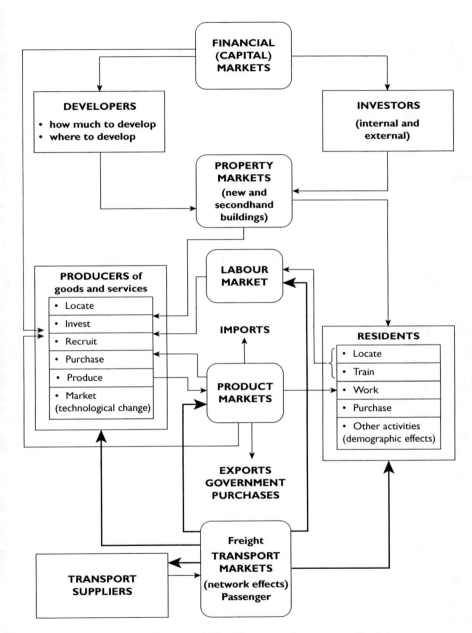

Figure 15.1 Flow chart for a Land-Use Transport Interaction Model
Source: Reproduced from Department for Transport, WebTAG Unit 3.1.3, p. 5, fig. 2.2.

The probability of all of these data being correct is nil; but that is not the important point: many of them are fuzzy representations of an unknown range of data and so are inherently 'inaccurate'. The prime importance is to know if the model is delivering outputs that are misleading. The usual method of testing complex models is to use them to 'backcast' – to enter data for some years previously and then to check whether the model 'forecasts' the known realities of the present. Something must be amiss if the disparities between the results from the model and contemporary reality are unacceptably large. There is no evidence to suggest that a 'backcast' test has been carried out on a LUTI in use within a Multi-Modal Study. The absence of that reassurance, coupled with the extent and complexity of the input data and calculations, creates a risk that outputs may be misleading. In general it is better to have simpler, cruder models in which errors and biases are recognisable and may be allowed for.

The root cause of the intricacies of the flow chart in Figure 15.1 is the reliance upon the five market mechanisms in the spine of the model. Any analysis of the global financial crisis of the first decade of the twenty-first century shows the fallibility of markets: no doubt economists will argue at length whether markets really are infallible but misunderstood, or whether they are, indeed, fallible – and still misunderstood. Whatever their intrinsic merits, the markets for property are particularly awkward to measure, let alone forecast. In part, prices and values are not fixed by common consent but by negotiations beyond the public gaze, making it very difficult to collect good data. As anybody who has bought or sold a house knows, prices may appear to be illogical, since no one property is an exact replica of another and the differing characteristics are weighted differently from person to person; in any event, values and rents are self-referential.[16] Any computer model to the design in Figure 15.1 is bound to have inputs that rely upon a mixture of assumptions and unverifiable data, making the results intrinsically doubtful.

Nonetheless, it is undeniable that some way of modelling credible reaction in land-use reactions to changes in absolute and relative accessibilities is required. Travel demand models (described later in Chapter 19) are designed to make predictions of movement and traffic between different places. To do this they require the input of some sort of land-use budget for each place to be used in conjunction with a tariff of generated movement per unit of each land-use type. Traditionally, the land uses specified by the approved statutory local plan were used as the input. This was acceptable for so long as the purpose of the town and country planning system was to steer anticipated growth into desirable locations. That task changed once economic growth faded and unemployment rose: growth was no longer waiting to be steered. Statutory plans changed their character from having a definitive role describing what was expected to happen, into a permissive role describing what would be desirable should the opportunity arise and, by implication, also describing what was undesirable. That trend then continued further into plans being an advocacy describing what should be striven for but no longer preventing all else – even Green Belts and Sites of Special Scientific Interest, once sacrosanct, are no longer off-limits to development. The pragmatic aim of the planning system is no longer to guide development but to engender it.

Modern statutory plans still define a desirable option for future land use, but how much of it will come into being is uncertain, and using plans as definitive maps of the future is no longer reliable. That leaves only one option: to take the present land-use pattern and try to estimate the most likely changes to it, accepting that this is more likely to be due to the collected decisions of developers than to the objectives of the local planning department.

GOMMMS includes a technique for converting land uses into the future demand for movement. The National Trip End Model (NTEM) works in concert with the Trip End Model Program (TEMPRO),[17] to produce estimates of the future population, dwellings, households, jobs and car ownership, together with the numbers of trips arriving and leaving by each of the 'main modes'. The model uses a 'Russian doll' structure to describe the country's geography: it uses 2496 zones, each one a collection of census 'output areas' and is also a subdivision of 'district control areas': these cover one or more local authority areas. District control areas are grouped into nine 'study areas' which are identical to the British regions, with the single exception of the 'Wider Southeast' which is a combination of three regions: London, East and Southeast.[18] This nested structure is necessary, since the input data to the NTEM come from a wide variety of sources, many of them unaligned to the 2496 modelled zones. Figure 15.2 shows the study areas shaded over the skeleton of the zones.

Forecasts are made in a cyclical series of leaps (usually each of five years) with the outputs from each leap being the input to the next. Inputs and outputs are at the district control area level, the outputs being the sum of the previous cycle's forecasts for each of the component zones and the inputs to the zones for the next cycle being a proportionate distribution of the previous output. This allows for an arbitrary shifting of the balances between zones from one cycle to the next.

The inputs to the NTEM are:

- households by size in the study area (region) for each forecast year;
- population by gender and age for each control area in each forecast year;
- jobs by sector, gender and working status in the control area for each forecast year.[19]

These input data are typically government-provided trend-based projections. In addition, there are projections of dwellings and growth factors representing expected/ likely patterns of development influencing the distribution of population and workers:[20]

- dwellings in each control area in forecast year;
- expected growth factors in each zone for employment type for the time period.

NTEM forecasts are a mixture of:[21]

- raw census and employment data;
- trend analyses (the source of estimates of future populations, households and employment (para 1.1.4));

250 Supporting the economy

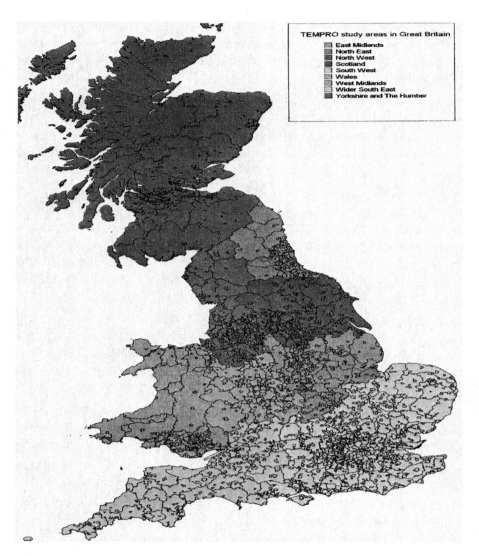

Figure 15.2 National Trip End Model: zones and study areas
Source: Reproduced from *NTEM Guidance* (www.dft.gov.uk/tempro), fig. A.2.

- local authority plans (the source of data on the future numbers of dwellings (para 1.2.11));
- arbitrary parameters (for example, the ratio of jobs to workers (by sector, gender and working status for the study area) (together with 15 others listed in Appendix D));

- statistical corrections (for example, shifting the gender balance in the employment forecasts and reconciling the numbers of households and dwellings);
- expected growth factors used particularly to divide the predicted change in the numbers of jobs and households for complete district control areas over the component zones;
- the trip rates reported in the National Travel Survey.[22]

Forecasts exclude any sense the actual transport system. Consequently the TEMPRO/NTEM process cannot help untwine the relationship between transport and accessibility. Changes in employment are reliant upon government-provided forecasts based on trends for the regional effects combined with the expected growth factors used to distribute changes at district control level across the component zones, not upon improvements to the transport system.

TEMPRO/NTEM is a very earnest process, concerned to be precise, but doomed to be otherwise – for example, it strives to correct population estimates to account for the 1.9 per cent of the population unfortunate enough to find themselves living outside normal households in prisons, boarding-schools, barracks and care homes, and also strives to resolve the statistical incongruities between the numbers of households and the numbers of dwellings by corrections based on a convoluted statistical process. If it really is vital for a transport model to map the numbers of households on to the numbers of dwellings, then a sub-model on household formation would be more informative. There is little point in trying to make an innately inaccurate process marginally less inaccurate: trying to compress Britain's complex geography into 2496 zones is a crude business (for example, the average population of 22,600 cannot be that precise, and correcting it to account for the 1.5 per cent living in institutions rather than in households is giving it a misleading patina of accuracy. Worst of all, TEMPRO/NTEM ignores transport service levels, the engine of travel demand and density (a major driver of mode use). For example, the trip rates derived from the National Travel Survey are held to be constant for all addresses within a zone; thus members of a household living near a railway station and with a bus-stop within 20 metres of their front door will be assumed to generate the same number of trips by public transport as another, otherwise identical, family living in the same zone but in an area without a bus service and a long walk from the station. Worse, there is no method of relating or placing jobs. GOMMMS/TEMPRO/NTEM is incapable of testing the government policy of generating economic growth through the selective improvement of the transport system.

So far, two methods seeming to relate to land use and transport have been introduced: the LUTI and TEMPRO/NTEM models. Both are extremely complex and have to be fed with large amounts of data, and yet neither method creates the needed linkage between accessibility and development. TRICS (Trip Rate Information Computer System) is a simple database containing actual, not modelled, data. It has the considerable merit of being designed for a specific, limited purpose, an objective which it achieves, and achieves well. Planning applications have to be for very specific and detailed developments within precisely defined sites. Local planning authorities will grant or refuse permission having considered whether the local road system will be able to carry the extra traffic. This will require data on existing and future traffic flows based on trip rates observed in the past at similar, newly constructed developments and then analysed by the nature of the development and its use to give a trip rate of the number of trips per day per employee or per square metre of floor space. The use of such rates stored in TRICS or similar databases is very simple, robust and focused, and able to provide credible estimates of the effects of development upon the transport system; however, it does not and cannot provide an answer to the puzzle of how to forecast the effects of changes in the transport system upon development.

There is a trip-wire hidden in the proposition that improved transport will enhance economic activity. The Queen said in her speech on opening the Forth Road Bridge in 1964 that economic benefits would be felt throughout that part of Scotland now brought closer to the capital. Her speech writers made the same point two years later at the opening of the Severn Bridge, although this time it was South Wales that was to be the beneficiary. In both cases the improved accessibility proved to be a mixed blessing. Some industries in the areas served by the new bridges did benefit by having their transport costs and transit times reduced and, no doubt, there will have been examples of new industry developing and thriving that would not have grown had it not been for an improved cost profile, but there is also no doubt that some industry and distribution centres were drawn away from the remoter areas to be concentrated at sites able to serve much wider areas once the bridges were opened. This happened in Italy where better communications to Abbruzzi and beyond to Apulia caused some larger enterprises to shift north to concentrated locations from which they then served the original, but now satellite, activities. In reverse, there has been considerable growth in smaller, newer enterprises.

This suggests complex effects which may be neither described nor analysed simply. This complexity is apparent at a global scale where international freight rates have fallen to a fraction of what they were 60 years ago, radically changing global accessibility. The effect upon economic activity has been revolutionary and far from simple. In the past, world trade was concentrated upon winning raw materials and transporting them to countries with historically high rates of both manufacturing and consumption. World trade is now dominated by the transport of part-finished goods and components manufactured in countries with low wage rates to areas of consumption where industry is focused upon assembly and finishing rather than manufacturing.

To have forecast that reorientation of the global economy would have been masterful: to have forecast that changing conditions would not preclude such a reorientation would have provided a basis for constantly monitoring and updating what was likely and unlikely to happen. It is a reiteration of the need for fuzzy rather than deterministic forecasts, not to try to predict too much with too much accuracy but to provide an outline capable of being refined and updated in the light of events.

This chapter began with the view that transport had to provide the means for the factors of production to be assembled at sites where efficient activity could take place and from which products could be distributed to consumers. It ends with the view that poor accessibility will certainly hobble economic activity, and that activity needs to be sustained by better freight transport, but economic growth cannot be guaranteed by improvements in accessibility.

The General Urban Model revisited

The assertion that neither GOMMMS/TEMPRO/NTEM nor complex LUTIs based on miming markets are not fit for purpose provokes the question of how they could be improved or, should that be impossible, by what they should be replaced. The first task is to define the purpose for which a model should be fit. There is one overriding purpose:

- to assess whether proposed policies and actions are effective in delivering their objectives.

For many economists, 'effectiveness' will be translated as a measured value for money. That translation should be rejected, since it requires costs and benefits to be placed on a scale of values facilitating the calculation of a rate of return. It has already been argued that putting arbitrary quasi-monetary values on intangibles such as pollution, for which no natural market exists, is a confusing charade which pretends that benefits and disbenefits may be ranked and valid trade-offs made. Trade-offs such as the increases in fuel burn and pollution created by taking advantage of the flexibility of private cars need to be set by debate, not by a technical process using embedded parameters. Each objective should have its own unit of measurement and a desirable target level. This implies that a General Urban Model should be designed to inform political debate about relative values, not replace it.

This creates an immediate, but familiar, difficulty in scale. It was argued earlier that travel choices are made in response to the perceived transport landscape, a landscape composed of a range of possible destinations, reached by a number of possible journeys, each made up of a string of segments by various modes, each segment tied into sequence at interfaces. That landscape will vary extensively and subtly from place to place: the walk to a point served by public transport is a crucial component in travel choices and varies sensitively from one address to another. It follows that travel demand models must be very aware of distance. At its limit, every address is unique, but collecting, analysing and updating descriptive data to that detail would be too expensive and time consuming. Some aggregation is necessary.

The traditional approach described in Chapter 19 is to divide a study area into zones. The problem of scale then appears as the choice of zone size. The problems and advantages of having a fine mesh of small zones or a coarse mesh of large zones is discussed in GOMMMS.[23] Many small zones are better at detailing the variations in transport landscapes and theoretically better at predicting journey-making, but gleaning data on property values, land uses and propensities down to individual site level is far more difficult. This creates the quandary of choosing a large number of small zones to support the prediction of travel demand, or a small number of large zones supporting predictions of land-use change outlined in Figure 15.1.

The quandary is best resolved by avoiding it. The need for large zones is due to the market-based complexities shown in Figure 15.1, and if this methodology were replaced by a simpler one, designed to cope with the use of many, smaller zones, then both forecasting land use and travel demand may be based upon the same inventory of zones. The result will be akin to pointillism,[24] with the massing of small zones creating a larger image.

To achieve this, a General Urban Model would have to include a land-use budget for each zone showing the area used for each of the major land uses linked to a tariff of travel demands (for example, the number of car journeys per hour or per dwelling as a function of car ownership, etc.). This is a feature of existing models such as NTEM, but a General Urban Model would have to be extended to include a probability of land-use change, not constructed from a mathematical representation of markets, as shown in Figure 15.1, but as a function of non-monetised accessibility. This would give the desired feedback between transport and land use. If transport service levels improve due to road improvement, service revisions, a new tram route, etc., the accessibilities to each zone will shift, dragging the probabilities of land-use change with them. If new developments generate more transport demand on the existing network, accessibilities will deteriorate due to congestion and overloading, reducing accessibility and cutting the probability of further development.

This suggested model architecture is only feasible if accessibilities by all transport networks are included. This must be comprehensive, covering the movement of people, freight, information, energy and waste through inter-modal networks that incorporate interchanges and waiting buffers. The algorithm calculating the probabilities of land-use changes would be the defining nub of a General Urban Model and should be the focus of research and development.

The use of small zones enabling a subtle sensing of transport landscapes,[25] coupled with modelling detailed accessibility as an input to land-use change, could be supported by the vast amount of data based on the postcode system: the census itself is related to postcodes and a wide range of marketing profiles are available to augment other data. On average, each postcode has 19 delivery points, so the shading of the transport landscape from one part of a postcode to another would not be too misleading. Moreover, there is a good foundation for the development of models using the currently available accessibility models.[26]

The difficulties cannot be overestimated. The first is intellectual inertia. Current methodology, epitomised in GOMMMS, is fundamentally based on concepts and models used 60 years ago and updated but unquestioned since then. Suggestions that it is totally unfit for purpose, unable to reflect government policy and needs to be rethought *ab initio* will be scoffed at. Concepts such as modal split and modal choice are embedded, despite their obvious irrelevance to real travel choices. A General Urban Model is bound to be data-voracious and claims will be made that the necessary computing power is unavailable, despite abilities such as inputting a postcode into Google Maps and getting a map showing roofed space and road layout: it is even possible to 'drive' along the road. Existing models are hungry for computer resources, but it is for the calculations rather than the detailed data storage.

There will be objections based on trying to make a General Urban Model do too much to too great an accuracy and detail, and too soon. Development should begin with a crude 'toy' model based on enabling assumptions which may be refined later. Most importantly, it must be constantly verified by 'backcasting', since it must have the credibility to encourage decision-makers at political, administrative and technical levels to use it to test out potential policies and actions. It must slot into the model of policy-making shown in Figure 3.3.

Notes

1 Ministry of Transport (1970), Paragraph 2.
2 Department of Transport (1980), Paragraph 1.
3 Ministry of Transport (1989).
4 See e.g. www.bartlett.ucl.ac.uk/CASA (the website of the Centre for Advanced Spatial Analysis).
5 Ministry of Transport (1963a), Paragraph 469.
6 One of the aims of this book, perhaps the prime aim, is to revive that vision.
7 DETR (2000a). Still live (2012) in Department for Transport, *Transport Analysis Guidance* (www.dft.gov.uk/webtag/).
8 Department for Transport (current) nts2010-notes.pdf.
9 Department for Transport (current) *Transport Analysis Guidance Unit 3.1.1*, Paragraph 1.2.35.
10 www.bartlett.ucl.ac.uk/CASA.
11 Department for Transport (current) *Transport Analysis Guidance Unit 3.1.2*, Paragraph 5.1.2.
12 Department for Transport (current) *Transport Analysis Guidance Unit 3.1.3*.
13 Department for Transport (current) *Transport Analysis Guidance Unit 3.1.3*, p. 5, fig. 2.2.
14 Department for Transport (current) *Transport Analysis Guidance Unit 3.1.3*, p. 19, table 3.1.
15 Department for Transport (current) *Transport Analysis Guidance Unit 3.1.3*, p. 21, table 3.2.
16 In Cairo there is an edict against buildings of more than nine storeys: it is an edict that is often ignored. Developers claimed that they had to build high because land was so expensive that they could not make a profit on anything lower. But land was so expensive because developers were allowed to build high. In the property market the price is sometimes determined by the amount of property on offer, but at other times the amount of property on offer determines the price. That happens everywhere, but in Cairo the expense of circumnavigating the nine-storey rule has added little extra uncertainty into exactly what is determined by what.
17 Department for Transport (current) *Transport Analysis Guidance Units 3.15.1* and *3.15.2*.
18 Planners' jargon for this area is 'Roseland' (Rest of Southeast England).
19 *NTEM Guidance 6.2*. (available on www.dft.gov.uk), Paragraph 2.3.5.
20 *NTEM Guidance 6.2* (available on www.dft.gov.uk), Paragraph 2.3.6.
21 Specified in *NTEM Guidance 6.2* (available on www.dft.gov.uk).
22 Department for Transport (current) www.dft.gov.uk/statistics.
23 Department for Transport (current) *Transport Analysis Guidance Unit 3.1.1*, Paragraphs 1.2.6–8, p. 2.
24 A style of painting developed by Seurat using small dots of pure colour rather than larger areas of mixed colours similar to the modern use of pixels to create a large picture from a matrix of individual dots.
25 Reminder: transport landscapes are the perceptions held by individual people at specific places of the range of opportunities presented by the transport system and the destinations to which it provides access.
26 See Titherage (2004).

Chapter 16

Road vehicle design

Construction and use regulations: the legalities

In Britain, as in many other countries, laws are made by two, interlinked processes. Primary legislation first appears as a Bill which is initially presented to Parliament and is then refined by amendments being formally proposed, debated and then either accepted or rejected by vote. A final vote transforms the Bill into an Act with the full force of law. Primary legislation often contains clauses enabling responsible ministers to propose secondary legislation designed to clarify, interpret, modify or extend the primary Act. In some instances the primary Act imposes duties upon a minister which will have to be discharged through making secondary legislation.

In Britain, this secondary legislation is in the form of regulations contained within 'Statutory Instruments' (SI). These are 'laid before Parliament' by putting the draft on a table where it may be perused by Members who then have 40 days to raise queries or objections. In the absence of any dissent, the secondary legislation becomes law by default and then has the same power as the original primary Act.

In Britain the primary, enabling Act covering the sizes and other characteristics of road vehicles is the Road Traffic Act (1972), but the Act itself does not specify any dimensions; Section 40 gives the Secretary of State for Transport the power to make the necessary regulations within a Statutory Instrument. This primary + secondary process of making law is designed to allow the regulations to be easily edited. For example, SI 2009/2196 extends the law to cover the retro-fitting of air-conditioning units using greenhouse gases, something that was not thought of back in 1972 when the primary Act was passed, but which has now been done without the time and expense of passing new primary legislation.

The 1972 Road Traffic Act included a provision unseen in previous legislation. Section 199 (2) states that before writing draft regulations to be laid before Parliament:

> The Secretary of State shall consult with such representative organisations as he thinks fit.

Although the Secretary of State may think that nobody is 'fit' to be consulted, this is extremely unlikely: interested representative organisations are consulted and make submissions in their own interests. This is the 'stakeholder' approach in which legislation is reviewed, and perhaps edited, by those who will be affected by it. It is in contrast to the former practice in which Members of Parliament were expected to voice the concerns of both the public at large and sectional interests, in the course of normal recorded parliamentary business. Providing opportunities for off-the-record, private lobbying of government ministers by 'representative groups' was a radical shift in governance, circumventing previous parliamentary procedure.[1]

Basic vehicle dimensions were established in SI 1986/1078, but there have been many amendments since then. For example, in 1986 the maximum gross lorry weight was set at 38 tonnes; SI 1994/329 increased this to 44 tonnes, but only for lorries hauling international containers to a port or railway terminal. That condition was removed by SI 2000/3224.

The legal situation is clouded by Britain's membership of the European Union. In general, the EU produces two types of legislation. Directives are binding instructions to member nations to pass national legislation to achieve EU objectives. For example, European Commission Directive 91/440 required railways to provide open access to operating companies, implying the separation of the managements of infrastructure and operations, but the Directive did not specify how this should be done. Each member state was able to pass its own legislation to achieve the common objective.

In contrast, European regulations are legally binding and have to be implemented as they are, although they only apply to activities that cross the borders between member states – they do not apply to in-country activity. 85/3/EEC set the maximum weight of goods vehicles at 40 tonnes at a time when the legal limit within the UK was 38 tonnes, producing a significant difference between vehicles on international and local journeys, and presenting the enforcement agencies with an unenviable task. The national and European regulations have now been aligned, although they are all very complex. Maximum gross vehicle weight is set at 44 tonnes with the weight taken by each individual axle limited to 10 tonnes (11.5 tonnes if it is the sole powered axle), but these limits are conditional upon complex combinations of suspension and tyres.

The most important European regulations are those on emissions and pollution. In Britain, the Vehicle Certification Agency (VCA)[2] is responsible for the application of the EU regulations and issues certificates to confirm compliance. A second agency, the Vehicle and Operator Services Agency (VOSA),[3] is responsible for testing vehicles when they are first registered and then at regular intervals during their lifetime. VOSA is also responsible for ensuring that vehicles in use comply with the regulations, and their staff, working with the police, carry out random checks, mainly on commercial vehicles to detect overloading.

To avoid the need to test each individual new car prior to it being first registered, the regulations are enforced through 'type approvals'. An example of each model produced by each manufacturer is tested and, if approved, the approval is deemed to have been given to all vehicles with the same specification.[4] The system covers, with detailed modifications, small, specialist product runs of just a few vehicles or even a single vehicle built by hand by an enthusiast. It also covers components such as tyres. The testing is arranged by VOSA and the results handed on to VCA.

As explained in Chapter 5, fuel consumption for each type of car is measured in the laboratory according to a speed cycle defined by European regulation (shown in Figure 5.3), with the objective of comparing makes and models to a common benchmark, not to produce data on real on-the-road use. VCA/VOSA publish these laboratory data on their website and all new cars offered for sale have to have the consumption data displayed on the windscreen. Strangely, fuel consumptions to a standard, legally defined regime are not required for vehicles other than cars, and so the published data do not include freight or other vehicles.

Lorries and buses are tested by VOSA before they are registered, paying particular attention to their physical dimensions and, in the case of lorries, to their laden and unladen weights. Lorries and trailers have individual 'plates' affixed to them which specify the legal maximum vehicle and axle weights. All vehicles must undergo an annual check to ensure that compliance with the regulations is being maintained: these checks are made either by VOSA staff or, in the case of cars, by firms franchised by VOSA.

A third agency, the Driver and Vehicle Licensing Agency (DVLA),[5] is responsible for taxing and licensing vehicles, for testing and licensing drivers and for recording violations of the regulations.

Managing pollution

The annual vehicle checks (colloquially called the 'MOT' – a remnant of the Ministry of Transport's introduction of annual tests in 1960) includes a test on exhaust tailpipe emissions, the criteria for which are specified in a VOSA manual (*In-service Exhaust Emission Standards for Road Vehicles*). Vehicles failing the test cannot be licensed or used on the roads. The test is implicitly on the exhaust system, and is concerned with smoke and particulates rather than with engine performance. This is sensible, since exhaust systems are replaced at regular intervals and all vehicles change from their original condition in which they were approved.

The major change over recent years has been in vehicle design as evidenced in type approvals and in the fuel consumption rates published by the VCA. Engine design and management, particularly electronically controlled engine management, has improved fuel-burn rates, and five- and six-speed gearboxes have reduced the average engine revolutions per unit distance. Electronic engine management has reduced urban fuel consumption partly by adapting gear ratios to relate engine and road speeds more efficiently, partly by switching off the engine while the vehicle is stationary and partly by squeezing more effective energy out of the fuel. These trends must be expected to continue, although at an ever-reducing rate.

Hybrid vehicles are driven partly by electric motors fed from on-board batteries and partly by internal combustion engines used both to power the vehicle directly and to drive a generator to recharge the batteries. The electric motor is efficient in stop/start, slow-moving, congested traffic, consuming no fuel at all when stationary and then using its innate high-torque to restart and crawl at slow, congested speeds. The internal combustion engine kicks in when moving at higher, more consistent, uncongested speeds, conditions in which some of its power is used to recharge the batteries. Hybrids must be expected to continue the reduction in average consumption rates per vehicle-kilometre, and they have the secondary advantage of moving tailpipe pollutants away from congested areas. However, care must be taken not to over-emphasise the improvements in fuel consumption per kilometre, welcome though they are. Despite more efficient engines being developed within the past decade, the total fuel burn is still rising as the reductions due to better vehicle performance are more than outweighed by increases in the total vehicle mileage due to the ever longer journeys being made as urban densities reduce and urban areas increase in size – by the continuous enlargement of the virtual city.

Successive governments have used the manipulation of costs as the prime method of implementing policy. At present, 60 per cent of fuel price is tax. If a car does 12,000 miles per year at an average of 30 miles/gallon the fuel bill will be close to £2500, of which £1500 will be tax. The annual Vehicle Excise duty is £135, although this varies with the CO_2 emission rate. This gives a total tax bill of £2635, of which just 5 per cent is attributable to the annual duty. Although it is necessary to maintain a register of vehicles in order to trace vehicles involved in traffic violations or in vehicle theft, and to ensure that a vehicle conforms with current construction and use regulations, trying to influence car ownership with minimal variations in duty seems to be a policy of gesture rather than effect. A simple, cheap, flat-rate licence charge would appear to be efficient with the prime taxation being upon fuel: this would make taxation reflect the propensity to pollute (since fuel pollutes at the same rate per litre no matter whether it is burned in a large, posh guzzler or in a dainty, frugal eco-vehicle). The pollution is pro-rata with the fuel consumption rate and distance driven, so making the tax burden a function of the fuel burn makes sense.

Our policy should aim to:

- ensure the fuel consumption rate per vehicle-kilometre reduces by:
  – striving to continue reductions in the fuel burn per vehicle-kilometre through improved vehicle and engine design;
  – reducing the proportion of vehicle-kilometres driven in congested conditions (in which fuel consumption is inefficient);
- reduce mean journey length by containing growth of the virtual city with its implied reductions in density;
- reduce the fuel burn per person-kilometre by encouraging improved vehicle occupancy and to do so by:
  – encouraging the use of public transport, particularly in urban areas with a tendency towards congestion in which person journeys in cars with low occupancies and high fuel-burn rates due to the congested speeds are converted into person journeys by public transport protected against congestion and with high occupancy rates to give minimal pollutions per person-kilometre.

Notes

1 In a project concerned with the published data on emissions, the suggestion was made that the printed information pasted by law on the windscreens of new cars should be emphasised by barcoded data on vehicle licences, enabling the detection of vehicles

transgressing the rules in low-emission zones. An 'interested representative group' (the Society of Motor Manufactures and Traders) objected successfully. The public and Parliament were unaware of this.

2 The VCA was established in 1990 by separating off the responsible department within the then Department for Transport. It became an independent agency in 1993. This may be seen as part of the changing nature of governance evidenced by the inclusion of the 'stakeholder' consultation built into the 1972 Road Traffic Act. Government responsibility and direct accountability has been spread, even out-sourced.

3 Founded in 2003 after their activities had been spun off from the Department for Transport.

4 The type approval reference will be found under paragraph K on the UK Vehicle Registration Certificate (form V5).

5 Like the VCA, it was founded as an independent agency in 1990. It had been formed as a centre within the Ministry of Transport in 1965 before which vehicle licensing had been the responsibility of 81 local authorities.

Chapter 17

Public transport

The definition

The definition of public transport is usually confined to the network of those passenger-carrying services used by the public on payment of a fare. By convention, air services are often excluded and the status of taxis and private hire cars is ambivalent. Three common attributes are important:

1. The great majority of services are run at published times over set routes, although taxis, hire cars and some mini-bus services are demand-responsive with individual ad-hoc arrangements made between the passenger and the provider.
2. Operators are paid from the collected fares, often augmented by monies arranged by the state.
3. Crucially, the use of public transport avoids the need for parking space at destinations.

Monopoly

In 1285, the Statute of Winchester created the King's Highway in England, a 'right of passage and re-passage by His Majesty's subjects without let or hindrance' on 'rights of way' across land in private ownership. This created a distinction between the ownership of land and the unfettered right of way across it. Today, the distinction between ownership and control is lost on many people: there is a common confusion that regulations restricting the free deployment of privately owned assets are either impossible or should be subject to the payment of compensation for lost 'rights'. That confusion has led some to assert that regulation may only be imposed if accompanied by either state ownership or compensation: that assertion was disproved by the legal basis of the King's Highway in the thirteenth century. Unregulated freedom is a definition of anarchy: the principles of freedom are concerned with the extent to which freedom is restricted and by whom. In practice, the many restrictions on individuals' behaviour are combinations of social conventions and the law of the land.

The medieval law of the King's Highway prevented land-owners from erecting toll bars and charging travellers to cross their land. Wherever the Highway was interrupted by river crossings, the 'right of passage and re-passage' across privately owned land became impossible. The law made two provisions: the construction of toll bridges could be covered by specific exemption from the general rule preventing the imposition of tolls, and ferries could be granted a licence or charter. The tolls were fixed by legislation in both cases. This is instructive: the law recognised that bridges were constrictions which created a local monopoly but, by setting tolls, the law also ensured that such monopolies were not exploited. In the case of ferries, the charters deliberately created artificial monopolies by preventing competition between ferries but also regulated the fares.

Regulation of transport by the state has an unavoidable ambivalence. The state was, on the one hand, creating monopolies, but, on the other, was limiting the prices they could charge. In later centuries the regulation of trade and transport grew, a trend seen latterly as an ideology, mercantilism, but was more a contemporary pragmatism. State control and regulation, often through the creation of trading monopolies such as the East India Company, formalised transport and trade so that it could be more easily taxed. Cynics will see this as a manifestation of the self-referential Matthew effect: the state needed to regulate in order to create a revenue stream to pay for the regulation. The fundamental undesirability of such state intervention is a basic plank of the platform of those arguing for the minimalist state. However, financial, legal and political stability is vital to the founding and growth of trade and industry, and the mercantilist monopolies provided that stability, fostering the early global economy to the great benefit of the European trading nations.

Regulation of British public transport

The regulation of British public transport has been continuous since the seventeenth century. The concern has been twofold:

1   to ensure the security and safety of passengers;
2   to prevent exploitation of the tendency towards monopoly.

These two concerns are linked. If passenger security and safety are to be safeguarded, controls have to be imposed upon vehicles and operators: the obvious way of doing this is by licensing. 'Quality licensing' tries to ensure safety and security by setting tests as a condition of the licence, with violations of the regulations being penalised by the removal of the licence. 'Quantity licensing' features a limit upon the number of licences issued in an attempt to ensure that service quality does not slip into undesirable competition during day-to-day operations, although, in practice, such licensing may be no more than a tax.

Both quality and quantity licensing in transport reinforce transport's inherent tendency towards monopoly. To be effective, competition must be between products which may be substituted, one for the other: for instance, consumers selecting products from a supermarket shelf, will tend to buy the cheapest from the set that are seen to be equally satisfactory – any one of the brands in the set may be substituted by any other. There is a major paradox in markets: firms are generally antagonistic towards both regulation and competition. They strive continuously to thwart competition by undermining substitutability through branding their products and then advertising them in an attempt to persuade consumers that their product is unique and may not be substituted by another, similar product. Real competition cannot happen without a variety of products perceived by consumers to be mutual substitutes.

In transport, possible substitution is extremely limited: a service running at the time and to the destination suited to a passenger cannot be substituted by one that runs at a different time or to a different place. If there were real competition between two services running at the same time and on the same route, it will almost certainly mean that there is over-capacity – a large number of the seat-kilometres will be unused. The operators will then strive to reduce their costs and increase their revenues by seeking to destroy the competition, either by a price war leading to the demise of the weaker company or by a take-over bid. This process is emphasised by timetabled services being infinitely perishable: their use may be planned before departure time but they cease to exist beyond recall immediately after departure – any possibility of substitution is fleeting: it is as though the goods on a supermarket shelf are there to be bought at one minute but vanish the next.

Effective substitutability in transport is a chimera. Later in this chapter it will be shown that the attempts to engender competition in the transport industry through deregulation and privatisation have failed: competition has rarely appeared and, when it has, it has been unstable, short-lived and has self-destructed.

Hackney carriages and taxis

Regulation was a feature of public transport from its very inception: it may even be claimed that regulation first defined and then fostered public transport. The original Hackney[1] Carriage regulations which were imposed in London in 1654 were an example of both 'quantity' and 'quality' licensing. The number of licences was limited and the suitability of the drivers was ensured by initial testing, and by an identifying badge to enable dishonest drivers to be traced and punished by a committee of aldermen. At the time there was no police force, and so passengers had to be protected from 'undesirable competition' such as refusing to take passengers to their destination unless they paid more money – a form of piracy that was to provoke further legislation in 1930.[2]

Subsequent Hackney Acts in London changed the tests and the limit on the number of licences. The limit was lifted altogether in 1833, causing a flood of licensees and fierce, chaotic, on-street competition. The limit on the numbers was restored and still exists today, although there is now a two-tier system. Throughout the country, taxis (often called black cabs) are legally required to have a Hackney Carriage licence issued by the local authority which also tests and licenses drivers. These taxis are permitted to pick up passengers without prior arrangement either when stationary at designated stands on the street or by passengers flagging them down while moving. The number of taxi licences in each local council area is limited, creating a weak monopoly, but, harking back to medieval tolls and the fear of monopolistic exploitation, the fares are fixed by law. The second tier are 'private hire cars' which are also licensed, but their numbers are unlimited. They have to be prebooked at individually negotiated fares (although the 'negotiation' is likely to be abruptly truncated by a take-it-or-leave-it fare being quoted).

Horse-drawn buses

Horse-drawn buses were introduced in London in 1829, covered by the Hackney Carriage regulations: they were treated as shared taxis at fares fixed by the local authority along with the other taxi fares. Soft, muddy, churned-up roads, conditions to which they themselves contributed, meant that buses needed two horses to haul quite small, 15-seater buses. Surfacing urban roads created a need for drainage, adding to the expense of the surfacing itself which was usually in the form of granite setts (called cobblestones in Britain and pavé on the continent), but surfacing was confined mostly to well-used streets with a cross-flow of pedestrians. The first London bus service was from Paddington to the Bank via Euston and King's Cross as a means for the rich to travel from the affluent suburbs of the Paddington area to the City, but later it became a service to carry passengers arriving at the newly built mainline stations. Today this is called 'down-town distribution', enabling people to complete their journey by getting much nearer to their final destination – it was an early demonstration of modes meshing with one another to provide transport all the way from an origin address to a destination. Costs and fares of these first buses were very high: 18 pence inside or 12 pence on the roof for five miles.[3] By comparison, the driver's wages were 3 pence per hour – travel by bus was only for the affluent.

The limited number of hackney licences could be traded. A French company (it renamed itself the 'London General Omnibus Company') dominated the London bus industry by buying all the licences it could, and by the 1850s it had 13,500 horses and operated three-quarters of London's buses. The year 1851 was an important one, with the Great Exhibition in Hyde Park generating a surge in traffic and giving considerable impetus to the bus operators' demands that more streets be surfaced, not with cobblestones but with a running surface of coal-tar or asphalt laid either upon wooden blocks where the weight of traffic justified the cost or directly on the compacted ground. In this case the surface was not there to provide strength but to waterproof the road and to prevent it from deteriorating into cloying mud. Given a better surface, the horses could haul bigger, more efficient buses with 26 seats.

Horse trams

Trams appeared first in Britain on the streets of Birkenhead in 1860 and in London the following year. In both instances an Act of Parliament was needed to authorise the construction of the track within the highway. It was a solution to the limitations upon the size and weight of buses imposed by the poor road conditions: the track meant that the strength of the horses could be used to pull trams that were bigger and heavier than the buses. Trams and their operating staff were licensed under the Hackney Carriage regulations in the same way as horse buses. Each tram was hauled by two horses at a speed of 11 km/h which, with stops for passengers to get on and off, gave a journey speed little faster than walking. These early trams were highly unpopular with other road users, since the rails were not well aligned with the road surface. The need for an individual Act for each tramway was replaced in 1870 by an Enabling Act.[4] Local authorities were responsible for the highways, and they, having received a proposal from a private company to build and operate a tramway, had to apply to the Board of Trade (the government department responsible for railways among other things) for permission to allow the company to break open the highway. The permission could be on condition that specified road improvements were made at the tram company's expense. The specification and construction of the track and of the trams were inspected and licensed by technical officers at the Board of Trade, but operations and fares were regulated by the local magistrates and, after 1888, by the newly created local councils. Under the 1870 Act, the track, although built at company expense, became the legal property of the local authority as the body responsible for the highway in which it was embedded. The track was then leased back by the local authority to the tram company on terms specified within the Act. These terms made the tram company, rather than the local authority, responsible for the cost of the maintenance of the highway within the track and for 18 inches (45 cm) to either side. One surprising element in the legislation was that the leases had an automatic limit of 21 years, at the end of which the local council retained its legal ownership of the track but also had to be given the opportunity to buy the rest of the tram operation in its entirety. Local councils then had the choice of renewing the lease, leasing it to another company or buying out the entire operation themselves. Many councils did exert their right to buy the tram system in their area and became public transport operators, although public ownership of tram operations had not been the original intention of the 1870 Act: that had been to include ownership of the track in with the fabric of the highway as well as emphasising the existing Hackney regulations on fares and safety. In later years many of the municipal tramway operations expanded into running buses, first as feeders to the trams and then as city-wide networks – municipalities became bus operators almost by accident.

After the 1870 Tramways Act, events moved extremely quickly; for example, in Edinburgh, a new company and the local authority had made the necessary written agreements, obtained authorisation from the Board of Trade, built the first line, had it inspected and licensed, and had carried the first passengers, all before the end of 1871. The line was through the affluent Southside and a ticket for the five-mile return trip to the city centre was 3 pence, equal to the hourly wage rate for the tram driver: today's bus fare on the same basis would be £12. Paying that amount for a journey at the speed of a walking horse was ostentatious rather than practical – the equivalent of driving a Ferrari to the local supermarket. Fares were high because costs were high: each tram was hauled by two horses able to work no more than three hours a day, so needing 12 horses per tram for a day's work. When it was built, the track cost £7500[5] per kilometre, the trams were £200 each and the horses £28 each, making a capital cost of £536 per tram. Providing a tram every five minutes needed two trams for every track-kilometre. Trams cost £830 each, and this, together with the £7500 for the kilometre of track itself, needed a capital outlay of £8332 per kilometre. The loan charge upon that was £1000 per kilometre per year. Add the wages of the driver and

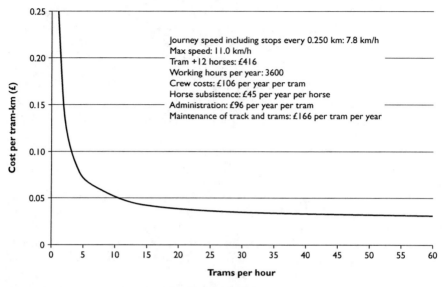

Figure 17.1 Total cost per horse tram-kilometre (1880 prices)
Source: Archived records for the Edinburgh horse trams.

conductor (6½ pence per hour) and feed for the horses, and the cost totalled £0.043 per tram-kilometre. That would need 10 or so passenger fares to cover it. Horse trams were a very expensive and exclusive means of transport only bettered by having one's own carriage or using a hackney.

Figure 17.1 is important, not for the data about horse trams but as a simple demonstration of an aspect of the costing of any form of transport using a fixed track or any other heavy capital cost. Track was expensive to construct and to maintain. If it were only lightly loaded with, say, a tram every 15 minutes, the proportion of those heavy costs borne by each movement along the track was very high, and easily outweighed the operating costs of wages for the operating staff and feed for the horses. However, the more the track was used (represented by the frequency of trams per hour in Figure 17.1), the lower the impact of the capital cost upon the cost per tram-kilometre: in Figure 17.1 this relationship creates an L-shaped curve with a critical frequency around a headway of six minutes (10 trams per hour). Although the precise arithmetic changes from mode to mode and from date to date, the principle remains that transport with high capital costs are very expensive to operate if underutilised, but become relatively cheap if used intensively.

The matter is rather more complex than that because tracked systems enable faster travel and are more efficient in the power used per hauled tonne, so there may be some justification for incurring high track costs. In the case of horse trams, the speeds and loads were not spectacularly high but they were better than horse buses running upon badly kept or unsurfaced roads. This simple, obvious principle meant that it was only commercially sensible to build horse tram tracks where demand justified a frequent service: elsewhere the untracked horse bus was more efficient, since it avoided the capital burden of the track, despite needing more horsepower per passenger to operate.

Two important and enduring principles were apparent from these early horse-powered beginnings:

1   A single mode was not suitable for all travel in all parts of a city: horse trams worked in areas of dense, affluent demand; horse buses served less dense but still affluent areas; hackneys in still less dense but even more affluent areas; railways were used for very selective traffic where track costs were met by freight haulage; and everyone else walked as they had done for centuries, obliged to live in the dense, crowded Victorian slums within a kilometre or two from wherever they worked.
2   The differences between the appropriate modes were related to the local, detailed geography and, in particular, to the density of demand.

There was, and still is, no universal solution to the provision of urban transport by any one mode of public transport. All modes have geographies to which they are suited and others to which they are certainly not.

Powered trams

At the turn of the century, the economics, role and influence of the tram changed completely with the replacement of the horse by mechanical power, usually by electric motors.[6] The extra power allowed trams to be heavier and faster. The capacity was doubled from 50 to 100 persons per tram, axle loadings rose to 6 tonnes and speeds more than doubled, requiring much stronger and more expensive track. There also had to be the means to supply power to the moving trams. The capital costs of the track more than doubled,[7] but the higher speeds and the shedding of the need for horses, which were expensive to buy, house and feed, reduced the cost per tram-kilometre to a quarter of their previous levels. Since powered trams had at least double the capacity of the old horse trams, the costs per place-kilometre[8] were reduced to one-eighth or even one-tenth of horse tram costs. Fares were reduced to such a level that the coinage could not cope – there were no coins small enough to charge per distance carried and most operators charged a flat fare of a penny return for the whole length of a route.[9] By 1905, one hour's pay for a tram driver (5.7 pence) would cover the tickets for 40 kilometres of travel, four times as far as with the pay of a horse tram driver.

The result was a complete redrawing of urban isochrones[10] and accessibility maps. Working people could now afford to travel to work and were no longer confined to the slum conditions within walking distance of their jobs. Landowners in areas on the edge of the Victorian city were quick to switch from agriculture or market gardening to being the landlords of new terraced housing. Unlike the slums, the houses in the new, extending suburbs[11] were heavily regulated, built in conformity to strict building regulations contained within council 'by-laws'. The resulting form (now called 'by-law housing') was in terraces, but with small gardens, accessed by council-provided roads under which there were municipal gas, water and sewer pipes. The nearby main road would probably have had a municipal tram service to the older commercial and industrial areas of the city. The physical differences between the slums and by-law housing were due in part to more affluence and more economic opportunity, but they were primarily due to municipal government. It was an era of massive civic pride, corporate activity and municipal responsibility characterised by the impressive municipal offices built in Glasgow (1888), Leeds (1858), Sheffield (1897) and Manchester (1877). Each became the centre of municipal electric tram networks built in the first decade of the twentieth century.

The high capital cost of the track and the need to run frequent, well-loaded services to cover those costs meant that tram networks tended to show two common characteristics:

1   In the dense city core built before the arrival of the electric tram, the network was comparatively dense and diffuse, with lines running along many of the major roads.
2   Outside the city core the routes were long, radial fingers providing access to the developing, lower density suburbs being built on previously agricultural land.

By-law housing provided the density of demand which justified the service frequencies needed to sustain the new tram routes. Frequencies were astonishing by today's standards: many tram managers boasted that if you had just missed a tram the next one was always in sight. For example, the 20-kilometre route from central London to the satellite town of Croydon was served by a tram every three minutes (1400 seats per hour), needing 50 trams working continuously, a frequency that was maintained until 1951. The intermediate fields were quickly filled with housing, creating a continuous strip of residential development linking Croydon to London.

The link between electric trams and new housing extending the city outward into the surrounding areas was exemplified by the official opening in May 1903 of the very first electric tramline in London. The Prince of Wales (the Future King George V) dutifully bought two halfpenny tickets (£0.0021 each) for himself and his wife for the 6-kilometre ride to Tooting and, once there, officially inaugurated the Totterdown Fields municipal housing estate, an area of 1261 dwellings built upon market gardens and specifically planned to be served by the new tramline.[12]

Three other trends completed the developing urban geography:

1   Industry remained where it was. Factories were still largely powered by belts and pulleys driven by stationary steam-engines. The coal required by the engines was brought from the mines by rail and so factories were reliant upon rail services, not only for the supply of coal but also to carry inward raw materials and outward products. Road freight was still by expensive, inefficient horse and cart: factories were tied to where they had been built, near the railways, although their employees could move to the new suburbs, commuting by tram.

2   The isochrones were now lozenge shaped, pulsing in sympathy with tram service frequencies and focused upon the very centre of the city which became the most accessible area by a very wide margin.[13] Retailing was becoming an ever-more important part of the growing economy and shops requiring high sales revenue could thrive only at a focus of tram routes. Similarly, offices, with their need for literate staff who were unlikely to live in the old, dense Victorian slums relied on their employees commuting by tram from the suburbs. City centres came to be dominated by retail and commercial activity.

3   Lower turnover shops selling food, etc. also had to locate where they could attract sufficient customers. Unlike the city centre shops, they did not need a flood of customers to provide the required cash flow but needed to have a threshold number of people within walking distance. For them, the best place was along the tram route where the pavements were thronged with people attracted by the tram service. Even today, the old tram routes may still be identified by the flanking lines of small shops. Today's bus-stops for routes into town are often sited at the same places as the old tram stops, and many still have nearby shops selling the newspapers, sweets and cigarettes then needed for the journey.

The very sudden arrival of the electric tram had an immediate and powerful effect on the geography of urban areas: the Edwardian city grew quickly to become a completely different structure to its immediate Victorian predecessor. The exact relationship is less important than the principle that urban structure depends on the means by which mobility and accessibility are provided.

Motor buses

Just as horses were replaced by electric motors in powering trams, so horses were replaced by petrol motors in powering buses. The motor bus first appeared in numbers on London's streets in 1904, the year after the first electric tram. They were operated by three or four new companies. London General, the major horse-bus company, reacted quickly, buying out the new companies and acquiring their hackney licences. In 1909 London General even established its own bus-building plant, a plant that went on, under the name of AEC, to build London's buses for the next 60 years, culminating in the iconic 'Routemaster'.

The First World War demonstrated how both armies and productive industries were dependent upon good transport. The development of the internal combustion engine had been proceeding quickly before the war, but became even faster in the war years: it was clearly the motive power of the future, replacing the horse almost entirely and eroding the use of the railways. The apparent problems and opportunities led the government to create the Ministry of Transport in 1919 within weeks of the end of the war. It faced two immediate problems: first, accommodating the expected flood of lorries, buses and cars, and second, addressing the parlous financial state of the railways.

The Ministry of Transport was the brainchild of Sir Eric Geddes who had been deputy general manager of the North Eastern Railway before, and Director-General of Transport of the British Army in France during the War. He was elected as the Conservative Member of Parliament for Cambridge, drafted the Transport Bill, and then became the first Minister of Transport, a good example of planning your own luck. During the War the entire railway system had been taken into state control (but not ownership), but dividends had fallen and the system required renovation after the wartime overuse and lack of maintenance. Share prices were not healthy and shareholders were becoming restless. The railways were never returned to their control but were compulsorily reorganised into four umbrella companies; the shareholders were bought out, much to their common delight, although with the obligatory veneer of outraged discontent.

A new Housing Act was passed in parallel with the Transport Act. A connection was seen by some Members of Parliament:

> Lastly, the Government has decided to bring in what is an absolutely essential concomitant of the Housing Bill that is a Transport Bill. It may be that other projects have failed because they were not accompanied by transport facilities, but to-day we may go forward with more hope than we ever had before in this matter.[14]

The next major piece of legislation was the 1930 Road Traffic Act which differentiated between hackney carriages (taxis and trams) and a new category of 'public service vehicles' (PSV) covering buses and long-distance coaches, but not trams or trolleybuses.[15] The 1930 Act established 13 Commissioners, each responsible for a traffic area within which they managed the licensing of bus routes, timetables, fares, vehicles and operating staff, and also lorries and their operators. The then Minister of Transport[16] Herbert Morrison was a staunch member of the Labour Party, but he was a minister in a coalition government which also imposed the speed limits, driving tests, driving licences and controls upon vehicle size and weight, still in place in principle, if not in detail, today. Deaths in road accidents prior to these regulations were over double the numbers today, even though the amount of traffic was far less. The 1930 Act with its heavy regulation was not enacted from political ideology but to organise a road transport system amidst dangerous chaos.

The problem had its roots in the First World War. In 1914, armies were dependent upon the horse – in Britain horses were requisitioned into army service well before men were conscripted. But the needs of war resulted in the swift development and refinement of the internal combustion engine and, towards the end of the War, the Army had become reliant upon lorries in their hundreds. In 1919 many of these vehicles were sold off very cheaply, with many of them bought by otherwise jobless ex-servicemen. Some were used to haul freight, but the inter-city road network was still weak and the railways were well organised to carry long-distance traffic, albeit with very long transit times. Many of the ex-army lorries were re-bodied as buses and operated in competition with the motor-bus services licensed under the Hackney Carriage Regulations, and run either by established bus companies, by local councils or by the railway companies. The Hackney Regulations could not keep pace, and unlicensed vehicles were being driven recklessly and with little concern for passengers.

It was not uncommon for lightly loaded buses to decant their passengers without refunding their fares and head off in another direction if a goodly number of people looked as though that was where they wished to go. It was not for nothing that these effectively unregulated buses were called 'pirates', and their activities caused considerable public and political disquiet.

The 1930 Act remained in force for over 50 years and moulded the bus and long-distance coach networks into patterns which may still be seen today. The traffic Commissioners very rarely granted licences to competitive services. There were a number of examples where licences were given to more than one operator to provide a joint service, but the basic tenet was that direct competition implied duplication and so was a waste of resources. It was regulation through imposed monopoly, just as it was with medieval ferries and seventeenth-century hackneys. It could be argued that this was taken to extremes. It was common for the licences for inter-urban, out-of-town routes to contain a provision to prevent them from picking up passengers and then setting them down within the same area if it were served by a local, in-town operator. Furthermore, in accordance with the tenet of avoiding 'wasteful competition', these in-town operators were often forced by the terms of their licence to wander off into side-roads and housing estates rather than staying on the major radial roads, spreading bus-kilometres to serve the suburban housing estates rather than duplicating services on the main road. Since fares were regulated as part of the licensing process, the route monopolies created by the system were not milked for monopoly profits.

Fare regulation was not only extensive but also intrusive. Companies wishing to raise their fares had to argue their case in a public hearing before the traffic Commissioner: that case was required to divulge information about the operating costs and profitability. The Commissioner could also hear objections from the public, from other operators and from British Railways. In one famous case in 1960, Midland Red began operating coaches between London and Birmingham along the newly opened M1 to an approved timetable and at approved fares well below train fares. There was no motorway speed limit and the coaches consistently arrived early to such a notorious extent that they actually – although unofficially – bettered the train times. British Railways complained to the traffic Commissioner and Midland Red was instructed to keep to the licensed timetable.

Buses had their effect on urban geography just as trams had had two decades previously, but bus economics were radically different. Bus operating costs (the vehicle, fuel and crew) were higher than those of trams, but the track costs were almost negligible, limited to the vehicle licence. That exempted them from the financial need to run high-frequency routes and the cost curve shown in Figure 17.1 became irrelevant. Nonetheless, although high frequency was not a financial imperative, buses could provide a high-frequency service – London's spine route 11 famously ran every two minutes until well into the 1960s, and even today has an eight-minute headway (800 places per hour in each direction).

The ability of the bus to run at low frequencies meant that it did not have to serve areas of dense demand, and so, unlike the trams, it could spread a public transport service over time and space: the route network was diffuse and bus-stops could be provided within walking distance of dwellings at much lower densities and spread over much wider areas than were required to sustain the tram network. This ability was related to a further change in residential development. The by-law terrace housing of the 1910s and 1920s gave way to the ubiquitous 1930s semi-detached with larger gardens and, probably, a bus-stop within walking distance served by two, maybe three buses an hour.

There is a threshold at about five buses per hour (a 12-minute headway) at which passengers begin to manipulate their time budgets to arrive at a bus-stop to catch a particular, timetabled service: at higher frequencies they arrive at stops at random.[17] These random arrivals create an average waiting time of half the headway while frequencies of fewer than five buses an hour produce a skewed pattern of waiting times, with a surge of passengers tending to arrive at the stop shortly before the expected arrival of the bus. This hints at waiting times being a crucial component of passengers' perceptions of service levels. If passengers arrive at random, they are implicitly accepting the possibility of a wait lasting up to the known headway, although hoping it will be less. Service quality will then be judged by the maintenance of the headway, with a low probability of waits being extended beyond the published headway. If passengers arrive at a stop in a non-random pattern, they are deliberately timing their arrivals to match the timetable, and service quality will be judged by the adherence to the timetable rather than by the frequency/headway. In either event, the perceived service quality will be a product of unexpected, extended waits due to not keeping to the headway (for service intervals of under 12 minutes), or being late (for less frequent services).

The railways

From their very beginning in the early years of the nineteenth century until the 1960s the major work and the major source of revenue of the railway network as a whole was to haul freight. Paradoxically, the first railway in London was built as a passenger line from London Bridge to Greenwich, duplicating the passenger boats on the Thames, but, like so many railways, it was built in anticipation of an unlikely volume of traffic and was a commercial disaster. It was then bought and extended to bring agricultural produce from Kent into a large goods yard built at the Bricklayers Arms. Although the expense of the track was met largely by freight traffic, the image of the train focused on the passenger services. This dichotomy resonated right through the detailed operation of railways and, it will be argued, still has to be fully resolved.

Initially, the track enabled trains to move at hitherto unbelievable speeds: in 1829 the Rocket had whirled people along at nearly 50 km/h and, by the late nineteenth century, 60 km/h was a common operating speed for passenger trains, but the major constraint was, and still is, the rate of acceleration and braking rather than the top speed. In Victorian times this limit was set by the rather crude train mechanics, the power of the locomotive to accelerate and the efficiency of the brakes to stop. In 1829 only the locomotive at the front and a guard's van at the back had brakes and so the working speed had to be restricted to well below the possible top speed.

The matter became a paradigm of the need for, and objections to, regulation. Early Victorian government was committed to 'soft regulation' and persuasion. Following a number of accidents, not all due to poor brakes, the Board of Trade issued a recommendation that passenger trains should have brakes fitted to every coach, and then, in 1875, it established a Royal Commission to look at the whole matter of railway safety. It set about its work in a commendable way, testing a number of commercially available braking systems, all using pipes along the length of the train to carry either air at pressure or a vacuum capable of applying a brake to every wheel, and to do so automatically should one part of a train become uncoupled from the rest. The Commission's report was quite clear about what needed to be done, but it was merely a repeat of advice which had already been given on 'best practice' 15 years previously.

Fewer than five years after the publication of the Commission's advice, an accident occurred just after lunch on 11 August 1880 at Wennington Junction in Lancashire, killing seven people and severely injuring many more. In a lesson that could well do with being copied, an inquest was convened that same afternoon, and a jury was empanelled and at the scene of the accident before nightfall. The verdict was returned nine days later after hearing much technical evidence: it found that the accident was due to excessive speed at the foot of a gradient over which the driver had lost control due to having brakes only on the tender of his engine and on just one of the nine vehicles it was pulling. The Board of Trade wrote to the directors of the railway company, pointing out that the accident would not have happened had the train been fitted with adequate brakes (as had been advised 20 years previously, advice that had been repeated and supported by experimental evidence by the more recent Royal Commission). The response by the company has a familiar ring: 'The company is fitting brakes to its rolling stock as a matter of urgency.'[18]

Nine years later another accident, this time at Armagh in Northern Ireland (then under the jurisdiction of the Westminster government), killed 87 people. This time the cause was even more inexcusable – the brakes were so ineffective that they were unable to hold the train at rest on a 1-in-75 gradient and the train ran backwards into the following train. In a subsequent parliamentary debate on railway safety, it was suggested that:

> It would be a very serious thing if the Government in its attempt to protect the lives of passengers by rail, and the lives of working men, should take on itself to decide what form of carriage, what form of coupling and brake, is the proper form for railway companies to use. I am of opinion that the lives of passengers and railway men will be safer in the long run, if these matters are left in the hands of those who understand them best.[19]

It is the argument that has been voiced in recent years about state regulation of all sorts, an argument steeped in an ideology claiming that regulation leads to inefficiency. At the time of the debate 87 people were in their graves as proof that companies could be selectively deaf to 'advice', gentle regulation and even to experimental evidence.

The Conservative government of the time, led by the Marquis of Salisbury,[20] realised that compulsion would be more effective than persuasion and passed the Regulation of Railways Act (1889) which forced companies to provide brakes on all passenger trains, and also stringent, detailed signalling practices. It is this Act that is the foundation of the safety culture which has made British railways the safest in the world.

Incredibly, poor, even absent brakes on freight wagons continued for another century. Until the 1980s many freight trains were running as they had been on the first railways 150 years earlier, with brakes on the locomotives at the front and a guard's van at the rear, but not on the loosely coupled wagons in between. It resulted in a maximum speed of 40 km/h, extended transit times, extremely poor use of rolling-stock, passenger train speeds and frequencies held back by lumbering freight trains, and with repeated derailments and accidents resulting in more disruption than injury. The Beeching Report of 1963, largely a compendium of facts and statistics devoid of any analysis of the causes behind the statistics, reported that:

> Without freight the main railway network could not exist. Although passenger trains can be operated profitably over main routes where they have to contribute only a part of the route cost, they would, on their own, be capable of supporting only a small fraction of the existing route mileage outside the London suburban area. It is encouraging to see, therefore, how well freight traffic is spread over all the routes on which passenger train services are likely to continue.[21]

At the time this was a justified analysis, but Beeching ignored the fact that network capacity was dominated by freight, not because of its volume but because of the primitive methods of working freight trains. The statistics were reported:

> The average turn-round time between one loading and the next for British Railways' wagons is 11.9 working days. The average loaded transit time is about 14.2 days, with an average journey length of 67 miles, but individual transit times are bound to vary over a wide range, not merely because of variations in distance but also because of variations in route and in marshalling delays.[22]

The analysis of the causes behind these facts was woefully inadequate: Beeching suggested that British Railways was striving to provide a service to carry freight traffic as it had been in the 1890s, before the development of motor vehicles. That may have been so, but the real problem was that the railways were trying to do it with a technology that had been created in the 1830s, and this was inhibiting the viability of the railways as a whole. Not only did the Beeching Report fail to address the fundamental causes of the railway's problems rather than describe their statistical effects, but it made the classic error of segmenting an overall problem into separate components and then attempting to create targeted policies and actions to resolve each without considering their continuing interaction. Subdividing the railway problems into freight and passenger and then resolving each independently was done in the face of the initial declaration that track costs were shared and that freight and passenger costings were interactive. The failure was in not understanding the basic technical problem behind the financial statistics, that sharing track capacity between freight and passenger was prejudiced by freight trains crawling at speeds of less than one-third of passenger trains. Such myopia is with us still: there is a consistent failure to see the transport system and the geography it serves as an organic whole, not a bundle of separate issues.

The rates of acceleration and braking are still the fundamental controls upon capacity and therefore upon costs. Passenger trains are limited by comfort and safety to a rate of approximately 1 metre per second per second (a change of 3.6 km/h during every second of braking or acceleration). Although most are mechanically capable of higher rates, a limit is set by the need for passengers to remain on their feet and for their luggage to stay on the racks.

Figure 17.2 is important, since it shows the effect of the constraint of acceleration and braking upon the distances between stops and the effect of that upon the maximum mean operating speed. It applies not just to trains but to all passenger vehicles unless passengers are belted into their seats and their luggage is securely stowed. Figure 17.2 assumes that a vehicle starts from rest at one stop, accelerates constantly at a rate compatible with passenger comfort and safety to the top speed, and then immediately starts to brake to come to a halt at the next stop. A train capable of a top speed of 75 km/h may only use that capability if the stops are at least 0.5 of a kilometre apart and even then it will only travel at its top speed for a metre or two before it has to start braking for the next stop. Similarly, trams with a top speed of 60 km/h may have stops no closer together than 260 metres.

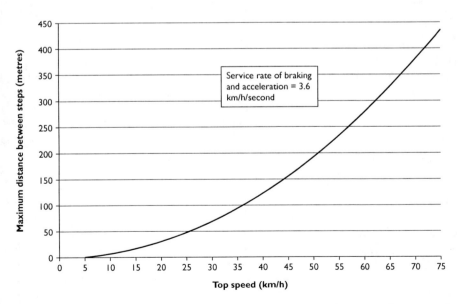

Figure 17.2 Maximum distance between service stops as a function of top speed

The curve demonstrates a characteristic that makes different modes of transport suitable for different conditions. Railways, having a reserved and engineered track, are capable of much higher speeds than the other public transport modes but those speeds may only be utilised if the stations are well-spaced out. Since each station will serve an area limited by the distance that passengers are prepared to walk to it, there has to be a trade-off between station spacing, operating speeds and the densities of the areas served – these densities are the drivers of demand which, in turn, drives frequency. It is clear that railways may only provide for in-town passenger traffic in large urban areas where travel distances are long enough for the speeds at which rail is capable to be used.

In the 1930s this led to a personal transport hierarchy:

- Walking. No waiting. Suitable for ultra-short distances at the start, end and within journeys, but distances and speeds are limited by individual physical capabilities.
- Trams. Very frequent with minimal waiting but a limited number of routes and so of stops. If the numbers of passengers necessary to justify the track costs were to be carried, residential densities within walking distance of the stops had to be high.
- Buses. No track costs and could run at lower frequencies upon a wider spread of routes serving many stops. Waiting times are dependent upon reliability rather than frequency. Economic viability is dependent upon adequate loadings and so could serve a wide range of densities of demand by matching frequencies to the demand.
- Rail. Major attribute of speed but that could only be delivered given substantial distances between stations and journey lengths by passengers.

The impact of the private car

Public transport in the 1930s through to the 1950s was dominated by the regulations imposed by the 1930 Road Traffic Act and administered by the traffic Commissioners. But the world changed to an extent quite unforeseen by Parliament in 1930. In the rising prosperity of the 1960s, cars ceased to be a mode of travel confined to the affluent and became increasingly popular, eroding the use of public transport, as shown in Figure 17.3.

Figure 17.3 shows the use of the railway and bus. Public transport reached its zenith in the 1950s, but from then on increasing car ownership pushed the use of both bus and train into steep decline. For rail, the problems were exacerbated by the simultaneous loss of freight traffic, particularly coal, due to a fundamental change in the supply of energy. The geography of electricity generation changed radically in the 1950s and 1960s and, with it, the movements of coal trains. Many small local power-stations were replaced by a few, very large multi-megawatt stations transmitting power at high voltages over long distances through the National Grid. The coal traffic became concentrated upon relatively few trunk routes feeding the new large stations rather than spread more widely over the entire rail network: the diffuse movement of energy by rail was being replaced by an expanding network of pylons and cables.

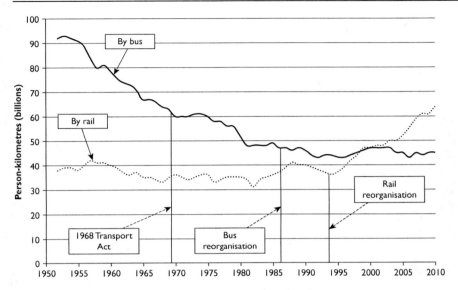

Figure 17.3 Person-kilometres (billions) by bus and rail
Source: Department for Transport, *Transport Statistics Great Britain* (2010), table 0101.

Later, local coal-gas plants were supplanted by North Sea gas transported by another new national network, this one of yellow pipes, and another source of traffic was lost to the railways. That was then followed by coal losing the domestic heating market. The need to supply coal to individual homes by road from local, rail-connected coal yards was replaced by the new national network of yellow pipes delivering natural gas to the great majority of British homes.[23] The massive reduction in the tonne-kilometres of coal by rail coupled with the concentration of the remaining traffic upon a few selected routes, leaving the majority of the network without any coal traffic at all, meant that the considerable track infrastructure costs had to be covered primarily by the passenger traffic which itself was declining due to increased car use. The railways hit the large and continuing crisis analysed in the Beeching Report which concluded that much of the rail system had been overtaken by events and was redundant, effectively replaced by new networks of pipes and wires to transport energy, and of cars to transport people. The situation was bad, but was made much worse by the railways failing to update the operation of freight trains, which dominated the network capacity, denying the opportunity to improve passenger speeds and frequencies.

Figure 17.4 shows in more detail the effects of increasing car ownership and use. The curve showing the downward trend in public transport patronage is a combination of the person-kilometres by rail and bus previously shown separately in Figure 17.3, but is now shown as a percentage of the total number of person-kilometres rather as absolute number. It also shows the comparable percentages by car and by pedal bicycle. Figure 17.4 displays not only the ever-increasing dominance of car travel but also how that dominance has caused a massive increase in the total

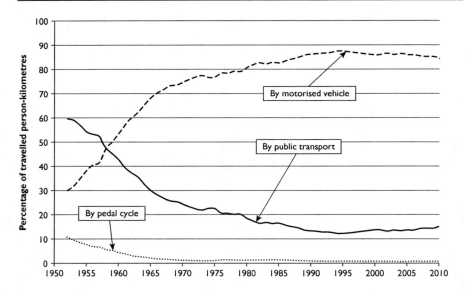

Figure 17.4 **Percentage of travelled person-kilometres by mode**
Source: Department for Transport, *Transport Statistics Great Britain* (2010), table 0101.

amount of travel. Figure 17.3 shows that there were 109 billion person-kilometres by public transport in both 1963 and 2010. In 1963 this was over 35 per cent of all travel, but by 2010 the same number of person-kilometres by public transport was only 15 per cent of the total. Figure 17.3 shows that travel by bus had declined more steeply and more constantly than travel by rail, both absolutely in the numbers of people carried, and relatively in the proportion of all travel.

Figure 17.4 should be regarded with a tinge of scepticism on two grounds:

1   The travel of which these are percentages excludes the distances walked either as a complete journey on foot or as an integral part of a journey using other modes. Consequently, the total distance travelled of which Figure 17.4 shows the percentages is an underestimate.
2   It is a picture for the whole of Britain from which there are wild variations from place to place. Some of these are just a matter of common sense: areas with few stations or bus services will show a percentage use of public transport well below the national average. Conversely, the areas with a good public transport service will exceed the national average. Of course, there would not be a good public transport service if it were not for the demand generated by the good public transport service[24] – this is yet another example of cause and effect (or of the independent and dependent variables) swopping places to create the self-referential 'Matthew' effect.

The data in Figure 17.5 show bus workings[25] and the mean number of boardings per working for the counties in just one English region. It is not directly related nor

	Route workings/ week (Tab BUS1001b)	Person boardings/ year (millions) (Tab BUS0109a)	Person boardings/ route working
East of England	**187000**	**179.2**	**18.4**
Bedford	9000	7	15.0
Cambridgeshire	16000	22.5	27.0
Central Bedfordshire	5000	1.4	5.4
Essex	49000	42.7	16.8
Hertfordshire	33000	25.9	15.1
Luton	10000	10.1	19.4
Norfolk	27000	29.9	21.3
Peterborough	8000	10.7	25.7
Southend-on-Sea	5000	8.5	32.7
Suffolk	20000	17.3	16.6
Thurrock	4000	3.2	15.4
London	**739000**	**2269.1**	**59.0**

Figure 17.5 Route workings and passenger boardings for a selection of local government areas

Source: Department for Transport tables.

Note: A route working is a bus traversing a route from one end to the other. Boardings are the numbers of passengers getting on the bus along its route.

comparable with Figure 17.4, but it serves to show that transport data, and public transport data in particular, vary widely. The data in themselves are not significant and neither are the reasons for the differences: they are shown just as a demonstration that countrywide generalisations such as those in Figures 17.3 and 17.4 hide radical differences from place to place.

The differences between parts of Eastern England range from an average of 5.4 boarding passengers in rural central Bedfordshire to 32.7 in Southend: even this is considerably fewer than the 59.0 in London. Within each of these local authority areas there will be much greater variation over quite small distances. Figure 17.6 shows data replicated from Chapter 4, reporting the modes used in four demonstration census output areas, all within the area served by one bus company but showing very wide differences between localities.

The purpose of Figures 17.3 and 17.4 is to show the national data, but Figures 17.5 and 17.6 are there to remind us that national data cannot be used to represent local areas. Although the figures are in no way comparable with one another, they serve, in combination, to demonstrate that the provision, use and perception of public transport varies from place to place, from locality to locality, even from address to address. This continuum is demonstrated by the public transport accessibility level (PTAL)[26] which consists of a combination of the walking distance to a public transport access point (a bus-stop or railway station) and the numbers and frequencies of services available there. It is used to calculate an 'equivalent doorstep frequency', a measure of public transport provision comparable with a private car parked outside

Figure	Persons per household	Cars per household	Cars per person	% j-to-w by 'soft' mode	% j-to-w by public transport	% j-to-w by motor vehicle
4.6	2.11	0.68	0.32	42.11	23.16	20.70
4.7	2.01	0.77	0.38	14.44	17.69	25.27
4.8	3.16	1.82	0.58	17.69	10.06	50.47
4.9	1.62	1.01	0.63	18.40	19.79	37.15

Figure 17.6 Census data showing use of mode for the journey to work for the examples given in Chapter 4

Notes:
'Soft' modes are walking and cycling.
j-to-w = journey to work.

the front door. PTALs vary from address to address pro rata with the walking distance to public transport. It is a part-measure of the transport landscape as perceived by individuals when standing on their doorsteps.

The conclusions are clear:

- The perceptions and uses of public transport vary in very subtle, detailed ways.
- The government objectives of 'managing travel demand' by encouraging the use of public transport must reflect these variations, precluding one-size-fits-all country- or even city-wide policies.

The Transport Act (1968)

The Act was a brave attempt to stem the loss of public transport patronage shown in Figures 17.3 and 17.4. It retained the previous regulation of routes and fares by the Traffic Commissioners which had been established by the 1930 Act but it made three radical changes:

1 The great majority of private bus and coach companies were bought out and amalgamated into the National Bus Company, although most of the earlier local names and brands were retained as operating subsidiaries. The municipal operators were left as they were, each in their own locality, but long-distance coach operations were bundled under one flagship name, 'National Express'.
2 Passenger Transport Authorities (PTA) were established in each of the major conurbations (London, the West Midlands, Manchester, Merseyside, West Yorkshire, South Yorkshire, Tyneside and Glasgow). These authorities were responsible for all public transport, by bus and by train, in their area. For buses this implied combining the operations inherited from the constituent municipal authorities together with the operations that would otherwise have been taken over by the National Bus Company. Some rail services were operated by the PTA itself, leasing track and trains from British Rail, and others were operated by British Rail under contract with the PTA.

3   For the first time, local councils were permitted to subsidise buses. Railways had been implicitly subsidised by financial reorganisation and nationalisation since 1923, but the bus industry, even though most of it was owned and operated by municipal authorities, was unsubsidised. Municipal operators were required to keep separate accounts to prevent any covert leakage of money across the boundary between public transport operations and the other municipal services.

Although history has been subsequently rewritten, the drive behind the 1968 Act was, like the 1930 Act, not one of ideological principle but a quest for a solution to the complex amalgam of:

- the public's desire to acquire and use cars;
- the resultant congestion and parking problems in city centres threatening their economic viability;
- the consequent loss of public transport revenue;
- the increases in bus costs due to congestion;
- the increases in rail costs due to the high, fixed infrastructure cost being spread over declining traffic.

Significantly, the 1968 Act was passed under a Labour government which was replaced less than two years later by a Conservative administration which not only retained the Act but introduced a system of transport supplementary grants (TSGs) to fund comprehensive transport planning. The combination of legislation enacted by two successive governments of opposing parties was an intelligent way of addressing the combination of transport problems confronting them.

Transport supplementary grants

The incoming Conservative government of 1970 retained and strengthened the policies within the 1968 Act, but did so through the medium of a complete restructuring of local government. The motives were, in part, political: many major cities tended to have Labour administrations but were surrounded by rural counties of the opposite political persuasion. The new local government structure[27] was based on county councils which now included the previously independent cities which had been demoted to second-tier district councils.[28] Whatever the agenda, hidden or otherwise, behind local government reorganisation, it made a great deal of sense. The changing isochrones and accessibilities implicit in car use were generating further, radical changes in urban geography. Just as electric trams had loosened the ties of housing to the city core and stimulated by-law housing and the later expanding bus networks had made more land accessible, triggering another drop in density and prompting the 1930s semi-detached revolution, so cars had brought swathes of the countryside within realistic commuting range. Densities were not just lowered by the conversion of agricultural land into developments of detached houses, each with its own parking space,[29] but the development was discontinuous, tending to flocculate around existing rural villages and towns while leaving intervening areas undeveloped. The fragmented, virtual city was becoming apparent. The boundaries between urban areas and the countryside surrounding them became a matter of history rather than of function.

The 1972 reorganisation of local government reflected this change in urban geography. Counties were more aligned with the virtual city – with the areas from which cities drew their commuters. This change was accompanied by a complete restructure of transport planning and finance.[30] Grants from central government for specific projects to construct and maintain roads (under the Highways Act (1959)), to build public transport infrastructure and to subsidise rural bus services and ferries (all under the 1968 Transport Act), plus the general support for transport within overall funding of local government, were bundled into a new transport supplementary grant (TSG). This was revolutionary, quite apart from the change in the nature and extent of county council responsibilities:

- The grants were to be made on the basis of a single document to be submitted by each county council, not as previously of separate documents asking for support for each individual project. This single document, a 'Transport Policy and Programme' (TPP), was required to contain:[31]
  - a statement of the transport objectives and strategy to cover the next 10 to 15 years;
  - a five-year programme of proposed expenditure on actions designed to deliver the declared objectives;
  - a statement of past expenditure, of the physical changes wrought by that expenditure and the extent to which those changes had delivered the desired objectives.
- TPPs were submitted annually with reports about the effectiveness of the previous year's expenditure and with any necessary updates to both the five-year rolling programme of expenditure and actions and the 15-year strategy and objectives.
- TPPs were to cover all expenditure on both the capital and current accounts on all aspects of inland transport specifically including airports, harbours, canals, freight and passenger transport, roads, parking and traffic management.
- Unlike previous grants, the money was granted before, not after, policies and actions were instigated, giving councils time to adjust their expenditure to fit changing circumstances.
- This flexibility was underlined by the freedom for councils to spend their allocated monies in whatever ways they deemed appropriate without being tied to the action list in their previous year's TPP submission. However, there was a sting in the tail because any deviation had to be explained and justified in the following year's submission and could result in a reduction in the next TSG.
- The level of grant in each year was to reflect the performance of the previous year's expenditure.

This entirely new and radical system had well-explained objectives of its own which actually reflected, even enhanced, the objectives which had been set for the Passenger Transport Authorities by the previous government in 1968:[32]

- Local transport problems increasingly involve decisions on the allocation of available resources between different modes of transport and about interrelated policies; for example, parking, traffic management and public transport.
- Therefore transport problems need to be viewed comprehensively and set in the wider context of land-use planning.
- The task of the councils (and of their TPPs) is to develop policies that promote the provision of efficient and coordinated systems of public transport and the power to support them financially.
- Eliminate bias towards either capital or current, or any other form of expenditure.
- Use government monies to solve local problems.
- Reduce the detailed supervision by central government over individual projects.

The programmed projects did not have to be capital investments in infrastructure such as roads (as they were in Bristol) or a new metro system (as it was in Newcastle): it could be a fare subsidy (as it was in South Yorkshire). The annual progress report and updated objectives, shifting policies from those that were not working to those that were, created a sensible steerage mechanism based on the cybernetic principle of error-actuated feedback. This, in itself, was really radical – it transformed the practice of planning from devising a definitive, idealised plan for some 'design year' in the long-distance future (the practice in command economies as well as in contemporary British town planning) into an organic, self-monitoring management system (as had been advocated by market-orientated gurus). It is the model for Figure 3.3 and the fundamental structure and advocacy of this book – a system to constantly monitor and steer the transport system and of the areas it serves.

The recursive TSG/TPP system was well conceived, coherent and inclusive, and also enjoyed wide political support. But it failed, and some would say that it failed comprehensively. The 1970s was a period of political oscillation with no fewer than four successive switches between left and right administrations. Despite this, the basic process of TSGs made on the basis of submitted TPPs, was retained throughout the bumpy political storms, although the emphases within the plans and in the criteria used to determine the grants shifted. But then the system had been designed to accommodate year-on-year shifts in objectives, in policies and in the list of projects. However, the original, overarching and unchanging purpose of TPPs was to plan the transport system as an entity, including both passenger and freight, by all modes and including all interfaces, and then to link it to urban planning. This was an imaginative purpose that was, and still is, beyond the comprehension of many people: it must have been the brainchild of a visionary person or group within the Ministry of Transport, people who had the ability to brief ministers of all persuasions. However, many politicians, professionals and public alike were wedded to a perception of the transport system, not as an entity through which individuals threaded their way from place to place, but as a bundle of modes – rail and road, bus and train, private and public, freight and passenger, stationary and moving. The inertia which sustains this perception is surprising, since everybody's day-to-day experience is quite the opposite – people make journeys from A to B by a combination of modes, a combination that always includes, at the very least, some walking to, from and between interlinked modes.

The strongest inertia was, and still is, in the ranks of professional transport planners. They had developed computerised models to predict private car traffic, models whose parentage could be traced back to the ideas developed by the Chicago School of Mathematical Geography in the 1950s and then built into early computer programs predicting traffic flows included with the main-frame computers sold to local authorities in the early 1960s. By the time the 1968 Act arrived, the models had become the centre of a methodology to assess the para-monetary value of road schemes, a procedure focused upon the travel-time savings due to improved traffic speeds: there was very considerable intellectual capital and inertia built into the system.

The TSG/TPP system required a largely unrecognised need for a radical modification of this assessment mechanism. If the projects listed in a county's TPP, including improvements to public transport as well as road schemes, were to be appraised properly, the methodology would have to be based on forecasted travel times and costs of travel by all modes rather than a prime focus upon cars and traffic. That really required a radical shift in the nature and purpose of travel-demand models, followed by a complete rewrite of the system analyses and software that had been developed over the past decade. It was a step too far for a profession that, since its inception, had perceived transport as essentially a matter of roads and traffic. The technical response was not the rewrite that was needed but a modification of the earlier traffic-oriented software to incorporate a 'modal split'. This retained the previous premise that the predicted number of trips between each pair of zones was a function of the numbers of households, jobs, etc. in both the origin and the destination zones, coupled with the travel distance between them by car, but then to 'split' that number between private and public transport using comparative travel times. It was an arcane nonsense enshrined in computer code that was never robustly evaluated by 'backcasting'.[33]

Prior to the 1968 Act, the bus system was perceived by many to provide mobility for those who had yet to acquire a car. The rail system was seen to be a lost cause – the retrenchment of the railways following the Beeching Report was still being digested. It appeared to be logical to believe that the trend to switch from public to private transport was unstoppable, and therefore planning for any major future role for public transport would deflect interest and resources away from the prime task of coping with traffic. The analysis at the time was that there was a vicious circle, as is shown in Figure 17.7.

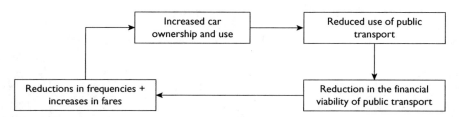

Figure 17.7 The vicious circle

The transport planning professionals' view seemed to be that the circle was the inevitable process of an unstoppable shift towards increasing car use, and breaking the circle was unrealistic. Hence, travel demand forecasting should strive to predict the effects of the circle rather than to reflect the objectives of the TSG/TPP system. However, this view failed to appreciate three related issues:

1 Urban road building was expensive and politically fraught, and was never likely to provide the accessibility to town centres that was needed to sustain them commercially. Hence, some alternative was needed.
2 Although the national trends shown in Figures 17.3 and 17.4 were clear and pressing, they were very far from uniform.
3 The changes in car use and traffic were not the only fundamental changes that were afoot: urban geography was moulding itself to accommodate car use.

The Nottingham Zone and Collar experiment

The objectives, faults, attitudes and failure of the TSG/TPP process were epitomised by the landmark Nottingham 'Zone and Collar' experiment (Figure 17.8). The scheme had been designed by the City of Nottingham Council when it was a separate county borough as a response to the spirit rather than to the detail of the 1968 Act. Nottingham had not been included in any of the new Passenger Transport Authority areas established by the 1968 Act but strove to emulate their set objectives, in particular to manage buses and general traffic together as the means to access the city centre. The Council's attitude was driven by an implicit theory that there was a set amount of road space and traffic capacity on the approaches to the city centre and, if this resource were to be used efficiently, the balance between accessibility by bus and by car would have to be managed.

The City Council, encouraged and supported by the Ministry of Transport, designed an experiment with the aim of testing the theory by a practical example. The experiment actually anticipated the TSG/TPP mechanisms which were created after the experiment had been arranged but before it was carried out. At the same time Nottingham City Council was demoted to be a second-tier authority and responsibility for the experiment passed to the newly designated County Council, making it into a test case at the very start of the development of radical new policies and of their administration. Unsurprisingly, the government arranged for the experiment to be thoroughly monitored and reported.[34]

The objectives of the experiment were explicit:

- to reduce congestion on bus routes by controlling non-bus traffic;
- to reduce traffic on residential roads;
- to protect pedestrians from heavy vehicular flows along unsuitable routes;
- to lessen the need for major highway schemes.

The experiment focused on two residential 'zones' on the western flank of Nottingham's city centre, barely two kilometres – but a cultural world – apart:

1   Bilborough is a classic 1930s geometric council estate.
2   Wollaton is an affluent area of detached houses built in the 1960s and 1970s.

The experiment was a combination of four interventions:

1   Traffic-signalled exit gates from the zones (eight exits for Bilborough and five for Wollaton); all other road entrances and exits were blocked. This was designed to limit the rate at which traffic left the origin zones to join the main roads, so that main road traffic, including buses, could run freely while making car use by local residents less attractive.
2   A 'collar' of traffic-signalled gates on the six radial roads providing access to the city centre from the west with the intention of limiting the traffic entering or passing through the inner city area.
3   Bus-only lanes on the approaches to the 'collar' signals to allow buses to bypass the queues of traffic waiting to pass through the collar controls, so giving a very demonstrative priority to buses.
4   Three park-and-ride sites outside the collar and served by special coach services into the city centre. These were largely intended for out-of-town commuters.

The experiment was monitored by a suite of surveys conducted in April and May 1975 before the scheme was initiated on 1 August and then repeated in April and May 1976 after the scheme had been in operation for 10 months. The scheme was abandoned in the following July almost immediately after the second set of surveys. It had been in operation for slightly under a year. The surveys comprised:

- home interviews;
- bus journey times, including dwell times at stops and times to travel the bus lanes;
- traffic delays at the zone exit gates;
- traffic flow studies by a 'floating car' to measure delays and journey times and speeds;
- traffic flow counts past a number of fixed survey stations;
- roadside driver interviews;
- counts of violations of the traffic control regulations (in the after-survey only);
- use of the park-and-ride facilities (in the after-survey only).

The purposes, design and monitoring of the experiment were both deliberate and thorough, but they carried the burden of contemporary professional attitudes rather than the objectives of the politicians who had initiated the experiment. The surveys reflected the professionals' concern with traffic flow rather than personal movement. Stemming the decline in the use of public transport as shown in Figures 17.3 and 17.4 was a marker, but this was not the real objective which was a far longer-term target: namely to manage the road space used to access the city centre. Implicitly this mapped on to the objectives of the TSG/TPP system devised by the new Conservative government, specifically:

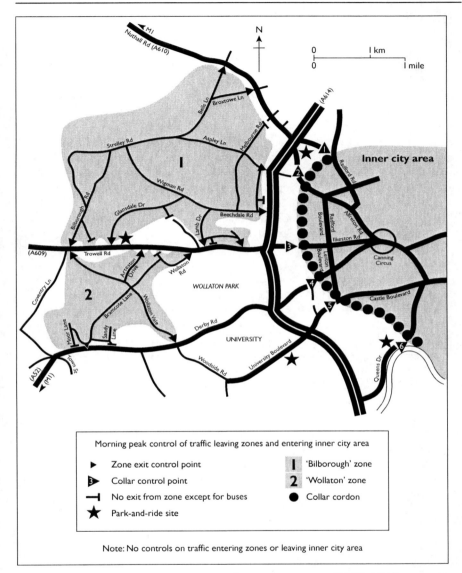

Figure 17.8 The Nottingham Zone and Collar experiment (1975–1976)
Source: Adapted from Layfield and Bardsley (1977), fig. 1.

Transport problems need to be viewed comprehensively and set in the wider context of land-use planning.[35]

The blinkered professional world was still immersed in the traffic modelling used to assess the value for money of road improvement schemes, hinging largely upon the time savings calculated as the difference between traffic speeds and volumes measured before the start of scheme construction, and the speeds and volumes predicted to occur once the scheme had been completed. The dominant concern with speeds and journey times reflected the 'modal split' theory that the proportion of people using public transport was in proportion to the ratios of travel times by public transport and private car. The technical reports on the Nottingham experiment assumed that the objective was to massage this ratio by slowing cars down and speeding buses up by traffic management.

The surveys were designed around this assumption and the final assessment[36] concentrates on the changes in speeds and travel times by both cars and buses, using the survey data to try to explain the changes. In retrospect the professional preconceptions that dominated the experiment were at fault for the following reasons:

- The data focused on three zones: the city centre and the two residential areas of Bilborough and Wollaton. In the style of the times, each was represented by a zone centroid, an arbitrary point at which all the activity of the zone was deemed to take place, making it impossible to conduct any research into the possible differences between parts of a zone.
- The conviction that relative nominal travel times explained modal choice blinded the researchers to any other explanations: there is only one set of figures which sought to compare travel by car and bus; this is reproduced in Figure 17.9. It concentrates on changes in travel times but fails to consider any other perceptions of the relative merits and demerits of the use of buses and cars.
- The time costs were those as used in the then standard road scheme assessments, but, despite all the effort put into the surveys, the walking, waiting and parking times are all arbitrary assumptions in the absence of any collected data.
- Strangely, very detailed data were collected on bus running times between road junctions but not between bus-stops.
- The reports show neither the bus routes nor the frequencies, nor the bus-stop locations: there is no obvious basis for the seven-minute walk plus wait for a bus shown in Figure 17.9. Even if there were it would be wrong, since there could not possibly have been a fixed walk plus wait time covering all 14,600 households in Bilborough and 3450 in Wollaton.
- The city centre appears to be a large, amorphous zone of which there is no geographical description whatsoever and so, once again, there can be no justification for the assumed two-minute walk from bus-stops to final destinations, nor for the two minutes needed to park a car and walk to a destination door.

The household before- and after-surveys would have been an opportunity to collect data about people's perceptions of the relative travel opportunities presented by car and bus use. Instead, the surveys copied the techniques used a decade earlier when traffic was the focus and the use of public transport was of little interest. The data collected were about the number of journeys made, their purposes and the main mode, data which showed little change from the first to the second survey. A question

Bus journey	Journey time (min)	Valued at (pence per hour)	Journey cost (pseudo-pence)
Walk to bus-stop	3.0	70	3.5
Wait at bus-stop	4.0	70	4.5
Ride time in bus	17.5	35	10.0
Bus fare (real pence)			8.5
Walk to destination	2.0	70	2.5
TOTAL	**26.5**		**29.0**
Car journey (driver only)			
Walk to car and start	1.5	70	2.0
Ride time in car	14.5	35	8.5
Car running cost			13.0
Park and walk to destination	2.5	70	2.5
TOTAL	**24.5**		**26**

Figure 17.9 Comparative journey times and costs from Bilborough/Wollaton to Nottingham city centre

Source: Reproduced from Layfield and Vincent (1977), table 9.

was tacked on to the second survey asking for people's attitudes and assessment of the scheme, but not about the scheme's objectives, nor about their perceived options and choices. Unsurprisingly, only 15 per cent of car travellers and 35 per cent of bus travellers thought the scheme should be continued unmodified: only 22 per cent of bus users thought their journeys had been improved.

A question put to car users about parking was extremely illuminating. No less than 62 per cent had free parking provided or had their parking costs reimbursed, and a further 23 per cent parked free on the streets or on vacant land. Only 8 per cent paid for parking. However, no data were collected on how much was paid, nor on how long it took to find, capture and retain a parking space. Those figures will have changed completely in the 30+ years since the experiment, years during which increased car ownership has placed on-street parking under severe pressure, but the reports give no clues as to the possible future responses to such changes.

There are two grounds for thinking it to be rather churlish to criticise the Nottingham experiment:

1   The survey techniques and the data collected were well conducted by the standards of the time. Public transport had only really become an issue with the 1968 Transport Act, and creating the necessary new methodology to sense the choices about using it or not would have taken time, even if the realisation that it was necessary had been fully appreciated. Those arranging the surveys would have had to fight considerable battles to upset the technical conventions, even if they themselves had not been trapped in them.

2   The scheme failed totally to achieve its objectives, limited though they were. Those failures were nothing to do with the surveys, which served their purpose in identifying the failure.

The morning peak bus travel times were reduced by 4 per cent and the evening peak by 11 per cent. Car travel times were changed by trivial percentages; perversely, many of them were small reductions in travel time. Unsurprisingly, the use of cars was unchanged, although there were a significant number of people who had previously travelled as car passengers but had switched to travelling by bus.

The park-and-ride scheme which absorbed over 50 per cent of the cost of the scheme carried around five persons per bus and the buses added more vehicles to the traffic flow than they abstracted.

The prime analysis of the entire scheme used the methodology for assessing road improvement projects to the letter. The criterion was in-vehicle travel time costed at the pseudo-cash rates shown in Figure 17.9: the time saved by bus travellers was valued at £8000 per year but the time lost by car users was valued at £48,000, a net dis-benefit of £40,000. When the effects of the park-and-ride scheme and of the delays to goods vehicles are added, the overall annual effect was assessed to be £54,000 of dis-benefit.

The report was overtly damning and extremely influential. For professional transport planners it served to confirm the belief that the prime means of transport was the private car and the prime objective was to manage traffic. From that it followed that forecasting travel demand should continue to focus upon traffic, and that demand models should remain focused upon the movement of vehicles rather than of people. As a result, the opportunity to devise a new generation of models focused upon predicting personal travel through a transport system planned and managed as an entity disappeared and, with it, any hope of providing decision-makers with any numerical justification or support for any policies or actions other than to improve traffic flow.

For politicians, it showed that tampering with car use was not only a political minefield but would probably be ineffective: there would be none of the prizes that drive politicians to make their decisions.

The Nottingham experiment is crucial to the structure of this book. If it showed a fundamental flaw in policies attempting to induce the use of public transport in preference to using a car, then the basic objective of sustainable transport planning becomes unattainable. This is not a matter of the objective of the experiment itself which was to reverse the decline in the use of public transport – to test whether the vicious circle shown in Figure 17.7 could be broken. Now the prime objective is to sustain the commercial functions of the city centre by ensuring future high levels of accessibility and so prevent the dispersal of its functions into the suburbs and beyond to create an urban form with a reducing density and ever-increasing travel distances. Now the logic is as follows:

- The overarching aim of sustainable transport planning is to reduce the amount of emitted CO_2. This serves both as an end in itself and as a proxy for the emission

of other pollutants and for the destructive use of other resources such as land and fuel.
- This overarching aim is best achieved by reducing the aggregate person- and tonne-kilometres, an aim driven by the density of development – the tighter the weave of the urban fabric, the shorter the distances travelled.
- Car use not only enables the loosening of the urban fabric by providing the accessibilities characterised by widely spread, stable isochrones, but actually demands that loosening, since car use needs parking space and a diffused traffic pattern avoiding concentrated, congested flow.
- Public transport provides very selective, targeted accessibilities characterised by elongated, pulsing isochrones. Locations well served by public transport are not only capable of being developed at high density but need to be dense to sustain public transport through high levels of demand.
- Hence the urban fabric may, and must, remain tightly woven.
- The overall argument is not that public transport has intrinsically desirable values that warrant its support and retention, nor even that it may produce lower CO_2 emissions per person-kilometre than cars, but that it is the determinant of the centrality of urban structures, of land values in central areas and of its commercial viability.
- That control is focused upon those urban centres which cannot provide sufficient parking space to sustain their financial viability. Elsewhere, public transport is unable to compete with the flexibility of the car and there is no need for it to try. The overall policy should be neither pro-car nor pro-public transport but should be to prefer the most appropriate mode to match local densities.

This advocated policy bundle depends on the public acceptability of public transport to access areas with a density that precludes the provision of adequate parking space. There are no prizes for flying in the face of reality and, if the Nottingham experiment were to show conclusively that it would be impossible to mould travel demand for journeys to urban centres in favour of public transport, then the whole logic of the proposed policy bundle would unravel. That makes the analysis of the failure of the Nottingham Zone and Collar experiment very significant:

- In 1975 national politicians had placed their faith in the continuing need and use of public transport: a Labour government through the 1968 Transport Act and the following Conservative government through the TSG/TPP funding system.
- The public were, and are, unconvinced. In the early 2000s there was an extensive debate about the need to control climate change by reducing traffic. This policy was well supported in principle but only provided that the detailed reductions did not affect the individual's car use.
- In the face of this complex attitude, politicians need the support of robust, defensible professional predictions of the desirable outcomes of unpopular policies.
- This must presume that professional transport planners have the travel demand models at their disposal by which those predictions may be made. The lack of an

ability to forecast policy outcomes was a major component of the failure of the Nottingham experiment. It was conceived in the dark, driven by political aspirations to unpick the 'vicious circle' as shown in Figure 17.7. The City of Nottingham Transport Committee instituted the scheme as an act of faith that turned out to be political suicide: the Chair of the Transport Committee was abruptly deposed at the conclusion of the experiment.

- The professional theory was that the choice of public transport was rooted in comparable in-vehicle ride times and the experiment effectively demolished the assumption that manipulating comparative ride times was an effective policy lever. In hindsight, the experiment was a doomed amalgam of a political decision based on aspiration rather than theory, and a technical theory devoid of aspiration. Had the politicians and the professional practitioners met before the experiment was designed, there may have been an investigation into the criteria and thresholds used by people in making their decisions whether to use public transport or not, followed by the design of a set of actions to influence those decisions and a monitored experiment to test the effects. As it was, the four components of the experiment were premised upon a theory that failed to reflect people's decision mechanisms.
- The outcome should have been the definition of a process by which the effectiveness of efforts to persuade people to choose to use public transport could be analysed and forecast: as it was, the report was about the extent, but not the nature, of the failure of a conjectured set of arbitrary actions. Unfortunately, neither the Transport and Road Research Laboratory nor anybody else made any assessment of why the actions that were taken were ineffective, nor whether any other actions could have been effective.
- It may have been that the experiment was before its time, particularly when the pressure upon parking was so limited that the majority of car users had access to a free parking space. That is unlikely to be true 30+ years later. The data collected at the time gave no hint of what people would do if the privilege of free parking were removed
- There was no analysis of the perceptions of bus service quality, of frequency, of reliability, nor of the relevance of the locations of bus-stops at either end of the ride, nor of full car costs, either as they are or as they are perceived to be; nor of the need to find, capture and retain a parking space. The professional myopia towards any choice mechanism other than crude comparative travel times still needs to be cured.
- Later in this chapter there are some suggestions as to how to make public transport the mode of choice of access to densely developed areas, but these suggestions cannot be definitive. They must be tested by predictive modelling and then assessed by experimental work. That work must have two purposes: first, to assess the methodology of prediction; second, to test the effectiveness of the experimental measures.
- The final problem with the Nottingham experiment was its very limited, truncated nature. Both the 1968 Transport Act and the TSG/TPP system had the linkage between transport and planning as objectives and, as the above logic trail

suggests, this remains as the prime aim. The relationships between transport and development were not known then, nor are they known now with sufficient clarity for policies based on the linkage to be defined. Certainly a project lasting just one year could not provide any illumination. Longer-term projects may show changes but would not necessarily demonstrate the reasons behind those changes. The only way forward is to experiment, but to do what should have been done at Nottingham: to learn enough from events to establish a theory and then design experiments to test that theory leading to its validation, modification or rejection. There is little opportunity to make meaningful, robust experiments in real time and therefore we are obliged to analyse historical changes and test theory by backcasting, trying to answer questions such as what our urban areas would have looked like under various policy regimes.

After the Nottingham experiment

The very public, well-published failure of the Nottingham experiment had an immediate effect. The annual advice given on the actions that would attract TSGs drifted away from the original vision of a comprehensive, coordinated transport policy into a view of separate development of each of the modes. The TPPs written in the summer of 1975 and in the following summers did not strive to implement the cohesive aspirations that had been set out in Circular 104/73. Travel demand models continued to use a multi-modal approach in which the prime, default mode was the private car, with public transport being seen as a weak competitive alternative: the alternative view of an inter-modal system of complementary modes went uninvestigated, leaving a fault line between the political objectives and the assessment methodology. Budgets became stratified by mode and gradually fell back to being essentially road programmes with public transport providing the back-stop for those journeys which could not be satisfied by road and car use.

After four years during which the radical objectives of the TSG/TPP system were gradually whittled away, the final nail in the coffin of this brave perception of an integrated transport system was driven home in 1976 by a consultation paper[37] and by a White Paper[38] the following year. A significant organisational change occurred in the gap between the two papers. The Department of the Environment, which had been created in 1970 in keeping with the ideals of the 1968 Act and had the responsibility for the environment, for planning, for transport and for their interlinkage, as characterised by the TSG/TPP system, was split, and the responsibility for transport was shifted back to a revived Ministry of Transport. The consultation paper had been produced by the unitary Department of the Environment but the subsequent White Paper was a Ministry of Transport document and the focus shifted away from the processes of urbanisation towards the immediately apparent problems of the transport system. The change was almost certainly driven by the Treasury in response to the massive expenditure on TSGs that had built up, particularly on the subsidy to the bus network. This was certainly poor value for money but that was primarily due to the lack of realistic objectives, apart from a politically driven desire to retain an unchanged bus service in cities which, under the influence of growing car use, were rapidly changing their urban form. Without any way of predicting the results of implementing such policies, councils were spending TSG money on buses in the dark.

Bus deregulation and privatisation

Less than two years later in May 1979, an ideology arrived in Westminster that was completely different to the mixed economy strategies espoused by previous administrations, no matter which colour flag they had sailed under. A government headed by Margaret Thatcher was driven by a belief that private ownership and enterprise were inherently better than organisations under the auspices of the state, a belief that was expressed in governance by accountancy rather than by political priority. It was a creed based on the tenet that competition created efficiency and that public ownership and state regulation hampered competition, and therefore were inherently inefficient, but it also carried the corollary that competition, and therefore efficiency, would be fostered by private ownership and deregulation. The initial tenet may contain elements of truth, but the corollary does not necessarily follow.

In transport, the first change occurred very soon after the new government came to power. The Transport Act of 1980 deregulated long-distance coach services which had been licensed by the traffic Commissioners under the 1930 Act and operated since 1970 by the National Bus Company under the brand name of 'National Express'. In practice the deregulation made very little difference, although there were later noisy claims that fares were reduced and the route network extended. Some competitive services appeared, but entrants to the industry had considerable difficulty in making their presence felt. National Express had built up a very efficient network of ticket agencies reinforcing the brand name and offering through tickets across the comprehensive network. National Express changed itself from the owner and operator of coaches into a management system to deliver a branded network by using competitive bids from small operators to provide coach services in National Express livery to carry passengers who had bought tickets through the National Express marketing network. The pre-deregulation image of on-road competition eroding the National Express monopoly failed to materialise: if anything, the monopoly was strengthened by National Express being able to undercut prices offered by competitors and then contract them to supply services under the National Express brand. Rather than competition, the new Act fostered the franchising of a monopoly brand, and National Express, now privatised, still continues to dominate English long-distance coach services.

As part of the 1980 Act the regulations covering ordinary bus stage carriage services were loosened as a test in four rural counties and the effects were monitored by the Transport Research Laboratory.[39] They found that patronage continued to decline and this led to a reduction in services, but there was no noticeable evidence that service provision had been held in check by the imposition of the regulations under the 1930 Act.

The *Buses* White Paper

A White Paper on the bus industry was published in 1984.[40] *Buses* is a very important document, since it set out the basis of deregulation and reorganisation of the bus industry and, by extending the general principles, to the later re-reorganisation of the railways. It is the explanation behind the current organisation of passenger transport in Britain. It advocated the changes that appeared a year later in the 1985 Transport Act:

- *Deregulation:* the removal of the system of the licensing of routes and timetables and of the control of fares by the Traffic Commissioners under the terms of the 1930 Act.
- *Privatisation:* the breaking up of the National Bus Company into smaller companies (often the subsidiaries that had been compacted into the NBC in 1968), followed by their subsequent sale. Municipal bus operators were detached from their council parentage and sold, but with the opportunity for councils to buy them and become formal shareholders.

Buses was mainly based on an ideology that efficiency is largely the automatic product of competition and, conversely, that any faults must be the result of a lack of competition. That the industry was in decline was self-evident. The trends shown in Figures 17.3 and 17.4 were presented in *Buses* together with the observation that bus-kilometres had declined by 50 per cent since 1953 and the 'market share' of all passenger-kilometres taken by buses had slumped from 42 per cent to 8 per cent. As Figures 17.3 and 17.4 show, this is a grossly misleading figure, since the surge in car ownership had created much more travel and, even if public transport had retained its patronage intact, the 'market share' statistic would have fallen very substantially. It was also undeniable that the financial support given to bus services under the TSG was wildly out of control: it had risen from £10 million to £520 million in the years 1972 to 1982, a 13-fold increase in real terms, while the number of passenger-kilometres had fallen by 20 per cent. Some action was clearly necessary to address three issues:

1. the failure of the policy to manage the transport system as a whole;
2. the decline in the use of public transport which seemed to reflect the increase in the use of cars;
3. the poor value for money being gained from TSG monies.

Buses ignored the first problem and made two fundamental errors in addressing the second:

1. It ascribed the ills of the industry (ever-increasing subsidies upon services that were losing patronage) as damning evidence condemning all regulation.
2. It had an overwhelming faith in the ability of deregulated competition to provide the necessary changes in bus services to meet the needs of a population with rising levels of car ownership. It was claimed that:

> Free and fair competition will bring great benefits to many travellers and to the community at large (para 8.1).
>
> The main network will continue and will better meet the needs of travellers. On many well-used services fares will go down (para 8.2).

It was claimed that 'Britain needs good bus services', since 39 per cent of households did not own a car (by 2011 this was 25 per cent[41]), displaying the major misconception that buses and cars were alternatives – that there was a 'market for personal travel' of which the bus 'market share' was 8 per cent. This was, and still is, wrong. There is not a 'market' for personal travel like there is for cornflakes or washing machines within which there is acceptable substitutability. *Buses* hinted that there was an element of differentiation with the assertion that most of the households without cars were in urban areas and that therefore most of the demand for bus travel was urban. This, too, is wrong. Car ownership in London is high, but so is bus use, disproving the simplistic claim that bus use is in inverse proportion to car ownership.

The analysis showed other gross misapplications of market theory. Markets are only able to exist where there is substitutability, but that requires a product which is perceived to be homogeneous. There was no attempt in *Buses* to establish what the 'product' to be provided by competitive firms actually was. Is the bus 'market' for single tickets to ride from one place to another? Or is it for a timed return journey? Or is it an enhanced mobility, perhaps constrained in time and space in some way? The question is important, since it defines limits to the nature of possible competition. For example, if there were a real choice between two equally acceptable buses in the morning but one company did not provide an acceptable return service, the choice may be between rides that, despite appearances, would not be substitutable for those wanting a flexibly timed return. The same limit on perception would be imposed if the desired return route did not match the outward one: an apparent competitive choice would hinge upon which company had the most desirable network. This leads to the conclusion that competition cannot be confined to a particular timed journey, but must be between substitutable networks over time and space. If that is so, the easy entry of new competing operators into the market suggested by *Buses* must be a fantasy. *Buses* suggested that lifting the 1930s regulations would induce a range of new operators providing new services:

> If operators are to stay in a free market, they will have to meet the needs of the customers as the need arises (para 4.14).
>
> It is for passengers to demonstrate what they want and for operators to respond (para 3.5).

This theory may have worked had the marketed product been single point-to-point rides, but even that is doubtful. The fantasy skips over the process by which potential passengers would 'demonstrate their needs' to operators. *Buses* was confused over this: on the one hand claiming that applicants to the traffic Commissioners for a route licence under the 1930s regulations had to demonstrate 'need' and that this inhibited network development (para 4.2); but, on the other hand, stating that new operators 'would not be slow to find what passengers want' (para 1.6). It then compounded the confusion by stating:

> It is impossible to forecast how many people will use buses more as fares decline and service improves (para 49).

The image in *Buses* is of potential customers investigating alternative choices by standing at a bus-stop, in the same way as customers graze supermarket shelves, and that this is the way in which 'passengers demonstrate their needs'. This is a fantasy. Even if the 'product' were a journey offered by substitutable alternatives, the act of standing at a bus-stop is based on some pre-knowledge of the service timings, coupled with the knowledge that the services are infinitely perishable: once a service has departed it is of no further use or interest to potential passengers. The mechanisms of competition and choice are vital to any analysis of 'markets' and cannot be left to the blind assertions of *Buses*.

The only analysis of product and service levels contained in *Buses* was in the appendix about cross-subsidy which appeared to be window-dressing for the *ex-cathedra* assertion that competition would automatically provide a better, more efficient service. Cross-subsidy is when the surplus of revenue over cost for one activity is transferred to another activity where costs are greater than revenues, so that the combined account for the two services shows revenues covering costs, even though one component service does not. *Buses* argued fiercely that cross-subsidies are a market perversion, forcing people using cost-effective services to pay premium fares to subsidise those using unprofitable services. It even asserted that:

> The practice of cross-subsidisation has its origins in the Road Traffic Act of 1930.[42]

It was undeniable that the 1930 regulations had their faults, addressing the problems of the piracy of 1920s rather than the decline of the 1980s, but to assert that they had spawned cross-subsidisation is unthinking demonisation. The ends and branches of transport routes are always more lightly loaded and less profitable than the trunks and are 'cross-subsidised'. Peak-hour surpluses 'subsidise' off-peak services. In retailing, 'loss-leaders' are paid for by more profitable lines. Cross-subsidisation is not the child of the 1930 Act; it is a normal, sensible, commercial practice.

The theories espoused by transport economists which are at the root of privatisation and deregulation fail to recognise that time and timing are major characteristics of transport demand and supply. For example, *Buses* analysed the cost per bus-mile and showed that the costs in metropolitan and dense urban areas were higher than elsewhere, failing to realise that bus costs are incurred per hour, not per mile – crews are paid by time, capital servicing is by time, even the fuel consumption is related to time (at least for internal combustion engines with mechanical transmissions, although, in any event, fuel is a minor component of cost). Urban congestion can result ultimately in buses packed with fare-paying passengers actually running at a loss, since revenue is by distance but cost is by time. Hence high metropolitan bus costs were related to congestion, not to the inefficiencies of the municipal operators who ran them at the time.

This prompts questions about costings where economic theory sits uncomfortably with practice. Although *Buses* does not explicitly use marginal cost theory, the argument about cross-subsidisation tends towards the notion that prices should be a direct reflection of costs and that this should appear at disaggregated, route-by-route levels. One of the touchstones of economic theory is that the revenue gained from one extra unit sold (the marginal revenue) should be equal to the cost of delivering that extra unit (the marginal cost) because moving away from that optimum will either add more cost than the revenue gained or will subtract more revenue than the extra cost: a neat theory that econometricians are able to wrap up in a cocoon of mathematics only rarely illuminated by field data.

Attempts to apply marginal cost and revenue theory to transport in general and to buses in particular must be futile. The problem lies in the definition of the product being produced, consumed and costed. Ticket sales may relate to routes and times, but they may well be passes giving network access. Costs come in completely different units: buses deliver 100 places at specific times but passengers travel singly or in small groups in a range of different rhythms. Neither costs nor revenues may be disaggregated down to sub-network levels which would permit the equation of cost and revenue, route by route, time by time, place by place. The theory of cross-subsidisation is a theoretical mirage.

A paradox in both *Buses* and in the consequent legislation was that, despite the assertion that the 1930 regulations were the root cause of the problems of the bus industry and should be swept aside, substantial regulations were retained with objectives which were very similar to those of the 1930 Act. The testing and monitoring of vehicles and crew to ensure passenger safety were retained and, as far as vehicles were concerned, strengthened. New legislation was enacted to monitor and regulate the companies providing bus and coach services to ensure that managers and companies of doubtful probity using cheap, second-hand vehicles did not work as pirates, as happened in the 1920s. Routes and timetables no longer have to be licensed but they do have to be registered, and they are monitored to ensure their delivery with the explicit requirement to be no more than one minute early or four minutes late for 95 per cent of the time; otherwise the operator may be fined.[43] The proposition that the inefficiencies of the bus industry in the 1980s were due to regulation seemed to have been nullified by the retention of much of the regulation.

Another strange *non-sequitur* was that *Buses* used taxis as an exemplar of the delivery of unsubsidised transport whose fares had not escalated in the previous 10 years, and yet taxis had been firmly regulated in their quality, quantity and price since the seventeenth century: they were hardly an argument for unlimited entry to a travel market at fares set by the driver.

The final conundrum in *Buses* was the problem of over-provision or, in the words of the 1930 Act, 'wasteful competition'. *Buses* suggested that this was not likely to be a problem on two grounds:

1   There would be a tendency for the number of provided seat-kilometres to be much better distributed by the replacement of large double-decker buses by the smaller vehicles likely to be operated by new entrants to the market. This would spread seat-kilometres over time and space providing a better network. It was another fantasy. Minibuses did appear on the streets immediately after the 1986 Act but were quickly replaced by ever-larger buses. In part, this was probably due to the minibuses being 'converted bread-vans', with very poor access for burdened or disabled passengers but mainly because the majority of bus costs are due to the crew and minibus operations have high crew costs per place-kilometre.
2   Over-capacity would correct itself by operators going out of business (ironically, by the self-destruction of competition).

Bus deregulation and privatisation: the outcome

In 2011 the Competition Commission produced a substantial report[44] on the bus industry as it had become 26 years after the deregulation and privatisation advocated in *Buses* (1984). The Executive summary concludes:

> **Para 2:** We found that head-to-head competition in the supply of local bus services was uncommon. Many local markets exhibit persistently high levels of concentration. We found that on-going sustained head-to-head competition, where present, delivers significant benefits to customers. However, the process of competition could result in periods of intense short-lived rivalry, leading to the exit of one operator. This reduces the extent of head-to-head competition. The anticipation of costly rivalry creates a barrier to entry and expansion. Along with other barriers to entry and expansion, this reduces the competitive constraint from potential competition and new entry.
>
> **Para 3:** We also found that competition has been diminished by operator conduct leading to geographic market segregation. We have found that this conduct occurred in relation to two operators in parts of the North-East of England. This reduces the extent of head-to-head competition between operators and reduces the constraint from potential competition and new entry. Aspects of this conduct have been seen elsewhere and we remain concerned that such conduct may be more widespread.
>
> **Para 4:** We found that competition in the supply of local bus services is not effective in those local markets where head-to-head competition does not exist.
>
> **Para 5:** We concluded that there were four features of local bus markets which mean that effective head-to-head competition is uncommon and which limit the effectiveness of potential competition and new entry. These features are the existence of: high levels of concentration; barriers to entry and expansion; customer conduct in deciding which bus to catch; and operator conduct by which

operators avoid competing with other operators in 'Core Territories' (certain parts of an operator's network which it regards as its 'own' territory) leading to geographic market segregation.

Para 12: There are approximately 1,245 operators running local bus services in the reference area. Since privatization, there has been a process of consolidation which has resulted in the emergence of a small number of groups with geographically extensive local bus operations. The five largest operators are Arriva, FirstGroup, Go-Ahead, National Express and Stagecoach. We refer to these as the 'Large Operators'. They provide 69 per cent of all local bus services. Only five other operators have a share of services which exceeds 1 per cent of the reference area, and 95 per cent of all local bus services in the reference area are provided by 219 operators. Apart from the private-sector operators, there are also 11 municipally-owned operators.

Para 13: We found that the majority of local areas are highly concentrated, with most areas being served by just one or two operators with a significant share of supply. For example, the largest operator in an Urban Area runs, on average, 69 per cent of local bus services on all routes in that area (we have identified 239 Urban Areas around cities or towns corresponding to existing networks of local bus services). However, there is substantial variation across different areas and routes. It is very uncommon for one operator's route to overlap the route of another operator completely, and although almost every route is overlapped by the route of another operator at some point, many routes face only very limited overlap.

Para 17: We found that customers' choice of bus operator differed depending on whether they were planning a trip in advance or were waiting at a bus stop. We found that a substantial proportion of customers plan the bus they are going to use in advance, according to timetable, or fares, or the nature and quality of service and many would be willing to switch between operators on the basis of differences in their competitive offer. However, customers who have not already bought a particular operator's ticket usually choose to board the first bus to their destination that arrives at the bus stop.

Para 18: We also found that changes in the fare or service on existing services offered by local bus operators had little effect on passengers' overall use of the bus. In conjunction with the finding that many customers would be willing to switch between operators, this indicates a substantial 'business-stealing' effect, where if rival operators on a route improve their offer, any increase in revenue would largely be as a result of customers switching from other bus operators, rather than as a result of growing the overall demand for bus services.

Para 19: Most passengers with multi-trip tickets make substantial use of these. We found that network effects can be important and that passengers will often commit to an individual operator's services through the purchase of an operator-specific multi-journey ticket.

The conclusion must be that the aspirations and predictions of *Buses* have been proved wrong. There is very little on-road competition and, rather than the market being invaded by a range of competing operators, the exact opposite has happened. Sixty-nine per cent of all services are provided by just five large groups: the data on the route-, bus- and passenger-kilometrage is redacted[45] from the report, but they are all probably well above 69 per cent. The report seems to supply evidence that bus operators, in common with most firms, are antagonistic towards competition. Given their legal obligations to their shareholders, they strive to create monopolies by either preventing competitors from entering the market through aggressive pricing ('unhealthy bus wars') or by buying out the competition. The head-to-head competition advocated and predicted by *Buses* is shown to occur in only 3 percent of bus routes, and that, in all probability, means that fewer than 3 per cent of passengers have the realistic choice between operators which *Buses* thought would bring such great benefits.

The data on ticketing show clear evidence that the presumption that the 'product' being bought and sold is single-ride tickets, but the public do not share that presumption: they see public transport as providing mobility through a network spread over time and space. That makes 'head-to-head competition' at the bus-stop an illusion and the effects it is supposed to bring unattainable.

Current bus policy: *A Green Light for Better Buses*[46]

A Green Light for Better Buses (2012) misconceives the problem on its very first page:

> The demand for the type of service buses can provide is enormous. At a time when people more than ever need a reliable way to get to work, the need for the bus has never been greater. Nor has the desire for low carbon alternatives to the car. Since half of all car journeys are less than five miles in length, the bus is ideally placed to help the Coalition Government meet its challenging carbon reduction targets. After all, 85 per cent of households in England (not including London) live within a six minute walk of a bus stop. We just need to join the dots (p. 4).

This statement appears to see the bus as a low-carbon alternative to the car and, in particular, as an alternative for journeys of under five miles. Buses do have a lower emission of CO_2 per passenger-kilometre than a car, but only if the bus is carrying a good payload and if it is compared with a car with a driver but no passengers. The possible reductions in CO_2 are far from uniform and may even be negative for a poorly loaded bus. If bus rather than car use is to help meet 'challenging carbon reduction targets', then policy has to be spatially selective.

Carbon reduction will be at its height where travel is by a well-loaded bus rather than lightly loaded cars, and this is most likely to occur in the urban areas where:

- the geography of travel demand sustains the frequencies that make it attractive;
- parking and congestion problems make the use of a car unattractive and inefficient.

Better Buses seems to be based on a strange paradox. It shows very clearly that the competition expected to increase following privatisation has not emerged; nor have the effects it was supposed to bring, and yet the policy is to advocate more competition. It is redolent of the agricultural policy of the 1930s Soviet Union which failed catastrophically, a failure that did not lead to the sensible rejection of the background ideology but to the strengthening of the policy driven by the belief that the ideology must be right and the fault must lie in its application. Unsurprisingly, *Better Buses* advocates that more competition should be engendered, but singularly fails to identify ways in which this might be done.

In part this is due to misunderstanding the nature of the market and of the product being marketed. Nobody (with the possible exception of bus enthusiasts) buys bus journeys on impulse: it is not comparable with browsing supermarket shelves. As the Competition Commission reported, people have a planned destination and a planned sequence of later journeys. The 'product' is not one journey capable of being provided by one operator and characterised by one ticket – it is a flicker of mobility needed to achieve a personal goal.

Unlike the 1968 Transport Act and the subsequent TSG/TPP system, the link between public transport and land use has been lost. *Buses* made the error of thinking that bus services were there to remedy the lack of mobility of the 39 per cent of households without a car, and *Better Buses* repeats the mistake. Public transport as a whole, including the bus networks, is there to serve two purposes:

1 to provide mobility for those who do not have a car or the ability to cycle or walk to all their destinations – it is there to satisfy many of the travel needs of a significant section of society;
2 to provide access to areas of inadequate parking for all sections of society.

Better Buses repeats the failures of its predecessors by not addressing the fundamental differences between these two needs. The first is a community action to meet a social objective – to include those without the use of a car into society. The second requires the moulding of millions of personal choices into the delivery of a community objective – to sustain the economic viability of dense urban centres. Although these two needs are bound together by the shared objective of reducing GHG emissions, this is likely to be achieved to a far greater extent by moulding urban choices than the necessities of remedying the lack of mobility of those without access to a car. The differences serve to highlight the need for spatially selective actions.

The policy set out in paragraph 1.12 of *Better Buses* contains four strands:

1 reforming the payment of the bus service operators grant (BSOG), a subsidy to operators that makes more services viable, to ensure taxpayers get better value for the money put into each and every local bus market;

2   incentivising partnerships between local transport authorities and operators to improve the quality of bus services and attract more passengers;
3   improving competition in English local bus markets, and bringing local transport authorities and bus companies together to help develop effective multi-operator ticketing schemes, by adopting the Competition Commission's recent recommendations to government;
4   supporting local transport authorities in their ability to procure non-commercial services, including more flexible, innovative options such as community buses.

The BSOG is to be abolished in all but name. The money previously given to operators in the form of a partial rebate of the duty paid on their purchases of fuel is to be redirected to local authorities to be combined with the existing monies used to provide contracted non-commercial services. Local authorities typically provide two remedies to make good the shortcomings of the network of commercial routes: they contract with operators first, to run unprofitable routes which would not exist without subsidy, and second, to provide additional workings on commercial routes at unprofitable times. Provided that the money is not depleted in moving it from one budget to another, the redeployment of the BSOG money should be welcomed, since a fuel subsidy tends to blunt the urge to reduce consumption and, furthermore, local authorities are best able to target specific network deficiencies.

Nonetheless, it is typical of much of modern governance. Policy appears to be a matter of establishing systems of administration by which decision-making (and responsibility), rather than purposed actions, is devolved away from central government towards local authorities, firms and individuals. The tendency of government to outsource decision-making extends to the second policy strand: 'to incentivise partnerships between local transport authorities and operators'. The government has already established a fund used to create 'better bus areas' and part of the funds released by abolishing the BSOG fuel duty rebate are to be used to enhance this fund. 'Better bus areas' are designated areas within which the infrastructure for which the local authority is responsible is improved and, in response, bus operators contract to provide faster, more reliable services. One of the improvements is expected to be in ticketing, including passes acceptable by all operators within designated areas. However, local authorities will have to combine with operators to submit competitive bids for a share of the capped fund. Wherever there are multiple operators, even the writing of such bids could produce haggling conflicts.

This displays a belief in the efficacy of competitive bidding, although it is unlikely to ensure the best value for money from the available funds. It will ensure that operators will support bids with enthusiasm in proportion to the predicted effects upon their balance sheets and share prices. It is also evidence of government's faith in 'partnerships' between the private and public sectors. Partnerships of any sort work only if there is a congruity of aims, coupled with agreement upon how responsibility is to be shared. It is difficult to see how private operators with a prime, legal responsibility to their shareholders can combine effectively with local authorities with a prime, legal responsibility to their citizens: one will measure 'success' by the short-term balance sheet and the other by ongoing lobbying and longer term voting.

Numbers with an audited pound sign will always carry more weight than impressionistic political pressures, and this will inevitably skew decision-making. Nonetheless, the notion of 'better bus areas' is a useful one, and will be developed later in the chapter.

Buses, which set the scene for the deregulation and privatisation of the bus industry, was quite clear that competition was the solution to the high cost and low efficiency of the bus industry. To change that view now would be tantamount to admitting that the policies of yesteryear had failed, carrying an implication that the corrective powers of competition were much weaker than originally thought. It is unsurprising, but nonetheless unfortunate, that the third strand of the current policy bundle shows a strong emphasis on the power of competition and markets to correct the existing deficiencies of bus services. What is surprising is that the justification for this is taken from the Competition Commission report quoted in the previous paragraphs[47] which catalogues shortcomings of current bus services in terms not dissimilar to *Buses*. For example, in 1984 each route was licensed, effectively granting a monopoly for that route. This was held to be a basic root of inefficiency and poor service levels. *Better Buses* develops an impossibility:

> Our goal is for the majority of public transport journeys to be undertaken using smart ticketing technology by December 2014, a significant proportion of which will be on the bus. As set out in our Local Transport White Paper 'Creating Growth, Cutting Carbon' smart ticketing can play a crucial role in the co-ordination of public transport. It can improve boarding speeds for passengers and allow them to make more seamless through journeys on a single ticket or travelcard. There are also significant benefits for bus operators and local transport authorities in terms of data and information gathering and sharing.[48]

This is a sensible goal, but, since it implies the pre-purchase of 'smart-tickets', it implicitly precludes 'head-to-head competition' of the nature advocated by the Competition Commission and repeated in *Better Buses*. This is no great loss, since the 'head-to-head' competition which was advocated and fostered in the 1984 White Paper and in the subsequent legislation is not apparent 30+ years later: on the contrary, the industry is now dominated by five companies that have built themselves into a series of local monopolies.

Most of the remaining actions described in *Better Buses* are concerned with funding. The 'Green Bus Fund' subsidises the purchase of low-emission vehicles. It is an example of implementing policy through fiscal measures, a common technique in recent years. The full effects have yet to be seen: one of the motives is to pump-prime the production of low-emission buses, particularly hybrids, by boosting initial orders. This is a desirable objective which looks as though it is well on the way to being achieved.

A major channel for financial support of the bus industry is the concessionary travel for pensioners and others. *Better Buses* states neither how much this costs nor whether the objectives are being achieved.[49] It does report that it has given a significant boost to the numbers of journeys by bus, but whether this has been instead of, or in addition to, car travel is not known. Past experiments with free public transport had a major effect of people making more journeys rather than switching from car use. It has also induced people to make short hop-on, hop-off trips on the bus rather than walking. But the prime objective of the concessionary scheme to provide more mobility for the elderly has clearly been achieved.

In recent years government policy documents have tended to be little more than marketing literature, putting a gloss upon past decisions and making extravagant claims for the effects of proposed actions. *Better Buses* is no exception – paragraph 1.5 preens:

> In the most recent survey by Passenger Focus of bus users' satisfaction with their local services, an average of 85% said they were satisfied overall. Even in the area with the lowest satisfaction, it still stood at a very respectable 79%. In many ways, this is not surprising – thanks to a combination of bus company investment, local council infrastructure improvements and Government regulation and funding, buses are more accessible with more high-tech information and ticketing facilities for passengers than ever before.

Asking the purchasers of any product whether they are satisfied or not is an invitation to say they are, since to say otherwise prompts the silent, follow-up question, 'Then why are you buying it?' The people to ask are those *not* using the product. As far as public transport is concerned, country-wide non-users are in the majority but the vital fact is that the proportion of users to non-users varies over a vast range: 90+ per cent of those commuting into the City of London use public transport,[50] but in Cornwall just 3.4 per cent travel to work by public transport.[51] It follows that the levels of satisfaction and of dissatisfaction in Cornwall will be radically different to those in London, making the claim of 79 to 85 per cent satisfaction even more disingenuous than first appears.

Current policy is weak due to the combination of:

- objectives which are imprecise aspirations devoid of measures by which success or failure may be sensed;
- a misreading of the 'product' and 'markets' for public transport;
- a lack of awareness of the mechanisms people use in making their travel choices;
- a similar ignorance of the spatial differences in the data that people digest in making their decisions;
- a misperception of the transport network as a bundle of modes working in competition rather than in combination;
- a failure to understand the importance of walking as an integral part of bus journeys, as reflected by the PTAL measure;
- a set of actions which are only loosely linked to the objectives they are supposed to achieve.

Regulating the railways

The origins of the road system were simple: primitive tracks, initially created by popular use, became public rights of way over privately owned land. That process could not produce the turnpike, canal and railway systems because they involved physical construction and expense over a very long, narrow strip of land along which agreement had to be made with the owners: that could only be arranged with the insistent facilitation of the state. Laws had to be made to clarify the ownership of land and of the pathways constructed across it, laws which overrode normal property rights. Although the road network had informal roots with no commitment of state monies, in the fourteenth and fifteenth centuries its maintenance became a matter of official parish council liability and management.

State involvement in transport of all sorts was unavoidable, not just in the creation and maintenance of tracks but in the control of the endemic monopoly. On the first railways the sheer speed prevented drivers from driving by line of sight, making danger unavoidable. Government has a duty to protect its citizens from all manner of dangers and injustices, a duty it has to discharge by insisting upon standards and best practice: transport systems cannot work, or even exist, without state intervention.

That is abundantly true of railways: the only query is about the degree of intervention. Before 1914 the British state regulated passenger fares, freight rates and safety through Parliament, but disquiet over the ability of the 121 private railway companies to provide the necessary backing to the war effort induced the government to take over railway management too. In the 1920s railways were reorganised into the private ownership of four large companies established by the state with a fig-leaf of theoretical competition, although exactly how the Southern Railway with its monopoly of lines in the South of England could ever have engaged in competition with the London and North-Eastern's east coast route to Aberdeen is even beyond theory. The risks and commitments borne by the shareholders of the new companies were reduced by state-provided capital with repayments and interest covered by Treasury guarantee: this money was used to provide very frequent, if not fast, commuter services and to buy powerful locomotives to power fast but infrequent long-distance trains.

War intervened once more in 1939 and railway management was once again taken into the direct control of the state. In 1948 this was formalised by complete nationalisation. This history suggests a progression. The first railways were facilitated by Parliament but, once built, were owned and managed privately. There then followed almost a century during which the state regulated the private companies, at first by fixing fares and freight rates, then by facilitating inter-company traffic, and then exerting powerful controls over safety. In the 1920s and 1930s the state added considerable financial control followed by the six war years of total control culminating in outright ownership. This progression was not driven by ideology but by necessary pragmatism.

The war years had demanded service levels in which commercial considerations played no part: if the wartime transport was necessary then it was almost treasonable not to strive to provide it. Post-war, the wear and tear of war had to be repaired, but the 1954 Modernisation Plan produced by the newly nationalised British Railways was a sleep-walk into a disastrous political, financial and technical nightmare. The war years had numbed all sense of financial discipline and so the 'Plan' was no more than a very long, very expensive shopping list, devoid of objectives, devoid of forecasts of the effectiveness of the proposals and based entirely upon impressions of how pre-war traffic could have been better provided at the time. It was an object lesson in how not to plan and how not to write an investment programme.

One massive mistake had extensive ramifications. Just as the horse had been replaced by the internal combustion engine in the aftermath of the First World War, so electric motors replaced steam-engines after the Second World War. The wartime munitions factories were powered by electricity and did not have to be built adjacent to railways. They were case studies of a new economic geography in which industrial energy came by wire, not by rail: industry and employment had been given a new locational freedom.

That freedom was to apply to the generation of electricity itself. The National Grid had been inaugurated in 1926, but with the intention of linking local power-stations together so that surges in local demand and supply could be evened out. In 1949 a new strategy emerged: using a higher, more efficient transmission voltage the old local stations were replaced by ever-larger stations located at places away from concentrations of demand but where coal supply costs could be minimised and where cooling water was available. The Modernisation Plan failed to even consider the effects of the changes in the geography of the supply and demand for electricity and planned to build massive new marshalling yards to cope with soon-to-be non-existent coal trains. It also built a fleet of coal-fired steam locomotives. The last of them, built in 1960 with an expected life of 30 years, was scrapped five years later, hurriedly replaced by an ill-judged fleet of diesel locomotives, some of which had such poor brakes that they had to be assisted by special wagons weighted down with cast iron to provide more braking adhesion, and others which had to be paired with steam locomotives, not to haul the train, but to heat it. At the time, European railways were being rebuilt after the wartime destruction with a heavy emphasis on electrification and, where that was uneconomic, by diesel: the demonstration projects were a channel-ferry ride away.

The political, technical and financial fiasco of the Modernisation Plan made the shift in focus of transport policy to roads inevitable. For example, one component of the Plan was the electrification of the line to carry coal across the Pennines from the Yorkshire coalfields to the Lancashire power-stations, a project that cost over £48 million, including £3 million spent on a new tunnel. The first 72 miles of the M1 cost £50 million. There was no doubt in anybody's mind which was the better investment even before the railway line was prematurely closed and the empty tunnel used for a cable to carry electricity generated in new power-stations built on the Yorkshire coalfield to the consumers of Lancashire.

The Beeching Report of 1963 threw the Modernisation Plan into an abrupt reverse, closing 4000 out of 6000 stations, 6000 out of 18,000 miles of line and some of the new marshalling yards even before they were finished. The nature, as well as the extent of railway services was changed completely: small station-to-station freight consignments, until then a main source of revenue, disappeared. Even the stations still open to passenger traffic lost their goods-handling facilities and sidings serving individual factories were closed. The railways did more than retract: they were transformed from a freight network that also carried passengers into a passenger network that also carried bulk freight between a very limited number of selected points. The demise of the bumbling goods train released swathes of mainline track capacity which was used to improve passenger services to undreamt-of speeds and frequencies. In 1958 there were 14 trains per day running direct from London to Newcastle at a mean speed of 84 km/hour: by 2012 there were 31 trains moving at an average speed of 140 km/h.

Figure 17.10 shows the changes in patronage over the past 70 years. The data on average length of journey are important but opaque. Passenger traffic by rail is essentially a combination of:

- long-distance travel (dubbed 'Inter-City' by British Railways);
- commuter travel;
- local, non-commuter travel.

The third type is characterised by quite short distances and comparatively sparse traffic susceptible to competition by bus and car. It was the traffic identified by Beeching as being high cost and low revenue and a market from which British Railways should withdraw. This it did, largely through the closure of two-thirds of all stations, but the Beeching Report made wild over-estimates of the savings from these closures, and the hoped-for effects on the railway balance sheet never materialised. Lightly loaded local, non-commuter services are still an accountancy problem.

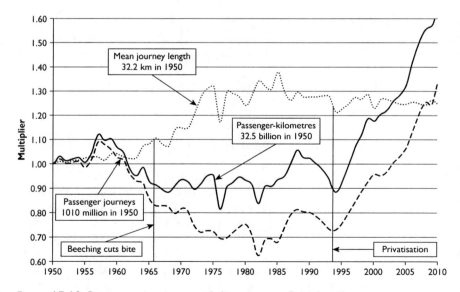

Figure 17.10 Passenger journeys and distances on British railways

Source: Department for Transport, *Transport Statistics Great Britain* (2011), table RA10101.

Before 1962 all rail fares were regulated at a fixed price per mile, although discounted fares with specific conditions of use were permitted. After 1962 British railways were able to tailor fares to demand, although it was a power used comparatively infrequently. Beeching was given a remit to make British railways profitable, and both he and his political masters believed this to be possible. It is a belief still harboured by many, a belief that somehow costs could be cut and fares raised within an accountancy ring fence to produce a surplus of revenue over cost. It is a delusion. Figure 17.1 may show horse-tram costs but the principle applies to modern railways too. Tracks have to be well used if their heavy costs are to be justified. Parity between costs and revenues may be approached only by reducing cost per train-kilometre to a minimum, either by cheap maintenance to cope with the very low but constant speeds of heavy, well-loaded freight trains or, alternatively, through expensive maintenance to allow high speeds but that expense to be spread over frequent, well-patronised services. The two options are technically incompatible, but either on its own makes railway costs very vulnerable due to the need to spread track cost over a large number of tonne- and passenger-kilometres and making the capture and retention of the necessary levels of demand vital. Perhaps using parity of costs and revenues as a measure of railway efficiency is mistaken.

An alternative is in the argument that transport is not, nor cannot be, an isolated, viable 'cost centre' but is an integral part of the life of the nation, incapable of being sensibly ring fenced. This seems to be accepted for the road network which is exempt from bringing costs and revenues into parity. There is no attempt to equate the 'costs' and 'revenues' of an office corridor or of a factory conveyor belt or any other integral component of the micro-transport system: they are seen as a necessary part of larger functions. This is not to say that they should not be assessed for financial or other quantitative justification, but only to argue, first, that such justification should not be based on a surplus, merely on efficiency in obtaining the best effects from the committed resources; and second, that the 'revenue' should include more than the financial income, including, perhaps, CO_2 emissions, the land-use budget, etc.

Rail privatisation

The continuing confusion between efficiency and profitability seems to have been the prime driving force behind the privatisation of the British railway system in 1993. It had been preceded by a White Paper *New Opportunities for the Railways* (1992) which echoed the mantra of *Buses* (1984):

> Privatisation is one of the great success stories of this government.[52]

New Opportunities then goes on to make exactly the same mistakes as the Modernisation Plan had done in 1954. A recitation, backed by statistics, of what was demonstrably wrong with the railway was used as justification for a set of proposals devoid of any expected indices of those performances expected to correct the listed problems. *New Opportunities* was an ideological belief in privatisation and competition just as the nationalisation of 1948 was an ideological belief that state ownership would be all the action that was necessary to deliver an efficient railway. The aspirations of the 1990s were that privatisation would generate competition and that the superior, motivated management of commercial companies would dissolve many, if not all, the railways' woes.

The infrastructure of the entire railway was given to a new company, Railtrack, whose shares sold well to people who could not have imagined that it would later fall into rancorous bankruptcy. The major competition that emerged was not seen by passengers at the station but in a convoluted, expensive Dutch auction of franchises, most of which have been won by large transport conglomerates established either within the regime created by *Buses* or are offshoots of foreign state-owned railways. The hoped-for use of 'open access' to the use of the tracks has flickered and died. The prime target of *New Opportunities* was the reduction of subsidy: in fact the subsidy per train-mile has doubled and the indebtedness of Network Rail (the new company created to replace the bankrupt Railtrack) is now seven times that of the state-owned British Railways in the last year of its life.[53]

Just as with the privatisation of the bus industry, the theory of competition has not delivered the predicted effects but has appeared to demonstrate that transport services are not suitable for sale within a competitive market because they are time-specific, unstockable and infinitely perishable. Those characteristics make them inherently monopolistic, and the job of the state is to recognise, control and organise that natural monopoly, not to ignore its existence. Transport's characteristics also make costing and accountancy fraught: the nature of the product, whether costs are time or distance based and the potent mixture of the capacities of track, vehicles and staff make optimising accounts very difficult indeed, quite apart from the collateral social benefits and costs.

In such a complex, volatile industry where external costs and benefits abound, using problematic measures of profitability as a proxy for efficiency is an impossible task. Efficiency should still be an objective, but, in order to be a useful concept it has to be measured by the resources used to achieve specific, defined objectives which are known and embraced by all the departments, agencies and actors concerned. For example, the minimisation of emitted CO_2, which could and should be an objective, cannot be delivered by measures of profitability even if imaginative games are played by putting a 'price' on it: all that will do is to allow failure to reach the objective, a matter of offsetting against other pseudo-prices.

Present and future uses of public transport

A contrast is usually drawn between public transport and the use of cars:

- Cars are always available, effectively providing an infinitely frequent service.
- Cars are difficult to cost per journey with the costs of debt servicing and depreciation being obscure. Although the cost per seat-kilometre by car is actually higher than those by public transport, it is often thought, or perhaps wished, to be lower.
- Car journey ends are fraught with the costs and problems of parking.
- The theoretical performance of cars is inhibited by congestion.

Given a choice between public transport and unfettered car use, the vast majority will choose to use the car, despite the real total cost per kilometre and despite the effect upon the environment. The convenience and flexibility of being able to choose time of travel, route and destination is overwhelmingly attractive. Any realistic policy has to recognise that cars appear to many people to be the most efficient and desirable method of transport and are the default choice.

This forces public transport to adopt the role of providing mobility wherever car use is impossible or has been rejected for some reason or another. In practice, public transport is perceived to be the remedial method of transport to be used only when necessary. To mount policies which try to make public transport a general mode will be to invite expensive failure: public transport has to be selective and targeted.

There are two clear targets:

1   to provide mobility for those without a car;
2   to provide an alternative wherever car use is seen to be undesirable.

These targets really consist of groups of people making choices to acquire a car and then, having done so, making choices whether to use it or not for specific journeys.

Acquisition and ownership

Non-car owners may be those who cannot use a car for financial or physical reasons or they may be those who choose not to own a car because it is an undesirable burden. The densely developed Edwardian tenements reported in Figures 4.6 and 17.6 have low car ownership due to two interlocked reasons: minimal parking space and excellent local public transport, both related to density. Of these two, the lack of parking space appears to be decisive, since another of the indicative examples, reported in Figure 4.9, also has good public transport and is about the same distance from the city centre, but is well provided with parking space and has significantly different car ownership and use.

This appears to suggest that car ownership will be reduced if densities preclude easy parking and also produce the demand to justify good, well-used public transport. But that points to a self-referential presumption: if an individual car owner moves house to somewhere where parking is easier, then a car may well be acquired, an action which, if repeated by a number of individuals, will erode the demand for public transport, leading to a reduced, less attractive service. If this logic is correct then there must be threshold densities and parking availabilities which, in combination, create sufficient stable travel demand to support public transport provision and use, but below which public transport may decline. This is no more than a rewrite of the relationship between Edwardian trams and by-law housing or between the 1930s semis and buses, although with different arithmetic. In effect it is also a definition of the permeable boundary between the first category, those who do not have a car, and the second, those who choose not to use a car.

It does rather more than that. It suggests a default propensity to acquire a car which will be done unless there is good reason not to. The history of the growth of car ownership supports this view: the financial constraints on acquisition and ownership seem to have been reflected in the age and purchase price of an acquired car rather than a decision whether to acquire a car or not. Consequently, the prime influence upon ownership open to policy levers is the provision of somewhere to keep a car for the 90 per cent of the time during which it will not move. This has important implications for land-use budgets.

Car use

The density threshold has another component which the Nottingham Zone and Collar experiment failed to explore. The public transport accessibility level (PTAL) is a function of the time/distance it takes to walk to a station or bus-stop and the service provided there. Hence, the position of stops will influence people's choices. These distances may be manipulated by housing form: if new residential areas are built along the line of a public transport route, as they were with Edwardian trams and railways, not only will the mean distance to a stop be minimised, but travel demand will be concentrated in that linear route. On the other hand, if housing is developed in an amorphous mass, filling up a field or two, then either public transport service will be restricted to nearby main roads with lengthy walks to the stops, or routes will have to be proliferated to provide lower frequencies to a spatter of stops nearer to people's front doors. This amounts to an argument in favour of linear or ribbon development rather than clumps of housing. This has been characterised by the difference between toad-spawn (in long lines) and frog-spawn (in shapeless clumps), but the distinction is far from absolute. In Edwardian times London's Metropolitan Railway was partly financed by property development along its length, but the development was not continuous as it was along the newly electrified tram routes: it was intermittent, clustered around stations – a combination of toad- and frog-spawn.

There can be no absolute arithmetic linking density, availability of parking, car ownership and use, walking distances to stops and frequencies, but there is an absolute, if unquantified relationship between the nature and size of residential areas and the use of public transport.

Thus far, the analysis has focused on the residential end of the journey to work, but, if anything, that is the less important end of the journey. There is a very good reason for not using a car if parking at the destination is difficult, expensive or impossible. Readily available city centre parking seemed to be a determining issue in the Nottingham experiment, and the provision of parking in suburban development appears to be a major determinant of the nature, size and position of decentralised development.

Figure 17.11 shows the main modes used for the morning commuter peak into the City of London. It reports the 'main mode' (the mode used for most of a person's commuting distance) and does not account for ancillary modes such as a bus being used to get from a railway terminus to the final destination. Only 11 per cent of people use the two modes needing parking space, namely car or motor cycle (powered two-wheelers (PTW)). Just slightly under 90 per cent travel by public transport, the great majority of them by rail (either the services provided by Transport for London (the

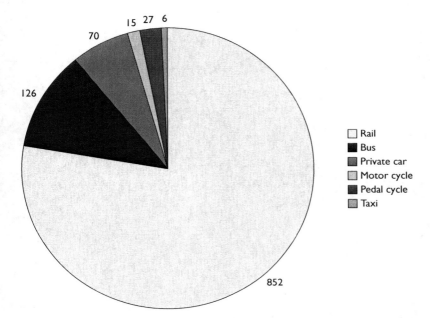

Figure 17.11 Numbers (thousands) commuting to the City of London in the morning peak in 2009, by main mode of travel

Source: Department for Transport, *Transport Statistics Great Britain* (2011), table 0106.

Underground and Overground) or by National Rail). London is an extreme case in which job densities are at their maximum, where parking is extremely limited and where commuting distances are extended. But there is nothing to suggest that the principles at work are not present in a diluted form wherever job densities are high and where parking is extremely difficult. Figure 17.12 shows that the minor use of private transport is stable with fluctuations in rail travel keeping in step with the total number of commuters, while buses and cycling show some growth.

London commuting distances are long and the proportion of car journeys that would be afflicted by congestion is high. Rail is unaffected by street congestion and the long distances between stations allow trains to reach good operating speeds, particularly since most of the London approach lines are multi-tracked, permitting fast skip-stop services. Other cities are not blessed with that advantage and, without the overtaking opportunities offered by multiple tracks, are limited to all-stations trains running at short headways (e.g. London's Underground) or have to sacrifice frequency to a mixture of skip- and all-stoppers. London also exhibits the advantages of multi-modal travel with car-parks at suburban stations and bus services providing feeders in the suburbs and distribution services in the centre. This works because frequencies are high and service rhythms interlock well. A major facet of London's commuting travel is the perception and use of the transport system as an entity with inter-modal journeys including interchanging. In recent years this has been helped by

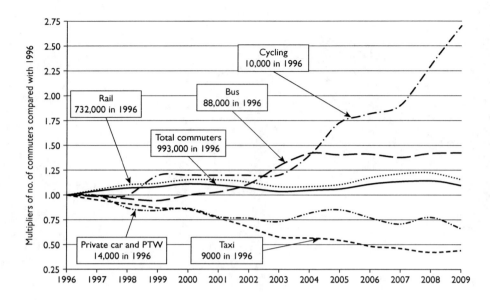

Figure 17.12 Trends in commuting mode used to access the City of London (1996–2009)
Source: Department for Transport, *Transport Statistics Great Britain* (2011), table 0106.

the Oyster Network ticketing scheme and its predecessor Travelcard, but inter-modal travel has always been a feature in the capital. This may have its roots in the fact that the main lines do not penetrate the city's heart, requiring ancillary modes to get people to their final destinations, one of the drivers in the formation of the London Passenger Transport Board in 1933 with responsibility for trams, trolleybuses, motor buses and the Underground. Whatever its reason, London's transport system has placed an emphasis on interchanges and the use of combinations of modes.

Commuter travel by rail has been characterised by comparatively short ride times and peak tidal movement, creating a cost burden through uneven utilisation of track and rolling-stock.[54] However, that has changed and is still changing. Four trends have been in evidence:

1 The surge in mainline speeds and frequencies has enabled long-distance commuting extending 'virtual London' (the area within which people both live and work) deep into East Anglia and the South Midlands; there is even significant commuter traffic from York, 300 kilometres north of London.
2 Britain has moved from a blue-collar to a white-collar economy with the relative importance of office rather than factory jobs producing more city centre jobs at densities which preclude car-parking.
3 Changes in the licensing laws and in the Shops Act have caused a massive shift in opening hours.

4   Young people have been leaving their family homes and setting up on their own, changing residential geographies with a trend towards small flats occupied by the yet-to-be-married.

The last three trends together have induced a shift in urban living with city centres being not only workplaces but recreational and retailing centres with a strong evening and night life, flattening and extending the evening peak. In the 1960 heyday of public transport it was comparatively empty in the evenings but is now crowded.

Whether the nature and timing of urban travel is changing or not, it has always been a matter of strong political concern. Beeching was fully aware that any attempt to apply his accountancy to commuter services would be politically rebuffed. The continuing political emphasis on commuter travel has ensured that there has been considerable investment in the refurbishment and electrification of lines, in new rolling-stock and signalling and the rebuilding of stations to accommodate longer trains. Virtual London has been the main beneficiary with massive investments in the Docklands Light Railway, the London Overground, local services on the Channel Tunnel high-speed line, and now Crossrail, but there have been significant investments in commuter services elsewhere too.

The isochrones focused on the areas dominated by white-collar office employment have been extended at the same time as their pulse representing service frequency has been quickened. This has sustained the accessibility to city cores and their commercial functions and land values, and has also maintained the high densities needed to support public transport.

The expansion of longer distance inter-city travel has led, first, to the growth in the amount of rail travel (measured in passenger-kilometres and shown by the solid curve in Figure 17.10), and also in the mean journey length (shown by the dotted curve). However, the growth in mean journey length has been muted, suggesting that the growth in long-distance inter-city travel is only partly responsible for the overall growth in passenger-kilometres: that view is reinforced by the dashed curve showing passenger journeys which is more in step with the overall growth.[55] This, in turn, suggests that the major growth is in the use of the railway for journeys with a mean of about 40 kilometres (the future for 1950 expanded by a multiplier of about 1.25). This is a fair representation of a mean commuting distance.

Commuting by bus is increasing in London due partly to policy decisions by Transport for London and partly by the changing household structure with young people occupying flats nearer the centre. But in London, buses still carry fewer commuters than rail: this is not a characteristic of smaller cities where demand is not sufficient to cover the railway track costs. Buses, in not having to cover track costs, are able to provide low-frequency services, but there will always be a floor frequency below which the service becomes unattractive, particularly when compared with the infinite frequency offered by the private car. The recursive Matthew principle will kick in: a low frequency, although theoretically possible, will fail to attract enough custom to sustain it and frequencies have to be reduced further in an attempt to reach viability. It follows that there will be a minimum residential density below which demand will be insufficient to sustain a consistently attractive service: however, this will never be a constant, since the threshold service will depend on the balance of advantages and disadvantages of the whole journey right through to the destination door, including the parking problems that will be avoided by the use of public transport. This requires consideration of the distribution network in the urban core and in the occurrence of congestion along the radial route.

In other towns and cities the crucial public transport provisions of access to the dense core without the need to park will lean more heavily on the bus unless the urban area is extensive enough to create the demand to sustain railway track costs and also to provide the inter-station distances which allow their higher speeds to be deployed.

Serving residential areas is not just a matter of frequency. Lower frequency services depend on adherence to the timetable for their perceived quality. There is also a need to provide a pattern of bus-stops and routes serving them to ensure acceptable walks from origin address to bus-stop. If the size and density of a residential area is insufficient to sustain an attractive service then the only alternative (apart from complete reliance upon the car) is a park-and-ride policy in which cars are used for that part of a journey passing through areas where an acceptable bus service cannot be provided, but buses are used for that part where cars would cause congestion.

Park-and-ride is usually perceived as a very large, formalised facility in which car-parks are large enough to support a dedicated, frequent bus service. In Virtual London these are related to railways stations[56] rather than radial bus routes, but the principle is the same. The arithmetic can be daunting. Large car-parks mean long walks from parking bays to the bus-stop; small car-parks fail to generate attractive public transport frequencies; car-parks sited too far out in the suburbs do not serve a large enough number of households; car-parks too close to the centre do not offer a long enough ride to create the attractive time savings.

Parking at some distance from the destination is common: it is a strong characteristic of major sports events and of airports, but it is also a characteristic of normal urban life. Side-streets on the fringes of urban centres are used as either park-and-walk or park-and-ride facilities. This is a good use of urban space and, although purists will deplore the use of cars at all, it serves to maintain the densities and viability of the urban core. This could be further stimulated by a combination of street parking charges with the sale of bus passes.

Insulating buses from congestion gives transport planners a major problem. The usual technique is to provide bus lanes which, theoretically, enable buses to 'overtake' congested queues of general traffic, but they are hobbled in five ways:

1 The bus lanes are usually immediately adjacent to the kerb.
2 They usually do not extend to the stop line at traffic signals where bus priority usually evaporates.
3 They are discontinuous with gaps wherever they cannot be fitted in and still leave a lane for general traffic.
4 Bus lanes are limited in their operating hours.
5 Bus lanes have to be shared with cyclists.

Urban kerb space is at a premium: it is used by stationary delivery and service vehicles, by parked vehicles, and by vehicles picking up and setting down passengers. In the past, these conflicts were the reason why tram tracks were built in the middle of the road, the place where they remain in European cities and where they have been built in the new British systems: if tram tracks were not in the centre of the road, trams would be blocked by dust-carts, delivery vans, rogue parkers, etc.

Bus lanes rarely run right up to traffic signal stop lines and this is probably partly due to their kerbside position, but the strongest reason, which also accounts for them being restricted in operating times and for their discontinuity, is that there is an inbuilt social and political bias in favour of car use expressed as an acceptance of bus lanes, provided that they do not over-inconvenience general traffic. It is an endemic bias manifested in bus riders' time being valued lower than car riders' time and in measuring traffic flow in 'passenger car units' (PCU), with constants that reflect the relative effects of different vehicles upon general traffic flow. If traffic were measured by relative efficiency, the PCU weighting would not reflect the effect upon traffic flow, but upon vehicle occupancy. Since this fluctuates and would be impractical to use operationally, the practical alternative would be to weight by the number of seats. This would rate a car at 0.25, a taxi at 0.2 and a bus at 0.001.

The recent White Paper *A Green Light for Better Buses* advocates the establishment of better bus areas. This is a useful concept but it needs strengthening. Unlike the official proposal which has no clear, testable objectives, 'public transport priority areas' would have the explicit objective of sustaining the economic viability of urban centres by providing excellent access for all members of society. Minimal car-parking would be provided in the centre itself, and would be replaced by parking on the periphery and in the suburbs, as well as by acceptable bus penetration into residential areas. In the centre itself low-floor minibuses would circulate to augment the range of normal stops served by the main radial routes. On the radial roads, buses would have priority, working as though they were trams in the centre of the road. Bus-stops would be protected by pedestrian signals triggered by the bus enabling alighting passengers to walk to either side of the road. This would be more than an operational procedure: it is a political statement that the buses and their passengers are more important to the commercial health of the centre than cars and their passengers. General traffic would be interrupted to the benefit of those using public transport. This reversal in current normal practice would be confined to the radial roads and to the centre itself where it would be illegal to impede a bus, just as it is illegal to impede a tram in European cities.

For this to work, buses would have to change their image and be more like trams. Bus interiors and levels of comfort have barely changed over the past 50 years, whereas cars are completely different. For some inexplicable reason bus operators pack as many seats as possible into their vehicles, providing a capacity which is only fleetingly used at the expense of knee room and circulating and luggage space. London's Routemaster became an iconic vehicle and a new icon is now needed.

The desirable objectives

Chapter 1 declared that the overall objective implicit in sustainable transport planning is to reduce the emission of CO_2. This is an objective in itself, but it is also a secondary measure of other objectives such as containing urbanisation (since this will reduce the amount of travel and will enhance the probability of the use of public transport).

It follows that sustaining the use of public transport is not an end in itself but is the means to an end. Public transport has no intrinsic value, but it can provide a direct short-term reduction in CO_2 coupled with a more important and potent long-term reduction by forestalling the congestion and parking problems that drive decentralisation and the development of the virtual city. But it has to be recognised that the geography of urban areas has changed considerably over the past 50 years or so, changes which have been partly driven by the changing economy and affluence, but the mainspring has been the rise in car ownership and use. The new urban geography reflects the virtual city with satellite towns and villages built to much lower densities, employment and retailing dispersed across wide swathes of countryside, but at its core is the new office-based service economy requiring more face-to-face contact in the workplace than in previous years and creating patches of high job density. Those densities cannot be supported by access by private car because the land budget of jobs per hectare cannot be matched with supporting car-park space.

The new urban geography cannot be reversed and is unsuitable for provision of a public transport system, in complete contrast to the central area which cannot be supported by anything other than public transport.

There are two interrelated objectives:

1   to provide access by public transport to areas in which sufficient car-parking cannot be provided in order to brake the decentralisation of the city;
2   to minimise the reduction of density in the rest of the city by providing public transport of sufficient quality to inhibit further switching to car use.

These two objectives in combination are designed to reduce the person-kilometres per head travelled by car both by direct effect and by the indirect brake on city expansions and lengthening journeys.

There is a subsidiary objective:

• to provide mobility for those without a car and, in so doing, to reduce the propensity for car acquisition.

A fundamental characteristic of policy must be for it to be spatially selective, targeted at local geographies. The definition of the differences can only be done by convincing, robust forecasts of the likely effects of interventions and policies, an ability good enough to provide support and numerical evidence for decision-makers at local and national levels. That need is addressed in Chapter 19.

Notes

1. 'Hackney' is derived from 'haquenée' – old French for an ambling workhorse.
2. This is still a problem: in New York recently the author's taxi driver pulled on to the hard shoulder on the way from the airport and refused to go any further without extra payment – old-fashioned extortion by ransom of the sort feared in seventeenth-century London.
3. Many bus drivers on modern double-decker buses still call the downstairs 'inside' and upstairs 'on top'.
4. An Enabling Act is one that does not authorise particular actions but establishes an administrative process to enable the authorisation of individual schemes. The 1870 Tramways Act is entitled 'An act to facilitate the construction and regulate the working of tramways'. The text of the Act itself is four pages long and laid the foundations for the organisation of urban public transport from the age of the horse to the diesel double-decker – an object lesson to legislators.
5. Clark (1894, p. 92).
6. Strangely, in Edinburgh the power was provided by steel cables running continuously in a channel under the tracks and powered by a central steam-engine. In 1923 the cable trams were converted to the normal practice of being individually powered by on-board electric motors.
7. The cost in London for track with an overhead cable to supply power was £24,500 per kilometre but the cost escalated to £32,700 with the preferred supply in a conduit between the rails See Harley (2002, p. 29).
8. In passenger transport the term 'place' covers both the seating and standing capacity; horse trams and buses were too small for any standing places but electric trams were far bigger.
9. Fifty years later London's tramways still offered as many miles as you could travel in a day for one shilling (£0.05).
10. Reminder: isochrones are imaginary lines passing through the places which could be reached in a given travel time from a defined origin.
11. A word with a less than attractive past. In Roman cities offensive activities ranging from slaughterhouses to brothels were clustered outside the city walls – literally 'sub urbs' (below the city).
12. Harley (2002, p. 18).
13. See Chapter 6 for an explanation of isochrones and how they pulse like heartbeats.
14. Hansard 1919.
15. The legal definition of a PSV excluded vehicles with an external power source.
16. He was the seventh minister. Transport became very quickly recognised as a poisoned chalice in which ministers would be necklaced with problems and failures, but unlikely to be recognised as effective. It has become a temporary staging post for those on their way up or down the political ladder. Three of the five ministers taking office in the first 11 years of the Ministry lasted less than a year.
17. Holroyd and Scraggs (1966).
18. Modern media relations would have added that 'We are learning from our mistakes and procedures are being improved; in the meantime our thoughts go out to the bereaved at this difficult time'.
19. Mr Brunner, Liberal MP for Northwich; House of Commons Debates, 2 August 1889, vol. 339 cc 228–30.
20. Hardly a political revolutionary, he was generally antagonistic to the advance of democracy by extending the right to vote, although he did say after the 1867 extension of the franchise that he found democracy to be less objectionable than he had expected. When pressed on votes for women, he said, 'When I am told that my ploughmen are capable citizens, it seems to me ridiculous to say that educated women are not just as capable'. It was to take until 1930 before women and ploughmen were to be treated as equals before the ballot-box.
21. Ministry of Transport (1963b, p. 24).

22 Ministry of Transport (1963b, p. 25).
23 The conversion of every gas appliance in the country to be fed from a new national natural gas network working to a higher pressure than the old coal-gas system was achieved quickly, efficiently and almost silently by a nationalised industry.
24 Economists use a good word hinting at this effect. 'Fructify' means literally to make fruitful, and is used to account for self-re-enforcing demand.
25 A 'working' is a timetabled movement of a bus from one end of its route to the other.
26 PTAL was a measure developed within the London Borough of Hammersmith and Fulham, and is now used throughout London.
27 Local Government Act (1972).
28 The administrative conflicts created by this two-tier system were amusingly illustrated in Ankers *et al.* (1979).
29 An example is given in Figure 4.7.
30 The changes were explained in full in Department of the Environment (1973a) *Circular 104/73*.
31 Annex to Department of the Environment (1973a) *Circular 104/73*.
32 Department of the Environment (1973a) *Circular 104/73*, Paragraph 3.
33 Feeding the computer model with historical data from some years back and seeing whether the predictions made from that base conformed with current reality.
34 See Layfield and Bardsley (1977); Layfield and Cooper (1978); Layfield and Vincent (1977).
35 Department of the Environment (1973a) *Circular 104/73*.
36 Layfield and Vincent (1977).
37 Department of the Environment (1976).
38 Department of Transport (1977b).
39 The TRL had started life as the Road Research Laboratory in 1933. It became the Transport and Road Research Laboratory in 1972 and then the Transport Research Laboratory in 1992. The changes in name signpost the changing government perception of transport.
40 Department of Transport (1984).
41 Department for Transport, *National Travel Survey*, table 9902.
42 Department of Transport (1984), Appendix B, Paragraph 2.
43 SI 1986/1671 as amended.
44 Competition Commission (2012) *Local Bus services: market investigation*.
45 An old word meaning 'worked into shape', but now meaning 'withheld from the public domain' – censored.
46 Department for Transport (2012b).
47 Competition Commission (2011).
48 Department for Transport (2012b), Paragraph 3.18.
49 Table BUS0502a in *Transport Statistics Great Britain* (Department for Transport) shows that the cost in England in 2010 to 2011 was £108 million.
50 *Transport Statistics Great Britain* (2011), table 0106.
51 Census (2011), table KS15.
52 Department of Transport (1992, p. 1).
53 Ford (2012).
54 Ministry of Transport (1958).
55 This should be treated with some scepticism, since it makes sense to cover long journeys by a series of tickets with breaks at changes from one company to another. Buying tickets that cross company boundaries often carries a premium and so the definition of a 'journey' may be contorted.
56 Usually in the converted coal yards which supplied coal for domestic heating and made redundant, not by Beeching, but by the yellow pipe network.

Chapter 18

Tolls, taxes and tariffs: fares, fines and fees

The paradigm shift[1]

That everything has to be paid for is a trite truism: the arguments arise over who pays whom for what, when and in which currency. The answers to those questions determine the processes for making the payments that are created by society. Most payments are made in money which is defined by fulfilling three basic functions:

1   a medium of exchange in which one person pays another for a good or service;
2   a common unit of account, enabling the values of goods and services to be summed;
3   a store of value representing either savings or debts.

Exchange, namely buying and selling, implies personal ownership: a good may only be rightfully sold by the owner and buyers may only become owners themselves through a legal transaction. It was a problem resolved in very early economies by assuming that everything belonged ultimately to the King, a personification of the state. Such absolute monarchs were often selected through a violent mixture of birth, inheritance and assassination, an inherently unstable, disruptive process which was gradually replaced by the democratic state, itself characterised by being a virtual, legal person able to own property, define the law, impose taxes and take actions in the citizens' interests. Latterly, the principle of the state as a legal person has been extended to companies which have become virtual legal persons too. This has led logically to the notion that a company may indulge in a criminal act and be punished for it: Network Rail, a legal person, has been fined for breaches of safety regulations which, had they been committed by a real person, might well have resulted in a prison sentence.

In recent years there has been a paradigm shift, not in principle but in intensity. Legal persons, including the large international companies, are now held to have 'rights' as though they were indeed real people, particularly the right to freedom of action. It appears in some political lexicons that both the state and numerous companies have not only become legal persons but have also acquired personal characteristics, bumbling in the one case and dynamic in the other, and are permanently engaged in some sort of personal vendetta.

Implicit to this paradigm shift is the corollary of the state changing into a business in Britain, often referred to as 'UK plc'. The shift into using numerical business techniques rather than political processes began, paradoxically, in the Second World War when business techniques were not much in evidence at the strategic level: there was no cost-benefit analysis of D-day. But the statistical analysis of the effectiveness of equipment and actions, at a tactical level, was developed as Operations Research. In step with war management in general, assessments did not use monetary values – the operations research into bombing was in terms of the effectiveness per bomb, not per pound spent on making and delivering the bomb.

After the War, operations research developed fast and spread wide, shedding the past military overtones of 'operations' by changing its name to 'operational research'. The change in character was closely related to the advent of the computer, itself spawned by the war, first as a decryption tool and, later, to create artillery tables laid out in pages of rows and columns, a form very similar to the 'analysis paper' used in business at the time to tabulate costs and revenues. Using the speed and flexibility of computers, this tabular form could be used, not just to analyse past costs and revenues, but also to predict future ones. While working on such scenario-driven business models in 1979, two students at Harvard Business School created VisiCalc,[2] the first spread-sheet, sparking a revolution in decision-making by providing an easy opportunity to score, rank and compare the predicted results of various possible options by simply changing the assumed input parameters.

The speed and adaptability of spread-sheets were used to change decision-making in two major senses:

1   Non-monetary quantities began to be converted into pseudo-money so that they could be aggregated in what appeared to be common units.
2   A completely new type of day-to-day variable appeared.

The conversion of non-monetary quantities into apparent money was demonstrated by the methodology used to assess road schemes initially published as Ministry of Transport (1967) Memo T5/67, and first used at the public inquiry into the Malton bypass in Yorkshire. The two assessment criteria were the predicted reductions in vehicle time and in accidents. The expected travel-time savings were not left in minutes and hours but were converted into what appeared to be money by using 'vehicle operating costs' calculated as a function of both distance and speed. Some of these costs were payments made in real cash for items such as fuel, but they also included drivers' time converted into 'money' at an assumed wage rate. Real money may be used as a medium of exchange but the pseudo-money representing minutes saved by drivers had no cash value – it could not be used to buy petrol or anything else: no drivers' pockets jingled with extra loose change as a result of using the bypass, nor would there have been any reductions in out-of-pocket expenses. The complaint made, and upheld, at the public inquiry in 1967 was that disparate units, money and something which was made to look like money, were being treated as though they were identical. Accidents were not given a 'value' in what appeared to be money and so there could be neither a summation nor a trade-off between time saved and the number of personal injuries and deaths. That was to come four years later in Memo H1/71 which placed a 'value' of £1150 upon all personal injuries irrespective of severity.[3] But this, too, was a disingenuous mixture of real cash costs (vehicle repairs, etc.) and unspendable pseudo-money.

The assessments made under Memos T5/67 and H1/71 were handwritten on analysis paper but it was an easy matter to write a computer program to do the job,[4] and then to include other, less tangible matters. Landscape quality scored by juries and community severance[5] were considered. Given the conversion of all quantities into a common unit, spread-sheets could be used to produce totals posing as facile indicators of 'worth'. The common unit of choice has been 'apparent money', but it is inherently misleading. The problem appeared in the Nottingham 'Zone and Collar' experiment reported in Chapter 17: minutes saved and lost were evaluated in what appears to be money, but it was pretend money, bearing little relationship to the actual coins paid in bus fares. The placing of a monetary value on accidents is worse. It is not real money — if an accident is avoided, there is no more money in anybody's pocket and the 'savings' cannot be used to pay the wages for those working on the road improvement.

The alliance between spread-sheets and business techniques has fundamentally changed decision-making with a strong emphasis upon numeric representation, summation and targets. Related to this is a tendency for the numbers to have a monetary appearance. A second, related tendency is for 'cost centres' for which the accounts, scores, targets and performance indices are calculated to become more numerous and isolated: decision-making has become fragmented to such an extent that some politicians have felt the need to counter it by asking for 'joined-up thinking', although without much success.

The drive towards numeric representations of opinions about intangible values such as landscape quality uses the oft-maligned boxes to convert assent or dissent into binary values, or scaling (on a scale 0–9, is this book worth reading?), by counting proxy events (how many times have you fallen asleep while reading it?)[6] or establishing a jury to create a subjective score.

The emphasis upon numeric representation, if possible in what appear to be monetary units, has extended to attributes which cannot actually be bought and sold, either because they cannot be owned, like an unpolluted atmosphere, or because they are intangible, like a sense of security or the grief resulting from a road traffic accident. Such things are now allotted a monetary value, tantamount to a price for the unpriceable.

Much of the difficulty in defining a 'price' for qualities for which markets do not naturally exist is related to security and risk. Maintenance is an expense incurred to reduce the risk of unwanted breakdown. As with other indeterminate products, what is being bought is not a quality in itself but the minimisation of an undesirable quality — the risk of breakdown — rather like security being an absence of insecurity. The problem with the accountancy is that it can never be known if the expenditure on maintenance has been effective or not; only with bad luck is it obvious that an expenditure has been inadequate: the Potters Bar and Greyrigg train derailments stand evidence to that. But the corollary, whether the expense of proper maintenance has been justified, is never known. That is a grave problem of accountancy which is resolved by constructing rules such as all vehicles will be serviced every fixed number of hours or miles, or all buildings will be painted every ten years, and then treating the cost of keeping to the rules as a cost of ownership, a cost which has no quantifiable 'product'. The stringency of the rules reflects a combination of the estimated risk of failure and of its effects: aircraft are subject to particularly stringent rules which are related to the terrible consequences of failure rather than to the probability of failure. The principle is that maintenance is a price which is paid for an intangible, unquantified, unaccountable product, not unlike a lottery ticket.

The need to build redundancy into transport systems is similar. An individual motorist would be unwise to plan a journey on the assumption that the maximum safe and legal speed will be possible from start to finish: it is much wiser to allow a safety margin to cover road-works, accidents, broken-down lorries, etc. Similarly, public transport timetables may be disrupted by unpredictable events, such as bad weather, trespassers and breakdowns, the effects of which will become unmanageable unless the system has some spare capacity. The back-up vehicles, staff or track capacity will cost money which will be 'wasted' for much of the time and will have an undefinable effect for all of the time. The extra capacity is there to protect service quality but, like preventive maintenance, it is hard to cost and evaluate.

The root of the problem is time. Unlike money, time is infinitely and abruptly perishable, causing considerable accountancy problems. If vehicles of any sort are delayed by congestion, accident or failure in traffic, the time during which they may have been productive is irretrievably lost, and the effects on overall costings are beyond correction.

The paradigm shift is from a world in which complex decisions were taken after debate and discussion to identify relative importance, into a world which is dominated by computerised numbers, many of them presented in what appears to be currency.

Prices

In economic theory prices are determined in a marketplace thronged with buyers and sellers. If the price is too low there will be more people wishing to buy than sellers wishing to sell, causing a dearth of the product and driving the price up: conversely, if the price is too high, there will be many more sellers than buyers, thereby creating a glut, and prices will be driven down. The theory posits that price will settle to a level at which the supply from sellers exactly matches the demand from buyers. No doubt Adam Smith, the doyen of market theory, observed such things 250 years ago in Edinburgh's Royal Mile. In such traditional markets, still seen in some poorer countries, prices are offered by the buyer, the person who has the money and is aware of the price at which they would get more satisfaction from the goods purchased than from having money in their pocket. It is up to the seller to accept the offer, or not, based on a judgement as to whether the price is as good a deal as they can get: hence prices are an outcome of a bargaining process initiated by the buyer and finalised by cash changing hands.[7]

That is not today's way. It is the supplier, not the buyer, who sets the price. Bargaining, with the implication that every deal sets its own price, could not work in today's commercial world except in the high-volume perhaps long-term transactions clinched in the form of contracts: goods' transport displays this tendency. Individuals making trivial purchases have to base their decisions on the price demanded. Markets as observed by Adam Smith have been replaced by the supermarket with fixed, barcoded prices and by specialised, high-volume, computer-driven virtual markets, all totally incomprehensible to a Scottish gentleman living while Louis XVI and his unfortunate wife still had heads upon which to wear their crowns and the North American colonies had the same status as Scotland. There seem to be grounds for thinking that seventeenth-century theory has yet to catch up with twenty-first-century reality.

Twenty-first-century practice involves stocks of goods in ways that were not that obvious in Edinburgh's Royal Mile of the 1760s. The vegetable sellers clustered around the site of Adam Smith's future statue would have had to sell all their produce at whatever price could be had because tomorrow it would have been worthless. Today, produce can be stored, but that is far more than a matter of refrigeration. In the modern world capital is plentiful and cheap, and so the money tied up in stock is much less of a burden than in the days when today's receipts were necessarily committed to buying the goods to be sold the following day.

It has already been asserted that transport is both timed and perishable, making substitutability a very rare attribute and storage impossible. Public transport cannot be bought and sold in a traditional market as described by Adam Smith. The amount on offer and the price charged are fixed by the operators and overseen by the regulators. There is no possibility of market equilibrium arrived at by the workings of market theory. It follows that transport prices are not set by negotiation in the marketplace but are unilaterally predetermined outside a market, a fact marked by all travel tickets bearing the note that they are 'non-transferable'; that is, they are not marketable.[8]

Tariffs

A tariff is no more than a price list, usually printed and published. The earliest examples were the lists of tolls charged on bridges and ferries, set by Act of Parliament or by Charter to prevent excessive monopoly profits or extortion. A later example is the list of fares to be found in taxis. Before 1952 all British Railways' fares and freight rates were fixed, listed as a tariff to be found on booking-office walls. After 1952 British Railways were able to charge fares that they, not the government, set according to the levels of demand apparent from their ticket sales, but the tariff was still stable, pasted on the station wall. In pre-broadband times passengers bought tickets in the ticket office immediately before travelling, accepting the price given to them by the booking clerk.

British Railways' ability to vary the price of travel was not used on a massive scale, but it did reflect price theory in two very important respects:

1   *Price elasticity* is a measure of customer reaction to changes in price. When fares are raised there is usually a reduction in the number of tickets sold as some customers decide to use another, now more attractive mode or route or perhaps not to travel at all. Total revenue will change under two contrary influences: revenue will increase because every ticket sold will yield more revenue, but revenue will fall because fewer tickets are sold. Elasticity is a measure of the strength and direction of the combined effect of these two changes. Elastic demand describes a strong consumer reaction to price rises with the effects of falling sales overwhelming the increase in revenue per ticket: revenue falls with a rise in fares. In contrast, inelastic demand is where total revenue rises as a consequence of a fares hike because the loss in sales has less effect on revenue than the increase in prices.

British Railways inherited a view from its predecessor companies that travel was a necessity rather than an option, and so the demand for travel was generally inelastic: fairly insensitive to price. The one very considerable exception was leisure and holiday travel which had grown in importance as disposable incomes rose. The railway industry responded to this by segregating demand into normal travel by timetabled trains at fixed, published fares and excursion travel at very low special fares strictly restricted to specified times and sometimes even to special trains. The Beeching Report found that British Railways had lost all sense in catering for this highly elastic holiday-leisure market and had complete trains that were only used for a few summer weekends, many of them traversing tracks to seaside resorts that were barely used for the rest of the year. Worse still, it was this traffic more than any other that was susceptible to erosion by the family car. Nonetheless, British Railways had come to understand that its customers were not one homogeneous mass but fell into groups displaying different elasticities and to be courted separately.

2   *Consumer surplus.* In any train load of passengers there will be some people who would still have bought their ticket had the price been higher. On the other hand, if the ticket price were set to the level these people were willing to pay, many of the other passengers would have stayed at home. Each individual has a different sensitivity to price – a different personal sense of elasticity. The difference between the price a person actually pays and the higher price they would have been willing to pay is called 'consumer surplus'. It is a bit of value that the customer has enjoyed without having to pay for it or, from the railways' point of view, some cash which has failed to make its way from the customer's pocket into their revenue account.

British Railways developed an old idea present in passenger transport for many years. Children's half-fares were developed, not to squeeze extra mobility from children's pocket-money, but in response to the fact that if people could not afford to travel *en famille*, revenue would be lost – that demand for family travel had a different elasticity to general travel. Children's fares are in effect a discount on the adult fare and so the problem of harvesting consumer surplus from those travelling without children was seen to be to charge a premium fare to be paid by those willing and able to pay it, but then to offer discounts to others, bringing the fare within reach of those more sensitive to price. Distinguishing those entitled to a discounted child's fare is obvious, but other groups offered a problem. British Railways' answer was to sell identity cards to those sensitive to price (student, senior and family railcards) while leaving high premium fares to be paid by others: the consumer surplus then became British Railways' revenue instead of remaining in the pockets of those who had been willing to pay more.

The use of discount cards to ensure that railway companies rather than their passengers glean consumer surpluses is still a feature of train travel, but the top premium fares are now the 'walk-on' fares bought at the ticket office immediately before travel. Discount travel has to be bought online through software written for the train-operating companies which incorporates 'yield management' routines. These sense the numbers and types of enquiries about fares and destinations and, in response, devise a flexible tariff of different fares for different departure times. Potential passengers know that the fares will change over time but do not know how or why. The system has some sort of negotiation between the buyer and the train operators' software so there is a hint of similarity to the markets familiar to Adam Smith, but buyers are dumb, able to accept or reject the company's fickle prices but unable to set a limit on the price they would personally be willing to pay. The proportion of consumer surplus which customers are able to retain depends entirely on the flexibility in their time of travel, larded by luck. The slight consolation is that having the bad luck to have paid a higher price than was really necessary will never be known unless fellow passengers are each quizzed about the fare they had paid, but, even then, it will afford no help in getting a better deal next time. It follows that even the use of the Web does not create anything like a market as perceived by Adam Smith. For that, tickets would have to be sold through e-bay.

Tolls

A toll is a sum of money paid to pass through a barrier: that, of course, has no intrinsic value – the toll is paid for access to what is on the other side of the barrier. In transport, tolls are functionally identical to fares, although the money is collected either upon entry (e.g. the New York Subway tokens) or exit (e.g. the French AutoRoute tolls). There is a break with theory in exit tolling, since payment is made after the consumption of the product and, unless care is taken well before entering the system, it is very likely that the price to be paid on completion of the journey will not be known until the end, by which time it will be too late for any rational choice about value for money.

Taxes

Taxes are sums of money paid to the state either at local or national level, in order to pay for state-provided services. Income, corporate and value-added tax are calculated at various percentages and the yield, together with taxes on specific goods such as alcohol and motor fuel, is credited in Britain to the 'consolidated fund'. This is the government's housekeeping account used to pay for defence, education, the health service and other government expenditure benefiting the public as a whole.

Licences are fixed sums demanded from only those wishing to use a particular service: the Vehicle Excise Duty is the prime transport example. The licence fee is payable per vehicle and is set by a tariff of charges varying with vehicle size and the propensity to pollute. Licensed vehicles are able to use the public highway without further charge. There are a few toll roads, bridges and tunnels, but, in law, these are not part of the legally defined public highway.

A hypothecated tax is one in which the revenue is not credited to the consolidated fund to be used for unspecified government expenditure but is earmarked for a particular use. The prime example today is the television licence, the revenue from which is used to create the broadcasting network and to cover the activities of the British Broadcasting Corporation. Up until 1927, receipts from vehicle licensing were hypothecated and credited to a road fund, used to pay for the surfacing and improvements of the road network. However, in the financial crisis of that year the contents of the road fund were transferred to the consolidated fund and thereafter road improvements were paid for from that general pool, breaking any equation between the licence revenue and roads expenditure.

Whether parking charges are fees paid for a service as specified by a tariff or a hypothecated tax is a moot point. There seems to have been a historical shift. At one time the control of parking was through the law of obstruction: the seminal Statute of Winchester, which established the right of passage and re-passage of His Majesty's subjects about their lawful business, was not only used to prevent toll bars but roadside stalls, hitching for horses, cattle pens, etc.: the medieval King's Highway was for movement, not for stopping. It followed that anything which obstructed movement along the Highway was illegal. That principle, rather modified, is still with us over 800 years later. In the early days of motor cars, parking was held to be an obstruction to the passage and re-passage of Her Majesty's subjects. However, cars were owned by the rich and influential, and the law was changed to permit 'authorised' parking, but, although a motorist was safe from prosecution in an authorised place, there were too few places, and those motorists parking in unauthorised places ran the risk of being charged with obstruction. In the days before traffic wardens, the law and traffic regulations were administered by the police, and motorists had to rely on their fine judgement as to what was and what was not 'obstruction'. It was a delicate relationship.[9]

As part of the paradigm shift towards numeric assessment and away from political debate, there is an increasing trend to argue in favour of relating charges of all sorts to the 'benefits' to be gained; it was a strong component within the *Buses* White Paper. This enables the accounts to report a relationship between costs and the value placed on the 'product', even if it is not bought in cash at a market 'price' and has to have a value ascribed to it. These 'value-for-money' scores need to be ring fenced if they are to be useful, but the fencing and the pricing within the fence are delicate.

A good example is the 'Polluter Pays' principle proposed in 1994 in Planning Policy Guidance Note #13.[10] The argument is beguiling, but raises some thorny problems. The proposition appears to be simple and just: there is one group of people, those using motor vehicles, who are imposing dis-benefits upon another group of people, perhaps the general public, perhaps a more limited group such as those living in houses fronting on to a busy road. The 'Polluter Pays' principle means there is no doubt about who is responsible – by definition it is the polluter, but then things get a little fuzzy. Chemical pollutants may be taken as pro rata with the amount of fuel burned – even that simplicity will be open to objection, since different fuels and different exhaust systems will have different tail-pipe emissions. For argument's sake, let us presume that agreement may be reached that pollution at both global and local level is near enough in step with fuel burn. To make matters easier, let us also assume that other pollutants such as noise, the sense of danger, visual intrusion, severance, etc. may all be covered by the proxy of the fuel burn. That has defined the polluter (the person who burns fuel) and the pollutants (the by-products of burning fuel). It also gives a heavy clue about a method of payment – a surcharge on the price of fuel. This is neat because such a tax may reflect the chemical effects of different fuels.

But the next problem is so much more difficult that it is hard the see how the justice of the principle may be retained. A surcharge on fuel prices will end up in the consolidated fund and may be spent at a government's whim upon waging unauthorised wars or any number of other possible uses that are at odds with the interests of those paying the surcharge. Alternatively, the revenue could be hypothecated and dedicated by some means to offset the effects of pollution – planting trees has been popular in recent years, although that poses problems over where and on whose land. A hypothecated fund could target particular groups. For example, grants could be made to those living near busy roads, a proposition that would delight researchers in the practice of economics. But it would not be a market. The polluter may be paying but not to the pollutee. Behaviours would not ape those in Edinburgh's Royal Mile as observed by Adam Smith: demand and supply would not tend to be at an equilibrium.

Instead, there would be two disconnected fiscal effects. A polluters' surcharge would encourage those buying fuel to strive to buy less, and so the demand for fuel-efficient cars (among those thought to be substitutable) would rise and people may drive fewer kilometres, all held to be desirable. The second effect would be, at best, a reduction in the household expenses of some people, perhaps pro rata with the traffic volume past their front door. That would make living on the flank of a busy road marginally more attractive: again desirable. But these two separate mechanisms would have to be constructed, defined and administered by the state: they would not emulate Adam Smith's principle of the 'hidden hand' bringing matters to an equilibrium. It is another example of markets being much less than omnipotent.

Fees

Fees are paid to professional providers for their services: they are effectively the prices charged by doctors, accountants, lawyers and the like. At one time the fees were in a published tariff set by each of the relevant professional societies, but this was outlawed in the 1990s in the name of competition, allowing lawyers to work on a 'no-win, no-fee' basis should they so wish. Tariffs still exist, but now they are set by individual practices and may be varied by negotiation: again, competition and markets are more apparent in name than in practice. Not only is substitutability compromised by advertising, but the choice of professional practice is heavily influenced by reputation rather than familiarity with the product.

The term is often stretched to cover office and administration as well as professional charges. It is common to refer to licence 'fees': in transport, the charges for vehicle, driving and operating licences, all of which are fixed by the state and hypothecated to pay for office costs.

Fines

Fines are penalties payable after an action that has breached the law. At one time penalties were imposed as the result of a court case at which the defendant had been found guilty of an offence, but the definition has shifted in recent years. The first shift was the publication of a tariff applied by a court upon receipt of a written guilty plea: a defendant could choose not to plead guilty and then appear in court to be dealt with summarily. The second shift has been for an authorised official to impose a fixed penalty according to a published tariff upon payment of which the matter is treated as a civil debt rather than a legally imposed fine. Payment clearly implies an admission that the unwonted action did occur but is not an admission of guilt in law.

This change has extended the common usage of the term 'fine' to include penalties that have been imposed as a matter of contract rather than regulations. Hence, railway companies may have to pay sums of money if their trains run late, but this is not because it is against the law to run late trains, only that it contravenes the signed contract. Blame for lateness and the charging of penalties has become a rich field for contract lawyers and accountants.

Policy levers

As part of the paradigm shift from state control by instruction to state influence by financial management, the levers of the transport system have been increasingly reliant upon changing cost profiles through combinations of fees, licences and tariffs. Nowhere has this been more apparent than in the control of pollution. The Clean Air Act (1956) made it illegal to burn anything other than smokeless fuel in domestic fireplaces: there were no overt public consultations and no exceptions. It was not a policy lever designed to institute a behavioural trend; it was a straight prohibition. The same approach was evident in the Civic Amenities Act (1967) which made fly-tipping a legal offence in pursuit of the Act's avowed intent to arrange for 'the orderly disposal of disused vehicles, equipment and other rubbish'.

The shifting paradigm has baulked at such draconian legislation, seemingly on the 'moral' ground that prohibition would impinge upon personal freedom – personal, that is, of firms in the form of legal persons. Prohibition has been replaced by financial encouragement, and so the control of the emission of CO_2 is not seen as the same sort of problem as the emission of smoke in 1956: it is seen as a matter of reduction through the buying and selling of 'carbon credits', effectively licences to pollute. Polluting motor vehicles are influenced by shifts in the tariff of licence fees, although there are criteria set by European legislation and applied through the annual vehicle tests.

In the main, the paradigm shift expects many problems to be addressed by the sum of personal decisions rather than by government edict and then to adjust the circumstances within which those decisions are made to achieve the desired objectives. It is a form of government that is new to the world.

The paradigm shift towards decision-making by the aggregate of a plethora of legal persons is characterised by the repeated proposal of road pricing, sometimes called congestion charging, but, more properly, road-user charging. The essential logic is as follows:

- The problem of congestion is a manifestation of more traffic than the capacity of the road system.
- The solution must be to either build more capacity or reduce the amount of traffic.
- Road construction is expensive and politically fraught, particularly in the urban areas where most of the congestion occurs.
- The only remaining option is to reduce the amount of traffic.
- That is best done by inducing change in travel choices, effectively in the myriad individual decisions, through manipulating the price of travel by imposing a cost surcharge.

The theoretical support for this logic is to be found in the Department for Transport's advice on transport modelling,[11] which is structured around Figure 18.1.

The text accompanying the figure notes that in 'classical' economics both supply and demand are functions of cost, although they are usually graphed with cost on the vertical axis (as shown in Figure 18.1), contrary to the convention that the independent variable is plotted on the horizontal axis.

Figure 18.1 shows that as travel gets cheaper people make more trips, but also, as trip costs rise so does the supply of the means to make them until, at some point, the number of trips made is equal to the capacity of the system. This is a straight transfer of Adam Smith's market analysis in the days of the Scottish Enlightenment 250 years ago. But trips are not physical goods like nails or vegetables, laid out in front of buyers to enable them to make a considered choice and to negotiate a price.

WebTAG Unit 3.1.2 does not offer any data or any references to data illuminating people's travel choice mechanisms, although it does acknowledge that choices include time of travel, route, mode, destination, frequency and trip suppression. In section 2.2 (of Unit 3.1.2) it suggests that the cost should be measured in 'effective minutes',[12] a sum of:

- for car journeys:
    - in-vehicle travel time;
    - vehicle operating cost;
    - parking time (finding a place and walking from it to the final destination)
    - any out-of-pocket expenses (converted into effective minutes using a value of time);

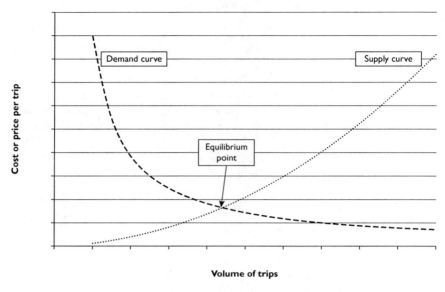

Figure 18.1 Supply and demand for trips
Source: Reproduced from Department for Transport, WebTAG Unit 3.1.2, fig. 2.1.

- for public transport journeys:
  - walking time to stop or station (weighted: 1 watch minute = 2 effective minutes);
  - waiting time (weighted: 1 watch minute = 2 effective minutes);
  - in-vehicle ride time;
  - out-of pocket fares, etc.;
  - interchange penalties (in effective minutes);
  - walking time to final destination (weighted: 1 watch minute = 2 effective minutes).

This does accord with past surveys of how people (on average) perceive the various components of their journeys but that does not make it a choice mechanism: as WebTAG Unit 3.1.2.1 makes clear, the choice of destination is a component issue and, worse, is likely to be self-referential – the choice of whether to make a journey at all or to choose one destination rather than another may reflect relative journey times and the rankings may change. That is, in effect, saying that 'trips' are not substitutable, and therefore, if Figure 18.1 is to have any value, it should refer to trips to particular places, not trips in general.

Nevertheless, the implicit generalisation that the more trips 'cost' (no matter what the units are) the fewer will be undertaken appears to be intuitively reasonable. The real problems come on the 'supply' side. WebTAG Unit 3.1.2 acknowledges that there cannot be a normal market response to rising demand for travel through an increase in supply. That would mean creating more capacity, which would certainly be oppressively expensive. It therefore argues that costs are self-referential – that if the number of trips shown in Figure 18.1 rises then the transport system will slow down due to the weight of extra traffic, precipitating extra cost which will then choke off some of the demand. This clearly hints at the notion that congestion mitigates itself by achieving an equilibrium at a point at which, if congestion lessened, reducing travel costs, more trips would be made up to the point where the rising congestion would suppress any more trips and, conversely, if actual congestion were worse than at the equilibrium, some trips would stop being made until demand returned to the equilibrium.

There are two large holes in this theory:

1 The equilibrium may be too congested to be acceptable by politicians or their constituents, demanding some intervention to move the equilibrium to a more acceptable level.
2 We know from past experience that the response to congestion is not to use public transport or to stay at home, but to change the ends of the trip – to develop a new urban geography that imperceptibly, insidiously reduces the demand at points of concentration in the network.

WebTAG Unit 3.1.2 reaches the notion of a 'point of equilibrium' through an impressive logical trick. It argues that the supply curve cannot be delivered by the expansion of the transport system to deliver an increase in capacity but that the inverse of the relationship is just as valid – that the cost per trip of meeting the demand for trips is a good proxy for the function for a normal supply curve. This is playing fast and loose with the theory by exchanging dependent and independent variables, arguing that demand is a function of cost, as shown by the demand curve, and then that cost is a function of demand, as shown by the supply curve: it is an arithmetic tautology. In practice this seeming impossibility is enabled as far as traffic is concerned by assuming that the increases in traffic which are due to increased demand cause a reduction in traffic speed,[13] which precipitates a rise in cost. Hence, it is argued, falling travel costs will cause a rise in demand but this will simultaneously cause delays and a rise in costs portrayed as a reduction in 'supply', bringing it all back to an equilibrium. There is a major problem with this argument: the assumption that speed is a function of flow is false, as was shown in Chapter 7.

In the case of public transport, WebTAG Unit 3.1.2 is diametrically wrong. Increased demand may lead to rising travel costs due to crowding and perhaps extra waiting time, but those effects only kick in at a very late stage when the system is already full to over-capacity. In general, increased demand for public transport leads to improvements in service through a combination of shorter headways, reduced waits and reduced walks due to the proliferation of routes and stops. Hence travel 'costs' measured in effective minutes fall with increased use, in contrast with car use, in which costs rise due to extra junction and parking delays.

A further, fundamental problem with Figure 18.1 is that it is based on 'trips' as the measure of travel rather than 'journeys'. A 'trip' is officially defined as the continuous travel by a specific mode from the 'trip origin' to the 'trip destination'. It is therefore just part – a 'stage' – of a complete journey from one address to another. Official statistics are bedevilled by crediting entire journeys to whatever mode is used for the major part of a journey: by pretending that entire 'journeys' are in fact 'trips' made by a single mode. In making that crude assumption, the ancillary, important stages in journeys are effectively ignored. This carries a crucial implication. In the minds of theoretical analysts, 'trips' are seen as 'products' to be independently demanded, produced and consumed, as shown in Figure 18.1. That is clearly wrong-headed. Nobody sees a trip by train from one station to another as a 'product' to be consumed in its own right: it is an integral part of a journey from one place to another, a journey which includes getting to and from the stations. This simple fact means that all journeys are unique, being made at specific times between specific places. The crucial characteristic of an economic 'product' is that all examples of the product are equally suitable and interchangeable – that one tin of beans may be substituted by any other. But that is not, and cannot be, the case for personal journeys. They are not mutually substitutable and therefore fail to meet the definition of an economic product. That indigestible fact makes a nonsense of Figure 18.1 and casts doubt on the market theory that works for real 'products' being used in transport.

The basic problem appears to be what Kuhn calls anomalies[14] – facts and conditions which do not fit in with existing theory and which have eventually to be accommodated by a new theory. The problem that Kuhn identified is that the adherents to an old theory strive to fit anomalies into their preconceptions. In the case of Figure 18.1 it seems to be a desire to take 'classical economic theory' as the initial and unavoidable template and force it upon an analysis of travel demand rather than research the decision mechanisms used in making travel choices, including the choice of origins and destinations, and then derive a theory to fit those observations.

The footprint of old theory is very apparent in Figure 18.2, a copy of fig. 2.2 in WebTAG Unit 3.1.2. Paragraph 2.1.7 which accompanies the figure includes an extraordinary statement:

> When assessing the impact of a policy, which means essentially changing the supply curve, the demand is held constant. Hence, the testing of strategies can be viewed as a comparison of two (or more) equilibrium points using a common demand curve but with each equilibrium point associated with a different supply curve.

This could be used as evidence to show that WebTAG is about 50 years out of date. The 'policy' to shift the supply curve was explicitly abandoned in 1968, when it was replaced by multi-modal policies in the TSG/TPP, and then explicitly rejected again when PPG13 was published in 1993 and 'predict and provide' was replaced by 'travel demand management'. Policy is not 'changing the supply curve' and has not been so for many years: the policy is to manage the 'demand curve', the very thing that WebTAG says should not be done.

Both Coombe[15] and Wenban-Smith and Van Vuren[16] have held that the Department for Transport WebTAG methodology is 'unfit for purpose'. But the truth

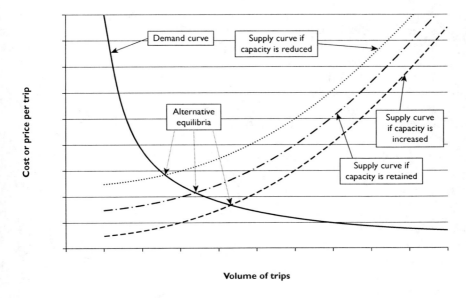

Figure 18.2 Effects of capacity changes
Source: Reproduced from Department for Transport, WebTAG Unit 3.1.2, fig. 2.2.

is that it cannot be fit for purpose because it has the wrong purpose. It was designed for the outmoded 'predict and provide' regime in order to predict the speed and volume of traffic resulting from changing the supply curve by providing more capacity, exactly as stated in the above WebTAG quote.

The incompatibility between the modelling epitomised by WebTAG Unit 3.1.2 and by post-1968 policy has been disastrous. Throughout the TSG/TPP era and during the later efforts to deliver travel demand management, decision-makers have been denied the tools to assess whether possible decisions are likely to have the desired results. Without such tools decision-makers have been keenly aware that any proposals to limit car use, either overtly by the dedication of road space to public transport, or covertly by stringent parking controls, will attract vehement criticism which will not be stilled without the presentation of convincing, robust forecasts of the anticipated effects.

The critical doubts over WebTAG Unit 3.1.2 and the theory it represents are:

- the initial assumption that classical economic theory will describe travel decisions;
- the use of 'trips' as a measure of the amount of travel, rather than person-kilometres;
- the validity of the coincidental assertions that the number of trips is a function of trip cost (in effective minutes) and that trip cost (also in effective minutes) is a function of the number of trips;

- the assertion that speed (and so cost) is a function of traffic volume;
- the apparent belief that modes are competitive and that travel choices are between them, excluding inter-modal choices;
- the assertion that service levels by all modes decay with increasing demand: this is clearly untrue for public transport;
- the apparent belief that policy is a matter of manipulating travel cost using road capacity as the policy lever;
- most importantly, the lack of recognition of the interactive relationship between changing patterns of travel and urban geography.

The last point is particularly relevant to road user charging.

Road user charging

Currently, motorists pay for their use of the transport system through the following measures:

- on acquisition: VAT on the purchase price;
- annual excise duty for cars in the range of £0 to £475 depending on CO_2 emissions;
- company car tax (a form of income tax on the benefit in kind provided by the private use of a company car);
- the duty payable on fuel (currently about 70 per cent of the pump price).

Of these measures, the annual excise duty is trivial at £0.025 or less per kilometre at the very highest rate. The tax paid on fuel is primarily a function of the distance travelled coupled with the power of the motor, but there is a significant surcharge for driving at low speeds in congested traffic at which internal combustion engines are inefficient (the rates are quoted in Chapter 5).

On top of the cash costs, travel takes time. By using a value of time the total cost may be summed in either 'effective minutes' as WebTAG suggests or in pseudo-money: either way, economic theory suggests that the higher the cost the less travel. That is intuitively true and it is certainly true for any one element within the transport system. If a particular section of road is congested, pushing up the time cost, motorists will strive to avoid it, and if a bus or train fare is raised, fewer tickets will be sold. Road user charging seeks to use this principle by imposing a tax on car-miles. This may take a number of forms:

- encircling an area by a cordon of gates and charging a toll to pass through them, effectively raising the cost per driven kilometre within the cordon;
- installing a cordon with gates which sense vehicles entering and leaving and imposing a time charge on the period spent inside the cordon;
- installing sensing points throughout an area and imposing a charge per calculated kilometre or per minute;
- selling licences entitling entry to an area.

All of these options require electronic sensing of particular vehicles, achieved through registration number plate recognition, although it could be done by tagging in the way that the London Oyster card works. There are no technical reasons why any of these systems cannot be made to work, although some will require payment in advance and the maintenance of a credit balance.

Moreover, the evidence is that they will be effective in reducing flow on those roads and in those areas where charges apply. The degree to which they are effective will depend on the elasticity of demand, represented graphically by the slope of the demand curve as shown in Figures 18.1 and 18.2. But that seemingly desirable result must be flawed because the effect of the charge will not be limited to the reduction in demand in one area or along one road but will ripple out into an ever-widening area. Driver response will, in the short term, be one or other of:

- Being deterred by the cost and not making a journey: this will have an impact on the activity that was the purpose behind the journey – that might be trivial or it might erode the turnover of a business and threaten its viability.
- Making the journey at a 'cheaper' time: an action which, if repeated by others, may just spread the problem over time rather than solve it.
- Use another route: this mitigates the problem by spreading it over space rather than time, but the effectiveness is limited by the ability of the other times and places to accept the diverted traffic.
- Use another mode: the evidence in Chapter 17 shows that the London congestion charge appears to have induced increased use of cycling and public transport.
- Choosing an alternative destination: this is the Achilles heel of road user charging. In the short term there has to be an available alternative destination which enables people to circumnavigate the surcharged route. This will be to the advantage of those places and businesses which are accessible without paying the surcharge and to the disadvantage of those places only accessible at extra cost.

It is the long-term effect that is the more important: businesses must maintain their accessibility if they are to thrive. If they think the road user charge regime is injuriously affecting their accessibility they will relocate to provide their customers with an alternative. Even if they do not, customers may well patronise those that do. This tendency will, over time, affect not only the location and choices of possible destinations but also the origins. In the case of residential areas, if householders think the costs of accessing the area in which they live are too high, they will move to somewhere better and, given the strength of that demand, house builders will strive to provide 'somewhere better', often in developments akin to the example given in Figure 4.8 of houses built on previously agricultural land in the extended 'virtual city'.

These geographical changes do not happen quickly, or by a simple process of firms and people making personal choices. They happen by churn: by some people in a group leaving and being replaced by others with a different set of choices. That makes forecasting difficult but far from impossible. Changes in fashion wrought by churn are almost impossible to predict in the long term, but short-term trends may be detected by effective monitoring (the 'steerage' shown in Figure 3.4), and these may be used to get a fuzzy picture of the future.

However, in the case of road user charging this is not necessary, because the changes in urban geography over the past 200 years show that urban areas have continuously adapted to the available means of transport, from horses, to electric trams, to the internal combustion engine, first in buses and then in cars. We know already that if car costs are driven up by congestion then corporate and individual decisions to react through relocation will change urban geography: the evidence is there, before our eyes and on every urban map. It follows that if motoring costs are driven upwards in a step change through the imposition of a road user surcharge then it will serve to accelerate the decentralisation and dispersal outwards into the virtual city. This will necessarily extend journey distances and so increase rather than decrease total vehicle-kilometres while spreading them over time and space, just as it has demonstrably done in recent history.

In addition to advocating a policy to reduce congestion and vehicle-kilometres but which is very likely to induce an increase, the concept of road user charging contains a political paradox. Government policy has been to improve road transport and cut transport costs as a stimulus to the economy, but road user charging relies on increases in costs as the prime policy lever. It appears that this is thought to be effective by replacing the costs of congestion by the cost of a tax surcharge. Theorists may well see this as the state harvesting consumer surplus.

Notes

1. Kuhn (1962). The term has since been clouded by a variety of meanings. Here it is used to cover the change in the conceptual framework of state decision-making from political edict to quasi-business numeracy.
2. Bricklin and Frankston (1979).
3. Department of the Environment (1971). A death is now scored at almost £1.5 million.
4. No doubt many people did so, including some in the Ministry of Transport. The author's version was written in Algol and made its debut at the Malton Public Inquiry.
5. Hutton *et al.* (1991).
6. Nurses in Devon and Cornwall were asked to report how many letters and bunches of flowers they received as a proxy for quality of service.
7. In Bristol the tradition was that cash covering the mutually agreed price was placed on a tall, small-topped table called a 'nail'.
8. See Sandel (2012) for a lively discussion of market limitations.
9. The author collected field data about the operation of the very first British parking meter scheme in London's Mayfair, and retains the memory of being confronted by a very angry man complaining that parking meters were no more than clockwork bribe takers.
10. Departments of the Environment and of Transport (1994).
11. *Transport Assessment Guidance Unit 3.1.2* (available online at www.dft.gov.uk/webtag).
12. This term is not used in the Unit but seems to reflect its intention.
13. WebTAG Unit 3.1.2, paragraph 2.1.4.
14. Kuhn (1962, Part VI, 'Anomaly and the Emergence of Scientific Discoveries').
15. Coombe (2009).
16. Wenban-Smith and Van Vuren (2009).

Chapter 19

Transport demand prediction

In Chapter 11 it was argued that any proposed intervention into the transport system should be properly assessed both before and after its implementation – before, so that the number of unwise interventions may be minimised; after, to establish whether the intervention had been worthwhile. This second analysis may appear to be no more than belatedly identifying regretted mistakes, but it is actually a very important contribution to recognising which sorts of interventions are likely to be the most effective – the popularly named 'learning curve'. The assessment rests on ten stages:

1. measuring the existing movement through the system;
2. forecasting the future movements if things are left as they are;
3. forecasting future movements once the intervention has been made;
4. estimating the movement costs, first with and then without the intervention;
5. hence, estimating the expected net change in movement costs wrought by the intervention; these are reckoned to be the 'benefits' to be credited to the intervention;
6. calculating the likely cost of the intervention;
7. estimating whether the cost of the intervention is likely to be justified by the estimated benefits;
8. making a go/no-go decision on whether to put the scheme into effect;
9. after the intervention has been made and has been working for long enough to have had a significant impact, measuring and costing the actual movement through the altered system and comparing it with the forecasts and estimates made in the original assessment;
10. striving to learn from the differences and, if necessary, modifying the assessment methodology.

It is important to realise that the differences between the initial forecasts and estimates and the later reality may disclose better-than-predicted benefits as well as worse and that such errors may be just as informative as the evidence of poor decisions. The 'errors' in error-actuated feedback may be positive as well as negative.

Measuring the existing movements

In the late 1950s and early 1960s Britain faced a rapid increase in car ownership and traffic. It was a hot political issue and widely agreed that the transport problem was actually a traffic problem – how to improve the road system to cope with the expected rise in the use of cars and lorries. The then Minister of Transport, Ernest Marples, oversaw the start of the construction of the motorway system but he also recognised the need for urban traffic management.[1]

Marples sent a copy of *Traffic Engineering* (Matson *et al.*1955) to every local authority, encouraging them to establish a Traffic Engineering Unit. Numerical analysis had always been used in the structural design of roads, and now engineers extended that numerical approach to the design of junction layouts, traffic-lights and other traffic engineering paraphernalia.

At first it was very simple.[2] When designing the improvement of a road junction, the volumes entering, leaving and turning within the junction were counted by observation and displayed, as shown in the hypothetical demonstration in Figure 19.1. The results of junction surveys were conventionally tabled as an 'origin and destination' (O+D) matrix similar to Figure 19.2.

Logging the existing traffic at a simple road junction could be done by roadside observers but they could not deal with busy, complex junctions: they could count vehicles entering and exiting the junction, but could not keep up with all the turning movements. A technique was evolved to record registration numbers of vehicles as they entered and exited the junction and then, back in the office, matching the entry

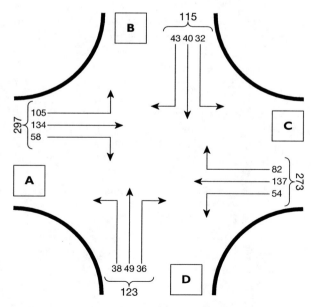

Figure 19.1 The hypothetical traffic at a simple four-legged, two-way road junction

Exit road	A	B	C	D	Total
Entry road					
A	–	105	134	58	297
B	43	–	32	40	115
C	137	82	–	54	273
D	38	49	36	–	123
Total	218	236	202	152	

Figure 19.2 The origin and destination (O+D) matrix from Figure 19.1

and exit records by the observer on an entry road calling out a registration number and the observers on the exit roads searching their field sheets for a match. It was derisively called 'bingo calling', and was expensive, tedious and inaccurate.

Relief came in the early 1960s with the arrival of main-frame computers in many local authorities. These machines were extremely expensive and the computer companies strove to justify the expense by bundling a range of free software within the price of the machine. This enabled local authorities to reduce the apparent cost by using their new machines on a wide range of tasks, often running them day and night. The software bundles always included traffic engineering packages. The initial packages did little more than make 'bingo calling' easier, producing O+D matrices of the existing traffic through busy, complex junctions. Future flows were estimated by simply multiplying all the numbers in the existing O+D matrix by a standard growth factor, usually derived from the rate at which current vehicle ownership was growing. The Ministry of Transport advocated a compound rate, giving a meteoric and, eventually, an infinite rise in traffic.[3] An economic analysis of the first stage of the M1[4] assumed a compound growth rate of 5.4 per cent per year, a rate which did much to justify an estimated 4 per cent per annum return on the capital cost of the motorway. Rumour had it that the first estimate was a politically indigestible negative rate of return. However, this assumed that the time saved by non-business users had no value. The Minister invited the RRL to change this assumption to a value of 2/- (10p) per hour, creating a much more acceptable 4 per cent.[5]

Enlarged origin and destination matrices

The computer companies were quick to develop more sophisticated programs, creating a completely new traffic engineering methodology. It is these programs, bundled in with the sales of main-frame computers in the early 1960s, that are the ancestors of today's techniques. The basic idea was carried over from earlier single junction analysis – the origin and destination matrix with the locations at which vehicles entered a road system down the side and those where they left along the top. The entry and exit roads were replaced by zones, each zone covering an entire section of the study area so that the cells of the matrix showed the zone-to-zone traffic. As an example, Figure 19.3 shows the zone structure for a small town, Kington in Herefordshire, population 2500.[6] The town straddled the A44 trunk road between the Midlands and Aberystwyth, and congestion was rife in its narrow streets. In 1972

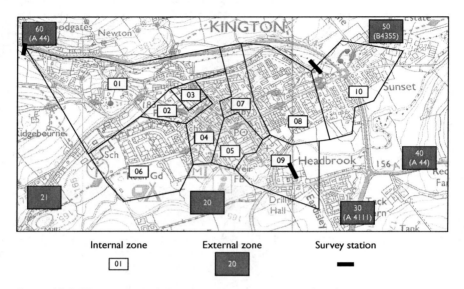

Figure 19.3 The origin and destination zone structure for Kington

a Local Public Inquiry was held into the relative merits of two alternative schemes to relieve the congestion. The first was an inner-relief road within the town itself proposed by the County Council and the second was a more expensive bypass advocated by a local action group.

The complex and extensive traffic between zones shown in Figure 19.3 could not be directly observed as it had been on single junctions: a new technique for gathering field data was needed. At first this was done by stopping vehicles at a string of checkpoints forming a cordon around the study area and presenting drivers with a questionnaire, including questions about the addresses between which their journeys were being made. Figure 19.3 shows Kington to have had a minimal cordon of just three checkpoints. Inside the cordon the town is divided into 11 'internal zones' (numbered 1 to 11), with seven 'external zones' (numbered 20 to 60) representing the areas outside Kington but linked to it by the main roads. It was a deeply flawed method: to avoid creating congestion, only a sample of traffic, moving in just the one direction, could be stopped for the drivers to be interviewed and traffic which happened not to cross the cordon could not be interviewed at all. Two major swathes of traffic, that inside the survey area and that leaving it, went unmeasured, while very variable sample rates affected the accuracy of the one remaining flow.

Although it would have been possible to have two different sets of zones, one for origins and one for destinations, it was usual to use the same for both: the zones in their role as origins listed down the side of the O+D matrix and the same set, now acting as destinations, listed across the top.

The County Council's origin and destination (O+D) matrix for Kington given in Figure 19.4 shows the results of the roadside interviews and has been divided into four

Destin zone	01	02	03	04	05	06	07	08	09	10	11	20	21	30	40	50	60	Total
Origin zone																		
01	0	0	0	0	0	0	0	0	0	0	0	0	0	0	0	0	0	0
02	0	0	0	0	0	0	0	0	0	0	0	0	0	0	0	0	0	0
03	0	0	0	0	0	0	0	0	0	0	0	0	0	0	0	0	0	0
04	0	0	0	0	0	0	0	0	0	0	0	0	0	0	0	0	0	0
05	0	0	0	0	0	0	0	0	0	0	0	0	0	0	0	0	0	0
06	0	0	0	0	0	0	0	0	0	0	0	0	0	0	0	0	0	0
07	0	0	0	0	0	0	0	0	0	0	0	0	0	0	0	0	0	0
08	3	1	0	3	1	0	1	0	0	0	0	1	0	1	0	0	0	11
09	0	0	0	1	0	1	1	0	0	0	0	0	0	0	0	0	0	3
10	28	3	1	43	9	0	16	8	0	0	0	20	5	0	2	1	13	164
11	0	0	0	0	0	0	0	0	0	0	0	0	0	0	0	0	0	0
20	37	19	3	64	22	2	12	18	11	18	6	0	13	10	4	29	156	414
21	32	21	8	41	54	5	48	17	3	3	2	0	0	0	0	16	220	481
30	3	2	2	5	2	0	3	3	1	2	3	0	0	0	13	22	151	213
40	4	2	1	7	5	0	8	3	0	0	0	1	1	7	0	8	197	245
50	29	10	3	76	17	0	13	0	4	1	0	37	8	40	1	0	15	262
60	37	20	29	56	11	12	8	21	4	7	5	202	49	205	230	12	2	910
Total	173	78	47	296	121	20	110	74	32	31	16	261	78	273	250	88	755	2703

Figure 19.4 The original but flawed origin and destination (O+D) matrix for Kington

sections: the top left section shows the movements from one internal zone to another (internal to internal traffic): virtually nothing is reported except movements from zone 10, a maverick internal zone which was actually outside the cordon. The top-right section shows traffic leaving Kington on its way elsewhere (internal to external). Since the survey only sensed traffic entering Kington, it is not surprising that this is almost entirely blank except for the peculiar zone 10. The bottom-left section reports the traffic from outside Kington on its way into Kington itself (external to internal): here the cells are quite well filled. Finally, the bottom-right section shows the through traffic from one external zone to another. Flows to and from external zones 40 and 60 are particularly strong; these represent the A44 trunk road between the Midlands to the east and Aberystwyth to the west.

Estimating traffic flow

Using O+D matrices as a data source for predictions of road flow depended on three further developments, all created by the computer companies and incorporated into their bundled traffic engineering packages, and all still in use.

1 The first was a method to describe the road network itself – essentially an expansion of the single junction into an area network.
2 The second was a technique to load the zone-to-zone movements from the O+D matrix on to the representation of the road network.
3 The third was to specify a route through the network from each origin to each destination. This enabled the number of movements in each cell of the O+D matrix to be added to the traffic on the links along the specified route. Loading all the cells on to the network created an estimate of the traffic flows over the whole network.

The description of the road network was achieved by identifying the major road junctions (in the network jargon these are called 'nodes' (lettered A to L in Figure 19.5)). Each section of road (called a 'link' in the jargon) between nodes was described by its length, its width, its 'capacity' (capacity is discussed in Chapter 7) and the average traffic speed (and therefore the time to travel the link).

The second development in the growing methodology to predict future traffic flows was a way to load the zone-to-zone traffic specified in the O+D matrix on to the road network. It was here that the computer models parted company with reality in a rather spectacular and bizarre way.[7] A point called a centroid was chosen to represent each zone. All movements to and from the zone were assumed to start and finish at the centroid. The centroid was therefore a proxy for all the precise origin and destination addresses within the zone and was arbitrarily chosen to best reflect this – despite the use of the term 'centroid', it was rarely at the geometric centre of the zone but was sited at the estimated centre of activity. Effectively, the actual geography of the zones was collapsed into a set of infinitely dense points, one for each zone.

These centroids were then linked to the computer representation of the real road network by fictitious 'dummy' links which connected each centroid to a nearby node in the real network: this often required the addition of fictitious 'dummy' nodes such as 'J' and 'C' (see Figure 19.5). Neither J nor C were actual, recognisable road junctions but were notional points at which traffic to and from zones 02, 03, 07 and 08 fed into the real network. Figure 19.5 also shows the two alternative proposals to alleviate the town centre congestion: the official inner relief road and the objectors' suggested bypass.

The third development was a method to allocate the flows identified in the cells of the O+D matrix to the road network. For example, the O+D matrix shown in Figure 19.4 gives a flow of 3 vehicles from zone 30 to zone 08. The only route for these vehicles before the construction of a new road was H → G → F → E → J. But once the bypass H→ K had been built, a second route H → K → J was available. The puzzle was as to which route the vehicles would take – in a more complex example than Kington, there may well have been a number of available routes. Wardrop[8] suggested that the road network could be likened to a net made of string with the knots representing the nodes and the string between the knots representing the links. If these lengths of string were proportional to the link lengths, then taking a pair of knots between finger and thumb and pulling the net taut would identify the sequence of links forming the shortest route between the two nodes. On the other hand, if the string representing the links were proportional to the driving time rather than the distance, pulling the net taut would identify the quickest, rather than the shortest, route.

These ideas were adopted by the authors of the traffic engineering packages bundled with main-frame computers. In Kington the volumes of traffic that would

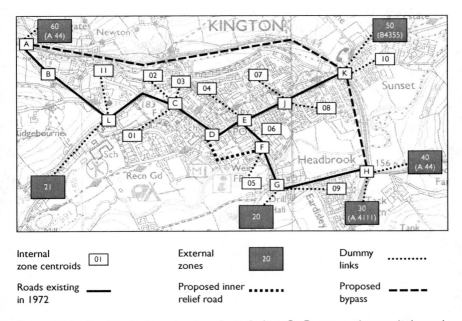

Figure 19.5 The Kington road network, including O+D zones, dummy links and road proposals

switch from the old roads to either the bypass or to the inner relief road were estimated by such programs and formed a large part of the choice between the two schemes. The assumption implicit in Wardrop's string analogy was that drivers would always choose the best route, itself based on the assumption that drivers would have pre-knowledge of the traffic conditions on all possible routes. Such assumptions may not always be absolutely true, but they were probably good enough: we know that drivers will strive to circumnavigate obstructive road-works by percolating through the road network as best they can, finding better, more reliable routes through trial and error. The identification of the 'best' (shortest, quickest, most likely) route has spawned a considerable volume of research and literature. No matter how the 'best' route is identified, allocating zone-to-zone traffic to it is termed 'Assignment'.

A methodology had now been created to estimate the flow of traffic along each link of a computerised network. The links comprising the shortest route from one zone to another could be identified. The numbers of vehicles estimated to move along that path could be read from the O+D matrix and assigned to the flow on each of the component links: once all the movements between zone pairs had been read from the O+D matrix, the total flow on each link in the network was complete.

The method as it existed at the time of the Kington study was very far from perfect, for three reasons:

1. The O+D matrix, derived from roadside interview surveys, was inherently incomplete and inaccurate – all local traffic between internal zones was ignored and the roadside sampling was unavoidably problematic.
2. The computer model of the road network included unreal, bizarre centroids and dummy links bolted on to an otherwise reasonable representation of the road system.
3. There was no immediately obvious method of extrapolating the link flows into the future. Just how inaccurate and unreliable this methodology was may be judged from Figure 19.6.

Link	Estimated vehicles per hour	Measured vehicles per hour	Error
A–B	129	237	1.84
B–C	129	310	2.40
C–D	218	324	1.49
D–E	242	335	1.38
E–F	226	376	1.67
F–G	218	373	1.71
G–H	113	435	3.85
E–J	123	163	1.33
J–K	17	151	8.71

Figure 19.6 Comparison between flows estimated from the Kington O+D matrix shown in Figure 19.4 and the actual flows measured by moving car observer

Figure 19.6 shows the flows along Kington's road network. The first column displays the estimates created by taking the O+D data collected by roadside interview (data which neglected movement from one internal zone to another), finding the shortest route through the network from each origin to each destination, and then allocating the flow in the O+D table to each link in the shortest route. The second column shows the actual traffic as measured on the street by moving car observers. It will be seen that the measured traffic is between 1.3 and 8.7 times greater than the traffic estimated by the computer model. It will also be seen that the size of the error related to the probability of a high proportion of local traffic – the element so badly represented in the O+D matrix.

Figure 19.6 illustrates a very common problem of the 1960s and 1970s. Because local traffic was underestimated, traffic speeds were overestimated, and much of the real congestion and delay went unrecognised, belittling the beneficial effects of a bypass. In Kington the action group's case in favour of a bypass won the day over the County Council's scheme for an inner relief road[9] and was built. There were similar outcomes in Frome, Trowbridge, Wells, Welshpool and other small towns.

The advent of household surveys and synthetic O+D matrices

The inherent inability of roadside interviews to sense the full range of traffic led them to be quickly supplanted by an entirely different technique. Rather than attempting to intercept trips at the roadside, samples of households were surveyed and asked to report all the trips made in a specific 24 hours. These field data were then analysed to create 'trip rates'. The rates created from data collected in Ponteland[10] were a very early example and are displayed in Figure 19.7. Such trip rates were, of course, specific to the place in which the field data were collected, but it was soon found that rates were very similar from place to place and rates relating to one place could be used in others without their credibility being compromised. That ability to transfer the rates from place to place was then extended to the notion that such rates were

Cars per household	0	1	2	3	4	Average
Persons per household						
1	0.06	0.65				0.25
2	0.21	1.42	1.85			1.13
3	0.36	1.75	2.80	1.33		1.72
4	0.38	2.30	3.53	3.00	6.00	2.25
5	0.57	2.61	3.81	1.00		2.48
6	0.40	3.00	4.29			2.76
7		1.60				1.60
8			3.00			3.00
Average	0.25	1.80	3.00	1.83	6.00	1.60

Figure 19.7 Numbers of car trips from the house per household per 24 hours
Source: Adapted from the Ponteland Study.

valid for the future too: the trip rates could be used at both different places and at different times. This was based on the assumption that future travel behaviour for a particular category of household would be similar to that recorded earlier for the same category: for example, any household comprising four people and four cars would in the future produce six trips per 24 hours, just as a similar household had been found to have done in Ponteland in 1963. Forecasts of trips for a future design year were then not directly dependent on traffic growth rates but were related to estimates of the numbers of households moving from categories with low rates of trip generation to categories displaying higher rates.

The Ponteland rates shown in Figure 19.7 presume that the number of trips per household per 24 hours were reflections of the numbers of people and of cars in each category of household: such quantities are called 'explanatory variables'. Trip rates combined with forecasts of the numbers of households within a zone classified by the numbers of cars and people enabled the calculation of the total number of trips generated by a zone for any date, now or in the future. For the present, the numbers of households in each category could be found from the census while for the future, household sizes and car ownerships had to be estimated. It was obvious that using just two explanatory variables was fairly crude, and later studies added other variables: the Leicester Traffic Plan[11] used no fewer than five, including rateable value and the income of the head of household; but, of course, this led to problems of predicting all five quantities before the number of future trips could be calculated.

Trip rates created a synthetic method of estimating the total number of trips starting at the households within a zone. If the existing numbers of household sizes and car ownerships were used, the result would be an estimate of the present number of trips and credibility could be cross-checked against data from other survey data, but there could never be absolute accuracy, partly because the original survey was only of a sample of households, and partly because travel patterns are constantly changing with differences between one day and the next. Unlike accuracy in structural engineering where catastrophic collapse due to inexact design is irreversible and even fatal, absolute accuracy in traffic engineering is unobtainable.

Having created a synthetic estimate of the numbers of trips originating at households within a zone, the next task is to establish where they are likely to go by creating an entirely synthetic O+D matrix. First, the zones have to be considered in their destination, rather than in their origin, roles, and estimates made of the numbers of trips arriving in each zone. This was done in much the same way as estimating the numbers of trips generated by households. Surveys were undertaken of shops, offices and other non-residential land uses, counting the numbers of trips and measuring the floor areas, numbers of employees and any other possible explanatory variables. The Leicester study concluded that floor area alone was the best explanatory variable of the numbers of attracted trips, in stark contrast to the five variables it used to estimate the household generations.

The new technique using trip rates rather than roadside interviews did not in itself create an entire synthetic O+D matrix but laid the foundations for doing so. Figure 19.8 shows a simple, hypothetical example of an O+D matrix with just four zones. It shows the total number of trips leaving each zone (the generations, in the column on

	Destination zones	Zone A	Zone B	Zone C	Zone D	Total
	Attracted trips	115	237	288	962	1602
Origin zones	Generated trips					
Zone A	287					
Zone B	594					
Zone C	486					
Zone D	235					
Total	1602					

Figure 19.8 A demonstration O+D matrix showing the number of trips starting and finishing in each of four zones

the left) and arriving (the attractions, in a row at the top). The generations and attractions shown in Figure 19.8 are not data from the Kington study, but have just been arbitrarily chosen. In reality, the origins will have been derived from the numbers of households in each zone stratified by their size and their propensity to own cars, multiplied by the types of trip rates shown in Figure 19.7. For the destinations, the numbers of attractions will be functions of the estimated floor space. For the moment, the cells of this initial matrix are empty, with no indication of where trips are either going to or where they have come from. The next task is to estimate the contents of the cells.

Without the ability to observe trips as they occur and with very limited data available from the household surveys, recourse had to be made to the creation of a completely hypothetical pattern of movement between zones. This was based on an adaptation of the gravity principle as adapted by Hansen and introduced in Chapter 13. In Newtonian physics the attraction between two bodies is held to be proportional to their masses (the heavier they are, the more mutual attraction is created) and in inverse proportion to the square of the distance between them (the further apart they are, the less mutual attraction). Without the stimulus of an apple falling on his head, Reilly[12] suggested, using floor space as an analogy for 'mass', that shoppers were more likely to use shops with large floor areas rather than smaller areas, but were less likely to patronise shops some distance away rather than local ones.

If the cells of an O+D matrix are to be filled using the gravitational principle that trips are more likely to go to large, 'attractive' places but less likely to go to places some distance away, then the distances between zones have to be measured. Figure 19.9 is a step development from the previous figure and now includes the distances from one zone to another.

There is an inevitable complication. There is a strong case for measuring distance in minutes rather than in miles or kilometres because that is how most people think of 'distance'. Journey times are certainly untidy – the time taken from A to B may well be different to the time from B to A, and both will continually vary. However, for simplicity, Figure 19.9 shows distances in kilometres rather than in minutes, and is naturally symmetric about the diagonal. In Newtonian physics the deterrent effect of the distance between two bodies is very powerful – the square of the distance between

	Destination zones	Zone A	Zone B	Zone C	Zone D	Total
	Attracted trips	115	237	288	962	1602
Origin zones	Generated trips					
Zone A	287	–	2	5	4	
Zone B	594	2	–	3	4	
Zone C	486	5	3	–	2	
Zone D	235	4	4	2	–	
Total	1602					

Figure 19.9 A demonstration O+D matrix by gravity model showing the distances in kilometres between zones

them. This means that the effect of each additional kilometre gains in deterrent strength; thus the effect of 2 kilometres is four times the effect of 1 kilometre but an extra kilometre, making a ground distance of 3 kilometres, raises the deterrent effect to nine times that of 1 kilometre. Empirical evidence showed that a power of about 1.3 (rather than the Newtonian power of 2) represents the effective deterrent of actual travel distance. Figure 19.10 shows this effect (measured in 'effective deterrent' distance) by increasing the ground distance in kilometres by a range of three different powers, including 1.3. (There has been a trend to supplant the Newtonian definition of the deterrent effect by entropy theory but, although the arithmetic is theoretically neater, the outcome is not radically different.)

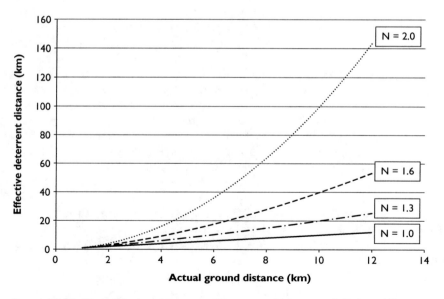

Figure 19.10 The effective deterrent distance = (the ground distance)^N

	Destination zones	Zone A	Zone B	Zone C	Zone D	Total
	Attracted trips	115	237	288	962	1602
Origin zones	Generated trips					
Zone A	287	–	2.462	8.103	6.063	
Zone B	594	2.462	–	4.171	6.063	
Zone C	486	8.103	4.171	–	2.462	
Zone D	235	6.063	6.063	2.462	–	
Total	1602					

Figure 19.11 A demonstration O+D matrix by gravity model showing the effective deterrent distance = (distance in kilometres between zones)$^{1.3}$

Figure 19.11 goes on to show the 'effective deterrent distances' for the four-zone worked example, achieved by simply raising the true distances in Figure 19.9 by a power of 1.3.

Figure 19.12 embodies the gravity principle itself. The 'likelihood' of trips being 'attracted' to a destination is held to be in proportion to its 'mass' (measured by the numbers of trips estimated to arrive in the zone) and in inverse proportion to the effective deterrent distance. The 'likelihood' is therefore equal to the number of attracted trips at a destination zone divided by the effective deterrent distance. For example:

L_{AB} = D_B / EDD_{AB}
D_B = the 'mass' of B (number of trips attracted) (= 237)
EDD_{AB} = the effective deterrent distance from A to B (= 2.462)
L_{AB} = the likelihood of making a trip from A to B (= 96.26). Note that this is just a number – it does not have any particular units of measurement.

The next stage in the calculation is rather more obscure. The weight of each 'likelihood' has to be calculated to give *relative* likelihoods'. This is done row by row,

	Destination zones	Zone A	Zone B	Zone C	Zone D	Total
	Attracted trips	115	237	288	962	1602
Origin zones	Generated trips					
Zone A	287	–	96.252	35.541	158.671	290.464
Zone B	594	46.705	–	69.045	158.671	274.421
Zone C	486	14.192	56.819	–	390.693	461.704
Zone D	235	18.968	39.090	116.964	–	175.023
Total	1602					

Figure 19.12 A demonstration O+D matrix by gravity model showing the 'likelihoods' of making a journey from one zone to another

	Destination zones	Zone A	Zone B	Zone C	Zone D	Total
	Attracted trips	115	237	288	962	1602
Origin zones	Generated trips					
Zone A	287	–	0.331	0.122	0.546	1.000
Zone B	594	0.170	–	0.252	0.578	1.000
Zone C	486	0.031	0.123	–	0.846	1.000
Zone D	235	0.108	0.223	0.668	–	1.000
Total	1602					

Figure 19.13 A demonstration O+D matrix by gravity model showing the 'relative likelihood' of making a journey from each origin zone to one or other of the destination zones

	Destination zones	Zone A	Zone B	Zone C	Zone D	Total
	Attracted trips	115	237	288	962	1602
Origin zones	Generated trips					
Zone A	287	–	95	35	157	287
Zone B	594	101	–	149	343	594
Zone C	486	15	60	–	411	486
Zone D	235	25	52	157	–	235
Total	1602	142	207	342	911	1602

Figure 19.14 A demonstration O+D matrix by gravity model showing the final synthetic O+D matrix

origin zone by origin zone. First, the sum of all the 'likelihoods' for each origin row has to be calculated; in Figure 19.12 these are already in place as row totals. To find the '*relative* likelihoods', each individual likelihood is divided by the row total to give a proportion between 0 and 1, with the row total being automatically equal to 1.00. This is shown in Figure 19.13.

The final calculation to complete the synthetic O+D matrix is to spread the total number of generated trips originating in each zone across all the possible destinations by simply multiplying the numbers of generated trips for each row by each of the 'relative likelihoods'. The result (Figure 19.14) is a complete O+D matrix (except for the diagonal of empty cells representing trips made entirely within a zone).

It will be seen that creating a synthetic O+D matrix using the gravity principle takes six steps:

1   The generations and attractions have to be calculated and set as row and column totals (Figure 19.8).
2   Distances between zones have to be entered into the cells of the matrix (Figure 19.9).
3   The distances must be converted into 'effective deterrent distances' by raising them to a power (Figure 19.11).

4 A 'likelihood' for each origin–destination pair must be calculated by dividing the attraction of the destination (measured in the total number of trips attracted to the zone) by the equivalent deterrent distance between the origin and the destination. The row total for each origin must be summed (Figure 19.12).
5 A 'relative likelihood' for each origin–destination pair must be calculated by dividing each 'likelihood' for an origin–destination pair by the row total of all 'likelihoods'. The result is a number between 0 and 1 and the sum of the relative likelihoods is always equal to 1 (Figure 19.13).
6 The O+D matrix is completed by multiplying the relative likelihoods by the total number of generated trips (Figure 19.14).

To demonstrate the gravity principle and its application, this chain of calculations has been explained as though the calculations were made by hand: of course, in practice they are always done quickly and invisibly by computer.

The problem of trips made entirely in-zone may be resolved by including an estimated local trip distance. There is one other, comparatively minor, problem. It will be noted from Figure 19.14 that, although the row total equals the number of generated trips, the sum of trips arriving in a destination zone at the bottom of a column is not exactly equal to the attracted trips at the top. This inaccuracy may be corrected by some iterative arithmetic. Whether the result is any nearer the real O+D matrix is debatable, but it is certainly tidier.

The three-stage land-use and transport prediction package

Once the creation of O+D matrices from data captured at roadside interviews had been replaced by synthetic matrices based on the gravity model, the bundled computer packages achieved a logical sequence:

1 A study area was divided into zones and the values of the descriptive variables (number of households, car ownership, floor areas in various uses, etc.) estimated both for the present and also for a future 'design year'.
2 Estimates of the numbers of trips generated and attracted by each zone were then created, using a combination of these descriptive variables and trip rates. This was known as the 'generation stage'.
3 Each zone was represented by a single arbitrary point called the centroid, and all the generated and attracted trips for the zone were assumed to start or finish there.
4 A computer model of the real road network was built using nodes to represent junctions and links representing the lengths of roads between junctions. Fictitious dummy links were added to act as connections from the centroids to the real network.
5 An O+D matrix was built starting with the distances between centroids as defined by finding the shortest routes from one zone to another through the model of the network. These were transformed into equivalent deterrent

distances and the numbers of trips originating in each zone spread over the possible destination according to the gravity principles described above. The result was a synthetic O+D matrix. This second phase was called the 'distribution stage'.

6   The distributed trips were then taken, cell by cell, and the shortest route identified through the road network from the origin centroid to the destination centroid. The number of trips in the cell was then added to the flow along each link in the identified route to create estimates of flow throughout the network. This third process was called the 'traffic assignment stage'.

7   Forecasting traffic in a specified 'design year' was achieved, not by using growth factors but by assuming that the descriptive variables for each zone would adopt new values – that car ownership, the number of employed persons and the floor areas for each zone would change.

The analysis of the original, simple junction shown in Figure 19.1 was concerned with counting and predicting the flow of vehicles, not people. The same was true of roadside interviews and studies such as that in Kington.

This could have been changed once household interviews based upon travel diaries had replaced roadside interviews as the preferred method of collecting raw travel data, but the change was not as radical as it could have been. Household surveys collected data about all person movement including that by foot, cycle and public transport, but all too often the data were converted from person movements to vehicle movements by disregarding reported movements unless they were made by a vehicle driver. The three-stage methodology (generation, distribution, assignment) retained the primary focus on the movement of vehicles: on traffic rather than on people.

The fourth stage: modal split

As explained in Chapter 7, government policy shifted radically in 1968 with the publication of *Traffic and Transport Plans*.[13] This recognised that urban traffic problems could not be solved by the construction of more road space and that public transport was necessary, not just to provide mobility for those who did not own cars, but to provide access for everybody, car owners and non-car owners alike, to those places where there was a dearth of parking space. A good example was, and is, the City of London, where over 90 per cent of people go to work by public transport, not because they like it, but because parking is impossible.

Traffic and Transport Plans required all local authorities to:

- create controlled parking zones with either meters or some other means to ration space;
- create clearway schemes for radial routes;
- improve and control road junctions;
- improve road safety;
- aid public transport;
- preserve or improve the environment.

This radical shift in policy was swiftly followed by the 1968 Transport Act, passed by a Labour government, and which authorised, for the very first time, the subsidy of the bus services thought to be necessary to achieve the objectives set out in *Traffic and Transport Plans*. A Conservative administration replaced Labour in 1970 and not only confirmed the new policy, but arranged for the subsidy of local public transport to be covered within a conglomerate transport supplementary grant (TSG). This was completely radical: the TSG wrapped into one package all the Whitehall contributions to local authority expenditure on transport, including local public transport by bus and rail, roads, car-parks and interchanges.[14]

The aims were explicit:

- to allocate available resources between the different forms of transport;
- to provide for the development and execution of comprehensive transport plans.

The three-stage traffic prediction process – 'generation', 'distribution' and 'assignment' – had been designed from the outset to provide the numerical justification for road schemes, not any scheme to improve the transport system. This was understandable for so long as the transport problem was perceived as too much traffic and too little road space, a problem that would grow as car ownership and use continued to expand. In the 1960s, before the change in policy marked by the introduction of *Traffic and Transport Plans*, it was assumed that predicting the use of public transport was unnecessary, since public transport was only needed to mop up the residual travel demand from those who had yet to acquire a car, a task that would gradually wither in the face of ever-increasing car ownership. Wherever new roads were unpopular, the traffic models could always be used to show that the scheme would affect flows in numerically precise ways and the benefits based on these predictions would outweigh the costs. But schemes to improve public transport could not be supported in this way – the analytical system had been designed from the outset to forecast traffic, not personal travel. Politicians were left in the dark, unable to quote forecasts of the likely effects of decisions to stimulate the use of public transport. Although it was possible to quote figures on the actual use of public transport, it was not possible to tell how much of that use was due to people leaving their cars at home – that would only have been possible if the data collection and analysis had covered all journeys by all means of transport. By default, and in the absence of a means to forecast the use of public transport, politicians used the transport supplementary grant to fund projects to the narrow, perceived advantage of their electorates, rather than deliver the objectives of *Traffic and Transport Plans*: in some cities this was done by freezing or even reducing fares; in others by continuing to ignore public transport, making plans for more road and parking space. The Ministry of Transport had been well aware of the dangers – hence the exhortation to provide for the development and execution of comprehensive transport plans, but their instructions went unheeded.

All three stages of the traffic prediction model had fundamental difficulties in predicting the use of public transport. Many 'generation' trip rates used in the 1970s were still based on the theory that the number of journeys made per household was a function of household characteristics, typically car ownership and some measure of the household size.[15] This was self-evidently partial. If the number of journeys by car is related to the availability of a car, then it follows that the number of journeys by public transport must be related to the availability of public transport. (The failure to recognise this relationship was one of the major deficiencies in the theoretical work related to the Nottingham 'Zone and Collar' experiment.) Many tariffs of trip rates took no account of the nature and quality of public transport service levels, continuing to assume that the travel generated per household was a function of household size and car ownership alone. This effectively assumed that trip-making was independent of location, and that a household in the remote countryside without adequate public transport would have the same trip-making characteristics as a similar household in an inner urban area with buses running past the front door. That assumption alone prevented any valid estimates of the changes in travel behaviour due to improved public transport service levels.

The 'distribution' phase was also gravely deficient. Gravity models estimate the number of trips between one zone and another as inversely proportional to the 'cost' of the journey. If this 'cost' is actually the airline, as-the-crow-flies, distance, then costs by car and by public transport may be similar, but if journey costs are measured more realistically by journey times, the 'cost' patterns of private and public transport are radically different.

A more sophisticated measure of journey cost, devised in the 1970s, lessened the gap between reality and the predictions made by computer modelling. 'Generalised travel cost' combined both the cash outlay and the time spent on the journey. Moreover, journey time was divided into ride time, waiting time and ancillary walking time, with a tariff of weights reflecting travellers' dislike of each of these elements, enabling the conversion of component watch times measured in 'real' minutes into a total of 'effective' or 'perceived' minutes. If ride time has a weight of 1 and waiting time of, say, 1.5, then a 15-minute journey composed of a five-minute wait plus a 10-minute ride will be logged as taking 17.5 effective minutes, whereas a 10-minute wait followed by a five-minute ride will be scored as 20 effective minutes. The components of conglomerate measures such as generalised cost have to be reduced to common units and considerable debate was held over whether these should be effective minutes or pseudo-money. Either way there has to be a presumed value of time to convert the cash spent on fares or parking meters into effective minutes or, alternatively, to convert effective minutes into a notional pseudo-cash value, itself composed of a nominal value of the time spent travelling plus the outlays of real cash on fares and parking, together with some less tangible real cash costs, like the cost per year of owning a car and the cost per kilometre of running it.

Whatever the method of calculating the 'costs' of zone-to-zone travel, there are very considerable differences between the patterns displayed in the matrices showing the generalised journey costs by car and by public transport. As shown in Chapter 2, cars are more or less equally efficient in all directions, able to take fairly direct routes without the constraints of timetables, interchanges and predetermined, indirect routes, and producing a fairly even spread across the cells of a journey cost matrix, but with a significant bias against driving to dense town centres due to the additional generalised cost of congestion, parking and getting from the parking place to the destination address. In complete contrast, the spread of generalised journey costs by public transport is very uneven, with wide differences between the cost of getting to town centres served by direct, frequent radial routes and the costs of reaching other places, involving indirect routes and awkward, time-consuming changes.

The conclusion is clear: given the radical differences in the patterns of journey costs between car and public transport, there need to be separate applications of both the generation and distribution stages of the travel demand model: one for journeys by public transport and the other for travel by car. First, in the generation stage there need to be separate estimates of the numbers of journeys by car and by public transport, both reflecting the provided service levels. Second, the distribution of car journeys should reflect a bias in favour of destinations with easy parking and little congestion, and the distribution of public transport journeys should be biased in favour of radial journeys along direct, frequent services. Both partialities may be represented by mode-specific measures of generalised costs.

Credible estimates of generalised cost must include estimates of walking and waiting times, and these are crucially dependent upon the whole journey between precise origin and destination addresses. Unlike cars, public transport cannot serve any address with almost equal facility. The assumption that all journeys begin and end at a zone centroid forces a presumption of mean service levels applicable to all addresses within a zone, making it almost impossible to estimate realistic public transport service levels and the reflected generalised cost. However, the obvious solution, namely to replace zones and their centroids by a more detailed geography of origins and destination, would have meant wholesale reconstruction of the distribution stage.

Creating a methodology capable of even very rough predictions of the cost-effectiveness of the policies and projects required by the TSG/TPP system was dependent on a basic rethink of the whole modelling process. Nonetheless, despite the government's realisation that there was a need to 'develop the means to forecast flows of people and goods both within urban areas and for regions as a whole',[16] the basic three-phase traffic prediction mechanism was perversely retained with a fourth stage, the 'modal split', added to the sequence of 'generation', 'distribution' and 'assignment'. The new modal split module was based on the notion that the total number of journeys between one place and another was fixed as predicted by the trip-end models reliant upon car ownership and usually ignoring the availability of public transport. This fixed number could be 'split' between the available modes of transport by the use of 'diversion' curves such as those shown in Figure 19.15.

Most diversion curves used the 'logit' model, a statistical technique to calculate the odds of an event happening.[17] Four fundamental problems disqualified diversion curves from being able to provide politicians with the clear, numerical support they needed to explain and justify decisions made to favour public transport as demanded by stated government policy.

1   The estimate of the total number of journeys between one zone and another by all modes, the total number to be 'split', were specified at the distribution stage by a gravity model using journey costs as the deterrence to travel. This posed the

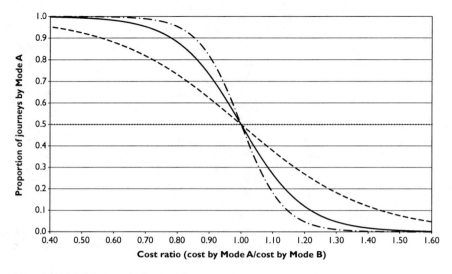

Figure 19.15 Theoretical diversion curves

problem of what measures of cost were to be used. If the journey costs were derived from the quickest route by car through the road network, then both the costs and the estimated total number of journeys would be biased against those places that are relatively difficult to reach by car. If the journey costs were those by public transport then the bias would be against those places that are relatively difficult to reach by public transport.

Unbelievably, many studies resolved this problem by using an average journey cost somewhere between the costs by car and by public transport and true of neither.[18] This made it impossible to assess any policy which set out to distinguish between the modes and to shift demand from one to another, and so impossible to give the required numerical reassurance to politicians charged with implementing the official policy.

2 The differences in travel costs to be used in diversion curves had to be based on the costs from one fictitious centroid to another. It was virtually impossible to estimate a cost of using public transport which was both realistic for a representative zone centroid and valid for all addresses within the zone. That lack of realism was unavoidably magnified by the variations in public transport travel times producing constantly shifting ratios.

3 Diversion curves gave a 'split' between modes which was based on the difference between private and public transport costs using measures of cost with different levels of accuracy and variation. The differences could vary wildly in line with different assumptions and different methods measuring average costs. This, together with the previous two problems, produced a doubtful estimate of the number of journeys between doubtful places, split by a doubtful diversion curve.

4 Both research and personal experience gives the lie that a destination is defined

first, followed by the choice of the method of getting there. Travel choices are made by sifting through possible destinations and selecting the most appropriate using a number of criteria, one of which is the practical possibility of getting there by one means or another. People do not choose to drive to destinations if there is little likelihood of finding a parking space, just as they do not travel by public transport it there is no service. Hence the sequential 'generation' and 'distribution' stages did not map on to the ways that real travel choices are made. Those defending the use of diversion curves will claim that generalised costs are able to include the collateral costs and inconveniences of parking, waiting and walking, and that is true; but that truth is clouded by other factors unless there is a clear distinction between private and public transport throughout the modelling process from generation to assignment.

The seemingly wilful retention of the three- (and then four-) stage travel demand model in the 1970s is a puzzle:

- Although government policy had shifted radically in 1968, the transport problem was still seen by many professionals and members of the public as essentially an imbalance between traffic and the available road space, an intractable problem to which public transport appeared irrelevant.
- This had the implication that the prime concern was movement, particularly the movement of vehicles – traffic – not the movement of people or of coping with stationary vehicles. Parking was seen as a separate, detached problem, leading to a failure to see the availability of parking as a major determinant of choices of destination.
- Walking was seen as a mode in its own right, an alternative to using a car or public transport. In fact, walking is a component of all journeys by whatever mode or combinations of mode.
- Hence walking must be a significant, weighted part of all estimates of generalised cost.
- The modes were seen as competitive alternatives, whereas modes are actually complementary. It was, and is, rare for an entire end-to-end journey to be made by one, single mode: even journeys by car imply some walking, but the insistence that walking was a separate mode to be used for entire journeys blinded transport planners to the importance of walking as a component part of all journeys. Most journeys, particularly in large cities, use multiple modes along their length, making them mutually supportive as well as being competitive.
- The fundamental, long-standing focus on roads and traffic prevented the consideration of the transport system as a whole as required by Circular 102/73:[19] on the contrary, the system was viewed as no more than a collection of separate, semi-autonomous modes – with very poor representations of the connections between them.
- Paradoxically, the retention of the three- to four-stage traffic model may have been due to the power of numerical justifications. Formal transport and planning inquiries could be struck almost dumb by technical evidence backed by piles of

computer print-out – the assumptions behind the calculations were rarely stated and, even more rarely, questioned effectively. The power of complex calculations and the amount of money spent on them may have numbed robust criticism and hobbled attempts to apply such power to support the new policies and actions rather than the old ones.

Another factor behind the apparent inability to create a travel demand model able to support a policy to provide access to town centres by public rather than private transport was perhaps a change in the funding of transport planning. Before the TSG/TPP regime 50 per cent of the costs of the transport planning studies, usually written by consultants, were paid by the Ministry of Transport. In addition, the Ministry maintained a 'Mathematical Advisory Unit' which focused on the theory and practice of demand modelling, providing advice to both the consultants and their clients. After 1973 the costs of such studies were no longer grant aided and the Mathematical Advisory Unit was disbanded. These two actions, in concert, appear to have stopped the development of travel demand theory in its tracks. Each consultant firm had invested in a programming suite based on four-stage architecture, and they were loath to volunteer to make it redundant.

The 1976 Consultation Green Paper[20] made a brave attempt to justify and prolong the 1968 policy of using public transport to support town centres, but it had to acknowledge that there was little evidence to show that the policy of coordinated budgeting and investment across the transport system as a whole, as organised under the TSG/TPP system, was actually effective.

> There is a widespread view that pricing and investment decisions for each mode are not taken within the framework of an integrated approach but in almost total isolation (para 1.3).

The prime reason for fragmented decision-making was the lack of an integrated, comprehensive methodology to predict travel throughout the transport system including parking, all modes and the interchanges between them. The absence of such a methodology prevented a credible estimation of the public's travel choices in reaction to modifications to the transport system, and so prevented any assessment of the cost-effectiveness of deliberate, targeted interventions. That, in turn, crippled any attempt to deploy an integrated transport budget.

Scheme assessment

This chapter began with the explanation that the assessment of any scheme to improve the transport system rests on ten steps:

1. measuring the existing movement through the system;
2. forecasting the future movements if things are left as they are;
3. forecasting future movements once the intervention has been made;
4. estimating the movement costs, first with and then without the intervention;
5. hence, estimating the expected net change in movement costs wrought by the

intervention; these are reckoned to be the 'benefits' to be credited to the intervention;
6 calculating the likely cost of the intervention;
7 estimating whether the cost of the intervention is likely to be justified by the estimated benefits;
8 making a go/no-go decision on whether to put the scheme into effect;
9 after the intervention has been made and has been working for long enough to have made a significant impact, measuring and costing the actual movement through the altered system and comparing it with the forecasts and estimates made in the original assessment;
10 striving to learn from the differences and, if necessary, modifying the assessment methodology.

At its simplest this process may be characterised by a 'before' study of existing movement and two 'after' studies, one assuming the system has been left unimproved and the other assuming the scheme has been implemented. In the Kington case study this was rather more complex, since two possible improvement schemes were considered: (1) the construction of the 'inner relief road' proposed by the Council, and (2) the 'bypass' proposed by the objectors. Rather than comparing them with each other, they were both compared with an unimproved system. The objectors' bypass scheme, although more expensive than the Council's inner relief road, was shown to yield considerably more benefit, sufficient to justify the extra cost.

The Kington case study raises two important questions:

1 What are the natures of the costs and benefits?
2 By what method are they compared?

The basic definitions of costs and benefits at the time when the scheme was first proposed (1970) and then assessed (1973) were set out in Department of the Environment Memorandum 1/71.[21] The benefits expected in the first year of use were the total savings in the movement costs of all the traffic forecasted to move through the assessed system (calculated by the difference between the costs of the traffic using the old, unimproved system and the new system), minus the extra costs of maintenance imposed by the new road, plus the expected savings from the reduced number of accidents. The calculations were primarily dependent upon predictions of the speeds and volumes of traffic along all the links of both the unimproved and improved networks. The volumes were estimated from a computer assignment, the speeds as a function of the volumes based upon the theoretically false assumption that speed is a function of volume rather than the reverse, as explained in Chapter 7. Vehicle operating costs were assumed to be a function of travel time along the links using a cost per hour and were therefore directly related to the link length and the traffic speed along it. It followed that the movement cost on both the unimproved and improved networks was the sum of the traffic movement costs on all links.

The benefits (the reduction in traffic costs) were created by diverting traffic from the old network to the new, reducing the volumes on the old network and increasing their speeds. That, in turn, reduced their movement costs. The movement costs on the new road had to be deducted from that benefit but, if the scheme has any merit at all, the sum of the movement costs of traffic diverted on to the new road would be substantially less than the costs of that traffic had it remained using the old ones.

The great majority of benefits on the Kington and all other, similar schemes stemmed from speeding traffic up and so reducing its operating costs. The accident savings were estimated by using a tariff of accident rates expressed as accidents per million vehicle-miles, stratified by road type, each with an implied traffic speed. A putative value was given to personal injury and fatal accidents, and the savings due to accident reductions were added to the benefits.

The assessment methodology was brutally simple. The expected benefits from the first year of operation were divided by the construction cost of the scheme, plus an allowance for the disruption caused by the road-works and expressed as a percentage termed the 'first-year rate of return'.

The basic structure of the assessment defined by Memorandum 1/71 was later embroidered by considering a sequence of years of benefits and costs, by replacing the first-year rate of return with more sophisticated financial arithmetic and including some appreciation of environmental issues, but the basic principle remains.[22]

It is self-evidently inadequate and unfit to assess any investment into the transport system with the possible exception of major road schemes, although even here it is unable to cope with end-to-end journeys by a combination of modes – it cannot deal with inter-modal journeys.

There is another major failing in its use. All it can do is establish, proposed scheme by proposed scheme, whether they achieve an arbitrarily defined surplus of benefits over costs. The system is designed to establish whether a scheme reaches a threshold profitability and, using that ability, may be able to illuminate the choice of one road scheme over another. But it is unable to help in decisions on what is the best use of a given sum of money. It seems that about £32 billion is available to build a high-speed railway through Middle England, but whether that money would be better spent on other projects has to be left to dogma and hope rather than to the evidence of calculated appraisals.

The intrusion of transport economics

The 1977 White Paper[23] offered three quite different objectives to those that could be traced back to 1968:

1   to engender economic growth;
2   to meet social needs, particularly by maintaining public transport to provide a reasonable level of personal mobility for those who did not have a car – a captive, declining market;
3   to minimise the harmful effects, in loss of life and damage to the environment, that are the direct physical result of the transport we use.

The second of these objectives is in total contrast to the previous policy, which saw public transport as the prime means of travel for everybody to particular places (the densely developed areas): now public transport was seen as the general means of travel for particular people (those without a car). Policy was now essentially back in step with the old four-stage travel demand methodology with the generation stage able to predict the demand from those households without the use of a car as a group likely to wither in numbers and for whom public transport was a stopgap.

The 1977 White Paper was also very clear about subsidy:

> Subsidy should be paid only where there is a clear requirement to meet social need (para 56).

> To use subsidies to disguise from people the costs of the services they are paying for is pointless and to subsidise richer people at the expense of poorer is perverse (para 57).

> Another test is value for money. It is sometimes argued that subsidies should be paid to public transport to attract travellers out of cars and so reduce congestion on the roads. But this can be a valid reason only where road congestion is a severe problem and where it would cost more to tackle it directly by traffic management or parking controls. The evidence is that there are few places where these conditions are met and that subsidies paid for this reason are, on the whole, misplaced (para 58).

The lack of evidence of the effectiveness of policies giving preference to public transport had a tinge of irony. Since modelling had failed to provide a mechanism to forecast the effectiveness of such policies, there was no benchmark against which value for money could be evaluated and hence there was an inevitable lack of evidence. Moreover, the major shift in policy from the 1972 TSG/TPP system to the 1977 White Paper removed any further need to provide politicians with data to support policies designed to favour public transport, so the benchmark was unlikely to appear in the future.

The 1977 White Paper was published by a Labour government dismayed that the emphasis on public transport as a solution to urban transport problems had been both expensive and ineffective. The 1977 White Paper marked a shift in policy focus away from urban transport problems towards inter-urban roads, a shift emphasised by the publication of the Leitch Report.[24] This effectively took up the development of estimating future road traffic from where it had been left in 1968 prior to the abortive diversion around urban transport policy and the use of diversion curves to create the modal split. The focus was now entirely on traffic rather than on travel, and assessing the pros and cons of dealing with this traffic through new road construction.

The TSG/TPP system was retained, but, in the Ministry of Transport's guidance on the contents of the first TPP submission after the change in policy marked by the 1977 White Paper, it belatedly regretted that past TPPs had failed to deliver proper transport planning which was defined as a sequence (Annex B):

- assessment of available resources;
- definition of present and future problems;
- objectives specified together with indicators which would measure the success in achieving them;
- options for action defined and evaluated;
- projects selected;
- programme costed;
- outcomes monitored.

This confirmed the view that the government had known what should be done, but recognised that the tools to do it had been unavailable: there was no method by which indicators, evaluations and monitoring could be arranged to cover an integrated transport system. In the following year, the last of the dying Labour government, there were more regrets of the same ilk:

> Only rarely are problems defined (in TPPs) in terms that can be measured and monitored.[25]

In May 1979 the incoming Conservative government echoed and amplified the 1977 White Paper, confirming the shift in focus from Urban transport to inter-urban roads. The next two White Papers[26] were both concerned with road, not transport, policy. The focus was very precisely upon stimulating the economy through developing the inter-urban road network:

> New road schemes can bring undoubted economic advantages. Exports can reach their markets more quickly: goods can be distributed more efficiently: traffic can flow more easily and fuel can be saved (para 1).

These priorities were no less clear than those of *Traffic and Transport Plans*, but could not have been more different:

- building roads to cut freight and distribution costs: for example, completing the M25;
- improving the environment of towns afflicted by heavy through traffic;
- enhancing the motorway network in order to reap more benefits from the network as a whole;
- ensuring value for money.

Although the incoming Conservative government surprisingly retained the TSG/TPP system, issuing year-on-year advice on what the plans could and should contain, the system gradually changed from the original purpose of providing an integrated budget supporting urban passenger transport, into a method by which central government could control expenditure on an inter-urban road system designed to support economic activity.

The withdrawal of bus subsidies began with Circular 1/81[27] which demanded very specific criteria for subsidy and assessment of the results, but in the following year there was an instruction to contain revenue support for buses and to demonstrate 'real value for money'. In contrast, there was an instruction to concentrate on urban and rural bypasses. The change of focus gathered force in Circular 1/85[28] which also introduced the notion of the primary road network (PRN). This was a significant step in the concentration on road traffic and construction. The country's inter-urban trunk road system had always been the responsibility of central government with the TSG/TTP grants supporting local authorities in their responsibilities for the local road system. The newly defined PRN consisted of the trunk roads, which continued to be the responsibility of the Department for Transport, and those other roads within local authority control which extended and thickened the trunk network. Circular 1/85 required local authorities to concentrate on improving the primary road network. Simultaneously, the Department for Transport de-trunked many roads, shifting the responsibility – and the cost – of maintenance and improvement to local authorities backed by TSGs, rather than central government funding the work directly.

The shift from urban transport to inter-urban roads was completed by Circular 1/87,[29] which required local authorities to include a five-year rolling programme of improvements to the PRN, each improvement accompanied by a full economic appraisal to the same standards as those used for trunk road improvements. This required measures of the changes in traffic routing and flow that a new road would engender, based on predictions of future traffic with and without the proposed improvement, predictions which were accomplished using the old four-stage methodology. The focus was less upon bypasses of small towns than on large, rural, road schemes. This had a profound effect on the size and shape of the areas to be studied: they became longer and thinner – typically corridors. In contrast to the lack of adaptation to public transport in the 1970s, transport planning methodology was adapted fairly quickly to this shift – yet more evidence that transport planning methodology was rooted in road rather than transport planning and assessment. Corridor studies implied that it was no longer necessary to divide the study area into zones and to identify centroids at which journeys were assumed to start and finish. Traffic growth was not estimated as a function of the changing characteristics of origins and destinations, but by growth rates – the methodology had reverted back to the pre-1960s simple techniques.

There were two, intertwined methods of finding a growth rate. The first and simplest was an estimate of growth published as the *National Road Traffic Forecasts* (NRTF). This was not the crude compound rate that had been advocated in 1961 in the Ministry of Transport's Memo 780 – the intervening rise in the use of computers and statistics had enabled a far more sophisticated range of growth factors with variations by type of vehicle and of road – but the basis was still questionable:

> Traffic is forecast to increase mostly because people are expected to become richer and to enjoy longer lives, because economic activity increases and because households are forecast to become more numerous.[30]

This was a declaration of the principle that was later to be tagged 'predict and provide'. Given the objectives in the series of White Papers in 1977, 1980, 1983 and 1989, all supporting the notion that economic prosperity depended on a good road system, it was a short step to the assertion that the road system should expand in step with traffic growth and that, if it did not, national prosperity would be threatened. The consequent technical agenda was clearly to identify unconstrained growth and to show where the economy was being hobbled. That agenda was explicit, and the means to achieve it was set out in very considerable detail in the *Design Manual for Roads and Bridges* (DMRB).[31]

The second, but related, technique of particular importance was identified in *Trunk Roads and the Generation of Traffic*.[32] This established the long-held suspicion that improving a road and reducing generalised traffic costs created an increase in total traffic. The assignment technique demonstrated in the Kington example established the transfer of traffic from unimproved roads to a new, faster alternative, but the report confirmed that new roads carried more traffic than just transfers from the relieved roads. Although the report was specifically about inter-urban trunk roads, it implied a general proposition that providing better transport creates more use. This shows that the numbers of trips are not the simple product of car ownership and household characteristics, as previously assumed, but also reflect the quality of the transport services on offer, be it in new, improved roads or a better bus or train service. This, quite incidentally, cast doubt upon the wisdom of diversion curves such as those shown in Figure 19.15 being used to divide a fixed number of trips in the cells of an O+D matrix between modes.

The somewhat obvious conclusion that better transport produces more movement resonated with economic theory – that reductions in price (or in generalised cost) create increased demand by a multiplier called the elasticity. *Trunk Roads and the Generation of Traffic* used elasticities to identify traffic growth rates, including the growth that could be expected to be created by road improvements. For example, it suggested an elasticity of about -0.16 for the short-term effect of a rise in the price of fuel (meaning that if the fuel price rose by 1 per cent then the quantity of fuel bought and used would fall by 0.16 per cent, an arithmetic demonstration that the total fuel burn is not that sensitive to price).

The second edition of the *National Road Traffic Forecasts*[33] took this approach to some lengths with a range of elasticities, but it also included a totally new technique which reflected another major shift in focus. Throughout the 1980s there had been a consistent emphasis upon the need for road use and investment to underpin the economy, implying a prime focus upon inter-urban transport. Urban transport policy in the 1990s was much more disjointed. Buses and then railways were privatised, carrying an assumption that the forces of supply and demand would achieve any appropriate coordination – a reliance upon the 'hidden hand' of market forces to relate supply and demand. In theory, but with virtually no practice, this was extended to traffic by road user or congestion charging – another example of economic theory and elasticities intruding upon the prediction of travel demand.

But four years previously, without the provocation of a change in government, transport policy had been given a substantial jolt with the publication of PPG13.[34] This added a completely new strand to government transport policy:

> An effective transport system is vital for the local and national economy. But continuing growth in road transport and consequential environmental impacts

present a major challenge to the objective of sustainable development. Traffic growth on the scale projected could threaten our ability to meet objectives for greenhouse gas emissions, for air quality and for the protection of landscape and habitats (para 1.1).

PPG13 marked the end of the 'predict and provide' roads policy. The major task of travel forecasting demand was no longer to estimate the unconstrained volume of traffic and to build roads to accommodate it: the task was to manage demand down to levels which the existing transport system could carry:

> The Government recognises that forecast levels of traffic growth, especially in urban areas, cannot be met in full and that new road building or the upgrading of existing highways will, in some cases be environmentally unacceptable. It is already Government policy not to build new trunk or local roads simply to facilitate commuting by car into congested urban centres (para 1.4).

> To maintain the effectiveness of the transport system, there are good reasons to place more weight on policies to manage demand, especially in urban areas, by:
> - promoting acceptable alternatives to the private car
> - enabling people to reach everyday destinations with less need to travel
> - reducing local traffic on trunk roads and other through routes (para 1.5).

PPG13 was long on objectives and aspirations but very short on the clear policies to achieve them. In the main, the document exhorted local authorities to manage property development and land use as a way to reduce the need to travel. It did recognise that tailoring traffic to match the capacity of the road system required more than reducing the total number of person-kilometres and that certain travel would need to be made on foot, cycle and public transport, but there were no explicit policies to encourage this. The flavour may be judged by:

> Local authorities should establish 'accessibility profiles' for public transport in order to determine those sites which could meet the policy goals set out in the guidance (para 4.23).[35]

This is an oblique, almost opaque, reference to the Public Transport Accessibility Level (PTAL) technique pioneered by Hammersmith Council. This provided 'equivalent doorstep frequencies' of public transport services at any particular point, and is an amalgam of the walking distance from the doorstep to the available public transport and service frequencies. It represented a break from previous travel demand modelling; it was concerned with a specific origin address, not an artificial centroid representing the multitude of addresses in a zone: it recognised that journeys have component parts but it ignored most of the parts, concentrating exclusively upon the segment between a doorstep and the entry point to the public transport system. It was the overture to a major shift in focus from the journey itself to the journey ends as presumed determinants of the choice of mode.

The major shift marked by PPG13 was a rejection of the notion that transport policy should be intent upon satisfying demand as best it could ('predict and provide') to managing demand to best fit the capacity of the network ('travel demand management'). This change in principle recognised the obverse of the finding that improved transport facilities generated increased travel demand: if new road capacity released increased demand then inadequate road capacity would suppress demand. This was reflected in the second characteristic of the 1997 *National Road Traffic Forecast*. NRTF 97 included a 'Fitting on' process, FORGE (Fitting on of Regional Growth and Elasticities), in which traffic growth on roads which had reached their capacity was deflected on to other roads or, if they too had reached capacity, was suppressed altogether. This was not done road by road: that would have been too complex and detailed. It was enabled, in the first place by measuring traffic, not by flow (the number of vehicles past a point) but in vehicle-kilometres. The road system was divided into a hierarchy of road types (motorways, the primary road network, urban main roads, etc.) and into geographical areas. Each type and area had a nominal ability to take a number of vehicle-kilometres before delay kicked in and, once this level had been reached, nominal mean speeds were considered to fall, forcing a rise in the travel time. Given an elasticity of the reaction to travel time, the percentage of the flow diverted to other roads or suppressed completely could be estimated. It was a predictive mechanism to express the real policy behind PPG13 which was to do as little as possible to the road system and let consumer reaction cope as best it could. Policy was now unrelated to the four-step methodology which was of little use in forecasting the effects of possible actions to implement the new travel demand management.

Although FORGE did recognise the PPG13 policy of managing travel to fit the system rather than extending the system to fit the traffic, it did so in a perverse way. The 'system' was confined to the road network, and management consisted of doing nothing and letting the hidden hand of supply and demand, as portrayed in Figure 19.16, sort the problems out. If the road system was predicted as unable to cope, the surplus traffic in the FORGE model was just suppressed – there was no mechanism and no suggestion that other forms of transport might provide an alternative. Public transport did not appear in the FORGE/NRTF mechanisms at all.

Figure 19.16, taken from DMRB and repeated in later documents, gives the standard economic theory that as cost falls so demand rises, the argument presented in the 1994 SACTRA report *Trunk Roads and the Generation of Traffic*. It suggests that any rise in cost will also cause supply to increase, creating a market equilibrium at a cost where supply and demand are equal. Clearly highways cannot be built to provide an exact adjustment of supply to match demand and so the argument is slightly shifted:

> The most well-known 'supply' effect is the deterioration in highway speeds as traffic volumes rise.

This argument reverses the usual relationship between the supply of goods and services in which volume supplied is held to be a function of the market price. In

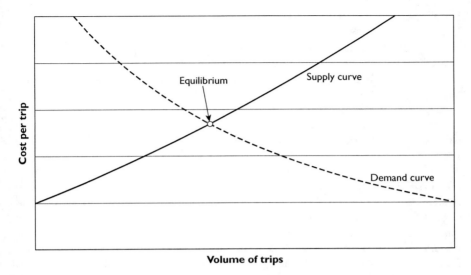

Figure 19.16 The classic economic theory of supply and demand curves

transport economics the argument is that, due to the escalating generalised cost of the congestion provoked by traffic volume, cost is a function of volume. There are two major flaws in this argument:

1 As shown in Chapter 7, volume is a function of speed – not the reverse.
2 Applying the general theory to all forms of transport is mistaken. Increased demand for public transport leads to improvements in frequency and route proliferation, so reducing waiting times and the generalised cost to the traveller – the reverse of what happens in road traffic. That precludes a sensible application of the classic theory of Figure 19.16 to public transport.

Two other seminal documents were published at the same time as the 1997 *National Road Traffic Forecasts* and FORGE. The National Trip End Model provided an alternative to the trip end generation models of yesteryear. It is a well-presented and easy-to-use model, particularly in its latest form, TEMPRO (Trip End Model Presentation Program) which may be downloaded off the Web. But it is flawed in the same way that the generation models of yesteryear were flawed. The primary focus is upon car journeys with travel behaviour focused upon variations due to household size and car ownership supported by an excellent basis for predicting the numbers of households and their characteristics. There is an element predicting the use of other modes but this lacks explanatory variables such as the available service levels. Instead, the analysis is by geographical area, which is not helpful in predicting the changes in the use of public transport in response to policies and actions designed to change travel behaviour.

The other model published in step with the 1997 *National Road Traffic Forecast* was the National Travel Model (NTM), which relies heavily on the National Trip End Model and therefore cannot itself predict changes in the use of modes, although it is able to reflect post-hoc reports of trends in modal use produced by the National Travel Survey, a small sample census of the use of transport.

Around the time that PPG13 was published, transport planning borrowed a technique from the marketing industry. 'Stated preference' was a market research technique in which potential consumers were interviewed and confronted with ranges of attributes of proposed products – cost, colour, performance, etc. – and were asked what their hypothetical reactions were likely to be. The results were analysed to create measures of elasticity – what percentages consumers would buy at various combinations of price, performance, etc. In transport the stated preference technique was used to predict the use of bus service frequencies, fares, comfort levels, etc. The actual demand as counted in practice was termed 'revealed preference'. The technique was statistically quite sophisticated, returning seemingly credible data from relatively small samples, but hypothetical questions are always dangerous and some respondents gave less than honest answers, sensing that if they said they would use a new service it was likely to materialise, giving them more choice although not committing them to actually using it.

The prime deficiency in this or any other method of forecasting movement by extrapolating from trends or from elasticities is that it cannot reflect deliberate attempts to modify the travel choices. That may only be done by modelling reactions to known explanatory variables and then, by design, massaging the values of those variables.

Lost in multi-modal integration

PPG13 was good on 'stated' policy but the later 'revealed' policy was weak: 'Traffic and Transport Plans' (Memo 1/68), written 30 years previously, had similar objectives, but, unlike PPG13, these were backed by clear policies plus the finance and procedures to deliver them. The failure at that time was the lack of a methodology to support the decision-makers with convincing predictions of the effectiveness of their decisions. That problem was to remain.

Post-1993, Britain had two strands to transport policy: first, an inter-urban roads policy underpinned by a methodology, well defined in the DMRB,[36] to predict future traffic flows and to evaluate the value for money spent on improvements to the network. The second strand was an urban transport policy driven by a need to reduce traffic and environmental damage. Differentiating urban and rural policy is a sensible reaction to their very different problems, with parking being at the core of the difference, and very different solutions, too – public transport is far more attuned to urban than to rural areas. However, in PPG13 the differentiation was more by accident than deliberation.

Environmental issues had climbed up the international agenda by the time the government changed complexion in 1997. A new Department for the Environment, Transport and the Regions (DETR) was created with John Prescott in charge, a politician with a declared mission to reduce environmental harm through integrated, sustainable transport and planning policies. The responsibilities of the new department were similar to those of the Department of the Environment in the 1970s and the new policy, published in a White Paper,[37] also harked back to the 1970s. It advocated two major themes:

1. An integrated transport policy (para 1.22) with:
   - coordination between all modes of transport: 'so that each contributes its full potential and people can move easily between them'
   - integration with the environment: 'so that our transport choices support a better environment'
   - integration with land-use planning: 'so that transport and planning work together to support more sustainable transport choices and reduce the need to travel'; this owed much to PPG13 published six years earlier by the previous government
   - integration with policies for education, wealth and wealth creation: 'so that transport helps to make a fairer, more inclusive society'.
2. A sustainable transport policy (para 2.12) with:
   - reduced pollution from transport
   - improved air quality
   - better lifestyles with less reliance on cars and easier travel by foot and bicycle
   - reduced noise and vibration
   - improved safety.

The new policies were clearly much closer to 'Traffic and Transport Plans' (Memo 1/68) and PPG13 than they were to the roads policies of the 1980s. However, the new policy was a collection of earnest, even naive, objectives with poor definition of any specific actions designed to deliver them. There was a major paradox: a key objective was transport coordination. The route to coordination was the establishment of an 'Integrated Transport Commission', in effect a detached, non-executive, government-funded think-tank charged with the task of lobbying the government with extensions to the theory and practice of integration, but with no ability to deliver either policies or actions: the Commission was not itself integrated.

One objective was to 'pursue the seamless journey' by:

- more through ticketing;
- better interchanges;
- better connections and coordination of services;
- wider availability of information on fares and timetables.

There were no suggestions on how the 'seamless journey' might be created, nor on how it might be known whether or not the 'seams' had been unpicked. This was particularly relevant because, over the previous 15 years or so, the public transport industry had been deregulated, privatised and fragmented, making integration very difficult – it could only be effected through the cooperation of a large number of actors.

This was just one aspect of the fragmentation of the transport industry, of its funding and of its administration which made 'integration' extremely difficult, if not impossible. During the 1970s and 1980s a reliance upon fiscal and financial market manipulation rather than direct regulation by government had swept through the world. New markets were created for energy, communications, transport and health. The effectiveness of government rather than market forces was constantly questioned, and decision-making and regulation was either relaxed or out-sourced to agencies. Market mechanisms work by multiple actors reacting to price and cost signals formalised through contracts, rather than by government instruction or decree, and administrative law had been insidiously replaced by civil and contract law.

The touchstone of coordination, the 'seamless journey' through ticketing, easy interchange and comprehensive information, required working agreements between multiple agencies and drawing upon multiple budgets designed to deliver a plethora of commercial objectives. In the 1970s, 1980s and 1990s the transport system had been deliberately designed to create competition, not seamless coordination. Estimating future travel demand was itself fragmented by mode and operator, each segment conducting its own surveys, defining its own market, driven by the commercial objectives of cost and revenue management. The policy declared in the 1999 White Paper advocated and required integrated decision-making, the very thing that had been designed out of the overall transport system. The panoply of the *Design Manual for Roads and Bridges*, the *National Roads Traffic Forecasts*, FORGE, the National Trip End Model, the National Transport Model and WebTAG were all strongly orientated to forecasting traffic, not the movement of people and goods.

The multi-modal studies

This fundamental problem came to be demonstrated by the multi-modal studies (MMS) initiated in 2000. These were planned to show the benefits of a coordinated approach, although their very conception did not inspire confidence. They were patterned upon the case studies within the 1998 Roads Review, studies that were aimed at specific problems on the trunk road network – the very limited image of the transport system that had prevailed from 1977 onwards. It was not the best progenitor of a method to:

> investigate problems on or with all modes of transport and to seek solutions to those problems.[38]

The definition of multi-modal studies fell at the very first hurdle:

> In seeking solutions to the problems to be addressed in Multi Modal Studies, the contributions of all modes should be considered, including walking, cycling, air transport, shipping and pipelines as well as roads, railways, buses and other forms of public transport.[39]

The perception from the beginning was of a set of discrete modes, each making a 'contribution' to satisfying transport demand. It was implied that the definition of 'multi-modal' was a collection of independent competitive modal systems. The idea that air transport and shipping could ever be free-standing modes, able to make a 'contribution' while unsupported by any other modes is clearly silly – it ignored the problems of getting to air- or seaports. By the same token, although with less obvious silliness, walking is not an alternative to bus travel but is an integral part of using all public transport. The inability to perceive multi-modal travel to mean the use of more than one mode along the length of a journey rather than a choice between one mode and another for a substantial part of a journey, destroyed any hope of creating 'seamless journeys'.

The whole MMS project was crippled by other fragmentations, quite apart from an inability to perceive the transport system as a whole rather than as a collection of semi-autonomous modes. Outputs from the MMS were expected to be a number of options, each option consisting of:

> a transport plan, that is, a collection of quite specific and individual interventions.[40]

On the contrary, as shown in Chapter 3, the very essence of a 'plan' is a collection of related and coordinated actions; otherwise it would be no more than a collection of fragmented, separate plans. The urge to fragment problems, solutions, organisations and finances appears to have overtaken reality. Docherty and Shaw[41] extend the same point: under the heading 'The Multi-Modal Studies – a problem of disintegration', they note that some studies produced a package of mutually supportive measures that could not be sensibly unpacked. But the government did unpack them, referring road interventions to the Highways Agency where they were welcomed and the rail proposals to the Strategic Rail Authority where they were not. Both of those organisations had their own budgets and their own objectives and their own criteria, conditions which ensured that neither had a concern for an integrated approach to a commonly understood problem. Neither organisation should be blamed: there was no reason why they should do otherwise in the fragmented world in which they battled.

The DETR years were particularly noted for a plethora of documentation. The year 1998 saw the White Paper and the 'New Approach to Transport Assessment'. This revised the methods by which projects were assessed for value for money and changed the definitions of what could be included as costs and of benefits. A series of 'daughter documents' were spawned by the White Paper, giving more detail, and more objectives, for buses, walking, cycling, etc. Then the methodology for the multi-modal studies was specified in considerable detail in 'Guidance on the Methodology for Multi-Modal Studies'.[42]

Nonetheless, there is still a gap between policy and technical methodology. Policy is aimed at reducing pollution by reducing travel (measured in person-kilometres) and by reducing the polluting fuel burn (measured in CO_2 per person-kilometre). Reducing the total distance travelled is to be achieved by land-use planning so that the mean journey distance is reduced. The methodology defined in WebTAG provides no way by which planning policies may be evaluated against the objective of reducing aggregate travel. To do so would require a combined land-use/transport model capable of estimating actual out-turn land uses. Fuel burn per person-kilometre requires a combination of changes to vehicle technology, of the type of fuel used and of vehicle loading. The techniques spelt out in WebTAG to estimate vehicle loading and fuel burn per person-kilometre, rather than per vehicle-kilometre, are either inadequate or absent.

The nub policy is to induce switching from car travel to the 'soft modes' – walking, cycling and public transport. For that policy to be accountable there has to be a model of travel demand that is able to identify journeys which could be induced to change mode from a mode with a high fuel burn per person-kilometre to one with a lower burn. That can only be done effectively by a model which includes all travel by whatever mode or combination of modes, and also includes the explanatory variables which influence that travel.

WebTAG Unit 2.11.3 (Mode Choice Models) is basically reliant on the notion that the modes compete for market 'share' and that this competition may be mimed by logit diversion curves, the methodology first used in the late 1960s. It assumes that there is a 'market' for travel between one zone and another, and that this market is shared by a comparison of the generalised costs of one mode against another. It is an inherently flawed concept:

- It assumes that generalised costs are homogeneous across a zone. Our own personal experience and the theory of PTALS and of effective doorstep frequency shows this to be untrue. Logit curves assume either that the generalised cost comparisons are between modes serving a real point (say, a bus-stop – but do travellers actually compare the cost of travel by bus and by car from a particular stop?) or a representative point (say, a centroid), but if this were done, the inaccuracy due to the differences between the real addresses at which the journey starts would be hopelessly biased, since cars are able to serve all the addresses within an area more or less equally, whereas public transport cannot.
- It either ignores the overheads of using public transport (the walk and wait) or it represents them by inaccurate surcharges.
- It cannot account for interchanging (except by crude averages). In particular, it cannot account for the final interchange from wheeled transport to foot. WebTAG Unit 3.7.1 suggests that a penalty should be added to the generalised cost of journeys using an interchange, but this is a crude generalisation – the penalties will vary with service frequencies and reliability. The penalty perceived by travellers cannot really be represented by an arbitrary standard surcharge.

During Ruth Kelly's brief occupation as the Cabinet Member responsible for transport (June 2007 to September 2008), she signed off yet another transport White Paper.[43] In the Foreword she wrote:

> I am determined to adopt a stronger passenger and user focus in our policies. We must increase our understanding of the needs of pedestrians, cyclists and road users, rail, bus, and aviation passengers and of international and domestic freight transporters. Our policies must improve every part of their travel experience,

from leaving their front door to arriving safely at their final destination. If we are to achieve that, we must understand the full end-to-end journey.

And in Paragraph 10:

> People travel daily and want a system that gets them from A to B safely, securely and without damaging the environment. If there are problems on their journey, they want to be told about them. They want predictable end-to-end journey times.

It was the first realisation that journeys are seen by those making them as a door-to-door movement through a transport system perceived as an entity, including the infrastructure of pavements, roads, car-parks, interchanges, and including the service levels provided by walking, cycling, riding and driving.

Unfortunately, Ruth Kelly's approach appeared to be stillborn. A number of end-to-end-studies were commissioned but they focused on freight. Freight transport has to include the penalties of handling at interchanges in a far more rigorous way than the penalties incurred by interchanging passengers are dealt with. Freight has also used the term 'inter-modal' to cover the fusion of more than one mode. Ruth Kelly's agenda clearly suggested that the theory and understanding of multi-modal freight should be extended to passenger travel, and she was right. The problems of interfacing modes and of people navigating through those interfaces from one mode to another are a crucial element within the transport system and of the uses made of it.

Fit for purpose?

Two fairly recent reports have cast considerable doubt upon transport planning methodology as defined in the WebTAG units. Wenban-Smith and Van Vuren[44] argued that effective predictions need to take account of the land-use changes which are one of the responses to transport problems. They cite three reasons:

1 The data show that mean trip lengths are increasing, evidence that land-use changes are a significant response to perceived deficiencies in the transport system. It appears that businesses relocate in order to sustain their accessibility and new businesses adopt sites which provide the required levels of accessibility.
2 Transport and land use have a symbiotic relationship: 'transport has shaped the city but the shape of the city influences the transport system.'
3 There is a need to assess value for money from interventions in the transport system and, if those interventions change land uses and the movements between them, then valid evaluations must account for land-use changes.

Wenban-Smith and Van Vuren claimed in a review of the Land-use and Transport Interaction (LUTI) model covering the Thames Gateway that it had not delivered credible forecasts. Their argument was therefore powerful – that LUTI models were necessary, but they had yet to provide acceptable results.

Coombe[45] reported to the Department for Transport on the dependability of a wide range of 30 models. In essence, the models were examined for their ability to assess the objectives identified in a further departmental paper[46] published a year after Ruth Kelly's White Paper. The revised objectives were:

- to *support* national *economic* competitiveness and *growth*, by delivering reliable and efficient transport networks;
- to reduce transport's emissions of carbon dioxide and other greenhouse gases, with the desired outcome of *tackling climate change*;
- to *contribute to better safety, security and health* and longer life-expectancy by reducing the risk of death, injury or illness arising from transport, and by promoting travel modes that are beneficial to health;
- to *promote* greater *equality of opportunity* for all citizens, with the desired outcome of achieving a fairer society;
- to *improve quality of life* for transport users and non-transport users, and to promote a *healthy natural environment*.

The bulk of the document is packed with anodyne platitudes, neither policies nor actions nor methods. The only issue it raised is the conflict between pollution and economic growth, but as a whole it was an unappetising menu. Nonetheless, reducing pollution using the touchstone of CO_2 emissions was recognised as a major objective. Coombe found that many models were unfit for purpose, implying that they could not define actions which would deliver this objective. Two deficiencies were noted: first, that the methodology set in government advice on modelling (mainly codified on the WebTAG site) was itself deficient, and second, that the advice, deficient or not, was not followed.

Coombe lists the deficiencies rather than explaining them, but the explanation appears to be that the models were not designed to fulfil the purposes to which they were now being put.

The objective of delivering a sustainable transport system has a prerequisite of understanding that it is a single, coherent system, much greater than the sum of its modal parts, through which personal travellers and freight shippers choose routes made of combinations of modes, including interchanges with their all-too-apparent costs and inconveniences. These interfaces include 'terminals' at which only the vehicles enabling movement terminate, not the movements themselves. They are a form of interface and together with all other interfaces, are crucial components facilitating the movements from A to B identified in *Towards a Sustainable Transport System*.[47]

This, in turn, implies that value-for-money assessments must be of the transport system as a whole, not of its separate parts. Hence the task of evaluation cannot be to assess whether a proposed intervention will reach a threshold value for money but whether the money spent could have been spent more beneficially upon some other improvements to the system.

If that be so, then there must be a single budget to enable the delivery of mutually supportive multi-modal bundles of interventions, a financial structure that had been specified 40 years ago in Department of the Environment Circular 104/73,[48] creating the TSG/TPP procedures.

Assessments of the effectiveness of interventions must be measurable requiring a fine-grained analysis of travel choices dependent upon perceived transport landscapes. In the long term such landscapes influence not merely transport choices but the development of land and understanding that process is a major need.

None of the models considered by Wenban-Smith were able to fulfil these needs and therefore could not be fit for purpose in the task of delivering a sustainable transport system.

Notes

1. Minister of Transport (October 1959 to October 1964). He opened the M1 in 1959 and commissioned both the Beeching Report on the Future of the Railways (1963) and the Buchanan Report on Traffic in Towns (1963)
2. See Matson *et al.* (1955, ch. 6).
3. Ministry of Transport (1961).
4. Road Research Laboratory (1960).
5. Road Research Laboratory (1960), table 33.
6. Transportation Planning Associates (1970).
7. See e.g. ICL (1970).
8. Wardrop (1952).
9. Department of the Environment (1973*)*.
10. Williams *et al.* (1963).
11. Smigielski (1964).
12. Reilly (1931).
13. Ministry of Transport (1968).
14. Department of the Environment (1973).
15. See e.g. table 2, in R Travers Morgan and Partners (1972).
16. Ministry of Transport (1967a), Paragraph 141.
17. At its simplest, the logit model takes the form $R=1/(1+e^{(-L*Z)})$ where R = the estimated likelihood of an event, e is the constant 2.71828, L is an arbitrary constant used to tweak the curve to fit empirical field data and Z is a measure of one choice compared with another. Logit curves always take the S-shaped form seen in Figure 19.15 which shows three versions of the logit curve, each dependent upon different values of Z, the 'tweaking' factor.
18. See e.g. Jamieson Mackay and Partners (1975).
19. Department of the Environment (1973a).
20. Department of the Environment (1976).
21. Department of the Environment (1971).
22. To be found on the Highways Agency website as the COBA (COst Benefit Assessment) methodology.
23. Department of Transport (1977b).
24. Department of Transport (1977a).
25. Department of Transport (1979), Paragraph 5.
26. Ministry of Transport (1980) and (1983).
27. Department of Transport (1981).
28. Department of Transport (1985).
29. Department of Transport (1987).
30. Department of Transport (1989), Paragraph 23.
31. Highways Agency. This was a continuously updated loose-leaf compendium of all the technical documents concerned with the design and economic appraisal of road schemes.

32 Department of Transport (1994).
33 Department for the Environment, Transport and the Regions (1997).
34 Departments of the Environment and of Transport (1993).
35 This is explained in Unit 2.1.4 in *Transport Assessment Guidance* (TAG) which itself is available online through the Department for Transport's WebTAG site.
36 The *Design Manual for Roads and Bridges* (Highways Agency) was originally published in 1992 as a series of loose-leaf volumes which included a volume of assessment. That has now been transferred to WebTAG which works in combination with the DMRB to provide definitive methodologies. Both are available through the Department for Transport website.
37 Department for the Environment, Transport and the Regions (1998).
38 Department for the Environment, Transport and the Regions (2000b), Paragraph 1.13.
39 WebTAG Unit 1.2.1, Paragraph 1.2.7.
40 WebTAG Unit 1.2.1, Paragraph 1.2.3.
41 Docherty and Shaw (2003).
42 Department for the Environment, Transport and the Regions (2000a). Available on the WebTAG (Transport Analysis Guidance) website.
43 Department for Transport (2007).
44 Wenban-Smith and Van Vuren (2009).
45 Coombe (2009).
46 Department for Transport (2008).
47 Department for Transport (2007).
48 Department of the Environment (1973a).

Chapter 20

The need for a new methodology to estimate travel demand

There has been a constant theme throughout the preceding chapters that the transport system should be treated as an entity, including all modes and the interfaces between them. The logic behind this stance is that the great majority of movements consist of a number of linked segments, often by differing modes, stretching from the journey start to its end and including the interfaces between segments. This system unity implies that investment should be from a single transport budget rather than individual modal budgets, and this, in turn, implies that there has to be a single assessment methodology. Chapter 19 described the development of the current methodology, but it is inherently weak, failing to reflect the need for interchange and making it impossible to mime inter-modal travel choices. Furthermore, the existing methodology focuses upon specific, often high-profile, modal projects such as the Edinburgh Tram, the London–Midlands high-speed railway and the third runway at Heathrow Airport, all projects which are restricted to providing just one segment within inter-modal journeys and which therefore rely on other modes to support them. This focus upon specific modal projects prevents the identification of the best deployment of a given budget over possible mixtures of other, perhaps smaller, but mutually supportive, projects. For example, the £600 million spent on the Edinburgh Tram may have been better spent on a range of improvements to the city's public transport, but there was no methodology to assess possible alternative bundles of actions. Exactly the same problem besets the investment of £34 billion in the London–Midlands high-speed rail proposal, an investment which will require improvements to the ancillary access modes with each supporting project having to be separately assessed. The existing methodology as described in WebTAG is designed to assess whether or not the investment in one project is likely to reach a threshold rate of return.

At the national scale, the inability of the existing methodology to cope with inter-modal journeys, including their embedded interchanges, prevents the proper assessment of actions to implement the contemporary policy of travel demand management: it is the fault-line between policy and its implementation. Before any projects or actions to manage demand may be assessed for their effectiveness, the present methodology as described in Chapter 19 must be abandoned and replaced by a new, purpose-designed methodology.

The objectives of a new methodology are as follows:

- To provide an ability to assess the value for money of any proposed modifications to the transport system presented as either a single, free-standing intervention or as a bundle of related actions.
- The modifications may range in scale from shifts in overall policy (e.g. changes in taxation) to simple, local improvements (e.g. a truck-climbing lane). The methodology must be adaptable in scale.
- The assessments must include the movement of both people and freight, since they share system capacity and cost.
- All modes and the interfaces between them must be included.
- The use of the 'soft' modes of walking and cycling must be included both as independent modes and as ancillary segments within inter-modal chains.
- Value-for-money assessments must be possible for all or any part of the transport system.
- The process must include changes in land use and the related trip ends, since land use both determines the geography of demand and is itself influenced by transport and utility services.
- The methodology must be robust and easy to use with minimal staff and computer resources.
- Resources should not be wasted on spurious 'accuracy': the need is for results of sufficient credibility to inform and validate decisions.
- Simple but credible results must be produced as soon as possible in order to convince decision-makers of the available support. Hence the whole structure must be designed to work, no matter how limited the data input but must be able to extend in area and detail. This suggests a programme of research, development, testing and refinement.

The structure of value-for-money assessments

Any policy or project assessment, large or small, requires:

- two descriptions of the transport network, the first without and the second with the intervention being assessed;
- predictions of the volume and patterns of movement through each of these two networks;
- predictions of the 'costs' of these movements in a number of different currencies: time, cash and, in particular, CO_2 emissions;
- by subtraction, the difference in the movement costs between the two networks – this is the 'benefit' to be credited to the intervention;
- estimates of the cost of implementing the intervention;
- finally, a calculation of the relationship between benefits and costs (the value for money).

The assessment process itself will be a fairly stable mechanism which will be gradually updated and refined, but which will retain its basic structure and function. In contrast, the database will be continuously updated as the transport system and the movements within it change.

There will be a number of differing possible approaches to this specification, but the continued adaptation of techniques which were originally created to assess, predict and provide interventions to improve traffic flows is not one of them. There now follows a suggested systematic technique which cannot be unique but which could initiate the development of the required methodology.

SALUTE: Simple Assessment of Land Use, Transport and the Environment

Development

- Development must begin with an initial, crude, 'baby-walker' version of SALUTE, eschewing complexity and subtlety, but sufficient to demonstrate whether the ideas are worthy of development.
- The crucial test is the description of the transport network. SALUTE will start with a very rough description of the transport network, although one that is able to be used for crude assessments. The description will be extended and refined over time and used for progressively better assessments.
- This means that the integrity of the network description must be maintained as the description fills out but without wholesale reconstruction of the database. Incremental additions and edits must be possible. This has a fundamental effect upon the design of the database.

The database: the system 'fabric'

- *Sections of 'way'*: lengths of the physical infrastructure of roads, railways, footpaths, pipes and wires which together make up the transport network carrying people, freight, energy, waste and information through from origin to destination. The entire set is needed, since, in combination, they both constrain and enable changes in land use.
  [Note: In current jargon representations of lengths of road within a computer model are called 'links', although the World Bank Highway Development Model does call them sections. 'Section' is preferred here as a general term to describe the lengths of track, pipe and wire that make the complete transport network.]
- *Nodes* are points defined by map coordinates and have two related roles. The first is to identify the ends of sections, pinning them to the map. The second is to mark places at which movement may switch from one section to another. A road junction will be a node, marking the end to the sections of road feeding it, but bus-stops and car-parks will also be nodes as places at which switches of mode take place.

The database: the system performance

- *Sections of mode*: reports of the performance (flows, times, speeds and capacity) of each of the sections of the infrastructure.
  [Note: the distinction between sections of 'ways' and of 'modes' allows some ways to carry more than one mode (roads – cars, trucks and buses) or railways (passenger and freight trains), but other ways will be mode-specific (footpaths, sewers). The distinction is necessary, since way capacity is shared and acts as an overall constraint, but each mode using the way has characteristics of its own.]
  A choice had to be made between:
  – assuming that all sections are two-way, one-way sections being represented by one direction being blanked off; *or*
  – assuming that all sections are one-way, two-way sections being represented by two complementary one-way sections.
  In some instances the section characteristics in one direction are different to those in the other: truck-climbing lanes are an example. These are important both in theory and in practice (because they generate very good values for money). This suggests that sections should be one-way.
  Single-track roads and railways work in alternating directions. This could be represented either by a two-way section with one direction or the other being made temporarily unavailable, or by two one-way sections, again with one direction or the other being alternately unavailable. Again, this is important, since the relief of such constrictions is very likely to be economically beneficial.
  Roads are usually two-way, with the flow in one direction influencing the flow in the other through the availability of opportunities to overtake. This does not have to be represented in detail: it is usual for roads to be given a ceiling capacity irrespective of the direction of flow.
  Although this seems to point to it being easier for all sections to be considered two-way, there are other complexities:
  – parking availability on one side of a two-way road may be different to the other so a road may be asymmetric;
  – although road traffic may be directional, footways are not, and sections including flanking pedestrian routes will inevitably have an element of two-way movement. This problem may be avoided by separating footways into separate way and flow sections.
  The quandary seems best resolved by describing the physical characteristics of sections of way independently of direction, but to distinguish directions when describing section performance.
- *Transfers*: these occur within nodes and report the time taken to transfer from an entry section to an exit section. The entry and exit may be of the same mode, as within a node representing a road junction, where the transfer would represent a turning penalty, or the transfer may be between sections of different modes representing an interface. The transfer will then report a delay time (which will be a function of disparate rhythms). Clearly, transfers are inherently directional and are performances, not physical fabric. Nodes may be simple such as a

bus-stop, or may be a complex collection of sub-nodes such as would be necessary to model a container port or an airport within which there were detailed micro-movements creating significant costs. Keeping transfer data separate from section data would enable the fabric and performance of the transport system to be easily updated and analysed.

The database: transport demand

The existing methodology of zones should be abandoned. It is geographically crude, reducing very important variations from address to address into a fudged, unrepresentative centroid. Worse, the related zone connectors and dummy nodes are fictions devoid of credibility.

Fortunately there is a ready alternative. Postcodes represent any number of delivery points from one upwards, with an average of about 12.5. Rich census data are published in the form of 'output areas' which are combinations of postcodes but with no postcode divided between output areas. There is a plethora of other available postcoded data, including the registered addresses of the keepers of motor vehicles, insurance, marketing and land use. Postcodes are also aligned to sections of road, although there is no exact mapping: roads may have different codes along their length and from one side of the road to the other, but it is not difficult to provide a table to proportion output area data over the constituent postcodes and then link those codes to sections of 'way' and 'mode'.

The need for zones to provide a location of origins and destinations would therefore be replaced in SALUTE by a combination of sections and postcodes. This implies that traffic entering a section through the entry node will be composed of traffic destined for the section plus through traffic on its way between other origins and destinations. The traffic leaving the section through the exit node will comprise the same through traffic plus the traffic originating in the section.

Polygons of land may be linked to each postcode which, in aggregate, will then cover the whole country. A land-use budget for each polygon will provide a country-wide pattern of land use. The performance of each mode and section serving a polygon of land uses will provide a comprehensive measure of accessibility by all modes, including services. The constraints and propensities to develop or redevelop land may then be related to these accessibilities.

The descriptive statistics used to calculate transport demand will cover all the property served directly or indirectly by the section, including not only the property fronting directly on to the section itself, but also the property served by minor roads accessed from the section, but not included within the network description. This definition assumes that all land and property within the entire study area will be allocated to one section or another, even in the early stages in the development of the database when the number of sections will be limited. As the network is extended by the inclusion of additional nodes and more side-roads, the transport demand data will be subdivided too – when a section is subdivided by a new node connecting to an additional side road, the transport demand data for the original, undivided section will be redistributed to the subdivided and additional sections.

Travel generation: at the simplest level the propensity to travel may be represented by trip rates in the style of those found in Ponteland and shown in Figure 19.7. However, these were unit rates per household defined by just two explanatory variables: household size and car availability. This should be expanded: car availability is a proxy for car service levels and similar measures of service by the other modes should also be included as additional explanatory variables. Bike ownership and the ability to ride it, constraints on walking time and distance and, crucially, public transport proximity and frequency should be considered. Research may show that the household is not the best basis for unit rates and that floor space is more appropriate and general. In the longer term modern satellite mapping may produce cheap, accurate data on roofed space, but, in any event, the need is for the generations of movement to be a predictable product of the nature and intensity in land use within each of the polygons.

Estimating the amount of movement will be simplified by a presumption that the number of journeys destined for a section per every 24 hours will exactly match the number of journeys originating along it. (In the terminology of traditional travel demand models, the number of generated trips will equal the number of attracted trips.)

[Note: this is *not* to say that all journeys are the one or other half of a return journey: although a journey from A to B must be balanced by another journey leaving B, the assumption does require this further journey to return to A. It may go to C and then on to D. The assumption is therefore no more than an extension of considering any journey as a chain of segments with the destination of one segment being the origin of the next. This has the sensible implication that nowhere do significantly more people arrive than leave.]

This leads naturally to a further extension. For any individual, the dwell time between arriving somewhere and leaving again becomes significant. For example, the numbers of people transferring to buses at a node representing a bus-stop will equal the numbers entering from other modal sections (usually pedestrian ways) and the dwell times at the node will reflect service rhythm. On the other hand, the numbers of people arriving at, say, a shopping mall will also equal the numbers leaving it, but the length and spread of dwell times will be completely different. Overall they will reflect the accumulation of people in the mall and will give an indication of parking demand.

In a still further extension of the same principle, if an individual's travel and dwell times are summed, the result should be exactly 24 hours. Detailed time budgets will be reflections of lifestyle and will also display the opportunity costs of changes in travel behaviour. This has the merit of providing a finite and checkable control. Opportunity costs in money terms are very difficult to determine, since an individual's travel budget is unknowable: the only certainty is that an unemployed man will have a far lower cash budget than Richard Branson. However, both have a common time budget of exactly 24 hours. It follows that a population of two million has an aggregate of 48 million hours per day, no more and no less, and this provides a very powerful constraint upon modelled estimates.

This is a universal constraint: people, freight, vehicles and the infrastructure all exist for 24 hours a day, every minute of which has a 'cost' and which may be used either in movement or be left fallow. Costs are driven by the proportion of time that vehicles and infrastructure are being used: time budgets within the working transport system are flags of productivity. Figure 10.5 shows costs per hour of modes and vehicles based on assumed hours of work, but if those hours are changed the rated costs will change too. Assessing opportunity costs and making adjustments to time budgets is a major component to decisions to relocate, be it household relocation to be 'nearer' to more suitable destinations, or a commercial relocation to improve customer footfall, supply costs, etc.

Distribution: origins are fixed by generating land use, although the locations are now proposed to be defined by sections of the network fabric rather than zones. Destinations are defined only by function, not location. This precludes the definition of routes and the estimation of flows along their component sections. Given that it would be impossible to gather data on every movement, the problem facing the transport planner is how to expand sample data into an estimate of the totality of movement and then to make a similar estimate for a future in which the land uses and possible destinations will have changed. The only way in which future destinations may be predicted, given that they may not yet even exist, is to derive some principles by which destinations are chosen, apply those principles to the status quo to create a hypothetical pattern of movement, compare that hypothetical pattern with the actual one as surveyed (the 'backcasting' test) and, if the patterns are more or less aligned, use the same principles to predict future movement between the origins and destinations implied by future land uses. If the current and hypothetical pattern does not align, the theory thought to be driving travel choice will have to be recalibrated.

The existing principle is that choice of destination is driven by 'gravity', that people are more likely to go to a larger destination than a smaller one and less likely to go to those further away than to those that are nearer. This principle is currently used to create hypothetical origin + destination matrices describing the movements between zones. Earlier chapters have found two faults with this theory, in addition to the fact that it has never been properly tested by 'backcasting'. The first fault is one of application: the definitions of 'nearer' and 'further away' are inadequate, being based either on generalised cost and travel times by car, or on some arbitrary hybrid of car and public transport costs. The second is one of principle: that a major influence upon the choice of destination is not just travel time or distance but the availability of parking. That view has been taken further with the assertion that much of the relocation of shops, offices, homes and employment which has changed the structure of urban areas over the past 50 years or so has been driven by the need for more parking space.

This suggests that the choice of destination and of mode, particularly the choice between car and public transport, is driven by an amalgam of parking availability and journey characteristics – between moving and stopping. More needs to be known about travel choices: it seems that for some choices the mode is chosen first followed by the destination, but in others the destination determines the mode. For example, a car owner living in the home counties and working in the London financial district has a fixed commuting destination, and the transport system makes the choice of public transport virtually inevitable, but for other journeys the choice of car will come first, colouring the choice of destination. Gravity principles do not appear to map very well on to this variability in choice. However, this may not matter. The fact that the principles behind the creation of hypothetical patterns of movement do not mime the actual choice mechanism is of no concern, so long as it produces results which are compatible with reality. This is no more that treating the ways in which travel choices are made as a black box, the contents of which are unknown, but which may nonetheless be represented by gravity principle without too much harm. However, the dearth of proper testing and validation must cast doubts upon whether methodology based on gravity really does produce credible synthetic origin + destination matrices.

It seems that some journeys made for a specific purpose and to a specific destination are prevented from being made by car either by the total realism of the lack of a car or by the lack of a parking space. It is another demonstration of transport not being entirely a matter of movement, but of pausing or stopping at interfaces, terminals and destinations, actions which define journeys rather than the journey itself. Lane argued that no journey was worthwhile unless the resultant dwell time was twice as long as the return travel time.[1]

If this is accepted, then the new version of the generation rates will be a list of destinations by their function but not by their location, coupled with the expected dwell times at each and the preferred mode of travel for the first segment of the journey. The rates will have to be based on new surveys similar in process to the ongoing National Travel Survey but seeking far more data about choice mechanisms rather than the outcomes of those mechanisms. It will be noted that the journey purpose is only inferred by the function at the destination: this reflects the proposition that the purpose behind a journey is of no significance compared to the characteristics of the destination: it does not matter to the transport system whether a journey to an office block is to work at a desk, to empty cash out of the coffee machine or to polish the floor. It is a journey to a place at which there is a function that makes the journey desirable.

This still leaves the location of the destination and the route to be travelled to be determined. In the existing methodology, using gravity principles to construct an O+D matrix, the cells of which are then 'assigned' to the network, requires swathes of computing time, making travel prediction an expensive exercise. One feasible alternative seems to be counter-intuitive. The purpose of the travel modelling exercise is to predict the section flows and their costs in travel time and CO_2 emissions. For this, the trace of individual journeys is unnecessary. For example, if a number of people arrive at a bus-stop from a variety of postcodes, exactly the same number will leave by bus, but they will get off at a number of different stops. There is no need to forge a link between a departure from a particular postcode with an arrival at a particular bus-stop: all that matters is that a person walked from a postcode to a bus-stop and a person travelled by bus from that stop to another. Whether or not they are the same person is immaterial.

This is tantamount to estimating flow volumes and costs by assigning disassociated segments of journeys to sections of the network rather than by assigning whole end-to-end journeys to complete routes. The aggregate effect should be the same: the total number of segments and their allocation to sections will be as it would be if the segments were to be chained in end-to-end journeys.

However, the location of destinations remains undefined. But that is right, because one of the required attributes of the model is to cope with an ever-changing urban structure in which functions and their associated journey destinations shift geographically. So far, the definition of SALUTE requires the predicted flows along sections between nodes to be recalculated at each successive node by the addition of transfers from other sections and the subtraction of transfers to other sections. The sources of the additions are irrelevant. At each node a proportion of the flow will transfer to another section: for a bus route the biggest proportion is likely to transfer to the next section along the route, with smaller proportions transferring to other sections connected to the node (effectively getting off the bus). This clearly requires a list of the proportions of entries into a node which transfer and exit by another section. That list is fundamental to the basis of prediction by segments rather than complete predetermined, end-to-end journeys.

These lists of proportions will reflect the functions served by the sections leading away from the node and therefore may only be calculated once the land-use budgets linked to all sections have been determined. It is here that a use for the gravity principle may be found. The land uses to which the exit sections from a node provide access need to be weighted; otherwise the accessible land uses would be unlimited. A weighting by time or distance using the gravity principle would be appropriate.

If all modal exit sections from nodes have proportions which sum to unity, then modal arrivals will transfer within the mode and will either find a destination function of the right nature in the land-use polygon served by that section or continue on to the next node. This effectively means that passengers, once they have set out from a postcode by a nominated mode along a relevant section, will repeatedly, node by node, transfer to new sections until a suitable destination is found. This 'organic' determination of destinations by extending routes node by node until a suitable destination is encountered is a reworking of the previous 'intervening opportunities' model.[2] Of course the result would not be known as a collection of 'routes' from given origins and destinations as it is in the existing methodology: it would be a pragmatic allocation of journey segments bundled together as section flows and split into proportions at each node for transfer to a subsequent section. It follows that the components of any flow along a section will not be identifiable by either the preceding section or by the location of its final destination.

The interrelated assumptions and principles are as follows:

- Movements of people and freight may be seen as a chain of segments.
- The destination of one segment is always the origin of the next.
- The numbers arriving at a node are always matched by the numbers leaving.
- Origins of journeys are always predetermined either by the generations calculated as a function of land uses or as an aggregate of previous arrivals.
- The dwell times may be no more than necessary to continue a journey, in which case they will reflect the interplay of modal rhythms at the time, or dwell times may reflect personal activity at a destination chosen by function but not location.

- The location will be identified by the model using intervening opportunities with the acceptance or rejection of each possible destination being determined by the proportionate transfers within a succession of nodes.
- In any event the sum of travel and dwell times in any one day must be exactly 24 hours per head of population.
- The aggregate 'cost' of movement will be the aggregate over all sections of the time, fuel and CO_2 consumed.
- The task is to design interventions which meet a defined thresholds level of cost: that is, to achieve desirable levels of performance.

Interchanges, car-parks and terminals: in the past, transport planning has been very concerned with moving traffic and has paid relatively little attention to the ends of journeys. This is unfortunate:

- Except for cruising in its various forms, there is little or no intrinsic value in travel – the purpose is to get to the destination, and so it is the attributes of destinations that create travel.
- The stationary vehicle at a destination demands space, very often road space, for parking or loading and unloading, and this restricts the amount of road space for moving traffic. Striking a balance between the needs of stationary and moving traffic is crucial, and adsorbs an immense and continuing resource in regulations, meters, enforcement and legal processes.
- Difficulties and costs of parking near the origin and destination doors are a major determinant of the choices of destination and mode.

The concentration on the movement of traffic flow in the past has precluded an analysis of door-to-door transport. It would be unwise to study railways by concentrating on the movement of trains to the exclusion of station working, and it is just as unwise to concentrate on traffic flow to the exclusion of the use of land and kerb space as destinations.

The suggested definitions of nodes and of the transfers within them would enable, but not require, the detailed workings of complex interfaces at ports and transshipment points. If short micro-movements were included as sections containing descriptions of rhythms, the throughputs and delays could be estimated, giving a far more accurate idea of transit times and costs. These would still not be precise, but they would be good enough to inform plans to update the system as a whole

Car-parking is the black hole in transport modelling. Experience shows it to be a crucial component in travel choices and, by aggregation of those choices, in land use and development. It is a major component of the decentralisation and dispersal of land uses that has created the virtual city. Detailing these effects is difficult: micro-detail would require volumes of data and computer time but, looking towards other terminal facilities for inspiration, by fitting the number of required platform or quay hours into the number of available space hours offers a clue. Trains and ships require known dwell times for loading, unloading and servicing which, in aggregate, have to be satisfied: efficiency depends on predict and provide.

The demand for parking cannot be met through a predict-and-provide mechanism. The number of space hours required to satisfy unconstrained demand cannot be provided within the land-use budgets of dense central areas – it has been asserted that the shortfall may only be met by public transport and its attribute of avoiding the need for parking space. In modelling terms the availability of space hours would have to be a variable used in the tactical calculation of the proportions of in-node transfers to exit sections by car. The problem with that in anything but the short term would be too near the truth. Car flows would be repeatedly diverted away from areas with inadequate parking, creating additional car kilometrage in the search for an acceptable destination.

Land-use dispositions

In reality, longer term, corporate decisions to relocate away from congested areas to suburban, even peripheral, malls, office parks, etc. with more parking space hours has relieved the pressure on inadequate parking in central areas. Consequently, the model structure of SALUTE may be able to ape the trends that are apparent on the ground by two interconnected mechanisms. First, to estimate the pressure to relocate by sensing whether the numbers of people arriving at a location with parking and access problems are sufficient for it to remain viable. The methodology being suggested does not predetermine journey destinations: journeys are extended without constraint until an acceptable destination is found. Inadequate parking will effectively deter arrivals. Second, to estimate the land-use changes to respond to the pressures to relocate. The land-use polygons related to each postcode and section will report land availability and the section characteristics will define its 'accessibility', not only by roads and vehicles, but also by the pipes and wires providing services and utilities. These data could well provide relative propensities to develop which could be used to update the land-use map represented by the polygons.

The real problem facing us is not to model and predict the development of the virtual city, but to assess the effectiveness of policies to prevent it. The migration of activity away from city centres may be driven by the aggregation of a multitude of personal and corporate decisions which cannot be dictated by edict. Individuals will have to be presented with transport landscapes which induce them to use the functions in the dense central areas – in practice this implies the use of public transport to avoid approach congestion and difficulties in parking. If successful, that will sustain the footfalls necessary to maintain the economic viability of the functions within the central area and relieve pressures for them to relocate.

British town and country planning appears to be at something of a crossroads. The roots were in countering poor living conditions both within dwellings and in urban areas in general. Undesirable crowding and the proximity of noxious land uses were major initial concerns. But the prevention of undesirable aspects of the environment grew to include fostering desirable features such as adequate recreation and leisure facilities, and ensuring that schools, shops, hospitals, etc. were provided. The agenda has changed: car use changed the impact of distance and expanded the areas served by functions. This has resulted in facilities becoming larger and serving wider areas.

Schools, hospitals, shops and firms have all grown in size and in the range of their functions, while at the same time requiring more person-kilometres to get to them. Dispersal rather than congestion has become the background to planning.

The reduction of the slum housing problem, the lack of recreational space and horrendous industrial pollution has resulted in planning being loosened from its roots while other, more modern concerns have taken their place. Full employment which seemed assured in the middle years of the twentieth century has vanished and one objective of town planning is now to provide sites and services to generate jobs. Linked to that is a drive to foster rather than contain development. Surprisingly, the worldwide concern with pollution and climate change has not been the prime concern of the planning system. Most plans mention it, but decisions and permissions do not appear to be driven by an objective to slow or reduce CO_2 emissions, and yet recent history has shown the rise in travel, in the fuel burn and in the land take which are related to decentralisation and dispersal of urban functions into the virtual city – issues that have not been adequately addressed by the planning system.

If we are to mount the control of CO_2 emissions as a major national objective, town and country planning has to be mobilised to manage the trend towards the virtual city. This needs the CO_2 budget associated with major applications for planning consent to be an element in the determination of the application. In turn this would demand some estimate of the journey to work by mode, speed and emission, and that would have to be done by a model of the SALUTE style. That is in effect an assertion that major land-use developments are interventions in the transport system in the same way as is a road proposal or any other change in the transport system.

Transport landscapes

This term, first introduced in Chapter 2, covers the travel opportunities and choices that are perceived by people who are about to embark upon a journey. The landscape will change by time of day, by the reasons for the journey, by personal attributes and abilities, and, most of all, by the services on offer. Perceptions will not be of the real facts, but will be coloured by prejudice and ignorance: car owners may well be ignorant of public transport services, an ignorance sustained by prejudices barring them from even investigating service levels. Such attitudes may only be counteracted by publicity and marketing, and that means good market research feeding aggressive promotion. The objective is not to improve public transport patronage and revenues per se, but to support the urban centres and the functions and businesses within them.

Making people aware of service levels is necessary but incomplete. The services themselves must induce travel choices which discourage further growth of the virtual city. The usual approach is stick and carrot – to make unsustainable choices less attractive and sustainable ones more attractive. The difficulty is to get the balance right: car travel is undeniably attractive – infinitely frequent at all hours to any destination of choice, attributes which public transport cannot possibly match. Use of cars is therefore the default which the public will inevitably adopt unless there is reason not to. The only reason not to is the difficulty of parking. Policies to sustain central areas must therefore not lean too heavily on the stick but make sure that the carrot is attractive enough for people to respond by leaving their cars at home and using public transport instead.

The perceptions of transport landscapes must be investigated, but enhancing the use of public transport has been dogged by the failure to recognise that the choice is not between public transport and cars in principle but in travel to a limited number of destinations and at a limited range of times: policies to change service levels and the perceptions of them need to be geographically selective. Transport landscapes are not pictures; they are movies which zoom on to very specific places.

The responses to transport landscapes are represented in travel demand models of the traditional type by the generation rates akin to those shown for Ponteland in Figure 19.7. The suggestion for SALUTE is that there should be tariffs of dynamic rates reflecting shifting service levels and representing the perceived transport landscape. These would be more responsive to the geographical differences in possible destinations and would thereof make the testing of policy options more defensible. SALUTE, or something similar, is necessary to define the interventions most likely to be successful and to demonstrate the consequences of not doing anything, or of doing something that is ineffective.

Notes

1 Lane (1972).
2 Haggett (1965, p. 46).

Chapter 21

Planning sustainable transport
The agenda

The objective

The objective is to contain the growth in the emissions of CO_2, both an objective in its own right and as a proxy for other objectives such as restraining the urban invasion of agricultural land. The strategy is to assess the aggregate emission due to the use of the transport system as an entity and to have an ability to predict the changes in emissions created by transport policies, schemes and actions, and then to monitor the subsequent effects in order to judge whether wise decisions have been made. This highlights the need for a methodology to predict and monitor.

The planning methodology

The transport system and the land uses it serves are constantly changing. If circumstances and problems are dynamic, then the methods of dealing with them have to be dynamic too, with policies and actions being adjusted to meet changing circumstances. The need is for an ability to steer decisions to cope with constant change rather than the traditional, fixed plans to be delivered by a set date – good management rather than designing a rigid outcome. The fundamental component of methodologies able to cope with incessant change is effective monitoring and feedback to sense both the problems and the effectiveness of the actions designed to cope with them, a cybernetic system based on error-actuated feedback.

Day-by-day changes in the land-use/transport system are small and insignificant, but they may sum to an important, although, at the time, almost imperceptible, trend: for example, the changes in urban structure since car ownership first began to expand have been very substantial, obvious now in retrospect but far less obvious as they occurred. Such trends need to be recognised early, since they may have become irreversible by the time they are obvious. The early detection of significant trends is only possible by, first, constant monitoring, and, second, by having the means to test hypothetical scenarios based on the current small changes expanding later into a significant trend.

Figure 21.1 is a copy of Figure 3.4 and displays the architecture of such a dynamic planning and management system.

Planning sustainable transport: the agenda 393

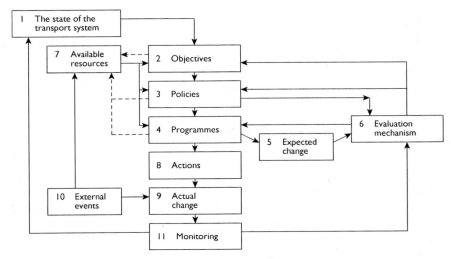

Figure 21.1 A recursive, flexible planning process (based on Figure 3.4)

The state of the transport system (Figure 21.1, box 1)

Chapter 1 asserted that the description of the transport system and the uses being made of it should include all the modes by which people, goods, energy, information and waste are moved, together with the interfaces between modes and terminals. The reasons behind this were as follows:

- All movements are from a starting point through to a finishing point.
- With very few exceptions, end-to-end movements by both passengers and freight are not confined to a single mode throughout their length. Even simple car journeys involve the finding, capturing and retention of a parking space and then walking to the destination, all crucial segments within a complete door-to-door journey.
- The quest for sustainability requires the use of non-car modes for all or part of many journeys with a consequent focus upon interchanges of all types from the almost trivial, such as parking places or bus-stops, through to complex railway stations, airports and park-and-ride sites.
- All transport modes have their signature rhythms characterised by the frequency and capacity of service. The disparity between rhythms at interfaces implies unavoidable delays which influence decisions and costs.
- Such delays are an important component of people's perceptions of the 'transport landscape' within which they have to make their transport choices.
- Their choices of end-to-end movements are perceived as a chain of segments, each linked to those before and after at interchanges.
- Both passenger and freight movements thread their way through the transport system seen as a whole, not as a bundle of separate modes. The state of the

land-use/transport system will be sensed at a particular point in time and then repeated at regular intervals in order to monitor changes in the system due to deliberate interventions (the actions described in Figure 21.1, box 8) and to the underlying trends in external imposed events (described in Figure 21.1, box 10).
- Over time there have been substantial shifts in the uses of modes. Energy, in the form of coal which used to be delivered by wheeled vehicles to nearly every address in the country, is now delivered by pipe and wire; information used to be dependent on letters and newspapers transported by train and lorry, and then delivered on foot, but now much of it is transmitted by cable; retailing and industry are being transformed by electronic ordering, logistics and payment. Any system designed to forecast uses of the transport system must cater for scenarios which include similar future changes of mode.
- Transport demand is a derivative of constantly changing land uses with site developments, each heavily influenced by the available service levels by roads, pipes and wires. Comprehensive measures of accessibility are therefore needed to estimate the probability of land developments which will later generate movement. Any transport model must cope with the interactive, self-referential relationships between land use and transport, and should therefore sense the quality and extent of accessibility by all modes.

The state of the transport system (Figure 21.1, box 1) must be in a form which will enable the assessment of future patterns of both land use and movement driven by:

- trends due to the myriad immediate, short- and long-term decisions made by individuals and by organisations;
- external events such as changes in global fuel prices;
- deliberate interventions, actions and policies – these may range from small, detailed projects, such as a road improvement, through to a nationally pervasive change, such as an alteration in taxation, or it could be a set of interlinked actions, such as a raft of railway electrification schemes.

This suggests a methodology that is able to describe the state of the transport system at differing times and at different scales ranging from a 'National Transport Model' supplanting the existing model,[1] down to small interventions such as a truck-climbing lane. This implies a structured database designed to store detailed local data which may then be aggregated up to a national level. This sounds daunting, but it is no different to the Census or to the geographical database held by the Ordnance Survey.

A methodology to describe the present or to predict the future state of the transport system was suggested in Chapter 20 and is radically different to the conventions set out in the official WebTAG site and described in Chapter 19. That comprises four distinct stages:

1 A description of the numbers of journeys (trips) starting and finishing in each one of a set of zones, estimated as a function of the land uses (either directly or as

represented by populations, floor spaces, etc.). This is called the trip-generation stage.
2   The allocation of the number of trips calculated in the trip-generation stage to the cells of an 'origin + destination matrix' with the rows representing origin zones and the columns the destination zones. The allocation is made by a mathematical model based on the gravity principle in which the probability of a trip starting in a particular origin zone and going to a particular destination zone is held to be in proportion to the 'attractiveness' of the destination zone (measured in the numbers of trips estimated to arrive there as predicted by the 'trip-generation stage'), but in inverse proportion to the cost of getting there. The creation of an origin + destination matrix in this way is called the 'trip-distribution stage'.
3   The splitting of the numbers of trips in each cell of the origin + destination matrix between different main modes of transport (particularly between public and private transport). This is called the 'modal split stage' and is based on some arcane mathematics designed to reflect relative journey costs.
4   The allocation of the trips in the origin, destination and mode matrix (after the previous stage it now has three dimensions) to particular routes from the origins to the destinations. This requires a computer description of the transport network made up of sections of road (called 'links' in the jargon) between pairs of nodes (junctions). This network has to be supplemented by imaginary links between arbitrarily nominated points at the centre of each zone at which all the generations of the zone are concentrated (called zone centroids), and equally imaginary nodes in the real network at which the real and imaginary links connect. This process is called the 'assignment stage'. At the end of the assignment stage there is an estimated traffic flow along each link.

This four-stage structure cannot possibly represent reality. It cannot cope with multi-modal journeys, nor with freight movements, nor with interchanges, nor, consequently, with whole end-to-end journeys and their costs.

The alternative being proposed is crucially based on an ability to describe and forecast inter-modal movements using a realistic description of the complete transport system, including all interfaces. The first step in achieving this is to split the description of the transport system into two parts:

1   the system fabric – a description of the physical infrastructure in the form of sections of 'way' (roads, tracks, paths, pipes and wires);
2   the system performance – a description of the speeds and volumes carried along each section by each 'mode' (private cars, lorries, buses, trains, etc.).

Although 'ways' and 'modes' may be similar, even coincident, they are, nonetheless, distinct: 'ways' are sections of infrastructure, but 'modes' are sections of use and performance. A section of road will be a 'way', but the flows of cars, public transport and freight are all separate 'modes' using the same 'way', each with their separate but related volumes, speeds, performances and pollutions.

Both the fabric of the ways and the performance of the modes are described by 'sections', each one linking a pair of 'nodes', characterised by their geographical position, and so pinning the sections on to the map. Nodes may represent either junctions within the fabric of ways, or they may be interfaces including bus-stops, stations, car-parks, ports, etc. Every node will have entrances and exits formed by modal sections. Within each node there will be 'transfers', each linking an entry section to an exit section. These are not representations of physical fabric, but of performance. Where a transfer is between sections of the same mode, as in a road junction, it will report the turning delays incurred within the junction; if it is between sections of different modes, as in an interface, the transfer will report the sum of the times taken within the node to move from the one modal entry to the modal exit plus the waiting times due to disparate modal rhythms.

Movement origins are to be calculated as functions of land use in a similar way to previous models. However, the locations of these land uses are not to be given by zone (a concept to be abandoned), but by the sections of fabric that serve them. The easiest method of doing this is to provide look-up lists of the postcodes within each census output area and to identify the sections of fabric that serve them. (In many instances, where postcodes are linked to road names, the sections and the postcodes they serve will be obvious.) Such lists will link census data to sections of the transport network. Data for non-residential modes will have to be gleaned, as at present, from rating and employment records, etc. These are all postcoded and therefore capable of being allocated to sections. By allocating all polygons of land served, either directly or indirectly, by particular sections, this process will create a complete inventory of land uses and of the infrastrucure serving them. This should be capable of being checked by modern satellite technology. The land-use inventory will identify vacant and underused land, with predictions of the likely changes in use being facilitated by the data about the infrastructure serving it, including the pipes and wires.

The numbers of movements, their timings, their initial modes and their destinations by function (but not by location) will be estimated by using look-up tables containing the estimated numbers of movements per item of land use using methods similar to the existing generation rates. However, the range of explanatory parameters must be extended to include all transport service levels, no longer confined to car availability. In combination, these parameters will describe the perceived 'transport landscape'.

The distribution stage (based on the gravity principle) together with both modal split and assignment is to be abandoned completely, being replaced by an entirely new, organic modelling architecture designed to mime the use of the entire, coherent inter-modal transport system, incorporating the interfaces and their use. This is to be based upon the following principles:

- The inclusion of modal choice within the initial estimates of the numbers of movements generated by land uses. This is vital, since modal choice is, first, a reflection of the transport landscape, and, second, is a major policy target to be reached by the deliberate manipulation of that landscape in order to engender the use of modes with lower emissions.

- A rejection of the concept of the origin + destination matrix created by mathematical model. Destinations by location would not be predetermined, although destinations by function would be produced by the generation rates associated with land uses. These rates will have to be created by extending the existing empirical data.
- Counter-intuitively, attempts to model entire movements from origins to destinations – from A to B – will be avoided since it would need massive databases feeding large, complex and expensive computer models. The vital task is not to predict such journeys per se but to estimate the vehicle- and person-kilometres, speeds, delays and CO_2 emissions spawned by the movements generated by a particular pattern of land uses as they move through a particular transport network. That is best done by aggregating data for each of the sections and interfaces of which the transport system is composed.
- The characteristics of the flow along each section of fabric will begin by predicting the movement from one node to the next along the section linking them, effectively treating the nodes as localised origins and destinations. This implies that the strings of segments of which complete A to B movements are composed, are being uncoupled and predicted independently. This is no more than asserting that, for example, it is not important to know whether a person alighting at a particular bus-stop is the same person as that boarding at a particular previous stop: all that a model needs to predict is the numbers boarding and alighting at each stop, and riding along each section, not where each of them is coming from or going to.
- This implies a crucial focus upon the function and activity at each of the nodes, requiring an expansion of the data describing the transfers within the nodes. The performance of the transfers, expressed as the time taken to move from an entry section to an exit section plus any waiting time provoked by disparities of rhythm, must be extended to form a table which includes estimates of the numbers making the transfer. This may be done by including the proportions of those entering a node by one entry section and leaving by each of the possible exit sections. For example, if the node were a road junction, the transfer table would show not only the turning penalties as surcharges in time, but also the proportion of entering vehicles making each of the possible turns. If the node were a bus-stop, the transfer table for each of the bus-mode entry sections would show, not only the time penalties incurred in transferring to each of the possible exit sections, but also the expected proportions of passengers making that transfer. One transfer is likely to be dominant, that on to the onward section of the route. This will be reported as the proportion of the on-board passengers staying on the bus: their transfer cost will be no more than the dwell time. Passengers getting off the bus will be proportionately divided between transferring to one or other of the exit sections: these may be pedestrian paths or, perhaps, another bus route, or a train. The table of proportions of each entry flow transferring to each of the exit sections will amount to a node-specific origin + destination matrix displaying the proportions of each entry flow transferring to the available exit sections. These tabled proportions of entry movements making transfers are crucial. They

could, of course, be derived from observations, but collecting field data on all possible transfers would be a mammoth task. A more tractable technique would be to calculate hypothetical proportions as a function of the land uses to which each of the exit sections provide access.
- This architecture, using the fabric sections to replace zones in describing the geography of land uses and of their related origins and destinations, means that the flow entering a section from the node at one end will be composed of the movements destined for that section, a number determined by the attributes of the land uses it serves, plus the movements using the section as part of a through route. Similarly, the flows leaving the section will be the sum of those through movements plus the movements generated by the land uses served by the section. The total flow exiting from a section will form the entry flow into the terminating node within which the flow will be distributed to the exit sections. This architecture avoids identifying the complete origin to destination flows characterised by origin + destination matrices, replacing it with organic estimates of flows section-by-section.

Time budgets

A further major suggested difference between the old four-stage methodology and the new proposal is an extension of the generation data to include dwell times in addition to the times on the move. This then accounts for the whole 24-hour day. The reasons for this are as follows:

- Everything and everybody exists for 24 hours per day which provides an accountable cross-check.
- This, in itself, provides a fixed constraint upon alternative deployments of time: for people, for equipment and for cargo-in-transit.
- Personal time budgets showing the deployment of each day's 24 hours are a measure of lifestyle and therefore a method of detecting changing lifestyles. If, for instance, a family move from a suburb to a low-density development in the countryside – into the virtual city – they will have to spend more time travelling, and may well alter the range of their activities and the destinations they visit. They will react to their altered transport landscape, perhaps in ways that are desirable and for which they made the move, perhaps in ways they had not considered.
- The aggregates of dwell times at destinations will give an estimate of the on-site population at any one time, creating a measure of parking demand.

From this it follows that the demand for travel, movement and dwell times will provide measures of the volumes of traffic and loadings but also of stopped and delay times – a major explanatory variable ignored by existing methodology.

The prime objectives (Figure 21.1, box 2)

The touchstone of sustainability, established in Chapter 1, is defined as the containment of CO_2 emissions, recognising four related attributes:

1. Although the relationship between CO_2 emissions, the increase in atmospheric CO_2 and climate change is not definitively proven, there are strong possibilities that links of some sort do exist. It is wise to assume that human activity is causing climate change through CO_2 emissions since, if that assumption were to be shown later to have been wrong, little harm will have been done: however, if the assumption turns out to have been correct, but no remedial action had been taken, then irreversible, even terminal damage will have been done to the planet.
2. CO_2 is important in its own right, but it could also reasonably stand proxy for other pollutants which, if not exactly pro rata with CO_2, are close enough for the proxy to be valid.
3. Policies to contain the emission of CO_2 would collaterally achieve other targets. In particular, efforts to reduce person- and vehicle-kilometres would imply the control of the density and spread of urban development – objectives in their own right.
4. CO_2 emissions are best expressed as an aggregate quantity measured in tonnes per annum rather than as a rate of grams per vehicle- or person-kilometre, although such measures may be components of the overall emission. This is because rates are too easily fudged – for example, the rates could be reduced by vehicle design and loadings, but the aggregate emission would be driven up by extended travel distances.

The objective of containing CO_2 emissions subsumes a general principle of avoiding the segmentation of overall issues into their component parts and then setting independent measures of effectiveness for each. For example, if reduced emission per vehicle-kilometre is treated as an independent objective, it could be achieved by reducing congestion, so raising fuel efficiency, but that would be best done by dispersing traffic over wider areas, increasing the number of vehicle-kilometres and nullifying part of, or even all, the improvements in the rate of fuel burn. Setting specific, self-contained targets may have contrary results: for example, road user charging may reduce congestion and low, inefficient speeds, but if it does so by pushing traffic out into relatively undeveloped areas, the total fuel burn may well rise.

There will be other objectives, both national and local, defined in box 2, some of which may be implied by the prime aim of controlling CO_2 such as limiting 'food miles'.[2] Other objectives may be separate: reducing the dangers and consequences of road traffic accidents will have only a loose connection with CO_2 emission. In any event, two principles have been offered:

1. Each objective should have a related measure by which the effectiveness of actions may be assessed.
2. There should not be a tariff of relative worth through which lack of effectiveness of one action may be offset by the success of another. This merely obscures failures to meet some objectives, hiding the failure behind the success in meeting others. In particular, pseudo-cash values should not be used: putting a currency symbol in front of a number does not make it into a unit of account.

Policies (Figure 21.1, box 3)

The authorities responsible for the development and management of the land-use/transport system will have to define policies designed to deliver the objectives. These will provide the framework for specific actions, schemes and projects: an example would be that contained in PPG13, to manage the volume of movement so that it fits into the system capability rather than expand the capability to accommodate unmanaged growth, or a policy to simulate international trade. Such policies should have measures by which the effectiveness of the programmes and actions designed to deliver them may be monitored.

Programmes (Figure 21.1, box 4)

These are the proposed projects, schemes and legislative changes designed to deliver the policies specified in box 3. Once again, they should be married to criteria by which their success or failure may be judged.

The predictive methodology (Figure 21.1, boxes 5 and 6)

The backbone of this book is formed by a set of interlinked propositions:

- That society, both as individuals and through the medium of the elected government, should pursue comprehensive polices of sustainability.
- That the touchstone of those policies should be minimising the emission of CO_2.
- In transport there are no easy panaceas because transport and land use are inextricably intertwined so that policies have repercussive effects which may be complex and even counter-intuitive.
- The complexity is reinforced by transport movements themselves being inter-modal combinations of segments on foot and by vehicle interconnected at interchanges which are themselves crucial parts of the transport system.
- Hence, sustainable transport planning must be concerned with the entire transport system, not with separated modes and projects.
- Given that land use and transport are fundamentally interlinked, the prediction of consequential changes in land use must be an integral part of the assessment policies and of any of the actions taken to implement those policies.
- Such assessment is vital for three clear reasons:
  1. The complexity of the land-use/transport system ensures that the results of decisions and actions may differ from the intentions, and so some predictive assessment is necessary before actions are taken.
  2. Identifying actions which will implement effective policy cannot be a matter of hunch – there has to be rigorous assessment of the effectiveness of past decisions. A memory of past successes and failures must inform future decisions, but it must be done within the context of the deployment of limited resources within the overall transport system.

3   The assessment mechanism must be able to assess scenarios of change driven, not by policy, but by underlying, perhaps insidious, trends and external forces.

The nub of this book is not the suggested policies, programmes and actions but the methodology to assess their predicted and actual effectiveness. The basic question to be asked of any proposed intervention is: 'What will be the net effect upon the tonnage of emitted CO_2?' and then later, 'What was the effect?' The answers to these questions are not needed to enable political preening or media finger-pointing, but must be fed back to adjust, clarify and refine policy as shown in Figure 21.1. The crux is not just the identification of CO_2 as the touchstone, but the identification of a methodology to predict it.

The total emission of CO_2 due to transport is the product of:

- The method of transport used. This is best measured in the emissions per kilometre of unit capacity (per available place- or tonne-kilometre). These emissions are shown in Figure 10.5.
- The vehicle occupancy. If fuel-efficient modes are only lightly loaded, their apparent efficiency vanishes: for example, although a bus emits less CO_2 per seat-kilometre than a car, it will only produce less CO_2 per passenger-kilometre if it is well loaded.
- The number of vehicle-kilometres.
- Vehicle speeds. All vehicles have an optimum speed at which emissions per vehicle-kilometre are minimal, but fuel burn and emissions increase faster as speeds fall below the optimum than when they rise above the optimum, except with very fast, impractical speeds. Those vehicles with continuously running motors, namely most internal combustion engines, have an infinitely large consumption when brought to a halt. The relationship between speed and emissions is discussed in Chapter 5.

If the total fuel burn and pollution is to be predicted without and then with a proposed action policy in order to assess its effectiveness, the predictions must cover all movements by all modes.

Actions (Figure 21.1, box 8)

The overall objective of a sustainable transport system is not that controversial. It is to support a declared effort to avoid undesirable climate change. Problems arise due to the conflicts of interest within the necessary actions. In particular, overt restrictions upon car use are political fireworks: it appears not to be a matter of an acknowledged efficiency of the car but of its image of untrammelled freedom, an image assiduously promoted in car marketing. Attempts to contain car use prompt media phrases such as 'declaring war on the motorist' and 'fascist controls'. Faced with this antipathy, decision-makers need numerical and technical support to explain and justify their decisions as demonstrably effective steps towards the realisation of a reasonable objective. It has been argued in previous chapters that the failures of past policies, particularly those following the 1968 Act and the TSG/TPP system, were due to decision-makers being unable to fully assess and explain proposed actions or assess the alternative policies proposed by objectors, or even demonstrate the results of a 'do-nothing' policy. It is for this reason that heavy emphasis has been placed on an improved methodology for assessing policy, programmes and actions, a methodology able to account for all movement through a comprehensive transport system. The policy proposals now put forward are much less important than having a proper transport planning system able to provide defensible evidence that actions are effective.

Urban structure

A major need is to reduce the total amount of travel. This reduction is not to target the comparatively infrequent long-distance journeys but the day-to-day, fairly short-distance movements, particularly within urban areas. This cannot be achieved in the short term or within the life of a Parliament: it has to be a determined, constant effort requiring political stamina. Over the past 50 years or so, urban areas have undergone considerable geographical expansion with associated reductions in density and a tendency towards decentralisation and dispersal. This has been characterised as the development of the discontinuous 'virtual city'. That clock cannot be put back, but it can be slowed down by using the town and county planning system to much greater effect.

This is a political trip-wire at the ideological heart of contemporary government. When the existing planning system first came into operation in July 1947 it was portrayed as being repressive but necessary to ensure that the considerable, if haphazard, housing developments of the 1930s were not repeated, that the desperately needed houses to replace those lost in the Second World War and to supplant the terrible conditions in the slums were built to a good standard and with supporting schools, shops, hospitals and recreational spaces within easy reach: in much of the private housing of the 1930s the seemingly unprofitable uses of land had been overlooked. Statutory town planning was also seen as a way to prevent the continued disorganised urban expansion into the countryside, primarily through the imposition of Green Belts and by strict controls over rural development.

The spirit and purpose of town planning was questioned but accepted, although the detail of its implementation later shifted. The ability of the system to invoke positive change was gradually weakened, leaving it with the essentially negative role of preventing the undesirable, about which there was considerable agreement – encroachment into the countryside; violation of the Green Belt and bad-neighbourly developments that undermined property values. The default decision was to refuse permission unless the proposed development conformed with the approved local plan. Although the prevention of undesirable developments ensured the retention of the regulatory planning system in the face of the paradigm shift that was moving government towards a business attitude, the incoming Conservative government of 1979 shifted the definition of 'undesirable' by reversing the default to refuse permission unless it conformed with the approved plan, to the granting of permission unless it could be shown that the development would be damaging. At a stroke this disabled longer term strategic planning and moved the emphasis on to tactical, shorter term issues, effectively releasing the brake on the construction of out-of-town shopping centres and semi-rural housing. It was the turning point in the advance towards the 'virtual city'.

Since then, the objectives of the planning system have steadily altered under the paradigm shift towards 'business enterprise' as the mainspring of government.[3] The prime driver was the radical change in circumstances from the days of full employment in the 1950s and 1960s when the task was to guide economic growth, into the days of rising unemployment of the 1980s when the task changed to stimulating economic growth. Local authority Planning Departments were charged with the task of capturing any local growth for their area. This task itself then gradually shifted to the current stance in which any form of regulation or negative control is held to be harmful to the business activities which are believed to be the source of economic vitality. The prime role of the planning system has become the facilitating of land development.

The difficulty of changing that attitude must not be underestimated. Sustainability, characterised by the control of the emission of CO_2 through land-use policies targeted at the reduction of urban travel, may only be achieved by an element of regulation, by limiting the freedoms of developers in favour of enriching the environmental future. Political attitudes need to revert to those of the days of the Clean Air and Civic Amenity Acts in which personal and business freedoms were subordinate to socially desirable environmental issues. That is no less than a counter-paradigm shift in which the needs, methods and objectives of 'business' are replaced by government in the interests of the future of the planet and its population.

Given that change in stance, planning applications should be accompanied by an estimate of the net change in CO_2 emissions to be debited against the development. This is impossible using current methodology, since it would require predictions of the travel generated, the modes used (which may well include inter-modal journeys), the changes in vehicle-kilometres, the speeds and the consequent rates of fuel consumption, all beyond current methodology. However, if logical decisions are to be made, such predictions must be made possible, since, without them it would be politically impractical to refuse permission. The grave danger is that the necessary predictive methodology will be too involved, too accurate, too slow and too expensive. This need not be so: the accuracy and complexity should be no more than that necessary to provide credibility, not absolute proof.

This is a demanding suggestion, since changes in land-use and transport patterns are an amalgam of innumerable minor changes, making it very difficult to manage them into the comprehensive assessment and shift needed to achieve sustainability. The mechanism shown in Figure 21.1 will have to be reduced to a commonly used test. This is no mean requirement, but it must be feasible – if it is possible for a camera in a police car to provide instant information on whether vehicles passing by at high speed are licensed, insured or stolen, databases accessed from a desk in a planning office must be within the bounds of possibility.

If CO_2 emissions are to be managed through the use of the town planning system to mould urban geography, then the assessment system must be used to study policy scenarios producing the most favourable results. The possible components are as follows:

- *Set criteria for desirable densities.* The primary criterion is the reduction of the mean walking distance between addresses and bus-stops or other public transport access points: this is a combination of the detailed layout and of the route and stop patterns reflecting the volume of demand. A possible stumbling-block is the provision of parking space. Cars are a sensible mode of transport for some trips, and there is no denying that the freedom to travel in any direction at any time is an attractive luxury. Restricting car ownership, rather than car use, is most unlikely to be either popular or effective. Limiting parking space in newer residential areas to the levels that are accepted in many of the older areas, such as that shown in Figure 4.6, may be possible, but only if good public transport provides acceptable mobility.
- *Foster residential forms to support public transport.* Historically there has been a close relationship between the nature and density of new residential areas and the transport that serves them. The isochrone analysis given in Chapter 3 demonstrated that public transport is at its strongest along linear routes, since this minimises the average walk from front door to boarding point, and coincidentally concentrates travel demand to create attractive high frequencies and low waiting times.

  This suggests linear development, either in a continuous strip along the lines of routes with lowish speeds and frequent stops in the pattern of the Edwardian tram routes, or in the interrupted, beaded form along railway routes with a station at the core of each bead. This was the basis of London's Metroland along the line of the Metropolitan Railway. The present structure of greater London is a variation upon this theme. The suburban stations are not just interchanges between walking segments from local addresses but also have park-and-ride facilities (often in converted coal trans-shipment yards) to serve longer segments providing access from other residential areas.

  These linear or beaded patterns conflict with many more recent housing developments which are in amorphous estates shaped to fit the previous field pattern. These are more suited to high car use, since they have road patterns which disperse traffic. Breaking the link to previous field patterns is difficult, since they usually reflect landownerships which are difficult to supplant.
- *Non-residential parking.* Terminal facilities are a crucial element in all transport modes: without them the purpose of movement cannot be fulfilled. Just as stations express the fulfilment of movement by train and ports by ship, so car travel is pointless without parking space. It follows that parking provision is the key to managing car traffic. As explained in Chapter 17, constraints on the land budget in some densely developed areas prevent the provision of sufficient parking space to meet demand. Only two solutions to that problem present themselves: either functions are dispersed to areas in which sufficient parking may be provided, or accessibility is sustained by the provision of public transport. An apparent, intuitive third way of building multi-storey off-street parking is actually impossible, partly because of the cost but mainly because the streets around the car-parks are unable to cope with the concentrated flows generated by the parks. A belief in an ability to satisfy in-town parking demand is commonly held and needs to be disproved by robust, numerical analysis and modelling.

- *Make spatially selective policy.* The continuing failure to provide adequate, acceptable public transport over the past decades has meant that the dispersal of city centre functions has become the default, leading to the virtual city, longer journeys, greater fuel burn and increasing emissions of CO_2. The conclusion must be to adopt transport policies matching density, parking and public transport in combinations suitable for particular parts of urban areas. Blanket policies to favour either car use or non-car use are doomed to failure. Public transport cannot match the flexibility of the car and to try to do so would be an expensive flop. On the other hand, car use cannot match public transport's ability to dispense with the need for parking space. Policy should play to these respective strengths and weaknesses. This leads to a clear conclusion: the provision of good public transport is the true alternative to the expense of out-of-town developments with their hectares of parking and tonnes of pollution, but identifying a stable and demonstrable balance between the two will need a new assessment methodology.

    It is a tenable hypothesis that the provision of adequate, acceptable public transport will need continuing subsidy, but that this will be less of a drain upon the nation's resources than the continuing conversion of agricultural land into an expansion of the virtual city with its implied fuel burn and pollution. That hypothesis needs evaluating, but that may only be done by the new, suggested land-use/transport model.

    There is a tinge of irony about this stance being seen to be radical; it is exactly the policy being implemented in London, although it is a policy probably born of a series of disjointed decisions by a variety of agencies rather than deliberate intent. The development of the Docklands into a new financial district has been fostered by billions of pounds of transport investment in the Docklands Light Railway, the Jubilee line, London Overground and in the future, Crossrail, all creating high levels of accessibility for car owners choosing to leave their cars at home. This policy has been applied in a more diluted form throughout Central London where low car use is not primarily due to the congestion charge but to the sheer inability to satisfy the demand for parking. The basic argument being offered is that this very successful London policy be adapted and extended to other areas wherever full parking provision is impossible.

- *Develop park and ride.* This is a marriage of private and public transport and an exemplar of inter-modal transport. As such, it cannot be realistically assessed by current methods. Park-and-ride policies have been implemented in a piecemeal, trial-and-error fashion, some successful and some not. The theory is clear: cars are at their best in low-density, residential areas with no concentration of traffic, but they are at their least efficient in dense areas typified by congestion and a dearth of parking. Public transport characteristics are the complete reverse. It therefore makes sense to use cars and public transport where they both work at their best and to build a contrived interface between the two.

    The devil is in the detail: the car-parks must be large enough to generate sufficient demand to justify an attractive public transport frequency extending for an attractive length of time, but it must not be so large that it creates flows which are beyond the capacities of the approaches. The car-parks must be sited at distances from the final destinations which create 'rides' that are attractive in comparison with using the car. The costs and probabilities of capturing an in-town parking space have to be balanced against the costs (in time and money) of using park and ride. It is a mixture of attributes which is difficult to get right, but it is a difficulty best addressed by a proper analysis and forecast rather than by the trial and error, as happened in the Nottingham 'Zone and Collar' experiment.

A possible variation may be to introduce normal suburban kerb-side parking regulated by parking charges, including a public transport ticket.

- *Research the nature of adequate, acceptable public transport* (perhaps this may be more usefully rewritten as 'research the nature of unacceptable public transport'). It cannot be denied that the car is the default to be used if public transport is seen to be inadequate. This is partly a matter of image rather than efficiency with choices influenced by relative attributes. Parking problems have been seen to be vital – it is the one major distinction between car use and all forms of public transport. But there are differences in attitude towards different forms of public transport. The list of public transport provisions to the Docklands are all forms of rail, and the lions' share of the dominant use of public transport by London commuters is by rail. There has always been a tendency for trains to be considered more acceptable than buses: in British class imagery they appear to be more middle class, more white collar. In part, it is an image that the bus industry has made little effort to dispel. Photographs of the interiors of the cars, trains and buses of, say, the 1950s compared with those of the 2010s show a massive change in space and comfort in cars but almost none in buses. The changes in the bus have been in their operation, with the engine moved to the back and the door to the front, but the seats are almost identical, still built with inadequate leg-room and luggage space, still with crude ventilation through the windows. But this is an image chosen by the industry showing that the customers are regarded as captive riders. The much-vaunted effects of competition had had little or no effect: any change in on-bus comfort levels have been due to disability legislation rather than bus operators striving to provide comfort for their passengers. This has to change.

It is often imagined that there is a 'sparks' effect – that electrically powered public transport has a better image. This seems to be unlikely: random chats on trains disclose that many people have no idea whether they are aboard an electric, diesel or diesel-electric train – and there is no reason why they should. The image is more about frequency, speed, timekeeping and comfort, attributes which may be influenced by the motive power but are not directly linked in passengers' minds. Perhaps a major component in the poor image of the bus is that there is an obvious and continuous comparison with cars: they both share the same road space and the same traffic restrictions. In contrast one cannot have a personal train.

It appears that public transport by rail is more 'adequate and acceptable' than by bus, but this is cold comfort. Tracks are expensive to build and maintain, and require heavy use for their justification, levels of use only possible to, from and within large cities. The flexibility and cost-effectiveness of the bus ensures it is the preferred mode for the great majority of urban travel both in its own right or as an ancillary role providing collection and distribution links to rail. This reflects the ability of the bus to reach towards a high proportion of people's front doors. Service frequency is very attractive, especially when compared to the infinitely effective frequency of the car, but people are able to adjust their personal timetables to some extent to fall into step with a bus timetable. The critical attribute is reliability, particularly with comparatively infrequent services – waiting times should never be longer than the published headway. Two remedial policies are necessary to suppress the worst effect of service perturbations; first, and obviously, public transport should be protected against congestion and its ability to disturb the timetable. Second, the schedules should have some redundancy built into them to enable recovery from delays. Both involve extra costs which undermine the financial viability of the service but enhance the service levels, making public transport more attractive and so able to support the economic viability of town centre functions.

- *Create public transport priority areas.* A fundamental component in enhancing the image of urban public transport by bus is to inoculate it against congestion. This not only makes a direct improvement to the image by making buses appear to be superior to general traffic, but it also enhances their cost profile. Urban bus costs are basically per hour,[4] and the higher the mean speed, the more financially efficient they are. Areas where accessibility is threatened by both an endemic lack of parking and a tendency towards congestion on the approaches require good remedial public transport and should be designated as public transport priority areas. Priority may be given in two primary ways, both common for trams but strangely denied to buses:

1 Public transport should be provided with its own lanes (either tram tracks or bus lanes) extending right up to signal stop lines.
2 At signals public transport should have priority starts triggered by transponders or selective presence detectors and the length of green time shown should be in proportion to the numbers of seats, not, as at present, in proportion to the physical size and acceleration of the vehicles (crudely in proportion to their effect on the general flow of traffic).

Public transport in priority areas should not be trapped against the kerb where priority will be compromised by parked and stationary vehicles. Kerb-space time is a very limited commodity and making public transport share it by siting dedicated lanes against the kerb will mean that any disruption caused by stationary vehicles will be borne by public transport and its users, rather than by cars and their occupants.

If the tram track or bus lane is a lane width away from the kerb, leaving the kerb-side lane for general traffic, then either stops will have to be sited on peninsulas extending across the nearside lane or there will have to be signalled pedestrian crossings triggered by approaching public transport vehicles. They are both interruptions to the flow of general traffic, one in space and the other in time. This is not just for the safety and convenience of public transport users but is a demonstration of their importance. It should be noted that the siting of public

transport priority lanes away from the kerb is not intended to be a general proposition but is limited to public transport priority areas.
- *Encourage and facilitate walking.* Walking is particularly important because it is not only a mode in its own right but it is a component segment within the vast majority of journeys. Clearly, urban pedestrian ways[5] should be properly lit, drained and maintained, but the major problem lies in the conflicts with vehicular traffic; these cannot be avoided completely, but they do need to be mitigated. Pedestrian crossings, whether signalled or not, should be enforced. A small minority of motorists use their vehicles as threatening weapons and wherever this occurs the same rules should apply as with other threatening weapons – they should be confiscated.

    Pedestrian areas within town centres, once rare with proposals meeting vociferous objections, are now more common. The endemic problems of servicing flanking properties by vehicles is usually overcome be allowing access at restricted times.

    Two modifications are proposed, both with the objective of reducing or codifying the conflicts between vehicles and pedestrians:
    1   An ability to specify 'Pedestrian Priority Areas' similar to the 'woonerf' in the Netherlands. Within these areas pedestrians and cyclists would have priority with a presumption of fault against the driver of any powered vehicle causing threat, harm or damage to any person or unpowered wheeled vehicle such as a pram or bicycle. The rules would be enforced primarily by the knowledge that any insurance claim or legal case against the drivers of powered vehicles would be successful. 'Pedestrian Priority Areas' could be used to cover residential areas and to emphasise and clarify the regulations under which motor vehicles are now allowed in existing pedestrian areas. Transgressions would have to be penalised severely by the impounding or confiscation of the vehicle. These areas could supplant the physical hazards of road humps, etc.
    2   Pedestrian-controlled powered trollies should be allowed in such areas to facilitate the delivery and collection of goods and wastes. It would sensible, but not compulsory, for such vehicles to be electrically powered. They are needed to reduce the number of heavy powered vehicles used in pedestrian-preferred areas.
- *Facilitate cycling.* Cycling has a useful but necessary minor role to play. At present it accounts for about 2 per cent of person-kilometres, so even if it doubles or triples, cycling will always provide a minority of urban travel. It will be forever constrained by the age and fitness profile of the population and by their willingness and ability to carry shopping, children and other burdens. This is not to say that cycling is not an important component of planning sustainable transport, but it will always be a minor component.
- *Integrate freight transport into general transport policy and investment.* The major problem in the public mind seems to have been the apparent excessive pollutions due to:
    - the use of the motorway network for over-long transits;
    - the use of 'juggernauts', particularly in urban areas.

The second problem appears to have dropped out of the public consciousness. The use of large lorries for the multiple drops that are typical of urban deliveries is intrinsically uneconomic, since it involves running part-loaded. The only use of large lorries in urban areas is to make single drops: this confines them to delivering to large shops which are either restricted by planning conditions or by practicalities to night or early morning drops, or they may be located out of the centre. In any event, very large lorries are not often seen on city streets during the daytime. Most urban deliveries are made by smaller lorries or vans working out of local distribution centres which are supplied by the large vehicles typically using the motorway network.

The 44-tonne six-axle lorries which earned the name 'juggernauts' present yet another self-generating paradox. Their operating costs and CO_2 emissions per tonne-kilometre are better than any other road vehicle. But this has ensured that the distribution depots and warehouses between which they operate are sited along the motorways and are sized to be at their optimum with large through-puts. This minimises their numbers which, in turn, lengthens the distances between them. Hence the low fuel burn and operating costs of the largest vehicles actually lead to an increase in tonne-kilometres.

The usual offered solution to the increases in tonne-kilometres is that freight should be transferred to rail. The difficulty in pursuing this policy is two-fold:

1. Railways, with very few exceptions, cannot provide a door-to-door service, so requiring inter-modal movement with lorries hauling the first and last segments of the journey. That requires two trans-shipments with their unavoidable costs and delays.
2. Lorries have a totally different rhythm to trains, roughly 30-tonne payloads as against hundreds of tonnes. Consequently trains must run either part-loaded or have to be delayed until a full train-load can be built up. Either way, the cost savings once the train is on the move are eroded, and the haul has to be quite long for the haulage savings to be large enough to offset the trans-shipment costs and delays.

The way forward appears to be counter-intuitive. Railways are at their best hauling heavy freight of low-value bulk cargo such as coal, oil or stone in which the costs of delay are very low. This is a far cry from the cargo carried by the motorway jugger-nauts. The possibility that presents itself is to build the large loads to which rail is suited by consolidating a large number of small loads – the antithesis of the railway's natural market. The model seems to be akin to passenger traffic. Trans-shipment stations similar to the Parkway stations could be constructed where the railway and major roads intersect. Here the normal cages and pallets used for general freight could arrive by road and be handled on to rolling-stock that is very similar in size and performance to passenger stock, with places booked in the same way as passengers book seats. Transit times would be similar to passenger trains and the similar speed profiles would mean that the freight movements would not take an undue proportion of track capacity. This is no more than a reworking of the Rail Mail operation of some years ago, but instead of the traffic being confined to the mails, the cages and pallets would be loaded with any mix of products. The rolling-stock would be similar in its floor space, volume and weight capacity to a conventional semi-trailer as seen on the motorways. The design and costs of the handling equipment and of the trans-shipment stations would be crucial, but with the rhythms of arrival by road and departure by train brought to near conformity, the delay and handling costs should not be so large that they could not be offset against the savings in fuel and staff. Handling could borrow some of the minimal cost efficiencies of air-freight handling.

The stumbling-block is not working out the detail from the theory: it is in the complexity of the organisation of the railways. Track costs would have to be shared with passenger operations which are already mired in complexities of organisation.

Postscript

Planning sustainable transport, judged for its success by the management of CO_2 emissions, needs a many-faceted approach. Better vehicle and motor design, the use of more CO_2-efficient fuels, the reduction of congestion with its poor fuel burn per vehicle-kilometre and more walking and cycling are all important components. But the major task is the control of the physical size and structure of urban areas with two major sub-objectives: first, to reduce the length of journeys and of the aggregate distance travelled; second, to provide the densities, layouts and parking space budgets which combine to enhance the probability of the use of non-car modes. However, this should not and cannot be applied to all journeys. Cars will always be the preferred and most efficient method of travelling between low-density, dispersed parts of the urban structure, in contrast to public transport which is best suited to provide access in those dense areas with a deficiency of parking. The long-term aim is to increase the proportion of the built-up area providing an environment suited to public transport while reducing the areas which require car use.

This agenda may only be knowingly and demonstrably delivered if the effects of the necessary policies are first predicted and then monitored to test their effectiveness and to improve decision-making in the future.

Notes

1 Department for Transport (2012c). Despite the title, this is not a transport model at all – it is confined to a traffic forecast.
2 'Food miles' is a popular shorthand to describe the extensive mileage covered by some supermarket products as a result of their logistics and supply chains. A commonly quoted example is baked beans, most of which are manufactured and tinned near Wigan and are distributed first to very large retail distribution centres from which they are carried to smaller, more local centres and then on to the shops. In the extreme case, tins of beans bought by somebody living in the shadow of the factory where they were baked may have been carted hundreds of miles.
3 The depth and extent of this shift is very considerable. Recently (summer 2012), the London Olympics and a Royal Tour of the South Sea Islands were both presented as business opportunities. It would have been unthinkable to present the 1947 Royal Tour of South Africa and the 1948 Olympics in such terms.

4   A bus trapped in stationary traffic has an infinite cost per kilometre and may, ultimately, make a loss, even if it were fully laden.
5   There is a clash between vernacular and technical language. In law and in technical jargon the pedestrian paths flanking roads are legally part of the 'highway' and are called 'footways', rather than the vernacular 'pavements'. Confusingly, the word 'pavement' does have a technical meaning, but it is the hard bitumen or concrete surface of the vehicular part of the highway. A 'footpath' is a separate route for pedestrians only.

Bibliography

Acemoglu, D. and Robinson, J. (2012) *Why Nations Fail.* Profile.
Ackroyd, P. (2000) *London: The Biography.* Chatto & Windus.
Adams, D. (1979) *The Hitch-Hiker's Guide to the Galaxy.* Pan.
Aldcroft, D.H. (1975) *British Transport Since 1914.* David & Charles.
Aldous, T. (1972) *The Battle for the Environment.* Fontana.
Allen, G.F. (1966) *British Rail after Beeching.* Ian Allan.
Ankers, S., Kaiserman, D. and Shepley, C. (1979) *Planning in Crisis: The Grotton Papers.* Royal Town Planning Institute.
Ball, S. (2009) *Branches.* Oxford University Press.
Banham, J. (1994) *The Anatomy of Change.* Orion.
Banks, N., Bayliss, D. and Glaister, S. (2007) *Roads and Reality: Motoring Towards 2050.* RAC Foundation,
Banks, R.V. et al. (1977) *Can Bus Replace Train?* Railway Invigoration Society.
Barker, T.C. and Robbins, M. (1963) *A History of London Transport (Vol 1. The Nineteenth Century).* George Allen & Unwin.
Barney, G.O. (ed.) (1982) *The Global Report to the President.* Penguin.
Beesley, M.E. and Kettle, P B. (1985) *Improving Railway Financial Performance.* Gower.
Bell, G., Blackledge, D.A. and Bowen, P. (1983) *The Economics and Planning of Transport.* Heinemann.
Bendtsen, P.H. (1961) *Town and Traffic in the Motor Age.* Danish Technical Press.
Bibby, P.R. and Shepherd, J.W. (1997) 'Projecting Rates of Urbanisation in England, 1991–2016: Method, Policy Application and Results'. *Town Planning Review,* Vol. 68, No.1, pp. 93–124.
Bowers, P.H. (1994) *Managerial Economics for the Service Industries.* Chapman and Hall.
Bradbury, M. (1975) *The History Man.* Secker and Warburg.
Bradshaw's (Various) *British Railways* Timetables. Henry BlackLock.
Breheny, M. and Hall, P. (eds) (1996) *The People – Where Will They Go?* Town and Country Planning Association.
Bricklin, D. and Frankston, R. (1979) *VisiCalc.* Software Arts.
British Transport Commission (1956) *Book of Stations.* BTC.
Brooks, D. (2011) *The Social Animal.* Short Books.
Bruton, M.J. (1985) *Introduction to Transport Planning.* Hutchinson.
Bryan, T. (2004) *All in a Day's Work – Life on the GWR.* Ian Allan.
Buchanan, C.D. (1958) *Mixed Blessing.* Leonard Hill.
Cairns, S., Goodwin, P. et al. (2004) *Smarter Choices – Changing the Way we Travel.* Department for Transport.

Carlstein, T. (1982) *Time Resources, Society and Ecology*. Allen & Unwin.
Carlstein. T., Parkes, D. and Thrift, N. (eds) (1978) *Timing Space and Spacing Time (Vols 1 and 2)*. Edward Arnold.
Carson, R. (1962) *The Silent Spring*. Houghton Mifflin.
Chapin, F.S. (1965) *Urban Land Use Planning*. University of Illinois Press.
Chernichewski, V. (1935) *Anthropological Report on a London Suburb*. Grayson and Grayson.
Clark, D. K. (1894) *Tramways, Their Construction and Working*. Crosby Lockwood.
Clark, J. and Hutton, B. (1991) *The Appraisal of Community Severance (TRRL Report CR 135)*. Transport and Road Research Laboratory.
Clemens, M. (2007) *The Withered Arm*. Ian Allan.
Collins, S. (1977) *The Wheels Used to Talk to Us*. Sheaf Publishing.
Competition Commission (2011) *A Report on the Supply of Local Bus Services in the UK*. HMSO.
Cooke, M. *et al.* (2004) *Reducing Waits in Emergency Departments*. NHS Report SDO/29/2002.
Coombe, D. (2009) *Regional and Local Strategic Modelling*. Department for Transport.
Cooper, T. (ed.) (1977) *The Wheels Used to Talk to Us*. Sheaf Publishing.
Cornwall County Council (1952) *The Development Plan: Report of Survey*.
Cowan, P. (1970) *Developing Patterns of Urbanisation*. Oliver and Boyd.
Cullingworth, J.B. (1964) *Town and Country Planning in England and Wales*. Allen & Unwin.
Davies, T. and Mayer, R. (2003) *Economics of Bus Drivelines*. Department for Transport.
Day, A. (1963) *Roads*. Mayflower.
De Neufville, R. (1975) *Airport Systems Planning*. Macmillan.
De Neufville, R. and Stafford, J.H. (1971) *Systems Analysis for Engineers and Managers*. McGraw-Hill.
Department for the Environment, Food and Rural Affairs (DEFRA) (2005) *Securing the Future* (Cm 6467). HMSO.
Department for the Environment, Food and Rural Affairs (DEFRA) (2010) *Factors for Converting GHG into CO_2 Equivalents*. HMSO.
Department for the Environment, Transport and the Regions (DETR) (1997) *National Road Traffic Forecasts*. HMSO.
Department for the Environment, Transport and the Regions (DETR) (1998) *A New Deal for Transport: Better for Everyone* (Cm 3950). HMSO.
Department for the Environment, Transport and the Regions (1999) *Breaking the Logjam*. HMSO.
Department for the Environment, Transport and the Regions (DETR) (2000a) *Guidance on the Methodology for Multi-modal Studies (GOMMMS)*. www.dft.gov.uk.
Department for the Environment, Transport and the Regions (DETR) (2000b) *Guidance on Local Transport Plans*. www.dft.gov.uk.
Department for Transport (2004) *The Future of Transport: A Network for 2030*. White Paper (Cmd 6234). TSO.
Department for Transport (2005a) *Inclusive Mobility*. HMSO.
Department for Transport (2005b) *Smarter Choices – Changing the Way We Travel*. HMSO.
Department for Transport (2006) *General Principles of Traffic Control by Light Signals Traffic Advisory Leaflet 1/06*. Department for Transport.
Department for Transport (2007) *Towards a Sustainable Transport System: Supporting Economic Growth in a Low-carbon World* (Cm 7226). HMSO.
Department for Transport (2007a) *Guidance on Transport Assessment*. Department for Transport.
Department for Transport (2008) *Delivering a Sustainable Transport System*. HMSO.
Department for Transport (2009) *WebTAG Unit 3.4.1. Accidents Sub Objective*. HMSO.
Department for Transport (2010) *Short-haul Rail Freight: On Track for Profits in Scotland*. HMSO.

Department for Transport (2011a) *Rail Benchmarking*. HMSO.
Department for Transport (2011b) *Transport Assessment Guidance Unit 3.5.6*. HMSO.
Department for Transport (2012a) *Reforming our Railways* (Cm 8313). HMSO.
Department for Transport (2012b) *A Green Light for Better Buses*. Department for Transport.
Department for Transport (2012c) *Road Transport Forecasts: Results from the National Transport Model*. HMSO.
Department for Transport (annual) *Transport Statistics Great Britain (TSGB)*. Department for Transport.
Department for Transport (online) *Traffic Analysis Guidance* (TAG). WebTAG, www.dft.gov.uk/webtag.
Department for Transport (online) *National Transport Model: FORGE (Fitting On Regional Growth and Elasticities)*, www.dft.gov.uk.
Department for Transport (various) *National Travel Survey; Notes and Definitions*. Department for Transport.
Department for Transport (various) *National Travel Survey*. www.dft.gov.uk.
Department of the Environment (1971) *The Economic Appraisal of Inter-urban Road Improvement Schemes* (Technical memorandum H1/71). DoE.
Department of the Environment (1972) *How Do You Want to Live?* HMSO.
Department of the Environment (1973) *Relocation of A 44 Decision Letter PEI/1281/223/2*. DoE.
Department of the Environment (1973a) *Local Transport Grants; Circular 104/73*. DoE.
Department of the Environment (1975) *What is our Heritage?* HMSO.
Department of the Environment (1976) *Transport Policy: A Consultation Document*. DoE.
Departments of the Environment and of Transport (1994) *Planning Policy Guidance Note #13: Transport* (PPG13). DoE.
Department of Transport (1977a) *Report of the Advisory Committee on Trunk Road Assessment (The Leitch Report)*. HMSO.
Department of Transport (1977b) *Transport Policy* (Cmnd 5836). HMSO.
Department of Transport (1979) *Submissions of Transport Policies, and Programmes for 1980/81. Circular 4/79*. DoT.
Department of Transport (1980) *Policy for Roads: England 1980* (Cmnd 7908). HMSO.
Department of Transport (1981) *Bids for Transport Supplementary Grants 82/83 Circular 1/81*. DoT.
Department of Transport (1984) *Buses* (Cmnd 9300). HMSO.
Department of Transport (1985) *Bids for Transport Supplementary Grants 86/87 Circular 1/85*. DoT.
Department of Transport (1987) *TPP Submissions for Transport Supplementary Grants 88/89 Circular 1/87*. DoT.
Department of Transport (1989) *National Road Traffic Forecasts*. DoT.
Department of Transport (1992) *New Opportunities for the Railways* (Cmnd 2012). HMSO.
Department of Transport (1994) *Trunk Roads and the Generation of Traffic*. DoT.
Department of Transport (1999) *Traffic Capacity of Urban Roads Traffic Advice Note* TA 79/99. Online.
Devas, N. and Rakodi, C. (eds) (1993) *Managing Fast Growing Cities*. Longman.
Docherty, I. and Shaw, J. (eds) (2003) *A New Deal for Transport*. Blackwell.
Docherty, I. and Shaw, J. (2003) *Traffic Jam*. The Policy Press.
Dorn, L. (ed.) (2000) *Human Factors in Road and Rail Transport*. Ashgate.
Durkin, J., Lane, P. and Peto, M. (1992) *Transport and Works Act*. Blackstone.
Eddington, R. (2006) *The Eddington Transport Study: The Case for Action*. HMSO.
Editorial Committee, Institute of Traffic Engineers (1950) *Traffic Engineering Handbook*. Institute of Traffic Engineers.

Elliott, J.A. (1994) *An Introduction to Sustainable Development*. Routledge.
Fairlie, S. (1996) *Low Impact Development*. Jon Carpenter.
Ford, R. (2012) *Railway Costs*. Modern Railways (July).
Freeman, M.J. (1999) *Railways and the Victorian Imagination*. Yale University Press.
Freeman, M. and Aldcroft, D. (1985) *The Atlas of British Railway History*. Croom Helm.
Freeman, M.J. and Aldcroft, D.H. (eds) (1988) *Transport in Victorian Britain*. Manchester University Press.
Freese, S. (1932) *The Ten-year Plan: A Dream of 1940*. Cecil Palmer.
Freidman, M. and Freidman, R. (1980) *Free to Choose*. Secker and Warburg.
Friend, J.K. and Jessop, W.N. (1969) *Local Government and Strategic Choice*. Tavistock.
Friend, J.K., Power, J.M. and Yewlett, C.J.L. (1974) *Public Planning: The Inter-corporate Dimension*. Tavistock.
Gardiner, D. (2009) *Risk: The Science and Politics of Fear*. Virgin Books.
Garnett, A.F. (2005) *Steel Wheels*. Cannwood.
Geddes, P. (1915) *Cities in Evolution*. Williams and Norgate.
Gill, P. (1987) 'Clearing up Crime'. *Journal of Law and Society*, Vol. 14, No. 2.
Glasson, J., Therivel, R. and Chadwick, A. (2012) *Introduction to Environmental Impact Assessment*. Routledge.
Gleick, J. (1988) *Chaos*. Cardinal.
Goldberg, J. (2007) *Liberal Fascism*. Penguin.
Goodman, R. (1972) *After the Planners*. Penguin.
Goodwin, P. (2008) 'Charging Economics'. *Local Transport Today*, 13 June.
Greenberg, M.R. (2012) *The Environmental Impact Statement after Two Generations*. Routledge.
Gritten, A. (1988) *Reviving the Railways: A Victorian Future*. Centre for Policy Studies.
Grodon, A. (1988) *To Move with the Times*. Aberdeen University Press.
HM Government (1994) *Sustainable Development: The UK Strategy* (Cm 2426). HMSO.
Haggett, P. (1965) *Locational Analysis in Human Geography*. Edward Arnold.
Hall, P. (1990) *Cities of Tomorrow*. Blackwell.
Hall, P. (1998) *Cities in Civilisation*. Phoenix.
Hall, S. (1999) *Hidden Dangers*. Ian Allan.
Hall, S.S. (1993) *Mapping the Next Millennium*. Vintage.
Hanley, N. and Spash, C.L. (1993) *Cost Benefit Analysis and the Environment*. Edward Elgar.
Hansen, W. (1959) 'How Accessibility Shapes Land Use'. *Journal of the American Institute of Planners*, Vol. 25, pp. 73–76.
Harley, R.J. (2002) *LCC Electric Tramways*. Capital Transport.
Harris, D. *et al.* (1966) *The Humberside Study*. Leeds School of Town and Country Planning.
Harris, N.G. and Godward, E. (eds) (1992) *Planning Passenger Railways*. Transport Publishing.
Harris, N.G. and Godward, E. (1997) *The Privatisation of British Rail*. Crystal Palace.
Harvey, D. (1973) *Social Justice and the City*. Edward Arnold.
Harvey, D. (2005) *A Brief History of Neoliberalism*. Oxford University Press.
Harvey, D. (2012) *Rebel Cities*. Verso.
Hathway, T., Lawson, D. and Hutton, B. (1981) *Communication Patterns in Local Authorities*. Bristol Polytechnic.
Headicar, P. (2009) *Transport Policy and Planning in Great Britain*. Routledge.
Hepworth, M. and Ducatel, K. (1992) *Transport in the Information Age: Wheels and Wires*. Belhaven.
Hibbs, J. (ed.) (1971) *The Omnibus*. David & Charles.
Hibbs, J. (1974) *Minutes of the Liberal Party Advisory Panel on Transport*.
Hibbs, J. (2000) *Transport Policy: The Myth of Integrated Planning*. Institute of Economic Affairs.
Hicks, J.R. (1960) *The Social Framework*. Oxford University Press.

Higginson, M. (ed.) (1993) *Tramway London: Background to the Abandonment*. Light Rail Transit Association.
Highways Agency (online) *Design Manual for Roads and Bridges* (DMRB).
Hillier, J. (2007) *Stretching Beyond the Horizon*. Ashgate.
Hillman, M. (2004) *How We Can Save the Planet*. Penguin.
Hobbs, F.D. and Richardson, B.D. (1967) *Traffic Engineering (Vols 1 and 2)*. Pergamon.
Hobsbawm, E. (2011) *How to Change the World*. Little Brown.
Holroyd, E. and Scraggs, D. (1966) 'Waiting Times for Buses in Central London'. *Traffic Engineering and Control*, Vol. 8, No. 3.
Houghton, R.W. (ed.) (1970) *Public Finance*. Penguin.
Hunter, D.L.G. (1992) *Edinburgh's Transport: The Early Years*. The Mercat Press.
Hunter, D.L.G. (1999) *Edinburgh's Transport: The Corporation Years*. Adam Gordon.
Hutton, B. (1967) *Evidence to the Public Inquiry into the Malton Bypass*.
Hutton, B. (1972) *Evidence to the Public Inquiry into the Hook Road in Cardiff* (commissioned by the Coordinating Committee of Objectors).
Hutton, B. (1973) *Evidence to the Public Inquiry into the Kington Inner Relief Road* (commissioned by the Kington By-Pass Association).
Hutton, B. (1978) *Evidence to the Public Inquiry into the Demolition of Listed Prior Park Cottages* (commissioned by Bath Preservation Trust).
Hutton, B. (1980a) *Evidence to the Public Inquiry into the City of Wells Inner Relief Road* (commissioned by the Save Wells Action Group).
Hutton, B. (1980b) *Report upon the Buchanan Road Plan for Bath*. The Bath Preservation Trust.
Hutton, B. (2002) *Cutting Through Congestion*. Holyrood.
Hutton, B. (2005) *Evidence to the Public Inquiry into the East Lothian Local Plan*.
Hutton, B. (2006a) *The Multi-modal Sustainable Transport Plan for Kosovo*. Ministry of Transport Kosovo.
Hutton, B. (2006b) *Fuel Burn by Cars at Low Speeds in Urban Areas*. Department for Transport.
Hutton, B. (2007) *Sustainable Multi-modal Transport Plan for Kosovo*. European Union.
Hutton, B. *et al.* (1969) *Master Plan for the Mosborough Extension to the City of Sheffield*. City of Sheffield Council.
Hutton, B. *et al.* (1974) *Master Plan for Martlesham Heath New Village (Suffolk)*. Clifford Culpin and Partners.
Hutton, B. *et al.* (1991) *The Appraisal of Community Severance* Report CR135. Transport and Road Research Laboratory.
Hutton, W. (1996) *The State We're In*. Vintage.
Hutton, W. (2011) *Them and Us*. Abacus.
ICL (1970) *Compact 2: A Program for Transportation Planning Studies*. ICL.
Irvine, K. (1988) *Track to the Future*. Adam Smith Institute.
Jackman, W.T. (1966) *The Development of Transportation in Modern England*. Frank Cass.
Jacobs, J. (1961) *The Death and Life of Great American Cities*. Random House.
Jacobs, J. (1970) *The Economy of Cities*. Jonathon Cape.
Jamieson Mackay and Partners (1975) *The Bristol Land Use Transportation Study*. Bristol City Council.
Jeffreys, R. (1949) *The King's Highway*. Batchworth.
Jones, G. (2006) *75 Years of Traffic Commissioners*. Road Transport History Association.
Jones, I.S. (1977) *Urban Transport Appraisal*. Macmillan.
Jones, P. (ed.) (1990) *Developments in Dynamic and Activity-based Approaches to Travel Analysis*. Avebury.
Joy, S. (1973) *The Train That Ran Away*. Ian Allan.
Joyce, J. (1967) *The Story of Passenger Transport in Britain*. Ian Allan.

Judt, T. (2009) *Reappraisals*. Vintage.
Keynes, J.M. (1936) *The General Theory of Employment Interest and Money*. Harcourt Brace.
Kimber, R.M., Barton, P.J. and Giokas, C. (1986) 'Predicting Time-dependent Distributions of Queues and Delays for Road Traffic at Roundabouts and Priority Junctions'. *Journal of the Operational Research Society*, Vol. 37, pp. 87–97.
Kimber, R., McDonald, M. and Houndsell, N. (1986) *The Prediction of Saturation Flows for Road Junctions Controlled by Traffic Signals* (TRL Report No. 67). TRL.
Kirby, H.R. and Hutton, B. (2003) *Structure of the Vehicle Market Model: Modelling the Effects of Transport Policy on National Fuel Consumption*. Transport Research Institute, Napier University, Edinburgh.
Kuhn, T.S. (1962) *The Structure of Scientific Revolutions*. University of Chicago Press.
Kwarteng, K. and Dupont, J. (2011) *Gridlock Nation*. Biteback Publishing.
Lal, D. (2006) *Reviving the Invisible Hand*. Princeton University Press.
Lambden, W. (1969) *Bus and Coach Operation*. Iliffe.
Lanchester, J. (2010) *Whoops: Why Everyone Owes Everyone and No One Can Pay*. Penguin.
Lane, C.J.D. (1972) *ALSER: Laboratory Report 478*. Transport and Road Research Laboratory.
Layard, R. (ed.) (1974) *Cost Benefit Analysis*. Penguin.
Layfield, R. and Bardsley, M. (1977) *Nottingham Zones and Collar Study: Results of the Before Surveys* (Supplementary Report 343). Transport and Road Research Laboratory.
Layfield, R. and Cooper, B. (1978) *Nottingham Zones and Collar Study: Results of the After Surveys* (Supplementary Report 365). Transport and Road Research Laboratory.
Layfield, R. and Vincent, R. (1977) *Nottingham Zones and Collar Study: Overall Assessment* (Laboratory Report 805). Transport and Road Research Laboratory.
Leadbeater, C. (2009) *We-Think*. Profile Books.
Litchfield, N. (1956) *The Economics of Planned Development*. The Estates Gazette.
Litchfield, N. and Marinov, U. (1977) 'Environment and Planning A'. *Land Use Planning and Environmental Protection*, Vol. 9, No. 9, pp. 985–1002.
Litchfield, N. and Proudlove, A. (1976) *Conservation and Traffic: The York Case Study*. Sessions Book Trust.
Lloyd, P.E. and Dicken, P. (1977) *Location in Space*. Harper & Row.
London and Home Counties Traffic Advisory Committee (1951) *Report*. Ministry of Transport.
MacKay, D.J.C. (2009) *Sustainable Energy: Without the Hot Air*. UIT.
Maling, D.H. (1989) *Measurements from Maps*. Pergamon.
Martin, A. (2012) *Underground Overground*. Profile Books.
Matson, T.M., Smith, W.S. and Hurd, F.W. (1955) *Traffic Engineering*. McGraw-Hill.
McKean, C. (2007) *Battle for the North*. Granta.
McKinnon, A.C. (2005) 'The Economic and Environmental Benefits of Increasing Maximum Truck Weight: The British Experience'. *Transportation Research Part D*, Vol. 10, pp. 77–95.
McKinnon, A.C. and Piecyk, M.I. (2010) *Moving Freight by Road in a Very Low Carbon World*. Green Logistics.
McLoughlin, J.B.(1969) *Urban and Regional Planning: A Systems Approach*. Faber & Faber.
McLoughlin, J.B. (1973) *Control and Urban Planning*. Faber & Faber.
Ministry of Housing and Local Government (1944) *The Control of Land Use* (Cmd 6537). HMSO.
Ministry of Transport (1958) *Crush Hour Travel*. HMSO.
Ministry of Transport (1961) *The Design of Roads in Rural Areas Memo 780*. HMSO.
Ministry of Transport (1963a) *Traffic in Towns (The Buchanan Report)*. HMSO.
Ministry of Transport (1963b) *The Reshaping of British Railways (The Beeching Report)*. HMSO.

Ministry of Transport (1965) *Urban Traffic Engineering Techniques*. Floating Car Studies.
Ministry of Transport (1967) *The Economic Appraisal of Inter-urban Road Improvement Schemes. Memo T5/67*. HMSO.
Ministry of Transport (1967a) *Public Transport and Traffic* (Cmnd 3481). HMSO.
Ministry of Transport (1968) *Traffic and Transport Plans (Roads Circular 1/68)*. HMSO.
Ministry of Transport (1970) *Roads for the Future* (Cmnd 4369). HMSO.
Ministry of Transport (1983) *Policy for Roads* (Cmnd 9059). HMSO.
Ministry of Transport (1989) *Roads for Prosperity* (Cmd 693). HMSO.
Monbiot, G. (2006) *Heat*. Allen Lane.
Moran, J. (2010) *Roads: A Hidden History*. Profile Books.
Morgan, E. (1978) *Falling Apart: The Rise and Decline of Urban Civilisation*. Abacus.
Moroney, M.J. (1951) *Facts from Figures*. Penguin.
Morris, A.E.J. (1994) *History of Urban Form before the Industrial Revolution*. Longman.
Murphy, S. (2005) *Northern Line Extensions*. Tempus.
Murray, A. (2002) *Off the Rails*. Verso.
Network Rail (2008) *A Consultation on Consumption Rate Methodology for Freight Operating Companies*. Network Rail.
Newkirk, R.T. (1979) *Environmental Planning for Utility Corridors*. Ann Arbor Science.
Nock, O.S. (1957) *Branch Lines*. Batsford.
Nock, O.S. (1966) *Britain's New Railway*. Ian Allan.
O'Brien, L. (1992) *Introducing Quantitive Geography*. Routledge.
O'Flaherty, C.A. (1967) *Highways*. Edward Arnold.
O'Riordan, T. and Voisey, H. (eds) (1997) *Sustainable Development: Coming to Terms with Agenda 21*. Frank Cass.
O'Sillivan, P. (1980) *Transport Policy – An Interdisciplinary Approach*. Batsford Academic.
OECD (1978) *Environment and Energy Use in Urban Areas*. OECD.
Openshaw, S. (1995) *Census Users' Handbook*. Geoinformation.
Ormerod, P. (1994) *The Death of Economics*. Faber & Faber.
Orr, S.C. and Cullingworth, J.B. (1969) *Regional and Urban Studies*. Allen & Unwin.
Parris, H. (1965) *Government and the Railways in Nineteenth Century Britain*. Routledge.
Peeters, P.N., Middel, J. and Hoolhorst, A. (2005) *Fuel Efficiency of Commercial Aircraft: Report NLP-CR-2005-669*. National Aerospace Laboratories.
Peters, G. and Beishon, J. (eds) (1981) *Systems Behaviour*. Open University.
Plowden. S. (1972) *Towns Against Traffic*. André Deutsch.
Plowden, W. (1971) *The Motor Car and Politics 1996–1970*. The Bodley Head.
Ponting, C. (2007) *A New Green History of the World*. Vintage.
Porter, M. E. (1990) *The Competitive Advantage of Nations*. Palgrave.
Quarmby, D. A. (1987) *Developments in the Retail Market and their Effects on Freight Distribution*. PTRC Summer Conference.
R Travers Morgan and Partners (1972) *The Cambridge Transportation Study*. Cambridge City and County.
RAC Foundation (2007) *Roads and Reality*. RAC.
Raper, J.F., Rhind, D.W. and Shepherd, J.W. (1992) *Postcodes: The New Geography*. Longman.
Rapoport, A. (1974) *Conflict in Man-made Environment*. Penguin.
Rasmussen, S.E. (1960) *London: The Unique City*. Penguin.
Reilly, W.J. (1931) *The Law of Retail Gravitation*. Privately published.
Relf, B. (1973) *Models in Urban and Regional Planning*. Leonard Hill.
Reynolds, D.J. (1966) *Economics, Town Planning and Traffic*. Institute of Economic Affairs.
Richards, M.G. (2006) *Congestion Charging in London*. Palgrave.

Rigney, D. (2010) *The Matthew Effect: How Advantage Begets Further Advantage*. Columbia University Press.
Road Research Laboratory (1960) *The London–Birmingham Motorway – Traffic and Economics: Technical Paper #46*. TRL.
Road Research Laboratory (1965) *Research on Road Traffic*. HMSO.
Roberts, P. (2005) *The End of Oil*. Bloomsbury.
Robertson, C.J.A. (2003) *The Origins of the Scottish Railway System*. John Donald.
Royal Commission on Environmental Pollution (1994) *Transport and the Environment*. HMSO.
Royal Commission on Environmental Pollution (1995) *Transport and the Environment* (2nd edn). Oxford University Press.
Samuelson, P.A. (1948) *Economics*. McGraw-Hill.
Sandel, M. (2012) *What Money Can't Buy*. Allen Lane.
Saul, J.R. (2005) *The Collapse of Globalism*. Atlantic.
Schaeffer, K.H. and Sclar, E. (1975) *Access for All*. Penguin.
Schaffer, F. (1970) *The New Town Story*. Paladin.
Schiller, P.L., Bruun, E.C. and Kenworthy, J.R. (2010) *An Introduction to Sustainable Transportation*. Earthscan.
Schmidt, R.E. and Campbell, M.E. (1956) *Highway Traffic Estimation*. Eno Foundation.
Schreiber, A.F., Gatons, P.K. and Clemmer, R.B. (1971) *Economics of Urban Problems*. Houghton Mifflin.
Scola, R. (1992) *Feeding the Victorian City*. Manchester University Press.
Scottish Executive (1999) *Tackling Congestion*. The Scottish Executive.
Scottish Government (2009) *Climate Change Delivery Plan*. The Scottish Government.
Scottish Office (1998) *Travel Choices for Scotland*. White Paper (Cmd 4010). HMSO.
Sharp, C. (1967) *Problems of Urban Passenger Transport*. Leicester University Press.
Sherlock, H. (1991) *Cities are Good for Us*. Paladin.
Smeed, R.J. (1962) 'The space requirements for traffic in towns' in T.E.H. Williams (ed.) *Urban Survival and Traffic*. Spon.
Smigielski, W.K. (1964) *The Leicester Traffic Plan*. Leicester City Council.
Smith, A. (1776) *An Inquiry into the Nature and Causes of the Wealth of Nations*. Strahan & Cadell.
Smith, A. (1795) *Essays on Philosophical Subjects*.
Snell, J.B. (1973) *Railways: Mechanical Engineering*. Arrow.
South-East Lancashire and North-East Cheshire Area Highway Engineering Committee (1962) *SELNEC. A Highway Plan 1962*. William Morris.
Southgate, G.W. (1965) *English Economic History*. Dent.
Steel, C. (2008) *Hungry City*. Chatto & Windus.
Stephen, W. (ed.) (2007) *A Vigorous Institution: The Living Legacy of Patrick Geddes*. Luath Press.
Stephen, W. *et al.* (2004) *Think Global, Act Local: The Life and Legacy of Patrick Geddes*. Luath Press.
Stern, N. (2006) *The Economics of Climate Change*. Cambridge University Press.
Stewart, I. (1990) *Does God Throw Dice: The Mathematics of Chaos*. Penguin.
Stewart, M. (ed.) (1972) *City: The Problems of Planning*. Penguin.
Stiglitz, J. (2002) *Globalization and its Discontents*. Penguin.
Stradling, S. *et al.* (1999) *Factors Affecting Car Use Choices*. DETR Contract (GE136NK).
Surowiecki, J. (2004) *The Wisdom of Crowds*. Abacus.
Surrey County Council (1993) *The Draft County Structure Plan*. Surrey County Council.
Tavis, C. and Aronson, E. (2008) *Mistakes Were Made but Not by Me*. Pinter & Martin.
Tawney, R.H. (1921) *The Acquisitive Society*. Harcourt Brace.
Taylor, N. (1998) *Urban Planning Theory Since 1945*. Sage.

The Standing Advisory Committee on Trunk Road Assessment (SACTRA) (1994) *Trunk Roads and the Generation of Traffic (The Wood Report)*. HMSO.
Thirlwall, A.P. (1972) *Growth and Development*. Macmillan.
Thomas, D.St J. (1973) *Summer Saturdays in the West*. David & Charles.
Thomson, A.W.J. and Hunter, L.C. (1973) *The Nationalised Transport Industries*. Heinemann.
Thomson, J.M. (1974) *Modern Transport Economics*. Penguin.
Timmerman, W.A. (1946) *Railway Expenditure and the Volume of Traffic*. Locomotive Publishing.
Titherage, H. (2004) *Accessibility Planning and Accessibility Modelling: A Review*. University College London.
Toledo, T. (2007) *Driving Behaviour: Models and Challenges*. Transport Reviews.
Tolley, R. and Turton, B. (1995) *Transport Systems, Policy and Planning*. Longman.
Townroe, P.M. (1974) *Social and Political Consequences of the Motor Car*. David & Charles.
TransPerth (1990) *The Corporate Plan*. City of Perth (Western Australia).
Transportation Planning Associates (1970) *Kington – Relocation of A 44*. TPA.
United Nations (1993) *The Global Partnership: A Guide to Agenda 21*. United Nations.
United Nations (1998) *Kyoto Protocol To The United Nations Framework Convention On Climate Change*. United Nations.
Victor, D.G. (2004) *The Collapse of the Kyoto Protocol*. Princeton University Press.
Vinen, R. (2000) *A History In Fragments*. Little Brown.
Walker, C. (1969) *Thomas Brassey: Railway Builder*. Frederick Muller.
Wardrop, J.G. (1952) *Some Theoretical Aspects of Traffic Research*. Proceedings of the Institution of Civil Engineers (Part II), Vol.1, No. 2.
Watson, G. (1957) *The Unservile State*. Allen & Unwin.
Webb, B. and Webb, S. (1913) *English Local Government: The Story of the King's Highway*. Longman.
Weiner, N. (1948) *Cybernetics: Or Control and Communication in the Animal and the Machine*. MIT Press.
Wenban-Smith, A. and Van Vuren, T. (2009) *A Review of the London Land-use Transport Interaction (LUTI) Mode*. European Transport Conference.
White, H.P. and Senior, M.L. (1983) *Transport Geography*. Longman.
White, P. (1976) *Planning for Public Transport*. Hutchinson.
White, P. (2002) *Public Transport: Its Planning, Management and Operation*. Spon.
Whitelegg, J. (1997) *Critical Mass: Transport, Environment and Society in the 21st Century*. Pluto Press.
Whitelegg, J. (1993) *Transport for a Sustainable Future*. Belhaven.
Whitelegg, J. (ed.) (1992) *Traffic Congestion: Is There a Way Out?* Leading Edge.
Whitelegg, J. and Haq, G. (eds) (2003) *World Transport Policy and Practice*. Earthscan.
Willbern, Y. (1964) *The Withering Away of the City*. Indiana University Press.
Williams, H.S. and Webb, A.Y. (1992) *Outcome Funding: A New Approach to Public Sector Grant Making*. Rensselaerville.
Williams, T.E.H. (ed.) (1962) *Urban Survival and Traffic*. Spon.
Williams, T., Dobson, G. and White, P. (1963) *Traffic Generated by Households*. Traffic Engineering and Control 2, pp. 176–181.
Willumsen, L.G. and Ortuzar, J. (1994) *Modelling Transport*. Wiley.
Wilson, A.G. (1970) *Entropy in Urban and Regional Modelling*. Pion.
Wilson, A.G. (ed.) (1971) *Urban and Regional Planning*. Pion.
Wistrich, E. (1983) *The Politics of Transport*. Longman.
Wolmar, C. (2001) *Broken Rails*. Aurum Press.
World Commission on Environment and Development (1987) *Our Common Future (The Brundtland Report)*. Oxford University Press.
Wylde, J. (2007) *Integrated Transport: A Will-o-the-wisp*. Jojm Wylde.
Yelton, M. (2004) *Trams, Trolleybuses and Buses and the Law*. Adam Gordon.

Index

accessibility 15, 42, 56, 290, 394; bridges 252; businesses 375; definitions of 89–90, 99–100, 202, 212; GOMMMS 245; isochrones 91–2; land-use change 254; planning 207–12; positive and negative effects 221; public transport 279–80, 367; relative 90, 93, 95–6, 248; road-user charging 337; SALUTE 389; supply-chain efficiency 98; theory of 212–16; urban structure 269
accidents 15, 188, 270, 362, 399; conflict points 120–2, 124; deaths in 219, 220; railway 183, 184, 273
accounting 160–5, 219–25, 323–4
Agenda 21 2–3
air quality 4, 371
air transport: costs 172–3; dwell times 172; fuel consumption and emissions 84, 199; load factor 87, 172; multi-modal transport 373; steerage 45–6; stringent aircraft rules 324; waiting time 27
airports 28, 36, 150, 173, 216–17
Alexander, Douglas 197
amortisation 164–5, 168, 222
assessment of interventions 339, 360–2, 377, 400–1; SALUTE 381–91; value-for-money assessments 375, 376, 380–1
average cost 227–8, 229

backcasting 248, 254–5, 284, 385
barcodes 147, 148
Beeching, Richard 58–60, 66, 309, 315
Beeching Report (1963) 58–60, 274, 277, 284, 307, 308, 326
behavioural churn 133, 134
Bibby, P.R. 51
Birmingham 149, 151, 179
Blair, Tony 8

bottom-up approaches 8, 211
braking: buses 77; cars 103–4, 126; trains 81, 82, 272–3, 274, 275
bridges 252, 262, 325
British Railways 97, 187, 205, 223–4, 234–5, 271, 274, 280, 307–8, 310, 325–7
Brundtland Report (1987) 1–2, 5, 16, 17, 29
Buchanan, Colin 58
Buchanan Report 241
bus lanes 286, 316–17, 407–8
bus service operators grant (BSOG) 302–3
bus transport 23–4, 159, 269–72, 284, 406–7; accessibility 202–3, 209, 281; commuting 313, 314, 315–17; competition 238; concessionary fares 203–4, 304–5; costs 166, 169–71, 281; current policy 301–5; decline in use of 276–7, 278, 295; deregulation and privatisation 186–7, 204–5, 294–301, 366; East of England 278–9; fuel consumption and emissions 76–8, 84–5, 199; hierarchy of personal transport 276; horse-drawn buses 264; hybrid buses 77–8, 86, 166; isochrones 91–2; layover times 232–3; Nottingham 'Zone and Collar' experiment 285–92; position of bus-stops 312, 316; subsidies 355, 364–5; transfers 387, 397; Transport Act 280–1; transport supplementary grants 293–4; urban development 41, 96–7; waiting times 26–7, 100n4, 149
business-driven approach 10, 403

canals 58, 181–3, 224–5
capacity: planning 33–4; public transport 88n18; rail transport 156–7; redundancy 324; roads 102, 106–7, 109, 116–20, 153–5; Transport Assessments 209, 210; WebTAG 333, 335; *see also* load factors

capital recovery factor (CRF) 165
car industry 235
carbon dioxide (CO_2) emissions 4, 69–87, 158, 220, 309, 405, 410; aggregate cost of movement 388; air transport 84; assessment of interventions 380; buses 76–8, 84–5, 301; cars 70–4, 84–5, 190; congestion 137; economic theory 185; figures for 69–70; Kyoto Protocol 6–8; licences 178; lorries 409; methodology to predict 401; planning objectives 37, 290–1, 318, 390, 392, 398–9, 403; policies 21, 376, 400; profitability measures 310; rail transport 78–84; road freight 74–6, 85–7; Stern Review 190–4; Strategy Indicators 13; *see also* greenhouse gases
carbon pricing 186
cars: acquisition and ownership 311–12; area density 243; availability 384; bus use related to car ownership 295, 296; changes in car use 284–5; commuting 281, 312–13, 314; costs 158, 160–5, 166, 169, 214–15, 259, 310, 358; demand 206, 216, 217, 369; destination choices 385–6; energy distribution 66; fuel consumption and emissions 70–4, 84–5, 190, 199; generalised travel cost 356; GOMMMS 244; growth in number of 49–51, 56, 57, 340; Heathrow Airport 216–17; hybrid vehicles 258–9; impact on public transport 276–80; 'modal-split' myth 148–9; Nottingham 'Zone and Collar' experiment 285–92; 'polluter pays' principle 328–9; public transport compared with 310–11; reducing use 4, 178; road capacity 153–5; spatially selective policy 405; stick and carrot policies 390–1; Strategy Indicators 13; sustainable transport planning 404, 410; taxes 336; Transport Assessments 209; trends 52–7, 66, 133; urban development 41–2, 43; vehicle design 256–60; WebTAG 331; *see also* congestion; parking; traffic
Carson, R. 194
centroids 288, 344–6, 353–4, 357–8, 365, 374, 383, 395
China 2, 147
choice 9, 179–80, 300, 331–2; destination 24, 132, 337, 358–9, 385–6; lifestyle 132, 133; mode of transport 24, 244, 396

Churn, behavioural 133, 134
city centres 52, 157–8, 269, 281, 389; commuting 314; Edinburgh 41; Nottingham 'Zone and Collar' experiment 288; parking 312; pedestrian areas 408; trends 314–15; *see also* urban areas
Civic Amenities Act (1967) 191, 330, 403
Clean Air Act (1956) 3, 191, 330, 403
Clemens, M. 28
climate change 3, 17, 37, 198, 212, 399; economic theory 185, 186; Kyoto Protocol 5–8; LA21 5; policy objectives 376; Rio Conference 2; Stern Review 190–4; traffic reduction 291
Climate Change (Scotland) Act (2009) 199, 200, 201
coaches 271
coal 22, 27–8, 58, 65–6, 90, 94, 172, 268, 276–7, 307, 394
communication 176, 184, 190
commuting 43, 53–6, 281, 305, 312–17; park-and-ride schemes 286, 290; railways 308; trams 269
competition 10, 236, 237–8, 262–3, 372; bus transport 186–7, 295–6, 297, 298–301, 302, 304; railways 309–10; Thatcherism 294
computer models 16, 24, 244, 245, 248, 254, 284, 344–6, 353
computer technology 147, 341
concessionary fares 203–4, 304–5
conflict points 120–6, 127–8
congestion 36, 41, 56, 58, 101–40, 259, 310, 410; buses 281, 297–8; carbon dioxide emissions 74; conflict points 120–6; Eddington Report 186, 188, 189; London 313; Nottingham 'Zone and Collar' experiment 285; public transport priority areas 407; public transport subsidies 363; road capacity 116–20, 136–7, 138; road-user charging 336–8; tackling 129–36; *Towards a Sustainable Transport System* 198; traffic flow 102–11, 112–16; WebTAG 333
congestion charging 102, 206–7, 209, 331, 337, 366; *see also* road-user charging
consultants 360
consumer surplus 326, 327, 338
containers 20, 22, 24, 78–81, 141–8, 168, 170–1
Cooke, M. 177
Coombe, D. 334, 376
coordination 371, 372

Index 423

costs 95–6, 159–74, 322; assessment of interventions 339, 360–2; buses 297, 298, 407; cars 158, 166, 169, 310; coal transport 90; congestion 129, 130, 137; containers 143, 144–5, 146–7; controlling 219–38; cost contours 93–4; cost of a journey 212–16; electricity 97; freight 21–2; handling 145, 146; horse trams 265–6; isochrones 93; lorries 409; measures of 356, 357–8; passenger interchanges 150; rail transport 309, 310; retail distribution 62; supply and demand 369; time budgets 384–5; waiting time 26, 27; WebTAG 331–6
cranes 143–4, 172, 173
cross-subsidies 297, 298
customer satisfaction 305
cybernetics 46, 181, 283, 392
cycling 23, 214, 374, 380, 408; commuting 313, 314; decline in use of 277–8; London 337; roundabouts 125; Transport Assessments 209, 210; trends 52–6

DDT 194
delays 132, 393; *see also* waiting times
Delivering a Sustainable Transport System (2008) 198–9
demand 137, 200, 206, 207, 217, 394; bus transport 301; forecasting 35–6, 248, 285, 290, 291–2, 339–78, 394–8; multi-modal approach 293; need for new methodology 379–91; planning 34; prices 324, 326; public transport 280, 369; road-user charging 337; Transport Assessments 210; travel demand management 99, 216, 241, 242–3, 368; WebTAG 332–3, 334, 335
density 13, 106, 216–17, 243, 281, 315, 318, 404
Department for the Environment, Transport and the Regions (DETR) 370–1, 373
Department for Transport (DfT) 25, 36, 109–10, 120, 138; congestion 130; primary road network 365; Transport Assessments 208; WebTAG 331–6
Department of the Environment 293, 361
depreciation 161–3, 164, 222
deregulation 186–7, 263, 294–301, 304, 371
Design Manual for Roads and Bridges (DMRB) 366, 368, 370, 372
destination choices 24, 132, 337, 358–9, 385–6
deterrence 213, 349–51, 352–4

diesel: buses 77; carbon dioxide emissions 70; trains 78, 79, 81, 82, 83
disabled passengers 202–3
discount cards 204, 327
discounted cash flows 163–4
disruptions 232–3
distance 349–51, 352–4
district control areas 249–51
Docherty, I. 373
Docklands 405, 406
Driver and Vehicle Licensing Agency (DVLA) 258
drivers: conflict points 123–4; decision times 126–9
dual carriageways 62–3
dwell times 156–8, 169–74, 384, 386, 387–8, 398; *see also* waiting times

economic growth 185–6, 188, 251, 252, 362, 376, 403
economic theory 185–6, 190–1, 195, 228, 298; prices 324; time cost 336; travel demand 334, 366
economy 239–55
Eddington Transport Study (2006) 185–7, 188–90, 194–8
Edinburgh 37–40, 42–3, 44, 54, 200, 265, 319n6, 324, 325, 379
electric vehicles 258–9; hybrid buses 77–8, 86, 166; trains 81–2, 83, 87n15; trams 96
electricity 13, 64, 65, 70, 78, 97, 307
employees 229–30
'end-state' planning 44–5, 46
energy consumption 13, 17, 21
energy distribution 64–6, 394
energy efficiency 200
European Commission 236, 257
European Union (EU) 16, 177, 178, 257
externalities 220–1

'fabric' 381, 395–6, 398
factories 37, 60–1, 95, 268
fares 67n6, 203–4, 261; buses 271, 294, 296; horse-drawn buses 264; rail transport 309, 326–7; taxis 263–4, 298, 325; trams 96, 265, 267, 319n9; *see also* tickets
feedback 45, 46, 94, 175, 181, 183, 283, 392
fees 329–30
ferries 262, 325
financial crisis 190, 219, 248
fines 330
First World War 11, 45, 96, 97–8, 269–70
Fitting on of Regional Growth and Elasticities (FORGE) 110, 120, 368, 372

'forced flow' 113, 114–15, 116
forecasting 34, 35, 89, 149, 206; bus use 297; carbon dioxide emissions 86, 192–3; changes of mode 394; demand 248, 285, 290, 291–2, 339–78, 394–8; multi-modal 244, 395; NTEM 249–51
fork-lift trucks 20, 21, 25–6, 141, 167, 172
Forth Bridge 223, 232, 252
'free flow' 114–15, 116, 117
freight 20, 21–2, 23, 97, 375; congestion 137; costs 235; dwell times 172; energy distribution 64–6; fuel consumption and carbon dioxide emissions 74–6, 78–82, 85–7; integration into general transport policy 408–9; inter-modal 24, 141, 145–8, 149, 151; international rates 252; policy 241; rail 21, 22, 58, 59, 60–1, 95–6, 97, 274–5, 307–8, 409–10; retail distribution 61–3; transport rhythms 25–6, 27; trends 48–50, 58–61; *see also* containers
frequency of services 217, 316, 393; buses 97, 100n4, 210, 271–2, 276, 302, 312, 315–16, 407; commuting 313, 314; density of areas 243; isochrones 202, 216, 315; modal rhythms 149; public transport accessibility level 279; trains 156, 276, 306, 309; trams 96, 100n10, 266–7, 268, 269, 276
fuel consumption 5, 399; air transport 84; buses 76–8, 84–5; cars 70–4, 84–5, 257–8; hybrid vehicles 258–9; rail transport 78–84; road freight 74–6, 85–7

gap acceptance 127–8
gap supply 128–9
gas 64, 65–6, 70, 277, 320n23
Gatwick Airport 236
Geddes, Eric 269–70
Geddes, P. 43–4
General Urban Model 242, 246, 253–5
generalised travel cost 212–13, 356–7, 359, 374
Glasgow 268
global economy 235–6, 252
global warming *see* climate change
'Goldilocks effect' 207, 216, 217
Goodwin, P. 133
gravity principle 349–53, 354, 356, 385–6, 387, 395
greenhouse gases 17, 68–88, 89, 198–9, 376; air transport 84; cars 70–4, 84–5; figures for 69–70; Kyoto Protocol 5–8; rail transport 78–84; Rio Conference 2; road freight 74–6, 85–7; road passenger transport 76–8, 84–5; Strategy Indicators 13; *see also* carbon dioxide emissions
gridlock 101–2, 132, 136, 137
gross domestic product (GDP) 14, 48, 49, 67n1
Guidance on the Methodology for Multi-modal Studies (GOMMMS) 242–52, 253, 254
Gummer, John 3

Hackney Carriages 263–4
Haddington case study 199–201
handling equipment 20, 21, 27, 141, 148, 410; containers 142, 144; costs 145, 146, 173
Hansen, W. 212–14
Harvey, D. 12
Heathrow Airport 216–17, 379
Highway Code 103, 126
Highways Act (1959) 282
Highways Agency 373
Hoon, Geoff 198
horse transport 94, 96, 97; horse-drawn buses 264; towpaths 92–3; trams 264–7
hotels 27
households 14, 52–6, 251; car ownership 50–1; definition of 67n2; size 249, 355–6, 384; surveys 347–8, 349, 354
housing 267–8, 270, 312, 337; bus-stops near 272; dockside 147; Haddington case study 200; planning 402; transport trends 52–6; urban development 37–8, 41, 43, 96, 97
Humber estuary 22
Huskisson, William 183, 236
hybrid vehicles 77–8, 86, 166, 258–9

industrial estates 42–3
industrial revolution 94
infrastructure 4, 90, 99, 381, 395; Eddington Report 189; maintenance 165–8; rail transport 236, 237; Transport Assessments 210; transport supplementary grants 282, 283
insurance 229
intangibles 219–22
integrated policy 370–2
Intelligent Transport Systems (ITS) 210
interchanges 141, 149–51, 156, 371, 388, 393, 400; *see also* transfers
interfaces 24, 152, 174, 206, 375, 380; freight 145–6, 148; terminals 376; transfers 382, 396; waiting time 26–7

inter-modal transport 24–5, 235–6, 243, 283–4, 400; forecasting 395; freight 141, 145–8, 149, 151, 375, 409; London 313–14; travel demand models 293; walking 244; *see also* multi-modal transport
Internet 147
iron industry 94–5
isochrones 91–2, 93, 96, 97, 99–100, 202; cars 291; commuting 315; cost of a journey 214, 216; public transport 291; trams 267, 269

journey time 68, 92, 134–6, 138, 158, 198
junctions: capacity 120, 136–7, 138; conflict points 120–6, 127–8; measuring movements 340; nodes 381, 397; transfers 382, 396; urban roads 119–20
'just-in-time' principle 67n8, 98, 147–8

Kelly, Ruth 197–8, 374–5
Kimber, R. 116
'King's Highway' 10, 17n12, 92, 182, 261–2, 328
Kington 341–7, 361–2, 366
Kosovo 151–2
Kuhn, T.S. 334
Kyoto Protocol (1997) 5–8, 16, 29

land budgets 154–5
land use 5, 89–100, 241–2, 400; changing patterns of 92–5, 206; Eddington Report 189–90; General Urban Model 254; GOMMMS 245–6, 249; integrated transport policy 371; inventory of 396; planning 30, 33–7, 205; SALUTE 389; Strategy Indicators 13; travel demand 248, 375, 380, 394; urban development 95–8
Land-Use Transport Interaction (LUTI) Models 241, 245, 246–8, 251, 253, 375
Lane, C.J.D. 386
leasing companies 225, 229
Leeds 268
legislation: Civic Amenities Act (1967) 191, 330, 403; Clean Air Act (1956) 3, 191, 330, 403; Climate Change (Scotland) Act (2009) 199, 200, 201; Highways Act (1959) 282; London Transport Act (1933) 11; Railways Act (1921) 11; Railways Act (1993) 205, 234; Railways Acts (1821/1826) 183; Regulation of Railways Act (1889) 274; Road Traffic Act (1930) 204, 270–1, 276, 295, 297, 298; Road Traffic Act (1972) 256, 260n2; Statute of Winchester (1285) 10, 92, 261–2, 328; Town and Country Planning Act (1947) 30–3, 44, 46; Tramways Act (1870) 10, 96, 100n11, 265, 319n4; Transport Act (1968) 99, 277, 280–1, 282, 284, 289, 291, 292, 302, 355, 402; Transport Act (1980) 294; Transport Act (1985) 295; Turnpike Acts 182; *see also* regulation
Leitch Report (1977) 363
licences: bus services 271; carbon trading 7, 69, 178, 330–1; taxes 328
licensing, quantity and quality 262, 263
'life-hours' 168, 170
Litchfield, Nathaniel 180
Liverpool 183
load factors: air transport 84, 87, 172; buses 76–7, 84–5; cars 84; costs 168; hybrid vehicles 86–7; lorries 74–6, 85–6, 230–2; trains 78–81
loans 164–5, 168, 222–3, 229
Local Agenda 21 (LA21) 4–5
local authorities 100n11, 251–2, 265, 303, 354, 367
location 89, 90, 93, 98, 146, 245
logistics 98, 394
logistics centres 28, 61, 62, 63, 66
London 101, 133–6, 138, 156, 160, 187; buses 269, 271, 296, 317; commuting 312–14, 315; congestion charge 206–7, 337; horse-drawn buses 264; linear development 404; London–Birmingham high-speed rail link 149, 151, 179, 379; Metropolitan Railway 36, 404; property development 312; public transport 305, 354; railways 272, 308; spatially selective policy 405; trams 268, 319n9
London Transport Act (1933) 11
lorries 4, 21, 97, 142, 145, 408–9; costs 22, 167, 226–8, 230–2; dual carriageways 62–3; energy distribution 66; ex-army 270; fleet capacity 63, 64; fuel consumption and emissions 74–6, 82, 85–7, 199; maximum gross weight 257, 258; maximum loading 62, 230; motorways 118; redundancy 232; road capacity 109; transport rhythms 25–6; trends 58, 60, 66; VOSA testing 258; waiting time 27; *see also* freight

M25 34–6, 216
maintenance 165–8, 323–4
Major, John 3

Malins, William 101
Malton bypass 322
management 12, 17, 176, 179, 225
Manchester 155–6, 183, 268
manufacturing 146–7, 235
marginal cost 227, 228, 298
market failure 186, 190
market forces 7, 9–12, 17, 46, 219, 372; Eddington Report 186–7, 189; financial crisis 190; privatisation 204, 205; Turnpike Acts 182
Marples, Ernest 58, 60, 340
Matson, T.M. 116, 126
'Matthew effect' 207, 216, 217, 231, 262, 278, 315
McKinnon, A.C. 231
McLean, Malcolm 141–2, 143
methodology 357, 360, 370, 373, 394–8; assessment of interventions 339, 362; need for new 379–81; planning 37, 392–3; 'predict-and-provide' 240–1; predictive 206, 400–1, 403; SALUTE 381–91; three-stage 353–4
metro systems 23
minibuses 171, 261, 299, 317
mobility 14, 90–1, 99, 202–4; bus transport 302; public transport 311, 318; urban structure 269
modal split 254, 284, 288, 357–9, 395
modes 23–4, 25, 45, 132, 395–6; changes of 394; cost of a journey 214, 216; GOMMMS 244, 245; multi-modal studies 372–3; NTS 243–4; perception of transport system 283; SALUTE 382; WebTAG 336; *see also* inter-modal transport; multi-modal transport
money 178–9, 221–2, 322–3
monopoly 261–2, 271, 294, 304, 310
Moroney, M.J. 193
Morrison, Herbert 270
motorways 28, 58, 240, 409; M25 34–6, 216; road capacity 118, 119, 153–4; slip roads 121; speed limits 200; traffic flow 115, 116
Moving Car Observer 138–9
multi-modal studies (MMS) 372–3
multi-modal transport 25, 148–51, 359, 375, 393; GOMMMS 242–52, 253, 254; London 313; travel demand models 293; *see also* inter-modal transport

National Bus Company 204–5, 280, 294, 295
National Express 294

National Road Traffic Forecasts (NRTF) 365, 366, 368, 372
National Transport Model 23, 372, 394
National Travel Model (NTM) 370
National Travel Survey (NTS) 23, 57, 243–4, 251, 370, 386
National Trip End Model (NTEM) 249–51, 253, 254, 369, 372
nationalisation 65, 187, 233, 234, 306, 309–10
Network Rail Ltd 224, 310, 321
nodes 344–5, 381–4, 387, 388, 395, 396, 397–8
noise levels 4, 371
Nottingham 'Zone and Collar' experiment 285–93, 312, 323, 356, 406

objectives 175–7, 205–6, 237, 292–3, 362–3, 376, 410; criteria 177–9; economic 240–1; planning system 403; public transport 290–1, 318; sustainable transport planning 392, 398–9; Transport Policy and Programmes 282; *see also* targets
offices 134, 157, 158, 269, 314
opportunity cost 195–6, 384
optimisation 179–80
origin and destination (O+D) matrices 340–54, 385, 386, 395, 397
overtaking 113–15
Oyster card 313–14, 337

pallets 20, 21, 25–6, 141
park-and-ride schemes 286, 290, 316, 404, 405–6
parking 24, 66, 150, 310, 317, 354; charges 328; city centres 281; demand for 388–9, 398; disabled drivers 203; free 292; housing types 53, 54, 55, 56; influence on car ownership 311; influence on destination choice 359; Nottingham 'Zone and Collar' experiment 289; space needed for 42, 155–8; sustainable transport planning 404, 410; time 331
partnerships 303
passenger car units (PCUs) 317
passenger carrying vehicles (PCVs) 76–8, 84–5; *see also* bus transport
Passenger Transport Authorities (PTAs) 280, 282
passenger travel: rhythms 26–7; trains 82–3; trends 48–9
peak times 132

pedestrians 23, 125, 285, 408; *see also* walking
performance indicators 12–16, 17
Perth 233–4
petrol 70, 190
PIEV analysis 126–7, 128
pipelines 58, 59, 64, 173, 277
planning 29–47, 242, 248–9, 363–4, 389–90, 402; accessibility 99, 207–12; change in scale and time frame 205–7; definitions of 29; funding changes 360; link between land-use planning and transport 33–7; process of 43–5, 47; rail transport 307; steerage 45–6; sustainable 392–411; TRICS database 251–2; urban areas 37–43
Planning Balance Sheet 180
Planning Policy Guidance Note 13 (PPG13) 205–7, 366–70, 371, 400
Plato 43
policy 4, 8–16, 211–12, 217, 363–70, 373–4, 394, 400–2; assessment of options 180; bus transport 301–5; carbon dioxide emissions 73–4, 399; congestion 137–8; demand management 99; economic theory 185–6; Eddington Report 188; effectiveness 253; integrated 370–2; levers 330–6; multi-modal transport 25; objectives 177, 178, 205–6, 240–1, 290–1, 362–3, 399; spatially selective 405; stick and carrot 390–1; *Traffic and Transport Plans* 354–5; WebTAG 334–5, 336; *see also* regulation
pollution 2, 4, 221, 371, 373, 390; DDT 194; freight 408; Kyoto Protocol 7; LA21 5; legislation against 191, 330; 'polluter pays' principle 194–5, 196–7, 328–9; trade-offs 253; vehicle design 258–9; *see also* carbon dioxide emissions; greenhouse gases
ports 28, 93, 146; containers 142–5, 147, 170–1, 173; trends 58; urban development 95
postcodes 254, 383, 386, 396
Potters Bar rail accident (2002) 183, 184, 323
powered two-wheelers (PTWs) 50, 199, 312, 313, 314
'predict-and-provide' policy 99, 240–1, 335, 365, 367, 368, 389
Prescott, John 101, 129, 130–1, 132, 370–1
prices 7, 9, 10, 11–12, 17, 324–5; competition 237; costs distinction 159;

price elasticity 326, 366; Stern and Eddington Reports 188, 190, 195; tariffs 325–7
primary production 90, 239
primary road network (PRN) 365
principal roads 118
privatisation 186–7, 204–5, 263, 366, 371; bus transport 294–301, 302, 303, 304; railways 224, 234–5, 237, 308, 309–10
productivity 14, 21, 92–3, 385
public rights of way 92, 182
Public Service Agreements (PSAs) 12, 13–15
'public service vehicles' (PSVs) 270
public transport 10, 23, 158, 261–320, 389; area density 243; capacity issues 88n18; commuting 312–17; costs 215, 358; demand management 216; demand prediction 355–6; Eddington Report 186; encouraging the use of 259; generalised travel cost 357; Heathrow Airport 216–17; impact of the car on 276–80; integration 371; isochrones 91–2; journeys to work 52–6; lack of knowledge about 132, 390; linear development 404; London 133–4, 138, 337, 354; 'modal-split' myth 148–9; monopoly 261–2; network tickets 160; Nottingham 'Zone and Collar' experiment 285–93; objectives 318, 362–3; priority areas 407–8; redundancy 232; regulation 262–76; spatially selective policy 405; stick and carrot policies 390–1; supply and demand 369; sustainable transport planning 404, 406–7, 410; Transport Act 280–1; Transport Assessments 209, 210; transport supplementary grants 281–5; urban development 41, 43; walking to public transport points 253, 279–80, 332, 404; WebTAG 332, 333, 374; *see also* bus transport; rail transport
public transport accessibility level (PTAL) 279–80, 305, 312, 320n26, 367, 374

quality licensing 262, 263
quality of life 4, 5, 376
quantity licensing 262, 263
Quarmby, D.A. 62–3

rail transport 11, 23, 267, 272–6, 406–7; accounting for expenditure 222–4; Beeching Report 58–60, 284; capacity 107; commuting 312–13, 314, 315; competition 237–8; containers 142; costs

166, 167, 281; dwell times 156–7, 171–2, 388; energy distribution 65, 66; European Directive 257; factories dependent on 268; First World War 270; freight 21, 22, 58, 59, 60–1, 95–6, 97, 274–5, 307–8, 409–10; fuel consumption and emissions 78–84, 199; geography of development 240; government control 187; Heathrow Airport 217; hierarchy of personal transport 276; high-speed routes 68; infrastructure 236; iron industry 94–5; London Metropolitan Railway 36, 404; London–Birmingham high-speed rail link 149, 151, 179, 379; nationalisation 187; privatisation 205, 234–5, 237, 309–10, 366; regulation 183–4, 306–9; subsidies 234–5, 237; systems approach 181–2; targets 16; transport rhythms 25–6; urban development 37; use of 276–7, 278; waiting times 27, 149–50
Railtrack plc 224, 237, 310
Railways Act (1921) 11
Railways Act (1993) 205, 234
Railways Acts (1821/1826) 183
redundancy 232–3, 324, 407
regulation 11, 186, 187–8, 262, 403; European 257; public transport 262–76; rail transport 183–4, 273–4, 306–9; Victorians 10–11; *see also* legislation; state intervention
Regulation of Railways Act (1889) 274
Reilly, W.J. 349
renewable energy 66, 177, 178
retail distribution 61–3, 394
'revealed preference' 370
revenue 228–9, 298, 309, 326
Reynolds, D.J. 129, 130
rhythms 25–8, 142, 144, 149, 393
Rio Conference (1992) 2, 3, 16, 29
risk 220, 323
rivers 37, 92–3
Road Research Laboratory (RRL) 108, 153, 292, 320n39, 341
Road Traffic Act (1930) 204, 270–1, 276, 295, 297, 298
Road Traffic Act (1972) 256, 260n2
road vehicle design 256–60
roads 23, 36, 92, 153–5, 285; conflict points 120–6; energy distribution 66; FORGE 368; freight 59, 60–1; Heathrow Airport 216–17; infrastructure 236; origin and destination matrices 340–54; policy 364, 365–7; road improvement schemes 206, 210, 287–8; SALUTE 382; subsidies 234; systems approach 181–2; Transport Assessments 210; *see also* congestion; junctions; traffic
road-user charging 102, 137, 206–7, 331, 336–8, 366, 399; Eddington Report 186, 189; Transport Assessments 209; *see also* congestion
roundabouts 124–5
route changes 131
rural areas 117–19, 130, 370
Russell, Bertrand 193

safety 10, 262, 273, 274, 371, 376
SALUTE (Simple Assessment of Land Use, Transport and the Environment) 381–91
satisfaction, concept of 195–6
scheme assessment 360–2
school transport 15
Scotland 199–201, 203, 204
'seamless journeys' 371, 372
Second World War 8, 11, 30–2, 45, 65, 98, 141, 191, 192, 306, 322
sections 381, 382, 383, 384, 396, 397, 398
Securing the Future (2005) 12
segments 253, 386–7, 393, 397, 400
Severn Bridge 252
share capital 223
Shaw, J. 373
Sheffield 268
Shepherd, J.W. 51
ships 22, 142–5, 168, 187, 232; costs 93, 167; dwell times 388; fuel consumption and emissions 78–9, 199; multi-modal transport 373; Suez-Mediterranean pipeline 173; trends 58, 59, 60
shopping 61–2, 63, 158, 269, 314
shopping malls 33, 42, 158, 384
signals 116, 125–6
'smart choices' 24, 211
Smeed, R.J. 153–5, 157
Smith, Adam 46, 195, 324, 325, 327, 329, 331
space 153–8
space-headway 103–5, 108, 110–11, 113, 115–16
speed: carbon dioxide emissions 401; conflict points 120–1, 123–4; congestion 129–31, 138; definitions and measures of 111–12; fuel consumption 70–4, 77; speed limits 200; traffic flow 102–3, 104–11, 112–16, 133; trains 272, 275–6
spread-sheets 179, 232, 322, 323

staff costs 167, 168, 170, 171, 225–6, 229
stakeholder approach 256–7
state intervention 187, 211–12, 262, 306; *see also* regulation
'stated preference' 370
Statute of Winchester (1285) 10, 92, 261–2, 328
Statutory Instruments (SI) 256
steerage 45–6, 175, 176
Stern Review (2006) 3, 185–7, 190–8
storage 28, 98, 142–3, 145–6, 148
Strategic Rail Authority 373
Strategy Indicators 12, 13–15
subsidies 9, 233–8, 281, 363; bus transport 302, 304, 355, 364–5; cross-subsidies 297, 298; rail transport 310
substitutability 263, 296, 325, 330
suburban areas 42, 134, 267–8
'sufficing' 180
supermarkets 42, 98
supply 332–3, 334, 335, 366, 368–9
supply chains 98, 145, 146, 147–8
sustainability 3, 11, 29, 37, 219, 393, 400; Brundtland Report 1, 2; definition of 1, 16, 17; greenhouse gas emissions 68–9; policy 8, 9; regulation 403; Rio Conference 2–3; sustainable transport policy 371; Transport Assessments 209
sustainable development 3–4, 6, 366–7
system performance 382–3, 395–6
systems 181–4

targets 4, 16, 68–9, 177, 399; *see also* objectives
tariffs 325–7, 329–30
taxes 9, 190, 196, 259, 327–9, 336
taxis 188, 261, 263–4, 298, 313, 314, 325
Tay Bridge 232
technology 66, 97–8, 147, 209
terminals 376
Thatcher, Margaret 294
tickets 160, 243, 300–1, 304, 326; *see also* fares
time 324, 336, 356, 384–5, 388, 398; *see also* dwell times; waiting times
time-headway: cars 103–8, 110–11, 113, 115–16, 128; trains 156, 157
timetables 272, 298, 324
tolls 92, 182, 234, 262, 325, 327
top-down approaches 8, 211
Towards a Sustainable Transport System (2007) 197–8
Town and Country Planning Act (1947) 30–3, 44, 46

towpaths 92–3
traffic: demand prediction 339–78, 383; flow 80, 102–11, 112–16, 117, 128, 133, 138–9, 344–7, 397–8; forecasting 34, 35–6; Nottingham 'Zone and Collar' experiment 285–93; trends 48–50; *see also* cars; congestion; roads
Traffic and Transport Plans (1968) 354–5
trams 10, 96–7, 100n10, 267–9, 281, 317, 407; costs 166; Edinburgh 39–41, 47n9; fares 319n9; hierarchy of personal transport 276; horse 96, 264–7
Tramways Act (1870) 10, 96, 100n11, 265, 319n4
transfers 382–3, 384, 387, 388, 396, 397–8; *see also* interchanges
TransPerth Corporate Plan 233–4
transport, definition of 19
Transport Act (1968) 99, 277, 280–1, 282, 284, 289, 291, 292, 302, 355, 402
Transport Act (1980) 294
Transport Act (1985) 295
Transport Analysis Guidance (TAG); see WebTAG
'Transport Assessments' 208–12
Transport for London (TfL) 76, 77, 149, 312–13, 315
'Transport Impact Analyses' 205, 208
transport landscapes 99, 202, 253, 255n25, 377, 389, 390–1, 396
Transport Planning Society 242
Transport Policy and Programmes (TPPs) 282–5, 286, 291–3, 360, 363–5, 402
Transport Research Laboratory (TRL) 292, 294, 320n39
transport supplementary grants (TSGs) 281–5, 286, 291–4, 295, 355, 360, 363–5, 402
transport system 19–22, 393–8
trans-shipment 21, 24, 28, 98, 141–8, 409, 410
travel demand management 99, 216, 241, 242–3, 368
trends 48–67, 134, 392, 394; city centres 314–15; energy distribution 64–6; freight 58–61; personal travel 48–58; retail distribution 61–3
Trip End Model Program (TEMPRO) 249–51, 253, 369
Trip Rate Information Computer System (TRICS) 34, 47n6, 251–2
trips 23, 57–8, 134–6, 251, 347–53; assignment stage 354, 359, 395; distribution stage 353–4, 356–7, 359,

385–8, 395, 396; generation stage 353, 355–6, 357, 359, 363, 384–5, 394–5; GOMMMS 243, 245; public transport 355, 356; quality of services 366; WebTAG 331–5
trunk roads 118
Turnpike Acts 182

United Nations Framework Convention on Climate Change (UNFCCC) 7
urban areas 37–43, 281–2, 293–4, 338, 370; buses 296, 297–8, 301–2; commuting 312–17; congestion 119, 124, 137, 186, 259; increase in size 259; land use 95–8; lorries 409; new urban geography 318; public transport 291; road capacity 119–20, 136–7, 138; road-user charging 189; speeds 130; trams 267–9; trends 52–8, 66, 134, 392; urban structure 402–10; *see also* city centres; virtual city

value, monetary 178–9, 221–2, 322–3, 399
value-for-money assessments 375, 376, 380–1
Van Vuren, T. 334, 375
Vehicle and Operator Services Agency (VOSA) 257–8
Vehicle Certification Agency (VCA) 257–8, 260n2
vehicle design 256–60
vehicle leasing companies 225
vehicle occupancy 83, 85, 153, 259, 317, 401
Victorians 10–11, 19, 96, 183, 187–8, 212, 264–7, 272–4

virtual city 259, 337, 338, 389–90, 405; car parking 388; new urban geography 318; personal time budgets 398; urban development 43, 55, 57, 281–2, 402, 403

waiting times 26–7, 91–2, 93, 100n4, 149–50; buses 272; containers 142–3; Nottingham 'Zone and Collar' experiment 288, 289; *see also* dwell times
walking 19, 48–9, 95, 132, 149, 206, 373; as component of all journeys 359; cost of a journey 214, 357; encouraging 408; hierarchy of personal transport 276; inter-modal transport 244, 283–4; isochrones 91; new methodology 380; Nottingham 'Zone and Collar' experiment 288, 289; policy 374; to public transport points 253, 279–80, 332, 404; Transport Assessments 209, 210; trends 52–6
Wardrop, J.G. 129, 130, 345–6
warehousing 27, 28, 98, 146, 147, 240
water transport 92–3
ways 381, 382, 395–6
WebTAG 331–6, 372, 373–4, 376, 379, 394
weight of vehicles 257, 258
Weiner, N. 45
Wenban-Smith, A. 334, 375, 377
'work-hours' 168

zones 246, 253–5, 284, 394–5; Nottingham 'Zone and Collar' experiment 285–93; origin and destination matrices 341–54